Information Technology and Law Series

Volume 22

For further volumes:
http://www.springer.com/series/8857

Aurelio Lopez-Tarruella
Editor

Google and the Law

Empirical Approaches to Legal Aspects
of Knowledge-Economy Business Models

T·M·C·ASSER PRESS    Springer

Dr. Aurelio Lopez-Tarruella
Universidad de Alicante
Ap. 99
03080 Alicante
Spain

ISSN 1570-2782
ISBN 978-90-6704-845-3   e-ISBN 978-90-6704-846-0
DOI 10.1007/978-90-6704-846-0

Library of Congress Control Number: 2012930906

© T.M.C. ASSER PRESS, The Hague, The Netherlands, and the author(s) 2012

Published by T.M.C. ASSER PRESS, The Hague, The Netherlands www.asserpress.nl
Produced and distributed for T.M.C. ASSER PRESS by Springer-Verlag Berlin Heidelberg

Printed on acid-free paper

Springer is part of Springer Science+Business Media (www.springer.com)

Series Information

The *Information Technology & Law Series* was an initiative of ITeR, the National programme for Information Technology and Law, which is a research programme set up by the Dutch government and the Netherlands Organisation for Scientific Research (NWO) in The Hague. Since 1995 ITeR has published all of its research results in its own book series. In 2002 ITeR launched the present internationally orientated and English language *Information Technology & Law Series*. This series deals with the implications of information technology for legal systems and institutions. It is not restricted to publishing ITeR's research results. Hence, authors are invited and encouraged to submit their manuscripts for inclusion. Manuscripts and related correspondence can be sent to the Series' Editorial Office, which will also gladly provide more information concerning editorial standards and procedures.

Editorial Office
eLaw&Leiden, Centre for Law in the Information Society
Leiden University
P.O. Box 9520
2300 RA Leiden
The Netherlands
Tel.: +31-71-527-7846
e-mail: ital@law.leidenuniv.nl

A.H.J. Schmidt, *Editor-in-Chief*
eLaw@Leiden, Centre for Law in the Information Society, Leiden University, The Netherlands

Chr.A. Alberdingk Thijm, *Editor*
SOLV Advocaten, Amsterdam, The Netherlands

F.A.M. van der Klaauw-Koops, *Editor*
eLaw@Leiden, Centre for Law in the Information Society, Leiden University, The Netherlands

Ph.E. van Tongeren, *Publishing Editor*
T.M.C. ASSER PRESS, The Hague, The Netherlands

Contents

Chapter 1
Introduction: Google Pushing the Boundaries of Law

Aurelio Lopez-Tarruella

Allow me to recall the first time I heard about Google. It was in the beginning of 2000. I was working in Brussels. A colleague of mine recommended me a new web search engine that was far quicker than the ones we used to work with at that time. The first impression I got was not very good: the home page was all in white and not very attractive. But my friend insisted on how fast it was and he constantly made me check the upper side of the results where the astonishing figure of the approximate results and the time used to produce them are shown. Although the number of results was incredible and the time was usually less than a quarter of a second, I was not impressed. The reason might have been that, at that time, I was expecting an Internet portal to provide not only a web search engine but also content. Therefore, I kept working with other web search engines.

Little by little Google started to come up more often in conversations with my friends and colleagues. Due to this, and influenced by the need of being up-to-date, I started to use Google. More important than this was that, during those conversations, the same question always came up: how does Google make money? Only one of my friends had an answer—"thanks to advertising!", and he explained to us the Google AdWords service—"companies pay Google for displaying small ads in the right side of the screen related to the words you introduce in the search box". None of us could imagine that such a service might have the implications for trade mark law explained by Jeremy Phillips in Chap. 3 of this work. Basically, at that time, the only thing my colleagues and I thought was that our friend was "nuts"

Senior Lecturer Private international law, Lecturer and Coordinator of the IT Module of the Magister Lvcentinvs on Intellectual Property.

A. Lopez-Tarruella (✉)
University of Alicante, Alicante, Spain
e-mail: Aurelio.lopez@ua.es

A. Lopez-Tarruella (ed.), *Google and the Law*,
Information Technology and Law Series 22, DOI: 10.1007/978-90-6704-846-0_1,
© T.M.C. Asser press, The Hague, The Netherlands, and the author(s) 2012

1

and that such a web site could not survive. In our defense, it has to be recalled that that was the time when the "dot-com bubble" exploded.

Time has shown that my friend was right and I was terribly wrong. In February 2010, the company founded by Larry Page and Sergey Brin in 1997[1] had almost 20,000 employees and its market value was USD 136,383,466,440.[2] In Fiscal Year 2010, Google revenues amounted to USD 29,321 million (48% from the US, 10% for UK, 42% from the rest of the world). Ninety six percent of those revenues came from advertising, the remaining 4% came from licensing of its search technology to other companies.[3]

What I did not understand in 2000 but which Google did perfectly, was that, in today's knowledge economy, information has become a "commodity". There is plenty of information on the world wide web. Everyone has access to it. If your business is providing information (content), it has to be very good to make it valuable in comparison to the information provided by others. If not, you cannot make money with it.

What is valuable is the organization of that information. Google understood this from the beginning. In 2000, search engines were provided as ancillary to other services and content provided by Internet portals (and at least most of the people I knew at that time was expecting those other services). Google decided to focus on the thing they did best: search. Google became successful because they designed a search engine that was better and faster at finding the right answer than other search engines at the time.

Broadly speaking, the success of Google's search engine is founded on three elements. First, the use of very powerful software programs called crawlers or "Googlebots" to constantly search the web for updates of sites which they have already indexed and for new information uploaded. Second, a very efficient technology to index all the information found by these crawlers. Third, the use of more than 200 criteria that allows a user, when typing a word in the search box, to find the most relevant website related to that word. Among those 200 criteria, the most important is PageRank®, an algorithm protected by patent in the US, and which determines the relevance of a web site according to the links that other websites include to it. This is claimed to be a "democratic" way to establish the relevance of a website. Placement in search results is not sold to companies by Google. It is exclusively based on the popularity of the web site on the web. Search results are listed taking into account what users have linked to—which is usually an indication of their appreciation, not according to which company pays the most.

---

[1] "Google", is a play on the word "googol", the mathematical term for a 1 followed by 100 zeros. The name reflects the immense volume of information that exists, and the scope of Google's mission: to organize the world's information and make it universally accessible and useful. See Google History, available at http://www.google.es/intl/en/corporate/history.html (last accessed 29th August 2011).

[2] http://www.nasdaq.com/symbol/goog (last accessed 30th August 2011).

[3] http://investor.google.com/financial/tables.html (last accessed 29th August 2011).

Having attracted the attention of users thanks to the efficiency of their search engine, Google started to monetize its services in 2000 by selling advertising space to companies.[4] As previously mentioned, this is done by means of Google AdWords. In this service, advertisers select words and phrases that are relevant to their business as keywords. When people use Google to search for those keywords, up to 11 "sponsored links" are displayed alongside the search results. Each time a user clicks one of those sponsored links, the advertiser pays Google.

The idea of providing services for free and to indirectly generate revenues through advertising is not new. For instance, it is used by public TV channels and free newspapers. However, there are important particularities that make Google's advertising system particularly successful:

a) ads in Google are contextualized and personalized: they relate to the information in the web page where they are displayed and they are personalized to the searches made by the user accessing the information. AdWords only shows sponsored links that are related to the terms introduced by the user in the search box: if the user looks for shoes, "sponsored links" of shoe companies will be displayed. This is extremely interesting for companies—they have more possibilities to sell their products or services—and users—the ads they see are related to things they are interested in. While advertising on TV and other media can also be contextualized, the possibilities are much more limited. In addition to this, ads may change depending on the information Google has about the users visiting their web sites. As is explained later, Google works really hard in gathering this information since it is essential for their advertising services. As an example, ads might be personalized depending on the geographic location of the user: companies may decide that their "sponsored links" are only displayed if the user accesses Google from a computer with an IP address in a country where they offer their products.[5]

b) Google provides services worldwide. This means that companies interested in subscribing to the Google AdWords services are located anywhere in the world. At the same time, these companies know that by using these services, they can reach users anywhere. While in theory this is also possible in other media, only a few companies can afford to make the investment this requires. With AdWords, SMEs and individuals can easily promote their products and services anywhere in the world.

c) Prices of "sponsored links" are not fixed. In order to get a good position in the list of sponsored links companies have to bid. While Google provides an estimated minimum bid needed to get on the first page of search results, it does not ensure that the best bid will automatically get the first position. The ranking of the different sponsored links is determined by a combination of the bid made by the advertiser when selecting the keyword and the so-called "quality score",

---

[4] Internet advertising only represents 10% of the total advertising market, however Internet advertising keeps growing in comparison with other segments of this market.

[5] Peguera 2010, p 358.

based on relevance (how well the ad matches a user's query), the quality of the landing page that the ad links to (the value of its content and how quickly it loads), and the ad's past clickthrough rate (or, if it is new, the rate of a similar ad), along with other criteria Google does not want to reveal.[6]

d) Advertisers in Google AdWords only pay if users click on the ad ("cost per click"). This last characteristic distinguishes Google from most online and traditional media advertisers and makes the service extremely attractive. Furthermore, Google enables advertisers to easily track the results of their campaigns—thanks to Google AdWords or Google Analytics, and helps them to improve their advertising strategy.

Since 2000 Google keeps improving its search engine with technologies like "autocomplete" or "Google Instant" having in mind that the most important thing is to provide users as fast as possible with what they are looking for. Thanks to this, at present, Google's global search engine's market share is 90.59%.[7] In February 2010, it was reported that, worldwide, there were more than 3 billion searches on Google per day.[8]

But more important than this, Google has impressively expanded its offer of services and applications with one and the same idea in mind: attract Internet traffic to their web sites. This offer includes web-applications—Gmail, GoogleCalendar, GoogleReader, GoogleDocs or GoogleMusic—improvements or specific applications of the search engine—GoogleNews, GoogleImages, GooglePatents, GoogleScholar, etc. – a social network—Google + - or a combination of services and content— GoogleMaps, GoogleStreetView, GoogleEarth, YouTube or GoogleBooks. It also provides tools for users that want to publish their own content—Blogger for blogs, GoogleSites for personal web sites or YouTube for audiovisual works—helping with the development of the so-called Web2.0.[9]

Attracting Internet traffic is also the reason why Google provides the Chrome web browser, the Chrome operating system[10]—for PC, laptops and netbooks—and the different versions of the Android operating system—for smartphones and

---

[6] See "Anatomy of an Auction", Wired Maganize, Issue 12.06, available at http://www.wired.com/special_multimedia/2009/nep_googlenomics_auction. (last accessed 29th August 2011).

[7] http://gs.statcounter.com/#search_engine-ww-monthly-200807-201108-bar. (last accessed 29th August 2011).

[8] http://searchengineland.com/by-the-numbers-twitter-vs-facebook-vs-google-buzz-36709 (last accessed 29th August 2011).

[9] A complete list of Google services and products is available at http://en.wikipedia.org/wiki/List_of_Google_products (last accessed 29th August 2011).

[10] The Chrome OS is open-sourced under the Chromium OS project, available at http://www.chromium.org/chromium-os (last accessed 29th August 2011).

tablets—for free and under open source licenses.[11] At present, this latter software is used in 48% of new smartphones worlwide.[12] The fact that the software is given under an open source license allows third parties to have access to the source code in order to develop applications that are compatible with the operating system. Such applications can be published in the Android Market—for free or for remuneration. This benefits Google and the software developers.

The reason why Google keeps providing applications and services for free to attract Internet traffic is two-fold. First, the use of its services allows Google to collect much more information about users than that collected just with the different modalities of its search engine. Just as examples, Google keeps track of all the time we access its websites, collects the personal data we introduce to subscribe to its services, information on all our searches, on all the blogs and web pages we follow through GoogleReader and of the content of the e-mails we receive.[13] As it has been said, giving away all that data for free is the price users pay for enjoying Google services.[14]

The information collected by Google is essential to personalize advertising and it is extremely valuable for companies that want to advertise on the Internet. Certainly, the compilation of this information is the most valuable of Google's assets and it is easy to understand the relevance of maintaining its exclusivity.

The second reason why Google is so eager in attracting as much Internet traffic as possible is easy to understand: the more services provided by Google, the more websites there are to place "sponsored links". Furthermore, the more "sponsored links" are clicked, the more revenues for Google.

But Google's strategy to maximize profits does not only consist in attracting Internet traffic, it also consists in improving its advertising services. Besides AdWords, Google created AdSense, a system to embed advertisements into third parties' websites that have signed up to a partnership agreement with Google and, thus, belong to the so-called Google Display Network. These websites might belong to media companies (New York Times, El País), other service providers (eBay, Skype, MySpace), airlines web sites (RyanAir), or bloggers using Google's Blogger application. Google shares a portion of its revenues with each publisher.

---

[11] Other strategic movements of the American company can be similarly explained: the extraordinary improvement of Google's translation tools, agreements with software developers to provide the Google Toolbar bundled with software (Sun, Adobe, Firefox) or with browsers to embed the search engine in it (Firefox) or Google's investments in infrastructures such as WIFI (Fon), satellites (O3b Network). Google's frustrated adventure in the Chinese market is another example of this policy. 420 millions potential users was an attractive figure to accept the conditions imposed by China to provide its services. However it turned out that the censorship measures implemented by the Chinese government were unsustainable for Google.

[12] Android is already used in 40% devices worldwide. See Android market share nears 50% worldwide, available at http://www.networkworld.com/news/2011/080111-canalys.html (last accessed 29th August 2011).

[13] A list of the information Google collects is available at http://www.google.com/intl/en/privacy/privacy-policy.html (last accessed 29th August 2011).

[14] Wauthy 2008, p 72.

AdSense displays ads based on the content of each particular site and on the data Google has about the user accessing it. The position of the ads in the list of sponsored links follows the same system as AdWords.

To further develop its advertising service, in 2008 Google acquired Double-Click.[15] Thanks to this, Google now offers a technology that allows embedding graphical ads into webpages. The technology allows advertisers to manage and track their display advertisements.

In addition to the information Google gathers from users accessing its services, this US company also uses *cookies* and other technologies to keep track of the computers from which websites belonging to the Google Display Network are accessed—and their users. This information is compiled in Google's servers and it is used to make profiles of users in order to personalize the ads shown to them when they access websites of the Network. That is: Google can monitor your online behavior within the network of affiliated websites and, according to this, provide you with ads that may be of more interest to you. This is so-called online behavioral advertising. Thanks to this, Google can provide more efficient advertising services to the companies belonging to the Network. At the same time, the bigger the Network grows, the more information Google collects from users.[16]

The latest steps in Google's deepening of its business model are the acquisition of AdMob in 2009[17] and of Motorola Mobility in 2011. The first company provides mobile advertising services—"in-app ads" that is, ads embedded in applications downloaded in portable devices—a market that is expected to reach 3.3 billion dollars by the end of this year and 20.6 billion by 2015.[18] In part, this is due to the fact that more and more people are substituting computers by mobile devices as the main means to access the Internet. At present, AdMob worldwide market share is above 40%.[19] In October 2010, Google announced that mobile ad revenues would reach 1 million dollars on an annualized run rate.[20]

---

[15] Other Google acquisitions are listed at http://en.wikipedia.org/wiki/Category:Google_acquisitions (last accessed 29th August 2011).

[16] Peguera 2010, p 362.

[17] In 2010, Google tried to buy Groupon, "a mediation platform that connects people seeking bargains with merchants who are willing to provide them" (See Arabshahi, Undressing Groupon, An Analysis of the Groupon Business Model, available at http://www.ahmadalia.com/download/Undressing-Groupon.pdf,, last accessed 29th August 2011). After Groupon rejected the offer of Google, the American company announced the launch of the competing service "Google Offers". At the time of finishing this book, the service was not available yet.

[18] See Gartner: Global Mobile Advertising To Hit $3.3 Billion In 2011, available at http://www.mediapost.com/?fa=Articles.showArticle&art_aid=148308&nid=125564 (last accessed 29th August 2011).

[19] See What's in Store for Mobile Advertising in 2011, available at http://blog.buysellads.com/2011/02/whats-in-store-for-mobile-advertising-in-2011/ (last accessed 29th August 2011).

[20] See Unpacking $1 Billion in Google Mobile Ad Revenues, available at http://internet2go.net/news/ad-networks/unpacking-1-billion-google-mobile-ad-revenues (last accessed 29th August 2011).

The recent acquisition of Motorola Mobility (and its patent portfolio) by USD 12.5 billions should help Google to consolidate its position in this market for at least two reasons: it will provide Google the option of producing its own hardware devices and it will allow the company to fight the more and more frequent patent infringement claims against Android. Furthermore, Motorola owns technology which seems to be very useful for the development of other big project, Google TV, thanks to which the Mountain View's company might be able to expand its business model to television.

While there is no doubt that Google's business model has proved successful, it has also become obvious that it presents a challenge to the law. Google seems to be imposing its ambitious business model without taking into account restrictions, checks, and balances established by law. Therefore, it is not surprising that Google's activities have given birth to a great number of lawsuits and to a rich case law all over the world. In this sense it can be affirmed that Google is pushing the boundaries of the law.

The aim of this book is to provide a legal assessment of the most relevant disputes where Google has been, or is still involved in, mainly from a European and US law perspective. Some of them relate to the first and still best known service developed by the company: the search engine. As Sophie van Loon explains in Chap. 2, Google is accused of listing their partners' web sites higher in the results list to the detriment of its competitors. Could this conduct be considered an infringement of EU Competition rules? Are there other business practices of Google in danger of infringing these rules?

A second group of disputes concern the most important aspects of Google's business model. First, the AdWords service: in Chap. 3, Jeremy Phillips reviews the treatment of this, Google's core service, by the Court of Justice of the European Union. Second, the collection of users' information: in Chap. 4, Bart van der Sloot and Frederik Zuiderveen Borgesius discuss whether the tracking of users' online behavior by Google is in compliance with European privacy standards.

A third group of controversies relates to the services and applications developed by Google to attract Internet traffic. Bart van der Sloot and Frederik Zuiderveen Borgesius also deal in Chap. 4 with the problems concerning Google Street View: are the photographs showing people in this service an infringement of the right to privacy? In Chap. 5, Raquel Xalabarder explains whether the complaints of online newspapers towards the GoogleNews service are well founded. Miquel Peguera examines some of the most relevant case law in Europe and in the US concerning the compliance of Google Images and Google Cache with copyright law (Chap. 6). Annsley M. Ward deals with the "*YouTube v. Viacom*" litigation in Chap. 7: is Google liable for providing users with the tool to upload video clips in YouTube potentially without the consent of the copyright holders, or does it benefit from the safe harbor provisions in the DMCA? Finally in this group, Gary Rinkerman gives his opinion in Chap. 8 on what will happen now that the GoogleBooks Settlement has been rejected by Judge Chin.

A fourth group of questions relates to Google's software and APIs (application programming interfaces). Chap. 9, written by Malcolm Bain, analyzes the particularities of the free/open source licenses used by Google to release Android and Chromium. In Chap. 10, Andrew Katz explains how Google implements terms and conditions for access to their cloud services, the threats posed by closed APIs, and what legal regulation may exist to counter those threats.

Finally, the book includes three chapters that are not focused in one particular service or application, but focus on Google's activities in general. The first is written by Danny Friedmann and aims to identify the lessons we can learn from Google's frustrated adventure in China (Chap. 11). The second is written by me and its objective is to argue whether the existing rules of Private international law could become an obstacle for the provision of Google's services internationally? (Chap. 12). Finally, Marcelo Thompson departs from Google's position on the on-going Net Neutrality debate to evaluate what the very idea of neutrality means for the regulation of Google itself, and of "Search" in a broader sense (Chap. 13).

As it is expected from a Law book, most of the articles discuss whether Google's services are in compliance with the existing legal order. However, that is not our only purpose. More important than that, this book aims to provide a deeper reflection: are current legal systems adapted to the Google business model? Are they adapted to the business activities that are flourishing in the digital environment? Are the present rules conceived for an industrial economy? Do they obstruct the development of businesses in the knowledge economy? Do the various lawsuits involving Google show an evolution of the existing legal framework that might favour the flourishing of these businesses? Or do they simply reflect that Google has gone too far? What lessons can other knowledge-based businesses learn from all the disputes in which Google has been or is involved?

I hope this book gives you the answers to these questions or, at least, makes you reflect on them.

I do not want to finish this introduction without recalling a verse in Tom Petty's song, *American Girl*: "God, it's so painful when something is so close and still so far out of reach". That's how I felt the first time the idea of editing this book came to my head. Fortunately, I found a bunch of devoted colleagues who made it possible. I thank them for that.

Alicante, 30th August 2011

References

Peguera Poch M (2010) Publicidad online basada en comportamiento y protección de la privacidad, in: Rallo Lombarte, A/Martínez Martínez, R., Derecho y redes sociales, Thomson Reuters, pp 355 and ff
Wauthy X (2008) La gratuité c'est le vol payant! Google, le Web2.0 et le modèle économique du gratuit : une industrie à réguler? In : Strowel, A/Triaille (dirs) Google et les nouveaux services en ligne, Larcier, pp 51 and ff

Chapter 2
The Power of Google: First Mover Advantage or Abuse of a Dominant Position?

Sophie van Loon

Contents

S. van Loon (✉)
Attorney-at-law with Kennedy Van der Laan, Amsterdam, The Netherlands
e-mail: s.van.loon@kvdl.nl

A. Lopez-Tarruella (ed.), *Google and the Law*,
Information Technology and Law Series 22, DOI: 10.1007/978-90-6704-846-0_2,
© T.M.C. ASSER PRESS, The Hague, The Netherlands, and the author(s) 2012

2.1 Introduction

On November 30, 2010, the European Commission announced the opening of formal antitrust investigations into acts performed by Google Inc. Google allegedly violates Article 102 TFEU[1] (prohibition on the abuse of a dominant position) by engaging in anti-competitive conduct.

The start of formal investigations by the European Commission underlines the image change that the ubiquitous search engine has undergone since its introduction. When Google was first introduced years ago, it was welcomed as a pioneer. As a general search engine displaying an almost blank starting page without advertisements and using an innovative indexing system to deliver highly accurate search results, it has brought many benefits to consumers.[2] By 2011, with an estimated market share of over 90% in the online search market in various European countries,[3] it is under the scrutiny of several European competition authorities as well as being criticized for—among other things—lack of transparency regarding its use of sensitive data.[4] Although the opening of antitrust investigations as such does not mean that Google will be held to have violated Article 102 TFEU, the investigation by the European Commission confirms Google's new reputation as one of the 'bad guys': companies with overwhelming market power that may exploit consumers and competitors and whose conduct should therefore be closely monitored.

Is Google therefore a victim of its own success? It would definitively not be the first company[5] to come within reach of European Competition law as a result of its rapid expansion. But as a first time Article 102 TFEU investigation into a search engine, the examination of Google's practices will involve complex issues related to the specific characteristics of search engines and the market(s) they operate on. In this respect, Google's position as a so-called first mover on this market will need to be addressed by the European Commission, and will have to be taken into account when assessing Google's market power. This market power largely follows from the fact that, as a search engine, Google was a first of a kind, due to its innovative indexing technology 'Page Rank'. Condemning Google for abuse of a dominant position therefore boils down to punishing a pioneer company for

---

[1] Treaty on the Functioning of the European Union.

[2] See, *inter alia*, Rosenberg 1998.

[3] Search engine market shares around the world, Q4 2010, available at http://blog.green lightsearch.com/greenlights_search_blog/2010/01/how-search-engine-market-shares-look-around-the-world-featuring-bing-yahoo-and-baidu-and-others.html (last accessed February 18, 2011).

[4] See, *inter alia*, *2007 Consultation Report of Privacy International*, available at http://www. privacyinternational.org/issues/internet/interimrankings.pdf (last accessed January 8, 2011), in which Google is ranked 'hostile to privacy'.

[5] For example French Wanadoo Interactive, which was the subject of antitrust proceedings due to its rapidly increasing market share in the market for high speed internet in France, *infra*.

finding a gap in the market, one may argue. Whether this is true or false, should the investigations lead to actual proceedings, it will be highly interesting to see whether the Commission will address Google's first mover status and the special characteristics of search engine markets, or if it will stick to its traditional assessment criteria for Article 102 TFEU cases.

This chapter will discuss whether the 'power of Google' amounts to a dominant position within the meaning of European competition law, and if so, whether Google may have abused such dominant position. In this respect, this chapter will examine what an Article 102 TFEU assessment of Google would entail, and will speculate on the outcome of possible 102 proceedings initiated against Google by the European Commission. To this end, it will first set out the legal framework of Article 102 TFEU and explain this framework in short (2.2). Second, it will discuss the complaints that were filed against Google and that gave rise to the investigations by the European Commission, as well as several other (pending) antitrust investigations into Google's market power (2.3). Under (2.4) it will be examined which relevant market(s) should be defined and whether Google would hold a dominant position in such market. Finally, it will be assessed whether Google's conduct should be considered abusive (2.5).

2.2 Article 102 TFEU

Article 102 TFEU (formerly Article 82 of the EC Treaty) contains a prohibition on the abuse of a dominant position. Together with the cartel prohibition (Article 101 TFEU) and the rules on State Aid (Article 107 TFEU) it embodies the core of the EU competition rules. The European Commission in its function as the European Competition Authority enforces Article 102 TFEU. Decisions by the European Commission may be appealed to the General Court and the Court of Justice. The European Commission may impose structural measures upon a company that has violated Article 102 TFEU in order to restore competition, as well as a fine.

2.2.1 Dominance

The prohibition on abuse only applies to the conduct of undertakings with a dominant position. Hence, the assessment of dominance is an essential requirement for its application. In order to determine whether an undertaking is dominant within the meaning of Article 102 TFEU, first a relevant market has to be defined, because dominance as such does not exist. The concept only has meaning in relation to an actual market. Google, for example, does not have a dominant position on the banana market, but it may very well be dominant on the market for search engines.

2.2.1.1 Relevant Market

Article 102 TFEU itself does not contain any rules on market definition. However, in 1997 the European Commission issued a notice on this subject, setting out the factors and circumstances it considers decisive.[6] These guidelines are still the main reference model for market definition, both for the European Commission itself and for national competition authorities.[7] The most important factor in market definition is demand substitution: which products (or services) does the consumer consider substitutable? Together, these products constitute the relevant product market, which is the starting point for the assessment of dominance.

The relevant market also has a geographic dimension. The relevant geographic market comprises the area in which the conditions of competition are sufficiently homogeneous and which can be distinguished from neighboring areas because the conditions of competition are appreciably different in those areas.[8] This area is assessed by measuring demand substitutability as well.

A dominant position within the meaning of Article 102 TFEU has been defined by the European Court of Justice as a position of economic strength enjoyed by an undertaking, which enables it to prevent effective competition being maintained on a relevant market, by affording it the power to behave to an appreciable extent independently of its competitors, its customers and ultimately of consumers.[9] Such position of economic strength may appear from various factors such as high market shares, barriers to entry and economies of scale. According to its 2009 Guidance document[10] in relation to the assessment of exclusionary practices, the European Commission will in particular take into account the following:

- constraints imposed by the existing supplies from, and the position on the market of, actual competitors (the market position of the dominant undertaking and its competitors),
- constraints imposed by the credible threat of future expansion by actual competitors or entry by potential competitors (expansion and entry),

---

[6] *Commission notice on the definition of the relevant market for the purposes of Community competition law*, Official Journal C 372, 9.12.1997, pp 5–13.

[7] *DG Competition Discussion Paper on the application of article 82 of the Treaty to exclusionary abuses*, available at http://europa.eu.int/comm/competition/antitrust/others/discpaper2005.pdf, para 12.

[8] *Commission notice on the definition of the relevant market for the purposes of Community competition law*, para 8.

[9] See Case 27/76, *"United Brands Company and United Brands Continentaal v Commission"* [1978] ECR 207, para 65; Case 85/76, *"Hoffmann-La Roche & Co. v Commission"* [1979] ECR 461, para 38.

[10] *Guidance on the Commission's enforcement priorities in applying Article 82 of the EC Treaty to abusive exclusionary conduct by dominant undertakings*, Official Journal C 45/02, 24.02.2009, pp. 7–20.

- constraints imposed by the bargaining strength of the undertaking's customers (countervailing buyer power).[11]

Although the European Commission's focus on market share has diminished in the last decade,[12] it still seems the main focal point for the assessment of dominance.[13] The existence of barriers to entry however has become more and more important as a factor in establishing dominance. If it is highly difficult for other undertakings to enter the relevant market, the allegedly dominant undertaking enjoys a safe position in which it may increase prices or otherwise act at its own will, without being held back by any competitive constraints. However, the European Commission adheres to a rather broadly defined concept of barriers to entry. In the aforementioned Guidance document, it clarifies that barriers to entry may also 'take the form (...) of important technologies or an established distribution and sales network. They may also include costs and other impediments, for instance resulting from network effects, faced by customers in switching to a new supplier.'[14]

This definition of barriers to entry may be criticized for including factors that can be a direct result of the undertaking's own investments and efforts. If an undertaking has invested much in the development of a new technology, or has made considerable expenses in order to enter the market itself, why should competitors not be required to do the same? Network effects, moreover, occur in many information technology-related markets (including—to some extent—in the market for search engines, as will be discussed later on) and may benefit consumers. By qualifying these factors as barriers to entry, the European Commission arguably lowers the threshold for dominance.

Barriers to entry play an important role in the assessment of Google's position on the relevant market(s), as will be discussed later on in this chapter.

2.2.1.2 Dominance in New Economy Markets

'New economy markets' is a phrase generally used to indicate markets within the knowledge economy, where fast succession of technological changes and product innovation play a key role. Characteristics of such markets are: products that have a short life circle and are technically complex, the occurrence of standardization

---

[11] *Guidance on the Commission's enforcement priorities in applying Article 82 of the EC Treaty to abusive exclusionary conduct by dominant undertakings*, para 12.

[12] Mrs. Kroes, at that time EU Commissioner for Competition, stated in 2005: '(...) high market shares are not–on their own–sufficient to conclude that a dominant position exists. (...) A pure market share focus risks failing to take proper account of the degree to which competitors can constrain the behavior of the allegedly dominant company'. Speech delivered on September 23, 2005 in New York at the Fordham Corporate Law Institute.

[13] *Guidance on the Commission's enforcement priorities in applying Article 82 of the EC Treaty to abusive exclusionary conduct by dominant undertakings*, par 13 and the case law mentioned therein.

[14] Idem, para 17.

and a large need for product compatibility and interoperability.[15] It is argued by both lawyers and economists that market definition and the assessment of market power in such markets should be dealt with differently.[16]

In many new economy markets competition no longer revolves around price, but around innovation. Rather than taking place on the market, the competition is for the market. This is called *dynamic* competition (as opposed to *static* competition: competition on price). Consequently, in this type of competition the winner takes all: the most successful competitor shall dominate the whole market. This process is often called 'tipping'. This dominant position is nevertheless fragile, because if another competitor innovates successfully it may in turn take over the whole market.

Focus on product substitutability and market share will often fail to acknowledge these dynamics of new economy markets. High market shares do not properly reflect the competitive constraints that the 'winner' of the market in question is under. Also, products in the new economy are often technologically complex and hence their characteristics differ to a high extent, as a result of which consumers will perceive certain products as non substitutable, even though they may be substitutable on the basis of their prices.[17] As a consequence, an assessment of product substitutability will make the market seem narrower than it actually is.

When traditional methods for market definition are applied to markets in the new economy, this may therefore lead to the conclusion that an undertaking is dominant, whereas in reality the undertaking involved may be under severe competitive constraints. The European Commission however adheres to demand substitution and market share when it comes to market definition and establishing dominance. Several authors have criticized this focus on 'traditional' methods and price competition.[18]

As the market(s) that Google operates on should be qualified as new economy markets, the European Commission will need to take this into account when assessing Google's market position.

2.2.2 Abuse

Having a dominant position as such is not prohibited by Article 102 TFEU. However, the dominant undertaking has a 'special responsibility' toward the competitive process.[19] This means that a dominant undertaking is not allowed to abuse its position by adopting conduct that may be considered abusive.

---

[15] Rahnasto 2003, para 1.08–1.13; Temple Lang 1996.
[16] Ahlborn et al. 2001; Teece & Coleman 1998.
[17] Ahlborn et al. 2006, para 5.1.
[18] Ahlborn, et al. 2006; Veljanovski 2001; Bishop and Lexecon 2001.
[19] Case 322/81, *"Nederlandsche Banden Industrie Michelin (Michelin I) v Commission"* [1983] ECR 3461, para 57.

Article 102 TFEU lists several practices that are considered abusive:

(a) imposing unfair purchase or selling prices, or unfair trading conditions;
(b) limiting production, markets or technical development to the prejudice of consumers;
(c) applying dissimilar conditions to equivalent transactions with other trading parties, thereby placing them at a competitive disadvantage;
(d) making the conclusion of contracts subject to acceptance by the other parties of supplementary obligations which, by their nature or according to commercial usage, have no connection with the subject of such contracts.

This list is nonexhaustive; practices not listed may also be considered abusive. Generally speaking, abusive conduct can be divided into two categories: exploitative conduct (such as imposing unfair prices or trading conditions) and exclusionary conduct (such as contractual tying or refusal to deal), which is aimed at excluding competitors from the market. Over the last years, the European Commission has focused its enforcement on the last category. According to the European Commission, exclusionary conduct may completely or partially deny profitable expansion in or access to a market to actual or potential competitors and often serves as a basis for subsequent exploitation of consumers.[20]

The conduct that Google has been accused of most likely falls into the category of exclusionary abuse. The paragraph below will discuss the complaints recently issued to the European Commission, and give an overview of both pending and completed antitrust investigations into Google's market power in various jurisdictions.

2.3 Antitrust Investigations into Google's Market Power

2.3.1 United States

In the US, Google has been the subject of several antitrust investigations in relation to alleged abuse of market power. Much publicity has been given to the examination of the Department of Justice with respect to the recently rejected Google Books settlement.[21] Although the Google Books settlement would have had implications for the European market as well, its effects on competition would have differed from the effects in the US due to the fact that the settlement allowed for the availability of

---

[20] Speech at Fordham Corporate Law Institute by Mrs. Kroes, *supra*; *DG Competition Discussion Paper on the application of article 82 of the Treaty to exclusionary abuses*, para 1.

[21] *Statement of Interest by the U.S. Dept. of Justice Regarding the Proposed Settlement, Authors Guild, Inc. v. Google, Inc.*, Case No. 05 CV 8136 (DC) (S.D.N.Y. Feb. 4, 2010), available at http://thepublicindex.org/docs/amended_settlement/usa.pdf (last accessed January 21, 2011). Other matters involve "*Kinderstart.com LLC v. Google*" (No. 5:06-cv-02057-JF (N.D. Cal. July 13, 2006)), and the merger between Google and Doubleclick (which was approved by both the FTC and the European Commission; see *infra* for the decision of the latter).

full book content in the US, UK, Canada and Australia only.[22] This in itself did not mean that the settlement was outside the grasp of the European Commission, since European competition law covers all conduct that is capable of affecting trade between Member States,[23] however the implications of the settlement for the competitive process would probably have been less far-reaching than in the US. As the settlement has recently been rejected[24] and the Google Book Settlement as such is dealt with in a different chapter of this book, this chapter shall not include an assessment of the Google Books settlement under European competition law.

Recently, it became known that the Federal Trade Commission ('FTC') has launched an investigation into Google's practices as well.[25] The FTC has not (yet) given any insight into the focus of its investigations, however, reportedly it is looking into similar behavior as the practices that are under the scrutiny of the European Commission.[26] These will be discussed below.

2.3.2 Article 102 TFEU Complaints with the European Commission

The complaints that have been filed against Google with the European Commission were initiated by three companies: Foundem,[27] a UK price comparison website, Ciao,[28] a German price comparison website (and Microsoft subsidiary) and eJustice,[29] a French search engine directed at legal search requests. All three complainants offer so-called vertical search services: search engines aimed at dealing with search requests for specific content rather than dealing with general search requests. Vertical search engines can be highly interesting for advertisers because of the opportunities for targeting a specific group of customers. For example, a travel agency would prefer to advertise on Expedia (a vertical search engine for travel related services) rather than advertise on a search engine such as Google, where it is less sure that its advertisement will reach consumers looking for travel services.

---

[22] *Amended Settlement Agreement*, http://www.googlebooksettlement.com/r/view_settlement_ agreement (last accessed January 21, 2011), para 1.19.

[23] Article 101 TFEU and article 102 TFEU both require that the agreement or conduct *may* affect inter-State Trade. See also *European Commission Guidelines on the effect on trade concept contained in Articles 81 and 82 of the Treaty*, Official Journal C 101/07, 27.4.2004, pp 81–96.

[24] *Opinion of Federal Judge Chin of March 22, 2011*, http://thepublicindex.org/docs/ amended_settlement/opinion.pdf (last accessed August 31, 2011).

[25] Google Confirms F.T.C. Antitrust Inquiry, New York Times June 24, 2011, http:// bits.blogs.nytimes.com/2011/06/24/google-confirms-f-t-c-antitrust-inquiry/ (last accessed August 31, 2011).

[26] Google confirms US antitrust probe, http://www.theregister.co.uk/2011/06/26/google_acknowledges_ ftc_review/ (last accessed August 31, 2011).

[27] http://www.foundem.co.uk/

[28] http://www.ciao.de/

[29] http://www.ejustice.fr/

The complainants have complained to the European Commission that Google downgrades their web pages in its search results, thereby placing its own competing services at a more preferential position. As advertisers will most likely prefer to advertise on search engines with a higher ranking in search results, a consequence of downgrading competitors' web pages will be that they are less attractive to advertisers. As a result, this practice eventually leads to the exclusion of competitors offering vertical search services—thus claim the three complainants.

The complaints about downgrading relate to *unpaid* Google search results: search results that are also referred to as 'natural' or 'organic'. Unpaid search results may be distinguished from *paid* results or 'sponsored links': search results generated as a direct result of advertisers' payments. Apart from their complaint about downgrading web pages in unpaid search results, the above-mentioned companies have also accused Google of influencing paid search results: they claim that Google lowers the 'quality score' of their services. The quality score plays an important role in determining the price to be paid for advertising under Google's advertising service Adwords. It rates an advertiser's advertisement, webpage and/or keyword[30] in terms of relevance, and influences the 'CPC' or 'cost-per-click': the price that an advertiser has to pay when a user clicks on its advertisement. The higher the quality score, the lower the CPC and vice versa.

Apart from these complaints relating to paid and unpaid search results, the European Commission made clear in its announcement of November 30, 2010 that it will also look into allegations that Google imposes exclusivity obligations on advertising partners. Such obligations would involve a prohibition for advertising partners to place advertisements by competitors of Google on their websites. Further, it will investigate alleged restrictions on the portability of online advertising campaign data to competing online advertising platforms.[31] From the documentation made available by the European Commission it is unclear whether these allegations also stem from the aforementioned three companies.

In December 2010 it was reported that the European Commission has added complaints with the German competition authority ('*Bundeskartellamt*') by a mapping company, Euro-Cities,[32] and two German associations for newspaper publishers and magazine publishers (B.D.Z.V.[33] and V.D.Z[34]) to its investigations.[35]

---

[30] The reference word or phrase that triggers the display of an advertisement in Google. Advertisers register keywords of their choice with Google AdWords.

[31] Press statement IP/10/1624 by the European Commission, 30 November 2011, http://europa.eu/rapid/pressReleasesAction.do?reference=IP/10/1624&format=HTML&aged=0&language=EN&guiLanguage=en (last accessed January 16, 2011).

[32] http://www.euro-cities-ag.de/

[33] http://www.bdzv.de/home-engl.html

[34] http://www.vdz.de/

[35] See Google antitrust inquiry in Europe becomes broader, New York Times December 17, 2010, http://www.nytimes.com/2010/12/18/technology/18google.html (last accessed January 16, 2011); German news media challenge Google, Der Spiegel January 18, 2010, http://www.spiegel.de/international/business/0,1518,672580,00.html (last accessed February 18, 2011).

Eurocities claims that Google has integrated Google Maps on other websites for free, thereby depriving Eurocities of its chances to make money by selling its own maps. The complaints by the publishers' associations relate to downgrading search results, just as with Foundem, Ciao and eJustice. In this respect, the publishers' associations have asked for divulgation of the Google search algorithm. A further complaint of the publishers' associations concerns Google's practices in relation to the display of content. According to the publishers, Google earns a lot of money by displaying advertisements in close proximity to hyperlinks leading to newspaper and magazine articles. In this way, they argue, Google benefits from the efforts made by the publishers without paying them any remuneration.

The European Commission will thus investigate the following practices that Google is allegedly involved in:

- downgrading competitors' web pages in its unpaid ('organic') search results;
- manipulating paid search results by influencing the quality score of competitors' services;
- imposing anti-competitive contractual restrictions on its advertising partners by prohibiting them to show advertisements of Google's competitors as well as by restricting the portability of their advertising campaigns to competing platforms;
- offering its own products for free, thereby putting its competitors out of business;
- using third party content to make money through advertisements, without paying any remuneration.

In spring 2011 it further became known that Google's competitor Microsoft has also submitted complaints with respect to Google's behavior to the European Commission. According to Microsoft, these complaints relate to alleged restrictions with respect to the access to and interoperability with You Tube, Google's alleged attempts to monopolize search results from "orphan books" and possibly anti-competitive contractual restrictions for advertisers and website owners.[36] At the time of writing of this chapter, the European Commission has not confirmed whether it has added these complaints to its investigation. If so, the investigation will become much broader and should be even more interesting than it already is. Especially the complaint in relation to lack of interoperability, which noticeably seems quite similar to the practice Microsoft itself was condemned for by the General Court in 2007, could be a challenge for the European Commission, as this complaint could involve forced access to Google's intellectual property.

Before examining whether Google indeed would be held dominant and if so, whether the above-mentioned practices would be considered abusive under EU law, we will first discuss the recent investigations into Google's market power by the French and Italian competition authorities.

---

[36] Adding our Voice to Concerns about Search in Europe, http://blogs.technet.com/b/microsoft_on_the_issues/archive/2011/03/30/adding-our-voice-to-concerns-about-search-in-europe.aspx (last accessed August 31, 2011).

2.3.3 *Investigations by European National Competition Authorities*

2.3.3.1 Autorité de la Concurrence *(French Competition Authority)*

In December 2010, the *Autorité de la Concurrence* concluded an investigation into the French online advertising sector. The investigation was triggered by a request of the Minister for Economy, Finance and Employment (*ministre de l'Economie, des Finances et de l'Emploi*) in accordance with Article L.462-1 of the French Code of Commercial Law (*Code de Commerce*).[37] This article provides for a consultation of the *Autorité* by parliamentary institutions. These are no 'real' antitrust proceedings as the *Autorité* does not issue an official decision directed at a specific company, but merely delivers an opinion.

The *Autorité* reached the conclusion that Google has a dominant position on the advertising market linked to search engines. According to the *Autorité*, search-related advertising represents a specific market that is not substitutable with other forms of communication.[38] In this respect, the *Autorité* considered it of crucial importance that the online advertising market allows advertisers to fine-tune the targeting of certain groups of consumers. Thus, advertisers are able to present consumers with an offer tailored to their needs, based on the consumer's search activity.[39] Google, which was heard by the *Autorité* as part of a large-scale consultation with entities in the online advertising sector, had argued that there is no separate market for online advertising, but rather a market for advertising in general, be it online or offline. Its main argument to support this view was that both online and offline advertising allow for cross-selling: many advertisers target several platforms (internet, mobile platforms, regular press) as part of the same campaign. However, the *Autorité* decided that this could also mean that online and offline advertising should in fact be regarded as *complementary*, and hence are to be dealt with as separate markets.[40]

---

[37] Article L462-1 reads: 'The Council on Competition may be consulted by the parliamentary committees with regard to bills and any issues relating to competition. It shall give its opinion on any competition issue at the request of the government. It may also give its opinion on the same issues at the request of the territorial authorities, professional associations and trade unions, approved consumer organisations, chambers of agriculture, chambers of trade or chambers of trade and industry, with regard to the interests for which these are responsible.'

[38] Press release of the *Autorité de la Concurrence* of 14 December 2010, available at http://www.autoritedelaconcurrence.fr/user/standard.php?id_rub=368&id_article=1514 (last accessed January 22, 2011).

[39] Press release of the *Autorité de la Concurrence* of 14 December 2010; *Opinion of the Autorité de la Concurrence on competition in the online search market*, available in English at http://www.autoritedelaconcurrence.fr/doc/10a29_en.pdf (last accessed August 31, 2011).

[40] *Opinion of the Autorité de la Concurrence on competition in the online search market*, pp 24–27.

With respect to the position of Google on the online advertising market related to search engines, the *Autorité* concluded that it holds a position of dominance. The *Autorité* based its conclusion on several observations:

- Google's high market share on the aforementioned market in France (over 90%) and the fact that it has held such market share for several years now;
- Google's high profits in comparison with its competitors' profits;
- the fact that Google can allow itself to largely ignore the dissatisfaction of its customers (the advertisers that it has a contractual relationship with);
- the existence of barriers to entry.[41]

The *Autorité* clarifies that Google's dominant position as such is not prohibited, as it stems from 'a great deal of innovation, supported by significant and continuous investments'.[42] However, it also identifies behavior by Google that may be deemed abusive, as both exclusionary and exploitative prohibited conduct. Several practices are highlighted in this respect:

- the artificial raising of barriers to entry through exclusionary (AdSense) contracts and by putting up technical obstacles (particularly making it harder for other search engines to index YouTube, Google's video service) (exclusionary);
- using leverage power: by manipulating competitors' quality scores, by favoring 'Google Maps' over competitors' mapping services when displaying geographic search results and by participating in AdWords biddings with its own services (exclusionary);
- lack of transparency and possible discrimination in relation to the AdWords mechanism[43] (exploitative);
- lack of transparency with regard to the calculation of revenues with regard to its AdSense services (exploitative).[44]

---

[41] *Opinion of the Autorité de la Concurrence on competition in the online search market*, p 48.

[42] Press release of the *Autorité de la Concurrence* of 14 December 2010. It has to be added that even if the Autorité would not have perceived Google's position the result of significant innovation, Google's position as such could not have been prohibited. French competition law (just as European competition law) does not prohibit a dominant position *per se*, only the abuse of such position.

[43] In June 2010, the *Autorité de la Concurrence* had already imposed interim measures on Google Inc. and Google Ireland as a result of such lack of transparency (*European Competition Network brief 05-2010*, available at http://ec.europa.eu/competition/ecn/brief/05_2010/fr_google.pdf (last accessed January 23, 2011). This decision was prompted by a complaint by Navx, a company selling databases for GPS navigation, indicating the localization of mobile and fixed speed traps. Navx's AdWords account had suddenly been suspended by Google because Google decided to change its policy for advertisers selling devices aimed at evading speed cameras. Google was instructed to restore Navx's account and improve transparency on its policy.

[44] *Opinion of the Autorité de la Concurrence on competition in the online search market*, pp 53–62.

As indicated above, the opinion of the *Autorité de la Concurrence* is not an official decision and the practices identified should be investigated in the context of a specific complaint. However, the *Autorité's* investigation was quite extensive, and despite the fact that it relates to French competition law, it will most probably be read with close attention by the European Commission in the course of its own investigations.

2.3.3.2 Autorità Garante della Concorrenza e del Mercato *(Italian Competition Authority)*

Finally, a short note on pending antitrust investigations into Google's market power by the Italian competition authority. The Italian competition authority (*Autorità Garante della Concorrenza e del Mercato* or 'AGCM') had opened an investigation in August 2009, looking into alleged tying between Google search and Google News. The Italian association of Newspaper and Periodical publishers had complained that publishers lacked control over their publications being used in Google News. Publishers were nevertheless forced not to extract their publications therefrom, as these would then also be excluded from Google search itself. To address the AGCM's concerns, Google proposed to introduce a new dedicated search functionality for Google News, so that publishers can exclude their content from Google News without the risk of excluding them from Google search.[45]

The AGCM also had another concern: the contract conditions imposed by Google in the framework of the AdSense program. It added these to its investigation, thus widening its scope. In this respect, Google proposed to increase transparency in the revenue sharing formula relating to AdSense and modifications thereto.[46]

In January 2011, it became known that the AGCM has accepted Google's commitments and has abandoned the case.[47]

---

[45] *European Competition Network brief 03-2010*, available at http://ec.europa.eu/competition/ecn/brief/03_2010/it_google.pdf (last accessed January 23, 2011).

[46] Idem.

[47] Press release of the AGCM of January 17, 2011, available at http://www.agcm.it/stampa/news/5194-a420-as787-antitrust-accetta-impegni-di-google-e-chiede-al-parlamento-di-adeguare-le-norme-sul-diritto-dautore.html (last accessed January 23, 2011). See also, the related news item at http://www.bloomberg.com/news/2011-01-17/italy-antitrust-accepts-google-commitments-for-web-publishers.html (last accessed January 23, 2011). The AGCM stated that it also submitted a report to the Italian government, recommending that Italian copyright laws be reformed in order to deal with the complex issues of the online dissemination of copyrighted works.

2.4 Google's Power

2.4.1 Initial Observations

Above, I have set out the contours of Article 102 TFEU and have given a brief overview of antitrust investigations into Google's market power. Now, I shall discuss whether Google's power would indeed amount to a dominant position within the meaning of Article 102 TFEU. As mentioned, this involves an assessment of the relevant product- and geographical markets.

With respect to the assessment of Google's dominance in relation to Article 102 TFEU, several observations may be made:

- The companies that have submitted complaints against Google with the European Commission do not compete with Google on the market for search engines itself, but on related markets;
- With respect to the Google/DoubleClick merger, in 2008 the European Commission has already defined several relevant markets in relation to Google[48];
- The market(s) Google operates on must be characterized as new economy market(s), where Google can be considered a 'first mover'.

These observations should be taken into account when assessing Google's dominance.

2.4.2 Google and the Relevant Market

What relevant market(s) should be distinguished in relation to the complaints that are now before the European Commission with regard to Google's alleged dominance? Below, we will examine several options for the definition of both the relevant product and the relevant geographical market.

2.4.2.1 Commission Decision in the Google/DoubleClick Merger

As indicated above, the European Commission has identified relevant product and geographical markets in relation to the Google/DoubleClick merger. Although in principle the relevant market has to be defined in each particular case separately and market definition with respect to merger control may differ from market

---

[48] *Commission Decision of 11.03.2008, declaring a concentration to be compatible with the common market and the functioning of the EEA Agreement, case No COMP/M.4731–Google/DoubleClick*, available at http://ec.europa.eu/competition/mergers/cases/decisions/m4731_20080311_20682_en.pdf (last accessed January 29, 2011).

definition in relation to possible abuse of dominance,[49] the Commission's market definition in relation to this merger could give some useful indications.

In its Google/DoubleClick merger decision, the European Commission identified several relevant markets. Just as with the investigation by the French competition Authority, Google/DoubleClick had argued that there is one market for both online and offline advertising. The Commission did not agree with this: offline and online advertising were perceived as separate markets by most of the Commission's respondents, and—it was argued—online advertising is much more capable of reaching a targeted audience. Also, the Commission stated, the measurement of the effectiveness of online advertising can be much more precise.[50] Thus, there is a separate market for online advertising. According to the Commission, it could be that the market for online advertising has to be further distinguished into separate markets for search- and non-search-related advertising,[51] but it did not reach a conclusion on this point.[52]

Further, the Commission identified a separate market for intermediation in advertising services, as it considers that the direct sale of advertising space ('inventory') is often not an option for smaller content publishers.[53] Third, it identified a separate market for the provision of ad serving technology (DoubleClick's core business),[54] which—according to the Commission—may be further subdivided into markets for ad serving technology for text advertisements and for display advertisements.[55] Within these subdivided markets, the Commission suggested that there might even be a further subdivision into the provision of the services to advertisers and to publishers.[56]

---

[49] For example, the SSNIP ('Small but Significant Increase in Price') test for product substitutability may provide better results within the context of merger control. The reason for this is that with mergers, generally the situation in which a dominant undertaking has elevated prices to such extent that every product will—unjustifiably—be considered a substitute (the so-called *Cellophane Fallacy*) will not occur as often as it does in relation to dominance.

[50] *Commission Decision of 11.03.2008, declaring a concentration to be compatible with the common market and the functioning of the EEA Agreement, case No COMP/M.4731–Google/DoubleClick*, para 45.

[51] 'Search related' advertising concerns advertisements that appear next to the results of search queries by internet users, such as the 'sponsored links' appearing after entering a search request in Google. 'Non-search related' advertising concerns advertisements that can appear on any webpage and are not triggered by search requests (such as banners).

[52] *Commission Decision of 11.03.2008, declaring a concentration to be compatible with the common market and the functioning of the EEA Agreement, case No COMP/M.4731–Google/DoubleClick*, para 48–56.

[53] Idem, para 57–73.

[54] Ad Serving technology is technology used to ensure correct placing of the advertisements, monitor their financial performance and manage the content publisher's inventory.

[55] *Commission Decision of 11.03.2008, declaring a concentration to be compatible with the common market and the functioning of the EEA Agreement, case No COMP/M.4731–Google/DoubleClick*, para 74–81.

[56] Idem, para 79–81.

With regard to the geographical market, the Commission ruled that this market consisted of—at least—the European Economic Area, except with regard to the market for online advertising. This market was deemed to be divided alongside national or linguistic borders.[57]

Does this market definition by the European Commission provide any leads for the definition of relevant market(s) with respect to the current complaints?

2.4.2.2 Product Market Definition

The Commission decision regarding Google/DoubleClick concerned the merger of two undertakings active in the field of online advertising—Google itself as a platform providing online advertising space and DoubleClick as a seller of ad serving services. Therefore, it is not a surprise that the relevant markets defined by the Commission all concern markets encompassing or related to online advertising.

However, not all of the companies complaining to the European Commission about Google's alleged dominance are also in this field. While eJustice, Ciao and Foundem all offer vertical search services and may therefore be considered to compete with Google on the market for providing online advertising space, the German publishers' association and Eurocities are content providers. As the investigation into Google would concern a market definition with regard to possible dominance, in principle the activities of the complainants are not decisive, however when choosing a starting point for market definition they are not entirely irrelevant either. For example, if the Commission would have to decide on the alleged dominance of a company producing and selling bananas, it would probably be quite pointless to test whether shoes constitute a substitute product. The question is therefore where to start when defining the relevant market in relation to the current complaints.

In this respect, it has to be taken into account that Google is much more than only a platform for online advertising space. Apart from its primary activity as a search engine, it also offers software (-applications) such as Gmail, Google Talk, Google Chrome and Google Maps, it exploits content (YouTube) and it offers services such as AdSense and Google Product search. One could therefore imagine that the Commission would define several markets.

It is likely that there are two 'main' markets that can be identified in relation to Google: the market for providing internet search results and the market for online advertising. These markets will be interrelated, as companies that offer search engines generally use a business model in which the search result services are financed by selling advertisements. As mentioned above, with respect to Google/DoubleClick merger the Commission suggested that this market could be (sub)-divided into a market for search-related advertising and for non-search-related advertising, because from a content publisher's perspective search-related

---

[57] Idem, para 82–91.

advertising and non-search-related advertising are not substitutable. The reason for this, it argued, is that search-related advertisements are generally shown on a different website and thus—so may be concluded—do not generate any income for the content publisher.[58] This assumption, however, is based on a rather narrow interpretation of the concept of search-related advertising, whereby (apart from search engines themselves) only embedded search engine boxes are connected with search-related advertising. However, in practice many content publishers offer search services that provide results for search queries within their own website.[59] Therefore, search-related advertising may be profitable for content publishers as well. The distinction between a market for search and non-search-related advertising should therefore in my opinion be abandoned.

With respect to the market for search results however, it could be argued that a separate market for the provision of vertical search services is to be distinguished. Although the search results that are generated through a vertical search service may also be found through a general search engine, it is likely that there is a specific consumer demand for vertical search engines. For example, Dutch internet users looking for houses for sale would rather use the vertical search engine 'Funda', than a general search engine, since such a search engine may not allow the user to fine-tune its search with regard to the price, location, etcetera. As the General Court has held with respect to *Microsoft*, the existence of a separate consumer demand may be decisive in respect to the existence of a separate market.[60] It could thus be argued that there is a separate market for vertical search engines.

In sum, with regard to the current antitrust investigation into Google, the following relevant product markets may be defined: the market for online advertising services, the market for internet search results and the market for vertical search results.

2.4.2.3 Geographical Market Definition

The definition of the geographical market will not be as straightforward as it may seem. Despite the world-wide accessibility of the internet, users' preferences are often nationally (or at least linguistically) oriented. Nevertheless, with respect to the market for search results I would argue that it is a world-wide market, as the conditions for competition are similar in each country (with the exception, perhaps, of countries where internet access and companies' online activities are restricted). However, the markets for vertical search engines and online advertising

---

[58] *Commission Decision of 11.03.2008, declaring a concentration to be compatible with the common market and the functioning of the EEA Agreement, case No COMP/M.4731–Google/ DoubleClick*, para 54.

[59] See, e.g., the Times' website (http://www.thetimes.co.uk/tto/news/).

[60] Case T-201/04, *"Microsoft v EC Commission"* [2007] ECR II-3601, para 917.

services identified above seem to be much more nationally oriented, as the conditions for competition (such as advertising prices) are likely to vary much more with respect to these markets. For these markets, I would think that the European Commission's decision in the Google/Double Click merger could be followed and that these markets should be defined along linguistic/national borders.[61]

2.4.3 Google and Dominance

Would the European Commission assess that Google is dominant in relation to the above-mentioned markets?

2.4.3.1 Competitive Restraints

As discussed earlier, when assessing Google's position, the European Commission will have to take into account the fact that market share may not be a useful indication for dominance with respect to the markets Google operates on. These markets qualify as new economy markets, where competition is all about innovation, and dominant positions may be highly transitory. Also, even though Google holds a large market share on the market for search results, this may be different in respect to the markets for online advertising services and vertical search engines.

A better way to measure Google's position on the identified markets, would be to analyze the competitive restraints Google is under. Does potential entry of Google's competitors to the market pose a serious threat to Google's position? The answer to this question is not a definitive 'no', and could even be a 'yes'. A few examples: Bing, Microsoft's search engine, has rapidly reached a market share of 12% in the US since its introduction in 2009.[62] Microsoft and Yahoo have started a 'search alliance', thereby cooperating in order to attack Google's position on the search engine and online advertising markets.[63] Companies that have market power in different but related markets, such as the market for internet browsers,

---

[61] *Commission Decision of 11.03.2008, declaring a concentration to be compatible with the common market and the functioning of the EEA Agreement, case No COMP/M.4731–Google/ DoubleClick*, para 82–91.

[62] ComScore reports of November 2010, available at http://www.comscore.com/Press_Events/ Press_Releases/2010/12/comScore_Releases_November_2010_U.S._Search_Engine_Rankings www.comscore (last accessed February 12, 2011). According to these numbers, Bing's market share in the US would even be almost 30%, if one would also count the market share of Yahoo's search engine (which uses Bing's algorithms as a result of the above-mentioned 'search alliance' between Microsoft and Yahoo). In Europe however, Bing's (and Yahoo's) market share is allegedly still small.

[63] http://www.searchalliance.com/home (last accessed February 18, 2011).

may use their position in those markets to enter the search engine market. The obvious example here is Microsoft's Bing, but one can imagine what could happen if Apple was to introduce a new general search engine.

Given these developments, it is not so self-evident that Google is under no competitive threat at all. As Google itself smartly remarked in its press statement after the European Commission announced that it would commence antitrust investigations: '(…) competition is only one click away'.[64] This may however not be too far from the truth.

Moreover: network effects, that characterize many new economy markets, play a less important role in the markets that Google is active on. For an internet user, the value of a search engine does not increase when more people start using it, as opposed to—for example—an operating system or word processor. On the other hand, network effects do occur with respect to Google's paying customers: the advertisers. However, these network effects are slightly different from 'ordinary' network effects: to the advertisers the value of the search engine does not increase when more advertisers start using it, but when more internet users start using it. In this respect, the search engine and related online advertising market resemble markets that need to have an 'installed base' before being able to function properly, such as markets for video games, where companies first have to attract a sufficient amount of console users before their can persuade game developers to build games for a certain platform. These markets are often identified as 'two sided industries'.[65] This characterization applies—to some extent—to the relationship between the market for online advertising services and the market for search results: before being able to attract sufficient advertisers, a search engine company has to have an installed base of customers using the search engine. However, it is important to note that—as opposed to, for example, the market for video games—this interdependence is not protected by a proprietary technology: both users and advertisers may switch to a different search engine without being restrained by proprietary lock-in effects. The fact that they have not done so (yet), could be the result of Google's first mover advantage rather than an indication of the existence of barriers to entry. In this respect, I disagree with the opinion of the Autorité de la Concurrence, where it states that high fixed costs for developing and testing new algorithms constitute a barrier to entry.[66]

It is argued that the specific characteristics of the market(s) that Google operates on should be taken into account when assessing its position, and here the absence of proprietary lock-in effects in these markets could indicate that barriers to entry may not be that high. This would mean that Google is under competitive constraint, even though it may have a high market share on the markets identified.

---

[64] Our thoughts on the Commission review, available at http://googlepublicpolicy.blogspot.com/2010/11/our-thoughts-on-european-commission.html (last accessed February 12, 2011).

[65] Jones and Sufrin 2011, p 79.

[66] *Opinion of the Autorité de la Concurrence on competition in the online search market, supra,* p 46.

The European Commission should arguably take this into account in its investigation.

2.4.3.2 Assessment by the European Commission

In the past, the European Commission has shown that it is not always susceptible to arguments relating to the special characteristics of new economy markets. In the *France Télécom* case, the Commission largely ignored the company's argument that its high market share on the—then emerging—market for high speed internet access was not representative, ruling that its increasing high market shares over a two-year period was a clear indication of dominance.[67] With respect to the *Microsoft* case, the Commission noted that it would not be hesitant in applying (traditional) antitrust analysis to 'hi-tech' markets, and that it even considered some aspects of such markets (such as network effects) as an especially strong indication of dominance.[68]

Also, the Commission has held undertakings to be dominant because they were an 'unavoidable trading partner'. As mentioned, the European Court of Justice has identified the criterion 'unavoidable trading partner' as the essential test for dominance,[69] but the Commission has deemed undertakings to be an 'unavoidable trading partner' merely because they became the most important trader in the field, not because competitors and consumers did not have any alternatives. Such has happened, for example, in the case of *Intel*, where the Commission ruled that for Intel's customers, a switch to a different supplier was 'unrealistic'.[70] Such assessment might be applied by the Commission to Google as well: despite the fact that customers and consumers are able to switch to a different search engine, it may rule that Google is still an 'unavoidable trading partner', merely by its current status in the market.

Considering the above, there is a fair chance that the European Commission will focus on Google's high market shares and the fact that it has become the most important player in the market when assessing Google's position in the market. However, it should also take into account the characteristics of the markets involved and perform an analysis of the competitive constraints that Google is

---

[67] Commission Decision of 16 july 2003 relating to a proceeding under Article 82 of the EC Treaty. (COMP/38.233 - Wanadoo Interactive), http://ec.europa.eu/competition/antitrust/cases/dec_docs/38233/38233_87_1.pdf (last accessed February 12, 2011), para 211–222.

[68] Commission Decision of 24.03.2004 relating to a proceeding under Article 82 of the EC Treaty (Case COMP/C-3/37.792 *Microsoft*), http://ec.europa.eu/competition/antitrust/cases/dec_docs/37792/37792_4177_1.pdf (last accessed February 12, 2011), para 470.

[69] Case 85/76, "*Hoffmann-La Roche & Co. v Commission*" [1979] ECR 461, *supra*.

[70] Commission Decision of 13 May 2009 relating to a proceeding under Article 82 of the EC Treaty and Article 54 of the EEA Agreement (COMP/C-3/37.990 - Intel), http://ec.europa.eu/competition/antitrust/cases/dec_docs/37990/37990_3581_11.pdf (last accessed February 12, 2011).

under, to see if this high market share is really a clear indication of dominance. This may be less self-evident than it seems.

2.5 Google's Abuse

As demonstrated above, it is argued that it is less sure that Google holds a dominant position within the meaning of Article 102 TFEU than it may initially appear. Let us assume, however, that the European Commission is to consider Google as being dominant in the relevant markets: will it then consider its behavior to be abusive?

2.5.1 Practices to be investigated

The following practices by Google that will be investigated by the European Commission have been identified previously in this Chapter:

1. downgrading competitors' web pages in unpaid ('organic') search results;
2. manipulating paid search results by influencing the quality score of competitors' services;
3. imposing anti-competitive contractual restrictions on advertising partners by prohibiting them to show advertisements of Google's competitors as well as by restricting the portability of their advertising campaigns to competing platforms;
4. offering products for free, thereby putting competitors out of business;
5. using third-party content to make money through advertisements, without paying a remuneration.

Below, we will address these practices and discuss whether they would constitute an abuse under Article 102 TFEU.

2.5.1.1 Downgrading Web Pages; Manipulating Search Results

The practices mentioned above under 1. and 2. are discussed simultaneously, as they both concern behavior where the dominant undertaking favors its own products or services on an ancillary market over its competitors products and services.

Both with respect to the first-mentioned practice, the downgrading of competitors' web pages in unpaid search results and the second mentioned practice, the manipulation of paid search results, it is quite likely that the Commission will consider this to be abusive—provided, however, that the complainants and the European Commission succeed in proving that Google actually and deliberately indeed downgrades their web pages. This could pose some problems, as Google itself denies this and claims that the complainants' websites do not obtain high search rankings because they copy most of their data from other websites.[71] 'We built Google for users, not for websites. (...) Not every website can come out on top' it stated in its response to the announcement by the European Commission of November 30, 2010.[72] In this respect, the European Commission may ask for disclosure of Google's algorithm (for the purpose of proceedings only).

If it is demonstrated that Google intervenes in its search results in order to give its own websites (such as Google Product, a vertical search engine that complainant Foundem has specifically protested about[73]) a higher ranking, this is likely to be considered abusive. The practice could be compared to a shop owner favoring its own products by giving them a much better display in the shop, even though there is a higher demand for its competitor's products. Whereas one may argue that this is normal competitive behavior, since the shop owner is the one investing in the shop and should therefore be able to favor its own products, the European Court of Justice's case law points in a different direction. In its leading judgment on this matter, *Commercial Solvents*,[74] the ECJ ruled that a dominant undertaking that refuses to supply a competitor in a derivative market because it wishes to enter this market itself, abuses its dominance. This situation is not entirely similar to the practice Google is allegedly involved in, because Google has not refused to display the complainant's websites altogether. However, it shows that behavior of a dominant undertaking which is aimed at excluding competitors from an ancillary market, because it wants to enter such market itself, is generally considered to abusive under Article 102 TFEU. Also, it is recalled that the *Autorité de la Concurrence* has identified exactly the same practices by Google as likely to be abusive.[75]

Further, there is a possibility that the European Commission would consider the above-mentioned practices by Google as abusive tying or bundling. In this respect, the Commission could consider that the supply of Google's search engine services and the supply of its products on the derivative market (the Google websites competing with the complainant's websites) are in fact tied together, so that consumers have less choice and competitors will be excluded from the market for the tied product. In its 2009 Guidance paper on exclusionary abuses, the Commission has identified the following requirements for abusive tying:

- the undertaking is dominant in the tying product market, and:
- the tying product and the tied products are two distinctive products, and:

---

[71] EU launches Google investigation after complaints, http://www.reuters.com/article/2010/11/30/us-eu-google-probe-idUSTRE6AT1L220101130 (last accessed February 18, 2011).

[72] See Google, Our thoughts on the Commission review, *supra*.

[73] Foundem has explained the backgrounds of its complaint to the European Commission on its website http://www.searchneutrality.org/, thereby comparing the search results for its own price comparison website with the results for Google Product.

[74] Cases 6/73 and 7/73, *"ICI and Commercial Solvents v Commission"* [1974] ECR 223.

[75] *Opinion of the Autorité de la Concurrence on competition in the online search market, supra.*

- the tying practice is likely to lead to anti-competitive foreclosure.[76]

These conditions could be deemed fulfilled with respect to the practices Google allegedly is involved in. However, in its *Microsoft* decision, the General Court identified a fourth requirement for abusive tying, namely that the dominant undertaking does not give consumers a choice to obtain the tying product without the tied product.[77] This requirement would be a particular impediment for a finding of abusive tying with respect to Google's alleged behavior, as consumers typically are under no obligation to use the Google search engine if they do not use Google's other products (and vice versa). However, the Commission could decide to 'incorporate' this condition of (lack of) consumer choice into the requirement of foreclosure: if in the end all competitors are removed from the market, consumers will have no choices left.[78] Nevertheless, the argument for abusive tying in relation to the above-mentioned practices seems less strong than the argument for foreclosure on the basis of the *Commercial Solvents* case law.

In sum, it is argued that—provided that Google will be held dominant and it is demonstrated that the alleged practices actually occur—both the downgrading of competitor's web pages in unpaid search results and the manipulation of paid search results will be deemed abusive.

2.5.1.2 Imposing Anti-competitive Contractual Restrictions on Advertising Partners

With respect to the allegations that Google has imposed exclusivity obligations on its contracting partners in the online advertising market, it is not unlikely that this behavior will be considered abusive as well. In the past, the European Court of Justice has severely condemned exclusivity obligations imposed on customers in derivative markets.[79]

The prohibition not to advertise for competitors of the dominant undertaking, as Google allegedly has imposed on its customers, has been specifically addressed in one of the ECJ's leading cases, *United Brands*.[80] In this case it was ruled that United Brands' refusal to supply a customer who had taken part in an advertising campaign for one of United Brands' biggest competitors was abusive. However, this concerned an absolute refusal to supply as a punishment for advertising for a

---

[76] *Guidance on the Commission's enforcement priorities in applying Article 82 of the EC Treaty to abusive exclusionary conduct by dominant undertakings*, para 50.

[77] Case 201/04, *"Microsoft v Commission"* [2007] ECR II-3601, para 864 and 962.

[78] Jones and Sufrin 2011, p 478.

[79] See, e.g., Case C-310/93P, *BPB*, and Case T-65/89, *"BPB Industries and British Gypsum v. Commission"* [1993] ECR II-389.

[80] Case 27/76, *"United Brands Company and United Brands Continentaal v Commission"* [1978] ECR 207.

competitor and not merely a contractual obligation. Moreover, the ECJ's ruling has been criticized on this point.[81]

Whether any exclusivity obligations imposed by Google will be deemed abusive arguably depends on the exact nature of these obligations. Exclusive (purchasing) contracts, obliging the customer to buy only the dominant undertaking's product or services, are generally considered abusive, as well as loyalty contracts, promising the customer priority deals or lower prices if it purchases exclusively with the dominant undertaking.[82] Restricting its customer's possibility to take its business to other companies offering online advertising services is likely to be deemed abusive if Google is considered to be an unavoidable trading partner.[83] However, with respect to a mere prohibition to advertise for competitors it may be argued that even a dominant company should be allowed to defend its commercial interests in this way. It is fully understandable that it could be quite destructive to a company's commercial policy if its customers engage in advertising for the company's competitors.

Therefore, it is hard to predict what will be the outcome of the assessment of Google's allegedly imposed exclusivity obligations without being familiar with the content of the contracts concerned. However, if such contracts would oblige the customer to purchase all its online advertising services with Google and would prohibit such customer to change to another supplier, it is not unlikely that this will be considered abusive.

2.5.1.3 Integrating Third Party Products on Other Websites for Free

The complaint issued by Eurocities relates to so-called predatory behavior: the dominant undertaking lowers its prices for a certain product to such an extent, that competitors are unable to compete and are driven off the market. Whether certain behavior should be considered predatory and therefore anti-competitive is often difficult to assess. The reason for this is not only that predatory pricing may benefit consumers in the short term (they receive the product at lower price or even—as is the case with Google Maps—for free), but also that there is a thin line between temporarily lowering prices as part of a normal business strategy and real predatory behavior.[84]

---

[81] Jones and Sufrin 2011, p 484, as well as the there cited article by P. Jebsen and R. Stevens 'Assumptions, goals, and dominant undertakings: the regulation of competition under the article 86 of the European Union', (64) Antitrust L.J. 1996, pp 510–511.

[82] Cases 40/73, "*SuikerUnie v. Commission*", [1975] ECR 1663, Case 85/76, "*Hoffmann-La Roche & Co. v Commission*" [1979] ECR 461, Case 322/81, "*Nederlandsche Banden Industrie Michelin (Michelin I) v Commission*" [1983] ECR 3461.

[83] *Guidance on the Commission's enforcement priorities in applying Article 82 of the EC Treaty to abusive exclusionary conduct by dominant undertakings*, para 36.

[84] Jones and Sufrin 2011, pp 392–393.

The European Commission and the ECJ have developed a test for predatory pricing in the case of *"AKZO"*,[85] which—in short—entails that if the company charges prices below average costs, these are presumed to be predatory, and that if prices are above average cost but below total costs, the prices are considered predatory if they are proved to be part of a plan to eliminate competitors. This test is however much disputed, as it may be difficult to assess whether costs are fixed or variable and also because there may be rational business reasons for pricing beneath average costs. In its Guidance paper, the European Commission states the following with regard to predation: '(…) the Commission will generally intervene where there is evidence showing that a dominant undertaking engages in predatory conduct by deliberately incurring losses or foregoing profits in the short term (referred to hereafter as 'sacrifice'), so as to foreclose or be likely to foreclose one or more of its actual or potential competitors with a view to strengthening or maintaining its market power, thereby causing consumer harm'.[86]

Would offering Google Maps for free amount to predatory pricing? The price Google charges is obviously below average costs as the product is offered for free, and one may argue that for this reason this practice thus falls within the test for predation as developed by the Commission and the ECJ. However this argument fails to take into account the fact that this is Google's business model. Google offers products for free, and makes money by selling advertisements related to these products. Google Search functions in the exact same way.

Moreover, an important requirement for the finding of predatory behavior is the existence of barriers to entry. Without barriers to entry, the eliminated competitors will immediately return to the market once the undertaking concerned raises prices. As mentioned above, it may be argued that in Google's case barriers to entry are not so high. This would plead against a finding of predatory behavior.

Finally, it is often argued that predatory pricing is a normal business strategy in new economy markets, as companies often lower their prices in order to win the competition race for the market. This reasoning could be applied to Google as well.

Considering the above, there are quite a few arguments against considering Google's behavior in relation to Google Maps abusive within the meaning of Article 102 TFEU. However, the European Commission has shown in the past that it is reluctant to take into account the 'new economy market' argument[87] and may still consider Google's behavior as a 'sacrifice' and therefore abusive.

---

[85] Case C-62/86, *"AKZO Chemie B.V. v Commission"* [1991] ECR I-3359.

[86] *Guidance on the Commission's enforcement priorities in applying Article 82 of the EC Treaty to abusive exclusionary conduct by dominant undertakings*, para 63. See also *supra*, Sect. 2.4.3.2.

[87] Commission Decision regarding *"France Télécom"*, *supra*.

2.5.2 Using Third Party Content to Make Money by Placing Advertisements, Without Paying a Remuneration

Finally, the complaint made by the German publisher's associations that relates to the use of content in order to generate advertising revenue, without paying remuneration. The exact nature of this complaint has not yet been disclosed, but according to several media the complaint revolves around Google's display of 'snippets' of third party content in Google News.[88] If so, this complaint relates to the practice that was also investigated by the Italian Competition Authority.[89]

Google News displays hyperlinks to news messages from different content websites, together with the first two or three lines of the message concerned. If the internet user clicks the hyperlink, it is guided to the corresponding page on the news source's website. The publishers allegedly are concerned about the fact that Google earns money by offering this service, whereas the content it revolves around is actually theirs.

I would argue that this complaint is more related to unfair competition (as opposed to unlawful competition within the meaning of the TFEU) or infringement of intellectual property rights rather than possible abuse of a dominant position. If Google is allowed to display the 'snippets' under the relevant intellectual property laws, the lack of remuneration to the publishers will arguably not be considered as abusive behavior. If the content is in the public domain, everyone is free to use such content without the obligation to remunerate the rights-holder for its use, and if there is no obligation to remunerate for the use of the content, then it is hard to imagine why there would be an obligation to share advertising revenue, even for a dominant company. Moreover, the service that Google offers by presenting an overview of news content, may bring benefits to consumers. To generate advertising revenue for this without remunerating the content owners should therefore be considered as competition on the merits (unless it infringes any intellectual property rights).[90]

Assuming that the complaint indeed relates to the above-mentioned use of snippets by Google News, I would therefore argue that this is unlikely to be considered abusive behavior within the meaning of Article 102 TFEU.

---

[88] See An Antitrust Complaint for Google in Germany, New York Times January 18, 2010, http://www.nytimes.com/2010/01/19/technology/19antitrust.html (last accessed February 18, 2011); German news media challenge Google, Der Spiegel January 18, 2010.

[89] *Supra,* Sect. 2.3.3.2

[90] *Guidance on the Commission's enforcement priorities in applying Article 82 of the EC Treaty to abusive exclusionary conduct by dominant undertakings,* para 1.

2.6 Conclusions

In this chapter it was examined whether the power of Google amounts to a dominant position within Article 102 TFEU and if so, whether Google will be held to have abused such position.

It is obvious that Google has a high market share on the search engine market, as well as on the market for online advertising. However this alone should not be decisive in the assessment of Google's alleged dominance. Google is a first mover in a new economy market, where high market shares are common and often do not properly reflect a company's competitive position vis-à-vis its competitors. The search engine market's characteristics are moreover different from many other new economy markets, as network effects and consumer lock-in situations are less present. This could indicate that barriers to entry are not so high, which would mean that Google is at least under some competitive constraints. Google's dominance may therefore be less self-evident than it seems.

If Google is held dominant, however, it is likely that at least some of the practices it has been accused of are considered abusive under Article 102 TFEU. The case law of the European Court of Justice and the European Commission shows that if a dominant undertaking uses its dominance in one market to eliminate competition in a related market it violates Article 102 TFEU. Practices whereby Google is proved to use its leverage on the search engine market to distort competition in related markets, such as influencing search results in order to favor its own services, are therefore likely to be considered abusive.

However, if Article 102 TFEU proceedings against Google actually take off, it is argued that—for the reasons mentioned above—the European Commission should first investigate closely whether Google may be under competitive constraints, and whether its behavior is not merely a reflection of severe competition on related markets. Because otherwise the European Commission would indeed punish a pioneer company that has made life easier, more efficient and arguably more fun for many consumers.

References

Ahlborn C, Denicolò V, Geradin D, Jorge Padilla A (2006) 'DG Comp's discussion paper on article 82: Implications of the proposed framework and antitrust rules for dynamically competitive industries'. Available at: http://ec.europa.eu/comm/competition/antitrust/art82/057.pdf

Ahlborn C, Evans DS, Padilla AJ (2001) Competition policy in the new economy: is European competition law up to the challenge? ECLR, pp 156–162

Bishop W, Caffarra Lexecon C (2001) Merger control in new markets. ECLR 2001, pp 31–33

Jones A, Sufrin B (2011) EU competition law, 4th edn. Oxford University Press, Oxford

Rahnasto I (2003) Intellectual property rights, external effects and anti-trust law. Leveraging IPRs in the communications industry. Oxford University Press, Oxford

Rosenberg S (1998) Yes, there is a better search engine. While the portal sites fiddle, Google catches fire, published 21 December 1998. Available at http://www.salon.com/21st/rose/1998/12/21straight.html (last visited on January 8, 2011)

Teece DJ, Coleman M (1996) The meaning of monopoly: antitrust analysis in high-technology industries. Antitrust Bull, Fall/Winter, pp 801–857

Temple Lang J (1996) European Community antitrust law–innovation markets and high technology industries, speech at the Fordham Corporate Law Institute at October 17, 1996 in New York. Available at http://europa.eu.int/comm/competition/speeches/text/sp1996_054_en.html

Veljanovski C (2001) E.C. antitrust in the new economy: is the European Commission's view of the network economy right? ECLR, pp 115–121

Chapter 3
Google AdWords: Trade Mark Law and Liability of Internet Service Providers

Jeremy Phillips

Contents

The author is a Honorary Research Fellow at Intellectual Property Institute, Professorial Fellow at Queen Mary Intellectual Property Law Institute, Editor at European Trade Mark Reports, blogmeistr IPK at weblog.

J. Phillips (✉)
Intellectual Property Institute, London, UK
e-mail: jjip@btinternet.com

J. Phillips
Queen Mary Intellectual Property Law Institute, London, UK

A. Lopez-Tarruella (ed.), *Google and the Law*,
Information Technology and Law Series 22, DOI: 10.1007/978-90-6704-846-0_3,
© T.M.C. ASSER PRESS, The Hague, The Netherlands, and the author(s) 2012

3.1 The Objective

So much has happened in so short a time, and so many words have been written, on the various legal issues arising from the creation, sale, purchase, use and abuse of AdWords that a thorough coverage of them would far exceed the length of this book. Accordingly this chapter will do no more than offer a few perspectives on the subject. Its objective is to raise awareness of problems and solutions; to offer some thoughts as to how the law and the market place may continue to respond to the AdWord phenomenon; and to stimulate enough momentum in the reader's interest to make him want to pursue the subject of AdWord liability beyond this chapter and into the future.

The focus of this chapter is on the development of themes of trade mark liability and liability of internet service providers as they appear through the case law of the Court of Justice of the European Union, since this is the stage on which the drama takes place. While the courts of European Union Member States offer some interesting diversions and side-shows, it is ultimately for the Court of Justice to determine the path which others must follow.

3.2 What is an AdWord?

The term "AdWord" is often used as a synonym for "keyword", the function of which is briefly explained in the next heading. In the plural, "AdWords" is a word which is a registered trade mark of which Google is the proprietor. The word, as of the date of writing of this chapter, is registered in the European Union only as a

Community trade mark for services in Class 35 of the Nice Classification. Thus Registration E2724672 of 5 June 2002 covers just "dissemination of advertising for others". Some national registrations for a range of Class 35 services are also in existence.

Whatever Google's strategy for its business development might be, a casual glance at the trade mark register suggests that the development of an all-powerful portfolio of trade mark registrations based on the core word 'AdWords' is not part of it. In 2007 a German resident, Hong Wu, applied to register the word ADWORDSHARE for 'business management; business administration; office functions' in Class 35, 'telecommunications' in Class 36 and 'scientific and technological services and research and design relating thereto; industrial analysis and research services; design and development of computer hardware and software' in Class 38. The mark was registered on 4 September 2010 as E6402705. A subsequent application, E9312232, has been filed by Francotel-Francophone Telecom SARL, for the registration of 'adwords' as a Community trade mark for 'insurance; financial affairs; monetary affairs; real estate affairs' in Class 36 and 'telecommunications' in Class 38, with a priority date of 11 August 2010. In reality, so long as keyword advertising is synonymous with the strongly-protected GOOGLE brand, time spent in seeking to retain exclusivity in the use of the word 'AdWords' for anything outside the narrow category of services for which it is registered is probably seen as a possibly costly distraction which confers no tangible benefit in terms of the company's bottom-line profits.

3.3 AdWords and Keywords

It is necessary to distinguish AdWords from keywords. A keyword is a word which, as the analogy suggests, operates as a key to unlock access to pages on the internet the precise location or even the existence of which may be unknown. The means by which it does so is by its being entered not into a lock but into an internet search engine, which will then endeavour to find and then list the web pages on which that word may be recorded as human-readable script or as meta-data which is readable only by a machine.

Advocate General Poiares Maduro explains the significance of the keyword in his Opinion[1]

> The act of typing a keyword into an internet search engine has become part of our culture, its results immediately familiar. The actual inner workings of how those results are

---

[1] Joined Cases C-236/08 to C-238/08, *"Google France SARL, Google Inc. v Louis Vuitton Malletier SA; Google France SARL v Viaticum SA, Luteciel SARL; Google France SARL v Centre national de recherche en relations humaines (CNRRH) SARL, Pierre-Alexis Thonet, Bruno Raboin, Tiger SARL"*, Opinion of Advocate General Poiares Maduro, 22 September 2009, [2010] E.T.M.R. 30, paras 1–4.

provided are, it is fair to say, mostly unknown to the general public. It is simply assumed that if you ask, it shall be given to you; seek, and you shall find.

In reality, for any given keyword typed into a search engine, that is to say, for any set of words entered, two types of results are usually provided: a range of sites relevant to the keyword ('natural results') and, alongside, advertisements for certain sites ('ads').

While natural results are provided on the basis of objective criteria, determined by the search engine, that is not the case with ads. Ads are provided because advertisers pay for their sites to feature in response to certain keywords; this is possible because the search engine provider makes those keywords available for selection by advertisers.

The present cases concern keywords which correspond to registered trade marks. More specifically, the proprietors of the trade marks are trying to prevent the selection of such keywords by advertisers. They are also trying to prevent the display by search engine providers of ads in response to those keywords, as this may result in sites for rival or even counterfeit products being displayed alongside natural results for their own sites. ...

3.4 Why are AdWords so Valuable?

Google's revenue from the provision of its AdWords service in 2010 amounted to some US$28 billion,[2] a remarkable figure if one considers that it does not generally constitute substantive advertising as such but merely a form of 'pre-advertising' which enables consumers, if they are so minded, to reach the advertising materials or website of an AdWords service purchaser. It is in effect an *hors d'oeuvre* which serves to stimulate the appetite of the consumer to the point at which he clicks a link from it to the main dish, as it were.

3.5 How Does the AdWords Service Work?

In short,[3] when an internet user performs a regular search, using Google's internet search engine, on the basis of one or more words which he uses as search terms, the search engine displays the sites which appear best to correspond to those words, in what Google's software calculates as being a decreasing order of relevance. The list of sites, in its decreasing order of relevance, is what the Court of Justice describes as the 'natural' results of the search.

Google's AdWords is what the Court terms a "paid referencing service". This service enables any "economic operator" (the Court's term for a business), by reserving one or more keywords, to obtain the placing of what the Court calls an "advertising link" to its site—assuming that there exists some sort of link between the user's search terms and the keyword for which Google has received payment.

Where a search throws up one or more advertising link, the latter does not appear together with the 'natural' results of the search. It is instead displayed under

---

[2] http://investor.google.com/financial/tables.html (last accessed 14 February 2011).

[3] This explanation is drawn from "*Google France*" Judgment, [2010] E.T.M.R. 30, paras H2–H3.

the heading 'sponsored links' and is normally situated either on the right-hand side of the user's screen display, to the right of the natural results, or on the upper part of the screen display, above the natural results.

Each advertising link is accompanied by a short commercial message; each combination of link and message constitutes an advertisement. Google charges a fee for the referencing service which is payable by the advertiser in respect of each click on the advertising link. That fee is calculated on the basis, in particular, of the 'maximum price per click' which the advertiser agrees to pay when concluding with Google the contract for the referencing service, and on the basis of the number of times on which internet users click on that link.

The profitability of this procedure for Google is enhanced by the fact that a number of different advertisers can reserve the same keyword. The order in which their advertising links are displayed is determined according to three criteria: the maximum price per click, the number of previous clicks on those links and the quality of the advertisement as assessed by Google. The advertiser can at any time improve its ranking in the display by fixing a higher maximum price per click or by seeking to improve the quality of its advertisement. Google has developed an impressively effective automated process for the selection of keywords and the creation of advertisements which enables advertisers to select keywords, draft a commercial message, and input the link to their site, while at the same time minimising the stress and labour-intensive exercise of dealing with individual bidders for reservation of a keyword in competition with one another, or may wish to remonstrate with Google for favouring one bidder over another.

3.6 AdWords and the Vocabulary of Trade Marks

The European Union is a complex organism. Its disjointed territories constitute a single, seamless market within which trade marks operate both transnationally and within national borders. Unlike the patent—which protects an invention which is not subject to purely local considerations of validity—the trade mark may exist either on a pan-European basis or as a legal phenomenon which is confined to one or more Member State for reasons of cultural relativity. This cannot be otherwise. A word which sounds exotic and fanciful in one of the Union's 23 languages may be descriptive or generic in another. The best-known example of this legal-cultural relativism in European jurisprudence is MATRATZEN, a meaningless word in Spanish but serving in Germany to designate "mattresses". Where the word is meaningless it may be registered as a trade mark for mattresses; where it means "mattresses" it may be registered as a trade mark too, for all goods and services that are not mattresses or obviously linked to them.[4]

---

[4] See *"Matratzen"*, paras 25–26.

The implications of this relativism for the utility of AdWords are immense. The same word, used by different consumers in search of their respective quarry, carries different meanings because it represents different markets, both across linguistic boundaries and within them. MATRATZEN might mean nothing to Spaniards and "mattresses" to Germans, but each may have mattresses in mind when selecting that word as a keyword for an internet search, so both Spanish and German consumers, and businesses purchasing that word as a keyword, might belong to the same market. Other examples suggest that the potential of the same word to serve a multiplicity of functions is great. For example, POLO is, among other things, the name given to two separate sports (regular and water polo), a trade mark for a mint-flavoured confection with a hole in the middle, a trade mark for leisure wear and the Italian word for 'pole'. This occurs even within the same language, where "apple" might equally be used by a consumer seeking a new computer or an item of fruit.

3.7 What is Surprising About AdWords?

The most remarkable feature of the use of AdWords is the relatively small number of occasions in which their sale or use has actually resulted in litigation of any description in any jurisdiction, particularly within the United States and the European Union. This article focuses only on liability for trade mark infringement in the European Union, and trade mark liability continues to be potentially the most likely area for the AdWord service to incur liability. While there are other issues, such as fraud[5] and 'click-fraud,'[6] which have also given rise to questions regarding Google's potential liability for content or unethical practices performed upon that content, it appears to be the cases involving liability for trade mark infringement which receive the widest publicity.

The paucity of reported legal decisions against Google is even more astonishing if one considers that, where online content has been furnished by an unscrupulous third party such as a fraudster or a dealer in counterfeit products, it is generally difficult if not impossible to identify and locate the party in question and bring him to court. Google, however, is omnipresent, almost by definition easily accessible and certainly possessed of adequate funds to compensate any successful plaintiff.

Explanations as to why such vast trade in AdWords has led to so little litigation are not difficult to hypothesise. They include:

- Reluctance to litigate against a corporation which has such a deep pocket for funding litigation and a determination to defend its position tenaciously since

---

[5] Goddard (2009).

[6] Sullivan D, Google Agrees To $90 Million Settlement In Class Action Lawsuit Over Click Fraud, 8 March, 2006, available at http://blog.searchenginewatch.com/060308-152034 (last accessed 14 February 2011).

any unfavourable ruling can stand as a precedent in literally millions of comparable cases;

- Reluctance to sue and thus antagonise a business upon which the aggrieved trade mark owner also depends for the promotion of its brands and the sale of its goods and services;
- A sense of defeatism based on the perception that whatever happens on the internet happens on so great a scale that any attempts to reduce alleged wrongful use are merely futile;
- Lack of awareness of the extent to which any potentially objectionable use is made of one's trade mark and trade name (this is manifested in many ways, one of which is the erroneous assumption that sponsored links have been purchased by one's own business or by a related one);
- Uncertainty as to which jurisdiction is the appropriate one in which to take proceedings;
- A determination that, on a cost-benefit analysis, there is insufficient benefit to be gained from even a successful litigation outcome.

There is however no systematic study or evidenced-based research to support the correctness and, if correct, the relevant significance of these various explanations.

3.8 Trade Mark Law: What are Its Functions?

Within the European Union, trade mark law is promoted as a means of enhancing consumer choice by enabling the consumer to distinguish between the goods and services of different and usually competing businesses. The national laws of 27 Member States are harmonised with regard to the main features of trade mark law, including what constitutes a validly registered trade mark, what acts infringe it and what acts may be lawfully performed even without the consent of the trade mark owner. The salient points of national law are also aligned with the corresponding provisions of Community law which create a single pan-European right, the Community trade mark.

The Court of Justice of the European Union is the sole judicial body charged with the ultimate and unchallengeable authority to interpret the provisions of both national and Community trade mark law in an authoritative manner which binds the courts of all the Member States. This Court has established that every registered trade mark possesses an "essential function",[7] which is to guarantee the identity of the origin of all goods and services in respect of which it is used as being that of the trade mark proprietor, who may have made, imported, licensed or selected the goods or services in question. In addition, a trade mark may possess

---

[7]   wCase C-206/01 "Arsenal Football Club plc v Reed" [2002] E.C.R. I-10273, [2003] E.T.M.R. 19.

other functions, in particular "that of guaranteeing the quality of the goods or services in question and those of communication, investment or advertising".[8]

Both European national and Community trade mark law contain the express requirement that any act which is mandatorily to be regarded as an infringement must be committed "in the course of trade".[9] This phrase has itself been treated to a number of interpretations by the Court of Justice and by national courts.

When the legality of Google AdWords is measured against the test of trade mark infringement, it must be borne in mind that a court is unlikely to conclude that any activity performed by an unauthorised person, whether a consumer, a competitor or an internet service provider (ISP), infringes a trade mark in the event that (i) the activity complained of does not affect the trade mark's essential or other functions or (ii) the use of which complaint is made does not constitute use "in the course of trade".

Irrespective of whether the law permits or prohibits the unauthorised use of a trade mark by anyone other than the trade mark's owner, the commercial reality is that for many businesses a trade mark that customers know and to which they respond positively is one of their main assets. For this reason many trade mark owners will react angrily even when a permitted use is made of their trade marks by anyone other than themselves and why they will resort to actions founded on grounds such as unfair competition or unfair marketing practices when trade mark law fails to protect their trade marks from what they consider unfair and wrongful usage.

3.9 Competition Policy: What are Its Functions?

The European Union currently holds itself out as being a cultural and political union. It was however originally an economic union, based on the perceived need to establish and maintain across its Member States a single market. In this single market, traders would be able to compete with one another in offering goods and services free from restrictions that were based, on the one hand, on national self-interest, and on the other hand, on the power of individual traders or groups of traders to control the market and bend it to their will.

Intellectual property owners have discovered that, even where their rights are purely national, those rights may not be employed in such a manner as to divide the market into national segments or to prevent or hinder competition. The supremacy of competition rules over intellectual property rights has been demonstrated by many rulings of the Court of Justice. In particular, the Court takes

---

[8] Case C-487/07, "*L'Oréal SA, Lancôme parfums et beauté & Cie SNC, Laboratoire Garnier & Cie v Bellure NV, Malaika Investments Ltd, trading as 'Honey pot cosmetic & Perfumery Sales', Starion International Ltd*", Court of Justice of the European Union, 18 June 2009; [2009] E.T.M.R. 55; [2000] E.C.R. I-5185, para 58.

[9] CTMR, Article 9(1), TM Directive Article 7(1).

very seriously the enforcement of any intellectual property right so as to prevent the establishment of a new market which is not the right owner's core market.[10] The Court has however taken a more ambivalent view of the need to inform the consumer about the existence of products that are comparable to, or compatible with, those bearing the trade marks of the brand leaders.[11]

3.10 Competition and Freedom of Expression

In "*Google France*" the Advocate General was particularly interested in the three-way intersection between the private property notion of trade mark protection, the wider public policy issue of fostering competition and the overlapping concepts of commercial and political freedom of expression. He said (with references omitted):

> 106. The question raised by the present cases is whether freedom of expression and freedom of commerce should also take precedence over the interests of the trade mark proprietors in the context of Google's uses of keywords which correspond to trade marks. Those uses are not purely descriptive; (nor do they constitute comparative advertising. However, in a manner comparable to such situations, AdWords creates a link to the trade mark for consumers to obtain information that does not involve a risk of confusion. It does so both indirectly, when it allows the selection of keywords, and directly, when it displays ads.
>
> 107. Google's uses of keywords which correspond to trade marks are independent of the use of the trade mark in the ads displayed and on the sites advertised in AdWords; they are limited to conveying that information to the consumer. Google does so in a manner which can be said to intrude even less on the interests of the trade mark proprietors than purely descriptive uses or comparative advertising. ... that point emerges more clearly if one reflects how absurd it would be to allow sites to use a trade mark for purely descriptive uses or comparative advertising, but not to allow Google to display a link to those sites. I believe, therefore, that the same principle should apply: given the lack of any risk of confusion, trade mark proprietors have no general right to prevent those uses. [...]
>
> 110. ... The internet operates without any central control, and that is perhaps the key to its growth and success: it depends on what is freely inputted into it by its different users. Keywords are one of the instruments—if not the main instrument—by means of which this information is organised and made accessible to internet users. Keywords are therefore, in themselves, content-neutral: they enable internet users to reach sites associated with such words. Many of these sites will be perfectly legitimate and lawful even if they are not the sites of the trade mark proprietor.

---

[10] See Joined Cases C-214/91 P and C-242/91 P "*Radio Telefís Eireann (RTE) and Independent Television Publications Ltd (ITP) v Commission of the European Communities*", 6 April 1995, [1995] ECR I-743.

[11] See eg Case C-487/07, "*L'Oréal SA, Lancôme parfums et beauté & Cie SNC, Laboratoire Garnier & Cie v Bellure NV, Malaika Investments Ltd, trading as 'Honey pot cosmetic & Perfumery Sales', Starion International Ltd*", Court of Justice of the European Union, 18 June 2009; [2009] E.T.M.R. 55; [2000] E.C.R. I-5185, ferociously attacked by the referring court: Meale and Smith (2010) but valiantly defended by Würtenberger (2010).

111. Accordingly, the access of internet users to information concerning the trade mark should not be limited to or by the trade mark proprietor. This statement does not apply only to search engines such as Google's; by claiming the right to exert control over keywords which correspond to trade marks in advertising systems such as AdWords, trade mark proprietors could de facto prevent internet users from viewing other parties' ads for perfectly legitimate activities related to the trade marks. That would, for instance, affect sites dedicated to product reviews, price comparisons or sales of second-hand goods.

112. It should be remembered that those activities are legitimate precisely because trade mark proprietors do not have an absolute right of control over the use of their trade marks.

...

113. It should therefore be concluded that the uses by Google, in AdWords, of key-words which correspond to trade marks do not affect the other functions of the trade mark, namely guaranteeing the quality of the goods or services or those of communication, investment or advertising. Trade marks which have a reputation are entitled to special protection because of those functions but, even so, such functions should not be considered to be affected. Thus, the uses by Google may not be prevented even if they involve trade marks which have a reputation.

These comments reflect the preference of the Court of Justice in a number of earlier decisions, cited by the Advocate General, for taking a "hands-off" and pro-competitive approach where the development of new markets, or new means of educating and guiding consumer choice even in old markets, are concerned. While this theme does not relate immediately to the questions referred for a preliminary ruling, and was not picked up by the Court of Justice, there is nothing in the Court's judgment to suggest that it has disassociated itself from either this expression of opinion or its relevance to the extent to which trade mark law should be allowed to prevail over freedom of commercial expression.

3.11 Balancing Trade Mark Rights Against Competition Policy in Google AdWords

Competition policy in the European Union is, unsurprisingly, in favour of the promotion of competition. This entails stopping Member States erecting blatant and concealed barriers to cross-border trade as well as the rendering unenforceable and indeed illegal a host of practices that fall within two broad headings: abuse of a dominant position and distorting competition in the market.

The three issues listed here are relevant to the sale and use of AdWords. Thus

- No Member State can state a convincing case to justify national legislation which regulates or inhibits the sale and use of registered trade marks as key-words if the effect of that legislation is to hamper Google from offering its referencing service within that market for the benefit of domestic providers of comparable services (which for these purposes probably include search engine optimisation services);
- An abuse of a dominant position is anathema to the European Commission which will, if the abuse is sufficiently egregious, root it out and make an order

which in theory has the effect of abating it. Competition authorities at national level have equivalent powers in respect of their own jurisdictions. A trade mark is capable of creating a dominant position within its market. Examples, all of which are of United States origin, are COCA-COLA for carbonated cola beverages, MICROSOFT WORD for word processing software, iPOD for personal media devices, eBAY for online auction services, AMAZON for online sale of cultural content and GOOGLE for search engine services and artificially intelligent advertising services. The existence of a dominant position does not of itself constitute an abuse of a dominant position, though, which means that the fact that AdWords have become the *de facto* market standard does not mean that any wrong has thereby been committed;

- Activity which distorts competition within the market, when carried out by two or more undertakings by agreement or merely in concert with one another is unlawful. Accordingly any pact between would-be customers of Google's AdWords service to avoid bidding against one another in order to reduce the expense to them of securing the benefit of the company's keyword referencing system, or perhaps to apportion between themselves the various calendar dates on which retention of a keyword is most profitable or propitious, might meet serious objections.

Competition law is rarely invoked within the field of modern trade mark law, and has yet to be invoked within the context of AdWord use. However, it must be borne in mind that the trade mark registration *can* partition the single market in some respects, since the same word or sign may be owned and used by traders who own unrelated trade mark registrations for it in different countries. The fact that a word is generic in one Member State but distinctive of the goods of a trade mark owner in another, with the result that goods marked with the generic term in their country of origin may be prevented from being imported into the country in which that term is a registered trade mark, has been held not to be an interference with the free movement of goods,[12] though it is unclear how this principle may be applied to the sale and use of words which are generic in some parts of the European Union but trade mark-protected in others.

3.12 Primary and Secondary Trade Mark Law Issues Arising from the Use of AdWords

A broad spectrum of possible heads of AdWord-related liability may be seen from the facts of "*Google France*" and from an appreciation of general principles of law and not merely trade mark law. This is because, where a consumer or a competitor of the trade mark proprietor performs an act which is demonstrably

---

[12] Case C-421/04 "*Matratzen Concord*" [2006] E.C.R. I-3657, [2006] E.T.M.R. 48, paras 28–29.

lawful, the ISP which facilitates the performance of that act may be jointly liable for that act or may incur a secondary liability for inciting, encouraging, facilitating, authorising or otherwise abetting the commission of that act in circumstances which prevent the ISP from relying on any immunity from liability which is based on its status as s service provider under the E-Commerce Directive. It is therefore necessary to take note of the acts which may give rise to such liability on the part of the ISP.

3.13 "Google France": the Factual Background

The first and so far most influential review of Google AdWords by the Court of Justice came in the form of a request for preliminary rulings in three separate cases before the French courts, which were heard together by the Court of Justice. In short their facts were as follows:

3.13.1 Case C-236/08

Louis Vuitton, which made and sold luxury bags and other leather goods, was the proprietor of various well-known Community and national trade marks for the words LOUIS VUITTON and LV. Early in 2003 Louis Vuitton discovered that internet users keying these trade marks in as search terms triggered the display of sponsored links to sites offering fake LOUIS VUITTON products. The trade mark in question actually appeared in the sponsored advertisements which were displayed in response to the computer user's search. It appears that Google offered advertisers the possibility of selecting not only keywords which corresponded to Louis Vuitton's trade marks but also those keywords in combination with expressions indicating imitation, such as 'imitation' and 'copy', though it was not shown that Google had advised the advertiser to do so. Louis Vuitton accordingly sued Google, seeking a declaration that Google had infringed its trade marks.

The *Tribunal de grande instance* de Paris held Google liable for infringement in a decision which the *Cour d'appel* de Paris upheld. Google's subsequent appeal on a point of law before the *Cour de cassation* led to that court staying the proceedings and asking for a preliminary ruling in the following three questions:

1. Must Article 5(1)(a) and (b) of [Directive 89/104] and Article 9(1)(a) and (b) of [Regulation 40/94] be interpreted as meaning that a provider of a paid referencing service who makes available to advertisers keywords reproducing or imitating registered trade marks and arranges by the referencing agreement to create and favourably display, on the basis of those keywords, advertising links to sites offering infringing goods is using those trade marks in a manner which their proprietor is entitled to prevent?

2. In the event that the trade marks have a reputation, may the proprietor oppose such use under Article 5(2) of [Directive 89/104] and Article 9(1)(c) of [Regulation 40/94]?

3. In the event that such use does not constitute a use which may be prevented by the trade mark proprietor under [Directive 89/104] or [Regulation 40/94], may the provider of the paid referencing service be regarded as providing an information society service consisting of the storage of information provided by the recipient of the service, within the meaning of Article 14 of [Directive 2000/31], so that that provider cannot incur liability until it has been notified by the trade mark proprietor of the unlawful use of the sign by the advertiser?

3.13.2   Case C-237/08

Viaticum was the proprietor of the French trade marks BOURSE DES VOLS, BOURSE DES VOYAGES and BDV, registered for travel-arrangement services. Luteciel, a provider of information-technology services to travel agencies, ran Viaticum's internet site. Those companies discovered that the entry, by internet users, of terms constituting Viaticum's trade marks into Google's search engine triggered the display, as 'sponsored links', of links to sites of Viaticum's competitors. It was shown that Google offered advertisers the possibility of selecting, to that end, keywords which corresponded to those trade marks. The Tribunal de grande instance de Nanterre held Google liable for trade mark infringement and ordered it to compensate Viaticum and Luteciel for the losses which they had suffered. Google appealed unsuccessfully to the Cour d'appel de Versailles, which ruled that Google had acted as an accessory to infringement. Google then appealed to the Cour de cassation, which decided to stay the proceedings and to refer the following questions to the Court for a preliminary ruling:

1. Must Article 5(1)(a) and (b) of [Directive 89/104] be interpreted as meaning that a provider of a paid referencing service who makes available to advertisers keywords reproducing or imitating registered trade marks and arranges by the referencing agreement to create and favourably display, on the basis of those keywords, advertising links to sites offering goods identical or similar to those covered by the trade mark registration is using those trade marks in a manner which their proprietor is entitled to prevent?

2. In the event that such use does not constitute a use which may be prevented by the trade mark proprietor under [Directive 89/104] or [Regulation 40/94], may the provider of the paid referencing service be regarded as providing an information society service consisting of the storage of information provided by the recipient of the service, within the meaning of Article 14 of [Directive 2000/31], so that that provider cannot incur liability before it has been informed by the trade mark proprietor of the unlawful use of the sign by the advertiser?

3.13.3   Case C-238/08

Mr Thonet owned the French trade mark EUROCHALLENGES, registered for matrimonial agency services. CNRRH, a matrimonial agency, was a licensee under that mark. During 2003 Mr Thonet and CNRRH discovered that the entry, by internet users, of terms constituting that trade mark into Google's search engine triggered the display, under the heading 'sponsored links', of links to sites of competitors of CNRRH, operated by Messrs Raboin and Tiger respectively. It was also shown that Google offered advertisers the possibility of selecting that term as a keyword for that purpose. In proceedings brought by Mr Thonet and CNRRH, Messrs Raboin and Tiger and Google were held liable for trade mark infringement by the *Tribunal de grande instance de* Nanterre, and subsequently, on appeal, by the *Cour d'appel de* Versailles. Google appealed to the *Cour de cassation*, which stayed the proceedings and referred the following questions to the Court for a preliminary ruling:

> 1. Does the reservation by an economic operator, by means of an agreement on paid internet referencing, of a keyword triggering, in the case of a request using that word, the display of a link proposing connection to a site operated by that operator in order to offer for sale goods or services, and which reproduces or imitates a trade mark registered by a third party in order to designate identical or similar goods, without the authorisation of the proprietor of that trade mark, constitute in itself an infringement of the exclusive right guaranteed to the latter by Article 5 of [Directive 89/104]?
>
> 2. Must Article 5(1)(a) and (b) of [Directive 89/104] be interpreted as meaning that a provider of a paid referencing service who makes available to advertisers keywords reproducing or imitating registered trade marks and arranges by the referencing agreement to create and favourably display, on the basis of those keywords, advertising links to sites offering goods identical or similar to those covered by the trade mark registration is using those trade marks in a manner which their proprietor is entitled to prevent?
>
> 3. In the event that such use does not constitute a use which may be prevented by the trade mark proprietor under [Directive 89/104] or [Regulation 40/94], may the provider of the paid referencing service be regarded as providing an information society service consisting of the storage of information provided by the recipient of the service, within the meaning of Article 14 of [Directive 2000/31], so that that provider cannot incur liability before it has been informed by the trade mark proprietor of the unlawful use of the sign by the advertiser?

3.13.4 The Advocate General's Opinion

The Advocate General advised the Court to respond to these questions as follows:

> (1) The selection by an economic operator, by means of an agreement on paid internet referencing, of a keyword which will trigger, in the event of a request using that word, the display of a link proposing connection to a site operated by that economic operator for the purposes of offering for sale goods or services, and which reproduces or imitates a trade mark registered by a third party and covering identical or similar goods, without the authorisation of the proprietor of that trade mark, does not constitute in itself an infringement of the exclusive right guaranteed to the latter under Article 5 of First Council Directive 89/104/EEC of 21 December 1988 to approximate the laws of the Member States relating to trade marks.
>
> (2) Article 5(1)(a) and (b) of Directive 89/104 and Article 9(1)(a) and (b) of Council Regulation (EC) No 40/94 of 20 December 1993 on the Community trade mark must be interpreted as meaning that a trade mark proprietor may not prevent the provider of a paid referencing service from making available to advertisers keywords which reproduce or imitate registered trade marks or from arranging under the referencing agreement for

advertising links to sites to be created and favourably displayed, on the basis of those keywords.

(3) In the event that the trade marks have a reputation, the trade mark proprietor may not oppose such use under Article 5(2) of Directive 89/104 and Article 9(1)(c) of Regulation No 40/94.

(4) The provider of the paid referencing service cannot be regarded as providing an information society service consisting in the storage of information provided by the recipient of the service within the meaning of Article 14 of Directive 2000/31/EC of the European Parliament and of the Council of 8 June 2000 on certain legal aspects of information society services, in particular electronic commerce, in the internal market ('Directive on electronic commerce').

3.13.5 The Court of Justice Ruling

The Court of Justice, in response to these questions issued the following ruling:

1. Article 5(1)(a) of First Council Directive 89/104 … and Article 9(1)(a) of Council Regulation (EC) No 40/94 … must be interpreted as meaning that the proprietor of a trade mark is entitled to prohibit an advertiser from advertising, on the basis of a keyword identical with that trade mark which that advertiser has, without the consent of the proprietor, selected in connection with an internet referencing service, goods or services identical with those for which that mark is registered, in the case where that advertisement does not enable an average internet user, or enables that user only with difficulty, to ascertain whether the goods or services referred to therein originate from the proprietor of the trade mark or an undertaking economically connected to it or, on the contrary, originate from a third party.

2. An internet referencing service provider which stores, as a keyword, a sign identical with a trade mark and organises the display of advertisements on the basis of that keyword does not use that sign within the meaning of Article 5(1) and (2) of Directive 89/104 or of Article 9(1) of Regulation No 40/94.

3. Article 14 of Directive 2000/31/EC of the European Parliament and of the Council of 8 June 2000 on certain legal aspects of information society services, in particular electronic commerce, in the Internal Market ('Directive on electronic commerce') must be interpreted as meaning that the rule laid down therein applies to an internet referencing service provider in the case where that service provider has not played an active role of such a kind as to give it knowledge of, or control over, the data stored. If it has not played such a role, that service provider cannot be held liable for the data which it has stored at the request of an advertiser, unless, having obtained knowledge of the unlawful nature of those data or of that advertiser's activities, it failed to act expeditiously to remove or to disable access to the data concerned.

3.13.6 "Double-Identity" Use of a Trade Mark as a Keyword by Someone Other than the Trade Mark Owner

Put simply, the first paragraph of this ruling imposes trade mark liability on the advertiser, Google's customer, only if he advertises—using a keyword identical to another's trade mark—goods or services which are identical to those for which that mark is registered, where that advertisement (i) does not enable an average internet user to ascertain whether the goods or services referred to in it originate from the trade mark owner or someone unconnected with him, or where it (ii) or enables that user to ascertain the source of those goods or services only with difficulty.

This part of the ruling does not address the liability of Google and therefore has no immediate bearing on Google's possible indirect liability for aiding or facilitating an infringement. The Court confined its words to a "double identity" situation in which the keyword is identical to the trade mark and the respective goods or services are also identical. However, while this is a situation in which neither Article 5(1)(a) of the TM Directive nor Article 9(1)(a) of the CTMR require proof of actual or likely confusion, the Court has surprisingly introduced a criterion (whether the advertisement "enables that user to ascertain the source of those goods or services only with difficulty") which appears to depart from the normal principle of liability which is that, where there is double identity, there is liability.

The consequence, on a literal understanding of the words, would appear to be as follows:

- Where X purchases Y's trade mark as a keyword and deploys it in a sponsored link which makes it plain that the goods sold are those of Y (for example it is clear that X sells second-hand products of Y), there is no infringement;
- Where X purchases Y's trade mark as a keyword and deploys it in a sponsored link which makes it plain that the goods sold are those of X (for example it is stated that X sells compatible parts for use with Y's products), there is no infringement;
- Where X purchases Y's trade mark as a keyword and deploys it in a sponsored link which states that the goods sold are imitation products, there is no infringement;
- Where X purchases Y's trade mark as a keyword and deploys it in a sponsored link which merely describes the type of goods sold (for example, "luxury goods", "alcoholic beverages", "camping equipment") and which will require the customer to make some effort to ascertain whether these items emanate from X, from Y or from neither of them, there is an infringement.

The reality is not so grim, however. We do not construe the words of the Court of Justice in the active part of their ruling literally but place them within a wider context, and it cannot be said that, within the framework of its reasoning, the Court intended the purchase of a trade mark as a keyword for the purpose of selling, say, "Imitation LOUIS VUITTON luggage" to be anything other than an infringement. In any event, regardless of the legality or otherwise of purchasing the LOUIS VUITTON trade mark as a keyword in order to sell counterfeit or infringing products, the act of sale is an infringement within the relevant Articles, whether the consumer knows they are fake, or can only find out with difficulty.

Behind the Court's curious verbal formula is its conviction that, even when the formal conditions for double liability are established, an unauthorised act on the part of a third party does not infringe the trade mark unless that act impinges in some manner on the essential function, or a court-recognised function other than the essential function, of the trade mark in question.[13] In this case the purchase and use of the LOUIS VUITTON do not of necessity have any effect on the various functions of the trade mark. Thus

- Such use need not prevent the words LOUIS VUITTON from indicating the identity and origin of genuine products sold under that trade mark by the Louis Vuitton company or any of its licensees. This is not, however, a particularly meaningful notion because it will usually be beneficial to everyone who uses the trade mark, including all infringers who are selling counterfeit products, for the customer to be encouraged to identify the trade mark, continually and convincingly, with the registered proprietor as the originator of the goods that bear it;
- The ability of the trade mark to indicate the quality of goods or services, rather than merely their source, does not depend on who uses the trade mark but on what it represents. So long as the use of a trade mark within the AdWords system does not cause the consumer to believe that there has been any diminution in such quality as he imputes to it, there should be no problem;
- The advertising function of the words LOUIS VUITTON is not impaired by their availability to a third party who buys them as keywords, since the use of those words as keywords does not prevent the trade mark owner using them for advertising. Additionally, it is open to the Louis Vuitton company to purchase the right to use these words as keywords itself, if it so desires;
- The communication function remains inherently unimpaired, as does the trade mark's investment function—in the absence, one presumes, of the sort of evidence which would lead a court to conclude that the unauthorised use of the trade mark disabled its function as a means of communicating a message to consumers or reduced its investment value. It is not easy to conceive of a scenario in which any honest use of another's trade mark as a keyword would have such an effect.

In result of this first ruling, there are two things which, while they are crucial to the issue of liability for wrongful use of another's trade mark as a keyword, lie outside the scope of a general proscription of such use because they are variable factors. The first of these variables is the textual context that frames the use of the trade mark within the sponsored advertisement which the customer's use of the search term generates. The second is the likely response of the customer himself.

With regard to the first of these variables, Stephan Ott and Maximilian Schubert[14] put the matter most succinctly:

> The ECJ focuses primarily on the text of the ad. Unfortunately for advertisers, the space in such an ad is strictly limited. AdWords usually consist of four lines. The title of the ad must only contain 25 characters and the two following lines 35 characters each. The last line contains the Display-URL. Top-Ads, which are displayed above the ('organic') search results, usually consist of only two lines, while the same character limitations apply.

---

[13] See 3.8 above.

[14] Ott and Schubert (2011) at p 27 (citations omitted).

Further restrictions limit the content of the ad; e.g. prices displayed must not be misleading, additional information about promotions must be provided with 1–2 clicks on the
landing site and the text should not contain certain call-to-action phrases, encouraging the
user to perform certain tasks, such as e.g. to click on to a link. The Display-URL shown at
the bottom of the ad also has to fulfil certain criteria. It need not be identical to the
Destination-URL to which the ad is linked, but it has to be a genuine URL that is part of
the advertiser's site. Thus an ad leading a user to the site http://www.linksandlaw.de/let-
me-out.htm might use the Display-URL http://www.linksandlaw.de, but not http://
www.austrotrabant.at.

This, it can be seen, gives little scope to the keyword purchaser to extol the
virtues of his own website or the goods and services that may be accessed from it.
With these restrictions it is likely that careful drafting is often needed to avoid "the
case where that advertisement does not enable an average internet user, or enables
that user only with difficulty, to ascertain whether the goods or services referred to
therein originate from the proprietor of the trade mark or an undertaking economically connected to it or, on the contrary, originate from a third party".

The second of these variables, the response of the customer on receiving and
reading the sponsored advertisement, has been given less space for analysis than it
deserves. There is no excuse for this. Not all advertisements are equal in their
impact and effect, and the sponsored advertisements which appear as though
conjured up by a genie in answer to the consumer's demand are unique in that—
unlike regular advertisements that appear in newspapers, on television, on bill-
boards or illuminated hoardings in public places—these advertisements do not
seek to create an interest on the part of a previously neutral or uninterested consumer but rather to respond to the expression of interest which he creates and
expresses through his own effort in searching. The customer who keys in "Louis
Vuitton" may be expected to have an interest in one or more items within that
brand's product range; "cheap flights" is an expression of interest in economy
class air travel, and so on. Accordingly there is a presumption that, unlike the
mythical monkey pummelling the keys of the typewriter for long enough to
reproduce the works of William Shakespeare, the person who types a search term
into a search engine's text bar and presses the "enter" key has a pre-existing and
positive expectation that the results of the search will be what he wants.

Since expectation of the user of the keyword is not easy to ascertain, the impact
of the appearance of any sponsored link generated by its use should be even harder
to ascertain. Does that expectation go only to the content of the sponsored advertisement or does it also take into account the keyword user's real, assumed or
absence of knowledge that the sponsored advertisement is not an authentic, natural,
organic product? Those of us who are online 12 h a day or more may fondly
remember the first time we encountered a sponsored search result in the early years
of this century and how, caught out once, we have had little or no trouble in
avoiding their unwanted, uninvited advances. Others click gamely through them,
marvelling at how their attempts to find one thing have led to quite the opposite
results, blaming either their ineptitude at searching or what they imagine to be
deficiencies in Google's own search software. So we can conclude that some people

know that they have reached a sponsored advertisement and others do not. If awareness of the existence of this phenomenon is not a question of law but a question of fact, we must be prepared for courts to take a different view, depending on the facts before them, as to whether the consumer knows what he has brought up.

In addition to the consumer's perception that he has reached either a natural search result or a link for which someone he is not seeking has paid, it is then necessary—as in all European trade mark infringement cases—to identify the relevant consumer in relation to the alleged infringing act. What are his or her assumed characteristics? Will these characteristics enable that consumer to avoid falling into any possible trap of confusing or linking one site, or one product, with another, or will they tend to have the opposite effect? The application of an objective test of what is inherently a subjective and infinitely variable commodity—human perception—is bound to produce decisions that are based more on the specific facts of each complained-of keyword use, rather than on the formulation and application of the sort of general rules that businesses with a major internet presence so greatly appreciate.

3.13.7 The Consumer and "Initial Interest Confusion"

When a pre-existing interest is stimulated by the display of a sponsored advertisement which appears to match that interest, the would-be customer may find his expectation unfulfilled after clicking the link to the advertiser's website. For example the would-be purchaser of GLENBLOGGER single malt whisky, searching for a good deal on his favourite tipple, might find himself led to a website offering GLENTWITTER whisky, which he does not enjoy, or to an e-tailer of expensive crystal glass products for use with spirituous products. In the latter case he may experience no more than momentary annoyance or inconvenience (or longer if his internet connection is running slowly); in the former case, since the distinctive part of the name of each whisky begins with the fifth letter and he is expecting to be offered GLENBLOGGER, he might not be immediately aware of the fact. Once the truth dawns on him, he departs the unwanted site and, now a little more carefully, makes tracks towards his intended destination.

At this point the question arises as to whether what in the United States is termed "initial interest confusion" is known also to the law of the European Union and to all and any of its individual Member States. Initial interest confusion has been defined in an International Trademark Association resolution as

> a doctrine which has been developing in U.S. trademarks cases since the 1970s, which allows for a finding of liability where a plaintiff can demonstrate that a consumer was confused by a defendant's conduct at the time of interest in a product or service, even if that initial confusion is corrected by the time of purchase.[15]

---

[15] INTA Resolution of 18 September 2006.

The conclusion that "initial interest confusion" exists in the doctrine of the Court of Justice of the European Union has been recently drawn by one of Europe's most cogent judicial analysts, Mr Justice Arnold (among other things, the trial judge in two major internet-related trade mark disputes which were both pending before the Court of Justice when this chapter was concluded[16]). In a recent decision,[17] following detailed discussion and substantial case citations on behalf of both parties, he said:

> My conclusion is that the weight of authority supports the conclusion that initial interest confusion is actionable under Article 9(1)(b) [of the CTMR]. Furthermore, I find the arguments of principle in favour of this conclusion ... more compelling than those against it .... Counsel for the Defendants had no convincing answer to the point that Article 9(2) shows that there may be an infringing use of a sign even if there is no sale, in particular in an advertisement. As discussed above, this analysis is supported by the [Court of Justice] decisions in "*O2*", "*Die BergSpechte*" and "*Portakabin*". Nor did he have a convincing answer to the point that confusion arising from an advertisement is capable of causing damage to the trade mark proprietor even if such confusion would be dispelled prior to any purchase. Although there will be no diversion of sales in such circumstances, there are at least two other ways in which the trade mark proprietor may be damaged. The first is that a confusing advertisement may affect the reputation of the trade marked goods or services. It is irrelevant for this purpose whether the defendant's goods or services are objectively inferior to those of the trade mark proprietor. The second is that such confusion may erode the distinctiveness of the trade mark ....[18]

3.13.8 Storage and Organisation of the Display of Advertisements Corresponding to Keywords

The second plank of the Court's ruling was its conclusion that Google, as an internet referencing service provider which stores trade marks as keywords and organises the display of advertisements triggered by the use of those trade marks as search terms, does not commit an act that can be characterised as a "use in the course of trade". If there is no "use in the course of trade", there can be no liability for trade mark infringement. This applies equally and without regard to whether the alleged infringement is of the "double-identity" variety, "identity/similarity of marks, identity/similarity of services plus likelihood of confusion" or "identity/similarity of marks and taking of unfair advantage without due cause of the

---

[16] Case C-323/09 "*Interflora Inc, Interflora British Unit v Marks & Spencer plc, Flowers Direct Online Limited*" Court of Justice of the European Union (pending).and Case C-324/09 "*L'Oréal SA, Lancôme parfums et beauté & Cie, Laboratoire Garnier & Cie, L'Oréal (UK) Limited v eBay International AG, eBay Europe SARL and eBay (UK) Limited*", Court of Justice of the European Union (judgment delivered on 12 July 2011).

[17] "*Och-Ziff Management Europe Ltd & Another v Och Capital LLP & Another*" [2010] EWHC 2599 (Ch),.

[18] *Och-Ziff*,n.17 *supra*, para 101.

reputation or distinctive character". As the Court explained,[19] while the storage and display in question are performed "in the course of trade", they are not a use of the trade mark in the course of trade; those uses do not fulfil the essential function of the trade mark, or indeed any other function (such as its advertising function). They are acts which are performed upon bare words, without reference to any specific goods or services: the value of those acts to Google does not depend on the distinctive character or reputation of any specific trade mark, but to the fact that it is a commodity upon which, irrespective of its quality or value, a set of bureaucratic functions are automatically performed.

This is in contrast with the activity of the would-be advertiser who selects a keyword for use in the AdWords referencing system (curiously, the Court of Justice does not appear to separate the act of selecting or 'reserving' a keyword from the act of using it: in theory it might be significant to distinguish the two, for example where a business selects and pays for a word in order *not* to use it— though it may be hard to imagine scenarios in which this makes commercial sense). Viewed from Google's perspective the system is neutral to the identity of the words it processes and administers, to the point at which it is actually indifferent to whether a word is registered as a trade mark, used as a trade mark but not registered as such, or quite devoid of legal protection or significance. For the advertiser it is quite the opposite. The advertiser bids for a word only because it is the word which, he believes, will trigger a response that will lead customers to his own websites and thence to sales. For the person who bids for APPLE, it cannot be said that PEAR is a substitute. The purchase of keywords is accordingly an activity which is a use in the course of trade.[20] And, if the use of the keywords refers customers to the goods or services of the advertiser, it is a "use in relation to goods".[21]

3.13.9 Google as a "Referencing Service Provider"

The Court interpreted Article 14(1) of the E-Commerce Directive as conferring an exemption from liability on a referencing service provider such as Google for trade mark infringement or indeed any other form of liability in respect of information which it stores, so long as it has played no "active role of such a kind as to give it knowledge of, or control over, the data stored".[22] Here we see the advantage of an

---

[19] Joined Cases C-236/08 to C-238/08, "*Google France SARL, Google Inc. v Louis Vuitton Malletier SA; Google France SARL v Viaticum SA, Luteciel SARL; Google France SARL v Centre national de recherche en relations humaines (CNRRH) SARL, Pierre-Alexis Thonet, Bruno Raboin, Tiger SARL*", Court of Justice of the European Union, 23 March 2010, [2010] E.T.M.R. 30, paras 55–57.

[20] "*Google France*" Judgment, paras 51, 52.

[21] "*Google France*" Judgment, para 60.

[22] See also E-Commerce Directive, recital 42.

automated system for enabling businesses to bid for and acquire the right to use as a keyword a trade mark, where the successful bidder prepares and posts its sponsored link advertisement without any human agency or intervention on Google's part. Google can only be liable where, according to Article 14(1) "having obtained knowledge of the unlawful nature of those data or of that advertiser's activities, it failed to act expeditiously to remove or to disable access to the data concerned".

The Court observed[23] the fact that a referencing service is provided in exchange for payment or that the service provider provides general information to its customers cannot of itself deprive that service provider from the protection provided by Article 14. However, any active role played by the referencing service provider in the drafting of the commercial message which accompanies the advertising link or in the establishment or selection of keywords—activities which Google does not provide and which, by all accounts, there is little likelihood that it will do so—may well be decisive in removing that protection. The service provider can no longer maintain that its function is technical, automatic and passive once it possesses actual knowledge or exercises any form of control of the data which it stores.

3.14 Subsequent Court of Justice Case Law

"Google France" has been considered in subsequent references to the Court of Justice for preliminary rulings. Some of these, at the time of writing, are still pending, while others have been ruled upon. This sub-section sets out briefly the parameters of each of them and the extent, if any, to which they embellish the "Google France" principles enunciated above.

3.14.1 "BergSpechte"

Decided just two days after "Google France", "BergSpechte" was a reference from the Austrian Oberster Gerichtshof. BergSpechte owned the figurative mark depicted on the right. This trade mark was registered for goods in Class 25

---

[23] "Google France" Judgment, paras 114–118.

(clothing), and for services in Classes 39 (travel services) and 41 (various teaching, entertainment and sporting services). Another company, trekking at Reisen, competed with BergSpechte in providing 'outdoor' tours. That company purchased 'Edi Koblmüller' and 'Bergspechte' as keywords for use as Google AdWords. The use by customers of those words as search terms generated the appearance of its own advertisements as sponsored links. BergSpechte sought and obtained an interim injunction which prevented trekking.at Reisen from directing users to its own home page by a link on the pages containing lists of hits obtained using internet search engines by entering those words as search terms. The action eventually reached the Austrian Oberster Gerichtshof (Supreme Court) which referred the following questions for a preliminary ruling:

1. Must Article 5(1) of the... Council Directive 89/104... be interpreted as meaning that a trade mark is used in a manner reserved for the proprietor of the trade mark if the trade mark or a sign similar to it (such as the word component of a word and figurative trade mark) is reserved as a keyword with a search engine operator and advertising for identical or similar goods or services therefore appears on the screen when the trade mark or the sign similar to it is entered as a search term?
  2. If the answer to Question 1 is yes:

(A) Is the trade mark proprietor's exclusive right infringed by the utilisation of a search term identical with the trade mark for an advertisement for identical goods or services, regardless of whether the accessed advertisement appears in the list of hits or in a separate advertising block and whether it is marked as a 'sponsored link'?
(B) In respect of the utilisation of a sign identical with the trade mark for similar goods or services, or the utilisation of a sign similar to the trade mark for identical or similar goods or services, is the fact that the advertisement is marked as a 'sponsored link' and/or appears not in the list of hits but in a separate advertising block sufficient to exclude any likelihood of confusion?

The Court of Justice ruled as follows:

Article 5(1)... must be interpreted as meaning that the proprietor of a trade mark is entitled to prohibit an advertiser from advertising, on the basis of a keyword identical with or similar to that trade mark which that advertiser has, without the consent of that proprietor, selected in connection with an internet referencing service, goods or services identical with those for which that mark is registered, in the case where that advertising does not enable an average internet user, or enables that user only with difficulty, to ascertain whether the goods or services referred to therein originate from the proprietor of the trade mark or by an undertaking which is economically connected to it or, on the contrary, originate from a third party.

This ruling related only to the first referred question since the Court concluded that, on the facts of the underlying dispute, it was not necessary to answer it in order to resolve that dispute. Its effect was to widen the application of the "*Google France*" ruling so as to apply it not only to a case of "double-identity" infringement but also to a "single-identity" situation[24] in which the allegedly infringed trade mark was merely similar to the keyword (in this instance, where the

---

[24] TM Directive, Article 5(1)(b); CTMR, Article 9(1)(b).

words were merely part of a complex trade mark). Unlike *"Google France"*, this was not an action in which the legality of Google's actions in facilitating the selection and use of keywords was called into question.

3.14.2 *"Eis.de"*

Three days after delivering its ruling in *"Google France"* and the day after doing likewise in *"BergSpechte"*, the Court of Justice published, in German only, an Order in *"Eis.de"*, a reference for a preliminary ruling from the German Bundesgerichshof. The operative part of this Order reflected the first paragraph of *"Google France"* (which was cited pretty well throughout the Order) and the ruling in *"BergSpechte"*. The question referred for a ruling in *"Eis.de"* was

> Is there use for the purposes of Article 5(1)(a) ... where a third party provides as a keyword to a search engine operator a sign which is identical with a trade mark, without the consent of the proprietor of that trade mark, so that, on inputting the sign identical with the trade mark as a search term into the search engine, an electronic promotional link to the third party's website advertising identical goods or services appears in an advertising block set apart from the list of search results, that link is marked as a sponsored link and the advertisement itself does not comprise the sign nor contain any reference to the trade mark proprietor or to the products it is offering for sale?

The reason why an Order was published, rather than a formal judgment, was that, according to the Court of Justice,[25] the question referred to it had been sufficiently answered by an earlier decision. The Court probably decided not to join *"Eis.de"* with the three *"Google France"* cases on the ground that the incorporation of a further set of background facts and submissions would have made its ruling cumbersome and even more unwieldy, while adding nothing of legal substance to the arguments and the outcome.

3.14.3 *"Portakabin"*

In this reference for a preliminary ruling from the *Hoge Raad der Nederlanden* (Netherlands) the plaintiff was Portakabin Ltd, which made and sold mobile buildings. Portakabin Ltd owned the Benelux trade mark PORTAKABIN for goods in Classes 6 (metal buildings, parts and building materials) and 19 (non-metal buildings, parts and building materials). Portakabin BV, a subsidiary, was the licensee of this mark.

---

[25] Case C-91/09 *"Eis.de GmbH v BBY Vertriebsgesellschaft mbH"*, Order of the Court of Justice of the European Union, 26 March 2010, paras 14–16.

An unrelated company, Primakabin, sold and let new and second-hand mobile buildings, both its own and those made by Portakabin. In respect of some of the second-hand Portakabin products, the PORTAKABIN trade mark was removed. Using Google's AdWords referencing service, Primakabin selected the keyword 'portakabin' which corresponded to the PORTAKABIN trade mark, as well as the mis-spellings 'portacabin', 'portokabin' and 'portocabin'. Originally, the heading of Primakabin's sponsored advertisement, which appeared once one of those words was entered into the search engine, was 'new and used units'. Later Primakabin changed this to 'used portakabins'.

Portakabin sued Primakabin for trade mark infringement, seeking injunctive relief, but failed, the trial judge taking the view that Primakabin did not use the word 'portakabin' to distinguish goods and was not gaining unfair advantage through such use: it was merely using the word 'portakabin' to direct interested parties to its website, on which it offered 'used portakabins' for sale. Portakabin appealed to the *Gerechtshof te Amsterdam*, which prohibited Primakabin from using advertising which contained the words 'used portakabins' and, in the event that it used the keyword 'portakabin' and its variants, from providing a link leading directly to pages of its website other than those on which units manufactured by Portakabin were offered for sale. However, since that court held that use of the keyword 'portakabin' and its variants did not constitute use in relation to goods or services, Portakabin appealed further to the *Hoge Raad der Nederlanden*, the Dutch Supreme Court. The *Hoge Raad* stayed the proceedings and referred the following questions to the Court for a preliminary ruling:

1. (a) Where a trader in certain goods or services ("the advertiser") avails himself of the possibility of submitting to the provider of an internet search engine [a keyword] ... which is identical to a trade mark registered by another person ("the proprietor") in respect of similar goods or services, and the [keyword] submitted—without this being visible to the search engine user—results in the internet user who enters that word finding a reference to the advertiser's website in the search engine provider's list of search results, is the advertiser "using" the registered trade mark within the meaning of Article 5(1)(a) of Directive 89/104 ...?

(b) Does it make a difference in that regard whether the reference is displayed:

– in the ordinary list of webpages found; or
– in an advertising section identified as such?

(c) Does it make a difference in that regard

– whether, even within the reference notification on the search engine provider's webpage, the advertiser is actually offering goods or services that are identical to the goods or services covered by the registered trade mark; or
– whether the advertiser is in fact offering goods or services which are identical to the goods or services covered by the registered trade mark on a webpage of his own, which internet users ... can access via a hyperlink in the reference on the search engine provider's webpage?

2. If and in so far as the answer to Question 1 is in the affirmative, can Article 6 of Directive 89/104, in particular Article 6(1)(b) and (c) [i.e. honest descriptive use], result in the proprietor being precluded from prohibiting the use described in Question 1 and,

if so, under what circumstances?

3. In so far as the answer to Question 1 is in the affirmative, is Article 7 of Directive 89/104 [exhaustion of rights] applicable where an offer by the advertiser, as indicated in Question 1(a), relates to goods which have been marketed in the European Community under the proprietor's trade mark referred to in Question 1 or with his permission?

4. Do the answers to the foregoing questions apply also in the case of [keywords], as referred to in Question 1, submitted by the advertiser, in which the trade mark is deliberately reproduced with minor spelling mistakes, making searches by the internet-using public more effective, assuming that the trade mark is reproduced correctly on the advertiser's website?

5. If and in so far as the answers to the foregoing questions mean that the trade mark is not being used within the meaning of Article 5(1) of Directive 89/104, are the Member States entitled, in relation to the use of [keywords] such as those at issue in this case, simply to grant protection—under Article 5(5) of that directive, in accordance with provisions in force in those States relating to the protection against the use of a sign other than for the purposes of distinguishing goods or services—against use of that sign which, in the opinion of the courts of those Member States, without due cause takes unfair advantage of, or is detrimental to, the distinctive character or the repute of the trade mark, or do Community-law parameters associated with the answers to the foregoing questions apply to national courts?

The Court of Justice reiterated its one-paragraph ruling in *"BergSpechte"* and continued:

2. Article 6 of Directive 89/104 ... must be interpreted as meaning that, where use by advertisers of signs identical with, or similar to, trade marks as keywords for an internet referencing service is liable to be prohibited pursuant to Article 5 of that directive, those advertisers cannot, in general, rely on the exception provided for in Article 6(1) in order to avoid such a prohibition. It is, however, for the national court to determine, in the light of the particular circumstances of the case, whether or not there was, in fact, a use, within the terms of Article 6(1), which could be regarded as having been made in accordance with honest practices in industrial or commercial matters.

3. Article 7 of Directive 89/104 ... must be interpreted as meaning that a trade mark proprietor is not entitled to prohibit an advertiser from advertising—on the basis of a sign identical with, or similar to, that trade mark, which that advertiser chose as a keyword for an internet referencing service without the consent of that proprietor—the resale of goods manufactured and placed on the market in the European Economic Area by that proprietor or with his consent, unless there is a legitimate reason, within the meaning of Article 7(2), which justifies him opposing that advertising, such as use of that sign which gives the impression that the reseller and the trade mark proprietor are economically linked or use which is seriously detrimental to the reputation of the mark.

The national court, which must assess whether or not there is such a legitimate reason in the case before it:

– cannot find that the ad gives the impression that the reseller and the trade mark proprietor are economically linked, or that the ad is seriously detrimental to the reputation of that mark, merely on the basis that an advertiser uses another person's trade mark with additional wording indicating that the goods in question are being resold, such as 'used' or 'second-hand';

– is obliged to find that there is such a legitimate reason where the reseller, without the consent of the proprietor of the trade mark which it uses in the context of advertising for its resale activities, has removed reference to that trade mark from the goods,

manufactured and placed on the market by that proprietor, and replaced it with a label bearing the reseller's name, thereby concealing the trade mark; and
- is obliged to find that a specialist reseller of second-hand goods under another person's trade mark cannot be prohibited from using that mark to advertise to the public its resale activities which include, in addition to the sale of second-hand goods under that mark, the sale of other second-hand goods, unless the sale of those other goods, in the light of their volume, their presentation or their poor quality, risks seriously damaging the image which the proprietor has succeeded in creating for its mark.

Paragraph 2 of the ruling is an "as-you-were" statement, confirming that (i) the application of the provision of the TM Directive that deals with honest commercial use of another's mark is not subject to blanket rules of applicability, since every alleged infringement which is met by an honest commercial use defence must be dealt with on its own facts and making it plain that (ii) this is so, whether the medium of the alleged infringing use is that of AdWords or an off-line scenario. The first part of para 3 of the ruling is equally non-contentious, applying existing Court of Justice case law on the use of trade marks when selling second-hand goods to online situations. The latter part of para 3 of the ruling however seeks to guide national courts in the exercise of their discretion to determine whether the keyword purchaser's use of AdWords is permissible when he is selling the trade mark owner's own second-hand goods—an issue that did not arise in any of the three "*Google France*" cases or in "*BergSpechte*". All three of the guides to assessment are stated in general terms that do not specify that they are only applicable in the case of the use of a keyword which represents a trade mark, which presumably means that the principles enunciated here are of general application, whether the allegedly infringing use is via a keyword or in a bricks-and-mortar shop.

"*Portakabin*" thus affirms the basic principles in "*Google France*" and extends their applicability in respect of the use of trade mark-related keywords for the sale of the trade mark owner's second-hand goods and de-branded goods.

3.14.4 "Interflora"

This reference for a preliminary ruling from the High Court, England and Wales, has been the subject of an exchange between the Court of Justice Registry and the referring judge, Mr Justice Arnold, which has resulted in the reduction of questions referred from ten[26] to four and in the redrafting of one of the surviving questions. This reference addresses the mechanisms for selling and using the AdWords system in more detail than any of the other post-"*Google France*" references but, in common with those other references, it arises from a dispute between a trade mark owner and the purchaser of a keyword which corresponds to a trade mark: Google again is not a party.

---

[26] The original ten questions remain posted on the Curia website http://curia.europa.eu/, accessed 15 February 2011.

Interflora owned the INTERFLORA United Kingdom and Community trade marks in respect of the sale and delivery of flowers. Marks & Spencer (M&S), a retailer of a wide range of goods and services, also sold and delivered flowers in direct competition with Interflora. Following the purchase and use by M&S of the word "interflora" as a keyword for Google's AdWords service, Interflora sued M&S for trade mark infringement. Curiously, since Google was not joined in these proceedings, Interflora's claim of trade mark infringement related to acts committed by M&S together with Google for which Interflora claimed M&S was jointly liable. M&S admitted both its own and Google's involvement in the acts complained of, but denied that either it or Google was in any sense liable.[27]

Having reviewed the position of the Court of Justice as expressed in "*Google France*", "*BergSpechte*", "*Eis.de*" and "*Portakabin*", Mr Justice Arnold stayed the proceedings and referred a series of questions to the Court, of which the four which remain are as follows:

(1) Where a trader which is a competitor of the proprietor of a registered trade mark and which sells goods and provides services identical to those covered by the trade mark via its website (i) selects a sign which is identical ... with the trade mark as a keyword for a search engine operator's sponsored link service, (ii) nominates the sign as a keyword, (iii) associates the sign with the URL of its website, (iv) sets the cost per click that it will pay in relation to that keyword, (v) schedules the timing of the display of the sponsored link and (vi) uses the sign in business correspondence relating to the invoicing and payment of fees or the management of its account with the search engine operator, but the sponsored link does not itself include the sign or any similar sign, do any or all of these acts constitute 'use' of the sign by the competitor within the meaning of Article 5(1)(a) of... the Trade Marks Directive and Article 9(1)(a) of... the CTM Regulation?

(2) Is any such use 'in relation to' goods and services identical to those for which the trade mark is registered within the meaning of Article 5(1)(a) of the Trade Marks Directive and Article 9(1)(a) of the CTM Regulation?

(3) Does any such use fall within the scope of either or both of:

(a) Article 5(1)(a) of the Trade Marks Directive and Article 9(1)(a) of the CTM Regulation; and

(b) (assuming that such use is detrimental to the distinctive character of the trade mark or takes unfair advantage of the repute of the trade mark) Article 5(2) of the Trade Marks Directive and Article 9(1)(c) of the CTM Regulation?

(4) Does it make any difference to the answer to question 3 above if:

(a) the presentation of the competitor's sponsored link in response to a search by a user by means of the sign in question is liable to lead some members of the public to believe that the competitor is a member of the trade mark proprietor's commercial network contrary to the fact; or

(b) the search engine operator does not permit trade mark proprietors in the relevant Member State of the Community to block the selection of signs identical to their trade marks as keywords by other parties?

---

[27] *Interflora Inc, Interflora British Unit v Marks & Spencer plc, Flowers Direct Online Limited*" [2009] EWHC 1095 (Ch), paras 39, 42, 52.

Questions 1 and 2 seek to unbundle the sequence of acts which leads from the selection of a keyword to the final stages of its use, a sequence which the Court of Justice has hitherto preferred to treat as a single act.[28] Questions 3 and 4 aim to test the applicability of the original *"Google France"* principle (subject to any refinement which it receives through the answers to questions 1 and 2) not only in the cases of "double-identity" and "single-identity plus likelihood of confusion" infringement but also to "unfair advantage/detriment" situations in which a likelihood of confusion is irrelevant, so long as the mark's reputation or distinctive character are jeopardised and there is no justification for this to happen.

The Advocate General delivered an Opinion on these questions on 24 March 2011 in Case C-323/09, in which the Court was advised to answer the questions posed by the referring court as follows:

(1) Article 5(1)(a) of First Council Directive 89/104/EEC of 21 December 1988 to approximate the laws of the Member States relating to trade marks and Article 9(1)(a) of Council Regulation (EC) No 40/94 of 20 December 1993 on the Community trade mark must be interpreted as follows:

– A sign identical with a trade mark is used 'in relation to goods or services' within the meaning of these provisions when it has been selected as a keyword in connection with an internet referencing service without the consent of the trade mark proprietor, and the display of ads is organised on the basis of the keyword.
– The proprietor of a trade mark is entitled to prohibit such conduct under abovementioned circumstances, in the case where that ad does not enable an average internet user, or enables the said user only with difficulty, to ascertain whether the goods or services referred to in the ad originate from the proprietor of the trade mark or an undertaking economically connected to it or from a third party.
– An error concerning the origin of goods or services arises when the competitor's sponsored link is liable to lead some members of the public to believe that the competitor is a member of the trade mark proprietor's commercial network when it is not. As a result of this the trade mark proprietor has the right to prohibit the use of the keyword in advertising by the competitor in question.
(2) Article 5(2) of Directive 89/104 and Article 9(1)(c) of Regulation No 40/94 must be interpreted as meaning that the use of a sign as a keyword in an internet referencing service in relation to goods or services identical to those covered by an identical trade mark with a reputation also falls within the scope of application of those provisions and it can be forbidden by the trade mark owner when

(a) the ad shown as a result of the internet user having typed as a search term the keyword identical with a trade mark with a reputation mentions or displays that trade mark; and
(b) the trade mark

– is either used therein as a generic term covering a class or category of goods or services;
– or the advertiser attempts thereby to benefit from its power of attraction, its reputation or its prestige, and to exploit the marketing effort expended by the proprietor of that mark in order to create and maintain the image of that mark.
(3) The fact that the internet search engine operator does not permit trade mark proprietors in the relevant geographical area to block the selection of signs identical

---

[28] *"Google France"* Judgment, para 52.

to their trade marks as keywords by other parties is as such immaterial in so far as the
liability of the advertiser using of the keywords is concerned.

The first part of the Opinion affirms the notion of "use in relation to goods or
services" and the "double-identity" principle which the Court of Justice had
previously articulated in *"Google France"*. However, where a proprietor's trade
mark is "mentioned or displayed" and "the advertiser attempts thereby to benefit
from its power of attraction, its reputation or its prestige, and to exploit the
marketing effort expended by the proprietor of that mark in order to create and
maintain the image of that mark", the Advocate General's Opinion seems mud-
dled. Since the user of a search engine has already selected the trade mark as a
keyword, on account of its power of attraction, reputation or prestige, there
appears to be little logic in inserting a further requirement that the mark which he
has already typed into the search engine should be mentioned or displayed in the
search result: it is too far removed from the allegedly infringing act. The
requirement can also be circumvented by the substitution of another trade mark
owned by the same proprietor (for example, the use of "Coca-Cola" as an AdWord
might lead to an advertisement in which the word "Coke" is used). The Court of
Justice may well wish to support the principle that an Article 5(2) infringement has
been committed while employing a different verbal formula.

3.14.5 *"L'Oréal v eBay"*

While the same trial judge delivered his judgments in this case and in *"Interflora"*
on the same day and both involved the reference of questions for a preliminary
ruling, this case has progressed more rapidly, since the Advocate General has
already given his Opinion.[29]
In short Paris-based L'Oréal, which had brought similar proceedings in several
European countries, argued that the online auction site eBay had not done enough
to prevent the sale of counterfeit goods, such as perfumes and cosmetics, for which
it owned a portfolio of well-known trade marks; the company also objected to the
sale, as though they were goods which had been placed on the market with its
consent, of items such as perfume testers, which contained genuine perfume but
lacked the packaging and presentation which was associated with the formal
marketing of such products. Broadly speaking L'Oréal's position was that eBay
should be liable for the sale of such goods sold via its website, and that eBay
should do more to prevent the sale of such trade mark infringing goods.
The reference concerns Google's AdWord service only indirectly, but in a
highly significant manner, since eBay had itself purchased some of L'Oréal's trade
marks in order to guide would-be customers more efficiently to its online auction

---

[29] After this chapter was completed, the Court gave judgment on 12 July 2011.

site. Of the ten questions referred to the Court of Justice for a preliminary ruling, the following concern the use of AdWords

(5) Where a trader which operates an online marketplace purchases the use of a sign which is identical to a registered trade mark as a keyword from a search engine operator so that the sign is displayed to a user by the search engine in a sponsored link to the website of the operator of the online marketplace, does the display of the sign in the sponsored link constitute "use" of the sign within the meaning of Article 5(1)(a) of [Directive 89/104] and Article 9(1)(a) of [Regulation No 40/94]?

(6) Where clicking on the sponsored link referred to in question 5 above leads the user directly to advertisements or offers for sale of goods identical to those for which the trade mark is registered under the sign placed on the website by other parties, some of which infringe the trade mark and some which do not infringe the trade mark by virtue of the differing statuses of the respective goods, does that constitute use of the sign by the operator of the online marketplace "in relation to" the infringing goods within the meaning of 5(1)(a) of [Directive 89/104] and Article 9(1)(a) of [Regulation No 40/94]?

(7) Where the goods advertised and offered for sale on the website referred to in question 6 above include goods which have not been put on the market within the EEA by or with the consent of the trade mark proprietor, is it sufficient for such use to fall within the scope of Article 5(1)(a) of [Directive 89/104] and Article 9(1)(a) of [Regulation No 40/ 94] and outside Article 7(1) of [Directive 89/104] and Article 13(1) of [Regulation No 40/ 94] that the advertisement or offer for sale is targeted at consumers in the territory covered by the trade mark or must the trade mark proprietor show that the advertisement or offer for sale necessarily entails putting the goods in question on the market within the territory covered by the trade mark?

(8) Does it make any difference to the answers to questions 5–7 above if the use complained of by the trade mark proprietor consists of the display of the sign on the web site of the operator of the online marketplace itself rather than in a sponsored link?

(9) If it is sufficient for such use to fall within the scope of Article 5(1)(a) of [Directive 89/104] and Article 9(1)(a) of [Regulation No 40/94] and outside Article 7(1) of [Directive 89/104] and Article 13(1) of [Regulation No 40/94] that the advertisement or offer for sale is targeted at consumers in the territory covered by the trade mark:

(a) does such use consist of or include "the storage of information provided by a recipient of the service" within the meaning of Article 14(1) of [the E-Commerce Directive]?

(b) if the use does not consist exclusively of activities falling within the scope of Article 14(1) of [the E-Commerce Directive], but includes such activities, is the operator of the online marketplace exempted from liability to the extent that the use consists of such activities and if so may damages or other financial remedies be granted in respect of such use to the extent that it is not exempted from liability?

(c) in circumstances where the operator of the online marketplace has knowledge that goods have been advertised, offered for sale and sold on its website in infringement of registered trade marks, and that infringements of such registered trade marks are likely to continue to occur through the advertisement, offer for sale and sale of the same or similar goods by the same or different users of the website, does this constitute "actual knowledge" or "awareness" within the meaning of Article 14(1) of [the E-Commerce Directive]?

(10) Where the services of an intermediary such as an operator of a website have been used by a third party to infringe a registered trade mark, does Article 11 of [Directive 2004/48 on the Enforcement of Intellectual Property Rights] require Member States to ensure that the trade mark proprietor can obtain an injunction against the intermediary to prevent further infringements of the said trade mark, as opposed to continuation of that specific act of infringement, and if so what is the scope of the injunction that shall be made available?

It may be that the first two questions invite the Court to consider whether the purchase and use of trade marks as keywords by eBay is a use in relation to goods in the course of trade, by analogy with *"Google France's"* view of purchasers, or whether eBay is to be regarded as dealing with trade marks as mere commodities, in the manner of a seller and administrator of a keyword referencing system. Given eBay's active role in selecting words for purchase and its benefit gained by selecting the right ones, it is unsurprising that the Advocate General has advised the Court to rule that eBay's use is a use in relation to the goods for which the trade marks are registered—subject to the now familiar rider that such use "does not have an adverse effect on the functions of the trade mark provided that a reasonable average consumer understands on the basis of information included in the sponsored link that the operator of the electronic marketplace stores in his system advertisements or offers for sale of third parties".

Turning to Article 14(1) of the E-Commerce Directive, on which Google has depended for its exemption for liability thus far, the Advocate General has advised the court that it may be necessary to split the activities of an "operator of an electronic marketplace" between those which are neutral, unknowing and therefore exempt from liability and those which are not so exempt, in respect of which alone a national court may impose damages or other financial remedies. In this context, says the Advocate General, the online service provider has 'actual knowledge' of illegal activity or information or 'awareness' of facts or circumstances where that operator has knowledge that goods have been advertised, offered for sale and sold on its website in infringement of a registered trade mark, and that infringements of that registered trade mark are likely to continue regarding the same or similar goods by the same user of the website.

There is however no hiding place so far as injunctive relief is concerned. The Advocate General recommends that, where the services of an intermediary such as an operator of a website have been used by a third party to infringe a registered trade mark, Article 11 of the IP Enforcement Directive requires Member States to ensure that the trade mark proprietor can obtain an effective, dissuasive and proportionate injunction against the intermediary to prevent continuation or repetition of that infringement by that third party, even if the identity of the third party infringer is unknown. Precisely how this is done is a matter for national law.

3.14.6 *"Wintersteiger"*

Google's search engine facility is global in its reach, but its sale of keywords is not. AdWords offers the ability to purchase words, including trade marks, on a country-by-country basis. This is not a *per se* abuse of Google's dominant position in the market for the supply of keyword services, but rather a reflection on the reality of a European Union in which (i) trade mark registration may cover the entire territory or only part of it, (ii) the same mark may be owned by different proprietors in different parts of Europe, (iii) the linguistic division of Europe is not coterminous with national borders and (iv) some countries share a language but do not share national trade mark systems. Thus, as is relevant to this reference for a preliminary ruling, Austria and Germany share a common language but each grants its own trade marks which are coterminous with its own territory, and the relevant Austrian and German consumers of products that are advertised via keywords can access the same websites, read the same advertisements and purchase the same products.

Products 4U reserved the keyword "Wintersteiger" for AdWords use on the German version of Google, Google.de, but not the corresponding keyword for use on the Austrian version of Google, Google.at. Keying the term "Wintersteiger" as a search term produced the result that the website of Wintersteiger itself appeared as the first natural result on Google.de. However, on the right hand side of the searcher's monitor and next to the natural search results, under the heading "Anzeige" (Ads) there appeared a text block with an advertisement by Products 4U. The text of this advertisement was headed by the word "Skiwerkstattzubehoer" (ski service station accessories). This word was in blue and was underlined. Underneath this heading, and in two lines were the words "Ski and Snowboardmaschinen" (Ski and snowboard machines) and "Wartung und Reparatur" (service and repair). The bottom line included Product 4U's internet address in green letters. By clicking the heading "Skiwerkstattzubehoer", one was led to the offer of "Wintersteiger-Zubehoer" on Product 4U's website. This sponsored advertisement did not include a note that there was no commercial link between Products 4U and Wintersteiger.

Wintersteiger maintained that Products 4U infringed its Austrian registered trade mark by employing its WINTERSTEIGER trade mark on Google.de since that website was accessible to consumers in Austria via the internet and was in the German language, the language spoken in Austria. Accordingly, Google's Google.de website, as well as advertisements which it contained, targeted Austrian users, it being irrelevant that accessibility of the website cannot be limited territorially for technological reasons. Products 4U disagreed. In its view the Austrian courts had no jurisdiction and that, in any event, it was not infringing the mark. This was because the Google.de website was directed exclusively at the German user, as was apparent from its layout. Accordingly its sponsored advertisement was only directed at German customers. If Products 4U had wanted to address Austrian customers, it added, it would also have reserved the use of "Wintersteiger" as a keyword for use on the Austrian Google.at website.

The trial court refused Wintersteiger's application for an interim injunction on the basis that, as Products 4U had argued, it lacked jurisdiction. According to that court, even though Google.de was accessible in Austria, since Google's services were offered under country-specific top-level domains the website Google.de was only directed at Germany, where Products 4U's activities were insufficiently connected to Austria to vest it with jurisdiction.

The appeal court accepted jurisdiction but nevertheless dismissed Wintersteiger's application for an interim injunction. While the fact that Google had country specific top-level domains did not mean that Google.de was only directed at internet users in Germany, the fact was that the website was accessible in Austria and in the German language. This being so, it was therefore also directed at the Austrian user. According to the appeal court it was not entirely out of the question that Austrian consumers, especially those near the Austrian-German border or who were interested in German products, would search for products or companies on Google.de. On this basis the court had international jurisdiction. However, Products 4U had not infringed the trade mark rights of Wintersteiger: the WINTERSTEIGER trade mark did not appear in Product 4U's sponsored advertisement, which in any event did not give the impression that there was any commercial link between Wintersteiger and Products 4U. On a further appeal to the Oberster Gerichtshof, that tribunal decided to stay the proceedings and refer the following questions to the Court of Justice for a preliminary ruling:

> 1. In the case of an alleged infringement by a person established in another Member State of a trade mark granted in the State of the court seized through the use of a keyword (AdWord) identical to that trade mark in an internet search engine which offers its services under various country-specific top-level domains, is the phrase "the place where the harmful event occurred or may occur" in Article 5(3) of Regulation 44/2001 ("Brussels I") is to be interpreted as meaning that;
> 1.1. jurisdiction is established only if the keyword is used on the search engine website the top-level domain of which is that of the State of the court seized;
> 1.2. jurisdiction is established only if the search engine website on which the keyword is used can be accessed in the State of the court seized;
> 1.3. jurisdiction is dependent on the satisfaction or other requirements additional to the accessibility of the website?
> 2. If Question 1.3 is answered in the affirmative: Which criteria are to be used to determine whether jurisdiction under Article 5(3) of Brussels I is established where a trade mark granted in the State of the course seized is used as an AdWord on a search engine website with a country-specific top-level domain different from that of the State of the court seized?

These questions do not directly affect the liability of Google which, to the extent to which it exists at all, is neutral in regard to the question of which country's court has jurisdiction to establish it.[30] The outcome may however have some bearing upon the functioning of Google's business model, in that keywords may be offered along linguistic lines rather than by, or in addition to, national top-level domains.

3.15 Some Closing Thoughts

3.15.1 Google's Business Plan: a High-Level Appraisal

Whatever one's personal opinions concerning the commercial activities of Google since its foundation in 1996, it is difficult not to admire not merely the scale of its success but the simplicity of its business plans and the single-mindedness and the efficiency with which they are executed.

---

[30] Further comments on the implications of the "Wintersteiger" case in the field of jurisdiction can be found in Chap. 12.

In less than a decade and a half Google has made itself the default search engine for the vast majority of internet users, with 90% of the market or more in virtually every country outside China, where it competes with local giant Baidu. Its AdSense and DoubleClick targeted advertising services claim between them nearly 60% of their market. AdWords enjoys around 70% of the pay-per-click market, as against 22% earned by closest rival Yahoo! In the provision of software for weblogs, Google-owned Blogger possesses 44% of the market, almost twice as large a share as second-placed MSN. Even in the browser market, which Google Chrome entered at the tail end of 2008, that service has now topped the 10% mark against industry standard Microsoft Explorer and continues to rise. The company also owns YouTube and, against the disunited opposition of much of the world of letters, has lifted GoogleBooks into a position of pre-eminence.

Each of these businesses feeds the others. One wonders whether there is any comparable company in which the degree of synergy between what the company gives away, what it stores, what it sells and what it provides is so great. From the outside one also gains the impression that Google has a very tidy, highly-focused business plan which involves making sure that no Google activity conflicts with another and that involvement or intervention in the activities and policy-making of others is carefully, and most sparingly, practised.

These factors may account for the fact that, despite its ubiquity and the fact that it is always in our faces and at our finger-tips, this global information behemoth is so rarely taken to court. A noteworthy feature of this chapter has been Google's low-key presence even when there is major litigation about and the stakes are high. The company does not seek to be joined as a litigant when users of its services are taken to court. It makes few pronouncements about its trade mark and brand-related activities

3.15.2 The State of Trade Mark Law in the European Union

1996 saw the great renaissance of trade mark law in Europe. On 1 April 1996 the Office for Harmonization in the Internal Market opened its doors to welcome the first Community trade mark applicants. By that year the 1988 TM Directive was largely implemented by EU Member States. It was also the year in which the Madrid Protocol commenced operation.

Sadly, the laws which we learned to operate in the 1990s were the laws which had been formulated in the 1980s, when computers were known—and indeed available—but their capacity was still small and their linkage via servers to the wealth of the internet was not yet appreciated by legislators.

Currently the trade mark law in Europe is pre-internet, while the E-Commerce Directive is not. The result of this is that, when we construe the relevant laws, the terminology of trade mark law and the situations for which it provides fit uncomfortably—if they fit at all—into the circumstances relating to paid referencing services, while those laws which seek to promote internet use by sparing common carriers of information from the worst risks of liability are in contrast relatively easy to apply.

The efforts made by the Court of Justice to bridge the gap between pre-internet law and post-internet infrastructure are immense, but we should question whether the referral of increasingly fact-specific and technical scenarios to a court which is best equipped to give general guidance is an inherently flawed way to proceed. To the extent that the rulings of the Court extend the principles of trade mark law, and its operation, into the furthest reaches of cyberspace, those rulings begin to look less like clarification and guidance on basic principles and more like judicial law-making.

3.15.3 Further Issues

So far, this author is unaware of any enterprise having sought to register its trade mark in respect of the provision of its use as a keyword for paid referencing services. If such a registration is possible, the proprietor could license the use of that word as a keyword not for ordinary, 'natural' searches but for the generation of sponsored advertisements. The trade mark proprietor could thus vet the identity and trade credentials of the licensed user, specifying the acceptable content of sponsored advertisements and defining their parameters of use. Anyone seeking to sell the use of the same word, now registered as a trade mark, would be performing the same service as that for which it was registered—which would in turn be a trade mark infringement. While there are some foreseeable difficulties in pursuing this path, it holds obvious attractions for any business which seeks to retain a higher degree of control over assets which, by definition, attract custom since they are the indicia by which customers seek to find what they are looking for in their online searches.

3.15.4 The 'Broad Match'

It has been remarked by one commentator[31] that a question which intriguingly remains unasked so far is that which relates to the 'broad match' As Google explains[32]:

> With broad match, the Google AdWords system automatically runs your ads on relevant variations of your keywords, even if these terms aren't in your keyword lists. Keyword

---

[31] Clark (2010) at 480.

[32] http://adwords.google.com/support/aw/bin/answer.py?hl=en&answer=6136 (last accessed 15 February 2011).

variations can include synonyms, singular/plural forms, relevant variants of your key-words, and phrases containing your keywords.

For example, if you're currently running ads on the broad-matched keyword web hosting, your ads may show for the search queries web hosting company or webhost. The keyword variations that are allowed to trigger your ads will change over time, as the AdWords system continually monitors your keyword quality and performance factors. Your ads will only continue showing on the highest-performing and most relevant keyword variations.

According to Clark it is at least arguable that Google's activities in this regard could be seen as more than being merely 'neutral'. If this is so, the corollary is that the Article 14 E-Commerce exemptions would not apply.

References

Clark B (2010) ECJ decides in French Google AdWord referrals: more seek than find? J Intell Prop Law Pract 5:477–480

Goddard (2009) Goddard v Google, Inc (ND Cal Jul 30, 2009) 640 F(supp 2d):1193

Meale D, Smith J (2010) Enforcing a trade mark when nobody's confused: where the law stands after L'Oréal and Intel. J Intell Prop Law Pract 5:96–104

Ott S, Schubert M (2011) It's the Ad text, stupid': cryptic answers won't establish legal certainty for online advertisers. J Intell Prop Law Pract 6:25–33

Würtenberger G (2010) L'Oréal v Bellure: an opinion. J Intell Prop Law Pract 5:746–747

Chapter 4
Google and Personal Data Protection

Bart van der Sloot and Frederik Zuiderveen Borgesius

*Google's mission is to organize the world's information and
make it universally accessible and useful.*
(About Google, corporate information).

*Whereas any processing of personal data must be lawful and
fair to the individuals concerned; whereas, in particular, the
data must be adequate, relevant and not excessive in relation to
the purposes for which they are processed (...)*
(Recital 28 of the Data Protection Directive).

Contents

B. van der Sloot (✉) · F. Zuiderveen Borgesius
Institute for Information Law, University of Amsterdam,
Amsterdam, The Netherlands
e-mail: b.vandersloot@uva.nl

F. Zuiderveen Borgesius
e-mail: F.J.ZuiderveenBorgesius@uva.nl

A. Lopez-Tarruella (ed.), *Google and the Law*,
Information Technology and Law Series 22, DOI: 10.1007/978-90-6704-846-0_4,
© T.M.C. ASSER PRESS, The Hague, The Netherlands, and the author(s) 2012

4.1 Introduction

4.1.1 Google

The stated aim of Google, one of the biggest, most important and most interesting companies of this age, is to "organize the world's information and make it universally accessible and useful."[1] This chapter discusses two Google services that have sparked much debate, Google's behavioural advertising program called "Interest Based Advertising" and Google Street View.[2] Can the services be reconciled with the requirements of the European Data Protection Directive?[3] The remainder of this section introduces the two services. In the second section, five aspects of the Directive are discussed, largely following the structure of the Directive. The sub sections focus on: the applicability of the Directive, the jurisdiction, the principles relating to data quality, the legitimate purpose and lastly the transparency principle in connection with the rights of the data subject. For each aspect its application to Interest-Based Advertising and Google Street View is discussed after a general introduction. Several aspects of the two services are not easy to reconcile with the requirements of the Directive, which was not written with the Internet in mind.[4]

4.1.2 Behavioural Advertising

Behavioural advertising entails the tracking of online behaviour of Internet users in order to build a profile of these users to target them with customised advertising.[5] In a highly simplified example, an Internet user who often visits websites with information about cars and football might be profiled as a male sports enthusiast. If this Internet user books a flight to Amsterdam on a website, advertising for tickets for a game of the local football club Ajax might be shown. Many Internet users are not aware to what extent their online behaviour is being tracked.[6]

---

[1] See Google's information Our Philosophy at www.google.com/corporate. (last accessed 31st August 2011).

[2] See Google, Interest-based advertising: How it works, at http://www.google.com/ads/preferences/html/about.html, and Google, Street View: Explore the world at street level, available at http://www.maps.google.com/help/maps/streetview (last accessed 31st August 2011).

[3] Directive 95/46/EC of the European Parliament and of the Council of 24 October 1995 on the protection of individuals with regard to the processing of personal data and on the free movement of such data (OJ L 281/31, 23 November 1995).

[4] See about the application of the Directive on the Internet: ECJ 6 November 2003, Case C-101/01, "Bodil Lindqvist", para 86.

[5] This description is loosely based on the definition used by the Article 29 Working Party (Article 29 Working Party, *Opinion 2/2010 on online behavioural advertising (WP 171)*. 22 June 2010, p 3).

[6] McDonald 2010, Chap. 5; Van Eijk et al. 2011.

Google obtains almost all its income from advertising.[7] For years Google concentrated mainly on small text ads next to search results, related to the search queries of users. It seemed that Google was not eager to enter the business of behavioural advertising.[8] In 2007, however, Google paid 3.1 billion dollars for DoubleClick, which was a leading company in the field of behavioural advertising for over fifteen years.[9] DoubleClick acts as an intermediary between website holders and advertisers, and places advertisements on websites for advertisers. These advertisements are often targeted on the basis of the online behaviour of Internet users. Among other tracking techniques, DoubleClick uses so-called cookies to monitor people's online behaviour. A cookie is a small text file that a website operator (or a third party such as DoubleClick serving content on that website) can store on a computer or a smart phone of an Internet user to recognise that equipment during subsequent visits. This way, a computer can be recognised when it visits another website on which DoubleClick serves advertising. As a result, DoubleClick can follow the online behaviour of an Internet user over all sites on which it serves advertising.

After the acquisition of DoubleClick, Google announced in March 2009 that it would start "making ads more interesting", and it launched its behavioural advertising program, called "Interest Based Advertising."[10] In order to build a profile of Internet users, Google tracks the browsing behaviour of Internet users over all the websites that are part of the Google Display Network, a collection of websites where Google serves advertising. As Google explains, this network "offers text, image, rich media and video advertising on Google properties, YouTube, and millions of web, domain, video, gaming and mobile partner sites"[11] and "reaches over 70% of unique Internet users around the world" from over 100 countries.[12] Internet users that do not visit any websites owned by Google are also being tracked. If somebody visits a website within the Google Display Network or a website where Google offers content such as an

---

[7] According to the annual report of Google, 97% of Google's revenue in 2009 came from advertising (See Google *2009 annual report*, p 37, available at http://investor.google.com/pdf/ 2009_google_annual_report.pdf. (last accessed 31st August 2011). See about the introduction of advertising to Google's business: Battelle 2005, Chap. 6.

[8] See about Google's shifting approach to behavioural advertising: Hoofnagle 2009.

[9] Google Investor Relations, Google to acquire DoubleClick. Combination will significantly expand opportunities for advertisers, agencies and publishers and improve users' online experience. 13 April 2007, available at http://investor.google.com/releases/2007/0413.html (last accessed 31st August 2011).

[10] Wojcicki S, Making ads more interesting. The Official Google Blog. 11 March 2009, http:// googleblog.blogspot.com/2009/03/making-ads-more-interesting.html (last accessed 31st August 2011).

[11] Google Adwords, Yankee Candle case study, available at http://static.googleusercontent.com /external_content/untrusted_dlcp/www.google.com/en//adwords/displaynetwork/pdfs/GDN_Case _Study_YankeeCandle.pdf (last accessed 31st August 2011).

[12] Google AdWords, What are the benefits of the Display Network? available at https:// adwords.google.com/support/aw/bin/answer.py?hl=en&answer=57174 (last accessed 31st August 2011).

embedded YouTube video, a cookie or other tracking device might be stored on his computer.

Google would have plenty of opportunities to enrich behavioural profiles with other data.[13] Google's databases might include data regarding with whom you communicate, what you buy, what you write, what you read, where you are, where you will go and of course what you search for.[14] If somebody provides Google with a name and address when registering for a service, Google could tie this information to the profile.[15] Furthermore, like many online email providers Google automatically scans the contents of email messages, for example, to filter out spam. Google also targets advertising in Gmail based on current and earlier email messages: "For example, if you've recently received a lot of messages about photography or cameras, a deal from a local camera store might be interesting."[16] Google could enrich profiles with data gathered like this. Research has shown that Google could even enrich profiles with information that users submit to social networks that are not related to Google.[17]

However, Google states that it does not tie a name to behavioural profiles: "Throughout this process, Google does not know [the Internet user's] name or any other personal information about her."[18] Furthermore, Google says that it "does not attach particular ads to individual messages or to users' accounts"[19] and that data collected for behavioural advertising are "intentionally kept separate from your Google Account."[20] Hence, Google does not add data that it could gather in, for example, a Gmail account to a behavioural profile.[21] It is difficult to deduce

---

[13] Krishnamurthy and Wills 2009b.

[14] See *inter alia* Google Chat (www.google.com/talk), Gmail (www.gmail.com), Google Voice (www.google.com/voice), Google checkout (http://checkout.google.com), Blogger (www.blogger.com) and Google Docs (www.docs.google.com), Google Books (www.books.google.com), Google Latitude (http://www.google.com/latitude), and Google Calendar (www.google.com/calendar) (last accessed 31st August 2011).

[15] For some services Google requires registration with correct name and address information (See Google Terms of Service, available at www.google.com/accounts/TOS (last accessed 31st August 2011).

[16] Gmail. Ads in Gmail and your personal data. http://mail.google.com/support/bin/answer.py?answer=6603 (last accessed 31st August 2011).

[17] Krishnamurthy and Wills 2009a.

[18] Google Ads Preferences, Interest-based advertising: How it works, available at www.google.com/ads/preferences/html/about.html (last accessed 31st August 2011).

[19] More on Gmail and privacy, available at http://mail.google.com/mail/help/intl/en_GB/more.html (last accessed 31st August 2011).

[20] Google Accounts: Is this everything? available at www.google.fr/support/accounts/bin/answer.py?hl=en&answer=162743 (last accessed 31st August 2011).

[21] It has to be noted that Google's adherence to its own privacy policies cannot easily be checked.

from the information Google provides to what extent it ties search queries to behavioural profiles.[22]

4.1.3 Google Street View

Why need a room with a view when the world with a view is within hand's reach? The concept of Google Street View is dazzlingly simple, as is the case with most good ideas. Take the roadmap of the world and allow people to zoom in, so that they may walk down Broadway, stop at Abbey Road's zebra crossing and drive down Route 66 in one day. All it takes to achieve this dream is a car and a circulating camera attached to it, or more specifically, several cars with several cameras attached to them.[23] Such techniques are of common use for smaller applications, such as virtual tour guides in famous museums.[24] The idea for Street View is perhaps more dazzling in bluntness than in originality, allowing for a virtual tour around the world. Still, Google has habituated projects larger than life as a company ethic, making the world's information available (Google Books, YouTube), easily accessible (search engine), understandable (Google translation) and visible (Google Street View, Google Earth).[25] Obstacles are of course inherent with projects larger than life, specifically legal problems, since law has a tendency to preserve rather than to change.

First some basic facts are provided. Street View was launched in May 2007 and allows users 360° horizontal and 290° vertical panoramic street level views.[26] In this sense, it is different from Google Earth, which makes it possible to zoom in on the earth from a bird's view perspective. With Street View, one sees the world through the eyes of the virtual person Pegman. Street View allows for zooming in on specific details, for the identification of a rare flower or the face of a man

---

[22] "The technical way that we're doing this is by associating the relevant query words in the referral URL with the existing advertising cookie on the user's browser." (Illowsky R, Better contextual matching. The Inside AdSense Blog. 10 February 2010, available at http://adsense.blogspot.com/2010/02/better-contextual-matching.html, last accessed 31st August 2011). The search history that is connected to a Google account is not added to a profile however: "Your ads preferences are not linked to your Google search history, Gmail, or other Google Account information in any way. Your ads preferences, including your custom list of interest and demographic categories, are only associated with an advertising cookie that's stored in your browser." Google Ads Preferences. Frequently Asked Questions. www.google.com/ads/preferences/html/faq.html (last accessed 31st August 2011).

[23] Anguelov et al. 2010.

[24] See for example: Louvre, Another Way to Visit the Louvre..., available at www.louvre.fr/llv/musee/visite_virtuelle.jsp?bmLocale=en (last accessed 31st August 2011).

[25] YouTube, www.youtube.com; Google Translate, www.translate.google.com; Google Earth, www.earth.google.com; Google Labs Mars, www.google.com/mars. See also Google Mobile. Google Sky Map (beta), www.google.com/mobile/skymap (last accessed 31st August 2011).

[26] Williams M, Google maps. Behind the scenes, available at www.google.com/intl/en_us/help/maps/streetview/behind-the-scenes.html (last accessed 31st August 2011).

leaving a strip club.[27] One may also click on a direction in the street and encourage Pegman to take a nice walk. Street View is active in every continent and although the 'Western' countries appear to be on the top of Google's wish list, in time, the whole world may be engulfed by it.[28] Biker tracks and ski slopes are covered by bikes and snow mobiles.[29]

Google's Street View cars have intercepted Internet traffic, including some email messages and passwords, transmitted via Wi-Fi networks, when driving around in neighbourhoods. After investigations by German Data Protection Authorities, Google acknowledged this problem. In a number of countries, investigations have been initiated to determine whether or not Google is violating privacy law, and many regulators concluded that it did.[30] Although it might be somewhat exaggerated to call Google's collection of Wi-Fi data "the largest privacy breach in history across Western democracies", this phenomenon is problematic.[31] The interception of Wi-Fi data is not discussed here *in extenso*.

4.2 Data Protection Directive

There are several major legal instruments on privacy-related matters in the European Union (EU).[32] Firstly, article 8 of the European Convention on Human Rights and article 7 of the Charter of Fundamental Rights of the European Union (EU Charter) provide that everyone has the right to respect for his private and family life, his home and his correspondence. Article 8 of the EU Charter provides a separate fundamental right to data protection:

> Everyone has the right to the protection of personal data concerning him or her. Such data must be processed fairly for specified purposes and on the basis of the consent of the person concerned or some other legitimate basis laid down by law.

---

[27] Schroeder S, Top 15 Google Street View sightings. Mashable. 31 May 2007, available at http://mashable.com/2007/05/31/top-15-google-street-view-sightings (last accessed 31st August 2011).

[28] Google maps, Where are our vehicles currently driving? available at http://maps.google.com/help/maps/streetview/learn/where-is-street-view.html (last accessed 31st August 2011).

[29] Google Maps, Cars, Trikes & More, available at http://maps.google.com/help/maps/streetview/technology/cars-trikes.html (last accessed 31st August 20011).

[30] See for an overview of national investigations of Google Street View: Electronic Privacy Information Center, Investigations of Google Street View, available at www.epic.org/privacy/streetview (last accessed 31st August 2011). See for the legal framework applicable to geolocation services: Article 29 Working Party, *Opinion 13/2011 on Geolocation services on smart mobile devices (WP 185)*.

[31] Australian Minister of Communications Conroy. Senate. Environment, communications and the arts legislation committee, Budget Estimates, p 159, available at www.aph.gov.au/hansard/senate/commttee/S13005.pdf (last accessed 31st August 2011).

[32] For easy reading, this chapter uses the phrases "EU" and "Community", also when the European Economic Area is meant.

Everyone has the right of access to data which has been collected concerning him or her, and the right to have it rectified. Compliance with these rules shall be subject to control by an independent authority.

This chapter focuses on the Data Protection Directive (Directive), which is the general instrument regulating the fair and lawful data processing of personal data. This chapter does not go into detail about specific implementations in Member States, but focuses instead on the Directive. Not all provisions of the Directive are discussed. The Directive contains an exemption for purposes of journalism, in particular in the audiovisual field, to reconcile the fundamental rights of individuals with the right to receive and impart information.[33] Although this may be relevant for Google, an in-depth discussion of this exemption falls outside the scope of this chapter. The right to freedom of expression is not discussed extensively in this chapter either.[34] Rights with regard to the commercial exploitation of one's portrait are not discussed in this chapter. The chapter does not discuss the e-Privacy Directive, which regulates data protection in the telecommunications sector and contains specific rules regarding the use of cookies and similar devices.[35]

When discussing the application of the Data Protection Directive, the opinions of the Article 29 Working Party are taken into account. The Working Party is an advisory body to the European Commission on data protection matters. It publishes opinions on all matters relating to the protection of persons with regard to the processing of personal data in the EU. The opinions of the Working Party are not legally binding. Nevertheless they are influential, since the Working Party consists of representatives of the data protection authorities of the Member States, and usually takes decisions by consensus.[36]

4.2.1 Applicability of the Data Protection Directive

4.2.1.1 Data Protection Directive

The Data Protection Directive protects the fundamental rights and freedoms of natural persons, and in particular their right to privacy with respect to the processing of personal data.[37] The applicability of the Directive is triggered when "personal data" are

---

[33] Article 9 and recital 37 of the Data Protection Directive.

[34] See about freedom of expression and the Data protection Directive: ECJ 6 November 2003, Case C-101/01, "*Bodil Lindqvist*", para 90; ECJ 16 December 2008, Case C-73/07, "*Satamedia*", paras 56 and 62.

[35] Directive 2002/58 of 12 July 2002 concerning the processing of personal data and the protection of privacy in the electronic communications sector (Directive on privacy and electronic communications) (OJ L 201, 31.7.2002, p 37), as amended by Directive 2009/136/EC of the European Parliament and of the Council of 25 November 2009 amending Directive 2002/22/EC.

[36] Article 29 and 30 of the Data Protection Directive; Gutwirth and Poullet 2008.

[37] Article 1.1 of the Data Protection Directive.

"processed" under the authority of the "controller" of the personal data.[38] Personal data are defined as "any information relating to an identified or identifiable natural person ('data subject'); an identifiable person is one who can be identified, directly or indirectly, in particular by reference to an identification number or to one or more factors specific to his physical, physiological, mental, economic, cultural or social identity."[39] The Working Party has elaborated on four elements of the definition: "any information", "relating to", "an identified or identifiable" and "natural person."[40] The information in question might relate either to objective or subjective information and might be kept in any form to be relevant for the Directive. Information may relate to a person either qua "content", such as medical records, qua "purpose", if it is used to evaluate or influence personal behaviour, or qua "result", if the consequence is that a person might be treated or looked upon differently.[41] Personal data may either be directly identifiable, such as a name, or indirectly, such as a telephone number.[42] To determine whether a person is identifiable, all the means likely reasonably to be used either by the controller or by any other person to identify a person should be taken into account.[43]

The concept of data processing is defined very broadly as any operation or set of operations which is performed upon personal data, whether or not by automatic means, such as collection, recording, organisation, storage, adaptation or alteration, retrieval, consultation, use, disclosure by transmission, dissemination or otherwise making available, alignment or combination, blocking, erasure or destruction.[44] In short, almost everything that can be done with personal data falls within this definition.

The Directive makes a distinction with regard to the actors processing the personal data. First there is the so-called "data controller", which is defined as anybody who alone or jointly with others determines the purposes and means of the processing of personal data. On him lie all the obligations under the Directive. A party that processes personal data on behalf of the controller is called the processor and has limited obligations under the Directive.[45]

The Directive distinguishes between non-sensitive data and sensitive data. The latter are data revealing racial or ethnic origin, political opinions, religious or philosophical beliefs, trade-union membership, data concerning health and sex life. There is a stricter regime with regard to the processing of sensitive data than there is with regard to non-sensitive data.[46]

---

[38] Article 2(d) of the Data Protection Directive.

[39] Article 2(a) of the Data Protection Directive.

[40] Article 29 Working Party, *Opinion 4/2007 on the concept of personal data (WP 136)*. 20 June 2007.

[41] Idem, p 10.

[42] Idem, pp 12–13.

[43] Recital 26 of the Data Protection Directive.

[44] Article 2(b) of the Data Protection Directive.

[45] Article 2(e) of the Data Protection Directive.

[46] Article 8.1 of the Data Protection Directive. This chapter uses the phrase 'sensitive data', while the Directive uses 'special categories of personal data'.

4.2.1.2 Behavioural Advertising

The first question that needs to be answered is whether personal data are processed for the behavioural advertising program. Google says that it "does not know Mary's name or any other personal information about her. Google simply recognises the number stored in Mary's browser, and shows ads related to the interest and inferred demographic categories associated with her cookie."[47] Perhaps Google assumes that because it does not collect a "name or any other personal information", it does not collect "personal data" as defined in the Directive, and that thus the Directive does not apply. Google defines "personal information" as "information that you provide to us which personally identifies you, such as your name, email address or billing information, or other data which can be reasonably linked to such information *by Google*" (emphasis added).[48] This definition is narrower than the Directive's definition of "personal data."[49] Google says that it does not "collect or serve ads based on personally identifying information without your permission."[50]

However, it is not decisive whether Google adds a name to a profile or not, as the Directive regards data that *can* lead to the identification of a person as personal data.[51] All the means that can reasonably be used by the controller *or any other person* to identify a person are relevant to determine whether a person is identifiable,[52] and it is often possible to tie "anonymous" information to a name.[53] According to the Working Party, behavioural advertising usually entails the processing of personal data, as a cookie can be used to "single out" one individual within a group.[54] After all, the profiles are built with the intention to target advertising to a specific (albeit nameless) Internet user. The purpose of behav-

---

[47] Google Ads Preferences, Interest-based advertising: How it works, available at www.google.com/ads/preferences/html/about.html (last accessed 31st August 2011).

[48] Google Privacy Center. Privacy FAQ, available at www.google.com/intl/en/privacy/faq.html. (last accessed 31st August 2011).

[49] See also: Lawford J, Lo J (2010) Consumer Privacy Consultations—Comments of PIAC. Public Interest Advocacy Centre (Canada). 15 March 2010. www.piac.ca/files/piac_comments_onlinetrackingconsultation.pdf (last accessed 31st August 2011).

[50] Google Privacy Center, Advertising and Privacy, available at www.google.com/privacy/ads (last accessed 31st August 2011).

[51] Bygrave 2002, p 318; Korff 2010, p 53; Article 29 Working Party, *Opinion 2/2010 on online behavioural advertising (WP 171)*. 22 June 2010, p 9; *Opinion 4/2007 on the concept of personal data* (WP 136). 20 June 2007, pp 12–21.

[52] Recital 26 of the Data Protection Directive. Article 29 Working Party, *Opinion 4/2007 on the concept of personal data* (WP 136). 20 June 2007, p 14.

[53] Ohm 2009; Toubiana and Nissenbaum 2011.

[54] Article 29 Working Party, *Opinion 2/2010 on online behavioural advertising (WP 171)*. 22 June 2010, para 3.2.2.

ioural advertising is influencing behaviour, as Google and advertisers hope that the targeted Internet users will respond to advertising. The discussion about cookie-based profiles resembles the ongoing discussion about IP addresses. The Working Party is of the opinion that IP addresses usually are personal data.[55] Many, including Google, do not agree: "IP addresses recorded by every website on the planet without additional information should not be considered personal data, because these websites usually cannot identify the human beings behind these number strings."[56] The matter is contentious, but many judges and data protection authorities in Europe tend to agree with the Working Party and consider IP addresses to be personal data.[57] It seems safe to assume that profiles tied to cookies or IP addresses should be regarded as personal data in most cases.

According to Google, it "will not associate sensitive interest categories with the anonymous ID (such as those based on race, religion, sexual orientation, health or sensitive financial categories) and will not use these categories when showing you interest-based ads."[58] Google's description of sensitive interest categories resembles the Directive's definition of sensitive personal data, but Google does not mention trade-union membership or political opinions. For its behavioural advertising program, Google can associate one's cookie with more than 1000 categories.[59] Although some might say that certain categories are sensitive, such as the category "parenting", with subcategory "adoption", there are no categories that squarely fall within the Directive's definition of sensitive data.[60] Nevertheless, adding the category "unions & labor movement" to a profile could be considered processing of personal data regarding political opinion. Someone's interest in the "labor movement" can imply a certain political opinion.

Furthermore, much depends on the question on which sites Google tracks browsing behaviour. Does Google process data concerning religion if it tracks daily visits to a website with kosher recipes?[61] However, when compared to other players in this field, Google stays away reasonably well from data that are

---

[55] Article 29 Working Party, *Opinion 1/2008 on data protection issues related to search engines (WP148).* 4 April 2008, para 4.1.2.

[56] Whitten A, Are IP addresses personal? Google Public Policy Blog. 22 February 2008, available at http://googlepublicpolicy.blogspot.com/2008/02/are-ip-addresses-personal.html (last accessed 31st August 2011).

[57] Kuner et al. 2009, 2010. The Advocate General of the ECJ is also of the opinion IP addresses are personal data (AG Opinion 14 April 2011, Case C-70/10, "*Scarlet/Sabam*", paras 75–78).

[58] Google Privacy Center. Privacy Policy for Google Ads and the Google Display Network. 29 September 2010, available at www.google.com/privacy/ads/privacy-policy.html (last accessed 31st August 2011).

[59] Krafcik J, Reach your audience with interest categories. Google Inside AdWords. 23 June 2011, available at http://adwords.blogspot.com/2011/06/reach-your-audience-with-interest.html (last accessed 31st August 2011).

[60] There is some debate about the question of whether the Directive lists categories of sensitive data exhaustively or not (Bygrave 2002, p 344).

[61] See e.g. Allrecepies.com, working with DoubleClick cookies (Privacy policy 2 February 2011), http://allrecipes.com//Help/aboutus/Privacy.aspx. (last accessed 31st August 2011).

considered sensitive in the Directive. Many other companies that engage in behavioural advertising are less restrained and target advertising based on categories such as "U.S. Hispanics",[62] "democrats", "Methodists"[63] or "cardiovascular general health."[64] Still, as the category "sensitive data" must not be interpreted narrowly, it could be argued that Google processes sensitive data.[65]

The collection and analysis of personal data of Internet users is a process that falls within the definition of processing of personal data in the Directive.[66] Google is the controller as it determines the goal of the processing, targeted advertising, and the means by which the data are processed, such as determining the data mining techniques. In short, the Directive is applicable.

4.2.1.3 Google Street View

Techniques used to capture, transmit, manipulate, record, store or communicate sound and image data relating to natural persons, fall under the scope of the Directive.[67] Hence, photographs with people that are processed for Google Street View fall under the scope of the Directive. Although the processing of personal data, photographs showing people, is not the goal of Street View, it is inherent to an online mapping service.[68] When Google registers and stores photographs with directly identifiable information, such as an individual's face, it processes personal data. However, Google erases most directly identifiable information.

> We have developed cutting-edge face and license plate blurring technology that is applied to all Street View images. This means that if one of our images contains an identifiable face (for example, that of a passer-by on the pavement) or an identifiable license plate, our technology will blur it automatically, meaning that the individual or the vehicle cannot be identified. If our detectors missed something, you can easily let us know.[69]

---

[62] Batanga Network Inc, About us, available at www.batanganetwork.com/about-us. (last accessed 31st August 2011).

[63] Graham R, Laredo Group, Getting Started with Behavioral Targeting (promotional video), available at www.youtube.com/watch?v=rqpd3O239qI. (last accessed 31st August 2011).

[64] Yahoo! Privacy, All Standard Categories, available at http://info.yahoo.com/privacy/us/ yahoo/opt_out/targeting/asc/details.html. (last accessed 31st August 2011).

[65] The European Court of Justice has ruled that "the expression 'data concerning health' (...) must be given a wide interpretation." In this light, the category 'sensitive data' must not be interpreted narrowly (ECJ 6 November 2003, Case C-101/01, "*Bodil Lindqvist*").

[66] Article 2 (b) and 3.1 of the Data Protection Directive.

[67] Recital 14 of the Data Protection Directive.

[68] Commission for the Protection of Privacy Belgium (2010) recommendation on mobile mapping, 05/2010, 15 December 2010, available at www.privacycommission.be/en/static/pdf/ recommendation-05-2010.pdf para 20.

[69] Google Maps, Privacy, available at http://maps.google.co.uk/intl/en_uk/help/maps/streetview/ privacy.html. (last accessed 31st August 2011).

Photographs of people make them identifiable, not only with regard to their faces but also with regard to their exceptional height, clothes, hair colour, physical handicaps or any other characteristics.[70] Photographs of people with a blurred face can constitute indirectly identifiable information, for example, when they are entering their own home. Different data put together (neighbourhood, colour of a car and a man seen knocking on a door) might paint a detailed picture (for example, a man secretly visiting his ex-girlfriend's house) and can also constitute indirectly identifiable information.[71] The Swiss Data Protection Commissioner has stated: "In outlying districts, where there are far fewer people on the streets, the simple blurring of faces is no longer sufficient to conceal identities."[72] Hence, the elements of "identified" or "identifiable" are often satisfied with regard to the photographs shown on Google Street View. Furthermore, the information relates to a "natural person" since it relates to the people walking, driving or standing in the streets. Thus, not all data protection authorities fully agree with the statement on the private blog of Peter Fleischer, Google's Global Privacy Counsel.[73] He does not think a person should be regarded as identifiable if the face is not visible.

> Basically, Street View is going to try not to capture "identifiable faces or identifiable license plates" in its versions in places where the privacy laws probably wouldn't allow them (absent consent from the data subjects, which is logistically impossible), in other words, in places like Canada and much of Europe. And for most people, that pretty much solves the issue. If you can't identify a person's face, then that person is not an "identifiable" human being in privacy law terms. If you can't identify a license plate number, then that car is not something that can be linked to an identifiable human being in privacy law terms. (...)
> Some privacy advocates raise the question of how to circumscribe the limits of "identifiability." Can a person be considered to be identifiable, even if you cannot see their face? In pragmatic terms, and in privacy law terms, I think not. The fact is that a person may be identifiable to someone who already knows them, on the basis of their clothes (e.g., wearing a red coat), plus context (in front of a particular building), but they wouldn't be "identifiable" to anyone in general. (...)[74]

However, the Directive states that "to determine whether a person is identifiable, account should be taken of all the means likely reasonably to be used either by the

---

[70] Article 29 Working Party, *Opinion 4/2007 on the concept of personal data* (WP 136). 20 June 2007, example 19.

[71] Idem, p 13.

[72] Federal Data Protection and Information Commissioner, Street View: FDPIC takes Google to the Federal Administrative Court, available at www.edoeb.admin.ch/dokumentation/00438/00465/01676/01683/index.html?lang=en. (last accessed 31st August 2011).

[73] The statements on this blog should not be attributed to Google: "Since I work as Google's Global Privacy Counsel, I need to point out that these ruminations are mine, not Google's. Please don't attribute them to Google, because they're just my views, and many people at Google may hold different views on the same topics." http://peterfleischer.blogspot.com. (last accessed 31st August 2011).

[74] Fleischer P, Can you "identify" the person walking down the street? Peter Fleischer: Privacy...? 23 October 2007, available at http://peterfleischer.blogspot.com/2007/10/can-you-identify-person-walking-down.html. (last accessed 31st August 2011).

controller or by any other person to identify the said person."[75] It is correct that most people with blurred faces will not be identifiable in most cases by most of the people. Still, some people might be identifiable, due to their unique qualities, such as celebrity status or remarkable body features. Moreover, many people with blurred faces will be identifiable by some of their close ones.[76] To refer to the famous quote attributed to Abraham Lincoln: "you cannot identify all the people all the time, but you can identify some of the people all the time and all of the people some of the time."[77]

Finally, the photographs shown on Street View may include sensitive data, such as data referring to race (with regard to the colour of the skin), religion (when walking out of a mosque) or sexual preferences (when walking out of a gay-bar).[78] For example, in a case between Google and the Federal Data Protection and Information Commissioner in Switzerland, the Federal Administrative Court ruled that in photographs of, for example, hospitals or prisons, not only faces but also features such as skin colour and clothing have to be blurred.[79]

In its notification to the Dutch Data Protection Authority, Google confirms processing sensitive data for the original unblurred photographs for its Street View service, both with regard to race and ethnicity and with regard to health-related information. According to the notification, Google processes the photographs (personal data) to use them in anonymised form for Street View.[80] It is not certain, but it seems that Google only regards the photographs as personal data before the faces are blurred.[81]

The personal data are processed by Google since it collects, records, organises, stores, adapts and alters data. As far as the blurred photographs contain personal data, Google discloses personal data to the public.[82] Google is the controller as it determines the goal and the means of the data processing, since it determines the techniques for processing and publication. In sum, Google processes personal data for Street View. In principle, the Directive applies.

---

[75] Recital 26 of the Data Protection Directive.

[76] Article 29 Working Party, *Opinion 4/2007 on the concept of personal data* (WP 136). 20 June 2007, p 21.

[77] It is doubtful whether Lincoln ever said this (Parker D B, A New Look at "You Can Fool All of the People." For The People, A Newsletter of the Abraham Lincoln Association, available at http://abrahamlincolnassociation.org/Newsletters/7-3.pdf. (last accessed 31st August 2011).

[78] Cf. Commission for the Protection of Privacy Belgium (2010) recommendation on mobile mapping, 05/2010, 15 December 2010, available at www.privacycommission.be/en/static/pdf/recommendation-05-2010.pdf, para 6.

[79] Federal Administrative Court Switzerland 20 March 2011, Case A-7040/2009, *"Eidgenössischer Datenschutz- und Öffentlichkeitsbeauf-tragter EDÖB vs. Google Inc. And Google Switzerland GmbH"*, Computer Law Review International 3/2011, pp 87–89.

[80] Notification of Google Street View to the Dutch Data Protection Authority, available at www.cbpweb.nl/asp/ORDetail.asp?moid=808084898f&refer=true&theme=purple. (last accessed 31st August 2011).

[81] See about anonymous data: Article 29 Working Party, *Opinion 4/2007 on the concept of personal data* (WP 136). 20 June 2007, pp 18–21.

[82] See also ECJ 6 November 2003, Case C-101/01, *"Bodil Lindqvist"* paras 24–27.

4.2.2 Jurisdiction

4.2.2.1 Data Protection Directive

This section discusses whether the Directive applies to Google, an American company.[83] The national provisions of each Member State apply to the processing of personal data in three circumstances. Firstly, the national provisions based on the Directive apply when processing is carried out in the context of the activities of an establishment of the controller on the territory of the Member State. When the same controller is established on the territory of several Member States, he must take the necessary measures to ensure that each of these establishments complies with the obligations laid down by the national law applicable.[84] Thus, the first circumstance under which the Directive applies is fulfilled when two criteria are met: "an establishment of the controller on the territory of the Member State" and "processing is carried out in the context of the activities." According to the European Court of Justice, an establishment requires "the permanent presence of both the human and technical resources necessary for the provision of [the] services."[85] This may be taken as a guideline for interpretation, says the Working Party. An establishment does not need to have a legal personality. With regard to the second criterion, relevant factors are the degree of involvement of the establishment(s) in the activities in the context of which personal data are processed, the nature of the activities of the establishments and whether an activity involves data processing or not. According to the Working Party, "the decisive element to qualify an establishment under the Directive is the effective and real exercise of activities in the context of which personal data are processed."[86] When applying the criteria, the goal of the Directive, an adequate protection of personal data, has to be taken into account.[87]

Secondly, the national provisions based on the Directive apply when the controller is not established on the Member State's territory, but in a place where its national law applies by virtue of international public law. An example where this criterion might be satisfied is the case of a foreign embassy.[88] This criterion is not relevant in the case of Google.

The final circumstance in which the national provisions based on the Directive apply, is when the controller is not established on Community territory and, for

---

[83] This section is largely based on Article 29 Working Party, *Opinion 8/2010 on applicable law (WP 179)*. 16 December 2010. The thorny question of which national law applies falls outside the scope of this chapter.

[84] Article 4.1(a) of the Data Protection Directive.

[85] ECJ 4 July 1985, Case C-168/84, "*Berkholz.*"

[86] Article 29 Working Party, *Opinion 8/2010 on applicable law (WP 179)*. 16 December 2010, p 11.

[87] Idem, p 14.

[88] Article 4.1(b) of the Data Protection Directive; Article 29 Working Party, *Opinion 8/2010 on applicable law (WP 179)*. 16 December 2010, p 18, example nr. 6.

purposes of processing personal data makes use of equipment, automated or otherwise, situated on the territory of a Member State, unless such equipment is used only for purposes of transit through the territory of the Community.[89] This last circumstance consists of four elements: "the controller is not established on Community territory", "and for purposes of processing personal data makes use of equipment, automated or otherwise situated on the territory of the Member State", "unless used only for purposes of transit through Community territory" and "must designate a representative established on the Member State's territory."[90] The criterion that "the controller is not established on Community territory" refers to the first circumstance, in which the processing is carried out in the context of the activities of an establishment of the controller on the territory of the Member State. The third circumstance thus only applies if the first one does not. For the second criterion, the controller needs to make use of the equipment on the territory of a Member State. The third criterion, "unless used only for purposes of transit through Community territory", refers to pure transmission services.[91] The final element is the obligation to designate a representative established on the Member State's territory, which is responsible for the activities of the controller throughout the Community's territory.[92]

4.2.2.2 Behavioural Advertising

As Google is an American company, a relevant question is whether the Directive applies at all to its behavioural advertising program. Is the processing carried out in the context of an establishment of Google on the territory of a Member State? Google has several offices in Europe. In an opinion regarding search engines, the Working Party has mentioned some factors to take into account when deciding if an establishment plays a relevant role in the data processing. For example, a relevant factor is whether a search engine provider complies with requests from the courts of a Member State. Another relevant factor is whether a search engine provider has an office in a Member State from where it sells advertising targeted to the Member State's inhabitants.[93] In many Member States such factors may apply to Google.

The third circumstance is also applicable. Google has several data centres in Member States, so it makes use of equipment on Community territory.

---

[89]   Article 4.1(c) of the Data Protection Directive.

[90]   Article 29 Working Party, *Opinion 8/2010 on applicable law (WP 179)*. 16 December 2010, pp 18–25.

[91]   Idem, p 23.

[92]   This is however without prejudice to legal actions against the controller himself. This was made clear, for example, in the controversial case of "*Italy v. Google*", before the *Tribunale Ordinario di Milano*, 24 February 2010, De Leon & Vivi Down/Google, available at

   http://speciali.espresso.repubblica.it//pdf/Motivazioni_sentenza_Google.pdf. (last accessed 31st August 2011).

[93]   Article 29 Working Party, *Opinion 1/2008 on data protection issues related to search engines (WP148)*. 4 April 2008, pp 9–12.

Furthermore, the Working Party has said several times that the Directive is applicable if companies store information on the computer of an Internet user which is located in a Member State, for example, when companies use cookies, web bugs or Javascript.[94] "The use of cookies and similar software devices by an online service provider can also be seen as the use of equipment in the Member State's territory, thus invoking that Member State's data protection law. (…) [T]he user's PC can be viewed as equipment in the sense of [the Data Protection Directive]."[95] In short: because Google places a cookie on computers of Internet users within the EU, the Directive applies. According to Google however, "concluding that a non-EEA controller is subject to the laws of every EEA member state as a result of the existence of a file in the terminal equipment of its EEA-based users seems very far fetched and beyond the aims of the Data Protection Directive."[96] Nevertheless, the Working Party is clearly of the opinion that the Directive applies to Google's behavioural advertising service.[97]

4.2.2.3 Google Street View

Does Google Street View fall under the scope of the Directive? As is the case with the behavioural advertising program, the first circumstance may often be applicable to Google: the processing is carried out in the context of the activities of an establishment of Google in a Member State. The third circumstance under which the Directive could apply is also applicable. Google makes use of equipment, situated on the territory of the Member State, namely cars, camera equipment and processing tools, for the purpose of processing data. The equipment is not solely used to transfer data through Community territory. The Working Party wrote a Street View specific example in its opinion with regard to this requirement.

> A company located in New Zealand uses cars globally, including in EU Member States, to collect information on Wi-Fi access points (including information about private terminal equipment of individuals) in order to provide a geo-location service to its clients. Such activity involves in many cases the processing of personal data. The application of the Data Protection Directive will be triggered in two ways:

---

[94] Article 29 Working Party, *Working document on determining the international application of EU data protection law to personal data processing on the Internet by non-EU based web sites (WP56)*, 30 may 2002, p 10–11, case A and B.

[95] Article 29 Working Party, *Opinion 1/2008 on data protection issues related to search engines (WP148)*. 4 April 2008, para 4.1.2.

[96] Google, Response to the Article 29 Working Party Opinion On Data Protection Issues Related to Search Engines, 8 September 2008, p 13, available at www.scribd.com/doc/5625427/google-ogb-article29-response. (last accessed 31st August 2011).

[97] Article 29 Working Party, *Opinion 1/2008 on data protection issues related to search engines (WP148)*. 4 April 2008, pp 9–12; Article 29 Working Party, Letter to CEO of Google, 26 May 2010, available at http://ec.europa.eu/justice/policies/privacy/docs/wpdocs/others/2010_05_26_letter_wp_google.pdf. (last accessed 31st August 2011).

- First, the cars collecting Wi-Fi information while circulating on the streets can be considered as equipment (…);
- Second, while providing the geo-location service to individuals, the controller will also use the mobile device of the individual (through dedicated software installed in the device) as equipment to provide actual information on the location of the device and of its user. Both the collection of information with a view to provide the service, and the provision of the geo-location service itself, will have to comply with the provisions of the Directive.[98]

In short, the Directive is applicable on Street View, even though Google is an American company.

4.2.3 Principles Relating to Data Quality

4.2.3.1 Data Protection Directive

The Directive lays down several rules under the heading "Principles relating to data quality."[99] The rather open norm that personal data must be processed "fairly and lawfully" is the overarching requirement of the Directive.[100] "Such data must be processed fairly for specified purposes and on the basis of the consent of the person concerned or some other legitimate basis laid down by law."[101] Data processing must abide by the purpose limitation principle, which stipulates that personal data must be "collected for specified, explicit and legitimate purposes and not further processed in a way incompatible with those purposes."[102] Not all Member States interpret "incompatible purpose" in the same way.[103] The Directive also requires that data should be accurate and, where necessary, kept up-to-date. Every reasonable step must be taken to ensure that data which are inaccurate or incomplete are erased or rectified, having regard to the purposes for which they were collected or for which they are further processed.[104]

Data minimisation is a core principle of the Directive. Although the principle is not laid down explicitly in the text, several requirements in the Directive together express the data minimisation principle.[105] Firstly, personal data shall only be processed where, given the purposes for which they are collected or subsequently processed, they are adequate, relevant and not excessive in relation to the specific purpose for which they are collected or further processed.[106] Secondly, personal data must be kept in a

---

[98] Article 29 Working Party, *Opinion 8/2010 on applicable law (WP 179)*. 16 December 2010, p 21.

[99] Article 6 of the Data Protection Directive.

[100] Article 6.1(a) of the Data Protection Directive.

[101] Article 8 of the Charter of Fundamental Rights of the European Union.

[102] Article 6.1(b) of the Data Protection Directive.

[103] Kuner 2007, p 100.

[104] Article 6.1(d) of the Data Protection Directive.

[105] Cf. Bygrave 2002, pp 341–348.

[106] Article 6.1(c) of the Data Protection Directive.

form which permits identification of data subjects for no longer than is necessary for the specific purpose for which the data were collected or for which they are further processed.[107] Thirdly, the word "necessary" in for example the phrase "data may be processed only if (...) processing is necessary for the performance of a contract" implies that the amount of processed data should be kept to a minimum as well.[108] Collecting data because they might prove useful in the future would be in breach of both the purpose limitation principle and the data minimisation principle. Finally, according to the European Court of Justice, the provisions of the Directive "must necessarily be interpreted in the light of fundamental rights, which, according to settled case-law, form an integral part of the general principles of law whose observance the Court ensures."[109] Hence, the European Convention on Human Rights and related case-law of the European Court of Human Rights should be considered when applying the Directive. As the proportionality principle takes a central position in this case-law, all data processing must comply with this principle.[110] A controller should always assess whether it is possible to achieve the purpose with less data.

4.2.3.2 Behavioural Advertising

To establish whether the data processing for behavioural advertising is legitimate, the first question is whether Google has a specified and explicit purpose. Google writes:

> How we use the DoubleClick cookie information. We use the advertising cookie information collected on AdSense partner sites and certain Google sites to: (...) Enable the following ad serving features: (...) Interest-Based Advertising: Allows advertisers (including Google) to serve ads to users on AdSense partner sites and certain Google services based on online activity and interests associated with the DoubleClick cookie and to serve subsequent ads to you after you leave that advertiser's website.[111]

According to the Working party, however, "the offering of personalized advertising" is not a sufficiently specified purpose, especially when a company also mentions other purposes for the same data.[112] As Google lists more purposes

---

[107] Article 6.1(d) of the Data Protection Directive.

[108] Article 7.1(b) of the Data Protection Directive. See also Bygrave 2002, p 341.

[109] ECJ 20 May 2003, Cases C-465/00, C-138/01 and C-139/01 "*Österreichischer Rundfunk*", para 68. See also ECJ 6 November 2003, Case C-101/01, "*Bodil Lindqvist*", paras 87 and 90.

[110] ECJ 29 January 2008, Case C-275/06, "*Promusicae*", paras 68–70.

[111] Google Privacy Center, Privacy Policy for Google Ads and the Google Display Network, 29 September 2010, available at www.google.com/privacy/ads/privacy-policy.html. (last accessed 31st August 2011). See also Google's main Privacy Policy: "We use cookies to improve (...) ad selection, and tracking user trends, such as how people search. Google also uses cookies in its advertising services to help advertisers and publishers serve and manage ads across the web and on Google services." (Available at www.google.com/privacy/privacy-policy.html. last accessed 31st August 2011).

[112] Article 29 Working Party, *Opinion 1/2008 on data protection issues related to search engines (WP148)*. 4 April 2008, p 16.

than just behavioural advertising, data protection authorities might not regard the purpose as sufficiently specified and explicit.

With regards to the accuracy of data, there is an inherent problem of profiling. For example, not everybody who lives in a poor town is a credit risk. An Internet user that visits websites about adoption or cars might be doing research for somebody else. Although sophisticated data mining software might be able to ignore certain false signals, wrongly inferred interests could be added to a behavioural profile. Google mitigates this problem by allowing users to edit their profile.[113]

The question of how Google's behavioural advertising program should be judged in the light of the data minimisation principle is difficult to answer, as it is not completely clear which data Google adds to a behavioural profile. An analysis of almost 400,000 unique domains by Gomez et al. showed that Google would be able to track browsing behaviour on 88% of the tested domains.[114] Many websites have installed Google Analytics, for example. However, this does not mean that Google enriches behavioural profiles with all these data. For Google Analytics, "[a] different cookie is used for each website, and visitors are not tracked across multiple sites."[115] Google's privacy policies preclude Google from adding a name or data from a Google account to a behavioural profile.[116] But, when an Internet user registers for a Google service (such as Gmail), Google reserves the right to combine that information with information it gathers from other sources.[117]

One of the most sensitive databases Google holds is the database with search queries. As Google stated in a court case: "There are ways in which a search query alone may reveal personally identifying information."[118] Google targets advertising based upon

---

[113] See para 2.5.2.

[114] Gomez et al. 2009, p 27.

[115] http://www.google.com/privacy/ads. (last accessed 31st August 2011). See also Google Ads Preferences, Interest-based advertising: How it works, available at www.google.com/ads/preferences/html/about.html. (last accessed 31st August 2011).

[116] Google's Knol service (an online encyclopaedia) is an exception. "Similar to other web services, Google records information such as account activity (e.g., storage usage, number of log-ins, actions taken), data displayed or clicked in the Knol interface (including UI elements, settings, and other information), and other log information (e.g., browser type, IP address, date and time of access, cookie ID and referrer URL). If you are logged in we may associate that information with your account." http://knol.google.com/k/privacy-policy. (last accessed 31st August 2011). See Toubiana V, A follow up on Google policies. Unsearcher. 15 June 2011, available at http://unsearcher.org/a-follow-up-on-google-policies. (last accessed 31st August 2011).

[117] Google Privacy Center, Privacy Policy. "We may combine the information you submit under your account with information from other Google services or third parties in order to provide you with a better experience and to improve the quality of our services." www.google.com/privacy/privacy-policy.html. (last accessed 31st August 2011).

[118] Declaration of Matt Cutts in "Gonzales v. Google", 234 F.R.D. 674 (N.D. Cal. 2006), p 9, available at http://docs.justia.com/cases/federal/district-courts/california/candce/5:2006mc80006/175448/14/0.pdf. (last accessed 31st August 2011).

earlier searches for "a short period of time (a few hours)."[119] It is difficult to deduce how much data are added to behavioural advertising profiles for this feature. It is obvious that Google tracks the surfing behaviour of Internet users over a large number of websites and that these data are added to the behavioural profile. Furthermore, many data are gathered and added to a behavioural profile when one watches YouTube videos, as it becomes clear from the following sentences from YouTube's privacy policy.

> YouTube is owned by Google and YouTube and Google share the same cookie technology in determining user interests.
> As you watch videos, or take actions (such as uploading) YouTube stores an advertising cookie in your browser to understand the types of videos you watch.
> Additionally, YouTube uses information based on the type of pages you visit on websites that are members of the Google content network.[120]

The statement that YouTube stores a cookie to understand what kind of videos an Internet user watches is somewhat confusing, when read together with Google's statements that it never ties a registered profile to a cookie-based behavioural profile. It is impossible to upload videos on YouTube without a registered profile. Google stores a cookie on the computer of an Internet user when he uploads a video to YouTube (this Internet user is logged into a Google service by definition). Perhaps the foregoing means that Google immediately separates data from the registered YouTube profile from data about which videos one watches or uploads. Since March 2010, Google also offers advertisers the chance to "retarget" Internet users. Google explains it as follows:

> Here's an example of how it works. Let's say you're a basketball team with tickets that you want to sell. You can put a piece of code on the tickets page of your website, which will let you later show relevant ticket ads (such as last minute discounts) to everyone who has visited that page, as they subsequently browse sites in the Google Content Network. In addition to your own site, you can also remarket to users who visited your YouTube brand channel or clicked your YouTube homepage ad.[121]

In short, a retargeted advertisement "follows" a user around, for example, after a user did not finish an online purchase. It is unclear what amount of data is added to the behavioural profile for this retargeting feature.

The requirement that personal data should not be kept longer than necessary for the specific purpose for which the data were collected or for which they are further processed is a rather open norm. In an opinion about search engines, the Working Party

---

[119] Illowsky R, Better contextual matching. The Inside AdSense Blog. 10 February 2010, available at http://adsense.blogspot.com/2010/02/better-contextual-matching.html. (last accessed 31st August 2011).

Google Ads Preferences. Frequently Asked Questions. www.google.com/ads/preferences/html/faq.html. (last accessed 31st August 2011).

[120] YouTube Advertising and You, available at www.youtube.com/t/interest_based_ads. (last accessed 31st August 2011). The Google Content Network is the old name for the Google Display Network.

[121] Weinberg A, Now available: Reach the right audience through remarketing. Google Inside Adwords. 25 March 2010, available at http://adwords.blogspot.com/2010/03/now-available-reach-right-audience.html. (last accessed 31st August 2011).

elaborated on how long search logs can be kept, and said that a longer retention period than six months could not easily be justified.[122] However, Google's privacy policies do not make clear how long a behavioural profile is kept. Most of Google's cookies expire in about 2 years, but some of them expire in 2038.[123] Furthermore, a cookie can be refreshed whenever an Internet user passes one of the millions of websites within Google's reach. According to Google however, a profile is lost when a user deletes the Google cookies or switches over to another browser.[124]

Some tentative conclusions can be drawn about which data Google adds to the behavioural profiles. Google's privacy policies preclude Google from adding a name or a registered profile to a cookie-based behavioural profile. But, Google does add the surfing behaviour over Google services and millions of websites to the profile, and enriches profiles with YouTube viewing data. Making an educated guess about the life span of behavioural profiles is difficult. Hence, Google may not comply with the data minimisation principle. The Working Party does not regard the purpose of the personal data processed for the cookie-based profiles as sufficiently specified and explicit.

4.2.3.3 Google Street View

With regard to Google Street View, personal data are gathered and processed for a specified and explicit purpose, namely, for the functioning of the Street View service, a cartography service that lets the public explore the world.[125] However, since the photographs of people with blurred faces are out in the open, all kinds of parties can use the personal data in Street View for their own purposes.[126] Personal data may not be further processed in a way that is incompatible with the original purpose and Google is responsible for publishing the data on the Internet. As Google can neither check nor control for which purposes third parties might use

---

[122] Article 29 Working Party, *Opinion 1/2008 on data protection issues related to search engines (WP148)*. 4 April 2008, p 19. Toubiana & Nissenbaum doubt whether the search logs are sufficiently anonymized (Toubiana and Nissenbaum 2011).

[123] The cookies that Google Scholar stored on the computer of one of the authors of this chapter have an expiry date in 2038.

[124] Google Ads Preferences. Frequently Asked Questions, available at http://www.google.com/ads/preferences/html/faq.html. (last accessed 31st August 2011).

[125] Information Commissioner's Office, *Google Inc.'s Notification for Street View*. Registration number Z2451429, available at www.ico.gov.uk/ESDWebPages/DoSearch.asp?reg=4923359. (last accessed 31st August 2011).

[126] See Rundle et al. 2011; Burdon 2010, para III. See also Mayer-Schönberger, who mentions the possibility of websites asking the public to report crimes seen on Street View: "law enforcement entertainment." (Wiser G, Google plans to launch Street View in Germany by end of year, Deutsche Welle, 10 August 2010, available at www.dw-world.de/dw/article/0,,5887193,00.html. (last accessed 31st August 2011).

the photographs published on Street View, questions regarding the purpose limitation principle may arise.[127]

To understand whether Google lives up to its requirements with regard to the data minimisation principle, the exact purposes for processing have to be established. In Google's notification to the Dutch Data Protection Authority, the purpose is described as taking panoramic photographs of public roads by means of camera cars, with the purpose of integrating these photographs in anonymized form into Google's Street View service.[128]

Hence, the question is whether it is necessary for Google to process personal data. Although the processing of personal data is a side effect of Street View, this question must be answered positively, since the Directive defines personal data very broadly.[129] Personal details, clothing and cars may indirectly lead to personal identification. Google has done a reasonable job to secure that the most direct and sensitive information is blurred, both with regard to faces and licence plates.

> We have developed cutting-edge face and license plate blurring technology that is applied to all Street View images. This means that if one of our images contains an identifiable face (for example that of a passer-by on the sidewalk) or an identifiable license plate, our technology will automatically blur it out, meaning that the individual or the vehicle cannot be identified.[130]

There may be an issue with regard to the requirement to stop processing data when it is no longer necessary for the purposes for which the data were collected or for which they are further processed. This regards the unblurred images, faces and licence plates. Google keeps the unblurred photographs for up to one year, for testing applications that are used for the anonymisation process and to "to build better maps products."[131] Members of the Working Party have asked Google to

---

[127] Cf. Kotschy 2010, p 52. Cf. the Article 29 Working Party in the context of social networks: "Personal data published on social network sites can be used by third parties for a wide variety of purposes, including commercial purposes, and may pose major risks such as identity theft, financial loss, loss of business or employment opportunities and physical harm." (Article 29 Working Party, *Opinion 5/2009 on online social networking (WP163)*, 12 June 2009, p 4).

[128] *Notification of Google Street View to the Dutch Data Protection Authority*, available at www.cbpweb.nl/asp/ORDetail.asp?moid=808084898f&refer=true&theme=purple. (last accessed 31st August 2011). The notification to the Information Commissioner's Office in the United Kingdom refers to the purpose 'cartography' (Information Commissioner's Office, *Google Inc.'s Notification for Street View, available at* www.ico.gov.uk/ESDWebPages/DoSearch.asp?reg=4923359. (last accessed 31st August 2011)).

[129] Commission for the Protection of Privacy Belgium (2010) recommendation on mobile mapping, 05/2010, 15 December 2010, available at www.privacycommission.be/en/static/pdf/recommendation-05-2010.pdf, para 20. (last accessed 31st August 2011).

[130] Google Maps Privacy. http://maps.google.com/intl/en_us/help/maps/streetview/privacy.html. (last accessed 31st August 2011).

[131] *Notification of Google Street View to the Dutch Data Protection Authority*, available at http://www.cbpweb.nl/asp/ORDetail.asp?moid=808084898f&refer=true&theme=purple. (last accessed 31st August 2011); Fleischer P, Navigating Europe's Streets, Google European Public Policy Blog, 7 October 2009, available at http://googlepolicyeurope.blogspot.com/2009/10/navigating-europes-streets.html. (last accessed 31st August 2011).

limit the period it keeps the unblurred photographs to six months.[132] Here, no definite answer to the question whether a shorter retention period would be possible can be given, since to a large extent the technological possibilities determine what is necessary and what is not. This information is however not publicly available.

Finally, Street View has published some incorrectly taken or processed photographs, which might come into conflict with the requirement of data accuracy. A further problem might be that some photographs may be outdated. "Our images show only what our vehicles were able to see on the day that they drove past the location. Afterwards, it takes at least a few months to process the collected images before they appear online. This means that images that you look at on Street View could be anywhere from a few months to a few years old."[133] But these are minor points. In brief, although there might be questions regarding the purpose limitation principle and the data minimisation principle, Street View complies with most of the principles relating to data quality.

4.2.4 Legitimate Purpose and Purpose limitation

4.2.4.1 Data Protection Directive

The Directive requires that personal data are processed on a legitimate basis as laid down by law and offers six possibilities to comply with this requirement. Firstly, a data processor may process personal data if "the data subject has unambiguously given his consent."[134] Consent is defined as "any freely given specific and informed indication of his wishes by which the data subject signifies his agreement to personal data relating to him being processed."[135] Consent can be given implicitly, but according to the Working Party, doing nothing can almost never be construed as unambiguous consent.[136] Consent should be freely given, so consent given under pressure is not valid. As consent also has to be specific, consent "to use personal data for commercial purposes" is not acceptable for example.[137] Finally consent has to be informed.[138]

---

[132] EDRI, Article 29: Reduce The Storing Period Of Google Street View's Images. 10 March 2010, available at www.edri.org/edrigram/number8.5/article-29-wp-google-street-view (last accessed 31st August 2011).

[133] Google Maps Privacy. http://maps.google.com/intl/en_us/help/maps/streetview/privacy.html. (last accessed 31st August 2011).

[134] Article 7(a) of the Data Protection Directive.

[135] Article 2(h) of the Data Protection Directive.

[136] Article 29 Working Party, *Opinion 15/2011 on the definition of consent (WP 187)*. 13 July 2011, p 12.
1/2008 on data protection issues related to search engines (WP148). 4 April 2008, p 17.

[137] *Landgericht* Bonn, LG Bonn, Urteil vom 31.10.2006, Az. 11 O 66/06.

[138] See about transparency and information duties: para 2.5.

Secondly data processing is allowed when it is necessary for the performance of a contract. This is for example the case when one pays with a credit card: certain personal data have to be processed. Thirdly, processing is allowed if it is necessary for compliance with a legal obligation to which the controller is subject. Fourthly, processing is allowed if it is necessary in order to protect the vital interests of the data subject. Fifthly, processing is allowed if it is necessary for the performance of a task carried out in the public interest or in the exercise of official authority vested in the controller or in a third party to whom the data are disclosed.[139]

Finally, under the so-called "balancing provision", data processing is allowed when the "processing is necessary for the purposes of the legitimate interests pursued by the controller or by the third party or parties to whom the data are disclosed, except where such interests are overridden by the interests for fundamental rights and freedoms of the data subject (...)."[140] When balancing the interests of the controller and the data subject, it has to be taken into account that the right to privacy and data protection are fundamental rights. As the proportionality principle guides the interpretation of the Directive, relevant questions are whether the processing of data is proportional to the specified purpose and whether there is another way of pursuing the purpose. The balancing provision is notoriously vague, and not all legislators and data protection authorities interpret it in the same way.[141]

The Directive provides for a separate regime for the processing of sensitive data, such as data revealing racial or ethnic origin, political opinions, religious beliefs, trade-union membership and data concerning health or sex life. In principle, the processing of such sensitive data is prohibited. This prohibition can only be lifted if certain specified conditions are met, which can be summarised as follows. Firstly, it can be lifted if the data subject has given his "explicit consent" to the processing of those data, except where the laws of the Member State provide that the prohibition may not be lifted by the data subject's giving his consent.[142] Secondly, processing of sensitive data is allowed if it is necessary to comply with employment law. Thirdly, processing is allowed if it is necessary to protect the vital interests of the data subject where the data subject is physically or legally incapable of giving his consent. Fourthly, processing is allowed if it is carried out in the course of the legitimate activities of a non-profit-seeking body with for example a political or religious aim. Lastly, processing is allowed if it relates to data which are manifestly made public by the data subject.[143]

---

[139] Article 7(b), 7(c), 7(d) and 7(e) of the Data Protection Directive.

[140] Article 7(f) of the Data Protection Directive.

[141] See Korff 2010, p 72.

[142] Article 8.2(a) of the Data Protection Directive. Some Member States require extra safeguards in their national laws, even when specific consent is obtained (European Commission, *Analysis and impact study on the implementation of Directive EC 95/46 in Member States*, p 12).

[143] Article 8 of the Data Protection Directive.

4.2.4.2 Behavioural Advertising

Like every controller, Google needs a legitimate basis for the use of personal data. There are no legal obligations for which the processing of personal data is necessary, and Google's behavioural advertising program does not serve the public interest or a vital interest of the data subject. Furthermore, Google cannot invoke a contractual relationship. Although search engine providers have suggested that the use of their service implies a contract on the basis of which they can process personal data for targeted advertising, the Working Party does not accept this reasoning.[144] Hence, in this case there are only two possible grounds to legitimize data processing: the balancing provision or unambiguous consent.

The balancing provision allows processing if it is necessary for the purposes of the legitimate interests pursued by the controller, unless the fundamental rights of the data subject should prevail. If behavioural advertising were not allowed, Google could still serve contextual advertising in many cases. Because the tracking of online behaviour can paint a highly detailed picture of an Internet user, which is often regarded as an invasion of privacy, the interests of the data subject should probably prevail.[145] According to the Working Party, "Covert surveillance of people's behaviour, certainly private behaviour such as visiting websites, is not in accordance with the principles of fair and legitimate processing of the Data Protection Directive."[146]

This means that in most circumstances the only possible ground to legitimize the processing of personal data for behavioural advertising is the "unambiguous consent" of the data subject.[147] Google's terms of service say: "You can accept the Terms by: (...) actually using the Services",[148] but such a 'browse wrap' license does not constitute unambiguous consent.[149] Merely using a Google service does not constitute a freely given, specific and informed decision to allow Google to collect personal data. Moreover, even visiting one of the millions of websites where Google serves content such as advertisements, can result in receiving a cookie and being profiled. It is not plausible that prior unambiguous consent is always obtained in such cases. Furthermore, it is possible that Google is

---

[144] Article 29 Working Party, *Opinion 1/2008 on data protection issues related to search engines (WP148)*. 4 April 2008, p 17.

[145] Idem, para 5.2. See also Article 29 Working Party, *The future of privacy (WP168)*. 1 December 2009, pp 16–17. The English Information Commissioner's Office seems to have a less stringent view ICO (2010) *Personal information online code of practice*. July 2010, available at http://www.gov.gg/ccm/cms-service/download/asset/?asset_id=13634136. (last accessed 31st August 2011).

[146] Article 29 Working Party, *Opinion 1/2008 on data protection issues related to search engines (WP148)*. 4 April 2008, p 23; See further about the requirements for valid consent: Article 29 Working Party, *Opinion 15/2011 on the definition of consent (WP187)*. 13 July 2011.

[147] Traung 2010, p 220; Koëter 2009, p 111.

[148] According to article 7.2 of Google's Terms of Service, accepting the terms of Service means that "You agree to the use of your data in accordance with Google's privacy policies." www.google.com/accounts/TOS. (last accessed 31st August 2011).

[149] See also ECJ 9 November 2010, Case C92/09 and C-93/09 "*Volker und Markus Schecke GbR*", para 63, and Opinion Advocate General, para 91.

processing sensitive personal data, such as data regarding political opinions. The mere fact that somebody uses the Internet does not entail he has manifestly made public his sensitive data. Therefore, in the case of behavioural advertising, the only relevant exception to the prohibition to process sensitive data appears to be the "explicit consent" of the Internet user. However, like most other companies that engage in behavioural advertising, Google does not obtain prior consent. Offering a possibility to opt out is not sufficient to obtain consent.[150] In October 2010, the Working Party sent a letter to several advertising network providers (possibly including Google), inviting them to come up with solutions for more transparency and suitable mechanisms for consent.[151] To conclude: in most cases Google needs the unambiguous consent of Internet users to legitimize data processing for behavioural advertising. Therefore Google may not have a legitimate basis for the processing of personal data for its behavioural advertising program.

4.2.4.3 Google Street View

Can Google rely on one of the grounds to legitimize data processing for Street View? There are neither contractual nor legal obligations for which the processing of personal data is necessary and Google does not serve the vital interests of the data subject. Google processes both ordinary and sensitive personal data for its Street View service. In principle the data subject's consent may be a legitimate ground for both the processing of ordinary and sensitive personal data. While data subjects have not consented explicitly to their data being processed, they might have done so implicitly. According to the American "reasonable expectation of privacy" doctrine, one may not reasonably expect full privacy when walking on the street. "Street View contains imagery that is no different from what you might see driving or walking down the street."[152] Google also writes:

> In the US, there's a long and noble tradition of "public spaces," where people don't have the same expectations of privacy as they do in their homes. This tradition helps protect journalists, for example. So we have been careful to only collect images that anyone could see walking down a public street. However we've always said that Street View will respect local laws wherever it is available and we recognise that other countries strike a different balance between the concept of "public spaces" and individuals' right to privacy in those public spaces. In other parts of the world local laws and customs are more protective of

[150] Article 29 Working Party, *Opinion 2/2010 on online behavioural advertising (WP 171)*. 22 June 2010, p 15. The new e-Privacy Directive (amended in 2009) only allows the use of tracking cookies on condition that the Internet user has given his prior consent, having been provided with clear and comprehensive information. Although Member States had to implement the rule in May 2011, it is not clear yet how this rule will be applied in practice.
[151] Letter from the Article 29 Working Party addressed to the Ad Network Providers, 29 October 2010, available at http://ec.europa.eu/justice/policies/privacy/docs/wpdocs/others/2010_10_29_letter_Ad_network_and_annex_en.tif. (last accessed 31st August 2011).
[152] Google Maps Privacy. http://maps.google.com/intl/en_us/help/maps/streetview/privacy.html. (last accessed 31st August 2011).

individuals' right to privacy in public spaces, and therefore they have a more limited concept of the right to take and publish photographs of people in public places.[153]

Indeed, in Europe the "reasonable expectation of privacy" doctrine is less influential; in certain circumstances one has a right to privacy in public.[154] Furthermore, according to the European Court of Justice, "a general derogation from the application of the directive in respect of published information would largely deprive the directive of its effect."[155] In principle the Directive applies when photographs that contain personal data are published on the Internet, also when they are taken in public.[156]

To invoke the consent of the data subject as the ground for data processing, it must either be unambiguous when it relates to ordinary personal data or explicit when it relates to sensitive data. An opt-out system that consists of blurring one's face if Google failed to blur it is not enough to construe unambiguous consent. The requirement for a legitimate purpose must be fulfilled before the data processing starts, not afterwards. The concept of implicit consent when walking in public or with regard to a less reasonable expectation of privacy in the public domain might also relate to another legitimate ground under the Directive for the processing of sensitive data, namely that personal data have been manifestly made public by the data subject. Although some people may have manifestly made public their (sensitive) personal data, it is unlikely that all people on the street have done so. Kotschy writes in another context: "'Making information public' requires a deliberate act by the data subject, disclosing the data to the public. Video surveillance can therefore not be justified by the fact that the data subjects 'showed themselves in public.'"[157]

Google might try to invoke the argument that its service is necessary for the performance of a task carried out in the public interest. Street View has indeed enriched the public life and might be said to be of such importance that it serves the public interest. However, this does probably not fulfil the requirements for a successful invocation of this legitimisation of the processing of personal data. This ground is primarily invoked by governmental organisations which serve the public interest. It may either relate to governmental organisations performing a public task or to private companies that fulfil privatised governmental tasks.[158] Neither is however the case with regard to Street View.

Finally the balancing provision allows data processing of non-sensitive personal data when it is necessary for the legitimate interests of the controller, unless these interests are overridden by the interests of the data subjects with regard to data

---

[153] Fleischer P, Street View and Privacy. Google Lat Long Blog. 24 September 2007, available at http://google-latlong.blogspot.com/2007/09/street-view-and-privacy.html. (last accessed 31st August 2011).

[154] ECtHR, 24 June 2004, application no. 59320/00, Caroline Von Hannover v. Germany, para 50.

[155] ECJ 16 December 2008, Case C-73/07, "*Satamedia*", paras 48–49.

[156] See ECJ 6 November 2003, Case C-101/01, "*Bodil Lindqvist*", paras 24–27.

[157] Kotschy 2010, p 62.

[158] Kuner 2007, p 244.

protection and privacy. Google has a legitimate interest in processing personal data, but the question is whether the fundamental rights of the data subjects should override this interest. To answer this question, there must be a balancing of the two interests of these parties. This weighing of interests must be done on a case-by-case basis, and all circumstances should be taken into account.[159] A fundamental right of the data controller would be an example of a legitimate interest that could override the fundamental rights of the data subject.[160] In general, fundamental rights carry greater weight than the interest for profit, which is Google's main interest. Therefore, it seems not evident that Google can rely on the balancing provision in the case of Street View. This conclusion appears to be in line with the fact that some national authorities asked Google to implement extra measures to ensure the privacy of the data subjects, such as prior opt-out options for houses, information distribution via media and more effective blurring methods.[161] These conditions may be set on the ground of a number of the Directive's requirements, but may also affect the outcome of the balancing act.

4.2.5 Transparency Principle and the Rights of the Data Subject

4.2.5.1 Data Protection Directive

Data processing should take place in a transparent manner. This is one of the key principles of data protection regulation.[162] In order for data processing to be fair the data subject has to be aware that data concerning him are being processed. The controller should at least provide information regarding his identity and the purposes of the processing. More information should be given when this is necessary to guarantee fair processing, having regard to the specific circumstances in which the data are collected.

---

[159] See Kotschy 2010, p 58; Kuner 2007, p 244.

[160] ECJ 6 November 2003, Case C-101/01 (Bodil Lindqvist) para 90; Kotschy 2010, p 58.

[161] See for example: Czech Office for Personal Data Protection, Annual Report 2010, pp 29–30, and Press Release 23 May 2011 (available at www.uoou.cz/files/rep_2010.pdf and www.uoou.cz/uoou.aspx?menu=125&submenu=614&loc=792&lang=en, last accessed 31st August 2011); Federal Administrative Court Switzerland 20 March 2011, Case A-7040/2009, *"Eidgenössischer Datenschutz- und Öffentlichkeitsbeauf-tragter EDÖB vs. Google Inc. And Google Switzerland GmbH"*, Computer Law Review International 3/2011, p 87–89; Hamburgischen Beauftragten für Datenschutz und Informationsfreiheit, Keine weiteren Veröffentlichungen von Bildern in Google Street View, Press release 11 April 2011, available at http://www.datenschutz-hamburg.de/news/detail/article/dies-ist-ein-pressebeitrag2-copy-3.html?tx_ttnews%5Bswords%5D=street%20view&tx_ttnews%5BbackPid%5D=129&cHash=1f64e5b4aebdf6d2d73d4107ca61491d (last accessed 31st August 2011); Türk A (2011) How many German households have opted-out of Street View?, Google European Public Policy Blog, 21 October 2010, http://googlepolicyeurope.blogspot.com/2010/10/how-many-german-households-have-opted.html (last accessed 31st August 2011).

[162] Gutwirth and De Hert 2006.

Some examples of this type of information are the recipients or categories of recipients of the data, the existence of the right of access and the right to rectify data. The information needs to be clear and precise. The Directive provides for an exemption from the information duty where the provision of information "proves impossible or would involve a disproportionate effort." In such cases Member States must provide appropriate safeguards.[163]

On the Internet, information is usually provided in privacy policies that are posted (behind a link) on websites. The Working Party emphasises that overly long privacy policies full of legalese do not provide information in a sufficiently clear manner and that is not acceptable if they are difficult to find on a website. Therefore, the Working Party calls for privacy statements written in "simple, unambiguous and direct language."[164] Indeed, there is abundant empirical research that shows that the current practice of posting privacy policies on websites largely fails to inform Internet users.[165]

Transparency is not only an obligation a controller must fulfil, it is also one of the rights the Directive grants the data subject. These rights are presented in somewhat summarised form below. Firstly, the data subject has the right to receive confirmation from the controller as to whether or not his data are being processed; information regarding the purposes of the processing; the categories of data concerned; and the recipients or categories of recipients to whom the data are disclosed. Secondly, the data subject has the right to obtain communication, in an intelligible form, of the data undergoing processing and of any available information as to their source. Thirdly, the data subject has the right to obtain from the controller as appropriate the rectification, erasure or blocking of data the processing of which does not comply with the provisions of the Directive, in particular because of the incomplete or inaccurate nature of the data.[166] Fourthly, a data subject has a general right to object on compelling legitimate grounds to the processing of his data.[167] The Directive requires Member States to grant this right at least when data are processed by a public authority or in the public interest, or when the processing is based on the balancing provision.[168] Where there is a justified objection, the processing may no longer involve those data. Fifthly, a data subject has a specific right to object to the use of his personal data for direct marketing.[169] Lastly, every person has the right not to be subjected to a decision which produces legal effects concerning him or significantly affects him and which is based solely on automated processing of data intended to

---

[163] Article 11 of the Data Protection Directive.

[164] Article 29 Working Party, *Opinion 10/2004 on More Harmonised Information Provisions (WP100)*. 25 November 2004, para V.

[165] McDonald 2010, chapter 5, with further references. See also Van Eijk et al. (2011).

[166] Article 12(a) and 12(b) of the Data Protection Directive.

[167] Article 14(a) of the Data Protection Directive.

[168] Article 7 (a) and 7(b) of the Data Protection Directive.

[169] Article 14(a) and 14(b) of the Data Protection Directive.

evaluate certain personal aspects relating to him, such as his performance at work, creditworthiness, reliability, conduct, etc.[170]

4.2.5.2 Behavioural Advertising

How should Google's behavioural advertising program be judged in the light of the transparency principle? Google provides more transparency than other companies that engage in behavioural advertising. Google did not launch its behavioural advertising program quietly, but announced it in a blog post.[171] Furthermore, Google releases videos on YouTube, explaining clearly how cookies are used and how behavioural advertising works (how Google makes advertising "more interesting").[172] In addition, Google presented a tool called the Ads Preferences Manager, "which lets you view, delete, or add interest categories associated with your browser so that you can receive ads that are more interesting to you."[173] Google also adds icons in advertisements based on behavioural targeting on which users can click to access their profile.[174]

There are also negative aspects in the light of the transparency principle. Google's privacy policies do not fully explain which data are added to a behavioural profile and to what extent one's online behaviour is monitored. Although Google's privacy statements are not typical legalese and not overly long, some questions remain about the data flows.[175] "Advertising and publishing customers may use web beacons in conjunction with the DoubleClick cookie to collect information about your visit to the website and exposure to a particular advertisement."[176] "We provide [personal] information to our subsidiaries, affiliated companies or other trusted businesses or persons for the purpose of processing personal

---

[170] Article 12(a) and 15 of the Data Protection Directive.

[171] Wojcicki S, Making ads more interesting. The Official Google Blog. 11 March 2009, available at http://googleblog.blogspot.com/2009/03/making-ads-more-interesting.html. (last accessed 31st August 2011).

[172] Google Privacy: Interest-based advertising. 2 March 2009, available at www.youtube.com/watch?v=aUkm_gKgdQc (last accessed 31st August 2011).

[173] Wojcicki S, Making ads more interesting. The Official Google Blog. 11 March 2009, available at http://googleblog.blogspot.com/2009/03/making-ads-more-interesting.html. (last accessed 31st August 2011).

[174] Shieh L, New In-Ads Notice Label and Icon, Google Inside Adwords, 21 March 2011, available at http://adwords.blogspot.com/2011/03/new-in-ads-notice-label-and-icon.html. (last accessed 31st August 2011).

[175] See also: Yang M, Trimming Our Privacy Policies. The Official Google Blog. 3 September 2010, available at http://googleblog.blogspot.com/2010/09/trimming-our-privacy-policies.html. (last accessed 31st August 2011).

[176] Google Privacy Center. Privacy Policy for Google Ads and the Google Display Network. 29 September 2010. www.google.com/privacy/ads/privacy-policy.html. (last accessed 31st August 2011).

information on our behalf."[177] Such phrases may confuse some readers. Which companies are deemed "other trusted businesses"? How many "affiliated companies" are there? Many companies reserve the right to change their privacy policies, and Google is no exception:

> Please note that this Privacy Policy may change from time to time. We will not reduce your rights under this Privacy Policy without your explicit consent. We will post any Privacy Policy changes on this page and, if the changes are significant, we will provide a more prominent notice (including, for certain services, email notification of Privacy Policy changes).[178]

Which changes would be "significant" is not clear. According to Google's terms of service: "The manner, mode and extent of advertising by Google on the Services are subject to change without specific notice to you."[179]

Although the Ads Preferences Manager is a step in the right direction, Internet users cannot see all data that are actually tied to their profile. The Ads Preferences Manager merely shows the interests that Google infers after monitoring the user's online behaviour. As Van Hoboken notes: "To some extent, the control and transparency is merely a façade, behind which a (for the end-user) opaque sophisticated data processing architecture is doing the real work."[180] For example, one cannot access information about the retargeting information. Likewise it is impossible to find out on what basis Google infers interests. Furthermore, ample research shows that most Internet users are not or only vaguely aware to what extent their online behaviour is tracked. The average Internet user does not understand how cookies work, and is not acquainted with the data flows behind behavioural advertising.[181] Such users might never see Google's Ads Preferences Manager or the possibilities to opt-out. An opt-in system would be a more transparent way of starting to track the online behaviour of an Internet user. The onus would be on Google to convince Internet users that the advantages of behavioural advertising ("ads that are relevant") outweigh possible disadvantages.[182]

In terms of the rights of the data subject, Google complies to a large extent with the requirements. The Ads Preferences Manager presents information in a user-friendly way and offers the possibility to rectify or erase categories Google has associated with a cookie. However, as there are much more data stored than one can see in the Ads

[177] Idem.

[178] Google Privacy Center. Privacy Policy. 3 October 2010, available at http://www.google.com/privacy/privacy-policy.html. (last accessed 31st August 2011).

[179] Article 17.2 of the Google Terms of Service. www.google.com/accounts/TOS. (last accessed 31st August 2011).

[180] Van Hoboken J, Google Rolls Out Behavorial Targeting. 19 March 2009, available at http://www.jorisvanhoboken.nl/?p=262. (last accessed 31st August 2011).

[181] McDonald 2010, chapter 5. See also Van Eijk et al. 2011.

[182] The e-Privacy Directive provides for a separate transparency regime. Article 5.3 only allows the use of cookies and similar devices "on condition that the subscriber or user concerned is provided with clear and comprehensive information in accordance with [the Data Protection Directive], inter alia about the purposes of the processing."

Preferences Manager, this may not be sufficient to comply with the right to access. For example, it is questionable whether Google provides sufficient information "as to their source" of one's data, as it is not completely clear which data are used to compile the behavioural profiles. Although it would be an interesting experiment, we have not tested if Google provides an overview of the personal data it processes for the behavioural profile upon request. Some practical issues might arise when doing such a request, as no name is tied to the profile, but a request to have access to all personal data tied to cookie "2vesgazbej45va555xsenyvs"[183] would be conceivable.

Google offers a user-friendly way to opt out of behavioural advertising. A common problem with such opt-out systems is that if a user clears his cookies, the opt-out cookie is deleted as well and the tracking starts again. Google also offers a plug-in for browsers to make an opt-out permanent.[184] According to Google, it will not only stop showing targeted advertisements after an opt-out, but it will also stop "collect[ing] interest category information."[185] In this respect Google offers users a broader opportunity to protect their data than many other behavioural advertising companies, which merely promise to stop showing targeted advertisements after an opt-out.[186] Although more transparency would make the rights of the data subject more meaningful, Google complies with a data subject's right to object.

Finally, every person has the right not to be subjected to an automated decision that produces legal effects concerning him or significantly affects him. This rule may seem relevant for some behavioural advertising practices. For example, banks might not advertise credit cards to people whose profile suggests that they live in a poor town. The targeting could limit the choices that are presented to a person. However, as such targeting does not constitute a decision that "significantly affects" a data subject, the prohibition does not apply.[187] In conclusion, Google's behavioural advertising program largely complies with the rights of the data subject, but it could do better with regards to the transparency principle.

---

[183] This is one of the cookies that Google placed on the computer of one of the authors.

[184] Wojcicki S, Making ads more interesting. The Official Google Blog. 11 March 2009, available at http://googleblog.blogspot.com/2009/03/making-ads-more-interesting.html (last accessed 31st August 2011). Harvey S, Moonka R, Keep your opt-outs, Google Public Policy Blog, 24 January 2011, available at http://googlepublicpolicy.blogspot.com/2011/01/keep-your-opt-outs.html. (last accessed 31st August 2011).

[185] Google Privacy Center, Advertising and Privacy, available at www.google.com/privacy/ads (last accessed 31st August 2011).

[186] Komanduri et al. (2011). See for example the opt-out page of the Internet Advertising Bureau, available at www.youronlinechoices.com/uk/your-ad-choices. (last accessed 31st August 2011).

[187] González Fuster G et al. 2010, p 115.

4.2.5.3 Google Street View

Does Google Street View comply with the transparency principle? In an opinion regarding video surveillance, the Working Party said: "Data subjects should be informed in line with Article 10 and 11 of the Directive. They should be aware of the fact that video surveillance is in operation (...); they should be informed in a detailed manner as to the places monitored."[188] Street View does not concern continuous filming, so it is not fully comparable with video surveillance.[189] Still, it is questionable whether the data subject is adequately informed about data processing. Many people do not know that they are on Street View. Google does publish on a website where it will be photographing in a certain period.

> This information shows a sample of the areas in which our cars are currently operating. We try to make sure the information is accurate and kept up to date, but because of factors outside our control (weather, road closures, etc.), it is always possible that our cars may not be operating, or be operating in areas that are not listed. In these circumstances, we'll try to update the list as soon as we can. Please also be aware that where the list specifies a particular city, this may include smaller cities and towns that are within driving distance.[190]

The user may click on a country and see in which areas Google is planning to photograph in the near future. However, a possibility for individuals to check Google Street View to see whether they might be or have been photographed may not suffice to comply with the Directive's transparency requirements. People cannot be expected to check Street View to see whether they will be or have been photographed either in their residential or working area, or in unusual places where they go to only once a month, a year or a lifetime. Moreover, the data specified on the website is not very specific. It may be possible to provide more information without a disproportionate effort. Several data protection authorities required Google to inform the public about photographing through the press as well.[191] Google grants data subjects the right to erasure of their personal data:

> If our detectors missed something, you can easily let us know. We provide easily accessible tools allowing users to request further blurring of any image that features the user, their family, their car or their home. In addition to the automatic blurring of faces and license plates, we will blur the entire car, house, or person when a user makes this request for additional blurring. Users can also request the removal of images that feature inappropriate content (for example: nudity or violence).[192]

---

[188] Article 29 Working Party, *Opinion 4/2004 on the Processing of Personal Data by means of Video Surveillance (WP89)*, 11 February 2004, p 22.

[189] See also: Information Commissioner's Office (2009) Letter regarding Privacy International's complaint about Google Street View, 30 March 2009, www.ico.gov.uk/upload/documents/library/data_protection/notices/response_to_pi_complaint_v1.pdf. (last accessed 31st August 2011).

[190] Google Maps, Where is Street View available?, available at www.google.com/intl/en_us/help/maps/streetview/where-is-street-view.html. (last accessed 31st August 2011).

[191] Article 11.2 of the Data Protection Directive. See Sect. 4.2.4.3.

[192] Google Maps Privacy. http://maps.google.com/intl/en_us/help/maps/streetview/privacy.html. (last accessed 31st August 2011).

To conclude, Google respects most of the data subject's rights, but there is room for improvement with regards to the transparency principle.

4.3 Conclusion

This chapter assessed the interplay of the European data protection regime and two services: Google's behavioural advertising program and Google Street View. The chapter focused on five aspects of the Data Protection Directive: the applicability of the Directive, the jurisdiction, the principles relating to data quality, the legitimate purpose and lastly the transparency principle in connection with the rights of the data subject.

The applicability of the Directive is triggered when "personal data" are "processed" under the authority of the "controller" of the personal data. Both "processing" and "personal data" are broadly defined in the Directive. Personal data is any information relating to an identified or identifiable natural person; an identifiable person is one who can be identified, directly or indirectly. Profiles without a name tied to them and photographs of people with a blurred face on Street View can also constitute personal data. Accordingly, Google processes personal data for both services. In the case of Street View, and possibly in the case of behavioural advertising, Google also processes sensitive data, such as data revealing racial origin, political opinions, religious beliefs, trade-union membership and data concerning health and sex life. As Google determines the purposes and means of the processing it is the data controller. Therefore, the first threshold is met for both services.

Secondly there is the jurisdictional threshold. The Directive applies, among other situations, when the controller is not established on Community territory and uses equipment situated on Community territory for data processing. For both services Google uses equipment on Community territory, by using cars for Street View, and—according to the Working Party—by placing cookies on computers for behavioural advertising. Hence, the Directive applies to both services. This chapter made an assessment with regard to three requirements: the principles relating to data quality, the legitimate ground for the processing, and finally the transparency principle in connection with the rights of the data subjects.

Firstly, the principles relating to data quality require that personal data be processed fairly and lawfully. Data must be collected for specified and explicit purposes and not further processed in a way incompatible with those purposes. Data must be accurate and not excessive in relation to the purposes for which they are processed, and retained no longer than is necessary for those purposes. Assessing Google's compliance with the data quality principle is not easy because not all aspects of its data processing practices are transparent. Google is more restrained than other companies that engage in behavioural advertising. Although Google does not add all information at its disposal to behavioural profiles, it does add large amounts of data, such as data regarding surfing behaviour and YouTube viewing data. Furthermore,

Google may not have a sufficiently specified purpose for this data processing. With regard to Street View, personal data are processed for a specified and explicit purpose. Street View largely complies with the principles relating to data quality.

Secondly, personal data may only be processed on the basis of a legitimate basis laid down by law. There are neither contractual nor legal obligations for which the processing is necessary and Google does not serve the vital interests of the data subject or the public interest with the services. As a result, there are only two possible grounds to legitimise data processing: the unambiguous consent of the individual and the so-called balancing provision. The Directive prohibits processing of sensitive data unless certain requirements are satisfied. In Google's case the most relevant exception to this prohibition is the individual's explicit consent. Google does not obtain prior consent for either of the two services. Offering a possibility to opt-out of a service is not sufficient for unambiguous or explicit consent. This would leave the balancing provision as the only possible legitimate ground for data processing. This provision allows data processing when it is necessary for the legitimate interests of the controller, unless the interests of the data subjects for data protection and privacy should prevail. Google has an interest in processing personal data, but this interest should be weighed against the fundamental rights of the data subjects. The Working Party does not accept the balancing provision as a ground for the processing of personal data for behavioural advertising. For Street View, the balancing act is somewhat more complex. Some data protection authorities only accept the balancing provision as a legitimate ground if Google takes additional measures to ensure that the privacy of the data subjects is adequately protected.

Thirdly and finally, this chapter has assessed whether Google lives up to its duties under the transparency principle and its duty to respect the rights of the data subject. In order for data processing to be fair the data subject has to be aware that data concerning him are being processed. The controller must provide clear, precise and comprehensive information. Furthermore, the data subject has several rights, such as the right to be informed, to consult the data, to request corrections and to object to processing in certain circumstances. With regard to its behavioural advertising program, Google respects most of the rights of the data subject. Google offers access to part of a profile and offers several user-friendly possibilities to opt out. In this respect Google is a forerunner in comparison with other companies. However, Google could do better in terms of transparency. Questions remain about how much personal data are stored, for how long the data are retained, and how the data are used. In the case of Street View, Google respects the rights of the data subject. People can request Google to blur their houses or their vehicles. Again, Google could do better in terms of transparency. In conclusion, not all aspects of the two services are easy to reconcile with the Directive's requirements. The Directive is under review at the moment, and issues such as jurisdiction, the definition of personal data, the requirements for consent and the application of the balancing provision may need clarification.

References

Anguelov D et al (2010) Google street view: capturing the World at street level. IEEE Comput Soc Comput 43(6):32–38

Battelle J (2005) The Search. How Google and its rivals rewrote the rules of business and transformed our culture. Penguin Group, New York

Burdon M (2010) Privacy invasive geo-mashups: privacy 2.0 and the limits of first generation information privacy laws. University of Illinois Journal of Law Technology & Policy. No. 1, 2010

Bygrave L (2002) Data protection law: approaching its rationale, logic and limits. Kluwer Law International, The Hague

Gomez J et al. (2009) Know Privacy, Final Report. UC Berkeley, School of Information. http://www.knowprivacy.org. Accessed 1 June 2009

González Fuster G et al (2010) From unsolicited communications to unsolicited adjustments. Redefining a key mechanism for privacy protection. In: Gutwirth S et al (eds) Data protection in a profiled World. Springer, Dordrecht, pp 105–117

Gutwirth S, De Hert P (2006) Privacy, data protection and law enforcement. Opacity of the individual and transparency of power. In: Claes E, Duff A, Gutwirth S (eds) Privacy and the criminal law. Antwerp, Intersentia, pp 61–104

Gutwirth S, Poullet Y (2008) The contribution of the Article 29 Working Party to the construction of a harmonised European data protection system: an illustration of 'reflexive governance'? In: Asinari VP, Palazzi P (eds) Défis du droit à la protection de la vie privée. Challenges of privacy and data protection law—Challenges of privacy and data protection law. Bruylant, Brussels, pp 570–610

Hoofnagle CJ (2009) Beyond Google and evil: how policy makers, journalists and consumers should talk differently about Google and privacy. First Monday, Volume 14, Number 4. http://www.firstmonday.org. Accessed 6 April 2009

Koëter J (2009) Behavioral targeting en privacy: een juridische verkenning van internet gedragsmarketing. Tijdschrift voor internetrecht 2009-4

Komanduri S et al. (2011) AdChoices? Compliance with online behavioral advertising notice and choice requirements. CMU-Cylab-11-005. http://www.cylab.cmu.edu/files/pdfs/tech_reports/CMUCyLab11005.pdf. Accessed 30 March 2011

Korff D (2010) Comparative study on different approaches to new privacy challenges, in particular in the light of technological developments, Working Paper 2.0. http://ec.europa.eu/justice/policies/privacy/studies/index_en.htm. Accessed 20 January 2010

Kotschy W (2010) Directive 95/46/EC—Data protection directive. In: Büllesbach A et al (eds) Concise European IT law. Kluwer Law International, Alphen aan den Rijn

Krishnamurthy B, Wills C (2009a) On the leakage of personally identifiable information via online social networks. WOSN'09: the second workshop on online social networks. http://www2.research.att.com/∼bala/papers

Krishnamurthy B, Wills C (2009b) Privacy diffusion on the web: a longitudinal perspective. In: Proceedings of the 18th international conference on world wide web. http://www2.research.att.com/∼bala/papers

Kuner C (2007) European data protection law: corporate compliance and regulation. Oxford University Press, Oxford

Kuner C et al. (2009) Study on online copyright enforcement and data protection in selected Member States. http://ec.europa.eu/internal_market/iprenforcement/docs/study-online-enforcement_en.pdf

Kuner C et al. (2010) Study on online copyright enforcement and data protection in selected Member States (Netherlands, Poland, UK). http://ec.europa.eu/internal_market/iprenforcement/docs/study-online-enforcement_042010_en.pdf

McDonald AM (2010) Footprints near the surf: individual privacy decisions in online contexts (diss.) Paper 7. http://repository.cmu.edu/dissertations/7

Ohm P (2009) Broken promises of privacy: responding to the surprising failure of anonymization. University of Colorado Law Legal Studies Research 2009 (Article No. 09–12), 13 August 2009

Rundle AG et al (2011) Using Google street view to audit neighborhood environments. Am J Prev Med 40(1):94–100

Toubiana V, Nissenbaum H (2011) An Analysis of Google logs retention policies. Journal of Privacy and Confidentiality. Volume 3, Issue 1, Article 2, 2011

Traung P (2010) EU Law on Spyware, Web Bugs, Cookies, etc., Revisited: Article 5 of the Directive on Privacy and Electronic Communications. Bus Law Rev 31:216–228

Van Eijk NANM et al (2011) A bite too big: Dilemma's bij de implementatie van de Cookiewet in Nederland (Dilemmas with the implementation of the Cookie law in the Netherlands), TNO-report no. 35473. http://www.ivir.nl/publicaties/vaneijk/A_bite_too_big.pdf. Accessed 28 February 2011.

Chapter 5
Google News and Copyright

Raquel Xalabarder

Contents

R. Xalabarder (✉)
Universitat Oberta de Catalunya, Barcelona, Spain
e-mail: rxalabarder@uoc.edu

R. Xalabarder
LLM Columbia Law School, New York, NY, USA

A. Lopez-Tarruella (ed.), *Google and the Law*,
Information Technology and Law Series 22, DOI: 10.1007/978-90-6704-846-0_5,
© T.M.C. ASSER PRESS, The Hague, The Netherlands, and the author(s) 2012

5.1 Introduction

News have always been compiled and reused. And copyright laws have always allowed it. Nevertheless, the social and economic significance of the news aggregation done online may require a re-assessment and adjustment of the copyright provisions governing news reuse.

Online news aggregators may take many forms.[1] *Feed aggregators* display contents from a number of different websites organized in "feeds" and usually arranged by topic, source, etc. Google News is a news-feed aggregator.[2] *Specialty aggregators* collect information from a number of sources but only dealing with a particular topic or subject. *Blog aggregators* use third-party content to create a blog about a specific topic (such as the Huffington Post[3]) thus, involving to some extent the creation of new "content".

They all have one thing in common: they use third-party pre-existing contents, such as newspaper articles, photographs and audiovisual recordings, which may be protected by copyright.

Google News was launched in September 2002 as an English-language "news service" to complement its general search engine. Today, Google offers more than 40 regional news services (Google News sites) in over 17 different languages. In Google's own words:

> Google News is a computer-generated news site that aggregates headlines from news sources worldwide, groups similar stories together and displays them according to each reader's personalized interests. ... On Google News we offer links to several articles on every story, so you can first decide what subject interests you and then select which publishers' accounts of each story you'd like to read. Click on the headline that interests you and you'll go directly to the site which published that story. Our articles are selected and ranked by computers that evaluate, among other things, how often and on what sites a story appears online. We also rank based on certain characteristics of news content such as freshness, location, relevance and diversity. As a result, stories are sorted without regard to political viewpoint or ideology and you can choose from a wide variety of perspectives on any given story.[4]

For copyright purposes, three elements in Google News must be distinguished:

- the Google News *website*: the site displays a pre-set compilation of links to the current and most popular news available online. The listing, showing the headline and a short extract of the linked work, is the automatic result from the Google news search engine. In addition, the links are classified under several

---

[1] For a general overview of different news aggregators, see Isbell 2010, pp 1–5.

[2] Yahoo! News also qualifies as a feed aggregator, albeit it only uses contents produced by press-agencies (not newspaper publishers) and recently it has started producing its own contents, thus resembling more a news-publisher than a "typical" news-aggregator.

[3] The Huffington Post was founded in 2005. Last February 2011, AOL bought it for $315 million.

[4] Source: http://news.google.com/intl/en_us/about_google_news.html Last visited 28 February 2011.

categories such as hot news, business, sports and entertainment. Google News aggregates news contents available online (and to a lesser extent, it also uses licensed material).[5] Google neither edits the content aggregated[6] nor includes any advertising on the News sites.[7]

- the Google News *search engine*: a complex algorithm that gathers, ranks and displays all the news available online on a particular topic, at the request of the user. The results are ranked according to pre-set criteria (such as relevance, freshness, diversity and users' preferences gathered from previous searches), showing the headline, a short extract of the located contents and a link to the full work as currently posted on the source webpage.
- its *cache* copy service: in addition to the above, the search engine offers a link to a *cache* copy of the located contents which has been previously stored in Google's servers. Through it, the user is able to access a newspaper article once it is no longer available on the original website.

5.1.1 The Economic and Social Impact of News Aggregation

The Internet is proving to be a catalyst for the news industry. Major newspapers have been suffering a negative trend in revenue[8] and aggregation sites with larger audiences[9] are identified as the cause of this decline, by taking further advertising share from newspapers.[10] As Rupert Murdoch bluntly put it:

---

[5] For instance, following the settlement reached in the U.S.A. with Agence France Press (see *infra*), AFP contents is reproduced in Google's servers and made available in full (not just a link) thru the Google News site. News served by other news agencies, such as Reuters, is linked to the original sites.

[6] Although the compilations listed in the Google News sites are the automatic result of the complex search engine algorithm, some editorial decisions are found in previously made choices: in the design of the search engine algorithm itself, in the identification of what is -and what is not- "news" that can be aggregated by the engine, and ultimately on the automatic ranking and classification of the results.

[7] Google's business model relying mostly on advertising, it is not unlikely that advertising might be included on Google News sites in the future.

[8] According to the Pew Project for Excellence in Journalism, advertising revenues for American newspapers dropped nearly 43% between 2006 and 2009. Print classified revenues, which used to generate 90% of newspaper revenues, have been steadily declining in the last decade. And so have online advertising revenues, with a 12% decline rate in 2010. See http://stateofthemedia.org/ 2010/newspapers-summary-essay/ (last accessed 28 February 2011).

[9] According to Nielsen/Netratings, Yahoo News is at the top of the list of the 20 most visited news websites, AOL News is the third, while Google News is ranking sixth. The remaining sites are major newspapers and broadcasting networks, such as MSNBC, CNN, New York Times, Fox News, ABC News, The Washington Post, USA Today, BBC and alike. Source: http:// www.stateofthemedia.org/2010/online_nielsen.php. (last accessed 28 February 2011).

[10] Source: http://stateofthemedia.org/2010/newspapers-summary-essay/ (last accessed 28 February 2011).

> Producing journalism is expensive. We invest tremendous resources in our project from technology to our salaries. To aggregate stories is not fair use. To be impolite, it is theft. Without us, the aggregators would have blank slides. Right now content producers have all the costs, and the aggregators enjoy [the benefits].[11]

The production and subsequent dissemination of news have always required large investments. Consequently these activities have merged in the exclusive hands of news agencies and publishing networks, respectively.[12] Internet and digital technologies have shaken the traditional formats of news production and distribution. On the one hand, the evolution of digital technologies (cameras, cell-phones, laptops, Internet, Wi-Fi access, etc.) and their social spread (also in developing countries) has opened up the sources of production of information.[13] The network of "informants" now includes every citizen of the world equipped with the right technological means.[14] On the other hand, different news agents have entered the market and are competing with (or at least, disrupting) traditional formats of news distribution and even news aggregation.[15] Individual blogs may be aggregated by sites such as Google Blog Search[16] or Global Voices[17]; Wikinews[18] allows major collaborative production of news through wiki technologies; Digg News[19] is a platform open to unedited submissions which are rated and graded by peers; and so on.

Despite that, traditional news production formats (news agencies, newspapers, TV and radio stations) keep providing the vast majority of "content" used by news aggregators. Google News[20] and Yahoo News[21] could not exist (in fact, they would make no sense) without the pre-existing content posted by news publishers, broadcasters and news agencies.

At the same time, the public interest of news aggregation is unquestionable: it affords a convenient and easy tool to allocate *all* the published news on a specific topic or event, thus avoiding time-consuming and burdensome visits to the

---

[11] Source: http://www.guardian.co.uk/media/2009/dec/01/rupert-murdoch-no-free-news (last accessed 28 February 2011).

[12] Albeit the separation is not clear-cut since a few large publishers may afford to produce its own news, in addition to relying on the news produced by agencies).

[13] We have recently seen how Facebook, Twitter and other social networks have become "the" place to get updated information concerning air-space closing or riots in Middle East.

[14] A major difference still exists between traditional and emerging news publishers: while the former are subject to professional liability rules, the later are still mostly unregulated.

[15] For a comparative survey of the performance and impact of these aggregators see Richter 2008.

[16] http://blogsearch.google.com (last accessed 28 February 2011).

[17] http://www.globalvoicesonline.org (last accessed 28 February 2011).

[18] http://www.wikinews.org/ (last accessed 28 February 2011).

[19] http://digg.com (last accessed 28 February 2011).

[20] http://news.google.com (last accessed 28 February 2011).

[21] http://news.yahoo.com/ (last accessed 28 February 2011).

multiple news sites. News aggregation (especially through news search engines) brings people broader access to more diverse, complete, richer and comprehensible[22] information, than any newspaper reader could gather at one time using other "traditional" means; and they bring it to more people.[23]

5.1.2 The Copyright Implications of News Aggregation

News aggregators improve accessibility of information over the Internet. But most *aggregated* content has *originated* from newspapers, broadcasters and news agencies[24] and comes in the shape of intellectual creations such as articles, photographs and recordings which are protected by copyright.

As we said, it is not the first time that informatory purposes and copyright must be leveraged. Within copyright history, at least three different forms of news "aggregation" may be distinguished:

- *Press summaries* (*revues de presse*) involve the selection, reproduction, display and distribution of relevant parts of previously acquired newspapers (traditionally, in print); these compilations are usually conveyed in paper formats, and are commonly carried out for in-house use (within companies, public administration, etc.). Press summaries have been traditionally permitted by copyright laws under statutory limitations (either as quotations or under specific limitations or fair use defenses). Whether or not these limitations also cover press summaries involving digital formats and online news aggregation depends on the interpretation of the language in the applicable statute.
- *Press-clipping* involves the selection, reproduction (and, sometimes, scanning), display and distribution by digital means, such as emailing lists or intranet posting (sometimes, the selection is also printed out and circulated in paper format) of indexed information (headline, source and a short abstract), including a website link or attaching a copy of the selected articles. These compilations

---

[22] In addition, Google offers automatic translation of all search results.

[23] News accessed through news aggregators reach a "new public"—beyond the public that would be commonly reached under the ordinary distribution (in print and online) policies of newspapers and broadcasters (i.e., an article published in a local newspaper or in a minority language would unlikely be visited by foreigners, yet it may be displayed and translated through Google's applications and—depending on the search criteria and ordering- it might be even ranked in a higher position).

[24] Nielsen classifies the top 199 news sites in three kinds: aggregators, commentators and originators of news. "Of the 199 news sites, 27 (14%) primarily aggregate information produced by others; 20 (10%) put most of their resources toward offering commentary about news events first reported on by others. The largest portion, 152 (76%) produces their own original content. ... Among those that originate content, the majority, 124, are affiliated with legacy media outlets. Of these sites the largest sub-group is newspapers, with 90 sites, followed by local TV-based sites, 10." See http://www.stateofthemedia.org/2010/online_nielsen.php (last accessed 28 February 2011).

are usually done by a media agency that produces the compilation for the client usually in exchange for a subscription fee. Press-clipping has generated abundant litigation and found different solutions in national laws: some countries permit it as press summaries or quotations, some allow it -subject to compensation- unless the authors have expressly opposed it, others allow it to the extent it clears fair use/dealing standards, while others subject it to voluntary licensing.

- *News aggregation*, as we currently know it, consists of locating, gathering and linking to information contents posted on online sites. News aggregators provide powerful *search engines* that enable users to automatically find, rank and display the information requested (according to their search criteria), among all the news available online. In addition, the *site* displays a selection of the most popular news with links to the original sites. News aggregation services may be offered for free (some include advertising on their sites) or under subscription. No copyright statute refers to news aggregation; its allowance under a limitation or fair use clauses depends on the interpretation of the specific statutory terms. In addition to its copyright implications, news aggregation raises issues connected with ISP liability and safe harbors exemptions, as well as with competition law.

Lacking a clear answer in current copyright laws, news aggregators have been sued on several occasions in different countries, with different outcomes (some settled out of court). For purposes of this chapter, we will refer to two major cases involving Google News.[25]

5.1.2.1 "Agence France Press v. Google, Inc."[26] *(USA)*

Many of the stories and photographs linked by Google News which appeared on the websites of major or local newspapers had been written by news agencies such as the claimant. AFP claimed that only licensed parties (the newspapers) were entitled to use their contents and sued Google in 2005 for copyright infringement. In addition, AFP claimed a tort of "hot news" misappropriation.[27]

---

[25] Beyond Google News, other news services have been brought to court with different outcomes. We will refer to them along this chapter.

[26] See "*AFP v. Google*", No. 1:05CV00546 (GK) (D.D.C. 29 April 2005), (D.C.C. 19 May 2005), (D.D.C. 12 October 2005), (D.D.C. 29 January 2007).

[27] The "hot news" misappropriation doctrine dates back to the 1918 Supreme Court decision *in* "*International News Service v. Associated Press*", 248 U.S. 215 (1918). The INS (owned by W.R. Hearst) and the AP were two competing agencies that provided news stories on national and international events to local newspapers throughout the United States. During World War I, the AP was best positioned to carry news from Europe, INS rewrote the AP news published in East Coast newspapers and sent them to the INS clients on the West Coast. The Supreme Court designed the "hot news" doctrine, as a variant of the common law tort of misappropriation: a competitor cannot free ride on another competitor's work (effort) when the later is expecting to benefit from it. INS was enjoined from taking facts from the AP's news until the commercial value of these facts "as news" had elapsed.

Google filed motions to dismiss based on the AFP failure to identify the works that had been infringed and on the grounds that the headlines and short paragraphs did not qualify for copyright protection. Furthermore, Google argued that AFP and its licensees could have easily opted-out (by using robots.txt and metatags to prevent automatic indexation by Google's search engines). Google also insisted that its service increased the traffic to the linked websites. In April 2007, after 2 years in court, the parties settled and reached a license agreement that entitles Google News to reproduce and make available AFP contents in full text on its servers.

5.1.2.2 "Copiepresse v. Google, Inc."[28] *(Belgium)*

In Europe, Google News has been brought to court in Belgium. In 2006, the Belgian French site of Google News ("Google News Belgique") was launched. Copiepresse, the collective management organization for Belgian newspaper publishers in French and German languages,[29] sued Google. On 13 February 2007,[30] the Court of First Instance of Brussels ruled in favor of the claimants on the following grounds:

- Google News is not a "mere" search engine but rather an online information website which enters into unfair competition practices with the original websites by providing direct access to their articles and skipping their advertising (thus, diminishing their advertising revenues);
- The headline and short extract of the articles linked by Google are reproduced and displayed without the copyright owners' consent; These may be protected by copyright and since no statutory limitation is applicable to allow it (neither quotations nor use by the press) Google is infringing their rights of reproduction and public communication;
- The Google *cache* service (which consists of storing copies of third-party content in its servers and later making them available to users) cannot be exempted either as a temporary copying in Article 5.1 of the Information Society Directive 2001/29/EC (hereinafter EUCD) or under the *cache* copying safe harbor in Article 13 of the e-commerce Directive 2000/31/EC (hereinafter ECD);
- Even the moral rights of attribution and integrity are being infringed since the name of the author does not appear on the search results list and the thematic

---

[28] See « *Copiepresse SCRL v. Google Inc.* », *Tribunal de Première Instance de Bruxelles*, 13 February 2007; confirmed by *Cour d'Appel de Bruxelles* (9eme Ch.), 5 May 2011. Unless otherwise indicated, references in this chapter are made to the appeal court ruling. For commentaries about the first instance decision, see Strowel and Triaille 2008, Dusollier 2007 and Laurent 2007.

[29] Copiepresse was joined by SAJ and Assucopie, the collecting management organizations of journalists and scholarly authors, respectively.

[30] See « *Copiepresse SCRL v. Google Inc.* », Tribunal de Premiere Instance de Bruxelles, 13 February 2007, available at http://www.juriscom.net/documents/tpibruxelles20070213.pdf. (last accessed 28 February 2011).

compilation of the extracts of articles done by Google might contravene the "editorial or philosophical line" of the original publication.

This ruling was confirmed and partially amended[31] by the Brussels Court of Appeal (9ème ch.) on 5 May 2011.[32] The court managed to brush off all the claims raised by Google:

- The *cache* service offered by Google is an infringement of the rights of reproduction and communication to the public because it cannot be allowed as a temporary copy under Article 5.1 EUCD and it cannot qualify as "proxy caching" under the safe harbor in Article 13 ECD; without Google's intervention the user could not access the page that is no longer available in the source website, thus conveying a prejudice to the normal exploitation and failing to clear the three-step-test.[33]
- As far as the *news* service (including the site and search engine), the court concluded that:
  - the headlines and the first three lines (extracts) of the linked articles are copyright-protected contents[34];
  - their reproduction and communication to the public cannot be exempted by any of the existing statutory limitations (including, quotations[35]) which have to be restrictively interpreted[36];
  - these acts are not done merely for purposes of indexation and reference but rather they amount to a *verbatim* and *in extenso* reproduction of a significant part of the linked articles which convey the essential information and, hence, substitute for the originals[37];
  - the moral rights of attribution and of integrity are being infringed[38];
  - no implied license derives from the mere fact that copyright owners have not implemented the technological measures that could have excluded indexation and caching by Google; Copyright is about "express, certain and previous licensing"[39];

---

[31] Idem, ruling (3). The appealed ruling was amended on two grounds: restricting it to the infringements committed within Belgian territory (that is, to the infringing contents on the News sites of Google.be and Google.com) and excluding the works of the periodical *L'Echo* which had expressly licensed Google.

[32] *See « Copiepresse SCRL v. Google Inc. »*, Cour d'Appel de Bruxelles (9ème Ch.), 5 May 2011, available at http://www.copiepresse.be/pdf/Copiepresse5mai2011.pdf. Last visited 23 June 2011.

[33] See *« Copiepresse SCRL v. Google Inc. »*, ## 21–23, # 44 and # 54.

[34] See *« Copiepresse SCRL v. Google Inc. »*, # 29.

[35] See *« Copiepresse SCRL v. Google Inc. »*, # 32.

[36] See *« Copiepresse SCRL v. Google Inc. »*, # 29; adding that it is not the role of the judge to convey new limitations, see idem # 45.

[37] See *« Copiepresse SCRL v. Google Inc. »*, ## 28–29.

[38] See *« Copiepresse SCRL v. Google Inc. »*, # 38–42.

[39] See *« Copiepresse SCRL v. Google Inc. »*, # 50–51.

- neither the hosting safe harbor nor the search engine one (inexistent in Belgian law) are applicable to exempt liability in the news site[40];
- the fundamental right of access to information (Article 10 European Charter on Fundamental Rights) is not an excuse for not complying with copyright law[41];
- it has not been proven that copyright owners are abusing their copyrights[42] or that Copiepresse is abusing a dominant position in the market by setting unreasonable licensing conditions and suing Google to avoid competition.[43]

- The court only referred to the general *search engine* (as "Google Web") to imply—by opposition to "Google News"—its lawful character to the extent that it involves the mere provision of links[44] and to explain that it would not be affected by an eventual denial of license from the copyright owners to the operation of the Google News service.[45]

Accordingly, the appeal court confirmed the previous ruling, and condemned Google for copyright infringement and ordered it to delete from Google.be and Google.com news websites any contents and links owned by the claimants, as well as to delete all links to cache copies of that contents, subject to a fine of 25.000 euros per day of non-compliance. All in all, although a blow for Google News and *cache* services, the ruling seems to condone the functioning of the general search engine.

We will revisit this case during this chapter. Let's now examine the several basic questions (not necessarily easy) that need to be answered to assess whether news aggregation is lawful or not in terms of copyright.

5.2 Copyright Subject Matter

The first question we need to address is whether news works as well as titles and short fragments of them are protected by copyright.

Copyright protects original creations. This is not the place to discuss the concept of originality and, specifically, its application to factual works. It suffices to state that the concept of originality is commonly built upon two requirements: that the work was not been copied and that it shows some minimal amount of creativity; how minimal the amount will depend on the kind of work as well as on different national traditions.

The concept of originality has been evolving over time according to technological, market and social changes. And this is especially true in the case of news and press works.

---

[40] See « *Copiepresse SCRL v. Google Inc.* », ## 53 and 55.

[41] See « *Copiepresse SCRL v. Google Inc.* », ## 56–58.

[42] See « *Copiepresse SCRL v. Google Inc.* », ## 59–60.

[43] See « *Copiepresse SCRL v. Google Inc.* », ## 61–63.

[44] See « *Copiepresse SCRL v. Google Inc.* », ## 30, 55 and 57.

[45] See « *Copiepresse SCRL v. Google Inc.* », # 62.

5.2.1 News Articles

A common principle accepted by all current copyright laws: facts and ideas are not protected by copyright, only the specific expression of these facts and ideas may deserve protection. Yet, the theoretical distinction between non-copyrightable facts and copyrightable factual expression did not (and does not) come easy.

At the end of the nineteenth Century, the protection of news articles under copyright was very limited and contested.[46] In fact, Article 7 of the original Act of the Berne Convention (1886) expressly stated that newspaper and magazine articles published in any Berne Union country could be reproduced, in the original language or in translation, unless the authors or editors had expressly reserved so.[47]

Times and markets have changed; news works are now fully acknowledged as protected copyright subject matter, as long as they constitute original creations.[48]

The Berne Convention (hereinafter BC) contains no definition of originality and Member States may have different thresholds for protection. In the U.K., the traditional threshold for copyright turns to "labor, skill and effort;"[49] while the U.S. refers to "independent creation and a modest quantum of creativity;"[50] and civil-law countries tend to look for the imprint of the author's personality in his creation.[51]

According to EU community *acquis*, the concept of originality has been harmonized as "the author's own intellectual creation" for three categories of works only: computer programs (Directive 91/250/EEC, Article 1.3), databases (Directive 96/9/EC, Article 3.1) and photographs (Directive 93/98/EEC, Article 6).

---

[46] For more information about the historic protection on news articles in the U.S.A. and the U.K., see Brauneis 2009. For France, see Lucas and Lucas 2006, para 105 (court decisions granting copyright protection to news articles date back to 1861).

[47] A similar provision existed in Article 31 of the old Spanish Law, of 10 January 1879, on Intellectual Property (currently derogated).

[48] Accordingly, the current Article 2(8) of the Berne Convention presents a different reading: "The protection of the Convention shall not apply to news of the day or to miscellaneous facts having the character of mere items of press information." This provision is explained to mean that while news *per se* (facts and mere information) is not protected, news articles may be protected to the extent that they constitute literary or artistic works. See Ricketson and Ginsburg 2006, para 8.104–106.

[49] See Bently and Sherman 2001, pp 88–90. This criterion applies to all works except databases and computer programs subject to the harmonized standard of "the author's own intellectual creation"; see idem, pp 101–106.

[50] See Leaffer 1995, pp 41–42.

[51] In Germany, the work must be a "personal intellectual creation" (Article 2.2); in Italy, the law requires some "creative character" (Article 1); in Spain, it must be an "original creation" (Article 10.1); in France, reference is made to "intellectual creations" (Article L.112-3); and the Dutch copyright act refers to "creation in the literary, scientific or artistic areas" (Article 10). This does not mean that "small works" (such as leaflets, instructions, classified ads, etc.) cannot be protected under copyright—in fact, in most of these civil countries, they are indeed protected.

Beyond these, the threshold of originality remains a matter for national laws.[52] This may have changed, unexpectedly, as a result of the ECJ's ruling in the "*Infopaq*"[53] case where the concept of "work" as "*a subject-matter which is original in the sense that it is its author's own intellectual creation*"[54] has been extended to all works—or at least, to newspaper articles.[55] Leaving aside any considerations as to the suitability of the "*Infopaq*" ruling,[56] its impact on harmonizing the concept of originality is uncertain.[57] It may well be a rather symbolic ruling since, at the end, the question of originality will remain subject to a case by case analysis and will be assessed by the national courts according to the concept of originality retained by each national law. And this holds true for news reports and articles as well as for any photographs and audiovisual recordings that may be

---

[52] In its 2004 Working Paper on the review of the EC legal framework in the field of copyright and related rights, the Commission stated that "(i)n theory, divergent requirements for the level of originality by Member States have the potential of posing barriers to intra-community trade. In practice, however, there seems to be no convincing evidence to support this." E.U. Commission, *Working Paper on the review of the EC legal framework in the field of copyright and related rights*, SEC (2004) 995, p 14; available at http://ec.europa.eu/internal_market/copyright/docs/review/sec-2004-995_en.pdf (last accessed 28 February 2011).

[53] See ECJ Judgement of 16 July 2009, *Infopaq International v. Danske Dagblades Forening*, (C-5/08), available at http://curia.europa.eu/. Infopaq International A/S is a media agency providing information services to its customers. Infopaq prepares lists of references to newspapers articles published in print which then sends to its subscribers. In order to do so, Infopaq scans the printed articles into an image format which is later converted into a text file; Infopaq then makes word searches into the text file and copies the results with a ten words margin (five words before and after the keyword searched). The resulting 11 words "captures" are listed, along with details of the source publication and page, on the summaries that are sent by email to its subscribers. Once it is converted into a text file, the image scan is deleted; and once the data searches have been "captured" the text files are deleted as well. The result from this "data capture process" is a list of fragments of news and press releases dealing with the issue or issues the subscriber has chosen to be informed about. Infopaq involves no linking (nor any making available online of the referenced articles) and is not open to the public in general: it is a subscriber service business that provides references to printed news and information. The professional association of Danish newspaper publishers (Dankse Dagblades Forening) sued Infopaq for copyright infringement. The questions submitted by the Danish court dealt with two main issues: the meaning of reproduction under Article 2 EUCD and the scope of the "transient or incidental reproductions" exempted under Article 5.1 EUCD. We will revisit both issues below. For a comment on this case, see Dercalye 2010, pp 247–251.

[54] See "*Infopaq*", para 37.

[55] A less disruptive reading of the ECJ ruling would apply the standard of originality to newspaper articles only (which constituted the factual basis for the "*Infopaq*" case) instead of extending it to all kind of works -as paragraph 37 of the ECJ ruling seems to imply.

[56] The ECJ may well be extra-limiting its competence. Had the E.U. Commission and Parliament desired to make such a concept applicable to all works, they could have done so in the EUCD articulate.

[57] It is not clear whether national courts will use this standard of originality when dealing with more "artistic" kind of works (such as novels and works of art, which are used to a very flexible yet traditional "artistic standard") or with the so-called small, sub-literary works (such as leaflets and classified ads which may be protected in many countries).

used in news aggregation. Yet, as we will see, the "Infopaq" ruling contains other elements that may be relevant for our analysis.

5.2.2 The Protection of Headlines and Titles

Far more difficult is to find a common playground for the protection of titles[58] and headlines *used* by news aggregators to display the search results and link to the original webpages. While in the U.S. and the U.K. the protection of titles and short phrases has been traditionally denied,[59] they may be granted protection in other European countries such as Spain (Article 10.2 TRLPI: titles of works are protected - if original- as part of these works) and France (the protection of titles as original works -independent from the work itself- has been generously granted by courts).[60]

Google has always argued that headlines are not entitled *per se* to copyright because they tend to encapsulate in a few words the factual content of the story, facts and expression merging into an indistinguishable unit that cannot be copyrighted. Courts have not always been persuaded by this argument. In one of the very first cases dealing with news aggregation, a UK court found an infringement by Shetland News using the headlines of The Shetland Times newspaper articles as pointers to the original site containing them.[61]

Similarly, the Tribunal de Première Instance de Bruxelles in *"Copiepresse"*[62] had already concluded that some headlines could meet the threshold of originality required to be protected as works. This is certainly so following the ECJ *"Infopaq"* ruling which found that a fragment of 11 words may be protected as an independent work.[63] The impact of the *"Infopaq"* decision should not be underestimated: even in the UK, where titles and headlines have not been traditionally

---

[58] It goes without saying, that titles may enjoy better protection as trademarks, as well as under unfair competition law against acts of imitation or unjust enrichment.

[59] For the U.S., see US Copyright Office, Copyright Basics p 3, at http://www.copyright.gov/circs/circ01.pdf (last accessed 28 February 2011).. For the U.K., see Bently and Sherman 2001, pp 61–62.

[60] See Lucas and Lucas 2006, para 108. Instead, in Spain, courts are reluctant to grant independent protection to titles (general words) which are not related to works. See AP Madrid (sec. 9), 12 November 2004 [*Crónicas Palestinas*] Westlaw.ES JUR2005/6645.

[61] See *"The Shetland Times Ltd. V. Dr. Jonathan Wills"*, Scottish Court of Session 24 Oct. 1996, [1997] E.I.P.R. 2: D-49. At the end, the parties agreed to include the notice "A Shetland Times Story" and the name of the newspaper, in addition to the headline, as pointers to the linked articles; *Apud* Strowel 2004, p 140.

[62] See « *Copiepresse SCRL v. Google Inc.* ».

[63] The ECJ conceded that "words … considered in isolation, are not as such an intellectual creation of the author who employs them. It is only through the *choice, sequence and combination* of those words that the author may express his creativity in an original manner and achieve a result which is an intellectual creation." See *"Infopaq"* (2009) ECJ para 45. Emphasis added.

protected under copyright, a recent court ruling (*"NLA v Meltwater"*)[64] concluded that news headlines may be copyrighted.

One cannot but wonder about the impact that the protection of titles and headlines *per se* may have on the making of general reference listings and indexation activities (such as bibliographical or otherwise) where titles and sources must be necessarily indicated in order to convey any information at all. This was precisely one of Google's defense arguments in the *Copiepresse* case, but it was expressly dismissed by the Appeal Court because Google was not only conveying the title/headline of the newspaper article but also a short extract which—according to the court- provided the reader with the *essential* information that the publisher intended to communicate, thus making it *unnecessary* to access the full newspaper article.[65] Certainly, instead of treading on the slippery slope of protecting titles *per se*, it may be wiser to protect titles and headlines only as part of their works and then assess whether its unauthorized use, together with the other fragments copied, is *substantial* enough to constitute an infringement. This is also what the French *"Microfor"* case did. This "old" case decided in 1983 and 1987 (in plenary assembly) by the French *Cour de Cassation*,[66] dealt with the limitation for quotations in Article L122-5-3a). The court concluded that the mere reproduction of titles and short extracts in an indexing document meant for information purposes would not be deemed a copyright infringement since the amount of copying did not substitute for the original work.[67]

---

[64] *"Newspaper Licensing Agency, Ltd. & Others v. Meltwater Holding & Others"*, [2010] EWHC 3099, 26 Nov. 2010), available at http://www.bailii.org/ew/cases/EWHC/Ch/2010/3099.html; *confirmed* [2011] EWCA Civ 890 (27 July 2011), available at http://britishcaselaw.co.uk/2011_ewca_civ_890. (last accessed 2 September 2011. It should be noted that both courts in this case ended up considering the aggregated results of the media monitoring service rather than examining whether a headline or an extract was original or a substantial copying; According to the appeal court: "What is in issue is not whether any particular extract is a substantial part of the original but whether the conduct of the business of Meltwater is such as, on a balance of probability, likely from time to time to cause its clients, *prima facie*, to infringe the copyright... (para 28). Furthermore, Meltwater had obtained a license from NLA to do its service but refused to obtain a second license to cover copyright uses done by its subscribers (albeit the first license required Meltwater to obtain it)—so the issue at stake was not so much Melwater's infringement but rather that of its clients.

[65] See « *Copiepresse SCRL v. Google Inc.* », # 28.

[66] Microfor created a database indexing (*"France actualités"*) all the titles of news articles published in the printed editions of major French newspapers (notably, Le Monde and Le Monde diplomatique). In addition to the headlines, a short fragment of the indexed articles were also shown. Le Monde sued for copyright infringement. The first instance and appeal courts ruled in favor of the claimant. The *Cour de Cassation*, in two different rulings (9 Nov. 1983 and 30 Oct. 1987), concluded that indexation for information purposes does not require any authorization from the copyright owner of the referenced work since it is a short quotation allowed by the law –as long as it does not substitute for the original work. See « *Microfor v. Le Monde* », *Cour de Cassation, Ass. plén.*, 30 Oct. 1987: JCP G 1988, II, 20932. Available at http://www.legifrance.gouv.fr/affichJuriJudi.do?oldAction=rechJuri Judi&idTexte=JURITEXT000007019548&fastReqId=615613219&fastPos=1 (last accessed 28 February 2011).

[67] Needless to say, the Microfor ruling by the Cour de cassation has been strongly criticized, on the grounds that the concept of work of "informatory character" is rather imprecise; see Lucas and Lucas 2006, para 400.

As explained in the recent ruling by the Federal Court of Australia ("*Fairfax v. Reed*") which denied copyright protection to newspaper headlines, the reason is obvious: "to afford published headlines, as a class, copyright protection as literary words would tip the balance too far against the interest of the public in the freedom to refer, or be referred, to articles by their headlines."[68] In short, what both rulings "*Microfor*"[69] and "*Copiepresse*"[70] have in common is that the key issue to decide infringement is not so much the copying (and independent protection) of headlines and titles *per se*, but rather the specific purposes and the amount of copying of extracts (rather than the headlines) and whether it substitutes for the original works.

5.3 Acts of Exploitation

We must now examine whether Google is undertaking any exploitation acts at all (reproduction, making available, transformation, etc.), and if so, which ones. Defining the acts involved in news aggregation is fundamental to assess whether a specific limitation or license will cover it or not.

5.3.1 Reproduction ... Temporary or Permanent ... in Whole or in Part?

Within the Google News services, reproduction must be examined on three different accounts: copying of headlines and extracts, linking to newspaper sites and *cache* copying.

There seems to be consensus in doctrine and case law that linking (be it manually or automatically generated) does not *per se* qualify as an act of reproduction.[71]

---

[68] See "*Fairfax Media Publications Pry Ltd. v. Reed International Books Australia Pty Ltd.*" [2010] FCA 984, 7 Sept. 2010.

[69] See « *Microfor v. Le Monde* ».

[70] See « *Copiepresse SCRL v. Google Inc.* ».

[71] In 2003, the German Federal Supreme Court had confirmed in the case "*Paperboy*" that the provision of a link to another webpage does not imply either an act of reproduction or an act of making available of the work, since it is the user who is making the acts of exploitation, and these uses were exempted as private uses (of course, the same conclusion may not hold true in other countries where the *private use* limitation only covers the reproduction right, not the right of making available (i.e., Spain Article 31.2 TRLPI). According to the *Paperboy* ruling, infringement only occurs if the link is made by circumventing any technological protection measures implemented against it (i.e., deep linking into an access-protected database). See "*Paperboy v. Urteil*", BGH, 17 July 2003, GRUR 2003, 958. For a complete analysis of the copyright implications of linking, see Chap. 6.

Yet, the use of pre-existing contents (i.e., headline and/or extract) as the pointer of the link may indeed involve an act of partial reproduction (or a reproduction in whole—if headlines are independently protected), unless it may be allowed under either the temporary copying in Article 5.1 EUCD or as a non-substantial use.

5.3.1.1 Reproduction ...in Whole or in Part?

Among the questions submitted by the Danish court to the ECJ preliminary ruling in the "*Infopaq*" case, two issues were fundamental: the meaning of reproduction under Article 2 EUCD[72] and the scope of the "transient or incidental reproductions" exempted under Article 5.1 EUCD. As to the first issue, the ECJ ruling should not come as a surprise: the concept of reproduction in Article 2 EUCD is a "Community" concept and must be given a harmonized interpretation throughout the EU.[73] Retaining a broad interpretation of reproduction, the ECJ concluded that the "storing (of) an extract of a protected work comprising 11 words and printing out that extract, is such as to come within the concept of *reproduction in part* within the meaning of Article 2 of [the] directive,"[74] as long as "that extract contains an element of the work which, as such, expresses the author's own intellectual creation."[75]

We may all agree that in some cases 11 words may be "the expression of the intellectual creation of the author." Yet, what is surprising is that the originality criterion was used to assess the existence of a "reproduction in part" under Article 2 EUCD,[76] instead of turning to other traditional criteria such as the substantiality/ *de minimis* test or the doctrine of "mere use" which are more appropriate to assess this issue (see *infra*).

5.3.1.2 Temporary Copying: Article 5.1 EUCD

Assuming that the reproduction of headlines and extracts amounts to a partial reproduction of copyrighted works, is it a copyright infringement?

Article 5.1 EUCD exempts the temporary acts of reproduction which are transient or incidental and an integral and essential part of a technological process,

---

[72] Article 2 EUCD: "direct or indirect, temporary or permanent reproduction by any means and in any form, in whole or in part".

[73] See "*Infopaq*", para 27. It is after all the same conclusion reached in terms of the concept of public within the definition of the exclusive right of communication to the public in Article 3 EUCD in Case C—245/00 *SENA* [2003] ECR I-1251, para 23, and Case C-306/05 *SGAE* [2006] ECR I—11519, para 31.

[74] See "*Infopaq*," para 33 and ruling (1).

[75] Idem, para 48.

[76] The ECJ chose to apply to the *part* the same originality requirement applied to the *whole*. Idem, paras 38–39.

whose sole purpose is to enable: (a) a transmission in a network between third parties by an intermediary, or (b) a lawful use of a work, and which have no independent economic significance. According to recital 33, this exemption is intended to cover reproductions on Internet routers, reproductions created during web browsing or copies created in Random Access Memory (RAM) of a computer, copies stored on local caches of computer systems or copies created in proxy servers.[77]

Google argues that the compilation of headlines and extracts done on the news site may be exempted under Article 5.1 EUCD because the list is automatically generated by the search engine. This may hold true as far as the general search engine (and regardless of the application of any search engine safe harbor): copying the headlines and extracts as pointers to enable the linking resulting from the search engine is an integral and essential part of a technological process to enable a transmission ...by an intermediary.[78]

However, by providing the news *site* and search engine Google may not be acting as a mere *"intermediary"* (as required by Article 5.1 EUCD) but rather as a *provider* of a different service itself, since it selects the pre-existing contents that qualify as "news" (to be aggregated and sought) and classifies it under pre-set categories.

Once again, the ECJ had something to say on this issue: in order to qualify as a "transient" copy the "process must be automated so that it is deleted automatically, without human intervention, once its function of enabling the completion of such a process has come to an end."[79] The ECJ's interpretation of Article 5.1 EUCD is better understood when considering the specific circumstances of that case, as well as of a similar U.K. case which retained it. In the *"Meltwater"* case the judge explained: "the temporary copies exception is solely concerned with incidental and intermediate copying so that any copy which is "consumption of the work", whether temporary or not, requires permission of the copyright holder... (unless) it was lawful for him to have made the copy. The copy is not part of the technological process; it is generated by his own volition. Making the copy is not

---

[77] Far more troublesome is whether *cache* copying is also exempted under Article 5.1 EUCD (see *infra*).

[78] Of course, one may also question whether showing the extract in the results list is necessary or instead the headline would suffice to achieve the purpose of locating the contents sought.

[79] See *"Infopaq"*, para 64. The ECJ agreed that some parts of the copying that took place within the "data capture process" could be exempted under Article 5.1 EUCD as transient or incidental (namely, the creation of the TIFF and text files) because they were automatically deleted from the computer memory; Instead, the printing of the titles and 11 word excerpts on paper might turn the copying into permanent (its deletion not being automatic but dependant on the human intervention) thus loosing the benefit of Article 5(1) EUCD.

an essential and integral part of a technological process but the end which the process is designed to achieve. ... Moreover, making the copy does have an independent economic significance."[80] However, if the *"Infopaq"* requirement of automatic deletion is retained for all purposes,[81] the scope of Article 5.1 EUCD will be dramatically restricted failing to exempt even the temporary reproductions necessary for the functioning of any general search engine, since the results may end up being printed or somehow saved by the user—its deletion depending exclusively on human intervention.

All this can only reinforce the conclusion that rather than being a true limitation, Article 5.1 EUCD completes (in negative terms) the definition of the reproduction right in Article 2 EUCD and that, as it stands today, Article 5.1 EUCD may soon be insufficient to balance the wide concept of reproduction in Article 2 EUCD and should be revised.[82] In the meantime, balance must be sought somewhere else.

5.3.1.3 Any Room for 'de minimis' and Non-substantial Uses?

After the *"Infopaq"* ruling, one wonders whether the only acts exempted from the broad scope of reproduction in Article 2 EUCD are the restrictive temporary, transient and incidental derogation of Article 5.1 EUCD or instead, there is still room for "mere use" and/or "non-substantial" reproduction also online.

As explained by professors Dreier and Hugenholtz, "it is widely accepted that the *mere use* of a work does not fall within the scope of any exploitation right under copyright law. However, the more the scope of the right of reproduction is extended, the more it covers the mere use of a work ... The Directive limits this undesirable

---

[80] See *"NLA v. Meltwater,"* paras 109 and 32. The Newspaper Licensing Agency issued on behalf of the newspaper publishers two different non-exclusive copyright licenses: the "Web Database License (WDL)" which allowed media organizations (such as the defendant Meltwater) using the copyrighted contents in the members' websites, and the "Web End User License "WEUL" intended to license the copyright use by the end-user, in this case, Meltwater's clients. Meltwater is a monitoring media website which searches the newspaper sites, creates an index of their contents and provides its subscribers with links to the original sites (either by email or via website) according to the search terms or words chosen by them; the headline and a short extract of the article is used to enable the link to the original site. Meltwater had obtained the WDL but refused to get the WEUL (despite the WDL required Meltwater's clients to hold a WEUL), claiming that it amounted to double licensing of the same acts already licensed under WDL (according to them, the provision and receipt of the service are but opposite sides of the same coin). The court denied (and the appeal court confirmed) that the temporary copying limitation in Sec. 28A UKCA (*ex* Article 5.1 EUCD) covered any copies done by the end-user and concluded that any such copies should be either allowed by law or covered by the WEUL.

[81] The appeal court in *"Copiepresse"* already applied the automatic deletion requirement when examining whether the Google *cache* copying qualified as a temporary copying; See « *Copiepresse SCRL v. Google Inc.* », ## 25–26.

[82] Furthermore, by being tagged as a limitation (under Article 5 EUCD), its interpretation under the three-step-test may unnecessarily restrict its application far beyond any logical mandate.

overextension of the right of reproduction in Article 5.1."[83] Yet, it remains to be seen whether Article 5.1 EUCD succeeds in excluding all the "mere" uses (as we saw above, the ECJ and UK courts have sanctioned the need of end-users licenses for uses that might have traditionally qualified as "mere" uses).

Case law retains the substantiality/*de minimis* test as the copying being so minor, insubstantial or insignificant that no finding of infringement may derive from it. In an early case, a Dutch court concluded that no copyright infringement resulted from the making of a list of links to news articles and sending it by email to subscribers, because it did not imply a *substantial* taking from the original webpages, and the service provided neither conflicted with the normal exploitation of the works nor unreasonable prejudiced the legitimate interests of the owners.[84] More recently, the Spanish "*Megakini*"[85] case concluded that the reproduction and making available of fragments of the webpage content displayed under the links resulting from the Google Search engine was temporary, incidental and *minimal* and, accordingly, lacked any infringing stature. Similarly, the "*Copiepresse*"[86] court seemed to retain the substantiality test when finding that the Google News site was not only "providing hyperlinks" but reproducing *significant fragments* of the works (conveying the essential information) and communicating them to the public. Accordingly, it has been suggested that the Google News site could avoid liability by merely reproducing the headlines or, even better, by merely linking (not reproducing) the headlines from the original websites (as it is done with the pictures and recordings listed by search engines which are not copied but merely embedded through an hyperlink to the source webpage).[87]

The substantiality test is also retained beyond the E.U.: an Australian court[88] rejected a claim of copyright infringement on the grounds that by using headlines combined with article extracts the defendant had not reproduced a *substantial* part of the newspaper articles (headlines alone were not copyrighted); And in the U.S., "most courts would treat an eleven-word fragment copied from a news article as non-infringing absent special circumstances."[89]

---

[83] See Dreier and Hugenholtz 2006, p 359 (emphasis added).

[84] See "Kranten.com," *Apud* Strowel 2004, p 143.

[85] See "*Pedragosa v. Google Spain, S.L.*", Provincial Audience of Barcelona (Sec. 15), 17 Sept. 2008, WESTLAW AC 2008/1773. The owner of a webpage (www.megakini.es) sued Google Spain for the unauthorized reproduction and making available of its contents, by means of the Google search engine and the Google Cache service, and sought damages for an amount of 2.000 € as well as an injunction to prevent Google Spain from further operating its search engines and services. Both parties (and the courts) agreed that Google's reproduction of the webpages html codes (and contents) in order for the search engines to operate was exempted under the temporary copies limitation of Article 31(1). This decision is currently under cassation at the Supreme Court.

[86] See « *Copiepresse SCRL v. Google Inc.* », #30.

[87] See Dusollier 2007, p 875

[88] See "*Fairfax Media Publications Pry Ltd. v. Reed International Books Australia Pty Ltd*". [2010] FCA 984, 7 Sept. 2010.

[89] See Moran 2011, p 251.

In view of all this, either the scope of Article 2 EUCD should be restricted by allowing *de minimis* and non-substantial copies or the scope of Article 5.1 EUCD should be interpreted more widely, for instance aligning the requirement of "no separate economic significance" with the scope of "lawful use," in the sense that "if a specific use of a work is lawful, technical reproductions necessary to enable such use should be deemed as not having independent economic significance".[90]

5.3.1.4 Cache Copies

Cache copying presents different issues. On the one hand, since copies are stored in Google's servers, it clearly involves an act of reproduction that can be hardly deemed temporary, transient or incidental.[91] On the other, it remains to be seen whether *cache* copying may benefit from any safe harbors exempting ISP liability for copyright infringements (see *infra*).

5.3.2 Making Available and Communication to the Public

Posting a work online is an act of *making it available* in a way that members of the public may access it from a place and a time individually chosen by them (*ex* Article 8 WCT, Article 10 WPPT, Article 3 EUCD). Since no exhaustion applies, the provision of a link to an online work might constitute an independent act of making it available online—if not a reproduction *per se* (see *supra*). As we mentioned, the question is no trifle and determines the scope of any license or limitation that may exempt it.

There may be two different ways of addressing this issue: either by considering the concept of "public" and its effects in terms of linking, or by examining the intrinsic relationship between the acts of making available online and reproduction.

On the one hand, by *linking* to the original websites of newspapers, news aggregators (and search engines) are indeed bringing the works to a "new public," a public that would not have accessed them otherwise—at least, not so easily accessed them. In fact, as we mentioned this is one of the public interest values of news aggregation. This "bringing" the work to a "new public" may qualify as a

---

[90] As proposed by the Institute for Information Law, see IVIR 2007, p 7.

[91] On appeal, the "*Copiepresse*" court concluded that the *caching* done by Google did not meet the conditions of the temporary copying exempted under Article 5.1 EUCD. See « *Copiepresse SCRL v. Google Inc.* »: it is not an integral and essential part of a technological process to enable a transmission by an intermediary (# 25) and cannot qualify as "transitory" since the copy is not automatically deleted after use but remains available once it is no longer so in the original website (# 26).

new act of making available or communication to the public—under the meaning of Article 11bis BC. Of course, the consequences of such a conclusion would be devastating for the functioning of the Internet, which basically relies on linking between sites and contents—and would force the finding of any legal solutions for it (be it, under statutory limitations or under safe harbors open to all internet operators and not only service providers).

On the other, a link may qualify as a mere provision of physical facilities which does not amount to an act of communication to the public.[92] The *"Copiepresse"* appeal ruling expressly rejected this argument when examining the cache copying done by Google[93]; but seemed to accept it for the operation of search engines and perhaps also news sites. As far as the news site is concerned, the *"Copiepresse"* court simply concluded that Google was not *merely providing links* but was *actively reproducing significant fragments* of protected works and making *them* (the fragments) available to the public.[94] Thus, it is difficult to predict whether by avoiding the "significant copying" (of fragments) the news site could still be lawfully linking to the original contents by only using the headlines[95] and whether the act of linking *per se* amounts to an act of making available to the public (despite not involving a reproduction).

Which leads us to the second issue: whether the act of making available (despite classified under the EUCD as a communication to the public) includes any acts of reproduction necessary for it or, instead, they are designed as independent separate rights (and therefore, subject to independent licensing and applicable limitations). If the acts merge, the exempting of the copying as either temporary (Article 5.1 EUCD) or non-substantial would also exempt its making available to the public. Instead, if the making available does not imply a reproduction, then the linking might still qualify as an infringement despite the reproduction being exempted as temporary and non-substantial.

The concept of making available online, its relationship with the concept of reproduction and the exempted temporary copying, as well as the legal qualification of links remain to be further examined by copyright doctrine and law.

---

[92] See Recital 27 EUCD and Agreed Statement Concerning Article 8 WCT.

[93] See « *Copiepresse SCRL v. Google Inc.* », # 23: "One should distinguish between the instantaneous search of a website currently available on the Internet *by means of the normal service of 'Google web' where Google only plays a role as search engine*, from the search of an old page, as it existed when it was accessed by Google's computer robots, which is thus offering a supplementary service" [translation by author] [*emphasis added*].

[94] See « *Copiepresse SCRL v. Google Inc.* », # 30.

[95] As concluded in the German "*Paperboy*" case where the provision of links to works made available on websites was not found to be an independent act of making available/communication to the public. See "*Paperboy v. Urteil*", BGH, 17 July 2003, GRUR 2003, 958.

5.3.3 Transformation

News aggregation activities may involve the transformation right on two accounts.

Aggregated news listings displayed (and classified) on the news site may indeed qualify as a derivative work, either as a compilation or a database, its exploitation requiring authorization from the original copyright owners.[96] Failing a license, the making of this derivative work will only be allowed to the extent permitted under an applicable limitation (i.e., quotations and press summaries—see *infra*).

Although none of the examined case law has dealt with the issue of translations, Google search engines offer automatic translation services which can be directly operated by the user. The unauthorized translation of a work may constitute an infringement of copyright. On Google's defense one could argue that the automatic translation is done by the user and for his or her private use only; the consent of the copyright owner of the translated work would be necessary not so much for the making of a derivative work (translation) but rather for its eventual subsequent exploitation.[97] It should be mentioned here that while the BC limitations are keen to include translations as implied within the same exempted scope of acts of reproduction and communication to the public, the EUCD and most national laws are silent (and sometimes contrary) regarding the extension of limitations to the right of translation (see *infra*). So, failing to be clearly exempted under a limitation, one wonders whether there should soon be a specific safe harbor for automatic translation services.

5.3.4 Moral Rights

Moral rights may also be affected by news aggregation.

The name of the author is often omitted in the list of aggregated news (it only appears—if so- on the linked original site). The "*Copiepresse*" ruling found an infringement of the moral right of attribution.[98] Yet, there are plausible reasons to defend that this omission can hardly amount to a moral right offence. Moral rights are not absolute; they are subject to market customs and technical requirements, and the listing of links requires that only the relevant and minimal information is given in

---

[96] Instead, the multiple different listings resulting from the (either news or general) search engines being operated by the users' specific queries could hardly be so, as long as displayed only in the RAM memory of the user's PC and strictly for private purposes. Instead, if the listing resulting from the search engine is exploited beyond that private sphere, infringement occurs but it is unlikely that Google have any liability on such downstream infringement.

[97] Such an automatic translation may hardly qualify as a derivative work itself, because it has been automatically done by a machine (thus, accruing no copyright protection in most countries); only when the user edits and modifies the automatic translation, it may turn into a derivative work and if subsequently exploited require authorization.

[98] See « *Copiepresse SCRL v. Google Inc.* », # 41.

the least space possible. Besides, the mentioning of the name of the author is not a constant when dealing with the reuse of news and current events reporting.[99] In fact, showing the name of the author with the extract automatically generated by a search engine might be even more infringing: if combined with the finding that an 11 words extract may be a protected work—ex *"Infopaq"*- then he might be credited as the author of a work not his own!

The Belgian court[100] also concluded that an infringement of the moral right of integrity occurred by showing only a few lines of the linked article and *in a different context* than that originally designed in a way that might contravene the "editorial or philosophical line" of the original publication. This seems to be an abusive interpretation of the moral right of integrity and virtually turns any partial use of the work into a moral right infringement. It seems advisable (so as not to abuse moral rights) to restrict the infringement of this moral right to cases where the alteration is prejudicial to the honor or reputation of the author, as envisioned in Article 6bis BC.

5.4 Applicable Limitations

Assuming that, by reproducing headlines and extracts and linking to the original sites of the works, Google News is involved in the exploitation of protected works, we must examine whether any or all of these acts of exploitation may be exempted under a statutory limitation or as a fair use. The BC, the EUCD and most national laws contain different limitations that might exempt news aggregators, namely the quotations and press summaries (1) or the limitations in favor of the press and media (2); Yet, since none of them expressly refers to news aggregation, its exemption depends on how the statutory language is construed and, for that matter, the three-step-test (specially in the E.U.) becomes crucial (3). In other countries, news aggregation practices may be examined under the fair use defences (4).

---

[99] For instance, Article 10bis(1) BC that permits reuse of news articles, photographs and recordings only requires that the source be indicated but—unlike under the quotation limitation-there is no requirement that the author be named. National limitations follow the same pattern.

[100] See « *Copiepresse SCRL v. Google Inc.* », # 42. The finding of an infringement of the moral right of integrity only concerned the acts involved in the news site, not the search engine itself. However, if Google's reproduction of the few lines of the work may amount to an infringement of the moral right of integrity, then search engines and in general any linking done online might well be infringing moral rights too, turning the whole internet operation into an unlawful activity—unless, of course, some sort of implied license was deemed applicable for the linking of posted contents.

5.4.1 Quotations and Press Summaries

Quotations are allowed by all national laws and international instruments. Some of them specifically allow the making of press summaries and press-clipping activities.

5.4.1.1 Article 10(1) BC

Quotations and, specifically, press summaries are permitted under a mandatory limitation in the Berne Convention. According to Article 10(1) BC:

> It shall be permissible to make **quotations** from a work which has already been lawfully available to the public, provided that their making is **compatible with fair practice**, and their **extent** does not exceed that **justified by the purpose, including quotations from newspaper articles and periodicals in the form of press summaries**.

The scope of this limitation is, in principle, favorable to news aggregation. It covers any acts of exploitation: reproduction, distribution, communication to the public (and making available, after the WCT), as well as translations.[101] It applies to all kind of works (provided they have been "lawfully made available to the public"), with no pre-set restrictions as to either the amount that may be quoted,[102] the beneficiaries or the means of exploitation (i.e., digital formats and online contexts), other than that the quotation is done *to the extent justified by the purpose* and in a manner that is *compatible with fair practice*. Article 10(1) BC does not impose any remuneration but nothing prevents Member States from subjecting the quotation limitation (or part of its exempted acts) to remuneration schemes (under a legal license)— which, "should more readily justify the requirement of compatibility with fair practice than would a free use."[103] The limitation is not restricted to any specific purposes and informatory purposes may clearly fit under it.[104]

---

[101] The right of translation under Article 8 is implicitly subject to the same exceptions as those of reproduction and broadcasting. See Ricketson and Ginsburg 2006, para 13.83–84: "the exclusion of translations from the exceptions provided in these Articles will lead to a manifestly absurd or unreasonable result."

[102] Of course, the term 'quotation' already suggests that what is quoted is part of a greater whole, but it was preferred to leave the length of the quotation as a matter to be determined *in casu* subject to the conditions of *"extent justified by the purpose"* and *"compatible with fair practice."* See also Ricketson and Ginsburg 2006, para 13.42 p 788.

[103] *See* Ricketson and Ginsburg 2006, para 13.41 p 786.

[104] This limitation originated at the Rome Revision Conference in 1928 with the following language: "analyses or short textual quotations of published literary works for the purposes of criticism, polemical discussion or teaching". The current language introduced in 1967 at the Stockholm Conference is not restricted to any specific uses (it was concluded that a list of specific purposes could never hope to be exhaustive), and quotations for "scientific, critical, *informatory* or educational purposes" fit clearly within its scope; See Ricketson and Ginsburg 2006, para 13.41 p 786.

And last, but not least, press summaries (*revues de presse,*[105] in the French text) are expressly allowed as quotations under Article 10(1) BC and subject to the same conditions.[106] Some scholars point out at the "linguistic difference" existing between the French and English texts of the Convention based on a prior definition of *"revues de presse"* as a collection of quotations from a range of newspapers and periodicals, all concerning a single topic, with the purpose of illustration how different publications report on, or express opinions about, the same issue.[107] We find no reason to adhere to such a restrictive reading of the French terms, especially one that will clearly distinguish it from its English counterpart and that directly derives from a very disputed interpretation of the terms in a *national* statute. Therefore, in principle, news aggregation could be exempted under Article 10(1) BC, either as mere quotations or as *quotations from newspaper articles and periodicals in the form of press summaries*, provided that it is done *to the extent justified by the purpose* and in a manner that is *compatible with fair practice*. In assessing the fairness of any particular quotation, the three-step-test in Article 9(2) BC would appear to be equally applicable.[108] According to Article 10(3) BC, mention shall be made of the source and the name of the author as it appears on the original.

A factor that must be highlighted and carefully considered is the *mandatory nature* of Article 10(1) BC and the implications it may have especially when dealing with national limitations which are wider or narrower in scope. According to its mandatory nature, when protecting foreign Berne Union authors and works, Member States are obliged to allow any uses exempted as quotations according to the scope of Article 10(1) BC; And this includes the making of press summaries. As a corollary, any national quotation exception that is more restrictive than Article 10(1) BC would only be applicable to purely domestic scenarios of copyright protection; While any domestic quotation exception broader in scope than what is exempted under Article 10(1) BC should still apply to foreign works and authors, as a result of the BC principle of national treatment (Article 5(1) BC). In short, any Berne Union Member is obliged to allow *quotations* and *quotations from newspaper articles and periodicals in the form of press summaries,* according to the scope of Article 10(1) BC regardless of what its national law says.[109]

---

[105] The French text of Article 10(1) BC refers to *"revues de presse"*.

[106] Although a fundamental difference applies: the making of press summaries is restricted to newspaper articles, while the quotation is applicable to all kind of works.

[107] See Ricketson and Ginsburg 2006, para 13.41 p 787. This interpretation of the BC terms seems to be directly influenced by the reading that some scholars do of the same terms in Article L-122-5-3b of French law (see infra).

[108] See Ricketson and Ginsburg 2006, para 13.41 p 786.

[109] It is surprising that Google has never raised this argument as a defense line, although of course, it would only affect the use of works which are "foreign" to the country of protection.

5.4.1.2 Article 5(3)(d) EUCD

The quotation limitation in Article 5(3)(d) EUCD is drafted in terms similar to Article 10(1) BC, but makes no express reference to press summaries. It allows Member States to exempt:

> *Quotations* for purposes *such as criticism or review*, provided that they relate to a work or other subject matter which has already been lawfully made available to the public, that, unless this turns out to be impossible, the source, including the author's name, is indicated, and that their use is in accordance with fair practice, and to the extent required by the specific purpose.

This limitation covers both the rights of reproduction and communication to the public (including the making available online) and -if the State so chooses- also the right of distribution (*ex* Article 4 EUCD). It is open-ended as to beneficiaries, purposes (the wording "such as" means that "criticism or review" are listed as mere examples) and as to the extent and nature of the quoted works.

Although not expressly contemplated, some scholars contend that reference to the "review" and "revue" purposes (in the English and French versions of the EUCD) implies the making of press summaries.[110] However, several arguments may be raised against it: the fact that other translations of Article 5(3)(d) EUCD refer to "recension" (in German, Spanish and Italian) or to "analysis" (in Portuguese) which better coincide with the sense of reviewing and making a critical analysis of a text[111]; the inherent connection between "criticism and review," in the sense of the quotation being used for some subsequent analysis, is far too strong to suggest another meaning for "review" and especially one so distant from criticism and analysis; and the very simple fact that had the EU legislator wanted, it could have easily mentioned press summaries in addition to quotations (as the BC does).

Having said all that, this reasoning is rather pointless since *criticism* and *review* are only mentioned as examples, and press summaries may be indeed allowed as long as they qualify as quotations for any other purposes (such as informatory).[112]

In addition, press summaries may also be allowed under domestic limitations restricted to non-digital contexts, which can be maintained under the "grandpa clause" of Article 5(3)(o) EUCD.

---

[110] See among others Marín López 2008, pp 14–15: "it is apparent from other language versions of the Directive that quotation for press review purposes is included in the scope of the limitation or exception for quotation".

[111] Furthermore, the French and Dutch versions of Article 21.1 of the Belgian Copyright Act refer to "*revue*" and "*recensie*," respectively.

[112] On the contrary, if too much weight is given to the examples of "criticism or review," they may be read so as to require that a new work is created which analyzes or reviews the quoted work, thus excluding the cases where the work is merely "quoted". Of course, several reasons discourage such a reading, among them, common sense, "*de minimis*" doctrines and compliance with the mandatory scope of Article 10(1) BC; Yet, it should not be entirely dismissed.

Perhaps the crucial issue is that the EUCD missed the opportunity to expressly make the BC quotation exception mandatory for EU members. Yet, as we already stated, EU Member States remain bound by the BC obligations toward each other and should therefore apply the mandatory limitation to permit quotations of at least foreign works under the scope of Article 10(1) BC.

5.4.1.3 National Laws

At domestic levels, news aggregation may travel differently under different limitations. Provided that the remaining requirements are met, news aggregation will likely be permitted under quotations limitations which are not restricted to specific purposes (i.e., Germany)[113] or which expressly refer to *informatory* purposes (i.e. France and Luxembourg).[114] Instead, the interpretation of the statutory terms becomes even more crucial when quotations are restricted to specific purposes such as criticism, review, research, teaching, or alike (i.e., Belgium)[115] or when the making of press summaries is expressly permitted either under a specific limitation (i.e., Portugal)[116] or as quotations (Spain and the Netherlands).[117]

News aggregation may still face other obstacles under domestic quotation limitations. Some of them require (or, at least, imply) that the quoted work is somehow incorporated in a subsequent "work"[118] and somehow analyzed in it; It could be easily argued that news aggregation listings constitute a new work where the quoted parts are integrated, but the requirement of a subsequent analysis in the new work could be hardly met by news aggregation.

As far as exempted acts of exploitation, the reproduction and making available are usually covered by the quotation limitations (some even cover translation).[119] And while most domestic laws allow quotations of any kind of works, a few prefer

---

[113] See Germany (Article 51).

[114] See France (Article L122-5(3)a), Luxembourg (Article 10.1).

[115] See Belgium (Article 21).

[116] See Portugal (Article 75.2 g).

[117] See Netherlands (Article 15a); Spain (Article 32.1).

[118] See France (Article L122-5(3)a), Germany (Article 51), Luxembourg (Article 10.1), Netherlands (Article 15a), Spain (Article 32.1: to include in one's work).

[119] By either referring to "quote" (permitting any acts of exploitation): see France (Article L122-5(3)a), Luxembourg (Article 10.1), Netherlands (Article 15a), Portugal (Article 75.2 g), Belgium (Article 21); or to specific exploitation acts: see Germany (Article 51: reproduction, distribution and communication to the public) and Italy (Article 70.1: abridgement, quotation, reproduction and communication to the public). Translations are expressly exempted in Luxembourg (Article 10.1), Netherlands (Article 15a). Since the transformation right was not harmonized by the EUCD, these provisions cannot be deemed out-of-compliance with it.

tailored formulas which impose restrictions depending on the nature of the work and even prohibiting the use of a whole work.[120]

Leaving aside the specificities of some national statutes, the most important test to be faced by news aggregators is whether the use is *compatible with fair practice* and the three-step-test (Article 5.5 EUCD). Let's see some examples.

French law permits quotations "justified by the critical, polemic, educational, scientific or informatory purpose of the work in which they are incorporated" (Article L122-5(3)a). The express reference to informatory purposes may be favorable to news aggregation.[121] According to the *"Microfor"* case[122] the limitation for quotations in Article L122-5-3a) allows the making of indexing listings of an informatory nature (à *un caractère d'information*) which merely consist of short quotations from preexisting works, and does not require that the quoted parts be analyzed or commented in the new work (it suffices that the "quoted" work is incorporated within a new work).[123]

Furthermore, in addition to quotations for informatory purposes, French law (Article L-122-5-3b) expressly permits the making of press summaries (*revue de presse*). The interpretation of this term is not pacific, let alone its survival in digital contexts. Some French scholars propose to distinguish between the *panorama de presse* (consisting of a compilation of news published in different newspapers) and the *revue de presse* (as a compilation of different articles on the same topic or event) so as to argue that the "panoramas *de presse*" are not exempted. However, and leaving aside the fact that it may not always be easy to distinguish between these two, there seems to be no reason to distinguish where the law does not,[124] especially not to restrict a limitation justified by the fundamental right of access to information. Despite that, this limitation could indeed allow news aggregation activities as long as conducted within the margins of the three-step-test, and this—as we will see- may require compensation. Yet, the

---

[120] This is the case in France and Luxembourg (Article L122(5)3a and Article 10.1: short quotations), Germany (Article 51: individual published works, passages from a work) and Spain (Article 32.1: fragments of written, sound or audiovisual character and isolated works of three-dimensional, photographic or art character). French case law has developed a very narrow interpretation of what is a short quotation (*courte citation*) excluding any use of an entire work and hence, *de facto*, prohibiting the quotation of works of art and photographs altogether. The same applies in Luxembourg: the quotation of an entire article or work (no matter how short) is deemed infringing.

[121] A similar result may be expected in Luxembourg, where according to Article 10(1) short quotations (also translations) justified by the critical, polemic, pedagogical, scientific or *informatory* nature of the work in which they are incorporated are permitted to the extent justified by the purpose, in accordance with fair practice, and provided that there is no commercial intent and no prejudice to the normal exploitation of the work.

[122] See « *Microfor v. Le Monde* ».

[123] Needless to say, the Microfor ruling by the *Cour de cassation* has been strongly criticized, on the grounds that the concept of work of "informatory character" is rather imprecise; see Lucas and Lucas 2006, para 400.

[124] See Lucas and Lucas 2006, para 401.

harder test for news aggregation under French law comes from the exhaustive list of limitations in Article 5 EUCD: since press summaries (and/or *revues de presse*) are not specifically listed there, any limitation on this account may end up confined to analog means of exploitation.[125]

Spanish law allows the making of press summaries (including *press-clipping*) as quotation, albeit subject to specific rules. According to Article 32(1), it is lawful to include in one's own work fragments of previously disclosed works "by way of quotation or for analysis, comment or critical assessment." Although the quotation limitation has always been restricted to "purposes of teaching and research," courts have so far granted flexible and broad constructions of these concepts, and have allowed quotations of all kinds as long as done "to the extent justified by the purpose of the inclusion" and within the parameters of the three-step-test (Article 40bis TRLPI).[126] Since this limitation does not formally exclude commercial purposes, news aggregation could be in principle exempted as long as complying with the three-step-test.

Furthermore, Article 32(1) *in fine* states that "Periodical compilations made in the form of press summaries or reviews (*reseñas o revistas de prensa*) shall be treated as quotations."[127] Before the implementation of the EUCD, this provision had been construed as allowing both press summaries as well as digital press-clipping.[128] However, this was modified by the Act 23/2006 implementing the EUCD[129] which restricted the scope of the exemption to press summaries done for

---

[125] Also Portuguese law, in addition to the limitation for quotations (Article 75(2)g), contains a specific limitation for press summaries in Article 75.2(c) subject to the three-step-test; its subsistence in digital contexts may face similar problems.

[126] See Pérez de Ontiveros 2007.

[127] This means that press summaries and reviews are permitted without needing to comply with the specific extent-conditions required for quotations (otherwise there would be no need to "treat them as" quotations). Of course, the parameters of the three-step-test (Article 40bis) may a posteriori impose some restrictions as to extent and kind of works used. See López Maza 2008, p 29. The same distinction between quotations and press summaries may be also seen in Portuguese law: while quotations (Article 75(2)g) should not be so long as to prejudice the interests of the right holder (Article 76.2), press summaries (Article 75(2)c) may obviously entail the reproduction of the whole article. Neither quotations nor press summaries are subject to remuneration or compensation in Portugal.

[128] See *Juzgado Mercantil No.2* Madrid, 12 June 2006, "*Periodista Digital*", Westlaw.ES JUR2006/183319: the court favored a broad interpretation of the former Article 32(1) in fine TRLPI under the light of the three-step-test (Article 40bis TRLPI). On appeal, the decision was reversed by interpreting the former Article 32(1) in fine TRLPI under the light of Article 40bis TLRPI (in short, via three-step-test the appeal court adopted a conclusion similar to what would have resulted under current Article 32(1) in fine TRLPI): see *Audiencia Provincial* Madrid (sec. 28) 6 July 2007, "*Periodista Digital*" Westlaw.ES AC2007/1146.

[129] Act 23/2006 added the following text: "Nevertheless, when a compilation of news reporting articles is made that basically consists of their strictmere reproduction and such activity is done for commercial purposes, the author who has not expressly opposed it will be entitled to obtain a fair compensation. When express opposition by the author exists, such activities will not be covered by this limitation".

non-commercial purposes and subject "strict reproduction"[130] of "news reporting articles" for commercial purposes to the will of their authors who can decide whether to allow it (by not expressly opposing it)[131] and receive fair compensation, or to oppose it and subsequently license (or prohibit) it.

This provision leaves many questions open: Who will decide, the reporter (author of the press article) or the publisher (owner of the newspaper as a collective work)? In principle, it seems fair to conclude that these rights belong to the authors only,[132] but newspaper publishers are already showing notices of opposition in their newspapers and they are claiming compensation.[133] Does "news reporting articles" include any article published in a periodical or news-related publication (reviews, magazines, etc.), in any format (printed or digital)?[134] What about photographs, recordings, etc.? Beyond press-clipping services provided by subscription which will be clearly commercial (and may, accordingly, be opposed), what is a non-commercial purpose?[135] How will the licensing be done?[136] How is the fair compensation established[137] and managed[138] (by CMOs or individually)? Can the 'right to oppose' and the compensation be waived and/or transferred?[139] In short, lobbying efforts were successful in preventing that press-

---

[130] That is, when no analyzing, commenting or criticism of the quoted work is done.

[131] This amounts to an "implied" statutory license.

[132] See Bercovitz et al. 2006.

[133] See, among others, www.elpais.es or www.lavanguardia.es.

[134] In favor of a broad interpretation, see Ribera Blanes 2008, pp 468–469.

[135] In favor of the non-commercial nature of in-house press-clipping, see López Maza 2008, pp 56–57.

[136] In 2004 (before the EUCD was implemented and the opt-out regime for commercial press-clipping introduced in Article 32.1), the major Spanish newspaper publishers and mass media created GEDEPRENSA, a commercial enterprise set to grant global licensing for commercial press-clipping. The competition court initially ruled that it was a horizontal agreement contrary to competition law, but this was reversed on appeal on the grounds that it would facilitate access to more efficient licensing (See Audiencia Nacional de Madrid, sala cont.-adm., 8 Feb. 2008; Tribunal de Defensa de la Competencia, 10 May 2004 (A 334/03); available at http://www.cncompetencia.es, last accessed 28 February 2011). See Marín López 2008, pp 25–37 and López Maza 2008, pp 45–53.

[137] One should expect that the remuneration is negotiated between the parties (or set under arbitration or by courts in case of disagreement). Fair compensation implies that the price agreed affords the sustainability of the press-clipping activity; See Bercovitz et al. 2006, p 56.

[138] Since it is not subject to compulsory collective management, each author may decide how to license the use and collect the compensation. This will require constant clearance and evidence of which authors have opposed and, if not, which association holds the mandate to do which licensing. On the long run, this regime is unsustainable. A binding limitation subject to a compensated collective management license (i.e., statutory licensing) would have avoided many of these problems. This is the solution adopted in Article 49(1) German Law.

[139] A priori, silence may be read to imply that both the opposition and compensation rights could be transferred and even waived (since the law does not preclude it). However, this may be contrary to the spiritu lege and goal of the legislator. See Marín López 2008, p 69 proposing that at least the authors' compensation be unwaiveable.

clipping fell straight under the press summaries limitation,[140] but one wonders whether this was the right solution. At the end, commercial press summaries and press-clipping services are subject to a voluntary (nonbinding) limitation similar to the one that applies under Article 33.1 in favor of the press and communication media (see *infra*), albeit within a very different and more complex context.

In the **Netherlands**, Article 15a(1) permits quotations (in original or translation) for purposes of *criticism and research* and expressly confirms (2) that the term 'quotations' shall also include quotations *in the form of press summaries from articles appearing in a daily or weekly newspaper or other periodical.* Unlike in Spain, the authors cannot oppose it; it is a binding limitation. The scope of this limitation has been assessed in several rulings dealing with press-clipping and since no compensation applies by law, its scope has been restricted to non-commercial press-clipping activities[141]; likewise, in-house digital press-clipping (within the administration) has been denied on the grounds that it may contravene the three-step-test.[142] Before the EUCD implementation, this limitation was applied to exempt the selection and linking (through the headlines) to articles on the original newspaper websites, arguing that no economic prejudice was caused to the copyright owner (*Kranteen.com*).[143] It is uncertain whether the same facts would now clear the three-step-test (*ex* Article 5.5 EUCD).

In **Belgium**, the quotation limitation is restricted to the specific purposes "*of criticism, review or teaching or in scientific works*" (Article 21.1). In "*Copiepresse*", Google argued that the exemption of press summaries is the only reason for the inclusion of "review"[144] among the purposes of the quotation. The lower Court was not convinced with this argument[145] and the appeal court bought it, albeit to no avail[146]: after accepting that the term "review" (*revue*) in Article 21.1 allowed press summaries (*revues de presse*), the court interpreted this non-statutory term (*revue de presse* is not mentioned in Article 21.1) by analogy

---

[140] The "right to oppose" was not included in the original draft presented by the government, and was only added later, after strong lobbying on behalf of the newspaper publishers.

[141] In "*Het Financieele Dagblad v. Euroclip*", the defendant was a press-clipping agency which scanned and reproduced in a database the press-articles published by the claimant, so as to provide their clients a selection of news requested. The court concluded that this was a commercial activity that could not be covered under Article 15a(1). See District Court of Amsterdam, 4 Sept. 2002, AMI [1995] p 116.

[142] See "*NDP v. De Staat*", District Court of Den Hag, 2 March 2005, Computerrecht [2005] p 143.

[143] See District Court of Rotterdam, 22 August 2000, available at http://www.ivir.nl (last accessed 28 February 2011).

[144] The EUCD implementation Act of 2005 brought the inclusion of the "*review*" purposes.

[145] In our view, the purpose of review does not refer to press summaries but rather to the making of a "*recension*": the French and Dutch versions of Article 21.1 of the Belgian Copyright Act clearly refer to "revue" and "*recensie*," respectively.

[146] See « *Copiepresse SCRL v. Google Inc.* », ## 32–33.

with French law and concluded that Google News could not qualify as a quotation since Google is not a press agency, the news listings are not organized by topic or event, the reproduction of extracts was not "accessory" to any criticism, analysis or comment at all, the moral right of attribution is infringed and the amount of the quotation substitutes for the reading of the original article. Furthermore, the court expressly accepted the reading of the French statutory term *revue de presse* to distinguish it from the commonly known *panoramas de presse*.[147] All this, based on a term inexistent in the Belgian statute! It would have been easier to simply accept that the aggregated uses were quotations and then examine whether they cleared the three-step-test. In fact, the court ended up doing so after this unproductive journey and with very little evidence[148]: according to the court, any user who accesses Google News is perfectly informed of the *essential* that is published in the press, making it unnecessary to access the original articles themselves and therefore causing a prejudice to the normal exploitation which fails to clear the three-step-test. We will come back to this issue later since it shows that what is really relevant is not so much the protection of the *work* but of the *information* it conveys.

A very last obstacle for the exemption of news aggregation as quotations comes from the very purpose (meaning) of quotation retained in some countries. In **Germany**, where the quotation limitation in Article 51 is not restricted to any specific purposes, the Federal Supreme Court in *"Vorschaubilder"*[149] denied that it could cover the display of thumbnails of online posted images by the Google search engine because it lacked the legitimate purpose of quotation -that is, to analyse or somehow elaborate on the quoted work.

In short, for many different reasons, news aggregation may hardly be exempted under the quotation and press summaries limitations existing in domestic laws.

5.4.2 Limitations in Favor of the Press and Media

Limitations set in favor of the press and communication media might also apply to Google News.

---

[147] The court even referred to the Wikipedia to stress the different meaning of these two concepts.

[148] The court went as far as concluding that "Google News aims, to a certain extent, at substituting the publishers' sites." See « *Copiepresse SCRL v. Google Inc.* », # 32.

[149] See *"Vorschaubilder"*, BGH I ZR 69/08, 29 April 2010, ## 10 and 26: the quotation requires that there is an *internal connection* between the work used (or parts of it) and the thoughts of the person quoting it.

5.4.2.1 Article 10bis(1) BC

According to Article 10bis(1) BC,[150] articles published in newspapers or periodicals as well as broadcasts on current economic, political or religious topics may be reproduced by the press as well as broadcasted and communicated to the public, provided that such uses have not been expressly reserved.

According to Article 10.2 WCT and its Agreed Statement,[151] nothing seems to preclude its extension to cover online publications and communications and to the right of making available online, provided that the requirements of the three-step-test are met. Translation would also be allowed, since this right is implicitly subject to the same exceptions to the rights of reproduction and broadcasting.[152] The source must always be indicated but—unlike under the quotation limitation-there is no requirement that the author be named. It is likely that photographs and other kind of works (beyond the press articles and broadcasts expressly mentioned) may be covered under Article 10bis(1) BC; However, the fact that these works must be "on current economic, political or religious topics," amounts to an important obstacle for news aggregation, since it leaves out non-current[153] topics as well as on art, sports and scientific or technical matters which are likely to be aggregated.[154]

In short, this limitation may exempt news aggregation (or, at least, part of it), but it is not mandatorily imposed on Member States (albeit most include it in their domestic laws) and only applies if the copyright owner has not *expressly* reserved it. In fact, the "opt-out" regime for news purposes can be traced back to the very first provision concerning news articles in Article 7 of the original Act of the Berne Convention (1886): newspaper and magazine articles published in any Berne Union country could be reproduced, in the original language or in translation, *unless the authors or editors*[155] *had expressly prohibited so.*

---

[150] The language of this limitation is the result of almost a 100 years of discussion over the several Acts of the Berne Convention. For more information on the several revisions, see Ricketson and Ginsburg 2006, para 13.48–13.53.

[151] See Ricketson and Ginsburg 2006, para 13.53 advising against it, although acknowledging that there is nothing in Article 10bis(1) BC that excludes such extensions.

[152] See Ricketson and Ginsburg 2006, para 13.84, quoting the report of the Main Committee I at the Stockholm Conference: "the idea that it was fairly obvious that exceptions to the other exclusive rights, such as the right of reproduction, implied corresponding exceptions in respect of the right of translation and that the Convention had generally been applied in this way".

[153] See Ricketson and Ginsburg 2006, para 13.53: "current" means "of immediate importance".

[154] See Ricketson and Ginsburg 2006, para 13.53.

[155] Unlike the original Berne Act language, the current limitation does not mention who is entitled to make such a reservation of rights.

5.4.2.2 Article 5(3)(c) EUCD and National Laws

Closely following the BC provision, Article 5(3)(c) EUCD allows Member States
to exempt:

> reproduction *by the press*, **communication to the public or making available** of pub-
> lished articles **on current economic, political or religious topics** or of broadcast works or
> other subject-matter of the same character, in cases where such use is not expressly
> reserved, and as long as the source, including the author's name, is indicated, or ... unless
> this turns out to be impossible;

Notice that unlike Article 10bis(1) BC, this limitation covers all kind of works and
other subject-matter (not only articles and broadcasts), and the author's name must be
mentioned together with the source. Despite this ample scope, the exemption of news
aggregation under the corresponding national limitations would find many obstacles
since most national laws require that the reproduction of news articles be done
"by the press" or by other media similar to the original source, and news aggregators
hardly qualify as "press."[156] But even in countries where the limitation is not
restricted to the press and media, such as in Germany,[157] it remains to be seen
whether *news aggregation* services would be permitted subject to compensation
schemes or permitted at all.

---

[156] In Spain (Article 33.1), "works and articles on current events" disseminated by the
communication media may be reproduced, distributed and communicated to the public by "any
other media of the same type", subject to compensation, unless the author has opposed to it. The
studies and articles on current events include those disseminated online, as well as in any other
format, and Google might qualify as communication media, but it will hardly benefit from this
limitation since it is restricted to "another media of the same type" that conveyed the original
news. In similar terms, see Article 65 Italian Law; Article 101(b) Italian Law expressly prohibits
the systematic reproduction of published or broadcast information or news, with gainful intent, by
newspapers or other periodicals or by broadcasting organizations. This has been confirmed by
courts, see *Corte di Cassazione*, 20 Sept. 2006, *apud* Ribera Blanes 2008, pp 476–477 and fn.70.

[157] Article 49(1) permits the reproduction, distribution and communication to the public of
articles from newspapers concerning current political, economic or religious issues; thus, already
falling short to cover the whole possible spectrum of works subject to news aggregation. This
limitation has been applied to permit *in-house digital press-clipping*, provided that it is duly
compensated (by means of compulsory collective management through V.G.WORT); instead, no
compensation is required when only short excerpts from several articles are used. See
"*Elektronischer Pressespiegel*", BGH, 11 July 2002, GRUR 2002, 963; The court argued that a
limitation must be construed according to the technological context existing at the time it was
enacted, although its goal and the benefit for the author must also be considered so as to assess
whether its scope may be extended beyond the initial scope. A few years later, an appeal court
ruled that Article 49(1) did not permit the making of *subscription press-clipping services*. See
López Maza 2008, p 69.

5.4.3 Fair Practice and the Three-Step Test

The so-called 'three-step-test' enshrined in Article 9(2) BC was originally envisioned in 1967 as a tool to guide national legislators, through a cumulative succession of steps, into designing statutory limitations to the reproduction right which were in conformity with BC standards.[158] More recently, the test has found a new meaning as an *interpretation rule* for the application of the statutory limitations to the factual circumstances involved in each case. This smooth "recalibration" of the three-step-test comes by the hand of the WCT and WPPT,[159] and has reached its zenith in Article 5(5) EUCD which, after setting an exhaustive list of limitations, mandates that they *"shall only be applied ..."*

The three-step-test in Article 9(2) BC was meant as an *enabling clause*—and as such, it was designed as *a cumulative test with a restrictive character.* The question that follows is whether the same requirements (accumulation and restrictiveness) should be retained when the three-step-test is used as an *interpretative tool* (like in Article 5(5) EUCD). Some scholars[160] contend that being the *exception* to the *rule* (the exclusive rights of exploitation), limitations must be restrictively interpreted and applied. The ECJ's *"Infopaq"* states so: "the provisions of a directive which derogate from a general principle established by that directive must be *interpreted strictly.*"[161] The same restrictive reading of the statutory limitations was retained by the Belgian appeal court in *"Copiepresse".*[162] Instead, more and more scholars[163] and courts are reluctant to accept this conclusion. In particular, the principle of restrictive *interpretation* of the limitations

---

[158] The three-step-test was first formally recognized in the Final Report of the Brussels Conference of 1948 of the Berne Convention, with regards to the "doctrine of minor reservations" which was meant to sanction the limitations to the right of communication to the public existing in domestic laws, and later in the Stockholm Conference of 1967 when it was enshrined in Article 9(2) BC regarding the limitations to the right of reproduction.

[159] Article 10(1) WPT and Article 16(1) WPPT extended the *enabling three-step-test* to all exploitation rights (beyond reproduction); the second paragraphs of these articles introduced a *new* three-step-test addressed to guide judges (rather than legislators) in the application and interpretation of the statutory limitations: "Contracting Parties shall, *when applying* the Berne Convention, *confine any limitations...*". See also Ficsor 2002, para C10.07: affirming that Article 13 TRIPs is both enabling and interpretative, at the same time.

[160] See Ficsor 2002, para C10.07; Reinbothe and von Lewinski 2002, p 132: Lucas 2010.

[161] See *"Infopaq"*, para 56; expressly referring to ECJ Judgement 29 April 2004, C-476/01, *"Kapper"*, para 72, and ECJ Judgement 26 October 2006, C 36/05, *"Commission v Spain"*, para 31.

[162] See « *Copiepresse SCRL v. Google Inc.* », # 29: "the exceptions and limitations [to the exclusive rights] must be restrictively interpreted and be expressly provided"; and # 45: "since the reproduction right is exclusive, any exception can only be restrictively interpreted".

[163] In this sense, see *Declaration for a Balanced Interpretation of the "Three-Step-Test" in Copyright Law*: http://www.ip.mpg.de/ww/en/pub/news/declaration_on_the_three_step_.cfm (last accessed 28 February 2011). For alternative readings of the three-step-test, see Geiger 2006; Gervais 2005; Koelman 2006.

not only lacks any historical basis in international instruments,[164] but is contrary to the general principles for the interpretation of laws based on the ordinary meaning of the terms, their context, their goals and purposes, etc.[165] In fact, plenty of examples may be found in national case law[166] granting flexible and sound constructions of the statutory limitations, as traditionally done when construing the exclusive rights. Furthermore, what some decisions (such as the *"Copiepresse"*[167] and *"Megakini"*[168]) show is that the statutory limitations existing in most national laws are insufficient to adjust to a rapidly evolving technological landscape; and that any exhaustive list of limitations is doomed to fail.[169] The BC legislator knew

---

[164] Nothing can be found in the Berne Convention Acts to support the reading that the three-step-test imposes a restrictive reading upon the application of all the limitations conveyed in domestic laws.

[165] See, for instance, Article 31 Vienna Convention on the Law of Treaties (1969).

[166] Domestic courts are already applying the three-step-test as a hermeneutic mechanism to "close" the copyright system and help compensate the lack of flexibility within it (perhaps more acute in *droit d'auteur* than in *copyright* systems), sometimes resulting in an "extensive" (rather than restrictive) interpretation of the statutory language. The German *"Elektronischer Presses-piegel"* case is a clear example of how the three-step-test may serve to extend the scope of a statutory limitation to accommodate technological progress (in that case, the limitation set for analog press-clipping uses was interpreted so as to also cover digital ones, provided the owners were duly compensated). See also Geiger 2007, p 491 (fn.43) and Leistner 2011, p 427. Furthermore, even in the more recent German *"Vorschaubilder"* ruling, despite acknowledging that the statutory limitations are generally narrowly construed, the Federal Supreme Court concluded that this should not prevent a general balancing of interests beyond the statutory provisions (para 27); See Leistner 2011, p 428.

For the U.K., see Derclaye 2010, p 250: "UK courts have interpreted the fair dealing exceptions broadly. They have repeatedly held that the terms "criticism", "review", "current events" must be interpreted liberally;" And citing *"Pro Sieben Media AG v Carlton UK Television Ltd"* [1999] 1 W.L.R. 605; [2000] E.C.D.R. 110.

[167] See « *Copiepresse SCRL v. Google Inc.* ».

[168] See *"Pedragosa v. Google Spain, S.L."* Provincial Audience of Barcelona (Sec. 15), 17 Sept. 2008, WESTLAW AC 2008/1773. Perhaps one of the most striking aspects of this decision is its interpretation that the three-step-test (Article 40bis TRLPI, which in fact is only a two-step-test, the first step being omitted) is set to guide the interpretation and application of the statutory exceptions in similar terms to what the 'fair use' doctrine does in sec. 107 USCA. Beyond this probably unhappy reference to a foreign fair use clause, this ruling shows the tendency of Spanish Courts to use the three-step-test as a flexible interpretative clause, and not only as a 'restrictive' instrument, in the application of the statutory exceptions.

[169] Although the harmonization of the national limitations is indeed necessary to build an effective internal market for the use and exploitation of copyrighted works, an exhaustive yet optional list of limitations is far from achieving any harmonization (unless to the top) and is crippled to adjust to an ever evolving technological world. The exhaustive list of limitations in Article 5 EUCD should be reconsidered as already proposed by some scholars; See IVIR 2007, proposing its modification into a shorter list of mandatory limitations reflecting fundamental freedoms, internal market considerations and the rights of consumers, accompanied by an open norm leaving Member States the freedom to provide for additional limitations subject to the three-step-test conditions. After all, this is what the original three-step-test in Article 9(2) BC was doing. If it was a good solution then, there is no reason to believe it should not be so now. See also Janssens 2009, pp 340–344.

better in 1967 when the BC three-step-test was designed to avoid any exhaustive list of limitations.

As things stand now in Europe, the introduction of any new limitation being ruled out, the correct interpretation of the existing statutory exceptions is even more crucial. In a time of constant technological development, the three-step-test is a precious tool to achieve sensible results in accordance with all the different interests at stake, not only of authors and copyright owners but also of third parties and the public interest, as it may be. And, for the same reason, any restrictive criteria that directly rules out taking into account the normative justification and purpose of any limitation should be discouraged. Instead, the three-step-test is nothing more (and nothing less) than an interpretative rule which will apply in addition to the traditional rules of interpretation applicable to all statutory terms, be it "exclusive" rights or "limitations".

With that in mind, we now turn to assess the three-step-test and fair practice implications of news aggregation.[170]

1. *Certain special case:* The first step is relevant in the *enabling* three-step-test since it helps the legislator to define the scope of the limitation in terms of limited, well defined, not arbitrary, etc.[171] Once the "certain special case" is already defined in the statute, the first step may still be useful to assess the quantitative and qualitative scope of the limitation, and must accordingly be examined together with the remaining steps, especially with the second: the broader the scope of uses exempted under the limitation the more likely it may be deemed to conflict with the normal exploitation, and vice versa. The scope of any limitation covering news aggregation must be assessed together with the next step.

2. *Do Not Conflict with the Normal Exploitation of the Work:* The two key elements here are "conflict" and "normal exploitation". Not every commercial use (that might yield some economic gain) will "conflict" with a normal exploitation of the work: only those uses that would deprive the owner of "significant" or "tangible" commercial profits are deemed to conflict with the normal exploitation.[172] Accordingly, news aggregation may conflict with the normal exploitation of the work, but only when this conflict results in a "significant" loss of commercial profits will it be contrary to the second step (... and even when it does, remuneration schemes under the third step may

---

[170] The *WTO Panel Decision* of June 2000, on section 110(5) of the U.S. Copyright Act may provide some non-obliging guidance to interpret the three-step-test. See *WTO Dispute Panel Report on United States—Section 110(5) of the U.S. Copyright Act, WT/DS160/R* (15 June 2000), available at http://www.wto.org (last accessed 28 February 2011).

[171] A "special case" is not synonymous with the "special purpose" behind the exception. The EC argued that for an exception to be justifiable under Article 9(2) BC, it must serve a public policy purpose, idem (6.105). The WTO Panel did not agree: the purpose behind the exception has nothing to do with the first step, although the specific public policy may be useful in determining the scope and preciseness of the exception, idem (6.111).

[172] Idem (6.180).

apply to clear the test). "Normal" exploitation, which may include actual as well as future potential uses, should be something less than the full scope of the exclusive right granted by law.[173] Furthermore, if all future potential uses are subject to the exclusivity scope of copyright, then the development of new commercial markets may be stalled (or at least, frozen) by the exercise of copyright. Although, the three-step-test does not formally call for it,[174] the concept of what constitutes a normal exploitation should take into account third-party interests as well as public interests, such as the development of the new potential markets.[175] Otherwise, a wide interpretation of normal exploitation as covering all and any forms of exploitation tends to "upset the balance of conflicting interests" struck by the limitations.[176] Furthermore, the assessment of the second step is intertwined with the third one: whether the conflict with the normal exploitation constitutes an *unreasonable* prejudice to the author/owner's *legitimate* interests.

3. *Do Not Unreasonably Prejudice the Author's Legitimate Interests:* The key words here are legitimate and unreasonable. Legitimate means lawful (from a positivist perspective), but "it also has the connotation of legitimacy from a more *normative* perspective."[177] In other words, it is within the third step that the normative justifications of the limitation are taken into account to decide whether the economic prejudice inflicted upon the author should stand and, if so, to what extent. In terms of legitimacy, then authors would have a stronger claim to oppose exempted uses for strictly entertainment purposes than uses for informatory or educational purposes—such as supplied by news aggregators. On the other hand, the degree of prejudice (significant loss of income)[178] that may be considered *unreasonable* can only be decided *in casu* and may be minimized (turned "reasonable") by requiring fair compensation schemes in favor of the author -a possibility that has always been accepted under the BC three-step-test.

---

[173] Idem (6.182–189). Idem (6.178): Each new means of exploitation must redefine the scope of what constitutes a "normal exploitation;" Otherwise, any new means of exploitation of works would be directly excluded from the copyright monopoly granted to the author.

[174] See Dreier 2010, p 52 pointing out that, unlike copyright, patent and trademark laws do mention the need to take third party interests into account when defining what constitutes a "normal exploitation".

[175] See Dreier 2007, p 253: when used as an interpretative (rather than enabling) clause, the second step should not be interpreted as comprising all future downstream exploitation possibilities of copyrighted material in value-added information services, such as news aggregators.

[176] See Dreier 2010, p 52.

[177] *WTO Panel Decision* (6.224).

[178] Idem (6.229): "In our view, prejudice to the legitimate interests of right holders reaches an unreasonable level if an exception or limitation causes or has the potential to cause an *unreasonable loss of income* to the copyright owner".

Accordingly, where news aggregation may benefit from a statutory limitation, what should be examined is whether the loss of income is significant or not, and unreasonable or not, and whether this loss may be compensated under remuneration schemes so as to clear the three-step-test. As we have seen, this is the solution adopted in some countries for press-clipping services (i.e., Spain and Germany). Yet the main problem remains in the origin since news aggregation can hardly find accommodation in any of the existing statutory limitations in the E.U. -unless in very specific cases and by means of interpretation of the statutory language.

Newspaper publishers' revenues have been steadily decreasing; however, whether (and to what extent) this is because of news aggregation is (rather, should be) a matter of evidence. Publishers argue that for many users news aggregators replace the need for the original articles (in fact, some media studies[179] show that though Google is driving *some* traffic to newspapers, 44% of Google visitors do not visit the original newspaper sites).[180] Instead, Google contends that news aggregation increases traffic to linked websites[181] and even that by using the extracts more traffic is generated to the original sites than by only using headlines.[182]

Yet, rather than looking at evidence some courts are satisfied with simple statements such as: "it cannot be questioned that the publishers, journalists and scientific authors suffer a prejudice in the normal exploitation of their work, to the extent that the users are not necessarily directed towards the original page were the article is published;"[183] or unless he wants "more detailed information", the user has no need to visit the original article/site since the extract reproduced is a "verbatim reproduction of the *significant part* of the referred articles."[184]

Interestingly, this shows that what is really at stake is not so much the protection of copyright itself but rather the conveying of information which is not protected by copyright. The production of information requires indeed a significant investment, and news aggregation may be diverting traffic and, accordingly, income. But we should be vigilant not to distort copyright law to

---

[179] See Outsell's *2009 News Users' Survey* at http://www.outsellinc.com/store/products/886?refid=pr886. Last visited 28 February 2011.

[180] Of course, this does not mean that all users who visit Google News would instead visit the original websites. Source: http://techcrunch.com/2010/01/19/outsell-google-news/ (last accessed 28 February 2011).

[181] According to Google, Google News sends one billion clicks a month to newspapers' sites; See http://www.editorsweblog.org/newspaper/2009/08/italian_antitrust_authorities_investigat.php. (last accessed 28 February 2011). Small and medium newspapers clearly benefit from a wider public by the fact that their articles are accessible through news aggregators; whether major newspapers may also benefit from the Google News service is disputed.

[182] See Travis 2008, p 194: according to Google, users visit linked sites 400% times more often when both the title and fragment of the article are displayed than when only the title is shown.

[183] See « *Copiepresse SCRL v. Google Inc.* », # 33 (translation by author).

[184] See « *Copiepresse SCRL v. Google Inc.* », # 28 (translation by author) (emphasis added).

protect interests which are alien to copyright and belong really in the realm of unfair competition.

5.4.4 Fair Use/Dealing and the "Hot News" Doctrine

Rather than (or in addition to) pre-tailored statutory limitations, Common law countries turn to fair use/dealing doctrines to assess whether a specific unauthorized use of copyrighted works may be deemed fair, thus avoiding an infringement of copyright. It should be pointed out that unlike under statutory limitations and three-step-test considerations (where remuneration may play an important role), fair use is merely a defense against infringement and involves no possibility to remunerate the author. As an example, we will briefly examine the U.S. fair use doctrine (being aware that fair use/dealing doctrines may differ -sometimes substantially- among countries).

The fair use provision in section 107 U.S. Copyright Act is an equitable rule of reason, a flexible and technology-neutral doctrine based upon the analysis of all factors and circumstances of the individual case, including "the purpose and character of the use," "the nature of the copyrighted work," "the amount and substantiality of the portion used," and "the effect of the use upon the potential market for or value of the copyrighted work." No single factor will determine whether the use is fair or not, and all must be weighed together in light of the particular circumstances of each case. When applied to news aggregation, the fair use factors may lead to the following considerations:

1. *Purpose and Character of the Use*: In considering whether the news aggregation is fair we must take into account the commercial or non-commercial character of the use (a free news aggregation service without advertising is more likely to be deemed fair than those which include advertising). Another issue to be considered is whether the use is "transformative", in the sense that it does not simply "replace" the original work but instead "adds something" to it. When sued by the *"Agence France Press"*,[185] Google argued that its actions were allowed under the fair use doctrine because indexing the internet was a beneficial activity and the search engine makes a fair, productive and non-competitive use of the indexed works. The same fair use claim was successfully made in *"Perfect 10, Inc. v. Amazon.com, Inc."*[186]: the thumbnail reproduction of copyrighted works posted online, as a result from the Amazon search engines, could be deemed a fair use because of the transformative character of the search engine result; The court mentioned that Google search engine was providing a significant public benefit by incorporating the preexisting work into a new one (an electronic reference tool) and concluded that "a search engine

---

[185] See *"AFP v. Google"*, No. 1:05CV00546 (GK) (D.D.C. 29 April 2005), (D.C.C. 19 May 2005), (D.D.C. 12 Oct. 2005), (D.D.C. 29 Jan. 2007).

[186] See *"Perfect 10, Inc. v. Amazon.com, Inc."*, 508 F.3d 1146 (9th Cir. 2007).

may be more transformative than a parody because a search engine provides an entirely new use of the original work, while a parody typically has the same entertainment purpose as the original work".[187] In similar terms, the same court had previously ruled in "*Kelly v. Arriba Soft Corp.*,"[188] that the use by a search engine of thumbnails of photographs available online was a fair use since rather than replacing the original work, it improved access to these pictures and such a use was deemed "transformative". Following this rational, news aggregation may be easily deemed transformative because by categorizing and indexing all the news available online from different sources, they are offering a different service rather than just replacing the original.

2. *The Nature of the Copyrighted Work*: Courts generally look at whether the work is creative or factual,[189] whether it has been published or not, and whether the work is still commercially available. Here, the factual nature of news articles, photographs and recordings, and the fact that they have been lawfully obtained would weigh in favor of a fair use defense—at least, as far as the search engines and news sites are concerned.[190]

3. *The Amount and Substantiality of the Use*: The third factor is addressed to ensure that only what is necessary to satisfy the specific purpose is taken. As a general rule, the smaller the portion used, the more likely it is to be fair. Yet the importance of this factor will depend upon the type of work as well as on the purpose and character of the use (first factor). Most news aggregators only use the headline and a few words (extracts) of the linked article, or a thumbnail link to the picture or recording; however, in some cases the headline alone entails a significant and substantial copying since it conveys the "core" of the article.[191] One may venture that if only headlines are used, news aggregation might be more easily fair than if also extracts are reproduced (especially if the extract conveys the *substance* of the news article), but this factor heavily relies on evidence and is related to the fourth one.

4. *The Effect of the Use Upon the Potential Market for the Work*: This turns out to be the most important factor of any fair use analysis and it depends upon the opportunities for sale or license of the work itself and its derivative works, the

---

[187] Idem, p 1165.

[188] See "*Kelly v. Arriba Soft Corp.*", 336 F.3d 811 (9th Cir. 2003).

[189] See "*Sony Corp. of Am. v. Universal City Studios, Inc.*", 464 U.S. 417 (1984). This means that a scientific work will be more easily subject to fair uses than a movie or a musical work.

[190] Instead, this factor would weigh against fair use when applied to the *cache* copying service, which links to works stored in Google's servers offering access after they are no longer available on the original sites.

[191] See "*Harper & Row Publishers, Inc. v. Nation Enters.*", 471 U.S. 539 (1985). This is the argument retained in the Copiepresse ruling -despite not dealing with fair use; see « *Copiepresse SCRL v. Google Inc.* », # 28.

availability of licenses for that use, or the denial of license,[192] the number of recipients, the character (commercial or non-for profit) of the institution using the work, and whether the use usurps the intended audience of the work (whether it substitutes for the purchase of a copy).[193] This fourth factor aims at protecting the commercial market of the work and, as it happened with the three-step-test, heavily depends on evidence and takes into account aspects of unfair competition law.

In the light of these factors, it is impossible to forecast a univocal solution to whether news aggregation as a whole is a fair use. When only headlines are used (no extracts copied) to link to the original sites (the source being clearly indicated) and the aggregation site is neither directly or indirectly commercial, the finding of fair use may be more likely. Yet, solutions will heavily depend on the facts and evidence presented in each case. In the case of Google News, the economic impact of its News aggregation service, as well as the company's commercial nature (although the service itself is not commercial) may weigh strongly against it; unless enough evidence is produced to support that news aggregation sites and search engines increase traffic to the original websites. Furthermore, a finding of fair use is more likely if only the search engine is considered, and less likely for the news sites and cache copying service. However, the fact that fair use excludes any compensation for it makes it rather unlikely to apply in the case of news aggregation which lacking any compensation, undeniably builds upon the use of pre-existing works.. Solutions must be, once again, found somewhere else. This leads us to the next issue.

In addition, the U.S. "hot news" tort of misappropriation may also be of interest for news aggregation. The Supreme Court designed the "hot news" doctrine in 1918,[194] as a variant of the common law tort of misappropriation. A competitor cannot free ride on another competitor's work (effort) when the later is expecting to benefit from it and enjoined the defendant from taking facts from the plaintiff's news articles until the commercial value of these facts "as news" had elapsed. Notice that the parties were two competing news agencies and that INS was not infringing AP's copyright but instead rewriting the news published by AP in the East Coast newspapers and sending them to the INS clients on the West Coast. In other words, the "hot news" claim of misappropiation is preempted by a copyright claim unless some "extra-elements" exist. In 1997, the Second Circuit explained these extra-elements (that could avoid preemption) as a five-part-test: the plaintiff has to show that it generated information at a cost, that the information

---

[192]   If copyright owners have opposed commercial uses, the finding of fair use is more difficult. In "NLA v Meltwater", the UK court concluded (and it was confirmed on appeal) that the press-clipping service could not qualify as a fair dealing since the websites of the newspaper publishers expressly stated that their contents could not be used for any commercial purposes. See "NLA v. Meltwater".

[193]   See, e.g., "Hustler Magazine Inc. v. Moral Majority, Inc.", 796 F.2d 1148, 1155-56 (9th Cir. 1986): the use will not be deemed fair when it diminishes (or usurps) the potential market for the sale of the original work.

[194]   See "International News Service v. Associated Press", 248 U.S. 215 (1918).

is time-sensitive, that the defendant is "free riding" on the plaintiff's work by passing it off as its own, that plaintiff and defendant are in direct competition and that the "free riding" threatens the quality or existence of the plaintiff's product.[195]

"*TheFlyOnTheWall.com*" case[196] considered the application of the "hot news" doctrine (and its preemption by copyright) on the Internet. The District court found that Fly engaged in hot news misappropriation as well as in copyright infringement for the unauthorized reproduction and communication of excerpts from the stock recommendations issued by some major Wall Street operators and required the financial news site to wait before reporting them: until 10 am for reports released before the market opens and at least 2 h for reports released after its opening. On appeal, the Second Circuit refused to rely on the NBA's five-part-test arguing that this test was specific to the facts in that case (and could not bind subsequent courts)[197] and that -unlike INS and Motorola- Fly was not free riding on the stock market operators' work but instead investing its own time and money in gathering and processing the information which was not presented as its own. Accordingly, the court reversed the ruling and allowed Fly to report on the recommendations as soon as it learns of them, as long as it does not violate copyright law.[198] The court understood that the brokers' reports were "news"[199] and Fly was gathering and conveying this news in a manner that was not free riding on the brokers' investment.

This ruling is good news for Google and bad news for the expectations of the major press agencies and newspaper publishers, which had all submitted *amicus curiae* briefs to the Second Circuit appeal.[200] It not only means that since the subject matter requirement for copyright preemption is satisfied (the headlines and extracts are protected under copyright law and the unauthorized acts are envisioned within copyright law) the publishers could not turn to the "hot news" tort as an alternative to seek the injunction eventually denied under copyright law (if, for instance, the unauthorized use of copyrighted material by Google News were deemed to be a fair use); But also that

---

[195] See "*National Basketball Association v. Motorola Inc.,*" 105 F.3d 841 (2d Cir. 1997).

[196] See "*Barclays Capital Inc. v. TheFlyOnTheWall.com*", 06 Civ. 4908 (S.D.N.Y. 18 March 2010); reversed by the Second Circuit Court of Appeals, 20 June 2011 (Case 10-1372), available at http://caselaw.findlaw.com/us-2nd-circuit/1571485.html (last accessed 28 June 2011).

[197] Concurring with the majority, circuit judge Raggi wrote that rather than rejected as dictum, the NBA's five-part-test could have applied to conclude that the "hot news" misappropriation claims were preempted by federal copyright law because plaintiffs failed to satisfy the "direct competition" requirement in that test.

[198] Fly stopped doing *verbatim* reproductions of the reports (since then, it now only publishes short summaries of them) and did not appeal the copyright infringement injunction.

[199] See "*Barclays Capital Inc. v. TheFlyOnTheWall.com*": "We conclude that in this case, a Firm's ability to *make news*—by issuing a Recommendation that is likely to affect the market price of a security—does not give rise to a right for it to control who breaks that news and how." (emphasis added).

[200] For a list of the *amicus curiae* briefs submitted see "*Barclays Capital Inc. v. TheFlyOn-TheWall.com*" available at http://caselaw.findlaw.com/us-2nd-circuit/1571485.html Last visited 23 June 2011.

when—and only when- the claim was not preempted by copyright law,[201] the publishers should then prove at least that Google is free riding on their investment by presenting the information as if it was its own; neither one condition is met in the Google News case. The Second Circuit's words sound quite instructive: "the adoption of new technology that injures or destroys present business models is commonplace. Whether fair or not, that cannot, without more, be prevented by application of the misappropriation tort."

5.5 Implied License, Opt-out and Abuse of Right

Failing any limitation (as a free use or statutory license) and—where applicable- of a fair use defense, one may turn to the existence of an implied license (or authorization) or even to the abuse of right doctrines (more aligned with civil-law traditions).

The implied license has traditionally been one of Google's strongest defenses by proving that the owner of the linked webpages had the possibility to easily prevent Google's software robots from automatically indexing their websites through simple technological means, such as implementing Robots Exclusion Standards Protocols[202] (which prevent that the contents of the webpage is cache-stored and/or used by search engines) or implementing password or otherwise protected access, as well as through more traditional means such as directly notifying Google; and that by having not done so, they were implicitly allowing indexation by Google.

The implied license has been recently enforced in several cases dealing with thumbnails of photographs resulting from Google's search engine in the U.S. ("*Perfect 10 v. Amazon*")[203] and France ("*SAIF v. Google*"),[204] on the grounds that the claimant failed to implement any technological mechanisms that could have avoided indexation by search engines.

Also in Germany, the Federal Supreme Court (*Bundesgerichtshof*) in the "*Vorschaubilder*"[205] concluded that Google was not infringing copyright by displaying thumbnail images of online posted photographs as its search engine

---

[201] As in the INS case, where facts and ideas—not works- were being copied; See *"International News Service v. Associated Press"*, 248 U.S. 215 (1918).

[202] See http://www.robotstxt.org/robotstxt.html (last accessed 28 February 2011).

[203] See *"Perfect 10, Inc. v. Amazon.com, Inc."*.

[204] See « *Société des Auteurs des arts visuels et de l'Image Fixe (SAIF) v. Google France and Google Inc.* », *Tribunal de Grande Instance de Paris*, 20 May 2008, available at http://www.juriscom.net/jpt/visu.php?ID=1067; confirmed by *Cour d'Appel de Paris*, 26 January 2011, available at http://www.juriscom.net/documents/caparis20110126.pdf (last accessed 28 February 2011).

[205] See *"Vorschaubilder"*. The lower court had decided in favor of Google; the appeal court concluded that an infringement existed but that the artist's claim was an abuse of right under Article 242 German Civil Code. The BGH concluded that no infringement existed since the claimant had implicitly consented (albeit not granting a copyright license) that the content of his website be available to search engines indexation by failing to use any technological means that could have avoided it.

results. However, the German ruling did not rely on the implied license (in fact, the court expressly denied it)[206] but rather on the general principles of contractual *bona fide* and *abuse of right*. According to the court, having made the works available online without implementing any technical impediment for indexation by search engines, the claimant *implicitly consented* to indexation by search engines; therefore, a subsequent claim of a copyright infringement is *inconsistent* with his previous conduct and consent implicitly granted (## 12 and 36) and breaches the general principle of contractual *bona fide* (## 32–33), thus incurring into an abuse of right (#12). Furthermore, the court added that since the *implicit consent* to indexation by search engines was granted in general towards the public (not to any specific operator), its revocation can only be done in public (that is, by implementing robots exclusion protocols)—rather than by exclusively addressing an opt-out notice to Google (# 37)

Yet, notice that these arguments only concern the functioning of the search engines. In fact, beyond them, the implied license defense has received some major blows recently. On the one hand, the New York Southern District Court denied the *Google Books* settlement agreement reached between Google and the Authors Guild,[207] on the grounds that it "is not fair, adequate and reasonable" because -among other reasons- "it is incongruous with the purpose of the copyright laws to place the *onus* on copyright owners to come forward to protect their rights when Google copied their works without first seeking their permission."[208] On the other, the appeal ruling in *"Copiepresse"* also denied the implied license argument, concluding that copyright is not exercised as a right of opposition, but as a right of "previous, express and certain authorization".[209]

Yet, opt-out doctrines are not so unknown to copyright as these rulings state. As we have seen, opposition or reservation by the copyright owner may invalidate

---

[206] See *"Vorschaubilder"*, ## 11 and 29: no copyright license can be implied from the fact that the claimant had his pictures posted on the Internet without any technical safeguards that could have avoided (indexation by search engines); the court also referred to the principle of restrictive interpretation in favor of the authors retaining copyright (#30). However, in practice, the result under a copyright license or consent for a use (simple authorization, no granting of right) may be similar since, after all, no one pretends that the "implied license" formally assigns any title of right upon the licensee; perhaps it may all be explained as a matter of translation of the term *license* in non-English civil-law regimes. See also Leistner 2011 pp 431–432, concluding that despite not being a "license", the "implicit consent" doctrine should not be read as not allowing fair compensation to authors/owners.

[207] The settlement granted Google a non-exclusive license to scan and use the books in its *Google Books* website, in exchange for a payment of 63% of all revenues received from these uses.

[208] See *"Authors Guild* et al. *v. Google, Inc."*, 22 March 2011(SDNY), available at: http://docs.justia.com/cases/federal/district-courts/new-york/nysdce/1:2005cv08136/273913/971/ (last accessed 28 February 2011).

[209] See « *Copiepresse SCRL v. Google Inc.* », # 50–51. It is difficult to ascertain whether when denying the implied license the court was referring to the search engine, the news site or a combination of them.

the otherwise applicable limitation[210] or even the finding of fair use. And this is nothing new when dealing with news: Article 7 of the Berne Convention Act of 1886 already provided for an implied license for the reuse of news articles unless the authors had expressly prohibited so. In other words, it is only a matter of legal interpretation whether this reservation or opposition is considered equivalent to opting-out from a previously granted statutory license. So, what should focus our attention is instead a question *de lege ferenda*: should the law establish a statutory license (with or without an opt-out scheme) for news aggregation?

5.6 ISP Liability Exemptions

News aggregation activities may benefit from the safe harbors[211] provided for in some national laws.[212] Google News has claimed the benefit of search engine/links and *cache* safe harbors to exempt some of the acts of exploitation done by means of its search engine and news sites. The safe harbors become especially important where all other defenses (namely a limitation, a fair use or an implied license) have been denied. Yet, as we will see, the existing safe harbors cannot fully satisfy Google's expectations.

5.6.1 Search Engine and Links

Section 512(d) DMCA establishes a safe harbor for the provision of information location tools (consisting of directories, indexes, references, pointers, or hypertext links); the e-commerce Directive does not,[213] but some EU national laws have enacted safe harbors for search engine and links, subject to different conditions.[214]

---

[210] For example, Article 5.3c EUCD permits reproduction and communication to the public of works on current economic, political or religious topics provided that "such use is not expressly reserved".

[211] For further study on Google's liability exemptions, see Chap. 6.

[212] See, for instance, the U.S. Digital Millennium Copyright Act (DMCA) http://www.copyright.gov, and the Directive 2000/31/CE, of 8 June 2000, on electronic commerce (e-commerce Directive) http://www.europa.eu.int/comm/internal_market/en/ecommerce/index.htm (last accessed 28 February 2011).

[213] So far, the only two reports submitted by the Commission (2003 and 2007) have been shy to suggest any need for extending the safe harbors to search engines and links (*ex* Article 21 e-commerce Directive). See COM(2003) 702 final and COM(2007) 1156 final, available at http://ec.europa.eu/internal_market/e-commerce/index_en.html (last accessed 28 February 2011).

[214] Spain and Portugal extended the *hosting* safe harbor to search engines and links; while Austria and Liechtenstein apply the *mere conduit* safe harbor to search engines and the *hosting* safe harbor to links. In a German case, the Federal Supreme Court has accepted that the conditions in the hosting safe harbor could exempt liability of the search engine for linking to third-party infringing contents; See "*Vorschaubilder*": a search engine will only be liable (for copyright infringement) when it has obtained knowledge of the unlawful nature of the content and does not act expeditiously to remove or disable access to it.

Safe harbors (at least, the ones for hosting and search engine/links) are intended to exempt secondary liability by the ISP for the infringements committed by their users (and they only serve as a first "filter," liability being decided in each case according to national applicable rules on liability). News and general *search engines* may easily qualify under these safe harbors (where existing) to avoid liability for providing search results and linking to infringing contents posted by third parties. In principle, this safe harbor does not exempt search engines from direct liability; yet, it is obvious that the acts of exploitation involved in the operation of search engines must be somehow (and subject to certain conditions) declared lawful if we want search engines to exist[215]; be it under a safe harbor exempting direct liability, a statutory limitation or the implied license (as we have already examined).[216]

In *"Copiepresse"*, the Belgian court refused to examine the application of the search engine and links safe harbor (arguing that the choice of the European legislator had been not to include search engines among the ISP benefiting from a safe harbor)[217] and dismissed the application of the hosting safe harbor in Article 14 EUCD because Google is not a "mere" and passive hosting service provider since it selects, classifies with a specific order and method and reproduces parts of the contents.[218] Instead, in *"SAIF v. Google,"* the French court ruled that Google was not liable for the unauthorized display of thumbnail images because its role as intermediary (in providing the search engine) was neutral, merely passive and automated,[219] and Google complied with the removal from the search engine operation of any infringing images when duly notified[220] (thusimplicitly applying the hosting safe harbor to exempt Google's direct liability for the functioning of its search engine)[221]; Furthermore, the court expressly mentioned that the use of thumbnails responds to the *necessary functionality* of the search engine.

All things considered, the chances for search engines and links to be somehow exempted of direct liability are higher than when the compilation on the news site

---

[215] Reproduction may be exempted under Article 5.1 EUCD (see *supra*), but the making available of the search results (be it images or texts) is not.

[216] In fact, if the whole Internet is to operate on a lawful basis, the act of linking itself should be allowed for all internet operators, be it an ISP or not (i.e., a business or a private individual), since linking—which is fundamental to the functioning of the Internet- is not only done by ISP, but by anyone who operates on it.

[217] See « *Copiepresse SCRL v. Google Inc.* », # 53.

[218] See « *Copiepresse SCRL v. Google Inc.* », # 55. It is unclear whether the court is referring to both the search engine and the news site, or only to the later.

[219] See « *SAIF v. Google* » p 7; despite no search engine safe harbor existed in France, the court treated Google according to the safe harbors principles since it is an internet operator which is what the safe harbors aim at regulating.

[220] See « *SAIF v. Google* » pp 8–9.

[221] As we saw, the German federal court reached the same result albeit under the abuse of right doctrine; See *"Vorschaubilder"*.

is considered (which is probably what the *"Copiepresse"* court had in mind when denying the application of the hosting safe harbor).

5.6.2 Cache Copying

Both the DMCA and e-commerce Directive provide for a specific safe harbor to exempt *caching*, albeit perhaps with a different scope.[222]

Google explores the web by means of a program called Googlebot, makes copies of the existing webpages and stores them in what is called "cache memory;" users can access these archive copies at any time (also after the original webpage is no longer available) by clicking at the link "cache memory" that appears under the more recent webpage of the listed results. Rulings are diverse. Both in France and Belgium,[223] the courts have denied that Article 13 e-commerce Directive could exempt Google's *cache* copying. Instead in the Spanish case "Megakini"—currently under appeal[224] the appeal court concluded that the Google *cache* service (despite not being exempted under the caching safe harbor) was not *substantial enough* to amount to an infringement, because it was a "socially tolerated" use not prejudicial to the interests of the webpage owner's, and because Google's Cache service facilitates precisely the further dissemination of the webpage as intended by its owner when posting it on the Internet. While in *"Field v. Google"*,[225] the US court concluded that cache copies could be exempted under sec. 512(b) USCA since the copies are available for approximately 14–20 days, and this may be deemed an "intermediate and temporary" storage.[226]

Yet, cache copying is indeed supplementary to the search engine and is not fundamental to news aggregation; Google could stop offering links to *cache* copies without affecting either the news aggregation site or the search engine services.

---

[222] Under Article 13(1) e-commerce Directive, this safe harbor strictly covers what is known as system and proxy caching aimed at making transmissions more efficient. Instead, the safe harbor in Sec. 512(b) DMCA may be read less restrictively.

[223] See « *SAIF v. Google* » p 8 and « *Copiepresse SCRL v. Google Inc.* », # 54. For a complete analysis of the Google cache service see Chap. 6.

[224] See *"Pedragosa v. Google Spain, S.L."*, Provincial Audience of Barcelona (Sec. 15), 17 Sept. 2008, WESTLAW AC 2008/1773. On the merits of that specific case, it may be pointed out that although *caching* the claimant's website may not be substantial in terms of copyright, the caching of other copyright-protected contents (such as news articles and photografs) may be indeed so.

[225] See *"Field v. Google"*, 412 F.Supp. 2d 1106 (D. Nev. 2006).

[226] See Peguera 2009.

5.7 Competition Law and Copyright

The copyright claims against Google News are usually accompanied or supplemented by claims of unfair competition and antitrust law.[227]

Google is currently facing investigation for anti-competitive practices for the Google News service: publishers accuse Google of free riding and abusing its market position by treating some search results preferentially.[228] In Italy, the Federation of Italian Newspapers Publishers (FIEG) complained that Google News was entering in unfair competition practices because when opting-out of Google News, their contents were also being excluded from the general Google search engine[229]; the parties settled but the court had the chance to state the need for a legislative solution to news aggregation.

To some extent, unfair competition concerns are already taken into account within copyright law. As we saw, the assessment of the three-step-test and—where existing- the fair use defense should involve the use of typical (yet difficult) competition concepts such as potential, incumbent or secondary markets, as well as the concept of normal exploitation. These concepts are not only foreign to copyright laws but can only be assessed a posteriori thus affording no predictability. Furthermore, whether the claims of copyright infringement and of unfair competition are cumulative or preempt each other will depend on each national law,[230] but courts tend to feel uncomfortable assessing them. As an example, in *"Copiepresse,"* the Belgian court expressly declined to assess any competition law issues, but was ready to find (without direct evidence to support it) that Google's services were replacing access to the newspapers' sites (thus, failing to clear the three-step-test).[231] Last but not least, competition concerns may also spawn from the other side: claims may be raised against an abusive *exercise* of copyright (*the existence* of the copyright being, in principle, at bay from competition law).

In terms of unfair competition, the basic question is whether news aggregators are engaging in parasite (*free riding*) practices. We already saw that there is no passing off (since Google is not showing the linked works as its own), that Google is adding its own effort in the development and maintenance of the news search engine and the news aggregation sites, and that there is not enough evidence to support that Google News is replacing access to the original contents (or rather,

---

[227] For a complete analysis of antitrust (competition) law see Chap. 6.

[228] Source: http://www.spiegel.de/international/business/0,1518,672580,00.html (last accessed 28 June 2011).

[229] Source: http://www.google.com/hostednews/afp/article/ALeqM5hyvoLee4fWQwavlZo3mwz1 pqGy2A (last accessed 28 June 2011).

[230] It is generally explained that unfair competition relates to specific behaviors, while copyright (and IP regimes, in general) deal with the protection of specific objects or subject-matter, and this is why they can cumulatively apply. In principle, within the E.U., the Directive 2005/29/EC on Unfair commercial practices seems to grant a general cause of action under unfair competition as complementary (or even overlapping) with copyright and IP protection.

[231] See « *Copiepresse SCRL v. Google Inc.* », ## 28–29 and ## 61–63.

bringing them more traffic). In the *"Paperboy"* decision,[232] the German Federal Supreme Court concluded against any finding of unfair competition taking into account the fact that this service offered *considerable added value* in terms of providing access to information. It is undeniable that search engines (and also news search engines) offer considerable added value and are not competing with the copyright owners' businesses; whether or not the same may be said about the news aggregation sites is more disputed. This leads us to another paramount question: whether news aggregators are *in direct competition* with the copyright owners or instead are they acting in different markets? Ultimately, this question may touch on the scope and goal of the exclusive rights granted by the law: can copyright be exercised in a manner that avoids (directly or indirectly) the development of new markets?[233] Usually, the exercise of copyright will not result in obstructing a whole new market (rather, it commonly affects the development of different means of exploitation within the same market); but when it does, competition law may intervene and force owners to grant a license -thus, *de facto* reducing the scope of their exclusive rights. Following the ECJ's *"Magill"*[234] essential facilities doctrine, when the copyright holder with a dominant market position on one market competes with other parties on a second market where the use of the copyrighted contents is necessary in order to build a position in (hence, an "essential facility"), a refusal to license these *essential facilities* to the competitor/s is considered to be unfair exercise of a dominant market position (this includes where the user depends on entering into an agreement with each of the several entities sharing the dominant market position, i.e., the copyrighted contents). If we accept that news aggregation amounts to a different market from the production and first distribution of news, then news works could be deemed an *essential facility* and copyright owners(newspapers, broadcasters and news agencies) be forced to license aggregators (as incumbents in the new market).[235]

This claim was made in *"Copiepresse"*. Google argued that Copiepresse's infringement claim was an attempt to prevent Google from entering a new market that would bring revenues that they could not otherwise obtain. The appeal court refused to enter "the intricacies of competition law," notably the definition of *the market*, and simply stated that had Google contacted the publishers, a license could have been granted thus avoiding the infringement claim. The court conceded that such a license—for the news site- is of a voluntary nature and that copyright

---

[232] See *"Paperboy v. Urteil"*, BGH, 17 July 2003, GRUR 2003, 958.

[233] Under the three-step-test, this concern is raised under the definition of "normal exploitation" (see *supra*).

[234] See ECJ Judgement of 6 April 1995, C-241/91 and C-242/92, *"Radio Telfis Eireann (RTE) and Independent Television Publications Ltd (ITP) v. Commission of the European Community"*.

[235] See Hoeren and Decker 1998, p 266, albeit referring to *press-clipping* services: "The exercise of their copyright in print products effectively keeps competitors from building up a position on the market which is separate from the market from which the dominant position of the rightholders results."

owners may choose not to license Google News.[236] In fact, the court operated on the assumption that Google was refusing to obtain a license which the copyright owners were eager to grant.[237] The reality is probably more complex, not all copyright owners being equally eager to license news aggregation.[238] Newspaper publishers probably believe that any income that may derive from news aggregation will be presumably smaller than incomes that may result from direct licensing of their contents,[239] and seem to be more interested in closed paying formats and platforms to license their contents.[240] At the same time, open web-based news aggregation—as we know it- may either disappear or be limited to the contents of small newspaper publishers which are not in a position to secure exclusive-licensing deals for other platforms[241]; thus, clearly diminishing the social value of news aggregation.[242] Hence, the *denial of license* for news aggregation is rather plausible and its effects are easy to foresee.

So the question remains: should copyright law ensure competition in new markets? By granting newspaper publishers an exclusive right to license their copyrights in all new markets (of any kind), copyright law is also granting them

---

[236] See « *Copiepresse SCRL v. Google Inc.* », # 62. Nevertheless, the court mentioned that the eventual denial of such a license for the news *site* would not affect the functioning of the *search engine* itself.

[237] See « *Copiepresse SCRL v. Google Inc.* », # 44: "the authors have a right to claim an equitable remuneration for a new publication of their work by means of a substantial extract, ... the litigation only exists because Google refuses to enter a reasonable agreement with the collective management societies, when largely having the means to do so;" and # 62: "Had Google contacted the publishers to request their authorization, it could have entered a general contract with the collective management societies and avoid exposing itself to the consequences of a judicial procedure for infringement."

[238] It is foreseeable that collective management societies and small publishers may be less opposed to license news aggregators, than larger newspaper publishers which may obtain more benefits from direct licensing.

[239] We all remember the music industry adopting the same approach when fighting Napster, Grokster and the P2P platforms, rather than licensing them; now, the license option (be it directly or indirectly, through the ISP services) does not seem so unacceptable.

[240] Murdoch recently announced the launching of the *The Daily* , a subscription service built for the iPad which will provide constantly updated daily news (including videos and pictures) to iPad owners. See http://www.guardian.co.uk/media/2011/feb/02/murdoch-daily-ipad-newspaper-review (last accessed 28 February 2011).

[241] For instance, Google is offering *Google One Pass*, a payment system that enables publishers to set the terms for access to their digital content by means of a purchase-once, view-anywhere functionality, that allows viewing the content bought in all the devices owned by the user; See http://www.google.com/landing/onepass Last visited 28 February 2011.

[242] Another foreseeable result from voluntary licensing is that predominant players (such as Google) might be in a position to obtain *exclusive* licenses for the aggregation of news, thus deterring competition in the news aggregation market.

vertical control over the technology (the platforms and the agents)[243] that will convey them. Of course, controlling the markets and means of exploitation (hence, its technology) naturally results from the exclusivity granted by the copyright laws. But perhaps not all markets should be treated equally? The dissemination of news-related articles and photographs (and the information they confer) entail a stronger public interest than the distribution of art works, musical works, movies and even books. If only for that reason, it may be justified to treat news works (and the market for news aggregation) differently—as copyright statutes have always done regarding news reuse in analog media.

In short, the survival of news aggregation (and its social and cultural benefits), as we know it today, is at stake; and if the exercise of copyright is allowed to prevent this efficient regime of news servicing, it may well do so "at the cost of distorting the market and impeding expressive diversity."[244]

News aggregation provides value-added services that satisfy a fundamental need in the information society. Accordingly, the question that the legislator should answer is whether the social and public interest of this new market should be secured by law or left to the exclusive interests of both the original upstream copyright owners and downstream platform operators. Perhaps competition law should not only have a role a posteriori but also a priori in helping define the scope of the exclusive rights granted by statutes.[245] It is uncontested that some statutory limitations (as well as safe harbors)[246] already regulate competition *per se*, by benefiting an intermediary (i.e., libraries, teaching and research institutions) or even a competitor (i.e., other press or media) who perform the exploitation acts in favor of the end-users.[247] It should be expected that the same competition law considerations be applied to design a statutory limitation for news aggregation.[248]

---

[243] See Netanel 2008, p 125: "Copyright has emerged as a significant bottleneck to competition from new media distributors in the digital arena. Moreover, the continued use of copyright as a vertical restraint threatens to extend media incumbents' control over distribution just when the economics of digital markets undermine the traditional bases and justification for that control."

[244] See Netanel 2008, p 126. In general, see Dreier 2007.

[245] See Dreier 2007, p 237.

[246] ISP liability exemptions also cut some beneficial treatment for the developing of intermediary services in the online market.

[247] See Dreier 2010, p 51: "copyright limitations and exceptions do not only benefit end-users. Rather, they help to define the delicate relationship between authors, rightholders and end-users and—which is often overlooked- they also define competition in the area of downstream information value-added production chains."

[248] In favor of a statutory license for news aggregation, see Netanel 2008, p 129. See also Dreier 2007, pp 239–240 favoring the consideration of competition law principles in drafting limitations to copyright, and Dreier 2010, p 52 referring to what he calls a "quadrupolar" copyright system where limitations and exceptions balance the interests of authors, rightholders, end-users as well as competitors, adding that "this is all the more true in the digital and networked information society, where copyright information is not only created and consumed, but constantly extracted, regrouped, repackaged, recombined, abstracted and interpreted".

5.8 Conclusions

Press summaries and, in general, the reuse of news-related works have always benefited from statutory limitations conveyed in international instruments as well as in domestic copyright laws. However, as technologies and markets evolve the reuse of news works has become more and more criticized. News aggregators are the latest challenge in the historical battle between copyright and access to information, and pose difficult questions in terms of the scope of copyright, access to information and competition law.

Both copyright and access to information are strong public interests, sanctioned by constitutional instruments. News aggregators are a fundamental tool for the development of a healthy society in the Internet age and, to the extent that they involve the use of copyrighted works, legislators should design how to balance both interests. However, news aggregation activities do not benefit from any specific statutory limitation and can hardly fit in the existing ones in favor of press summaries, quotations, or for communication media; Obstacles being diverse and varying according to the interpretation of the statutory language. Within the insufficient, uneven and uncertain regime of E.U. domestic statutory limitations applicable to news aggregation, the key element remains the three-step-test. Yet, a rather questionable trend in favor of a restrictive reading and application of the statutory limitations risks rendering them ineffective, making it almost impossible to consider their application to new technologies and evolving markets. In addition, the impossibility of enacting any new statutory limitations within European laws further aggravates the situation.

Fair use/dealing doctrines grant more flexibility to assess news aggregation, yet little precedent exists and the non-compensated nature of fair use makes it hard to conclude that news aggregation could be deemed fair.

Failing any limitation or defense to allow the operation of news search engines and sites, news aggregation turns to the existence of an implied license or consent (by failing to implement technical means that would prevent indexation by search engines) and to the (rather shallow) shelter offered by ISP safe harbors. Neither solution is completely satisfactory for news aggregation, since they could *in extremis* allow the functioning of the search engines (including news search engines) but would hardly cover the uses made on the news aggregated sites.

The lack of harmonized rules and the resulting legal uncertainty may be a deterrent for the provision of online news aggregation services. Rather than creating a solid basis for true competition to develop in this upcoming market, legal uncertainty not only endangers its survival but ultimately benefits larger agents (such as Google) who can afford the economic costs of the copyright infringement claims resulting from developing such a new market.

It is not so much a clash between traditional and new media business models as it is usually being portrayed, but rather an opportunity to design the "information society" we want for the future: with *access to information in the most efficient and diverse formats possible*, while protecting the copyright interests of the authors and owners who have produced this "information".[249] Whether this is done by means of carefully balanced statutory limitations (including remunerated compulsory licensing) or, instead, left for voluntary licensing (including non-binding limitations, implied licensing and opt-out schemes) will have significantly different results for the development of the so-called "information society".

In fact, if we pay close attention to news aggregation claims, we may see that what matters is not so much the copyright infringement (if existing) but rather the conveyance of the information contained in the copyrighted works and, of course, the recoupment of the investment made in its production. A spokesman for the German Newspaper Publishers Association made it clear: "the problem is that Google earns billions, and we earn nothing."[250] This is not (and should not be) a question for copyright alone. It is instead a question of fair (or unfair) competition. The mechanism to approximate both concerns has been used many times before: compulsory licensing to secure news aggregation services and ensure revenues to the news producers. And this should be a concern for legislators.

By failing to envision any solution (other than a theoretical voluntary licensing) we may be giving up some of the richest potentials of the Internet in exchange for a "pyrrhic victory" for newspapers[251] and the maintenance of the copyright regime *status quo* (which has always been evolving with technology and markets).

Technological changes always pose difficult questions to the law of copyright and to the assessment of the fundamental rights in our democracies. These challenges should not only be seen as threats to existing business models, but rather as opportunities to improve our copyright laws. News aggregation is one of these opportunities.

References

Bently L, Sherman B (2001) Intellectual property law. Oxford University Press, Oxford

Bercovitz R, Garrote I, Gonzalez A, Sanchez R (2006) Las reformas de la ley de propiedad intellectual. Tirant lo blanch, Valencia

Brauneis R (2009) The transformation of originality in the progressive-era debate over copyright in news, The George Washington University Law School, Legal Studies Research Paper n.463. http://ssrn.com/abstract=1365366. Accessed 28 Feb 2011

Dusollier S (2007) Le géant aux pieds d'argille: Google News et le droit d'auteur, Revue Lamy droit de l'immatériel 26:70–75. http://www.crid.be/pdf/public/5509.pdf. Accessed 28 Feb 2011

Derclaye E (2010) Wonderful or worrisome? The impact of the ECJ ruling in infopaq on UK Copyright law. EIPR 5:247–251

Dreier T (2007) Regulating competition by way of copyright limitations and exceptions. In: Torremans P (ed) Copyright law: a handbook of contemporary research. Edward Elgar, Cheltenhamp, pp 232–254

Dreier T (2010) Limitations: the centerpiece of copyright in distress—an introduction. 1 JIPITEC 50

---

[249] See Dreier 2007, p 238.

[250] Source: http://www.nytimes.com/2010/01/19/technology/19antitrust.html.

[251] See Turner and Callaghan 2008, p 34.

Dreier T, Hugenholtz PB (2006) Concise European copyright law. Kluwer Law International, Alphen aan den Rijn

Ficsor M (2002) The law of copyright and the internet, the 1996 WIPO treaties, their interpretation and implementation. Oxford University Press, Oxford

Geiger C (2006) The three-step-test, a threat to a balanced copyright law? IIC 37:683–700

Geiger C (2007) From Berne to National Law, via the Copyright Directive: the Dangerous Mutations of the three-step-test. EIPR 12:486–491

Gervais D (2005) Towards a new core international copyright norm: the reverse three-step-test. Marq Intell Prop L. Rev 9:1 (Winter 2005)

Hoeren T, Decker U (1998) Electronic archives and the press: copyright problems of mass media in the digital age. EIPR 7:256–266

Isbell K (2010) The rise of news aggregator: legal implication and best practices. http://cyber.law.harvard.edu/publications. Accessed 28 Feb 2011

IVIR (2007) Study on the implementation and effect in member States' Laws of Directive 2001/29/EC on the harmonisation of certain aspects of copyright and related rights in the information society. Institut for Information Law, University of Amsterdam. http://www.ivir.nl. Accessed 28 Feb 2011

Janssens MC (2009) The issue of exceptions: reshaping the keys to the gates in the territory of literary, musical and artistic creation. In: Derclaye E (ed) Research handbook on the future of RU copyright. Edward Elgar, Cheltenhamp. pp 317–348

Koelman K (2006) Fixing the three-step-test. EIPR 8:407–412

Laurent P (2007) Brussels high court confirms google news' ban—Copiepresse SCRL v. Google Inc. Comput Law Secur Rep 23:290–293. http://www.crid.be/pdf/public/5512.pdf. Accessed 28 Feb 2011

Leaffer M (1995) Understanding copyright law. Matthew Bender, New York

Leistner M (2011) The German Federal Supreme Court's judgment on Google's Image Search—a topical example of the "limitations" of the European approach to exceptions and limitations. IIC 42:417–442

Lucas A (2010) For a reasonable interpretation of the three-step-test. EIPR 6:277–282

Lucas H, Lucas HJ (2006) Traité de la Proprieté Litéraire et Artistique, 3rd edn. Litec, Paris

López Maza S (2008) Las revistas de prensa en el entorno digital. Los supuestos de "press clipping". Revista pe.i 30:13–84

Marín López JJ (2008) Derecho de Autor, revistas de prensa y press clipping. RIDA 215:2–101

Moran C (2011) How much is too much? Copyright protection of short portions of text in the United States and European Union after Infopaq International A/S v. Danske Dagblades. Wash J Law Technol Arts 6:247. Available at https://digital.lib.washington.edu/dspace-law/handle/1773.1/563. Accessed 28 Feb 2011

Netanel NW (2008) New media in old bottles? Barron's contextual first amendment and copyright in the digital age. Available at http://ssrn.com/abstract=1183167. Accessed 28 Feb 2011

Peguera M (2009) When the cached link is the weakest link: search engine caches under the Digital Millennium Copyright Act. J Copyr Soc USA 56:589, (Winter 2009). http://ssrn.com/abstract=1135274. Accessed 28 Feb 2011

Pérez de Ontiveros Vaquero C (2007) Comentarios a los Artículos 32 y 33, Comentarios a la Ley de Propiedad Intelectual (Bercovitz R., ed.), Ed. Tecnos, Madrid, 3ª ed., pp 548 – 610

Reinbothe J, von Lewinski S (2002) The WIPO treaties of 1996. Butterworths, London

Ribera Blanes B (2008) Recopilaciones periódicas, reseñas, revistas de prensa y press-clipping. Límites a la propiedad intelectual y nuevas tecnologías (Moreno Martínez JA, coord.) Dykinson. Madrid, pp 439–481

Richter W (2008) The performance of distributed news aggregators. OII DPSN Working Paper No. 9. Available at http://ssrn.com/abstract=1324462. Last visited 28 Feb 2011

Ricketson S, Ginsburg JC (2006) International copyright and neighboring rights—the berne convention and beyond. Oxford University Press, Oxford

Strowel A (2004) La responsabilité des intermédiares sur l'Internet: Questions laissées ouvertes par les textes législatifs. ALAI Study Days Oaxaca, Mexico DF, pp 123–150
Strowel A, Triaille JP (2008) Google et les Nouveaux Services en Ligne. Ed. Larcier, Bruxelles
Travis H (2008) Opting out of the Internet in the United States and the European Union: copyright, safe harbors and international law. Notre Dame Law Rev 84:1, 331–407. http://ssrn.com/abstract=1221642. Accessed 28 Feb 2011
Turner M, Callaghan D (2008) You can look but you don't touch! the impact of the *Google v. Copiepresse* decision on the future of the internet. EIPR 1:34–38

Chapter 6
Copyright Issues Regarding Google Images and Google Cache

Miquel Peguera

Contents

6.1 Introduction

It is hardly a novelty to note that the Internet conflicts with copyright—or at least with an idea of copyright based on rights holders' absolute control over copying in any manner of form. Indeed, if copying is essential for a computer to work,[1] it is

---

[1] See *e.g.* "*MAI Systems Corp. v. Peak Computer, Inc*". C.A.9 (Cal.), 1993, holding that "copying for purposes of copyright law occurs when computer program is transferred from permanent storage device to computer's random access memory (RAM)."

M. Peguera (✉)
Associate Professor of Law, Department of Law and Political Science,
Universitat Oberta de Catalunya, Barcelona, Spain
e-mail: mpeguera@uoc.edu

A. Lopez-Tarruella (ed.), *Google and the Law*,
Information Technology and Law Series 22, DOI: 10.1007/978-90-6704-846-0_6,
© T.M.C. ASSER PRESS, The Hague, The Netherlands, and the author(s) 2012

even more so when it comes to digital communications networks, and thus when it comes to the Internet. The way data packets travel through the net is by means of temporary reproductions made at the different gateways connecting the networks. In addition, end hosts are able to display the information received only by storing it in memory devices of different degrees of stability. Moreover, proxy caches, mirrors and content delivery networks replicate the contents in order to make them more accessible to final users. In a way, the whole operation of the Internet relies on the possibility of copying.

Copyright laws in various jurisdictions have tried to adjust to this phenomenon by allowing, or by exempting from liability under certain conditions, some types of ephemeral copies which may be necessary for carrying out technical functions or for enhancing their performance.

For instance, with regard to intermediate copies made by a provider of digital communications in the course of transmitting or routing third party material, statutory adjustments have been enacted in the US and in the EU, among other jurisdictions. Those provisions establish liability limitations or "safe harbours" that cover such types of reproductions. Section 512(a) of the US Copyright Act provides for a safe harbour for "transitory digital network communications", which exempts a service provider from liability for monetary relief for infringement of copyright "by reason of the provider's transmitting, routing, or providing connections for, material through a system or network controlled or operated by or for the service provider, or by reason of the intermediate and transient storage of that material in the course of such transmitting, routing, or providing connections".[2] Similarly, Article 12 of the European Directive on Electronic Commerce sets forth a safe harbour for "mere conduit", which includes "the automatic, intermediate and transient storage of the information transmitted in so far as this takes place for the sole purpose of carrying out the transmission in the communication network, and provided that the information is not stored for any period longer than is reasonably necessary for the transmission."[3] While the E-Commerce Directive does not focus specifically on copyright, its safe harbours apply horizontally to cover all kinds of liability, including that arising from copyright infringement.

Another safe harbour, both in the US and the EU, covers the so-called proxy caching, which refers to the activity carried out by some Internet access and transmission providers consisting of storing a copy of web pages frequently requested by their users in order to be able to serve that copy to ulterior users who request that same page. The US Copyright Act provides for this safe harbour in Section 512(b). In the EU, a very similar safe harbour, which again applies horizontally to any kind of liability, is laid down in Article 13 of the E-Commerce

---

[2] 17 U.S.C. § 512(a).

[3] Article 14(2) of the Directive 2000/31/EC of the European Parliament and of the Council of 8 June 2000 on certain legal aspects of information society services, in particular electronic commerce, in the Internal Market ('Directive on electronic commerce') [hereinafter E-Commerce Directive].

Directive. Both provisions subject the liability limitation to almost identical conditions, which are of a highly technical nature.

In addition, the EU has established a compulsory exception regarding the reproduction right, which allows the making of certain kinds of technical copies. This exception is set forth in Article 5(1) of Directive 2001/29/EC on the harmonisation of certain aspects of copyright and related rights in the information society (hereinafter, InfoSoc Directive). According to this provision, "[t]emporary acts of reproduction... which are transient or incidental [and] an integral and essential part of a technological process and whose sole purpose is to enable: (a) a transmission in a network between third parties by an intermediary, or (b) a lawful use of a work or other subject-matter to be made, and which have no independent economic significance, shall be exempted from the reproduction right".

Moreover, as we will see below, courts in some jurisdictions have found certain cases of copying to be a fair use, or to be lawful under a theory of implied license or other doctrines. However, not withstanding all those legal provisions and case law, the conflict between the technical functions carried out by some Internet operators and copyright law is still far from settled. On the one hand, some of those protections are not available in all jurisdictions, as is the case with fair use. On the other hand, the statutory provisions not always squarely apply to the new technical developments, or they may only allow some acts of exploitation, such as reproduction, but not others, such as the communication to the public. In addition, some of the legal protections only apply to direct infringement, leaving the possibility of finding secondary liability open.

This chapter will consider some copyright issues that may arise in relation with two specific and well-known functions performed by Google. The first one is Google Images—Google's search tool for images—which entails storing thumbnail images in Google's servers and showing them as search results, each thumbnail being a reference that links to the original full-size images located elsewhere in the Internet. The second one is a feature of Google Web Search that consists of providing a so-called "Cached" link along with the search results, which leads to a cached version of the page, stored in Google's servers—the Google Cache. Both functions are undeniably useful and very much appreciated by users, yet they may raise some legal concerns from a copyright perspective. While the two services are clearly different, some of the legal issues they present are intertwined enough as to warrant a parallel consideration within a single chapter.

6.2 Technology

Before describing the operation of Google Images and Google Cache it may be useful to briefly recall a few basic notions about the technology behind the World Wide Web which are relevant for the legal debate about both services. Specifically, it is important to bear in mind how web pages are built and how web browsers interact with them.

A web page is essentially a document that consists of text and strings of HTML or XHTML code—what is also known as the page's "source code". When this information gets to the user's computer, the web browser is able to interpret the HTML commands in order to produce the result intended by the author of the web page and to display it on the user's computer screen. While it is fairly common for a page shown on the screen to include images, a web page in itself—which, as noted, consists of no more than the source code—does not contain those images. Rather, the HTML code instructs the browser to download them from the location where they are hosted, in order to display them within the page on the screen. This process is known as "in-line linking".[4] Indeed, what the user perceives as a unity on the screen is in fact an aggregation of a number of elements taken from different places. Images are thus separate files, which have their own URL that determines their location, stored either in the same server that hosts the web page document or in a different one. As a consequence, if an image file—which may be for example a ".jpg" file—has been removed from the location to which the HTML instructions were pointing, the browser will not be able to find it, and thus it will not show up on the screen—instead, an icon indicating that the link is broken will normally appear. The directions included in the source code will determine where exactly the image must be displayed within the page, as well as its size. The size with which the image will be displayed is not necessarily the actual size of the image file. However, it is not that a copy of that image is shown; it is simply that the browser is able to show it in a smaller size—the information of which the displayed image consists is still taken from the original location of the image.[5]

6.2.1 Google Images

Google's robots crawl the Web and make small copies of the images they find. These copies, usually referred to as "thumbnails" due to their reduced size, are stored in Google's servers. They are indexed according to many factors, particularly the contextual information provided by the web page where the image was found. As of today, Google indexes over ten thousand million thumbnail images.[6]

Google Images, formerly Google Image Search, is the tool that allows users to search Google's index of thumbnail images. It was launched in 2001, and underwent a major revamp in July 2010 with a new graphic design and advanced new features. The basic operation is simple. Typically, users go to http://images.google.com and type in the search box the word or words they deem relevant for the image or images they are looking for. They may also limit the

---

[4] See Honkasalo 2010, p 441.

[5] For the sake of clarity I am not considering now the fact that normally a copy of the image will be stored on the local cache memory of the user's computer.

[6] The Official Google Blog, Ooh! Ahh! Google Images presents a nicer way to surf the visual web, available at http://googleblog.blogspot.com/2010/07/ooh-ahh-google-images-presents-nicer.html. Accessed 31 August 2011.

search to images that have a certain size, or a particular predominant colour, among other options. From June 2011 it is also possible to search by image, i.e., using an image instead of text as a search query. To do so a user may upload an image from his or her computer or paste an image's URL into the search box. When using Google Chrome of Firefox browsers a user may simply drag and drop an image into the search box or even using a browser extension to search by image on the web by right-clicking on the image.[7] The search engine produces a result page full of image thumbnails responsive to the user search query.[8] The current version of Google Images displays a dense layout with lots of images. The user may see several pages scrolling down the screen, getting hundreds of images in one scrolling page. These thumbnails are somewhat bigger, and of higher resolution, than they used to be in the old version. Besides, when the cursor is placed over an image, a hover pane pops up with an even slightly larger preview—which is the actual size of the thumbnail file stored by Google—along with some information about the original image, namely, the image's file name, its original size in pixels, a short text normally taken from the web page where the image was found that may be descriptive of the image, and the address of that web page. In addition, an option labelled "similar" allows the user to find images which are similar in appearance to the selected one.

The search result page of Google Images is therefore a web page created by Google that includes HTML commands instructing the web browser to download a number of image thumbnail files stored in Google's servers and display them in a particular layout. Each of these thumbnails has thus its own URL—for instance, under gstatic.com, a domain name owned by Google.[9]

When clicking on a thumbnail, the user is led to a new landing page. This is again a Google web page, which is divided in two vertical frames. The main, bigger frame shows the web page where the image was taken from. But it is shown only as a backdrop, for a hovering pane in the centre of it shows the selected image in a large size. This image is no longer the thumbnail stored by Google, but the actual original image hosted somewhere else on the Internet. This can be easily verified by right-clicking on this image to find the URL indicating its location. The size with which this image is displayed may or not coincide with its original size, as the hover pane must leave enough space surrounding it so that the backdrop web page can be seen. By clicking anywhere on the backdrop area that surrounds the floating image, the user leaves the Google frames and gets to the origin web page, where the image can be seen in its context, as intended by the author of the page. Besides this main frame, a small right-hand vertical frame provides some information about the original image. This information includes a link labelled "full

---

[7] See http://images.google.com/support/bin/answer.py?hl=en&answer=1325808 (last accessed 30 August 2011).

[8] When conducting a "search by image", the results page may look different than the normal Google Images results page, as it may provide links not only to images but also to webpages which may be relevant to the image used in the search.

[9] See http://www.whois.net/whois/gstatic.com (last accessed 31 August 2011).

size", that links to the place the original file is stored, and also a notice stating that "[t]his image may be subject to copyright."

6.2.2 Google Cache

Just like Google Images searches Google's index of images, Google's main search engine—Google Web Search—performs the searches over an enormous index of web pages and other documents. For the purposes of building this index, Google's robots constantly crawl the web and make a copy of the HTML code of every web page they find—unless instructed otherwise, as it will be discussed below, or unless they are not able to access the content because it is protected by a password or otherwise (e.g. encrypted). Each of these copies—or "snapshots" as Google calls them—is then stored in Google's servers and it is kept there until it is replaced by a new one—that made by the crawler the next time it visits the same web page. These copies are called "cached" copies, and this repository is referred to as the Google Cache.[10]

Google not only uses this information to build an index in order to perform the searches. Rather, it also makes those copies available to the users of its Web Search engine. This is made through a link labelled with the word "Cached", which appears in most of the search results, along with the title of the relevant web page and a short snippet from it.[11] When clicked by a user, this link shows the copy of the web page that was made by the search engine's robot last time it visited that page. As noted, the cached copy of a web page consists only of its HTML code. The images that may be embedded in that page are not stored in the cache. When displaying the cached copy on the screen, the browser will execute the HTML instructions, including those that in-line link to images located elsewhere, causing those images to show up within the page—as long as the images are still available at their original location.

Obviously, the cached copy is not necessarily identical to the current page, for the latter may have changed since the robot took the snapshot stored in the cache. This is clearly noted through a prominent disclaimer on the top of the page which stresses its character. The notice indicates that "[t]his is Google's cache of http://[url of the original page]. It is a snapshot of the page as it appeared on [date and GMT hour]." It also warns that "[t]he current page could have changed in the meantime." In that sentence, the words "current page" are again a link to the

---

[10] See http://www.google.com/intl/en/help/features_list.html#cached (last accessed 31 August 2011).

[11] To be sure, Google Web Search not only shows results for web pages but also for other type of documents, such as .pdf, .xls, .ppt, .doc or .rtf. Likewise, Google Cache not only stores copies of web pages but also HTML versions or these other type of files, which it uses to build the index and perform the searches.

actual web page. In addition, the notice includes a "learn more" link which explains the nature of cached copies.

By making available the cached copies to users, Google provides them with additional or alternative information about the relevant web page. Indeed, a user may find it useful to access the cache copy for several reasons. First, the original web page may be unavailable at that particular moment, whether temporarily or definitively. In that case, the cached copy will provide information that, while not always current, may be useful for the user's interests. Second, since the cached copy highlights in colour the terms used to perform the query, it makes it easier to identify why a particular web page is relevant to that search query. To be sure, this also could be easily found out just looking at the current page and performing a word search within it. However, since the search results are based not on the content of the current pages but on an index that stems from the copies stored by the search engine, it may be the case that the current page has changed and no longer includes the term used in the search query. In that case, when looking at the current page, the user will find it difficult to know why the page has been included in the search results, while she will find it out looking at the older version of the page accessible through the "Cached" link, where the search terms still appear. Third, in some cases the user may find it interesting to compare the current web page with an older version of it, such as the cached copy. The cached copies are indeed archival in nature. They are meant to show how the appearance of that web page was at a particular time in the recent past. This function, however, is better accomplished by an archive of web pages that keeps not just temporary but permanent copies, such as the Internet Archive.[12] In contrast, a cached copy stored by a search engine is deleted when replaced by the new snapshot of the web page taken by the crawler.

6.2.3 Opting Out from Google Images or Google Cache

As noted, unless instructed otherwise or being protected content, robots will make a copy of each web page they visit, and will make this copy available through "Cached" links. Nonetheless, webmasters may opt-out, specifying some directions so that robots do not index or archive their web pages. To be effective, these directions must adjust to the existent industry standards. There are two main types of standards widely accepted by the industry. One consists of the inclusion of meta-tags in the HTML code of the web page; the other consists of the placement of a "robots.txt" file in the server root.[13]

---

[12] See Internet Archive, http://www.archive.org (last accessed 31 August 2011).

[13] For a description of both standards, see e.g. The Robots Pages, http://www.robotstxt.org (last accessed 31 August 2011).

Meta-tags may be directed either generally to all the robots, or to specific crawlers, indicating then the name of the robot in the meta-tag. Through meta-tags, webmasters may direct robots, for instance, not to index the page, or follow its links. It is also possible to allow the robots to index the page, but not to follow the links it contains. Through a "noarchive" meta-tag, webmasters can also instruct the robots to index the page but not to make available a cached copy of it for users. Following this "noarchive" meta-tag, a search engine will include the web page in its search results, but will provide no "Cached" link. The inclusion of a "robots.txt" file in the server root is another widely known and accepted industry practice. The "robots.txt" file is a very simple text file that, again, can be directed either to any robot or to one or more specific robots.

In addition to meta-tags and robots.txt standards, web owners may also opt-out through other means. First, if the website is protected, by a password or otherwise, the robot will be unable to access it, and thus to make a copy of it. Second, a website owner may request the search engine not to display "Cached" links to particular web pages either contacting the search engine directly, or through a removal procedure established by the search engine. There is also a removal procedure to deal with Google Images.

6.3 Copyright Issues

The operation of the services described above may affect copyright law in several ways. First, the initial copying for the purposes of building the index—whether the index for Google Images or that for Google Web Search—obviously affects the reproduction right. Second, displaying the content stored by Google servers, whether image thumbnails or cached pages, may also affect other exclusive rights, such as the right of communication to the public—or, in the US, the display right and the distribution right. Third, in-line linking to images not stored in Google's servers causing them to be displayed within the cache page, or even simply linking to infringing images via normal links, might also be relevant, whether as primary or secondary infringement.

6.3.1 The "Server Test" as a Criterion for Distinguishing between Primary and Secondary Liability

Apart from the initial copying and storing for indexing purposes, the actions carried out by Google—whether through Google Images or through the Cached links feature of its Web Search service—may be distinguished in two categories depending on whether the material displayed is located in Google's servers or somewhere else. The first category includes the display of thumbnail images and cached web pages, as those elements are stored in Google's servers. The second category comprises the instances where the content is brought to the user's screen through in-line links. Embedding or in-line linking occurs, for instance, in the landing page to which a user is led after clicking on a thumbnail. As explained above, this page is Google's framing page that in-line links elements taken from someone else's servers: the larger image that appears in a hover pane, and the background vision of the web page to which the image belongs. Another instance of in-line linking takes place when a cached web page is displayed. While the web page is taken from Google's Cache, the images included in it, as noted, are actually coming from their original location through an in-line link.

This distinction has proved relevant in some jurisdictions for the purposes of direct infringement analysis, concluding that while the first category of actions may constitute a direct infringement, the second type of conduct—in-line linking—raises only secondary liability issues.

In the US, the relevant case regarding in-line linking—and specifically the in-line linking carried out by Google Images—is *"Perfect 10 v. Google"*,[14] which later on was renamed by the Ninth Circuit as *"Perfect 10 v. Amazon"*.[15] For what matters here, Perfect 10, a publisher of euphemistically called adult pictures, sued Google for copyright infringement on account of the thumbnails of Perfect 10's copyrighted images displayed on Google's Image Search results, and also on account of the in-line linked full-sized images. At the time, Google Image search engine would display a slightly different landing page once a user clicked on a thumbnail. That page had two frames. The upper frame would show the thumbnail image, along with some information about it. The lower frame would show the full-sized image alone by means of an in-line link. Perfect 10 sought a preliminary injunction to prevent Google from "copying, reproducing, distributing, publicly displaying, adapting or otherwise infringing, or contributing to the infringement of" Perfect 10's copyrighted images; and from linking to websites which display or make available such images.[16]

In order to determine whether or not in-line linking could be considered a display for the purposes of the Copyright Act, the district court discussed two possible approaches, which the court called a "server" test and an "incorporation" test.[17]

Under the server test, favoured by the defendant, "display" would be defined as "the act of *serving* content over the web—i.e., physically sending ones and zeroes over the internet to the user's browser",[18] and thus the originating server and not Google would be the one actually displaying the in-line linked image. Under the incorporation test, endorsed by the plaintiff, "display" would be defined as "the mere act of *incorporating* content into a web page that is then pulled up by

[14] *"Perfect 10, Inc. v. Google, Inc"*., 416 F.Supp 2d 828 (D. Cal. 2006).

[15] *"Perfect 10, Inc. v. Amazon.com, Inc"*., 508 F.3d 1146 (9th Cir. 2007).

[16] See *"Perfect 10 v. Google"* 416 F.Supp 2d at 834–35.

[17] Idem at 838–44.

[18] Idem at 839. Emphasis in the original.

the browser."[19] Hence, in the latter case, Google would be deemed to 'display' the in-line linked images, and therefore could potentially face liability for *direct* infringement. The district court concluded that "in determining whether Google's lower frames are a 'display' of infringing material, the most appropriate test is also the most straightforward: the website on which content is stored and by which it is served directly to a user, not the website that in-line links to it, is the website that 'displays' the content."[20] Applying thus the server test, the court found that "for the purposes of direct copyright infringement, Google's use of frames and in-line links does not constitute a 'display' of the full-size images stored on and served by infringing third-party websites."[21]

On appeal, the Ninth Circuit endorsed the server test and upheld the conclusion reached by the district court on this matter—finding that the court's analysis comports with the language of the Copyright Act.[22] The court pointed out that according to the Copyright Act, "[t]o 'display' a work means to show a copy of it, either directly or by means of a film, slide, television image, or any other device or process ..."[23] Regarding the in-line linking of the full-sized images, the Ninth Circuit reasoned that "[b]ecause Google's computers do not store the photographic images, Google does not have a copy of the images for purposes of the Copyright Act ... and thus cannot communicate a copy."[24] It held moreover that the same analysis is applicable to Google's cache "[b]ecause Google's cache merely stores the text of webpages."[25]

In reaching this conclusion, the Ninth Circuit followed a strictly technological approach: "[i]nstead of communicating a copy of the image, Google provides HTML instructions that direct a user's browser to a website publisher's computer that stores the full-size photographic image. Providing these HTML instructions is not equivalent to showing a copy. First, the HTML instructions are lines of text, not a photographic image. Second, HTML instructions do not themselves cause infringing images to appear on the user's computer screen. The HTML merely gives the address of the image to the user's browser. The browser then interacts with the computer that stores the infringing image. It is this interaction that causes an infringing image to appear on the user's computer screen. Google may facilitate the user's access to infringing images. However, such assistance raises only contributory liability issues ... and does not constitute direct infringement of the copyright owner's display rights."[26] Using a similar reasoning, the Ninth Circuit concluded that Google does not distribute those images either. Conversely, applying the same test to the use of the thumbnails stored on Google's servers, the Ninth Circuit—just like the district court—concluded that

---

[19] Idem. Emphasis in the original.

[20] Idem at 843.

[21] Idem at 844.

[22] *"Perfect 10 v. Amazon"* 508 F.3d at 1160.

[23] See 17 U.S.C. § 101.

[24] *"Perfect 10 v. Amazon"* 508 F.3d at 1160–61.

[25] Idem at 1162.

[26] Idem. (internal quotations omitted).

"Perfect 10 [had] made a prima facie case that Google's communication of its stored thumbnail images directly infringes Perfect 10's display right."[27]

While this reasoning is accurate from a technological perspective, the question remains as to whether it is the right approach, as it seems to disregard the fact that in-line links are activated automatically, without any decision taken by the user once the framed web page is generated. The explanation above stresses the fact that it is the user's browser that requests the image from the server that stores it. Though this is accurate, it should not be disregarded that this is so because the linking page causes the browser to request that image.[28] Still, it is undisputed that that image is not stored in Google's servers, and thus the questions regarding the display and distribution rights may turn out to be whether 'to show a copy' might also mean 'to cause a copy to be shown', or whether to distribute a copy may include causing a copy to be distributed.

So far, European case law does not seem to follow the "server-test" approach. A few cases in Europe have dealt with embedding links, yielding different outcomes. A criterion that appears to be relevant in order to assess whether embedding images may tread on rights holders exclusive rights is whether or not the linking page's layout clearly indicates the origin of the embedded image. In 2007, a Munich District court decided a case where the defendant's website had embedded an image in-line linking to the copyright owner's website.[29] The court took into account the fact that the image was embedded in a way that users were not able to identify its origin, and held that the defendant had engaged in a copyright infringement on the grounds that that incorporation affects the rights holder's exclusive right of making the work available.[30] Conversely, in a case where the linking page held a clear copyright notice indicating the origin of the embedded image, the Austrian Supreme Court held that defendant did not engage in copyright infringement.[31]

6.3.2 Direct Infringement Regarding Materials Stored in Google's Servers

While in-line linking raises the issue of whether or not it affects any of the copyright owner's exclusive rights, when it comes to copies of third-party

---

[27] Idem at 1160.

[28] See Honkasalo 2010, pp 443, 446 (arguing that "the 'object' element included by the linker is the very deciding factor that de facto contrives the reproduction" and that "[a]lbeit the data transmission in respect of the embedded material takes place between and end user and the origin server, it is the link provider that *causes* the automatic transmission.") (Emphasis in original).

[29] *Landgericht München* I (Munich District Court I) 10 January 2007, 21 O 20028/05 (*"Nutzung eines Werks im Internet mittels Framing"*).

[30] See Honkasalo 2010, p 446. See Article 3(1) of the InfoSoc Directive.

[31] *Oberste Gerichtshof* (OGH) (Austrian Supreme Court) 17 December 2002, 4 Ob 248/02b (*"MeteoData"*). Honkasalo 2010, p 447.

copyrighted material which are actually stored in Google's servers—such as
Google Images' thumbnails or the cached web pages kept in Google's Cache—
case law generally agrees that there may be a *prima facie* direct copyright
infringement. This is not perfectly settled, though, as some court has held that
there's not even a *prima facie* infringement because Google's conduct lacks the
level of volition which is necessary to find direct infringement.[32]

Deeming the conduct a *prima facie* infringement does not necessarily mean that
an actual infringement has in fact occurred, as the actions carried out by Google—
or for that matter, other search engines—may be considered a fair use and thus
noninfringing. In addition, some other theories—such as implied license—may
protect that use. Moreover, safe harbours from liability may apply.

6.3.2.1 Google Images

The landmark case that dealt with the use of thumbnails by an image search engine
in the US is *"Kelly v. Arriba Soft Corp"*.[33] Defendant Arriba Soft operated an
image search engine—that later on changed its name to Ditto.com. Leslie Kelly,
a professional photographer, filed a complaint for copyright infringement against
Arriba Soft on account of Arriba's use of thumbnail copies of his images. For what
matters here, the operation of Arriba Soft was similar to that of Google Images.
Arriba would make copies of the pictures found when crawling the Internet and
would create thumbnail versions of them for indexing purposes. Once the
thumbnail version was created and stored, the copy of the original full-sized image
was deleted from Arriba's server. When a user typed a search query, the search
engine would produce a result page of thumbnail images. The thumbnails were
also pointers linking to the full-sized image, located either in the plaintiff's website
or in third-party's websites. The plaintiff moved for summary judgment asserting
that Arriba's use of the thumbnail images violated his display, reproduction and
distribution rights. Arriba filed a cross motion for summary judgment, conceding,
for the purposes of the motion, that the plaintiff had established a *prima facie* case
of infringement, but contending that its use of the thumbnails was a fair use under
Section 107 of the US Copyright Act.[34]

The district court granted the defendant's motion for summary judgment and
held that Arriba's use of the thumbnail images was fair,[35] a conclusion upheld on
appeal by the Ninth Circuit.[36] Specifically, the Ninth Circuit held that "the
reproduction of Kelly's images to create the thumbnails and the use of those

---

[32] This was held in a case dealing with Google's Cache: *"Field v. Google Inc"*., 412 F.Supp.2d
1106 (D. Nev. 2006). We will deal with this case below, when considering Google Cache.

[33] *"Kelly v. Arriba Soft Corp."*, 336 F.3d 811 (9th Cir. 2003).

[34] 17 U.S.C. § 107.

[35] *"Kelly v. Arriba Soft Corp"*, 77 F.Supp.2d 1116 (C.D. Cal. 1999).

[36] *"Kelly v. Arriba Soft Corp"*. 336 F.3d 811, 817 (9th Cir. 2003).

thumbnails in Arriba's search engine" was a fair use.[37] The key finding to that effect was that the search engine's use of the thumbnail images was transformative. The Ninth Circuit held that "Arriba's use of the images serves a different function than Kelly's use—improving access to information on the internet versus artistic expression. Furthermore, it would be unlikely that anyone would use Arriba's thumbnails for illustrative or aesthetic purposes because enlarging them sacrifices their clarity. Because Arriba's use is not superseding Kelly's use but, rather, has created a different purpose for the images, Arriba's use is transformative."[38] Finding that the use was transformative implied that the first factor of § 107—the purpose and character of the use—weighed heavily in favour of Arriba. As to the other three factors of § 107, the court found that the factor dealing with the nature of the copyrighted work weighed only slightly in favour of Kelly; the factor regarding the amount and substantiality of the portion used was neutral; and finally, the factor that considers the effect of the use upon the potential market for, or value of, the copyrighted work weighed also in favour of Arriba.[39]

The Ninth Circuit deemed to be a fair use both the initial copying and the ulterior use of the thumbnails by Arriba. Thus not only the reproduction but also the display and distribution of the thumbnails by the search engine were a fair use. Apparently, moreover, these uses were considered fair uses irrespective of the source from which the image was taken by the search engine, that is, whether it was taken from a legitimate source—i.e. Kelly's website—or from an infringing source—i.e. a third-party website publishing the images without Kelly's authorisation.[40]

In the above-mentioned "Perfect 10" case, which dealt directly with Google Image Search, the district court distinguished "Kelly" and found that the use of thumbnails by Google was not a fair use. A key point to reach this conclusion was the fact that Perfect 10 had licensed to a third company—Fonestarz Media Limited—the right to sell and distribute reduced-sized versions of its images to download to cell phones. The district court found that because users could download the thumbnails displayed by Google to their cell phones, Google's thumbnails superseded Perfect 10's reduced-sized images and might have a negative impact on plaintiff's potential market. In addition, the district court found that Google's use of the images was more commercial than the use in Kelly. In particular, the court noted that some of the websites having infringing Perfect 10

---

[37]   Idem at 817.

[38]   Idem at 819.

[39]   Idem at 822.

[40]   As to the full-sized in-line linked images, the Ninth Circuit issued a first ruling holding Arriba directly liable for copyright infringement— "Kelly v. Arriba Soft Corp.", 280 F.3d 934 (9th Cir.2002). However, this ruling—very much criticised—was later on withdrawn on procedural grounds and a superseding decision was filed on 7 July, 2003—"Kelly v. Arriba Soft Corp"., 336 F.3d 811 (9th Cir. 2003). The new ruling left the issue of the full-sized images undecided. It reversed the district court holding that displaying these images was fair use on the grounds that the court should not have addressed this issue as the parties did not include it on their motions for summary judgment, and remanded for further proceedings.

images were partners of Google's AdSense program. Thus, it held that using the thumbnails to lead users to those websites directly benefit Google, which would increase the commercial nature of the use. As a result, the district court denied Google's fair use defence. On appeal, however, the Ninth Circuit reversed this holding, finding that Google's use of the thumbnails was indeed a fair use.[41]

Before examining how the court tackled the fair use issue, it is worth pointing out that—as noted when explaining the 'server' test—the Ninth Circuit deemed Google's use to be a *prima facie* infringement. Interestingly, since the thumbnail images are stored by Google out of its own initiative, the Ninth Circuit distinguished this situation from the one where an entity like a bulletin board passively stores and communicates the content uploaded by users: "[b]ecause Google initiates and controls the storage and communication of these thumbnail images, we do not address whether an entity that merely passively owns and manages an Internet bulletin board or similar system violates a copyright owner's display and distribution rights when the users of the bulletin board or similar system post infringing works. *Cf.* "*CoStar Group, Inc. v. LoopNet, Inc.*", 373 F.3d 544 (4th Cir. 2004)."[42] This holding strongly implies that Google's active role in storing the thumbnail images prevents reaching the conclusion that its conduct lacked the necessary volition to find a direct infringement—a volition that was missing in "*CoStar v. LoopNet*".

As to the fair use analysis, the Ninth Circuit stated that the superseding use was not significant, as the district court "[did] not find that any downloads for mobile phone use had taken place,"[43] and thus that potential harm to the plaintiff's market remained hypothetical.[44] In addition, it noted that the district court had not determined that the commercial dimension derived from leading users to AdSense partners with infringing images was significant.[45] Rather, the Ninth Circuit concluded that the "significantly transformative nature of Google's search engine, particularly in light of its public benefit, outweighs Google's superseding and commercial uses of the thumbnails in this case."[46]

Interestingly, the Ninth Circuit expressly rejected the plaintiff's contention that the use of images taken from infringing websites could not be deemed transformative and thus it was not a fair use. The court, distinguishing two cases on which the plaintiff relied,[47] stated that "[u]nlike the alleged infringers in "*Video Pipeline*" and "*Atari Games*", who intentionally misappropriated the copyright owners' works for the purpose of commercial exploitation, Google is operating a comprehensive search engine that only incidentally indexes infringing websites. This incidental impact

---

[41] "*Perfect 10, Inc. v. Amazon.com, Inc.*", 508 F.3d 1146, 1168 (9th Cir. 2007).

[42] Idem. at footnote 6.

[43] Idem at 1166.

[44] Idem at 1168.

[45] Idem at 1166.

[46] Idem.

[47] "*Video Pipeline, Inc. v. Buena Vista Home Entm't, Inc*"., 342 F.3d 191 (3d Cir.2003), and "*Atari Games Corp. v. Nintendo of Am. Inc.*", 975 F.2d 832 (Fed.Cir.1992).

does not amount to an abuse of the good faith and fair dealing underpinnings of the fair use doctrine. Accordingly, we conclude that Google's inclusion of thumbnail images derived from infringing websites in its Internet-wide search engine activities does not preclude Google from raising a fair use defense."[48]

Lacking a fair use defence, European courts have followed different approaches when confronted with lawsuits regarding Google Images.

Two cases in France have been decided in opposite ways. In a 2008 case— "*SAIF v. Google France and Google Inc*"—a Paris court of first instance, somewhat unexpectedly, reached the conclusion that the applicable law was the US law. It thus applied the fair use defence of the US Copyright Act to hold Google not liable.[49] The plaintiff was SAIF,[50] a French collective rights management society, who brought a copyright infringement lawsuit against Google France and Google Inc. on account of the reproduction and display of the thumbnail images in Google Images' search results. The court found that the French company Google France S.A.R.L.—a Google Inc. subsidiary created in 2002—lacked any power as to the administration of the search engine in France. It noted that Google Inc. was the entity that controls, directs and takes all decisions concerning the search engine's activity, including the French-written site accessible at www.google.fr. As a consequence it dismissed the action with regard to Google France for lack of standing.

Key to this case was the issue of which law should apply. According to article 5(2) of the Berne Convention, the applicable law is that "of the country where protection is claimed."[51] The court endorsed Google's view that the country where the protection is claimed is not the place where the damage arises but the place where the event giving rise to the damage occurs. In the case, the relevant acts of the alleged infringement were carried out by Google, which operates at its headquarters in the US. Therefore, the court concluded that the US Copyright Act was the applicable law. Then the court went on to analyse the fair use factors laid down in Section 107 of the US Copyright Act and ruled that Google had indeed engaged in fair use.

In 2009, however, the same Paris court—albeit a different section of it— reached the opposite outcome in the case of "*H&K v. Google*".[52] Here the court

---

[48] "*Perfect 10 v. Amazon*", 508 F.3d at 1164, footnote 10.

[49] *Tribunal de grande instance de Paris 3ème chambre, 1ère section*, Judgement of 20 May 2008, "*SAIF c. Google France, Google Inc*", available at http://www.legalis.net/spip.php?page=jurisprudence-decision&id_article=2342 (last accessed 31 August 2011).

[50] *Société des Auteurs des Arts Visuels et de l'Image Fixe*.

[51] Article 5(2) of the Berne Convention for the Protection of Literary and Artistic Works of 9 September 1886: "the extent of protection, as well as the means of redress afforded to the author to protect his rights, shall be governed exclusively by the laws of the country where protection is claimed.".

[52] *Tribunal de grande instance de Paris 3ème chambre, 2ème section*, Judgement of October 2009, "*H & K, André R. c. Google*", available at http://www.legalis.net/spip.php?page=jurisprudence-decision&id_article=2776 (last accessed 31 August 2011).

held Google liable for copyright infringement on account of the reproduction of a copyrighted photograph in Google Images. The plaintiffs in this case were Mr. André R., a photographer and author of the concerned photograph, and H&K, the producer of that photograph. They had found that, without their authorisation, someone had uploaded the picture to a website and that it was also accessible in Google Images. They notified the website about their rights on the photograph, and the site promptly removed it. However, it showed up again after some time. The right holders ended up filing a complaint for copyright infringement against the concerned website and also against Google Inc. and Google France. Google raised several defences, including the contention that the use of the photograph by Google Images was a fair use according to the United States Copyright Law, which should be applied to the case. In case this was not to be accepted by the court, Google argued that the use was lawful according to the principles governing search engines' liability under French Law as well.

The court rejected Google's arguments without much elaboration. It held that the US law was not applicable, as the country where the harmful event occurred was France, rather than the US. Applying the French law, the court held Google liable. First, the court held that the reproduction of the photograph on Google Image's website was infringing. It also noted that the information about the image lacked any mention to its author, and thus that Mr. André's moral rights were also infringed. In addition, the judgment stressed that the evidences revealed that the picture appearing in Google's website had been cropped. The court warned that trying to deny this would be to no avail, as the website clearly stated that "the image may have been reduced", and underscored that such a way of displaying the image allows only a visualisation of poor quality, mostly because of its reduced size. Accordingly, it held that the right to the integrity of the work had also been infringed.

More recently, the Paris Court of Appeals handed down its ruling on the appeal of the "*SAIF v. Google*" case—the case where the lower court had applied the US law.[53] In this ruling, of 26 January 2011, the court found that the applicable law was not US but French law. The court argued that the law of the country where the damage occurred can be applied when it is manifestly more closely connected with the lawsuit. In this sense, the court noted that while the infringing services could be generally accessed by a francophone public, they were specifically destined to the French public, noting that they were accessible at the addresses google.fr and images.google.fr. According to the court, in this case the country of reception constitutes a manifestly more pertinent link of proximity than the country where the event giving rise to the damage occurred. In addition, the Court of Appeals reversed the lower court's holding that Google France lacked standing to be sued. Nonetheless, the court found that neither Google Inc. nor Google France were liable, as they were protected by the liability exemptions laid down in the

---

[53] *Cour d'Appel de Paris, Pôle 5—Chambre 1*, Judgment of 26 January 2011. Available at http://www.juriscom.net/documents/caparis20110126.pdf (last accessed 26 February 2011).

E-Commerce Directive and in the French national transposition. This question will be examined below, in the part of this chapter dealing with the safe harbours as a defence from both direct and secondary liability.

Besides fair use and the safe harbours protection, other defences, such as implied license, abuse of right or exculpatory consent have been discussed in cases involving image search engines. Some German cases are relevant in this regard—particularly the case known as *"Vorschaubilder"* (thumbnails), decided by the German Federal Supreme Court in 2010.[54]

The claimant in the *"Vorschaubilder"* case was an artist who maintained a website where she displayed pictures of her paintings. She found out that when typing her name in Google's image search engine, some of her pictures were displayed in the form of thumbnails. She filed a complaint against Google seeking, inter alia, injunctive relief so that the search engine would stop indexing her website and making the pictures accessible via the Internet.

The court of first instance dismissed the claim.[55] It took into account the fact that the claimant could have easily prevented Google from crawling her web by implementing the robots.txt described above. The court held that in choosing not to do so, the claimant had in fact granted Google an implied licence in order to index her website and to make available the thumbnail images. Thus, though the display of the thumbnails by Google was *prima facie* infringing, because of the implied consent no real infringement took place.[56]

The claimant appealed the ruling. The Court of Appeals dismissed the claim as well, though on a completely different ground—abuse of law.[57] The court rejected the implied licence theory, holding that Google's acts were not covered by the claimant's consent. On the one hand, the court reasoned, there was no express declaration of consent, and on the other hand the mere fact of posting the pictures freely accessible on her website, without protective measures preventing the indexation by crawlers, is not enough to infer an implied consent. However, the court deemed that the claim was barred because the claimant was acting in abuse of law under Article 242 of the German Civil Code. The court found that the plaintiff had in fact engaged in search engine optimisation, and set her website's source code in a way that conveyed the impression that she was interested in attracting search engines to her page. Thus, complaining later on for the creation and use of thumbnails appears to be inconsistent with that previous conduct, as this is the normal way image search engines operate.

In yet another twist, following a further appeal, the Federal Supreme Court (BGH) dismissed the abuse of law theory applied by the Court of Appeals. The BGH held again Google not liable, but did so on yet a different ground—that of consent, as

---

[54] *Bundesgerichtshof* (BGH) (German Federal Supreme Court) 29 April 2010, I ZR 69/08 (*Vorschaubilder*).

[55] Regional Court of Erfurt, 15 March 2007, Az 3 O 1108/05 (*"A painter v Google"*).

[56] Allgrove 2007.

[57] Higher Regional Court of Jena, 27 February 2008, 2 U 319/07. See also Clark 2010, p 554.

different from implied licence. To begin with, according to the BGH, the display of
the thumbnails in the search result pages made by Google—if made without the right
owner's authorisation or consent—clearly would have constituted an infringement of
the making available right. The court underscored that by hosting the thumbnails in
its own computers, independently from their original source, Google was not just
providing the technical means but exercising control over the making available of the
pictures. The court further found that Google could not benefit from any copyright
exception or limitation in order to carry out such acts of making available without the
rights holder's consent. Moreover, the BGH agreed with the Court of Appeals in that
the plaintiff had not granted Google a licence, neither an express nor an implied one.
In rejecting a possible finding of implied licence, the BGH noted that the plaintiff had
placed a clear copyright notice along with the pictures on her website, which
excluded that her intention could have been granting a license to use the images.
On the contrary, the fixing of a copyright notice revealed plaintiff's intent of keeping
her rights for herself and arguably to assert them against any third party.[58]
Accordingly, the BGH concluded that the granting of an implied license could not be
inferred from the facts of the case.[59]

However, while not finding an implied licence, the BGH did find some sort of
simple consent on the part of the plaintiff. Such a consent does not entail a transfer
of rights. Rather, it is simply a permission that makes the use lawful, although the
user who benefits from such permission does not acquire a *ius in rem*, nor a claim
which could be enforced against the will of the right holder under the law of
obligations. Such a simple permission or consent does not require a legal declaration of intent, and can be inferred from the claimant's conclusive behaviour.[60]
Indeed, according to the court, the claimant's behaviour in designing the website,
resorting to search engine optimisation, and choosing not to make use of technical
means to prevent search engines from crawling the site, could be understood by
Google as a permission to use the pictures in the way it is usual for image search
engines.[61] This includes displaying the thumbnails of pictures that have been
already removed from the claimant's website during the usual period of time that
takes the search engine's crawlers to revisit the site and refresh the index.[62]

The BGH dismissed as well the claim for injunctive relief. The court reasoned that
the claimant's simple consent can certainly be revoked for the future. However, since
the consent was given by the fact of posting the pictures without technical means
against search engines robots, the revocation of that consent requires an opposite

---

[58] BGH 29 April 2010, I ZR 69/08, para 30.

[59] As noted by Zimbehl (2010), para 5, "[s]ince the licensing is a disposition of a right in rem,
the strict requirements of such a disposition must be met. This means in particular that from an
objective point of view it has to be clear that the copyright holder wants to license the use of the
work. Such a disposition cannot be seen in the mere act of putting pictures on a website. And
much less, if the applicant has used a copyright notice on the works."

[60] BGH 29 April 2010, I ZR 69/08, para 34.

[61] Idem, para 36.

[62] Idem, para 38.

behaviour—for instance, implementing the said technical means. Therefore, as long as the pictures remain unprotected on the claimant's website, her simple consent is still in force and thus the injunctive relief cannot be granted.[63]

Finally, in an interesting obiter dictum, the court considered the hypothetical case that the pictures had been taken by the search engine from an infringing website—rather than from the right holder's site. It pointed out that in such a case a search engine would still be free from liability as long as it met the requirements set forth in the E-Commerce Directive hosting safe harbour. I will comment on this below, in the part dealing with the safe harbours.

6.3.2.2 Google Cache

Just a few cases have dealt so far with Google Cache, that is, with Google's activity that essentially consists of storing "cached" copies of the web pages its robots crawl and, more importantly, providing access to those copies through the so-called "Cached" link shown in the search results page.

The most relevant case in the US specifically tackling the Google cache from a copyright standpoint is "*Field v. Google*".[64] The plaintiff, Blake A. Field, wrote 51 short stories over a 3-day period. He registered copyrights for each of them separately. Then he created a website where he uploaded these works, making them freely accessible on the Internet. Being aware of how to instruct Google not to show the "cached" links, he set out to make his web pages to be automatically included in Google search results, so that Google would provide a "cached" link to those pages as well. Once that happened, Field, acting as a *pro se* plaintiff, filed a complaint against Google for copyright infringement on account of those "cached" links. Not surprisingly, he did not seek actual but statutory damages.[65] The court immediately determined that the plaintiff was acting in bad faith.[66]

Field did not claim that Google was either contributory or vicariously liable, thus the case dealt exclusively with direct liability. Even with regard to direct liability, the plaintiff exclusively claimed that Google engaged in copyright infringement when it showed the cached copies to a user who clicked on the "cached" links.[67] He did not contend that the initial copies made by Google's robots and stored in Google's servers were infringing, and thus this point was not considered by the court either.[68]

---

[63] Idem, para 37.

[64] "*Field v. Google Inc*"., 412 F.Supp.2d 1106 (D.Nev. 2006).

[65] He requested $50,000 in statutory damages for each work, totalling $2,550,000 for the fifty-one short pieces he had written over a three-day period.

[66] See "*Field v. Google*", 412 F.Supp.2d at 1123.

[67] Idem.

[68] Idem at 1115.

Plaintiff Field specifically contended that Google's response to a user who clicks on a "cached" link entails both an unauthorised reproduction and an unauthorised distribution of the work.[69] The court dismissed this claim holding that Google lacked the necessary volition. The court stated that "when a user requests a web page contained in the Google cache by clicking on a 'cached' link, it is the user, not Google, who creates and downloads a copy of the cached web page. Google is passive in this process, as Google's computers respond automatically to the user's request. Without the user's request, the copy would not be created and sent to the user, and the alleged infringement at issue in this case would not occur. The automated, non-volitional conduct by Google in response to a user's request does not constitute direct infringement under the Copyright Act."[70] However, it is not clear whether this approach will prevail in the case law, since, as noted above, it stands in contrast with the Ninth Circuit decision in "Perfect 10".[71]

In any event, the court found as well that, even assuming that Google's conduct was a *prima facie* direct infringement, Google had successfully established four defences,[72] namely, implied licence, estoppel, fair use, and the caching safe harbour of § 512(b) of the Copyright Act.

Quoting a number of US cases, the court noted that an implied licence can be found where the copyright holder engages in conduct from which the other party may properly infer that the owner consents to the use. It further underscored that "[c]onsent to use the copyrighted work need not be manifested verbally and may be inferred based on silence where the copyright holder knows of the use and encourages it".[73] In this regard, the court specifically quoted "Keane Dealer Servs., Inc. v. Harts", which held that "consent given in the form of mere permission or lack of objection is also equivalent to a nonexclusive license".[74] This is thus a different approach than that followed by the German Federal Supreme Court in the "Vorschaubilder" case, where, as noted, the BGH distinguished between a licence and simple consent.

Similar to the "Vorschaubilder" case, though, the "Field" court inferred consent from the fact that the plaintiff knew that by using the "no archive" meta-tag, or a robots.txt file, he would have prevented Google from displaying cached links to his pages, and yet he chose not to do so, knowing that Google would interpret this as a permission to display the cached copies. As a result, the court held that plaintiff's conduct could be "reasonably interpreted as the grant of a license to Google for that use".[75]

---

[69] Idem.

[70] Idem.

[71] "Perfect 10, Inc. v. Amazon.com, Inc"., 508 F.3d 1146 (9th. Cir. 2007).

[72] See "Field v. Google", 412 F.Supp.2d at 1114–15.

[73] See "Field v. Google", 412 F.Supp.2d at 1115–16.

[74] "Keane Dealer Servs., Inc. v. Harts", 968 F. Supp. 944, 947 (S.D.N.Y. 1997).

[75] See "Field v. Google", 412 F.Supp.2d at 1116.

The estoppel defence was also accepted by the court. It found that the plaintiff was estopped from asserting his copyright claim, because (i) he knew of the allegedly infringing conduct before it took place, (ii) he "remained silent regarding his unstated desire not to have 'Cached' links provided to his Web site, and he intended for Google to rely on this silence", (iii) Google was not aware of Field's desire and (iv) Google detrimentally relied on Field's silence.[76]

Moreover, as noted, the court considered Google's use to be a fair use and thus noninfringing.[77] The court relied on the fair use analysis in *"Kelly v Arriba Soft"*, and noted that the use was transformative. The last defence accepted by the court was the protection granted by the DMCA caching safe harbour, a question that will be examined in the last part of this chapter.

Arguably, the first three defences—implied licence, estoppel and fair use— might not be available under different circumstances. In *"Field v. Google"* the content stored and made available through "cached" links was copied from the site where it had been legally posted by its copyright owner, who allowed free access to that material and did not exploit it commercially. Let us envision, however, a different situation. Imagine that the copyright owner of a work of authorship is exploiting it commercially and does not provide free access to it. Imagine as well that someone copies the copyrighted material and publishes it on a website without the authorisation of the copyright owner. Consider further that a search engine makes a copy of the material posted on the infringing website, stores it on its cache and makes it available through a "cached" link. Imagine finally that the copyright owner—and not the publisher of the infringing website from where the material has been cached—brings a lawsuit against the search engine.

A situation like this seems likely to affect the fair use analysis. Certainly, the mere fact that the cached copy has been taken from an infringing site does not in itself prevent the finding of a fair use.[78] However, the circumstances in this hypothetical situation could be relevant for the first statutory factor,[79] when assessing whether the use of the cached copies is superseding rather than trans-formative.[80] Second and most importantly, this could also affect the analysis of the fourth statutory factor which refers to "the effect of the use upon the potential market for or value of the copyrighted work".[81] The *"Field"* court held that "[t]he fourth fair use factor cuts strongly in favour of fair use in the absence of any evidence of an impact on a potential market for Field's copyrighted works."[82] It seems then that a different conclusion might be reached if the copyright owner was

---

[76] Idem at 1116–17.

[77] See 17 U.S.C. § 107 ("... the fair use of a copyrighted work,... is not an infringement of copyright.").

[78] See *"Perfect 10 v. Amazon"*, 508 F.3d at 1164, footnote 8.

[79] 17 U.S.C. § 107(1).

[80] See *"Perfect 10 v. Amazon"*, 508 F.3d at 1165–66.

[81] 17 U.S.C. § 107(4).

[82] See *"Field v. Google"*, 412 F.Supp.2d at 1123.

commercially exploiting the works unlawfully posted in the original website and then cached by the search engine. In addition, the *"Field"* court's analysis of an additional factor dealing with defendant's good faith suggests that this additional factor would be neutral in a case in which the copyright owner did not take any affirmative steps to have her works included in the search engine's cache, but the search engine's robot copied the works from an infringing website. To be sure, these elements would not necessarily preclude a fair use defence, but they might make the outcome even more uncertain.

In such a scenario, the availability of other defences would also be affected. Indeed, if the claim against the search engine is brought by a copyright owner who did not make the material freely available online—the search engine having taken the snapshot from an infringing website—it seems clear that neither the implied license nor the estoppel defence could be sustained.

In Europe, the well-known Belgian case of *"Copiepresse v. Google"* must be noted.[83] While the case focuses mainly on the legality of the Google News services, and as such is already examined in Chap. 5 of this book, it dealt partially with Google cache as well.

Copiepresse SCRL, a collective rights management society representing Belgian publishers of daily newspapers in French and German, filed a lawsuit against Google—joined later on by other collective rights societies—seeking an injunction to remove from Google News and from Google's Cache any articles and images owned by the publishers represented by Copiepresse. A preliminary injunction against Google was issued in 5 September 2006. For the most part, this injunction was upheld by the final ruling issued by the Court of First Instance of Brussels, of 13 February 2007. The Court held that the reproduction of articles' headlines and excerpts by Google News constituted violations of the Belgian Act on Authors' Rights and Neighboring Rights (*Loi relative au droit d'auteur et aux droits voisins*) of 30 June 1994. Moreover, it held that storing articles and documents, and making them available to the public through "cached" links, were infringing activities as well. It also held that Google could not rely on any exception provided by the statute. Google was ordered to remove all these materials from Google News and to remove also the "cached" links from its search results.

As for the Google cache, the court noted that Google's robots make a copy of each web page they visit, and that this copy is stored on Google's memory and made available to Internet users through a "cached" link—*"en cache"*. It held that this is a reproduction of the work and a communication to the public, in the sense of Article 1 of the Belgian Law on the authors' rights and neighbouring rights. This provision grants the author the exclusive right to reproduce or authorise the reproduction of the work in any way and under any form whatsoever. As amended

---

[83] *"Copiepresse v. Google"* (*Tribunal de Première Instance de Bruxelles*, 13 Feb. 2007, No. 06/ 10.928/C). Partially affirmed on appeal (*Cour d'Appel de Bruxelles 9ème chambre*, 5 May, 2011, available at http://www.copiepresse.be/pdf/Copiepresse5mai2011.pdf (last accessed 31 August 2011). For an in-depth analysis of this case see Chap. 5 in this book.

in 2005, following the InfoSoc Directive, that article also grants the author the exclusive right to communicate the work to the public by any means, including the making available to the public of the work in such a way that members of the public may access the work from a place and at a time individually chosen by them.

Like in the *"Field"* case, Google argued that it is the user, and not Google, who creates a copy of the work, and thus the user is the author of the eventual reproduction and communication to the public, while Google limits itself to the provision of the facilities that allow Internet users to make such a communication to the public. Unlike in *"Field v. Google"*, though, the Belgian court rejected this argument. It underscored that Google is the author of the first reproduction—the copy made by the robot and stored in Google's memory. It also pointed out that it is Google who makes available this copy on its own site through the *"en cache"* link—as opposed to the links that send the user to the originating site—and therefore Google's role is not limited to the mere provision of facilities. The court held thus that Google engages in a reproduction and in making available to the public the copy stored in its memory.

Google contended that by failing to adopt the technical measures to opt-out, website publishers had granted an implied license to index the pages and to make them available through "Cached" links, but—again unlike in *"Field v. Google"*—the court did not accept this argument, stating that the authorisation needs to be obtained with certainty and before engaging in the activity.[84]

On appeal, Google's arguments regarding the cached links were rejected again.[85] In particular, the Brussels Court of Appeals held that providing a link to a cached copy stored by Google cannot be equated to "[t]he mere provision of physical facilities for enabling or making a communication" in the sense of Recital 27 of the InfoSoc Directive.[86] It held as well that Google cannot benefit from the exception for transient or incidental copies (article 5.1 of the InfoSoc Directive and article 21 § 3 of the Belgian Copyright Act). According to the court, the provision of cached links by Google is not "an integral and essential part of a technological process" for the purpose of enabling "a transmission in a network between third parties [the publisher of the web page and the user] by an intermediary [Google]", and in addition, a cached copy stored by Google cannot be deemed "transient or incidental".[87]

Another interesting case was decided by the Barcelona Court of Appeals in Spain, which is currently pending before the Spanish Supreme Court. The case is *"Megakini v. Google"*, also known as the *"Google cache"* case.[88]

---

[84] For a comparison between *"Copiepresse v. Google"* and the *"Field v. Google"*, see Triaille 2008. On both cases see also Strowel (2011).

[85] See judgement of the *Cour d'Appel de Bruxelles 9ème chambre*, 5 May, 2011, available at http://www.copiepresse.be/pdf/Copiepresse5mai2011.pdf (last accessed 31 August 2011).

[86] Idem, numbers 21–23.

[87] Idem, numbers 24–26.

[88] Judgment of the Commercial Court No 5 of Barcelona, 30 March 2007; *affirmed* on different grounds by the Judgment of the *Audiencia Provincial* (Court of Appeals) of Barcelona, Section 15, 17 September 2008.

The owner of the website www.megakini.com sued Google, claiming the search engine had violated his copyright over the website. He alleged that the short excerpt or "snippet" appearing just below the main link to his website in Google's search results page was a copyright violation, as it was a non-authorised copy of part of the website's content. Moreover, he contended that Google's acts of reproducing and making available a *cached* copy of the website by means of a "Cached" link constituted a copyright infringement as well. The claimant requested an injunction so that Google stop performing these activities, and asked for a small monetary compensation for the allegedly suffered harm.

The court of first instance rejected the plaintiff's claim.[89] It held that the type of use Google was carrying out was protected under a joint interpretation of Article 31 of the Spanish Copyright Act (TRLPI),[90] which transposes the exception for temporary reproductions laid down in Article 5.1 of the InfoSoc Directive, and of the caching and linking safe harbours set forth in the Law 34/2002 of 11 July, on Information Society Services and Electronic Commerce—the Spanish transposition of the E-Commerce Directive.

The judgment was appealed by the plaintiff. The Court of Appeals confirmed that Google was not liable, but on different grounds.[91] On appeal, the plaintiff identified three types of uses of his work—the Megakini website—in which Google engaged. The first one related to the initial—and internal—copies that Google's robots make, for indexation purposes, of every web page they find. The plaintiff conceded that those copies are necessary for the search engine to perform the searches, and thus he did not question them. Actually, the plaintiff admitted that they fall under the exception of technical copies set forth in Article 31.1 TRLPI (Article 5.1 of the InfoSoc Directive), and thus they were not infringing. This was also accepted by the defendant, and therefore those copies were not an issue between the parties. The Court pointed out that indeed they seem to fall under the said exception. However, it did not elaborate much on this, concluding that "at least the parties have so agreed".[92] The second type of Google's use the plaintiff identified was that of showing a snippet from the website just below the main link in the search results page. The plaintiff-appellant insisted this was a copyright violation, but the Court of Appeals considered it to be *de minimis*.

The third type of use was that involved in the provision of the "cached" link. The plaintiff contended that this was a reproduction that was neither necessary to carry out the search function nor covered by any exception. As the court rightly pointed out, the discussion was actually about the legality of *making available* the

---

[89] Judgment of the Commercial Court No 5 of Barcelona, 30 March 2007.

[90] Royal Legislative Decree 1/1996, of 12 April, which enacts the *Texto Refundido de la Ley de Propiedad Intelectual* (TRLPI).

[91] Judgment of the *Audiencia Provincial* (Court of Appeals) of Barcelona, Section 15th, 17 September 2008.

[92] Idem, Legal Ground 2.

cached copy—a copy already made by Google's robots when crawling the web and stored in Google's servers.

The Court of Appeals held that the "cached" link feature is not protected by the safe harbours—a question we will consider below. It also held that the making available of cached copies is not covered by the exception of Article 5.1 of the InfoSoc Directive as it is not necessary to carry out the search function. Moreover, although the ruling did not point it out, this exception, even if deemed to be applicable to the making of the cached copies, would never cover the making available of those copies, as the exception concerns only the reproduction right.[93]

After excluding the applicability of all those protections, the Court of Appeals concluded nonetheless that, in that particular case, the making available of cached copies was not a copyright infringement. Essentially, the court held that Article 40 *bis* of the Spanish Copyright Act—which introduces the three step test into the text of the Act—may be not only an interpretation criterion to construe the scope of the exceptions set forth in the Copyright Act, but also a way through which courts may ask themselves about the limits of the concerned rights, beyond the literalness of the exceptions. The court asserted that something similar to the Anglo-Saxon doctrine of fair use should guide the court's interpretation of the scope of intellectual property rights. It held that, ultimately, courts should apply to the context of intellectual property rights a limit similar to that of *ius usus innocui* in the context of movable and real estate property—the right of using someone else's property in a way that does not harm its owner, whose rationale is to prevent an overreaching protection of the owner's right. While not explicitly mentioning the US Copyright Act, the court even briefly brought into consideration the four fair use factors of its Section 107. It concluded that, in the present case, Google's acts did not harm the plaintiff's rights, and were even implicitly accepted by the plaintiff as he published his website without restricting the access to it in any way. Therefore, defendant Google was held not liable of copyright infringement.

To sum up, the rulings considered thus far, with some exceptions, such as the Belgian "*Copiepresse*" case, tend to find that Google's activity—both as regards Google Images and Google Cache—is not a direct copyright infringement. Rather, it is justified under different legal theories such as fair use or some types of implied licence or consent. However, at least in some jurisdictions, the question may remain as to whether Google's use, while not constituting a direct infringement, may give rise to secondary liability.

6.3.3 Secondary Liability

Liability for copyright infringement is primarily imposed on the party that directly carries out an infringement of the exclusive rights which the law vests on the copyright owner. However, several legal theories extend liability to those that

---

[93] On the applicability of Article 5.1 of the InfoSoc Directive to Google's cache see Klein 2008.

contribute to, encourage, induce, or benefit from, the infringements committed by third parties. This "secondary" copyright liability depends on legal doctrines and approaches which differ from one jurisdiction to another.[94]

Case law dealing with secondary or derivative liability is particularly relevant in the US. With regard to Google Images and Google Cache, the issue of secondary liability relates mainly to the technique of in-line linking.[95] As explained above, under the 'server' test adopted by the US courts, Google is only deemed to display the images that are actually hosted in Google's servers. On the contrary, images hosted somewhere else that appear on the user's computer screen thanks to in-line linking are not deemed to be displayed by Google. As a consequence, Google's direct infringement is not at issue when it comes to in-line linked images, whether in the context of Google Images or in the context of cached web pages. Nonetheless, in-line linking to infringing images may raise the issue of secondary liability, that is, whether Google might be held liable under the common law doctrines of contributory or vicarious liability.[96]

The Ninth Circuit addressed this issue in "Perfect 10", when analysing the plaintiff's claim that Google should be held secondarily liable for in-line linking to the full-sized images located in infringing websites. The district court had ruled that Google was not likely to be secondarily liable under the doctrines of contributory or vicarious liability on account of those in-line links.

The Ninth Circuit agreed with the district court regarding vicarious liability. This form of liability requires that the defendant profits from third-party direct infringement and has the right and ability to control the infringing activity.[97] In this case, the direct infringement was the unauthorised reproduction, display and distribution of the copyrighted images by third-party websites. The Court of Appeals agreed with the district court that Google lacks the right to stop or limit the direct infringement of third-party websites. Although Google has contracts with some of those websites, which are partners of the AdSense advertising program, these contracts do not confer on Google the right to stop their direct infringement. Google lacks as well the practical ability to prevent that direct infringement.

---

[94] For an overview of theories of secondary copyright liability worldwide, See Dixon 2009.

[95] See Strowel and Hanley 2009.

[96] These forms of liability are not expressly imposed by the US Copyright Act. Rather, they have been developed by courts. See "Metro-Goldwyn-Mayer Studios Inc. v. Grokster Ltd.", 545 US 913, 930 (2005) ("[T]hese doctrines of secondary liability emerged from common law principles and are well established in the law").

[97] The traditional formula of vicarious liability states that "[w]hen the right and ability to supervise coalesce with an obvious and direct financial interest in the exploitation of copyrighted materials—even in the absence of actual knowledge that the copyright monopoly is being impaired—the purposes of copyright law may be best effectuated by the imposition of liability upon the beneficiary of that exploitation". "Shapiro, Bernstein & Co. v. HL Green Co"., 316 F.2d 304, 307 (2d Cir. 1963). The US Supreme Court in "Grokster" held that one "infringes vicariously by profiting from direct infringement while declining to exercise a right to stop or limit it." "Grokster", 545 US at 930.

With respect to contributory liability,[98] the Ninth Circuit reversed the district court's ruling. The first element of contributory liability, namely, the direct infringement by a third party, was satisfied, as the direct infringement by third-party websites was undisputed.[99] As to the other elements to find contributory liability, the Ninth Circuit, quoting from the well-known cases *"Napster"* and *"Netcom"*,[100] and taking into account the Supreme Court's opinion in the *"Grokster"* case,[101] crafted a specific test of contributory liability: "a computer system operator can be held contributorily liable if it 'has *actual* knowledge that *specific* infringing material is available using its system,' *"Napster"*, 239 F.3d at 1022, and can 'take simple measures to prevent further damage' to copyrighted works, *"Netcom"*, 907 F.Supp. at 1375, yet continues to provide access to infringing works."[102]

The district court had held that even assuming that Google had actual knowledge of the existence of infringing material, it did not materially contribute to the infringement, as it did not encourage visits to infringing websites. The Ninth Circuit found this analysis to be erroneous, and held that "[t]here is no dispute that Google substantially assists websites to distribute their infringing copies to a worldwide market and assists a worldwide audience of users to access infringing materials."[103]

It further stated that "[a]pplying our test, Google could be held contributorily liable if it had knowledge that infringing Perfect 10 images were available using its search engine, could take simple measures to prevent further damage to Perfect 10's copyrighted works, and failed to take such steps."[104] The Ninth Circuit found that the district court had "failed to consider whether Google … knew of infringing activities yet failed to take reasonable and feasible steps to refrain from providing access to

---

[98] According to the traditional formula of *contributory infringement* "[o]ne who, with knowledge of the infringing activity, induces, causes or materially contributes to the infringing conduct of another, may be held liable as a 'contributory infringer'" (*"Gershwin Publishing Corp. v. Columbia Artists Management, Inc"*., 443 F.2d 1159, 1162 (2d Cir. 1971)). In *"Grokster"*, the Supreme Court developed a new form of contributory liability in the field of copyright—that of inducement—taken from patent law. It held that "one who distributes a device with the object of promoting its use to infringe copyright, as shown by clear expression or other affirmative steps taken to foster infringement, is liable for the resulting acts of infringement by third parties." *"Metro-Goldwyn-Mayer Studios Inc. v. Grokster Ltd"*., 545 U.S. 913, 936–37 (2005).

[99] The plaintiff claimed other instances of alleged direct infringement by third parties. It alleged that individual users of Google Images stored full-sized images on their computers. However, the plaintiff failed to provide evidence supporting this claim. On the other hand, it claimed that individual users automatically made local cache copies of the full-sized images on their computers. This automated function, however, was deemed to be a fair use by both the district court and the Ninth Circuit (*"Perfect 10 v. Amazon* 508" F.3d at 1169).

[100] *"A & M Records, Inc. v. Napster, Inc."*, 239 F.3d 1004 (9th Cir.2001); *"Religious Tech. Ctr. v. Netcom On-Line Commc'n Servs"*., Inc., 907 F.Supp. 1361, (N.D.Cal.1995).

[101] *"Metro-Goldwyn-Mayer Studios Inc. v. Grokster Ltd."*, 545 US 913 (2005).

[102] *"Perfect 10 v. Amazon"* 508 F.3d at 1172. (Emphasis in the original).

[103] Idem.

[104] Idem.

infringing images."[105] In addition, there were factual disputes over the notices sent by Perfect 10 and Google's responses to those notices, as well as questions of fact as to whether there were reasonable and feasible means for Google to avoid providing access to those images. As a result, the court remanded the claim to the district court for further consideration on Google's contributory liability for in-line linking to full-sized images under the new test.[106]

Interestingly, the Ninth Circuit ordered the district court to consider as well whether Google could benefit from the DMCA safe harbours—a question that the district court had not analysed precisely because it found that Google was not likely to be secondarily liable in the first place. On remand, as we will see below, the district court granted Google summary judgment that it is protected under the DMCA safe harbours,[107] a ruling currently under appeal.

Though, as noted, different forms of secondary liability do exist in other jurisdictions, the European cases considered in this chapter that dealt with Google Images or Google Cache focused specifically on direct infringement. Arguably, the cases that dealt only with material actually posted by the copyright owner did not need to address indirect liability. And those that considered infringing postings by third-party websites either held Google directly liable—for instance the French case *"H&K v. Google"*, or the Belgian case *"Copiepresse v. Google"*—or held Google not liable resorting to the E-Commerce Directive safe harbours—for instance the French case *SAIF v. Google*, or the German case *"Vorschaubilder"*. In any event, at least in some jurisdictions, for the court to discuss secondary liability the plaintiff should specifically claim this type of liability, as it may constitute a different cause of action, based for instance on the general rules of tort liability rather than in copyright law.

6.3.4 Safe Harbours as a Defence from Both Direct and Secondary Liability

6.3.4.1 The Digital Millennium Copyright Act

In 1998, the US Congress passed the Digital Millennium Copyright Act (DMCA). This statute included a number of provisions seeking to limit the potential liability of internet intermediaries for online copyright infringements. Title II of the DMCA amended the US Copyright Act by adding a new section 512 titled "Limitations on

---

[105] Idem at 1177.

[106] Though the court only remanded the question of Google's contributory liability with regard to the in-line links to full-sized images, the court's analysis is arguably applicable to the thumbnails as well, as they are also links to the infringing websites.

[107] See *"Perfect 10, Inc. v. Google, Inc."*, No. CV 04-9484 AHM (SHx) (C.D. Cal. July 26, 2010), available at http://docs.justia.com/cases/federal/district-courts/california/cacdce/2:2004cv09484/167815/937/ (last accessed 13 March 2011).

liability relating to material online".[108] This section does not modify the general principles of liability; instead it creates a series of "safe harbours" for certain common activities carried out by service providers.[109] These activities are described in subsections (a) "Transitory Digital Network Communications"; (b) "System Caching"; (c) "Information Residing on Systems or Networks at Direction of Users"; and (d) "Information Location Tools".[110] Qualifying service providers for each of these safe harbours are shielded from liability for all monetary relief for direct, vicarious and contributory infringement,[111] by reason of carrying out the activity considered in each safe harbour. The safe harbours also limit injunctive relief against qualifying service providers, but only to the extent determined by section (j).[112]

In order to qualify for any of the safe harbours, a service provider must meet some general conditions for eligibility. These threshold conditions include having "adopted and reasonably implemented... a policy that provides for the termination in appropriate circumstances of subscribers and account holders of the service provider's system or network who are repeat infringers."[113] Apart from meeting the threshold criteria for eligibility, for a service provider to benefit from a particular safe harbour, the activity it carries out must meet the description provided by the pertinent safe harbour, and must comply with the specific conditions it establishes.

As noted, in the *"Perfect 10"* case, the Ninth Circuit remanded to the district court the question of whether Google could benefit from the DMCA safe harbours. Google claimed to deserve protection under the information location tools safe harbour, for its Web and Image Search services, and under the "system caching" safe harbour for its caching feature.[114]

---

[108] 17 U.S.C. § 512.

[109] See *Senate Report No. 105–190* at 19 (1998).

[110] See 17 U.S.C. § 512(a)–(d).

[111] See *House of Representatives Report No. 105–796*, at 73 (1998) (Conference Report) ("The limitations in subsections (a) through (d) protect qualifying service providers from liability for all monetary relief for direct, vicarious and contributory infringement."). The Ninth Circuit confirms this scope: "We have held that the limitations on liability contained in 17 U.S.C. § 512 protect secondary infringers as well as direct infringers. *"Napster"*, 239 F.3d at 1025". *"Perfect 10, Inc. v. Amazon.com, Inc"*. 487 F.3d 701, 732 (9th Cir. 2007) (citing *"A&M Records, Inc. v. Napster, Inc."*, 239 F.3d 1004, 1025 (9th Cir. 2001)).

[112] 17 U.S.C. § 512(j). See *House of Representatives Report No. 105–796*, at 73 (1998) (Conference Report).

[113] 17 U.S.C. § 512(i)(1)(A). This condition, however, does not apply to Google's Web Search, Image Search and the caching feature, as these services don't have account holders or subscribers. See *"Perfect 10, Inc. v. Google, Inc."*, No. CV 04-9484 AHM (SHx) (C.D. Cal. July 26, 2010) at 7.

[114] In addition, Google claimed to be protected under the hosting safe harbour for its Blogger service, regarding users' blogs stored by Google that may contain infringing images. The court agreed and granted summary judgment that Google is entitled to this safe harbour for its Blogger service. However, I will not address this issue here, as it does not relate directly to Google Images or Google Cache.

The safe harbour for information location tools exempts from monetary relief a service provider "for infringement of copyright by reason of the provider referring or linking users to an online location containing infringing material or infringing activity, by using information location tools, including a directory, index, reference, pointer, or hypertext link".[115] In order to benefit from this limitation it is required that the service provider (i) does not have actual knowledge that the material or activity is infringing; (ii) in the absence of such actual knowledge is not aware of facts or circumstances from which infringing activity is apparent or (iii) upon obtaining such knowledge or awareness, acts expeditiously to remove, or disable access to, the material. It is further required that the service provider "does not receive a financial benefit directly attributable to the infringing activity, in a case in which the service provider has the right and ability to control such activity." Finally, upon notification of claimed infringement the service provider must respond expeditiously to remove, or disable access to, the material that is claimed to be infringing or to be the subject of infringing activity; i.e., the link to the infringing content.

The parties debated whether Perfect 10's notices of infringement met the statutory requirements as to be relevant to confer actual knowledge on Google. The court found that most of them were defective, as they did not adequately identify the infringing object. Except for a few instances of adequate notices to which Google did not react expeditiously, the court granted summary judgment that Google was indeed entitled to the information location tools safe harbour set forth in § 512(d).[116]

Google had moved as well for summary judgment that, regarding its caching feature, it was entitled to the caching safe harbour of § 512 (b). However, the court held it did not need to assess this point, as in this case, the operation of Google cache was also covered by the linking safe harbour. This was so because the claims in this case related only to copyright infringement of the plaintiff's images, and, as it has been repeatedly noted above, those images were not hosted in Google's cache. Rather, the cached copies stored by Google only contained in-line links to the infringing images. Hence, Google's activity in this respect fell as well under the linking safe harbour.

In contrast, in the "*Field*" case, the claim did not relate to in-line linked images, but to the *text* of the cached web pages, which clearly fell outside of the linking safe harbour. In "*Field*", besides asserting other defences already mentioned, Google was granted summary judgment that it was entitled to the caching safe harbour of § 512 (b). This was somewhat surprising, as a careful analysis of the caching safe harbour shows that apart from using the word "cache", it has nothing to do with the operation carried out by Google. The function that is described under § 512(b) is that known as 'proxy caching'. This is an activity that some

---

[115] See 17 U.S.C. § 512(d).

[116] "*Perfect 10, Inc. v. Google, Inc*"., No. CV 04-9484 AHM (SHx) (C.D. Cal. July 26, 2010). This order of 26 July 2010 granting summary judgement was subsequently appealed by Perfect 10 before the Ninth Circuit.

access providers perform by means of a *proxy server*, consisting of keeping a copy of a web page that a first user has requested, so that when a subsequent user requests the same page the provider can show to this user the cached copy as a substitute for the original. This way, the ISP avoids having to fetch again the information from the origin source, and thus it saves time and bandwidth. This function is different from that performed by Google's cache. Google is not a transmission service provider that serves web pages requested from users. It does not create a cached copy of a web page while responding a request from a user; rather it copies all the pages in the first place on its own initiative. By means of "cached" links Google makes those copies available to users much in the way of an archive—acknowledging that the cached copy may not reflect the current state of the original web page, as this may have changed since that snapshot was taken by Google's robot. Almost none of the specific requirements to which the safe harbour is conditioned are met in the case of the Google Cache—simply because it consists of a different service.[117]

6.3.4.2 The Electronic Commerce Directive

As noted, the European Union legislated as well limiting the liability of Internet Service Providers through a series of safe harbours laid down in the E-Commerce Directive.[118] Sometimes, these limitations of liability have been claimed by Google in cases dealing with Google Images or Google Cache, with different outcomes.

In *"Copiepresse v. Google"*, a case presented above, the court held that storing the copyrighted works and making them available through "cached" links constituted a copyright infringement not covered by any exception or limitation.[119] The court rejected the argument that this "caching" activity could benefit from the "caching" safe harbour set forth in Article 13 of the European Directive on Electronic Commerce. While this safe harbour closely mirrors that of § 512(b) of the DMCA, the language of the European Directive when it comes to the definition of "caching" makes it even more straightforward that a search engine's cache falls outside its scope. The same outcome was reached on appeal.[120]

Similarly, in the Spanish case *"Megakini v. Google"*, the Court of Appeals rejected that Google's Cache falls under the caching safe harbour laid down in the Directive and transposed into national law by means of the Law 34/2002 of 11 July, on Information Society Services and Electronic Commerce (LSSICE).[121]

---

[117] For a detailed justification of this thesis see Peguera 2009.

[118] Articles 12 through 14 of the E-Commerce Directive.

[119] *"Copiepresse v. Google"* (*Tribunal de Première Instance de Bruxelles*, Feb. 13, 2007, No. 06/10.928/C).

[120] *Cour d'Appel de Bruxelles 9ème chambre*, judgment of 5 May, 2011, number 52–54.

[121] *Ley 34/2002, de 11 de Julio, de ser-vicios de la sociedad de la información y de comercio electrónico* (BOE 166, 12 July 2002, p 25388).

Interestingly, the Court of Appeals distinguished proxy caching from Google's Cache, and rightly concluded that Google Cache does not fall under the caching safe harbour of Article 15 LSSICE—against what had been held by the court of first instance. In addition—again in contrast with the lower court—it held that the linking safe harbour of Article 17 LSSICE did not apply either, as it relates to the searching function and not to the making available of the cached copies stored in Google's servers.

Regarding Google Images, the Paris Court of Appeals recently held in "*SAIF v. Google*" that Google was a neutral intermediary protected by the safe harbours of the E-Commerce Directive.[122] Unlike the DMCA, the E-Commerce Directive does not establish a specific safe harbour for information location tools to deal with search engines' liability. And while some Member States chose to incorporate such a safe harbour in their national laws, this was not the case of France, whose Act No. 2004-575 of 21 June 2004 on confidence in the digital economy, hereinafter LCEN,[123] only transposed the liability limitations established in the Directive.

In this case, however, the court noted that the LCEN was actually meant to govern the different Internet operators, and thus its rules should be taken into consideration to analyse Google's allegedly infringing activities. Google claimed that its service, consisting of indexing the contents uploaded by third-parties to the Internet, is of a merely technical, automated and passive nature, and that it qualifies as an intermediary hosting provider according the LCEN.

The court pointed out that the images are captured automatically by Google's robots when crawling the Internet, and that the websites' owners are the ones who have the ability to exclude the indexation of their images using the robots.txt standard, or utilising meta-tags. Thus, Google's indexation relates only to those images that a website owner chose not to prevent from being indexed. It further noted that the mere fact that it was Google who designed the algorithm used by its crawlers is not enough to exclude the neutral nature of the indexation system—in the absence of any evidence to the contrary. On the other hand, displaying the thumbnails on the results page would simply be part of the normal functionality of an image's search engine, as merely textual results would be ineffective for a user who is searching images. Thus, it cannot be deemed as something that exceeds the normal technical function provided by this type of search engine. In other words, according to the court, showing the thumbnails does not convert Google into a content provider, which is what the plaintiff was claiming.

The court considered as well the fact that the thumbnails stored by Google may remain in their servers even after the original image has been removed from its original location. Typically, the thumbnail will remain in Google's servers for a short period of time, until the crawler revisits the site concerned. The court

---

[122] *Cour d'Appel de Paris, Pôle 5—Chambre 1*, Judgment of 26 January 2011. Available at http://www.juriscom.net/documents/caparis20110126.pdf (last accessed 26 February 2011).

[123] *Loi du 21 juin 2004 pour la confiance dans l'économie numérique* (LCEN).

stressed that this storage is temporary, and seeks to enhance the performance of the search function. It even stated—somewhat recalling the wording of Article 5(1) of the InfoSoc Directive—that this temporary reproduction has a transient character, and constitutes an integral and essential part of an image search engine, and that, as such, "it must be tolerated" and cannot give rise to liability for the search engine provider.

As to the in-line liking to the actual full-sized images, the court held that this is just a means that allows users to access an image which has been made available to the public by the owner of the website where it is located. By providing such a means the provider remains neutral, as this does not exceed the limits of an intermediary's role.

The court pondered as well whether Google could be held liable on account of the eventual abusive use of the images that users could engage in—which would be a form of secondary liability. It held that this would not be the case, as Google clearly warns users that the images "may be subject to copyright." Besides, the court held the mere fact that Google is aware that automatic indexation may reach copyrighted images does not suffice to hold it liable, inasmuch Google accepts to de-index the images upon receiving a notification. The notification should contain information enough as to allow the identification and localisation of the image, and to give Google actual knowledge of the illicit character of the concerned images. In the case before the court, it appears that SAIF did not communicate the URL addresses of the images it wanted removed, or those of the infringing sites.

Summing up, the court appears to find that Google is no more than a neutral intermediary and therefore its actions do not suffice to give rise to copyright liability. The court certainly relies on the passive, automated nature of Google's services. The problem, however, is that the safe harbours contemplate very specific activities and arguably, Google's acts go beyond the case provided for by the hosting safe harbour.

In Germany, the *"Vorschaubilder"* case contains as well, albeit in *dicta*, a ruling that Google Images would fall under the hosting safe harbour.[124] Thus, had the thumbnail been taken from infringing websites, rather than from the copyright owner site, Google could not rely on the copyright owner's consent but still would be free from liability under the safe harbour. Like in *"SAIF v. Google"*, this arguably expands the safe harbour beyond its limits. The hosting safe harbour set forth in Article 14 of the E-Commerce Directive applies to the hosting of contents provided by the recipient of the service, which does not seem to be the case when it comes to a search engine that proactively crawls the web. The BGH explicitly relied on the judgment handed down by the European Union Court of Justice on the *"Google France"* case,[125] which nonetheless was considering a

---

[124] BGH 29 April 2010, I ZR 69/08, para 39.
[125] ECJ Judgment of 23 March 2010, C-236/08 to C-238/08, *"Google France and Google Inc. et al. v Louis Vuitton Malletier et al."*.

different set of facts, as it did not deal with thumbnails captured by Google but with the text of ads created by the recipients of the Adwords service.

References

Allgrove B (2007) The search engine's dilemma: implied license or crawl and cache? J Intellect Prop Law Pract 2:437–438

Clark B (2010) Google image search does not infringe copyright, says Bundesgerichtshof. J Intellect Prop Law Pract 5(8):553–555

Dixon A (2009) Liability of users and third parties for copyright infringement on the internet. In: Strowel A (ed) Peer-to-Peer file sharing and secondary liability in copyright law. Edward Elgar Pub, Cheltenham, pp 12–42

Honkasalo P (2010) Treatment of hypertext linking under copyright law. In: Sylvia M, Kierkegaard S (eds) Private law: rights, duties and conflicts. IAITL, Copenhagen, pp 436–450

Klein S (2008) Search engines and copyright: an analysis of the Belgian Copiepresse decision in consideration of British and German copyright law. IIC 39(4):451–483

Peguera M (2009) When the cached link is the weakest link: search engine caches under the digital millennium copyright act. J Copyr Soc USA 56:589–645

Strowel A (2011) Quand Google défie le droit. Plaidoyer pour un Internet transparent et de qualité, De Boeck & Larcier, Bruxelles

Strowel A, Hanley V (2009) Secondary liability for copyright infringement with regard to hyperlinks. In: Strowel A (ed) Peer-to-Peer file sharing and secondary liability in copyright law. Edward Elgar Pub, Cheltenham, pp 71–109

Triaille JP (2008) La question des copies "cache" et la responsabilité des intermédiaires. *Copiepresse c. Google, Field v. Google.* In: Strowel A, Triaille JP (eds) Google et les noveaux services en ligne, Impact sur l'économie du contenu et questions de propriété intellectuelle. Larcier, Bruxelles, pp 251–267

Zimbehl P (2010) Google images, BGH Entscheidungung vom 29.04.2010, I ZR 69/08 (Vorschaubilder), english introduction. J Intellect Prop Inform Technol E-Commerce Law 1:190–199, available at http://www.jipitec.eu/issues/jipitec-1-3-2010/2798. Accessed 31 Aug 2011

Chapter 7
The *"Viacom v YouTube"* Litigation and Section 512(c) DMCA: When the Safe Harbour Becomes a Permanent Mooring

Annsley Merelle Ward

Contents

A. M. Ward (✉)
Collyer Bristow LLP/IPKat, London, UK
e-mail: annsley.ward@collyerbristow.com

A. Lopez-Tarruella (ed.), *Google and the Law*,
Information Technology and Law Series 22, DOI: 10.1007/978-90-6704-846-0_7,
© T.M.C. ASSER PRESS, The Hague, The Netherlands, and the author(s) 2012

7.1 Introduction

The liability of online service providers in the era of user-generated content remains an ever central theme in the legal challenges faced by them and their legal adversaries. Prior to the Internet and social-media explosion during the 2000s, the US Supreme Court in 1997 heralded the Internet in *"ACLU v Reno"* as the "the most participatory form of mass speech yet developed".[1] With the later advent of social-media platforms such as YouTube, Twitter, Facebook, eBay, and the millions of discussion boards premised around user-generated and user-uploaded content, the "most participatory form of mass speech" has begun to be confronted with legal battles. The increased availability and ability for users to upload their own original content at a click-of-a-button onto service providers' platforms also increased the ability of users to upload unauthorised third-party copyrighted content. With millions of users uploading unauthorised copyright works onto the Internet at such a rapid speed, copyright owners' attention turned not to the vast number of unidentified primary infringers, but to the service providers who hosted, stored, and maintained the sites where the content resided. However, a year after *"ACLU"* and with the implementation of two 1996 WIPO treaties, the US passed the Digital Millennium and Copyright Act (DMCA) which created a series of "safe harbours" under Section 512 which enabled service providers to escape liability provided they complied with some minimum criteria. These safe harbours, although a blessing for service providers, have been legally problematic for copyright owners who have struggled against service providers in their fight in enforcing their copyright online. The 2010 case of *"Viacom v YouTube"*,[2] which at the time of writing is subject to appeal in the Court of Appeals for the Second Circuit, has illustrated the strength of these safe harbours and the up-hill climb that rights holders may face when enforcing their copyright against service providers in the user-generated digital environment.

7.2 A Brief History of YouTube

The staggering growth and popularity enjoyed by YouTube in a very limited space of time has contributed to making the up-hill legal battle faced by rights holders even more difficult. Viacom is, after all, not battling just any service provider; they

---

[1] *"ACLU v Reno"* 521 US 844 (1997).
[2] 2010 WL 2532404 at *11 (S.D.N.Y., 2010).

are battling a company that in less than a year from the domain name's (www.youtube.com) activation on 5 February 2005 would rank fifth as the most viewed website, after MySpace. Today, the video-sharing site receives around 100 million unique visitors per month, making it the third most accessed site in the world and the fourth in the United States.[3]

YouTube enables users to upload videos onto the website for other users to view. When users upload their content they can assign keywords to the video to enable it be found more easily in search results. Other users can post comments on the video, share the video's URL links with others and embed the content into other on-line publications. YouTube's business model, an advertisement-based model, earns the company a reported $15 million per month. These advertisements appear either on or alongside videos. With the most popular video—Lady Gaga's "Bad Romance"—receiving 185.39 million views in 2010, the ability for advertisers to reach a very large audience of potential consumers in one very discrete channel has made YouTube incredibly attractive to advertisers. In 2009, the number of advertisers on YouTube increased by ten times than that of the previous year. YouTube has also continued to increase the number of their official partners who have dedicated user accounts on YouTube, including EMI Music, NBC, and Universal Music Group.

The brain child of former PayPal employees Chad Hurley, Steve Chen, and Jawed Karim, the YouTube story begins like most technological success stories— in a makeshift office in a garage in the US. YouTube shares this trait with other technology giants such as Microsoft, Google, and HP, but unlike its formidable forefathers, the YouTube origin story is even more astonishing given the speed of its formation and of its astronomical growth. Only a few months after the registration of the now infamous domain name, YouTube's official public debut occurred in November 2005. That same month a venture capitalist firm, Sequoia Capital, invested an initial $3.5 million into the business and 5 months later injected a further $8 million with the help of Artis Capital Management. In the summer of 2006, less than a year after their public debut, YouTube ranked as the fifth most popular website, outpacing the then current forerunner—MySpace— and, again, less than a year after the site was launched, it was announced that Google was to purchase YouTube for $1.65 billion in stock.

Not only is the speed of YouTube's growth staggering, the sheer scale of the user-generated content being uploaded onto YouTube is equally bewildering. It is reported that every second 24 hour of video content is uploaded onto YouTube by its users.[4] However, the copyright in this content does not always vest with the user, nor does YouTubes users necessarily have permission from the copyright owner to upload the material. With such a high rate of content being loaded onto

---

[3] http://www.alexa.com/siteinfo/youtube.com (last accessed on 1 September 2011).

[4] O'Malley G (2006) "YouTube is the fastest growing website", Advertising Age, 21 July 2006 available at http://adage.com/article/digital/youtube-fastest-growing-website/110632/ and http://www.blogherald.com/2010/11/02/the-youtube-story/ (last accessed on 1 September 2011).

YouTube, it is not surprising that rights holders have been extremely concerned that YouTube continues to host infringing content and at an ever increasing rate. This concern has in turn resulted in rights holders taking legal action against the site in attempt to combat an infringement that knows no geographical, time, or financial limits. However, the DMCA's safe harbours, which came into effect 7 years before YouTube itself came into existence, has made this seemingly impossible according to rights holders.

7.3 The Digital Millennium Copyright Act

7.3.1 Legislative History to DMCA

On 28 October 1998, President Clinton signed into law the Digital Millennium Copyright Act (DMCA) which implemented two World Intellectual Property Organization (WIPO) treaties—the WIPO Copyright Treaty and the WIPO Performances and Phonograms Treaty—together with further home grown copyright legislation into US law. The DMCA's further provisions were implemented in recognition of the fact that the Internet was entering a realm of widespread use, and with it rights holders and service providers were beginning to face legal challenges with this new medium. The United States Congress recognised[5] that the application of the 'old' copyright laws in this new environment were insufficient in addressing the needs and concerns of these two disparate groups[6] who had two distinct copyright goals. The rights holders required robust laws that would serve to protect their intellectual property in the digital environment where infringement could instantaneously and often, namelessly, be perpetrated. The service providers on the other hand demanded legislation that would create certainty as to the extent of "their legal exposure for infringements that may occur in the course of their activities."[7]

Although these interests are competing, in the US legislature's mind these interests sought to cumulatively advance the goals of a new copyright legislation in the e-commerce environment—that of protecting intellectual property and promoting the growth of and investment in electronic commerce. In formulating this new copyright legislation the US legislature sought to balance these two goals by recognising that weak protection for rights holders may result in them hesitating "to make their works readily available on the Internet", while overly strong protection may hinder growth of the service providers who served as the Internet's "backbone".[8] The Senate Committee on the Judiciary Report stated that

---

[5] H.R.Rep.No.105-551 at 112 (1998)("House Report"); S. Rep. No. 105-190 at 1 (1998)("Senate Report").

[6] Senate Report at 2.

[7] Idem.

[8] Senate Report at 8.

"There have been several cases relevant to service provider liability for copyright infringement. Most have approached the issues from the standpoint of contributory and vicarious liability. Rather than embarking upon a wholesale clarification of these doctrines, the Committee decided to leave current law in its evolving state, and instead, to create a series of "safe harbours," for certain common activities of service providers. A service provider which qualifies for a safe harbour, receives the benefit of limited liability."[9]

The DMCA was also in part inspired by the *"Netcom"*[10] case where the court reasoned that businesses that undertake core Internet functions should not be liable for direct infringement for incidental infringement in the absence of volitional conduct. *Netcom* did however hold that such businesses could be liable under the higher threshold of contributory liability. As set out below, the DMCA's provisions therefore generally echo that of traditional secondary liability standards.[11]

7.3.2 Section 512(c) of the Digital Millennium Copyright Act

Like Europe's E-Commerce Directive, Section 512 DMCA or as it is most commonly referred to—the "safe harbour" provisions—acts by limiting a service provider's direct, vicarious, and contributory infringement liability in four general categories of activity—that of transmitting, caching, storing, and linking to infringing copyrighted content.

At issue in the *"Viacom v YouTube"* case is the interpretation of one of these limited liability Sections—that of Section 512(c)(1) which deals with the liability of a service provider who stores material, like user-generated videos, including infringing material, on their site as part of their service. Section 512(c)(1) reads as follows:

"(1)   A service provider shall not be liable for monetary relief, or, except as provided in Subsection (j), for injunctive or other equitable relief, for infringement of copyright by reason of the storage at the direction of a user of material that resides on a system or network controlled or operated by or for the service provider, if the service provider -

(A)   (i)   does not have actual knowledge that the material or an activity using the material on the system or network is infringing;

---

[9]   Idem.

[10]   *"Religious Technology Center v Netcom On-Line Communication Services, Inc.",* 907 F. Supp. 1361 (N.D. Cal. 1995).

[11]   *"Columbia Pictures Industries, Inc. v Fung",* No. CV 06-5578 (C.D. Cal. Dec. 21, 2009), slip op at 36 which states "In many ways, the digital Millennium Copyright Act is simply a restatement of the legal standards establishing secondary copyright infringement—in many cases, if a defendant is liable for secondary infringement, the defendant is not entitled to Digital Millennium Copyright Act immunity."

(ii) in the absence of such actual knowledge, is not aware of facts or circum-stances from which infringing activity is apparent; or

(iii) upon obtaining such knowledge or awareness, acts expeditiously to remove, or disable access to, the material;

(B) does not receive a financial benefit directly attributable to the infringing activity, in a case in which the service provider has the right and ability to control such activity; and

(C) upon notification of claimed infringement as described in paragraph (3), responds expeditiously to remove, or disable access to, the material that is claimed to be infringing or to be the subject of infringing activity."

Before benefiting from Section 512(c)(1)'s limited liability provisions a service provider must ensure that it has complied with two preliminary criteria. First, a service provider must adopt and reasonably implement a policy for the termination of repeated infringer account holders and/or subscribers, and must inform said account holders/subscribers of such a policy. Second, it must accommodate and not interfere with "standard technical measures".[12] These are measures whereby copyright owners identify and protect their copyright works and which have been developed with the consensus of service providers but without substantial costs to them.[13]

For a service provider to then benefit from the safe harbour protection afforded by Section 512(c)(1) it must satisfy three things: (1) that it does not have actual knowledge of the infringement or is not aware of facts or circumstances which would make the infringement apparent ("the red flag" test); (2) it does not receive financial benefit directly attributable to the infringing activity where the service provider has the right and ability to control the activity; *and* (3) upon notification of the infringement it acts expeditiously in removing the infringing content.

7.3.2.1 The Applicable Knowledge Standard: Actual and "Red Flag" Test Knowledge—Section 512(c)(1)(A)(ii)

The majority of service provider liability cases before the US Courts have focused on the interpretation of the requisite or "applicable knowledge standard" required by Section 512(c)(1)(A). As stated above, to fall foul of the safe harbour provi-sions a service provider must either have actual knowledge of the infringement or, under Section 512(c)(1)(A)(ii), be aware of facts or circumstances from which the infringing activity is apparent. This is what the House Report called the "red flag" test, in that it ensures that per Section 512(c)(1) a service provider is not required to monitor its service or to affirmatively seek out facts that identify infringing activity, but that if and when it becomes aware of facts that signpost or red flag

---

[12] Section 512(i)(1) DMCA.
[13] Section 512(i)(2) DMCA.

infringing activities and it does not act expeditiously in removing that content then it no longer benefits from the safe harbour.

The House and Senate Reports identified that there were two tests to consider when determining whether a service provider is aware of a "red flag": a subjective test and an objective test. The subjective test first asks what facts or circumstances the service provider actually knew of and then the objective tests asks whether these facts or circumstances constitute a "red flag", i.e. "whether infringing activity would have been apparent to a reasonable person operating under the same or similar circumstances."[14]

Under the knowledge standards laid down by Section 512(c)(1)(a)(i) and (ii) and by the Senate and House Reports, a service provider would have "no obligation to seek out copyright infringement" but it would also "not qualify for the safe harbour if it had turned a blind eye to 'red flags' of obvious infringement."[15] Further, there is no requirement under Section 512 that requires that the use of a "notice and take down procedure" by a copyright owner is necessary in order for a copyright owner to protect their copyright against a service provider. Although a service provider is not under a duty to police their site, if and when a service provider acquires actual or constructive knowledge of infringing content the service provider must remove or disable access to the offending material. That is to say that under Section 512 there is no prerequisite that a copyright owner must first notify a service provider in order for that service provider to be under a duty to remove content that it knows (actually or constructively) to be infringing. In fact, if a service provider wishes to benefit from Section 512, it must not to wait for a notification from a copyright owner—it must always first act independently. However, as stated above, that does not mean that the service provider has to "seek out copyright infringement"; it merely means that once it have actual or constructive knowledge of infringement it must remove the content even if it has not received a notice from the rights holder.

The Reports explain that a service provider is not deemed to have the requisite standard of knowledge merely because it has seen a photograph of a well-known celebrity on its site. The service provider cannot be expected "during the course of its brief cataloguing visit, to determine whether the photograph was still protected by copyright or was in the public domain; if the photograph was still protected by copyright, whether the use was licenced; and if the use was not licenced whether it was permitted under the fair use doctrine". Similarly, this reasoning can be extended, as was done in the *Viacom* case, to infer that Congress also did not intend service providers to be expected to satisfy the requirements of knowledge simply because it may have seen one or more well-known music or TV clips uploaded on their site. In short, the US legislature recognised that the number of permutations and variables that a service provider would be faced with when assessing whether or not particular uploaded content is or is not permitted under

---

[14]   Senate Report at 44–45; House Report at 53–54.

[15]   Senate Report at 48–49; House Report at 57–58.

the Copyright Act would be too onerous on a service provider. However, obvious content that identifies itself as infringing (i.e., with "bootleg" or "pirate" in its title or description) would be, Congress suggested, enough to bring a service provider into the sphere of the requisite knowledge demanded by Section 512(c)(1)(A)(ii) and (ii).

7.3.2.2 Financial Benefit: Section 512(c)(1)(B)

A service provider, who satisfies Sections 512(c)(1)(A) may nevertheless fall foul of the safe harbour protection if the service provider financially benefits from the activity. The House and Senate Reports identified that the courts, when determining whether the financial benefit criterion is satisfied, should take a "common-sense, fact-based approach, not a formalistic one." The Reports provided examples of the type of financial benefit that would and would not fall within the ambit of Section 512(c)(1)(B), but unhelpfully did not address whether third-party paid-for advertising on a service provider's site, such as on YouTube, was an example of such financial benefit.

7.3.2.3 Notification and Expeditious Removal: Section 512(c)(1)(C)

Although formal notification of infringing content to a service provider to remove infringing content is not a prerequisite to whether or not a service provider benefits from Section 512(c)(1)(A), knowledge of infringing content can be imputed onto a service provider if the service provider is served with a notice that infringing content is residing on its site. Notification under Section 512(c)(1)(C) requires a copyright owner to provide a service provider "with information reasonably sufficient to permit the service provider to identify and locate the allegedly infringing material", such as a description of the copyright work claimed to be infringed,[16] a description of the infringing copyright[17] and the URL location of the infringing content.[18] Where a notification fails to "substantially" comply with the requirements for notification under Section 512(c)(3)(A), the notification "shall not be considered" as determinative of whether a service provider has actual or constructive knowledge under Section 512(c)(1)(A).[19] Therefore, even where a copyright owner does notify a service provider of the existence of infringing content on the site, it may still be insufficient in imputing actual or constructive ("red flag") knowledge onto the service provider in instances where that notification is defective.

---

[16] Section 512(c)(3)(A)(ii).

[17] Section 512(c)(3)(A)(iii).

[18] Section 512(c)(3)(A)(i).

[19] Section 512(c)(3)(B)(i).

Where a service provider is notified of the presence of infringing content under Section 512(c)(1)(C) or where the service provider itself acquires actual or constructive knowledge of the presence of infringing material on its site under Section 512(c)(1)(A), it must expeditiously take down or disable access to the infringing material. No further guidance as to what "expeditiously" means was given in either the House or Senate Reports save that "the factual circumstances and technical parameters may vary from case to case",[20]

7.4 Viacom's Complaint

7.4.1 Who is Viacom?

Viacom was established in 1971[21] and is one of the biggest content owners in the world, with annual estimated revenue of £13.6 billion. It refers to itself as the "world's preeminent creators, producers and distributors of copyrighted television programing, motion pictures, short form audio-visual works and other entertainment programming."[22] Viacom distributes and publicly performs copyright works or licences such uses to cable and television companies, movie theatres and for DVD formats, Internet distribution channels, and portable devices. The company owns some of the world's most prominent film and TV production companies including MTV, Nickelodeon, Paramount Pictures, and DreamWorks and their copyright portfolio includes works such as SpongeBob's Square Pants, The Daily Show, An Inconvenient Truth, and The War of the Worlds.[23]

7.4.2 Background to Complaint

The formal dispute between Viacom and YouTube arose in March 2007 when Viacom filed copyright infringement proceedings against YouTube in a New York federal court after Viacom discovered its copyrighted episodes, movies, and substantial segments thereof were being uploaded onto YouTube without Viacom's authorisation by YouTube users. Viacom was joined in the action by its affiliates, Comedy Partners, Country Music Television, Inc, Paramount Pictures Corporation, and Black Entertainment Television, LLC whose copyrighted

---

[20] Senate Report at 44–45; House Report at 53–54.

[21] http://www.viacom.com/.

[22] Viacom's Complaint for Declaratory and Injunctive Relief and Damages dated 13 March 2007 ("Viacom's Complaint"), para 20.

[23] Viacom's Complaint, Exhibit A.

content, including television and film works, were also being uploaded onto YouTube without authorisation.

Unlike other media corporations, such as NBC and CBS, Viacom chose to take a more aggressive tact in their dealings with YouTube. NBC had been dealing with the infringing works on YouTube on a case-by-case basis. CBS, with arguably more foresight than its contemporaries, took a more permissive approach in countering the infringing uploads. Instead of taking more forceful action against users and the site, it instead established its own YouTube channel which in 3 months was viewed 90 million times. CBS also entered into a deal with YouTube in which it would receive a proportion of the advertising-revenue generated from the site.

Viacom, however, entered into several months of negotiations with YouTube. As part of these negotiations it was reported that Viacom had repeatedly demanded that over 100,000 infringing YouTube clips be removed.[24] The main contention, however, arose from the fact that Viacom had also asked YouTube to automatically filter out its copyright content, but that Google and YouTube reportedly failed to respond to this request. At the time YouTube was in the beginning stages of using filtering technology in conjunction with Warner Music. Under this arrangement, YouTube agreed to use their own filtering technology to identify potential infringing content owned by Warner Music, and YouTube would then potentially remove the offending clips. It was reported that YouTube stated that Viacom was welcome to enter into similar arrangements with them, however Viacom stated that it was wrong for YouTube to only deploy the filtering technology in circumstances where rights holders, such as Warner Music, were prepared to enter into an agreement with YouTube.[25] By this point a stalemate had been reached between the two parties and the next viable option for relief was to issue proceedings against YouTube for copyright infringement.

Even before Viacom launched their claim, legal academics were quoted in the US media as being sceptical of their chances of success. Tim Wu, a law professor at Columbia University, was quoted as saying that "It's a common misconception that YouTube is a big land mine of liability, but the law in this area favours YouTube much more than people realize."[26] John G Palfrey Jr of Harvard Law School's Berkman Center for Internet and Society also agreed that YouTube would benefit from the DMCA safe harbour, but that he did not "think the law is entirely clear".[27]

---

[24] Hau L (2007) Viacom demands YouTube remove Videos, Forbes, 2 February 2007, available at http://www.forbes.com/2007/02/02/viacom-youtube-google-markets-equity-cx_lh_0202 markets20.html (last accessed on 1 September 2011).

[25] Fabrikant G, Hansell S (2007) Viacom asks YouTube to remove clips, The New York Times, 2 February 2007.

[26] Musgrove M (2007) Viacom decides YouTube is a Foe: Videos reclaimed after talks fail, The Washington Post, 3 February 2007.

[27] Fabrikant G, Hansell S (2007) Viacom tells YouTube: hands off. The New York Times, 3 February 2007.

Following the commencement of the claim in March 2007 and 3 years of legal tos-and-fros, Viacom and YouTube cross motioned for summary judgment in March 2010.

7.5 Viacom's Arguments

Viacom's argument in their initial complaint and motion for summary judgment focused on four arguments in respect of YouTube's claimed liability—*"Grokster"* intent, vicarious liability, direct infringement, and the unavailability of the DMCA's Safe Harbours to YouTube.

7.5.1 *"Grokster" Intent*

Viacom's complaint and motion for summary judgment focused primarily on the knowledge and knowing intent of YouTube in inducing or encouraging the uploading of infringing content onto its website, i.e. *"Grokster"* intent.

The *"Grokster"* case[28] addressed the liability of Grokster, a distributor of free software products that enabled users to share files on a peer-to-peer network. Once a user downloaded Grokster's software, the actual process of searching, selecting and downloading a file did not involve any intervention by or involvement of Grokster. MGM sued Grokster for contributory copyright infringement and argued that because Grokster intentionally distributed software that could be used for the unauthorised distribution of copyright works, Grokster should be held liable. Grokster in turn relied on Section 512's safe harbour provisions.

The Ninth Circuit in *"Grokster"* was tasked with interpreting the extent of the Grokster's liability in light of the earlier Supreme Court case of *Sony*[29] which involved the Betamax video cassette recorder (VCR). Several Hollywood film studios, including Walt Disney, claimed that the Betamax VCR was being manufactured by Sony as an instrument to infringe copyright, and by extension Sony as the manufacturer of the Betamax should be liable for any copyright infringement perpetrated by those who bought VCRs. However, in extending a doctrine of US patent law, the Supreme Court held that a manufacturer of a product which is "capable of substantial non infringing uses" cannot be held liable for infringement even if it has constructive knowledge that users of the equipment might use it to infringe copyright. Likewise, the Ninth Circuit in *"Grokster"* held that secondary liability could only arise if Grokster had reasonable knowledge of specific

---

[28] *"Metro-Goldwyn-Mayer Studios Inc. v Groskter Ltd"*, 380 F.3d 1154 (9th Cir. 2004), rev'd 545 U.S. 913 (2005).

[29] *"Sony Corp of America v Universal City Studios, Inc."*, 464 U.S. 417 (1984).

instances of infringement and failed to prevent such infringement. The Court held that such knowledge was not present.

However, on appeal the Supreme Court in *"Grokster"* unanimously ruled that manufacturers of a product that could be used by its users to commit copyright infringement could be liable of contributory copyright infringement if the manufacturer *intended* it to be used for such infringing purposes. In other words, if the manufacturer induces users to conduct themselves in a way which infringes copyright, then a manufacturer could be held to be liable.[30] Further the Supreme Court held that it was an "error" to require "specific knowledge"[31] of infringement in order for a company to be liable. Instead, it may be enough for the service provider to be held liable where it acts with *an unlawful purpose* or intent irrespective of whether it has knowledge of specific instances of infringement.

In deciding whether a company should be held liable for the inducement or facilitation of copyright infringement by virtue of its business model having been built for an unlawful purpose, the Supreme Court focused on three possible factors: the defendant's communication to its users or otherwise that their service could be used for infringing purposes, the absence of filtering technology and their advertising-revenue model. The presence of communication to Groskter's users that their software was to be used in a manner similar to illegal file-sharing programs, such as Napster, was held by the Supreme Court to evidence inducement. Further, the fact that Grokster did not attempt to develop or institute filtering tools to address the scale of infringing activity underscored the "intentional facilitation of their users' infringement."[32] The final factor was the fact that Grokster achieved revenue from the sale of advertising space.

These three factors were also referred to by Viacom in their arguments to establish YouTube's *"Grokster"* intent. First, Viacom argued that it was not only direct messages or suggestions from a company about how their service or product should or could be used for infringing purposes that was necessary. Under the Ninth Circuit decision in *"Columbia Pictures Indus., Inc. v Fung"*[33] a court can also infer from a defendant's statements and actions the presence of a "patently illegal objective" to which a court can attach liability. This inference, Viacom argued, could be readily found in YouTube's communications and course of conduct which showed that not only did YouTube actively encourage that the growth of the site be sustained "as aggressively as we can through whatever tactics, however evil",[34] but that it had intended to "to bring about infringement" by failing to develop "filtering tools or other mechanisms to diminish the infringing activity" all of which generated "money by selling advertising space".[35] As evidenced by YouTube's internal

[30] Idem at 2780.

[31] *"Grokster"*, 545 U.S. 913 at 934.

[32] *"Sony Corp of America"*, 464 U.S. 417 at 2781.

[33] *"Fung"*, CV 06-5578, slip op. at 23 (quoting Grokster, 545 U.S. at 941.

[34] Statement of Undisputed Facts ("SUF"), para 85.

[35] *Grokster*, 545 U.S. at 939-940.

e-mails, if "the obviously copyright infringing stuff" was removed or blocked site traffic would drop by "maybe 20% of what it is".[36] Viacom argued that not only did YouTube turn a wilful blind eye to the infringement, but it went so far as to welcome the uploading of infringing content by users. As a result YouTube, Viacom argued, continued to host content in furtherance of the unlawful purpose for financial profit.

The second factor was YouTube's refusal until May 2008 to implement filtering tools and other mechanisms to reduce infringing activity which again "under-scor[ed] [their] intentional facilitation of...infringement"[37] and their "deliberate strategy of wilful blindness."[38] The final factor in *"Grokster"*, that of the presence of an advertising-based revenue model, was also present in YouTube's business model. Viacom argued that the description of Grokster's advertising-revenue model by the Supreme Court described YouTube's model: "YouTube also makes "money by selling advertising space, by directing ads to the screens of computers employing their [service]. The more the [service] is used, the more ads are sent out and the greater the advertising revenue becomes. Since the extent of the [service's] use determines the gain to [Defendants], the commercial sense of their enterprise turns on high volume use which the record shows is infringing."[39] If YouTube were to stop the on-going infringement and prevent future infringement Viacom argued that it would see its website traffic and advertising revenue greatly diminished. As a result of these factors, Viacom argued that under *"Grokster"*[40] these internal communications and business practices show "unequivocal indica-tions of an unlawful purpose" and it therefore established that the defendants "are liable for the infringement it intentionally made possible".

Viacom's argument under *"Grokster"* also emphasised that Google shared the requisite knowledge of YouTube. In May 2006, Google held a Google Product Strategy (GPS) meeting attended by top executives including Google CEO Eric Schmidt. At the meeting a final internal memo allegedly recognised that "YouTube is "a 'rogue enabler' of content theft" and its "business model is completely sustained by pirated content." Viacom allege that despite Google's "keen awareness that infringement was the linchpin in YouTube's success" it nevertheless went ahead with the October 2006 acquisition. Furthering Viacom's allegation of Google's knowledge and complicity in the mass scale of YouTube's infringement, Viacom pointed to a due diligence report prepared by Credit Suisse for Google which esti-mated that "54% of the video views in the due diligence sample were of premium copyrighted content that was admittedly unauthorised by the content owner."[41]

---

[36] SUF, para 54-58.

[37] 545 U.S. 913 at 939.

[38] Viacom's Memorandum of Law in Support of Viacom's Motion for Partial Summary Judgment on Liability and Inapplicability of the Digital Millennium Copyright Act Safe Harbour Defense ("Viacom's Memorandum"), p 29.

[39] *"Grokster"*, 545 U.S. 913 at 940.

[40] Idem. at 938.

[41] Viacom's Memorandum, p 16.

7.5.2 Vicarious Liability

Viacom argued that because YouTube derived direct financial benefit from copyright infringement, of which it had the right and ability to control, it was liable for infringement under vicarious liability. Vicarious copyright liability arises where a defendant has "the right and ability to supervise conduct with an obvious and direct financial interest in the exploitation of copyrighted materials—even in the absence of actual knowledge."[42] The common law vicarious liability test is mirrored by Section 512(c)(1)(B) DMCA.

Viacom argued that YouTube derived a direct benefit from the infringing activities occurring on its site because YouTube provided users with a space to upload and access infringing copyright material. These spaces were in turned used by companies to advertise their goods and/or services with a fee payable to YouTube. Thus, as in *"Shapiro"*, the infringement provided YouTube with a source of users, who in turn attracted advertisers who paid YouTube for advertising space.[43] YouTube itself, Viacom argued, admitted that the site's advertising drawing power was due to infringing videos as evidenced by their internal e-mails.[44] In fact, the Credit Suisse report estimated that between 57 and 80% of video views and site traffic on YouTube were of or due to infringing videos.[45] It is because of this "draw" that Viacom argued YouTube becomes vicariously liable.[46]

This "draw" was also present in the *"Napster"*[47] case, even though Napster had not actually received any direct revenue from their infringing activities. The Court in that case held that it was enough that there may be a realisation of potential future revenue as a result of the "increases in user base."[48] This premise was similarly applied in the *"Arista Records, Inc. v Mp3Board, Inc."*[49] and *"Arista Records LLC v Usenet.com"*[50] cases. It was this drawing ability, Viacom argued, which resulted in the site, "for legal reasons" stopping the practice of placing advertisements on pages of suspected infringing videos.[51] Although YouTube took this action in the beginning of 2007, Viacom argued that it did not detract for their liability even after this date. This is because YouTube still received direct financial benefit by "placing ads on the home, search browse and upload pages that are

---

[42] *"Shapiro, Bernstein & Co v H.L. Green Co"*. 316 F.2d 304 at 307 (2d Cir. 1963).

[43] Idem; C.f. *"Buck v Jewell-La Salle Realty Co"*, 283 US 191 at 198 (1931).

[44] Viacom's Memorandum, p. 16.

[45] SUF, paras.170-174;196-200; and 202.

[46] *"Fonovisa Inc. v Cherry Auction, Inc"*, 76 F.3D 259, 263–64 (9th Cir. 1996).

[47] *"A&M Records, inc. v Napster, Inc"*, 239 F.3d 1004, 1023 (9th Circ. 2001).

[48] Idem at 1023.

[49] *"Arista Records, Inc. v Mp3Board, Inc."*, No. 00 CIV 4660 (SHS), 2002 WL 1997918 at *11 (S.D.N.Y. Aug. 29, 2002).

[50] 633 F. Supp. 2d 124 (S.D.N.Y. 2009).

[51] SUF, para 250.

viewed by users drawn by infringement."[52] Established and new users are still attracted by the infringing content irrespective of where the actual advertisement happens to be located on the site, Viacom argued, and new users mean "more money" that YouTube can make through the sale of advertisement space.[53]

In order for YouTube to be vicariously liable, Viacom has to also prove that not only YouTube received a direct financial benefit for the infringement but that it had the right and ability to control the infringing activity on the site. Under *"Napster"*,[54] this requirement is satisfied where a defendant has the absolute discretion to block users or content. Viacom argued that YouTube routinely removed "videos containing adult material, hate speech, nudity, violence and any other content that Defendants, in their sole judgment, deem offensive."[55] Not only did it have the right and general ability to control the material, YouTube also possessed further techniques to control infringing items, such as human review, community flagging, manual, and automated searches through their index and digital fingerprinting for YouTube partners.[56] This "broad power", Viacom argued, was exactly what was envisaged by the *"Napster"* Court when assessing whether a defendant had the right and ability to control the infringing activity. Further, instances such as YouTube refusing to use digital fingerprinting technology for Viacom's copyright until "at least May 2008"[57] was argued by Viacom to be exactly what the *"Shapiro"* and *"Napster"* Courts had envisaged pointing to a finding of vicarious liability.[58]

7.5.3 Direct Copyright Infringement

As arguably one of their weakest arguments, Viacom's argument on YouTube and Google's liability for direct infringement was brief. Although direct copyright infringement is a strict liability tort, the Court of Appeals in the Second Circuit has held that some element of *de minimis* "volitional conduct"[59] on the part of a defendant is also required in addition to the acts of direct infringement.

Viacom argued that YouTube makes an exact copy of a video uploaded by a user and a further copy in a Flash format to make it easier for online viewing.[60]

---

[52] Viacom's Memorandum, p 40.

[53] *"Perfect 10, Inc v Cybernet Ventures, Inc"*, 213 F. Supp 2D 1146, 1181 (C.D. Cal. 2002).

[54] *"A&M Records, Inc. v Napster, Inc".*, 239 F.3D 1004 at 1023 (9th Cir.2001).

[55] Viacom's Memorandum, p 40.

[56] Idem at p 41.

[57] SUF, para 22,295–98.

[58] *"Shapiro"*, 316 F.2d 304 at 308 and *"Napster"*, 239 F.3D 1004 at 1023.

[59] *"Cartoon Network LP v CSC Holdings, Inc".*, 536 F.3D 121 at 130-131 (2d Cir. 2008), cert. denied, 129 S.Ct. 2890 (2009).

[60] SUF, paras 315–316, 318.

Further, Viacom argued that YouTube also performed the copyright works by streaming them on demand, as well as licensing the videos for use on handheld and wireless devices such as on iPhones.[61] Because these operations were being committed by and on YouTube facilities, and not by the users themselves, Viacom argued that YouTube is directly liable for these acts.

Turning to the point of YouTube's "volitional conduct", Viacom argued that although YouTube's acts in copying may be construed to be automated or to occur incidentally[62] when a user elects to upload a video, YouTube's volition was still present. Viacom argued that at least two judges in the Second District recognised that even in incidences of incidental or automated processes the "volitional conduct" standard in the *"Cartoon Network"* case is satisfied where the defendant possesses intentional conduct which transforms them "from passive providers of space in which infringing activities happened to occur to active participants in the process of copyright infringement."[63] Defendants who operate facilities where infringing acts occur and do so with the intent of providing a platform for this infringement, like YouTube satisfy the *de minimis* test of "volition" under direct infringement.

7.5.4 The DMCA Safe Harbour Provisions

Viacom's preceding three arguments repeatedly emphasised the intent of YouTube, as well as their wilful blindness to the ongoing infringing activity on the site. The reason for the emphasis was to cast a shadow onto YouTube's inevitable reliance on the DMCA's safe harbour. Viacom argued that Congress had not intended that the safe harbours be used to shield defendants from "extremely culpable conduct"[64] such as that in *"Grokster"*. Further, Viacom argued that unlike the position advanced by YouTube, the DMCA does not automatically immunize a defendant's liability by virtue of the defendant's removal of specific infringing videos identified by way of takedown notices from copyright owners, nor does the DMCA place the entire burden of monitoring copyright infringement on copyright owners. This Viacom argued was evidenced by the Senate Report which stated that the DMCA aimed to "balance the interests" of copyright owners and service providers[65] in order for them "to cooperate to detect and deal with copyright infringement."[66] Viacom's argument against the availability of the safe

---

[61] SUF, paras 324.

[62] *"Netcom"*, 907 F. Supp. 1361 at 1368–69.

[63] *"Usenet.com"*, 633 F. Supp. 2d at 148 (quoting *"Playboy Enters., Inc. v Russ Hardenburgh, Inc"*., 982 F. Supp. 503 at 513 (N.D. Ohio 1997)).

[64] Viacom's Memorandum, p 48.

[65] House Report at 21.

[66] Idem.

harbour defence to YouTube was set out in three Sections which echoed their earlier arguments—that of YouTube's intent, the direct financial benefit, and the fact that the infringement does not result from the specific Internet functions to which the DMCA applies.

7.5.4.1 Section 512(c)(1)(A): YouTube's Knowledge and Intent Defeat the DMCA Defence

Under the DMCA, an otherwise innocent service provider losses DMCA protection "the moment the service provider" loses its innocence.[67] The DMCA safe harbours were meant to provide a shield for service providers who conducted their business in good faith. Such a shield of innocence is removed when a service provider's conduct transforms to active bad faith. Viacom argued that YouTube lost its innocence as soon as it could be shown that it had an intent to provide a platform for infringing content. Such *Grokster* intent, Viacom argued, defeats any DMCA safe harbour because there is no good faith conduct on the part of YouTube if it knew of and maintained infringing content on its site. Further, Viacom argued that because it could be shown from the evidence (as referred to above) that YouTube had intent to operate a site rampant with infringing content, it therefore followed that YouTube had either "actual knowledge" or were "aware of facts or circumstances from which infringing activity" was apparent under Section 512(c)(1)(A). Given that YouTube knew that around 54–80% of the traffic on YouTube was as a result of the presence of infringing content on the site, Viacom argued it would be implausible that this type of evidence could not constitute a red flag for YouTube.

YouTube's argument (as set out below) was that general knowledge of infringing content being uploaded onto the site does not satisfy the definition of "actual knowledge" or the red-flag test. In their opinion, they need to have specific knowledge that a particular video was infringing. Without this specific knowledge the DMCA safe harbours were still available to it. Viacom argued that the law could not and should not be interpreted to allow a company to escape liability by turning a blind eye to the infringing content upon which its business reportedly depends. Judge Richard Posner in the Seventh Circuit had rejected the "specific knowledge" theory for contributory infringement in *"In re Aimster Copyright Litigation"* and stated that "[w]ilful blindness is knowledge, in copyright law…as it is in law generally."[68]

Viacom argued, that for the court in this case to find favour with YouTube's argument it would have to write out both the established concept of wilful blindness knowledge from copyright law and from the DMCA, as well as read into the DMCA that "specific" knowledge is required—a word that is not in the statute. As discussed

---

[67] *"ALS Scan, Inc. v RemarQ Communities, Inc."*, 239 F.3d 619 at 625 (4th Cir. 2001).

[68] 334 F.3d 643 at 650 (7th Cir. 2003).

above, the statutory language is whether or not a defendant has "actual knowledge" or is "aware of facts and circumstances from which infringing activity is apparent".[69] Viacom focused their attention on the word "activity" which it argued meant that YouTube need only have constructive or red-flag knowledge that there were infringing *activities*[70] occurring on the site, not that any specific *video* itself was infringing.[71] The Senate Report defined "activity" as "intended to mean activity using the material on the system or network" or "wrongful activity that is occurring at the site on the provider's system or network."[72] Therefore, where a defendant becomes aware of a 'red flag' of infringing activity on the site and fails to act, the safe harbour is no longer available to them.[73]

Once YouTube had awareness of infringing activity a "proactive obligation to block access"[74] was triggered in order for them to qualify for statutory immunity. This flew in the face of YouTube's pre-motion letter to the Court which argued that it had no obligation to take action in the face of red flags under *"Perfect 10, Inc. v CCBill, LLC"*[75] and *"UMG Recordings, Inc. v Veoh Networks Inc ("UMG II")"*.[76] Viacom argued that these cases did not involve intentional *"Groskter"* wrongdoing as was the case here. The *"Fung"* decision, of the same Circuit as *"Perfect 10"* and *"UMG II"*, made clear that those cases "do not stand for the proposition that the DMCA shields such intentional conduct from infringement liability."[77] Professor Jane Ginsburg indeed distinguished *"Perfect 10"* and explained that

> "'apparent' does not mean 'in fact illegal.' Nor does it mean "conclusively exists." Such an interpretation would allow the service provider to 'turn a blind eye' to infringements because the provider could claim that the possibility that some files might be fair use means that infringement can never be 'apparent' as to any file. By the same token, Section 512(m)'s dispensation of service providers from 'affirmatively seeking facts indicating infringing activity' should not entitle the service provider to remain militantly ignorant."[78]

In any case, Viacom argued, that when faced with a red flag Section 512(c)(1)(A)(ii) and (iii) makes it clear that a service provider must expeditiously remove material in order to benefit from the safe harbour defence. When it

---

[69] Section 512(c)(1)(A)(i),(ii).

[70] YouTube, as noted later, would focus their attention on the word "the" in arguing that it was knowledge of a specific infringing activity (*"the* infringing activity" as referred to under Section 512(c)(1)(B)) that was the requirement, not just knowledge of general *activities*.

[71] Viacom's Memorandum, p 52.

[72] Senate Report at 44.

[73] *"Cybernet"*, 231 F. Supp. 2d at 1177.

[74] Ginsburg 2008, p 596.

[75] 488 F.3d 1102 (9th Cir. 2007).

[76] 665 F. Supp. 2d 1099 at 1108 (C.D. Cal. 2009).

[77] Viacom's Memorandum, p 53.

[78] Ginsburg 2008, p 598.

does not, the defence is forfeited. This argued Viacom demonstrates that the DMCA does not sanction wilful blindness. To hold otherwise, Viacom argued, would contradict the policy reasoning behind the DMCA—that of balancing the interests of both the rights holders and the service providers—by placing all of the responsibility of policing the site not on YouTube who financially benefit from the infringement, but on the copyright owners who are the "victims".

Viacom argued that YouTube's reading of *"Perfect 10"* and *"UMG II"* could not be reconciled with the DMCA's statutory language or legislative history which incorporated actual and wilful blindness knowledge as prerequisites for the safe harbour defence. YouTube could not just sit "idly" by and wait for copyright owners to serve takedown notices and only at that point remove the content in order to benefit from the safe harbours under Section 512(c)(1)(C). The first hurdle that YouTube had to surpass was whether it has actual or red flag knowledge and if it did, as was the case here, it had a duty to remove the infringing material under Section 512(c)(1)(A) even if it was not first notified by the copyright owner. YouTube did not do this and in fact refused to remove infringing content unless it received a take down notice for a specific video.[79] This violated Section 512(c)(1)(A)'s requirement and therefore Viacom YouTube could not take refuge in the DMCA's safe harbour.

7.5.4.2 Section 512 (c)(1)(B): YouTube's Direct Financial Benefit and Right and Ability to Control Infringement Defeat the DMCA Defence

Viacom's arguments for YouTube's liability under Section 512(c)(1)(B) were identical to the arguments of liability under common law principles of vicarious liability. As noted above, Section 512(c)(1)(B) echoes the test for vicarious liability in that where a defendant receives a "financial benefit directly attributable to the infringing activity" and has "the right and ability to control such activity" it falls outside the safe harbour protection. Viacom argued that the common law principles of vicarious liability must be taken as being settled into statutory language, unless the statute "dictates" otherwise.

Further, case precedent held that the DMCA's statutory language should be interpreted consistently with principles of vicarious liability. The *"Perfect 10"* case held that in respect of the "direct financial benefit" prong of the test, Section 512(c)(1)(B) should be interpreted consistently with the "similarly-worded common law standard for vicarious copyright liability" and therefore the relevant inquiry is "whether the infringing activity constitutes a draw for subscribers."[80] The second prong, the "right and ability to control such activity", was held by the court in *"Io Group Inc, v Veoh Networks, Inc."* as also necessitating consistent

---

[79] SUF, paras. 38, 189, & 220.

[80] 488 F.3d 1102 at 1117.

interpretation with the common law standard. The case of *"Fung"* also granted summary judgment on the basis of applying the vicarious liability "right and ability to control" standard to Section 512(c)(1)(B).[81] A 2007 case involving YouTube, *"Tur v YouTube"*, held that if the evidence showed that YouTube had "the technical capabilities needed to detect and pre-screen allegedly infringing videotapes"[82] then YouTube would have the "right and ability to control" under the DMCA.

Viacom did recognise that *"UMG"* suggested that the DMCA "dictate[s] a departure from the common law standard" because the DMCA presupposes that a service provider can terminate repeat infringers and remove infringing content in response to takedown notices, and it recognises that service providers do not have to actively "monitor" infringing activity on their site under Section 512(m)(1). However, Viacom argued that these reasons do not permit a departure from the vicarious liability standard because the presupposition under Section 512(c)(1)(C) that a service provider has the ability to remove infringing material is only as a result of a *response* to a takedown notice, and not of a greater standard of control by the service provider.

Further, Section 512(m) was not intended to override the common law standard. In the House Report, Congress made clear that the DMCA's "right and ability to control language... codifies the second element of vicarious liability."[83] *"UMG II"* dismissed this Congressional intention because that Court held that the intention related to an earlier version of the DMCA.[84] However, Viacom argued that the earlier version contained the same provisions and language as in the current DMCA—that of the "right and ability to control" language and what later became Section 512(m). Viacom also criticised the *"UMG II"* court's reading of Section 512(m) as being "so sweeping"[85] that it deprived "the right and ability to control" standard of "all meaning". Section 512(m), entitled "Protection of Privacy" was "designed to protect the privacy of Internet users"[86] and it is in this context that the word "monitor" must be interpreted. It cannot be argued, therefore that the public infringement of Viacom's videos on YouTube could fall within the ambit of Section 512(m)'s ambit in protecting the privacy of Internet users. Because it cannot be said that the DMCA dictated a departure from the common law standard of vicarious liability, Viacom argued YouTube would fail Section 512(c)(1)(B).

---

[81] *"Fung"*, No. CV 06-5578 at Slip op. at 39.

[82] No. CV064436, 2007 WL 1893635 (C.D. Cal. June 20, 2007) at *3.

[83] House Report at 26.

[84] *"UMG Recordings, Inc., v Veoh Networks Inc."*, 665 F. Supp. 2d 1099 at 1115-16 (C.D. Cal. 2009).

[85] Viacom's Memorandum, p 59.

[86] House Report at 64.

7.5.4.3   Section 512(a)–(d): The Infringement on YouTube Does Not Result from the Specified Core Internet Functions to Which the DMCA Applies

Viacom's final and brief argument was that YouTube fell outside the DMCA safe harbour because the infringement was not a result of YouTube providing one of the four specified core Internet functions under Section 512(a)—(d). Viacom argued that YouTube is not transmitting material because it does not satisfy the definition of a "service provider". Under Section 512(k)(1)(A) a "service provider" is restricted to those who "play the role of a 'conduit' for the communications of others" such as telecommunications carriers.[87] Under Section 512(b) YouTube's activities do not include that of caching because it does not simply make an "intermediate and temporary copy" in the course of a requested transmission between one user and another.[88] Nor does YouTube's activities fall within Section 512(d)'s ambit of "referring or linking" to infringing material on other websites because the infringing material is actively present on their website.

The main provision of contention was Section 512(c), where a service provider stores infringing content at the "direction of a user". Viacom argued that YouTube was not a storage or web hosting service, but "a media and entertainment business no different from a TV station."[89] The word "storage" was not defined in the DMCA so the rules of statutory interpretation dictate that it takes on its natural and ordinary meaning which is "to record (information) in an electronic device (as a computer from which the data can be obtained as needed."[90] The House Report indicated that storage would also include the provision of website space for a chatroom or other forum.[91] Viacom argue that YouTube is doing more than just acting as a mere host of a forum—it acting as a "consumer media company"[92] which is evidenced by the public performance of the videos—not the storage of videos. Further, any storage present is not solely at the direction of the user because YouTube makes multiple copies of the videos and distributes them on "watch pages designed by Defendants in order to attract advertising revenue pursuant to advertising practices and deals that are determined, negotiation and priced by the Defendants, not their users."[93] Such an active role is also evidenced by YouTube negotiating distribution deals of the content with Apple and Verizon Wireless.[94] Such copying, active placement and licensing of the content, Viacom argued, takes

---

[87] House Report at 51.
[88] Idem. at 52.
[89] Viacom's Complaint, p 62.
[90] *Webster's Third New International Dictionary* (1986), p 2252.
[91] House Report at 53.
[92] SUF, para 15.
[93] Viacom's Memorandum, p 64.
[94] SUF, para 330.

YouTube out of the bounds of being a mere host of the content which takes itself outside the safe harbour.[95]

Viacom did note that the two courts dealing with the Veoh video website—"*Io*" and "*UMG I*"—interpreted "storage" broadly as meaning to cover any automatic action performed by a service provider's computer systems that facilitate access to the user-uploaded content.[96] However, Section 512(c) of the DMCA expressly state that the safe harbours are available for infringement caused "by reasons of" the specific function of storage, not any other function such as facilitating access to user-uploaded content. In any event, Viacom argued, YouTube operates without any user direction at all because it initiates the copy and distribution themselves, and therefore it does not perform one of the function covered by Section 512 (c).

7.6 YouTube's Defence and Motion for Summary Judgment

In response, YouTube's defence and motion for summary judgment, besides relying on the safe harbour defence, appealed to the intent of Congress in drafting the DMCA. In particular, YouTube emphasised the important and meritorious public function undertaken by YouTube in acting as a "backbone" to the Internet. YouTube stated that its service was a "prominent source of political information"[97] which it evidenced by citing the failed 2008 Presidential Republican candidate, Senator John McCain, whose campaign "congratulated YouTube for its "ground-breaking contributions" to the democratic process "by providing a platform for political candidates".[98] It also appealed to its "extensive efforts to help copyright owners" including providing "Copyright Tips", "reminding users that it are prohibited from uploading copyrighted content and terminating accounts of repeat infringers."[99] A quote from the Motion Picture Association of America (MPAA) was also cited in support of its contention that its activities were without fault: "YouTube has been a good corporate citizen and taken off copyrighted material."[100]

---

[95] "*Perfect 10*", 488 F.3D 1102 at 1117.

[96] "*Io*", 586 F. Supp. 2d 1132 at 1147; "*UM Recordings, Inc. v Veoh Networks, Inc*". 620 F. Supp. 2D 1081 at 1086 (C.D. Cal. 2008).

[97] YouTube's Memorandum of Law in Support of defendants' Motion for Summary Judgment ("YouTube's Memorandum"), p 6.

[98] Declaration of Zahavah Levine at paragraph 29 and Exhibit 13.

[99] YouTube's Memorandum, p 19.

[100] Declaration of Zahavah Levine at paragraph 32 and Exhibit 14.

7.6.1 Section 512(c): Threshold Qualifications

Prior to launching into its main argument, YouTube stated that it met the threshold conditions for protection under the safe harbour defence because it was a "service provider"[101] under the Act, was registered as an agent to receive notifications of claimed infringement,[102] had implemented a policy for terminating repeat infringers' accounts and did not interfere with copyright owners "standard technical measures".[103]

7.6.2 Section 512(c): "Storage at the Direction of the User"

YouTube argued that the disputed videos uploaded by YouTube users reside on the site at the direction of the users. Copies of the videos are automatically made by YouTube's systems in response to users' direction which are made for the "efficient storage and viewing of user submitted videos"[104] Although Viacom argued that the ambit of "storage" under Section 512(c) should be limited to only the mere storage of material, cases such as *"Corbis"*[105] and *"Costar Group, Inc. v Loopnet, Inc"*[106] affirmed that storage also includes online services that make user-uploaded material more readily accessible. Further, YouTube stated that unlike what Viacom argued, the two Veoh decisions—*"UMG I"* and *"Io"*—actually explained that "storage" need not be "limited to merely storing material"[107] but could also include other functions that are "directed toward facilitating access to materials stored at the direction of users."[108] YouTube argued that like Veoh, it also automatically created additional copies of user-uploaded videos, converted them into mobile-accessible Flash formats and allowed users to stream these video copies on their computers. Therefore, YouTube argued that the court must interpret their decision similarly with that of *UMG I* and hold that YouTube met the requirements for "storage" under Section 512(c).

---

[101]   Section 512(k)(1)(B).
[102]   Section 512(c).
[103]   Section 512(i).
[104]   YouTube's Memorandum, p 27.
[105]   351 F. Supp 2d 1090 at 1110–11 (W.D. Wash. 2004).
[106]   164 F. Supp. 2d 688 at 701–02 (D. Md. 2001), aff'd 373 F.3D 544 (4th Cir. 2004).
[107]   *Io*, 586 F. Supp. 2D 1132 at 1147.
[108]   *"UMG I"*, 620 F. Supp. 2d 1081 at 1088.

7.6.3 *Section 512(c)(1)(A): Knowledge*

YouTube again rested their argument on the "*UMG II*" case which held that it was not sufficient that a plaintiff could show a service provider's "general awareness of infringement",[109] what it had to have was knowledge of specific infringing activity. YouTube argued that without specific knowledge of an infringing activity that would, in the words of Section 512(c) enable them to remove "*the* material",[110] the presence of general knowledge of infringing material would not be enough for YouTube to act in removing "*the* material". Therefore it would not be enough for YouTube to fall foul of the safe harbour defence.

Turning to the "red-flag test", YouTube argued that there was no evidence that it had actually seen or had knowledge of any "red flags". This was because, most of YouTube's employees had "never even seen the overwhelming majority of the more than 500 million videos that have been posted to the service" and YouTube would not even be aware when a video is uploaded because the process is automated.[111] Without first being aware of these "facts and circumstances" from which alleged infringements are apparent, YouTube could not be held to have had notice of any "red-flags".

Even where it could be argued that YouTube had seen certain of the offending clips, the infringing nature of these clips would have had to have been "obvious"[112] to a reasonable person in order for a "red-flag" to subsist. YouTube argued that anything less than this 'obviousness' would be contradictory to the purpose of the DMCA in ensuring that service providers would not have "to make discriminating judgments about potential copyright infringement."[113] The "*Perfect 10*" case supported this view that a service provider was under no "investigative duties" to make such a determination,[114] as did the "*UMG*" case, which held that the "high bar for finding 'red flag' knowledge is yet another illustration of the principle underlying the DMCA safe harbours, that the burden is on the copyright holder, not the service provider, to identify copyright infringement."[115] Following this line of reasoning, YouTube argued that Viacom would therefore have to prove that YouTube had seen each clip or 'red flag' associated with each clip at issue and that it was able to immediately identify that the clip was an obvious infringement of Viacom's copyright. This would be near impossible, argued YouTube, because at the very minimum it would be uncertain whether any

---

[109] "*UMG II*", 665 F. Supp. 2d 1099 at 1111.

[110] Section 512(c)(1)(A)(iii).

[111] YouTube's Memorandum, p. 34; Levine Declaration at paragraph 29; Schaffer Declaration at paragraph 11; Hurley Declaration at paragraph 18.

[112] Senate Report at 44; House Report at 57.

[113] House Report at 58.

[114] 488 F.3D 1102 at 1114.

[115] "*UMG II*", 665 F. Supp. 2d 1099 at 1111.

clip on YouTube was or was not authorised by Viacom and if not, whether the use would be covered by fair use.[116]

The linchpin of Viacom's argument (as stated above) was that YouTube's internal e-mails and general business and marketing strategy (which seemingly to Viacom showed that YouTube fostered a platform for infringing content) evidenced "*Grokster*"'s intent under contributory copyright infringement which in turn evidenced its liability under Section 512(c)(1)(A). This is because, generally, intent must equate to knowledge. For ten pages in YouTube's Memorandum of Law, YouTube highlights Viacom's own marketing and business strategy on YouTube as evidencing not only culpable conduct on their part but in undermining any argument that YouTube could have been aware of legitimate "red flags". YouTube state that Viacom itself "uploaded video clips from their movies and television shows to YouTube for promotional purposes" which itself complicates whether or not the defendants could reasonably know which uploaded clips were authorised and which were not. YouTube argue that "much of its marketing activity [in placing materials on YouTube] takes place covertly." Such stealth marketing by Viacom, it was argued by YouTube, further blurs the lines between authorised and unauthorised content making it impossible for YouTube to possess any legal standard of knowledge of infringing content on the site. Further arguments were raised regarding Viacom's marketing policies including their "leave up"[117] practices.

The above arguments were a build up to YouTube's main point—that if even Viacom lacked the ability to distinguish infringing videos from authorised material on YouTube, and were unable to identify those videos which their own agents and employees uploaded from those that were uploaded without authorisation, how could YouTube be expected to discern these characteristics? YouTube argued that Viacom itself contributed to this difficulty by virtue of its own marketing practices.

7.6.4 Section 512(c)(1)(B): Ability to Control the Alleged Infringing Activity

YouTube argued that, as with knowledge of infringing activities needing to be specific, the service provider's control has to be control over the *particular* infringing activity at issue. The statutory support for this under Section 512(c)(1)(B) derives from the usage of the phrase "*the* infringing activity" in respect of which a service provider has the right and ability to control and has received a financial benefit. YouTube argued that, following on from "*Io*",[118] general control over the YouTube website does not necessarily mean that YouTube has control over "*the* infringing activity". For the DMCA to hold otherwise

---

[116] YouTube's Memorandum, p 37.

[117] YouTube's Memorandum, p 45.

[118] 586 F. Supp. 2d 1132 at 1151.

would mean that the test of "right and ability to control" would be illusory as every activity on the website would necessarily be able to be controlled by a service provider.[119] Further, the ability of a service provider to remove content following the service of a takedown notice also is not sufficient to show that it has the "right and ability to control" the infringing activity. Again, to hold otherwise would devoid the control test of content.[120]

YouTube argued therefore that there is a stark difference between the ability of a service provider to control their website and the ability of a service provider to control the infringing activity on their website. Because YouTube hosts "an overwhelming abundance of videos that no one has ever claimed (or could claim) are infringing YouTube's systems of control cannot be said to control *only* "the infringing activity." Further, there is no precondition under Section 512(m) that requires YouTube to actively monitor its site to seek facts indicating infringing activity.[121] Even if it were possible to individually screen the hundreds of thousands of videos that are uploaded onto YouTube every day, YouTube again argued that there would be no way to know for certain or if there was a 'red flag' that could indicate whether or not the clip being uploaded was infringing or not.

Turning to the financial benefit limb of the test, YouTube argued that it did not derive a financial benefit "directly attributable" to the alleged infringing activity. YouTube argued that it earns revenue when users watch or click on ads that run throughout locations on the site. It cannot be said that YouTube benefits directly from specific infringing videos, i.e. "*the* infringing activity". YouTube argued that although the financial benefit test included in Section 512(c)(1)(B) incorporated the common law standards for vicarious liability for copyright infringement, the DMCA did not "simply codify" the standards. Instead, Congress instructed the courts to "take a common sense, fact-based approach, not a formalistic one."[122] This, argued YouTube, meant that the courts must give "service providers greater protection from liability than it would have enjoyed under the common law of vicarious liability."[123] YouTube explained that this argument is supported by the legislative history of Section 512(c)(1)(B) where the Senate and House reports stated that "a service provider conducting a legitimate business would not be considered to receive a 'financial benefit directly attributable to the infringing activity' where the infringer makes the same kind of payment as non-infringing users of the provider's service."[124] That is to say, where the service provider accepts a different kind of payment from a non-infringing activity as it does from

---

[119] YouTube's Memorandum, p 59.

[120] "*Hendrickson v eBay, Inc.*", 165 F. Supp 2d 1082 at 1096' "*UMG II*", 665 F. Supp. 2d 1099 at 1113–15; Io, 586 F. Supp 2d 1081 at 1152; "*Corbis*" 351 F. Supp. 2d 109 at 110.

[121] Section 512(m).

[122] Senate Report at 44; House Report at 54.

[123] YouTube's Memorandum, p 73; Nimmer and Nimmer 2008, Section 12B.04[A][2][b].

[124] Senate Report at 44; House Report at 54.

an infringing activity, then this could be construed as a direct financial benefit. YouTube argues that there is no such distinction between how it receives its revenue.

The Senate and House Reports also distinguished financial benefit from those who conduct "legitimate business" and those whose value "lies in providing access to infringing material."[125] YouTube argued that their business is conducted legitimately because its revenue model did not favour infringing material, the site provided a platform for millions of non-infringing videos from which financial value was also generated, and the advertising-based business model is also an industry standard, including sites such as Daily Motion, Vimeo, Veoh, Atom, MySpace, and Facebook. Given these factors and the established industry standards YouTube argued it cannot be the case that "any service provider that hosts-user-submitted content and that makes money by running advertisements fails the DMCA's financial-benefit test."[126] To hold so would threaten the very business model of online service providers that the DMCA was created to protect.

7.6.5 *"Grokster" Intent*

YouTube's final argument was addressing Viacom's first argument—that YouTube's alleged *Grokster* intent trumped the availability of the DMCA's Safe Harbours. YouTube was quick to dismiss this argument saying that the DMCA's statutory language and legislative history clearly showed that the safe harbours applied to all forms of copyright infringement, including contributory infringement under *Grokster*. Further, there was no evidence to suggest that YouTube was a pirate site and actively encouraged users to infringe copyrights, as was the case in *Grokster*.

Grokster involved a pirate file-sharing site who, along with StreamCast, distributed over 100 million copies of file-sharing software programs that were used almost exclusively to illegally share copyright material. Grokster never implemented procedures to block or impeded the sharing of infringing material and in fact directly targeted users of Napster—a known source of infringing copyright content. In addition, by contrast with YouTube, it was showed that close to 90–97% of files shared through Grokster's software was infringing.

YouTube argued that it differed from Grokster in all of these respects. Its business model did not involve a "patently illegal object" geared towards infringing content, nor was it actively encouraging or soliciting users to upload infringing material, especially on the scale encountered in Grokster. Subsequent cases involving other Napster descendants also showed Grokster type behavioural characteristics, such as in Usenet.com where over 94% of the content was shown

---

[125] Senate Report 44–45; House Report at 54.

[126] YouTube's Memorandum, p 77.

to be infringing. In Fung it was between 90 and 95%.[127] Any evidence of the amount of infringing content on YouTube could not be said to even approach this level. YouTube closed its argument by stating that if their business model is said to be as illegitimate as what Viacom argues it to be to fall foul of the DMCA's safe harbours, then it should be examined why Viacom itself was using the platform to broadcast their own videos.

7.7 District Court Ruling in Summary Judgment

In June 2010, Judge Louis Stanton of the Southern District of New York granted summary judgment in YouTube and Google's favour. Despite the hundreds of pages of arguments before the court, Judge Stanton's decision was incredibly brief and was dealt with in thirty pages. Such a brief judgment was a result, not only of the nature of the motion—that of a summary judgment—but mainly of the fact despite tomes of legal arguments from the parties there was only one main question that needed to be answered to decide the case: whether under Section 512(c)(1)(A)(i) and (ii) meant that general awareness of infringements or actual or constructive knowledge of specific and identifiable infringements of individual items were required for a service provider to fall foul of the safe harbour provisions.

7.7.1 Legislative Consideration

Judge Stanton's Opinion, like the parties' file arguments before, again commenced with an analysis of the legislative intent in drafting the DMCA as set out above. Judge Stanton held that the tenor of the Reports indicated that the phrases "actual knowledge that the material or an activity" is infringing and "facts or circumstances" indicating infringing activity describe knowledge of specific and identifiable infringements of particular individual items; "[m]ere knowledge of prevalence of such activity in general is not enough."[128] Judge Stanton explained that the requirement that there be specificity as to infringing material "is consistent with an area of the law devoted to protection of distinctive individual works, not libraries. To let knowledge of a generalised practice of infringement in the

---

[127] *"Fung"*, CV 06-5578, slip op. at*66.
[128] *"Viacom"*, WL 2532404 at p 15.

industry, or of a proclivity of users to post infringing materials, impose responsibility on service providers to discover which of their users' postings infringe a copyright would contravene the structure and operation of the DMCA."[129]

Judge Stanton stated that this standard of knowledge was consistent with the *Perfect 10* case because in that case the burden of identifying copyright infringement under the DMCA was placed on the copyright owner, not the service provider. Further, he stated, that the DMCA itself explicitly states at Section 512(m)(1) that the Act should not be construed to condition the enjoyment of a "safe harbour" on a "service provider monitoring its service or affirmatively seeking facts indicating infringing activity". To illustrate the apparent efficiency of the DMCA notification procedure Judge Stanton stated that when Viacom sent a notice to YouTube about 100,000 infringing videos and that YouTube had removed almost all of them the next day.

7.7.2 Case Law Consideration of the Knowledge Standard and *"Grokster"* Intent

Turning to case-law on the issue of knowledge, Judge Stanton first applied *"UMG II"* which held that "if investigation of 'facts and circumstances' is required to identify material as infringing, then those facts and circumstances are not 'red flags'." Therefore, irrespective of a service provider's "awareness of pervasive copyright infringing, however flagrant and blatant"[130] this still does not impose liability on the service provider. Judge Stanton also referred to *"Corbis"* which equally held that a claimant had to prove that the defendant was aware of specific identifiable infringing activities.[131]

Although only a few months after the decision, Judge Stanton also referred to Judge Sullivan's opinion in *"Tiffany v eBay"*[132] which similarly held that generalised knowledge possessed by eBay that some portion of Tiffany goods being sold on its website might be counterfeit was insufficient to impose upon eBay an affirmative duty to remedy the problem. Judge Sullivan held that eBay would have to have knowledge of specific instances of actual infringement to be held contributory liable. The later Court of Appeals ruling also agreed with this interpretation. Judge Stanton noted that although the *"Tiffany"* case concerned trade mark infringement, he stated that "the DMCA applies the same principle, and its establishment of a safe harbour is clear and practical: if a service provider knows (from the notice from the owner, or a 'red flag') of specific instances of infringement, the provider must promptly remove the infringing material. If not,

---

[129] Idem.

[130] 665 F. Supp. 2d 1099 at 1108.

[131] 351 F. Supp. 2d 1090 at 1108.

[132] 600 F.3d 93 (2nd Cir. April 1, 2010).

the burden is on the owner to identify the infringement. General knowledge that infringement is 'ubiquitous' does not impose a duty on a service provider to monitor or search its service for infringements."[133]

Judge Stanton's opinion briefly focused on the Grokster intent issue as argued by Viacom. The *"Grokster"* Court had held that one is liable for the consequent acts of third-party infringement if it "distributes a device with the object of promoting its use to infringe copyright". YouTube had said that it did not exist "solely to provide the site and facilities for copyright infringement." However, the issue of whether it matters that the objective must be a sole objective or just one of several was never discussed by Judge Stanton, or in the *"Grokster"* decision. Judge Stanton went only so far as to state that *"Grokster"*-type cases, including *"Arista Record LLC v Lime Group"* and *"Fung"* were not ones of a service provider who furnishes a platform for users to post and access materials, of which the service provider is unaware. The facts of these cases were different. Therefore, he indicated that the *"Grokster"* cases were of little relevance in relation to application of the DMCA provisions.

7.7.3 Other Considerations

The final part of Judge Stanton's opinion considered Viacom's argument that the display of videos on YouTube fell outside the DMCA protection as it was not "storage" of the material. Judge Stanton held that Viacom construed the term "storage" too narrowly, especially in light of the definition of "service provider" in Section 512(k)(1)(B). This Section defined "service provider" as including "an entity offering the transmission, routing, or providing of connections for digital online communications." It was clear from this and the Senate Report indicated that YouTube's activities were caught by these provisions. Viacom's argument that because the infringing activities were a result of YouTube facilitating access to online videos and thus did not benefit from the safe harbour provisions also failed. Judge Stanton referred to the rulings in the *"Io"*[134] and *"UMG I"*[135] which held that even though service providers' activities may be in the pursuit of facilitating access to online content and not strictly just that of one of the four core Internet activities, it does not mean that it did not benefit from the safe harbour defence showed.

Viacom's argument that YouTube could not benefit from the safe harbour because it financially benefited from the infringing material being uploaded on the site also failed. Judge Stanton referred back to the knowledge criteria and stated that under Section 512(c)(1)(B) a service provider must not receive a financial

---

[133] *"Viacom"*, WL 2532404 at p 20.

[134] 586 F. Supp. 2 d 1132 at 1148.

[135] 620 F. Supp. 2d 1081 at 1089.

benefit directly attributable to the infringing activity, in a case in which the service provider has the right and ability to control such activity...". Judge Stanton held that the "right and ability to control" the activity requires item-specific knowledge of it and without such specific knowledge, YouTube did not fall foul of this section. It followed that he did not need to consider the direct financial benefit strand of the test.

The remaining pages of Judge Stanton's judgment was a summary of the several actions undertaken by YouTube which evidenced their positive conduct in respect of managing infringing copyright content on the site. Any criticisms yielded by Viacom in their complaint about YouTube's conduct in delaying removal of infringing content, deleting accounts of multiple infringers and not implementing digital finger printing technology was held by Judge Stanton to be reasonable given all the circumstances, i.e., the need for YouTube to monitor systems and to improve site functionality in identifying repeat infringers.

Although incredibly and woefully brief in its analysis and discussion of the relevant authorities and statute, the resounding message from Judge Stanton was that without specific knowledge of particular infringing videos on the site, You-Tube did not have either actual or "red flag" knowledge to fall foul of the safe harbour defence, despite general knowledge of infringing activity.

7.8 Viacom's Appeal

Expectedly following YouTube's summary judgment success Viacom, supported by several *amici curiae*, appealed Judge Stanton's judgment.

In its opening appeal brief Viacom called Judge Stanton's interpretation of Section 512(c) "absurd, disquieting and disruptive" and stated that the effect of this interpretation would be that even the most "piratical businesses held to account in *Grokster* could be immune with just minor tweaks to their business models."[136] The root of Viacom's argument was that the text of the DMCA, when properly interpreted, performed a function completely opposite to what Judge Stanton held. Viacom argued that the DMCA actually compelled service providers who are aware of pervasive copyright infringement, participate and profit from it, to be found liable for copyright infringement under the DMCA when it fails to act.

Before turning to the substantive legal arguments, Viacom's argument yet again addressed the legislative history of the DMCA which substantially repeated their arguments in support of their motion for summary judgment. Viacom also again referred to YouTube's internal communications and failure to implement digital fingerprinting technology which it argued evidenced YouTube's knowledge of the pervasiveness of infringement on the site and their conscious plan to evade lia-

---

[136] Viacom's Opening Brief for Plaintiffs-Appellants ("Viacom's Appeal"), p 3.

bility by placing the burden of policing infringement squarely on the shoulders of a copyright owner in an effort to maintain their site traffic.

7.8.1 The Section 512(1)(c)(A) Issues: The Knowledge Standard

Viacom argued that the district court erred in holding that YouTube could benefit from the safe harbour provisions, despite being "generally aware of" and indeed "welcom[ing]" of copyright-infringing material, because it lacked knowledge of the specific URL of each individual infringing video. Viacom argued that the evidence actually showed that YouTube did have item-and-location specific information in respect of some of the works complained of and, for those that it did not, YouTube chose to actively blind itself from assimilating specific information of infringement in order to benefit from the safe harbour, i.e. by not implementing infringement detecting software or a community flagging system for infringing videos. It was argued that the internal email evidence also indicates that, for years, YouTube's policy and practice was to take "no action". Viacom argued that because YouTube, in the district court's own words, "welcomed" "blatant" infringement, and turned a blind eye to such infringement it knew was occurring as evidenced by the internal emails, it cannot be said to not be "aware of facts or circumstances from which infringing activity is apparent" under Section 512(c)(1)(A)(ii). Viacom argued that YouTube's inaction while aware of widespread incidents of infringement should not be rewarded with a shield from liability.

Viacom also argued that the district court's higher standard of knowledge—that of knowledge of specific instances of infringing content—under Section 512(c)(1)(A)(ii) was not supported by the statutory language. Breaking down the provision, Viacom argued that the exclusion of the safe harbour depends upon the defendant's awareness of "facts or circumstances" that make the "infringing activity" "apparent". This does not mean that these facts have to automatically point to an activity being absolutely and conclusively illegal.[137] Further "facts and circumstances" suggests that Congress intended there to be a more holistic view of the origin, quality and quantity of information of infringement which a defendant may possess to fall within or foul of the provision. That is to say there is not just one type of specific information that is required for the inoperability of the safe harbour under Section 512(c)(1)(A)(ii) (i.e., the requirement of specific URL addresses) but a combination of information sufficient to raise a "red flag" of warning to the service provider. Holding that there has to be specific identifiable knowledge on the part of the defendant to find an ISP liable renders the purpose of 512(c)(1)(A)(ii) void. If the same standard of knowledge is required for _512(c)(1)(A) (i) as is for (ii), the (ii) would not serve any purpose.

Further, if the district court was held to be correct in its interpretation of Section 512(c)(1)(A)(i) and (ii), such a finding would be at odds with Congress's

---

[137] Ginsburg 2008.

intent in enacting the DMCA. Viacom argued that main purposes of enacting the DMCA was to provide reasonable assurance to copyright owners that their copyright would be protected, given the increased risk and ease that their works can be infringed online. Although Viacom hinted that the safe harbour provisions in the DMCA are appropriate for "innocent service" it argued that if the DMCA is to "conform to the central purposes of the statute, [it] must exclude at least those that 'welcome', and even intend, their users' infringement. To conclude otherwise would fatally undermine Congress's intent to address 'massive piracy', and it was argued, would immunize even entities such as Grokster itself.

7.8.2 *Wilful Blindness*

Turning to their argument relating to wilful blindness, Viacom argued that even if Section 512(c) excluded from liability those that do not have URL-specific knowledge of infringement, the district court erred by finding for YouTube where the evidence showed that it was wilfully blind to the massive scale of copyright infringement on the site. It was held "*In re Aimster Copyright Litigation*", cited in "*Arista Records v Doe 3*"[138] and in "*Tiffany v eBay*"[139] that "wilful blindness is knowledge in copyright law… as it is in the law generally." Wilful blindness occurs where a person engages in "deliberate avoidance" amounting to knowledge where "the circumstances were such to alert [the person] to a high probability" of the relevant fact, but the defendant "consciously avoided learning" that fact. A potential finding of wilful blindness can be defeated where a defendant is "continually taking steps to further refine its anti-fraud measures", as was the case of eBay in "*Tiffany v eBay*". Viacom argues that YouTube actually did the opposite of eBay by taking "affirmative steps to shut down any mechanism that might have provided the URL-specific knowledge YouTube claims is indispensable" for a finding of liability. It did this, Viacom argued, by removing the ability for community users to flag suspected infringing videos and only "selectively" implementing fingerprint technology.

7.8.3 *Section 512(c)(1)(B): The Financial Benefit Issue*

Under Section 512(c)(1)(B), Judge Stanton held that YouTube lacked the "right and ability to control" the activity because it did not have "item-specific" knowledge of the activity, but did not rule on whether or not it received a financial benefit. Viacom again argued that the touchstone of "item-specific" knowledge is

---

[138] 604 F.3d 110 at 118 (2d Cir.2010).

[139] 600 F.3d 93 at 109 (2d Cir. 2010).

not a pre-requisite for being able to control an activity. Viacom argued that YouTube had the "ability" to control third-party infringement by implementing Audible Magic filtering, but did not.

Viacom also argued that the effect of the district court's interpretation of Section 512(c)(1)(B) would hold 512(c)(1)(A)(ii) virtually meaningless. This is because if the "right and ability to control" under Section 512(c)(1)(B) requires an ISP to have "item-specific knowledge"—the same knowledge under Section 512(c)(1)(A)(i) and (ii)—then any service provider who has item-specific knowledge of users' acts of infringement automatically falls foul of Section 512(c)(1)(A) and thus never gets to Section 512(B). Viacom argued that the legislative intent of Section 512(c)(1)(B) was to follow the common law rule that a defendant may be found vicariously liable for copyright infringement where the defendant "derive[s] a direct financial benefit from the infringement and ha[s] the right and ability to supervise the infringing activity."[140]

Such an interpretation of Section 512(c)(1)(B) was confirmed by Congress in the House Report[141] at 25-26, by the courts in *"Perfect10"* and by academics such as in *Nimmer on Copyright*. Because common law vicarious liability turns on financial benefit and control, even in the absence of actual knowledge of infringement under *"Shapiro"* and *"Grokster"*, YouTube's activities clearly fall within the scope of Section 512(c)(1)(B). Viacom argued that YouTube had the right to control activities on the site by reserving editorial control in and the right to remove content and terminate accounts. It also has the ability to control the site by way of community flagging of suspected infringing videos, by way of its search feature and index and by implementation of fingerprint filtering technologies. YouTube also obtained a direct financial benefit attributable to the infringement because the infringing material acted as a "draw" or "major lure" for an ever-increasing YouTube audience.

7.8.4 Section 512(c): The "Storage" Issue

Viacom again revisited their arguments under Section 512(c). It restated that YouTube's reliance on the safe harbour provisions were not available because the infringing activities on their site were not occurring "by reason of the storage at the direction of a user" of the material. Viacom argued that its claims of infringement do not have anything to do with "storage" with or without the direction of a user: YouTube, in transcoding user-uploaded material into a standard format for display, distribution, and performance of the content from its site, does not just facilitate storage but facilitates broadcasting. Viacom argued that a

---

[140] *"Ellison v Robertson"* 1357 F.3d 1072 (9th Cir. 2004); *"Matthew Bender Co. v W. Publishing"* Co. 158 F.3d 693 (2d Cir. 1998).

[141] House Report at 25–26.

user's decision to upload a video on to YouTube is not a direction to YouTube to then make copies of the video in different formats, to index and feature the material, or to licence the material to third parties to make viewing of the video easier on hand-held devices of which Viacom licences out. Viacom argued that YouTube takes those actions independently and for its own benefit and profit.

However, the strength of this argument appears dubious, even on appeal. YouTube users use the site because they want their videos accessible by the public in formats that facilitate viewing. Had YouTube users just wanted their videos to be stored they would not be uploading them onto YouTube. Their direction must therefore be implicit from the mere fact they are using YouTube to upload their video.

7.9 Conclusion

The current status of the law on service provider liability, at least in the case of a business such as YouTube, has not altered greatly from the past cases on Section 512's safe harbour provisions. If a service provider does not possess specific knowledge of a particular infringement—even if evidence shows that rampant copyright infringement was apparent and that it "welcomed" infringement—it nevertheless may still benefit from Section 512's safe harbour defences as long as their business's sole objective is not to maintain and encourage infringement of copyright like that of Grokster. When YouTube filed its response to Viacom's appeal brief in March 2011, repeating much of the same arguments that were before the District Court, it again focused its response on this main argument—that the requirement of knowledge has to be knowledge of individual instances of infringement. It argued that Congress crafted such a high threshold for finding 'red flag' knowledge "because it recognised that it is challenging for service providers to distinguish infringing from non-infringing material". YouTube argues that it could not have been Congress's intention when drafting the DMCA that generalised information of occurrences of some infringing activity equates to 'red-flag' knowledge.

Although at the time of writing,[142] the final decision from the Court of Appeals for the Second Circuit is pending and despite Viacom's significant support of *amici curiae* including Microsoft, The Washington Post, Newspaper Association of America, the Associated Press (and a group of economic professors), this author does not believe that the Court of Appeals for the Second Circuit will arrive at an outcome any different from that of the lower court. Although, we may see more detailed analysis of the legal arguments, in particular of the knowledge requirement in Section 512(c)(1)(C)(i) and (ii) and its assumed duplication in Section 512(c)(1)(B), the appeals court is unlikely to alter the final result for the exact

---

[142] August 2011.

reason referred to by YouTube in its appeal brief The US Courts, as with some European courts such as Germany and the Court of Justice for the European Union, have been reluctant in finding YouTube or Google liable for copyright or trade mark infringement because there is an unspoken judicial intent, albeit a spoken US legislative intent, that YouTube and Google's services hold a vital societal importance. A finding that general knowledge of infringing activity is enough to attach liability to a service provider risks weakening service providers legal and economic position and the vital societal importance they provide in providing a "backbone" to the Internet.

This chapter commenced with providing a background of YouTube's business structure and its speed and success of growth. It is important to note these characteristics when assessing the legal merits of the parties' arguments, the brief opinion of the lower court and the pending decision of the Court of Appeals, because it is these economic and arguably valuable societal characteristics that appear to be informing the US courts discretion and altering the proposed balance of the DMCA. However, balance or not, the US Courts are very aware that a finding of liability against YouTube or Google will have far too many and too great ramifications for the legal and economic safe harbours currently being enjoyed by large service providers, as well as the drastic policy considerations that would accompany such a finding. As long as a service provider treads the fine lines between general knowledge of infringing activities and specific knowledge of individual infringements, and between "welcoming" infringing (and non-infringing activities) and having infringement as its sole intent, the "*Viacom v YouTube*" case clearly demonstrates that the safe harbour's robust defence can act as a permanent mooring for a service provider's immunity to reside.

References

Ginsburg JC (2008) Separating the sony sheep from the grokster goats. Ariz L Rev 50:577
Nimmer M, Nimmer D (2008) Nimmer on copyright

Chapter 8
Looking Beyond the Google Books Settlement

Gary Rinkerman

"We're trying for something that's already found us."
James Douglas Morrison.

Contents

8.1 Setting the Stage

It is customary in most legal and academic writing that the author avoids the "first person" voice. This avoidance of individual "personality" in the text is intended to create the impression of objectivity, lack of bias and, above all else, credibility. However, in practice, the approach is often used to mask bias and create false

Adjunct Professor at Queen Mary (University of London) Intellectual Property Research Institute, New York University Polytechnic Institute and the Technology Management ("TechMan") Program of George Mason University's MBA program. He also lectures frequently in the member institutions of The European Intellectual Property Institutes Network (EIPIN) and in other US and non-US universities and organizations.

G. Rinkerman (✉)
New York University, New York, NY, USA
e-mail: Gary.Rinkerman@dbr.com

G. Rinkerman
George Mason University, Fairfax, VA, USA

A. Lopez-Tarruella (ed.), *Google and the Law*,
Information Technology and Law Series 22, DOI: 10.1007/978-90-6704-846-0_8,
© T.M.C. Asser press, The Hague, The Netherlands, and the author(s) 2012

impressions of objectivity. In such cases, readers are better served by a frank admission that the author's experiences, subjectivity, and even biases are at work in the approach used and in the conclusions drawn. Therefore, in the interest of "full disclosure," I will outline briefly the experience and perspective that have somewhat shaped the approach I have used and the conclusions I have drawn in the following discussion.[1]

As the first Editor-in-Chief and co-founder of *Computer Law Reporter*, one of the earliest US legal journals to focus exclusively on computer technology and digital media, I enjoyed a unique advantage in observing, among other things, the development of the Internet. The technological, social, cultural, and legal issues concerning the Internet were among the daily topics to which my attention was drawn. Although there were significant privacy concerns, intellectual property concerns, access and use term enforcement concerns, information export concerns, and a host of other legal issues, no one seriously argued that the Internet was not a tremendous and advantageous development, nor did anyone seriously argue that we should wait until Congress or the international treaty process had fully vetted all of the issues (if that were even possible) before this important resource was implemented and expanded. In short, the general concept of, and the capabilities offered by the Internet were, a priori, beneficial on a groundbreaking order of significance. Also, the concepts and the implementing technology were already developed, and there was, at that point, neither the means nor the motivation to "put the genie back in the bottle."

On the other hand, I also watched as search engines, advertising techniques, and other technologies changed aspects of the Internet significantly in terms of utility, content presentation, and "user experience." By this I mean that, at least in its current state, a significant aspect of the Internet has evolved (or devolved) from, essentially, a well-stocked library to a shopping mall full of any number of advertising ploys and misdirection. Rather than an intelligently ordered offering of information and information resources, the user experience provided by many search engines would be comical if it were not so frustrating and deceptive. For example, years ago I did a search on the Internet to locate information about a serious illness suffered by a family member. The top results included incredibly and immediately helpful medical journal articles from top institutions in the US and England. Today, if I try to recreate the same search, I will likely have within the top results, short and relatively unhelpful articles by law firms that want to help me sue a medical service provider, a series of "pseudo sites" that offer the minimum amount of information (often copied from Wikipedia), and the maximum amount of wholly unrelated advertisements, brief and relatively unhelpful marketing swipes from sellers of books on the topic, etc.

---

[1] In addition to my lecture schedule, I practice law as a partner in a firm that has represented Google in certain unrelated matters. The analysis, opinions, and conclusions contained in this article are solely my own and do not necessarily reflect the views of any employer, partner, client, family member, friend, etc.

In essence, my earlier search is now a "cyberfossil." It is, in terms of the speed by which the Internet has developed, an ancient digital resource or experience that has lost out and become extinct as advertisers and accounting departments have displaced the original Internet visionaries and gained the upper niche in determining how much useless or unwanted content will be thrust upon the user. In short, my time is being wasted and an important resource has been diluted and invaded by "artificial ingredients." Yet, I am hopeful; I am waiting for the much touted "competitive process" to kick in and offer me an effective and practicable alternative to this "cyber clutter," an alternative for which, by the way, I would be willing to pay.

Now, to the Google Books Project, the Google Books Agreement, and the Google Books Settlement process.[2] It appears to me that, like the original concept of the Internet, Google's original concept of, through digitization and indexing, making so much content so much more "locatable" and ultimately accessible is a groundbreaking and beneficial development, *albeit,* admittedly, not anywhere near the same scale as of the Internet itself.[3] As such, Google's actions should not be lightly interfered with or discouraged. Moreover, waiting for the US Congress or the international treaty process to initiate, address, or "bless" such a robust "knowledge indexing" process would, in essence, likely be comparable to the nightmare–comic experience of *Waiting for Godot.* Perhaps unfortunately for presiding Judge Denny Chin, formerly at the U.S. District Court for the Southern District of New York and now a judge at the Second Circuit Court of Appeals, the task of "driving the locomotive," or at least approving its departure, in the matter of the Google Books Agreement was thrust upon him.[4] In essence, one US judge in New York City was presented with a massive and far-reaching blueprint for a major digital library as well as its implementing and regulatory processes. On March 22, 2011, Judge Chin issued his opinion rejecting the Google Books Agreement.[5] There are likely many sighs of relief in several sectors of the book publishing industry, but many of the fundamental issues recognized or raised in the process of considering the Google Books Agreement will not "go away," but rather will persist in the now-daily attempt to accommodate authors' rights, publishers practices, and end-users' concerns (privacy, intrusive advertising

---

[2] The term "Google Books Project" is used in this discussion to refer to the large-scale project by Google to digitize books for indexing purposes and to provide a platform for book sales and advertisements for other, likely related works. The term "Google Books Agreement" is used to refer to the proposed, amended settlement agreement in the case *"Authors Guild, et. al v. Google"*, 05 Civ. 8136 DC (SDNY), a copyright-based class action suit filed in 2008 against Google in the U.S. District Court for the Southern District of New York. The representatives of the plaintiff classes are the Authors Guild and the Association of American Publishers. The term "Google Books Settlement" is used to refer to the settlement process itself.

[3] For even more "good news," see Elhauge 2010.

[4] Although Judge Chin has been elevated to a seat on the appellate court, he continues to preside over a number of his district court cases, including the *"Google"* case.

[5] *"The Authors Guild, et. al. v. Google, Inc".,* Opinion, 05 Civ. 8136 (DC)(March 22, 2011).

practices, etc.) as digital distribution technologies evolve and create new revenue generation models.

It may be that the parties in the Google Books Settlement will persist and seek to further amend the Google Books Agreement, appeal Judge Chin's determinations, or have the matter reconsidered. There is also a chance that the parties will simply use the judicially-rejected Google Books Agreement as the template for a private business system along the lines of ASCAP or the Harry Fox Agency[6]— with "opt in" rather than "opt out" provisions—so that they can move forward with full text distribution of copyrighted works. Of course, the original issue in the case, the "fair use" issue, would still be there. Nonetheless, the question as to whether Google's indexing efforts, and the tremendous cultural benefits achieved by the concurrent archiving of the non-distributed digital copies of the indexed works, comprise a process that is sufficiently "transformative" to constitute fair use presents an issue that, in my view, can be dealt with fairly expeditiously and in a straightforward manner.

Like many others, I am anxious to at least have the benefit of Google's indexing system, and it is useful that the Google Books Agreement addresses "Orphan Works"[7] issues and shows some sensitivity to the "second generation" issues of content presentation as perceived by the end-user. We are nonetheless left somewhat uncomfortably with the feeling that the train needs to be on the right track, at least in a general sense, before it leaves the station. Actually, for those who feel they have been excluded from the process, it would, but for Judge Chin's rejection of the Google Books Agreement, have already left. In any case, as in the implementation and evolution of the Internet, "the devil is in the details" and some details do not become apparent until well after the system is in operation. Moreover, even if Google does not get to implement its plan, either in its entirety or in part, the concepts and implementing technology are now here and, as in the rapid development and adoption of the Internet, it is difficult to imagine that they will not be employed by someone, *albeit* perhaps after unnecessary delay. In short, the core questions raised by the Google Books Project, The Google Books Agreement and the Google Books Settlement process will need to be confronted irrespective of whether Google and the other parties to the Google Books Agreement succeed, fail, or simply become "mired" in the judicial process.

---

[6] ASCAP and The Harry Fox Agency are examples in the music industry where private business concerns have supplied the means, through voluntary contractual arrangements, for individual rights holders to offer and collect royalties from exploitation of their rights. *See* http://www.ascap.com/; http://www.harryfox.com/index.jsp (last accessed 29 August 2011). These private entities arose in large part to address the complexities and opportunities offered by new technological means of content distribution; the terms of the Google Books Agreement also attempt to address new technological means of content distribution, but through the technique of a class action settlement.

[7] The term "Orphan Works" refers to works for which the owners of copyright, if any, cannot be readily identified or located.

Therefore, the "second generation" issue of how digital works will be presented to end-users should not be overlooked.

8.2 Initial Developments and Some Core Questions

In an alternative, and in my view more perfect world, the original *Google* litigation would have resulted in the following determinations:

1. Google has the right to digitize, index, display, and otherwise act upon public domain works in the manner permitted in the jurisdictions in which Google seeks to offer its system. To the extent that, in some jurisdictions, there may be some "moral rights" or other doctrines that could impact upon Google's ability to aggregate public domain materials with certain third-party materials, which would be a matter for consideration in each specific jurisdiction.
2. As to works still under copyright, Google should have, at least in the US, the right to create digital copies solely for the transformative purpose of indexing, but not full text display. If ultimately some text is displayed, the question of how much text may be displayed for the purpose of providing a useful index might be a candidate for further clarification. However, this would not impact upon the ability to create the overall system. Moreover, whether or not photographs and images may be included as part of the indexing system could be addressed via application of the current and developing US case law on fair use and, perhaps in the future legislation.
3. Because whether or not a fair use defense applies to activities in the US is determined by applying US law, Google's activities would be, to the extent the activities and results are confined to the US, sheltered by US law. If another jurisdiction does not accept Google's digitization and indexing as "fair dealing," "fair use", or protected by some other principle, then that jurisdiction can forego or delay the benefits of the system and explain to its population why the need to compensate individual authors for indexing activities justifies the delay, inaccessibility, or incompleteness of the system in that jurisdiction.
4. As to "Orphan Works" that are included in the indexing process—works for which the owners of copyright, if any, cannot be readily identified or located—the fair use analysis provided above would fully apply. Again, to the extent that this approach is rejected by a particular jurisdiction, that jurisdiction can forego or delay the benefits of the system and explain to its population why the need to compensate individual authors for indexing activities justifies the delay, inaccessibility, or incompleteness of the system in that jurisdiction.

Of course, the above simply constitutes a "wish list" on my part. The list includes its own complexities and potential localized risks that, admittedly, could severely impact the implementation and utility of the system, at least in non-US jurisdictions. Nonetheless, in the course of the Google Books Settlement process, the matter has become somewhat more complex. A visit to the Google Books

Settlement web site[8] will assure even a casual observer that the current form of the Google Books Agreement looks more like a complex piece of privately-created intellectual property legislation or treaty than the typical fare of judicial opinions. In fact, Judge Chin noted that the Google Books Agreement is 166 pages long, not including attachments.[9]

The excerpt below from Google's description of one aspect of the Google Books Agreement should suffice to provide a glimpse of the complexity and intended far-reaching effect:

> Now, works are only included in the Amended Settlement if they were published by January 5, 2009 and either were registered with the U.S. Copyright Office by that date or their place of publication was in the United Kingdom ("UK"), Canada or Australia. A work will be considered to have a place of publication in the UK, Canada or Australia if its printed copy contains information indicating that the place of publication was in one of those two countries. Such information may include, for example, a statement that the book was "Published in [Australia] or [the UK] or [Canada]," or the location or address of the publisher in one of those three countries.
>
> If your work meets the criteria above, then you are a member of the Amended Settlement Class regardless of where you reside and regardless of whether your work may have been published outside the UK, Canada or Australia. However, if your works were not either (a) registered with the United States Copyright Office by January 5, 2009 or (b) published in Canada, Australia or the UK by that date, you are not a member of the Amended Settlement Class, even if you were a member of the original Settlement Class.[10]

Moreover, according to Google's settlement information site, the Google Books Agreement provides Google with the following core rights:

> "Under the Amended Settlement, Rightsholders authorize Google, on a non-exclusive basis, to:
> Continue to digitize Books and Inserts
> Sell subscriptions to an electronic Books database to institutions;
> Sell online access to individual Books;
> Sell advertising on pages from Books;
> Display portions of Book in a "preview" format to encourage sales of online access to Books;
> Display Snippets from Books; and
> Display bibliographic information from Books".[11]

The question that immediately comes to mind is how did this matter so rapidly evolve from a fairly basic "fair use" case to a relatively complex business blueprint of international proportions. The answer is that Google and the other participants in the case saw an opportunity to address and shape, in a relatively rapid fashion, a broad range of legal and logistical issues that could otherwise present obstacles to their now-

---

[8] http://books.google.com/googlebooks/agreement/index.html (last accessed 29 August 2011).

[9] Opinion, at p 5.

[10] Available at http://www.googlebookAgreement.com/help/bin/answer.py?answer=118704& hl=en#q21 (last accessed 29 August 2011).

[11] See http://www.googlebooksettlement.com/help/bin/answer.py?answer=118704&hl=en#q30 (last accessed 29 August 2011).

collective business model. Whether or not they will be successful, especially after Judge Chin's opinion and in non-US jurisdictions in which Google may offer its services and business model, is another question. Nonetheless, Google has "rolled the dice" and, win or lose, perhaps we should be thankful that Google and the other participants in the suit have expended so much of their resources in placing their bets "on the table." At the very least they have certainly framed and brought to the fore some issues that deserve very serious consideration. In an era where digital communications evolve so rapidly and have obliterated so many national, cultural, and social borders, perhaps waiting for each jurisdiction to weigh in via its legislative or treaty-making bodies prior to the implementation of a system such as the Google Books Project is an antiquated notion. Perhaps not. The ultimate fate of the Google Books Project, as well as the potentially separate fate of the Google Books Agreement, should shed some light on this issue.

As to its general nature and development, the Google Books Agreement raises a number of basic issues regarding where and how its terms should be shaped and sanctioned. Two major questions that have immediately arisen are: (1) Can and should a US District Court located in New York City be looked to as the proper forum to oversee the establishment of a system that has such significant national and international ramifications?; and (2) Is the US "class action system" an appropriate procedural vehicle for addressing the multitude of concerns, both domestic and international, raised by the Google Books Project and the Google Books Agreement?[12] Are we dealing with judicial legislation or even judicial treaty-making? Judge Chin has now weighed in on the above questions, and he has rejected both the terms of the Google Books Agreement and the attempt by the parties to morph a fair use dispute into a major business model that goes well beyond the original issues presented in the case.

Of course, there are numerous other issues to be addressed, perhaps in book-length detail.[13] On the other hand, rather than seek to expand this discussion beyond an appropriate length, I have provided some thoughts on the forum, procedure, and pace for the Google Books Settlement process as well as some thoughts on a potential issue that might not be readily apparent among the forest of other, perhaps, more immediately significant issues. This final issue arises from the placement of third-party content, particularly advertising, in association with, or

---

[12] In US jurisprudence, in a class action lawsuit, one or more "class representatives" sue on behalf of others who have similar claims. All such persons are, together, a "class" and each is a "class member." As an initial matter, the presiding court must determine whether if it will allow the lawsuit to proceed as a class action. If it does, any settlement will affect everyone who is a member of the class and must be approved by the court. See e.g., Google Books Settlement Notice to Class at http://www.googlebookssettlement.com (last accessed 29 August 2011).

[13] Among these many other issues are: (1) is Google inappropriately securing a monopoly position with judicially-sanctioned (and inappropriate) barriers to entry; (2) is the regulatory process proposed in the Google Books Agreement appropriate and adequate; and (3) even if the Google Books Agreement is implemented in its present form, will there be an appropriate mechanism whereby the terms can be challenged and changed by third parties or even by present parties to the Google Books Agreement?

even in digital displays of text and text excerpts. The question is whether creators of content will have some input into how the chief end-result of the process, digitized and searchable text, are presented. This concern goes well beyond the present implications of the Google Books Project and impacts generally the digital manipulation and presentation of text, images, and audio.[14] Certainly, creators of such content have an interest in the particulars of how their work will be presented and whether or not third-party content (such as advertising) will be jammed into or displayed in conjunction with their works.

8.3 Selecting the Appropriate Forum, Procedure and Pace: "Look Before You Leap" or "He Who Hesitates Is Truly Lost"?

As to two core issues—the appropriateness of forum and procedure— Google and the other participants in the Google Books Settlement process seem to have proceeded on the notion that, although potentially flawed, there is really no practicable alternative to the judicial process and the, at times, dubious benefits of the class action process. It is tempting to say they are correct. Notably, a number of scholars and other commentators have raised very insightful and, in varying degrees, meritorious objections to the process. Yet, if we accept that the overall conclusion that some or all aspects of the general concept are valuable and would have great and immediate social benefits, we must consider the various objections with the proper amount of respect and then simply ask: "What alternative system do you propose, who will develop it and how soon can it be expected?" In rejecting the Google Books Agreement, Judge Chin has said, essentially, "this is not my job." Instead, Judge Chin has pointed to Congress and also noted that, in his view, "many of the concerns raised in the objections [to the Google Books Agreement] would be ameliorated" if it were "converted from an 'opt-out' settlement to an 'opt-in' settlement."[15]

I have described a potential and, in my view, preferred approach earlier in this discussion. Perhaps an alternative would be a completely individualized, contract-based approach, with Google freely digitizing accessible public domain materials and, with regard to works that are still protected by copyright, having to secure specific licenses from the rights holders individually or through clearly appropriate,

---

[14] At present, Google's sample "snippet" for use in indexing and user display appears to be quite useful or, at least, benign. See representative "Snippet View" at http://www.google.com/ googlebooks/screenshots.html#snippet.view (last accessed 29 August 2011). Included in the snippet are links to sites where the subject book can be purchased and to libraries where the book can be borrowed. Other books that are determined to be related to the book that is the subject of the snippet are also listed. Of course, questions may arise as to, e.g., how the listed retailers and related books are selected, but these issues are beyond the scope of the present discussion.

[15] Opinion, at p 46.

representative bodies. This would, in effect, "scrap" the process whereby affected rights holders who do not feel properly represented in a class action have an affirmative duty to "opt out." This approach would be similar to the approach taken by the music industry when the proliferation of distribution technologies (piano rolls, phonograph records, radio, etc.) made it much more practicable for rights holders to voluntarily band together in their enforcement and royalty collection efforts. Thus, songwriters and other owners of rights in musical compositions can elect to join and delegate some of their rights to ASCAP, BMI, or SESAC, but no one forces these songwriters and rights holders to "opt out" of these private organizations rather than voluntarily "opt in." Nonetheless, it is notable that, rather than being created in the legislature or judiciary, these highly effective royalty collection agencies are essentially creatures of private business interests, commercial logistics, and contract law. They were not created by any legislation or class action.[16] Granted, however, antitrust law and other laws have "stepped in *ex post facto* to regulate or provide guidance to these organizations.[17] However, the question again arises as to who will implement this alternative system and how long will it take.[18] As Judge Chin may be hinting, the parties to the *Google* litigation have devised a complex model that might attract authors' voluntary participation.[19] In short, the system may already be here; the only thing for the parties to the *Google* litigation to do is to push the "fair use" issue to a judicial conclusion and offer the details of their now-cooperative business plan as a model for voluntary participation, perhaps with some agreement by authorities in academia and the industry that the model's approach to "Orphan Works" offers a method of "good faith" and "due diligence" that at least avoids willfulness with regard to the use of third-party materials and, also, should spur some further judicial or Congressional attention to the issue.

Another consideration is that the music-industry model does not present a perfect analogy to the Google Books Project, nor does it address Google's argument that it has a "fair use" defense to the digitization of copyrighted works for the purpose of creating useful indexes. Faced with the likely years-long ordeal that it would take for the courts, the legislature and the treaty-making process to address these issues, it seems like the temptation is to, as a major company's slogan puts it, "just do it." We can do the best we can on the "front end" and then see what aspects, if any, of the system need to be retooled or regulated after the process is up and running. Yet,

---

[16] The US Copyright Act does, however, provide for compulsory "statutory licenses" and a royalty rate setting process with regard to certain types of subject matter, such as "mechanical rights" that pertain to the recording of musical compositions. See e.g., Copyright Royalty Board at http://www.loc.gov/crb/.(last accessed 29 August 2011).

[17] See e.g., discussion of ASCAP and BMI antitrust consent decrees in The History of Broadcast Music Performance Rights at http://www.nrbnlc.com/?page_id=568 (last accessed 29 August 2011).

[18] The Google Books Agreement actually bears some resemblance to this system, although the mechanisms of the class action process might be viewed as "forcing the issue" as to what entities will collectively bargain for the rights holders.

[19] Opinion, at p 46.

unless carefully justified, such an approach might lead to determinations of willfulness (which I am not encouraging) and would not be appropriate if the subject involved matters of public health, environmental concerns, and the like. But in truth, the Google Books Project, and its massive digitization effort, is a "non-destructive" process and, even assuming their "compensation" (if they actually are entitled to any) is somewhat deferred as final judicial resolution of the "fair use" issue is pending, are these authors really being irreparably damaged? There are certainly mechanisms, in US and non-US jurisdictions, that can be employed to modify the system and even secure remedies after its implementation. However, is there true social utility in requiring US rights holders to expend funds and tie up future judicial resources in assessing, monitoring, and perhaps, forcing modifications to the Google indexing terms and practices? If we accept that the indexing portion of the Google Books Project is a unique and highly valuable social resource that should be provided without undue delay, the answer may be a plain (*albeit,* in some circles, very hesitant) "yes." To be clear, I am not suggesting that an "it's here, deal with it" approach is appropriate. Nor am I suggesting that vigorous comment, debate, and objection are not appropriate and constructive. Rather, simply put, there is nothing in the Google indexing project that cannot be undone, remedied, or modified in other judicial, legislative, or international forums.

In rejecting the full text of the Google Books Agreement, with its provisions that go well beyond the "fair use" issue, Judge Chin seems to have acceded to the chorus of objections that Google might well be trying to bully its way into an unwarranted monopoly position.[20] In other words, why does Google get to write the rules, or at least propose and shape them, in conjunction with the other organizations in the suit, simply because Google has broad ambitions, superior resources and, essentially, has blazed a path to a particular US courthouse? This is a serious question. For non-US rights holders affected by the Google Books Agreement, it is likely even more serious and, potentially, aggravating.[21]

As to US rights holders potentially affected by the Google Books Agreement if an appeal or other judicial processes go forward, the US legal system has shown itself to be quite robust and there is no shortage of lawyers who are willing to undertake to raise claims and vindicate rights. Anyone who lives in the US for even a brief time will recognize that the culture is quite litigious and one of its chief literary outputs consists of judicial opinions. Turning again to the history of, for example, ASCAP, we can see that large-scale pools of intellectual property rights are certainly not immune to developing principles of antitrust law and intellectual property law. However, again, is there true social utility in requiring US rights holders to expend funds and tie up future judicial resources in assessing, monitoring and, perhaps, forcing modifications to the Google Books Agreement

---

[20] See e.g., Peritz and Miller 2010; Grimmelmann 2010.

[21] A useful exposition of actual and potential "non-US" objections to the Google Books Agreement can be found in *Objections and Responses to the Google Book Agreement: A Report, Version 2.0, The Public-Interest Book Search Initiative*, New York Law School, May, 2010. Similarly, a helpful discussion is contained in Gervais 2011.

terms and practices? If we accept that the Google Books Project is a unique and highly valuable social resource that should be provided without undue delay, the answer may be a plain (*albeit,* in some circles, very hesitant) "yes." Yet, it is troubling to think that, on any given day, an author can wake up in the US (or outside of the US) to find out that, suddenly, he or she needs a lawyer to fathom the intricacies of a class action judicial proceeding and a proposed settlement agreement that relates directly to the author's rights. The counterargument is of course that a similar process actually does happen every day as cases involving other parties establish principles of fair use, appropriate damages calculations for species of infringement, and other precedents that directly affect that specific author's rights. From this point of view, the class action mechanism is actually more inclusive than routine litigation where in class action procedures attempt to provide notice to a larger number of affected individuals as well as an opportunity to participate in the process or, in the alternative, "opt out."

As to non-US rights holders affected by the Google Books Agreement, the picture is much more complex or, perhaps, much more simple. To the holder of US rights and non-US rights in the same work, the considerations with regard to the Google Books Settlement process and the Google Books Agreement present a host of thorny issues that can impact upon the value of the US rights; on the other hand, as to the non-US rights that may be impacted by the accessability of the Google index or other features in non-US jurisdictions, application of local law will likely cut the Gordian Knot as to whether Google's US actions, and their results, are acceptable in that jurisdiction. To the (inappropriately) light-hearted US intellectual property law practitioners, this development raises opportunities for burning in effigy, like a straw man, one of the currently circulating notions of trans-national intellectual property "progress." For example, the word *de jure* in many international intellectual property law circles seems to be "harmonization." The Google Books Agreement offers an opportunity for a species of "harmony." Why not simply take it? In another context, as defenders of the US patent system's requirements of a duty of candor and disclosure of the inventor's "best mode" are quick to point out when arguing against proposals that the US system be more closely "harmonized" with non-US precepts and processes, "harmonization" is not, by itself, a virtue.[22] The real issues are: (1) What is the nature of the system produced by "harmonization"?; and (2) Does it properly and fairly reflect the principles and serve the interests of each, individual participant? At the very least, we can expect these two questions to be raised whenever the "harmony" offered by the products, if any, of the Google Books Agreement are considered in non-US jurisdictions or the Google Books Agreement is offered as a model for local implementation.

---

[22] On the other hand, in the interest of presenting an "opposing view" in favor of the elimination of the "best mode" requirement and modification of the "duty of candor," see *A Section White Paper: Agenda For 21ˢᵗ Century Patent Reform, The ABA Section of Intellectual Property Law*, available at http://www.americanbar.org/content/dam/aba/migrated/intelprop/home/PatentReformWP.authcheckdam.pdf (last accessed 29 August 2011).

Yet, one of the more perplexing developments in the debate over the Google Books Settlement process is the notion in some circles that the results of a US class action lawsuit, or its settlement terms, can so significantly affect rights in other jurisdictions.[23] The issue of proper notice to non-US holders of US rights is a serious concern, but no more so than any judicial developments in the US that affect property interests in the US. The Google Books Settlement process can only concern itself with US rights that are the appropriate subject matter of the litigation. Moreover, even if the US judicial system ultimately concludes that full text digitization for indexing purposes constitutes "fair use," it is not at all clear that non-US jurisdictions will have to accept that determination with regard to the accessibility of the index in their jurisdiction. Again, the best approach for non-US observers may be to "let Google build it now, with the minimum of required interference, and we can reshape, regulate or even reject it later." Moreover, Google is expending time, effort, and money in developing an undoubtedly valuable resource along with a business model that is, at a minimum, potentially "at risk" in non-US jurisdictions if the details of the Google Books Agreement are presumed to encompass, or even provide a model for, the disposition of works outside of the US court's proper jurisdiction. It would be difficult to argue that the database being constructed by Google is not a tremendously valuable resource and it has been compared, in concept if not scale, to the project that resulted in the ancient Library of Alexandria. Yet, Bill Gates, former CEO of Microsoft, is one of the most qualified individuals to testify on whether non-US adjudicative forums are hesitant to heavily penalize US companies for inappropriate activities on non-US soil and, in some cases, to appropriate and open to local competition the results of the US company's development expenditures and activities.[24] In short, it is unlikely that, even if accepted in the US, the terms of the Google Books Agreement or Google's practices with regard to indexing will be immune from "more localized" scrutiny, adaptation, and even rejection in non-US forums if the results of the Google Books Agreement inappropriately impact local rights.

Before we leave this section, it is worth noting a final point on the notion that the legislative branch, at least in the US, is the more appropriate entity to address the many copyright and other issues raised by the Google Books Project and the Google Books Agreement. On a theoretical level, this proposition is attractive; on a practical level, it is not.

A useful area of focus on the likely inability of a distracted US Congress to timely address the complex issues raised by the Google Books Project and the Google Books Agreement is the proposed "Orphan Works" legislation that seems

---

[23] See references in footnote 15.

[24] ECJ Judgement of 17 September 2007, T-201/04, *"Microsoft Corp. v. Commission of the European Communities"*. EUR 479 million fine imposed on Microsoft, as well as requirement that corrective action be undertaken, for violation of Article 82 EC through abuse of dominant position.

to have languished and floundered through a number of Congressional sessions.[25] In a prior, vigorous and somewhat successful effort by the US to harmonize a portion of its copyright law with non-US precepts, the formality of copyright notice as necessary under US copyright law to preserve copyright rights was abolished.[26] Because the prior law regarding notice could be draconian, this elimination of the notice requirement was a welcome development in preserving the rights of copyright holders who lacked knowledge of copyright formalities and, therefore ran the risk of forfeiting their rights. However, this is where the law of unintended (or incompletely considered) consequences "kicked in." As for example, producers and distributors of documentary films can readily attest, the difficulties, expense and risks that can arise in identifying and locating the owners (if any) of rights in works that lack notice, have adversely impacted other creative individuals who wish to determine whether those works are in the public domain or, alternatively, can be licensed.[27] Similar difficulties arise with regard to the species of Orphan Works that have a copyright notice, but contact information for that individual or entity (or successor rightsholders) is not readily available or is not available at all. In a typical circumstance illustrating this point, works of historical significance, such as photographs, may be omitted from a documentary simply because no one can determine whether the works can be used without the risk of a lawsuit. (If at this point you are thinking "fair use," also think "uncertainty," "delay", and "expense.") Yet, the producers of documentaries, and the public that benefits from them, apparently must wait until Congressional relief is provided. This wait has already been a long one. Surely, these documentary film producers must look with envy upon the portions of the Google Books Agreement's "Safe Harbor" provision that addresses such concerns through a proposed rights-owner identification process and a limitation of liability.[28]

Operators of Internet services that receive qualified shelter and limited immunities from the "notice and takedown" procedures in the Digital Millennium Copyright Act[29] also frequently use those procedures to address third-party claims of trademark infringement, defamation and other species of torts that are outside the scope of the DMCA. At least, use of such procedures might provide a basis for a judicial finding of "due diligence" that can limit damages or obviate a claim of "willfulness." In other words, the US Congress has given us a "safe harbor" model for use in the US copyright context; many online service providers have resorted to the model in other contexts in the hope that adherence to its terms in non-copyright contexts might provide some benefit and evidence of "good faith"

---

[25] For an excellent summary of "Orphan Works" issues, see Peters 2008.

[26] See US Copyright Office Circular 3, Copyright Notice, available at http://www.copyright.gov/circs/circ03.pdf. (last accessed 29 August 2011).

[27] Aufderheide and Jaszi 2005.

[28] See Google Books Agreement, Sect. 3.2(d)(v)(3). Although the terms of the Google Books Agreement Safe Harbor may not be readily adaptable to the needs of filmmakers, the point is that, at least with regard to books, someone is trying to establish a workable mechanism.

[29] See 17 U.S.C. § 512.

and "due diligence." Similarly, now that the parties to the *Google* litigation have provided their version of a system to address Orphan Works issues, we might be able to point to it, in its present form or in a form that results from further industry comment and/or endorsement, as a good model to adopt to demonstrate good faith and, perhaps, ultimately, fair use or copyright abandonment. Again, "win, lose or draw," we owe the *Google* parties a bit of thanks for "putting the issues on the table" and trying to offer solutions. Hopefully, even if the *Google* litigation ultimately "sputters out," the numerous academics, industry groups, and government entities that have taken the time to comment on the Google Books Agreement will direct their attention to resolving the many issues it legitimately tried to raise and address.

8.4 Digital Book Content Presentation: Opening the Gate for a "Trojan Horse" or "Looking a Gift Horse in the Mouth"?

As noted earlier in this discussion, irrespective of the fates of the Google Books Project and the Google Books Agreement, they have served as useful "lightning rods" for a number of general issues that relate to the digital archiving, indexing, and distribution of copyrighted works. Yet the chief focus in the many comments on the process has been on the core issues of whether or not the class action process and the mechanisms for the creation of the digital archive itself are appropriate. Nonetheless, the issue of what actually appears on the screen in a digital content distribution process is a concern that touches upon the actual operation of the system and has, therefore, been a "less immediate" concern in the bulk of the comments, proposals, and counterproposals that comprise the "*Google* litigation literature." Yet, from authors' and system users' point of view, this can be a "first level" concern.

The following excerpt from the Google Books Agreement contains a restriction on the use of advertising content within the Google Books Project:

Advertising Content. Google may not place on, behind or over the contents of a Book or portion thereof (including on Preview Use pages or Snippet Display pages), as displayed to a user, any pop-up, popunder, or any other types of advertisements or content of any kind. In addition to a Rightsholder's right to exclude one or more of his, her or its Books from Advertising Uses pursuant to Section 3.5(b)(i) (Right to Exclude), the Unclaimed Works Fiduciary may exclude from Advertising Uses one or more unclaimed Books if Google displays animated, audio or video advertisements in conjunction with those Books and the Registry determines that exclusion from such Advertising Uses is in the best interests of Rightsholders of such unclaimed Books.[30]

---

[30] See Google Books Agreement, Section 3.10, Specific Prohibitions, for this provision and related provisions.

It is not the intention of this discussion to speculate on the scope and effect of the above-cited restriction or how it or the related provisions in the Google Books Agreement will be implemented if the system provided for in the Google Books Agreement is adopted via judicial or private arrangements similar to ASCAP or The Harry Fox Agency. Nonetheless, the inclusion of the term in the Google Books Agreement is indicative of a concern that authors will likely have whether they are included or not included in the arrangement described in the Google Books Agreement or in any process involving the digital distribution of their works.

When digital content is searched for and presented via a computer, an electronic book display device or similar technology, random advertising, behavioral advertising, demographic data collection, and other factors of potential concern to the user come into play.[31] Yet, the creators of the content to be displayed also may or may not have concerns about how, and with what other content, their works will be displayed. For example, teleplay writers for US network television shows must generally accept the fact that, to some degree, the resulting television programs will be "chopped up," framed, and otherwise overlaid and manipulated to accommodate advertisements. Put simply, this is the culture of the medium. On the other hand, such practices would not be expected in a Broadway theater or in a hard copy of even a William Burroughs "cut up" novel. In short, the question is whether authors of digitized books will now be placed in a position that more closely resembles the position of the teleplay writer. If this issue is left unaddressed by specific licensing language or otherwise left unattended, the answer, at least in the US, may now, or in the future, be "yes."

The premise, as described in an earlier section of this discussion, is that sooner or later (likely sooner or even now) we will have the system or a system fundamentally similar to at least several key features inherent in the Google Books Project or proposed in the Google Books Agreement. Whether or not Google wins the race to be the first provider of such a system is not necessarily a core concern. On the other hand, how and with what other materials the system presents the contents, is in light of the current "Wild West" advertising-driven state of the Internet, a potentially significant concern, especially to: (1) authors who want more control over how and with what other content their works (or excerpts for them) are presented; and (2) users who are still waiting for some workable, voluntary, or imposed, rational set of practices with regard to advertising associated with searches, sites, and other features of the Internet. In this context, significant questions arise as to who (if anyone) will address these concerns and who is qualified to address them. As noted earlier, most of the attention to the Google Books Agreement terms and the Google Books Settlement process focuses on core "first generation" issues as to the general character and internal operations of the

---

[31] See e.g., U.S. Federal Trade Commission, *Protecting Consumer Privacy in an Era of Rapid Change: A Proposed Framework for Businesses and Policymakers, Preliminary FTC Staff Report* (Dec. 1, 2010), available at http://www.ftc.gov/os/2010/12/101201privacyreport.pdf (last accessed 29 August 2011).

overall system. This is reasonable and appropriate. However, there are presently, or will likely be in the future, a series of "second generation" issues as to content presentation. These issues are, however, not confined to the Google Books Project, but, rather, affect digital book publishing in general.

As indicated above, each industry has its own culture, present issues, and business customs. This can have significant legal effects, including whether a particular business or industry organization is competent to anticipate, recognize, and properly frame issues that are not within its common activities or experiences. For example, because publishers of printed media did not have the experiences of the music, film, and television industries with regard to multiple means of content delivery, many book publishers were a bit "late to the game" in adopting license documents that covered digital media rights. On a less grand scale, it is almost impossible to read the arguments and opinion in the British *Apple Corps. v. Apple Computer*[32] case without suspecting that one of the parties who focused on current forms of recorded music simply did not fully appreciate the nature and pace of developments in the software and digital equipment industries and their implications with regard to radical changes in the recorded music industry. In other words, it is easy to overlook that which you believe you have no reason to see. It is not surprising therefore that questions have been raised regarding the ability of the class representatives in the *Google* case, and even the classes themselves, to anticipate and adequately address the broad range of issues concerning the Google Books Project and the Google Books Agreement. For example, one author has seriously questioned the ability of the Authors Guild, at least in its present posture, to properly represent academic writers as opposed to writers of fiction or mass market works.[33] So, who is going to fully appreciate and address circumstances where digitized books can be interspersed with third-party advertising content, obscured for a length of time by pop-up type advertising or placed in juxtaposition to advertising content that is an anathema to the authors of particular books? Is there, perhaps to a lesser extent, a similar set of concerns for book excerpts and indexing "snippets"? Do we care or should we? Clearly, this issue was significant enough for the representatives of authors in the Google Books Settlement process to consider and address. It will not "go away" if their efforts to obtain a judicial "imprimatur" on their approach fails.

Although not on the grand scale of many of the points raised by the Google Books Project, the Google Books Agreement and the Google Books Settlement process, it is interesting to wonder how authors who are unprotected by advertising restrictions will react to having their works placed in a context where positioning advertisements next to content, or even within content, is now, or likely will be, an attractive practice to operators of digital publishing and search technologies. As the current US book publishing industry operates, it would be a surprise to

---

[32] *"Apple Corps Ltd. v Apple Computer, Inc"* [2006] EWHC 996 (Ch) (08 May 2006), available at http://www.bailii.org/ew/cases/EWHC/Ch/2006/996.html. (last accessed 29 August 2011).
[33] Samuelson 2010.

purchase a hard copy, audio recording, or digital download of a Stephen King book and find its covers or contents blatantly cluttered with advertisements for unrelated products, services, and political causes. As it currently operates, this is not expected in the US book publishing industry. Yet, although the public, including authors, might be (unhappily) used to such intrusions into television programming, magazine articles, and newspaper articles, it is useful for authors of books to regard the Internet developments noted in the introduction to this discussion as a "cautionary tale" with respect to the development of any digital content location or distribution system. So too, in an era where a one-hour US television program generally consists of approximately 40 minutes of content interspersed with approximately 20 minutes of commercials, often in excruciatingly long blocks, the "piling on" of advertising in a "free for all" and consumer-alienating manner, should not be a surprising development in any US digital content distribution model. In short, for authors and publishers who "buy into" third-party digital display processes for content, it is not untoward to consider, and ask questions about how and with what third-party content the work will be displayed. To perhaps a lesser degree, authors whose works are excerpted or listed for indexing purposes may have similar questions and concerns.

As demonstrated in the case of *Gilliam v. American Broadcasting Co.*,[34] the exceptionally "severe editing" of a television program, may, if not expressly contemplated in the scriptwriter's agreement, violate the underlying copyright in the script. *Gilliam* dealt with an actual editing out of critical materials and truncation of the program, in part to make room for advertising content. This unauthorized and radical removal of copyrighted content is an unlikely scenario in the context of the Google Books Agreement or any other legitimate digital book display and distribution system. Moreover, there was a "gap" in the licensing process under consideration in the "*Gilliam*" case. The point is, even with the "*Gilliam*" precedent, under current Internet advertising practices, it should not be too much of a surprise to authors whose works are distributed digitally if advertising-related images, text, and even audio-visual content are inserted by the system to, depending on your point of view, "break up" or "enhance" the reading experience with advertisements. For example, if author James Patterson writes a passage about a car crash, does the operator of the digital channel of distribution get to insert into the margin an advertisement for automobile insurance or funeral home services? Would the author of a religious work feel comfortable having his or her text presented along with images or advertisements for products and services that do not comport with or may even contradict the principles set forth in the text. At the very least, unless authors simply do not care about or are willing to accept the prospect of such scenarios, we can expect, at least in the context of

---

[34] 538 F.2d 14 (2nd Cir. 1976). In an interesting and somewhat characteristically US approach, the Court rejected a general moral rights principle, but included contract interpretations and contract-related presumptions to decide the issue in the writers' favor.

works still under copyright, to see licensing concerns more frequently raised with regard to such issues.

The appropriately limited use of third-party content for the process of displaying search results or performing a linking function is generally not, under the current US approach, considered to be an infringement of copyright.[35] However, the leading cases are not analogous to the circumstances that may arise when advertising content is placed in or near to an author's full or excerpted work solely for advertising purposes, particularly if the advertising or its manner of presentation is reasonably objectionable to the author. So, it is possible that the fair use analysis and other principles usually relied on in the general trend of framing and other content-presentation fair use cases might not prevail. Alternatively, a determination may be made that the scope of a license was exceeded by subjecting the author to such advertising practices. Other theories, such as unfair competition, rights of publicity, and various types of torts might also be "thrown into the mix" with varying prospects for success. The key point is that the ability to freely place all types of advertisements in, or perhaps even in proximity to, an author's work should not be lightly assumed. On the other hand, authors (particularly in the US) should also not lightly assume that they retain control in such situations if the issue is left untreated in their agreements. In the past, especially in the hard copy book publishing industry, certain norms with regard to whether or not the publisher would place unrelated content on or in the book might have operated to prevent such "intrusions." Especially in light of the waves of advertising practices that have enveloped the Internet, we should not assume that the norm of hard copy book publishing will survive, currently or in the future, the migration into the digital distribution industry. As the Google Books Settlement process indicates, the migration and survival of such norms are best assured through recognition of the risk in the digital distribution environment and inclusion of "preemptive" terms to preclude or regulate forms of advertising and other types of third-party content.

In another context, the model and film actress Bettie Page unsuccessfully attempted, under a rights of publicity theory, to prevent the use of her image to advertise the full catalog of a videocassette seller called (unfortunately) Something Weird Video ("SWV").[36] Although her name and the image in the advertisement appeared on the cover of a videocassette recording of films in which she appeared, Page argued that SWV was exploiting Page's image to promote itself and advertise the availability of unrelated, third-party videos. According to the Court, however, the First Amendment protected SWV's use to promote itself and its wares, which legitimately included the videocassette recording of the Page films, especially

---

[35] See *"Kelly v. Arriba Soft Corp."*, 336 F.3d 811 (9th Cir. 2003) (search engine display of "thumbnail" images of third-party works); *"Perfect 10, Inc. v. Amazon.com, Inc."*, 508 F.3d 1146 (9th Cir. 2007) (framing and hyperlinking in the process of performing a search). Of course, if the display inappropriately suggests that the creator of the displayed content endorses or is affiliated with the entity providing the display, other potential causes of actions may arise.

[36] *"Page v. Something Weird Video"*, 960 F.Supp. 1438 (C.D. Cal. 1996).

because SWV did not falsely claim that Page endorsed SWV. Although the *"Page"* case involves a unique set of facts, and some would argue a unique jurisdiction (California), the underlying principles in the *"Page"* case may have applicability where an author's work is placed or listed in a set of recommendations for works that are, in the judgment of the distributor, similar with regard to topic, style, or some other characteristic. In short, depending on the facts of the case, the right of publicity might not provide full protection or any protection at all where an individual's name, image, or work is placed in proximity to advertisements for third-party products or services.

Again, reference to another industry that has some relevant experience might be useful. Provided that they have sufficient "leverage," composers and songwriters may require, in the context of synchronization rights, that their compositions not be associated with images or activities that the composer or songwriter finds unacceptable. Performers may also have similar concerns with regard to their recorded performances. For example, artists such as Tom Waits and Bruce Springsteen are notoriously selective about the context in which their work is presented and have turned down lucrative offers to use their songs in particular advertisements. Yet, it would beg credulity to suggest that those artists would be successful in trying to control the nature and content of the advertising on radio stations that play their music even if such control was, as a practical matter, possible. In a similar vein, it is unclear whether authors, Google, or anyone else can really monitor and fully control the advertising content that presently or in the future may flare across our computer screens, e-book readers, and similar devices. Yet, the Google Books Agreement indicates that the system, if sufficiently "closed," is capable of being regulated with regard to forms and content of advertising.

In the film industry, motion pictures are (except for the pre-show previews and advertisements) shown in theaters or on certain cable channels without being "encumbered" by advertisements, but are then treated as any other content when shown on network television. Expect advertisements—lots of them. Perhaps we will see the evolution of a multifaceted digital content delivery system where the amount you pay for a particular digital text, or whether you pay at all, will depend on how much advertising content you can tolerate or ignore. There are likely authors who would find such a multitiered digital book distribution system attractive or, at least, inoffensive. Other authors who are more comfortable with the current conventions of the hard copy book publication industry, or who simply do not want their works freighted with advertisements for third-party products and services, might envision such a multitiered digital distribution system as only feasible in their nightmares.

In conclusion, the Google Books Project, the Google Books Agreement, and the Google Books Settlement process have brought us to a crossroads, or perhaps a precipice, with respect to some core copyright issues and models for content distribution. On the other hand, one of the less apparent issues relates to how advertising content will shape our experience of digital literature. Unless an author or the author's representative is sensitive to this issue, it may simply be passed over in the "rush" of negotiations or (properly or improperly) left to market forces and developing conventions in the industry. As long as we are considering large-scale issues concerning book digitization and digital text presentation, it is interesting to wonder how most authors feel about the placement of advertising content in or in proximity to their works and how such issues will be addressed, if at all, in the interpretation of licenses, litigation, legislative proceedings, agency regulations, or through other means. The Google Books Agreement presents, at least, a proposed method to address this concern and it is worth keeping this concern in mind irrespective of the fates of the Google Books Project and the Google Books Agreement.

References

Aufderheide P, Jaszi P (2005) Untold stories: Creative consequences of the rights clearance culture for documentary Filmmakers. Center for Social Media, available at http://www.acsil.org/resources/rights-clearances-1/nps240.tmp.pdf

Elhauge E (2010) The Google books agreement is procompetitive. J Leg Anal 2(1):

Gervais D (2011) The Google books agreement and the TRIPS Agreement. Stan. Tech. L. Rev. 1, available at http://stlr.stanford.edu/pdf/gervais-google-books-and-trips.pdf

Grimmelmann J (2010) The amended google books settlement is still exclusive. New York Law School Legal Studies, Research Paper Series 09/10#25, available at http://ssm.com/abstract=1560242

Peritz R, Miller M (2010) An introduction to competition concerns in the Google Books Settlement. New York Law School Legal Studies, Research Paper Series 09/10#23, available at http://ssrn.com/abstract=1564363

Peters M (2008) The importance of orphan works legislation. register of Copyrights (September 25, 2008), available at http://www.copyright.gov/orphan/

Samuelson P (2010) Academic author objections to the Google book search settlement. J Telecommun High Technol Law, Forthcoming, available at SSRN: http://ssrn.com/abstract=1553894

Chapter 9
Google Chrome and Android: Legal Aspects of Open Source Software

Malcolm Bain

Contents

9.1 Introduction

On 12 August 2010, Oracle America Inc., a subsidiary of Oracle Inc. formerly known as Sun Microsystems Inc., filed a complaint against Google Inc. for patent and copyright infringement through Google's development of the Android mobile operating system.[1] Oracle seeks an injunction restraining Google from engaging in further infringements and damages. Google's defense, submitted on 4 October 2010, has been that the Oracle America's claim should be dismissed as baseless.[2]

---

[1] Documents relating to the *"Oracle America Inc. v. Google Inc."* case are available at http://www.groklaw.net/staticpages/index.php?page=OracleGoogle (last accessed 15 February, 2011).
[2] Available at http://groklaw.net/pdf2/OraGoogle-32.pdf (last accessed 15 February, 2011).

M. Bain (✉)
id law partners, Barcelona, Spain
e-mail: malcolm.bain@id-lawpartners.com

A. Lopez-Tarruella (ed.), *Google and the Law*,
Information Technology and Law Series 22, DOI: 10.1007/978-90-6704-846-0_9,
© T.M.C. ASSER PRESS, The Hague, The Netherlands, and the author(s) 2012

Google claims that it does not infringe any Oracle patents, and that the copyright claim is legally deficient as it does not sufficiently specify the infringement.[3] At the heart of Google's defense is its claim that Android was independently developed, except for a subset of (open source) Apache Harmony libraries: *"Other than the Harmony libraries, the Android platform, including, without limitation, the Dalvik VM, was independently developed by the OHA [Open Handset Alliance]."*[4] Google implemented its own Virtual Machine, Dalvik, as part of Android, purposely avoiding the Oracle Java Virtual Machine.

At the heart of this matter is Java, a programming language specified and created originally by Sun Microsystems and now frequently used in the development and running of many computer programs on diverse platforms. A key component of Java is a piece of software called the Java Virtual Machine. This case deals with one flavor of Java: Java ME (Java Micro Edition: a version designed for embedded and mobile applications), as the claims made by Oracle America relate primarily to Google's development of Android, an operating system for mobile devices and smart phones.

Java technologies are now basically "open source", as Sun Microsystems Inc. freed most of the Java platform technologies under free and open source software ("FOSS") licenses in 2007, before being purchased by Oracle Inc.. However, not all components are offered under the same license. In addition, Android itself is distributed under a FOSS license, the Apache Software License. So an interesting question arising in the context of this case is: if Java is freed under an open source license that allows third parties to use and redistribute the technology, on what basis would Oracle be suing Google for using it in Android?

Free and Open Source Software is increasingly present and relevant in the so-called "information society", not only constituting the backbone of the Internet (in the web servers which often run on GNU/Linux and the Apache Webserver, and the BIND internet domain name addressing system) and enterprise information processing systems, but also becoming a serious option for desktops, both at home and in business. In this chapter, we look at Google's use of FOSS and its involvement in the FOSS community, and how it leverages FOSS for the provision of its services and fulfilling its business strategy. We first give an overview of the legal aspects of free and open source software and FOSS licensing, illustrated by some interesting Google projects such as Android, Chromium and WebM, before looking at some legal questions emerging from the *"Oracle America Inc. v. Google Inc."* case.

---

[3] Since then, Oracle has provided further specifics, on 27th October 2010 (available at http://groklaw.net/pdf2/OraGoogle-36.pdf, last accessed 15 February, 2011).

[4] Paragraph 13, Google Defense. *See* Open Handset Alliance, http://www.openhandsetalliance.com/index.html, Alliance Overview, http://www.openhandsetalliance.com/oha_overview.html (last accessed 15 February, 2011).

9.2   Please Use My Software, Its Free (As in Freedom)

Free and open source software is software distributed under a free and open source license. This seems obvious, but it is important to highlight the fact that it is not the software itself but the licensing regime and rights attached to the software that are different from what is referred to as "proprietary software" (software licensed under a more traditional restrictive licensing regime).

9.2.1   The Legal Regulation of Software: All Rights Reserved

Software generally falls under the legal protection of copyright law, while patent rights may also cover software products and processes in certain jurisdictions, notably the USA. A brief explanation of the objectives and mechanics of copyright (and patent rights) help us understand those of free software.

Copyright or "author's rights" (*droits d'auteur*) grants the original author of a creative work and successive rights holders an exclusive right for the term of copyright to exploit the work or to authorize its exploitation—more specifically, its reproduction (copying), transformation (modifying or adapting) and distribution (both in physical and digital form).[5] Thus the rights holder has a monopoly in relation to the use of the work: without authorization, except in certain determined circumstances, a third party may not use it or he or she will be liable for copyright infringement.

Patent rights, while intrinsically different from copyright and often confused with it under the single title of "Intellectual Property Rights,"[6] protect what are known as "inventions", and operate in a somewhat similar manner: patent protection grants the inventor (and successive rights holders) a right to prevent others using his or her invention, i.e. from making, using, selling, offering for sale or importing the patented invention, for the term of the patent. Patent rights are exclusionary, i.e. a right to exclude others from using, making or selling a product or process embodying the invention, as opposed to the author's right or copyright which is exclusive.

These legal regimes are by nature restrictive. The basic purpose of the legal protection is to grant rights holders these monopolies over the exploitation of the work or invention so that they can authorize such exploitation in return for monetary

---

[5] These are the exclusive rights set out in the European legal framework under the Directive 2009/24 on the protection of computer programs (former Directive 91/250/EEC). Matching, though not necessarily the same rights, is listed in the US Copyright Act and in other jurisdictions, under the Berne Convention and WIPO Copyright Treaty 1996. In continental European jurisdictions, the legal regime for authors' rights grants certain moral rights to authors of works, including arguably software, for example rights to be recognised and attributed as author and to protect the integrity of the work.

[6] Commented in Stallman 2004b.

compensation. This financial incentive should, theoretically, lead authors and inventors to create further works or make further inventions, and enable editors and publishers to promote such works, thus contributing to enriching culture and society.[7] This system has been leveraged very successfully by software publishers such as Microsoft, Oracle, SAP, Adobe, Apple and numerous other software developers who license their software to users in return for license fees that can be either one-off (often for end-user licenses) or recurring. Proprietary licensors have used several mechanisms for determining the fees to be paid, whether per installation, per number of end-users, per CPU,[8] per quantity of data processed, etc.

License fees are not the only thing. These "proprietary" software licenses tend to be restrictive too: they grant users the minimum rights necessary for them to be able to take advantage of the functionalities of the software. Specifically, traditional software licenses do not grant any rights to reproduce or copy the software (other than internally or for back up purposes) and even less so to redistribute it. Redistribution would kill the business model, as it would enable third parties to have another (exact) copy of the software without paying license fees to the rights holder.

> Subject to Section 2(b), you may install and use the Software on a single computer; OR install and store the Software on a storage device, such as a network server, used only to install the Software on your other computers over an internal network, provided you have a license for each separate computer on which the Software is installed and run. Except as otherwise specifically provided in Section 2(b), a license for the Software may not be shared, installed or used concurrently on different computers....
> (Adobe® MACROMEDIA SOFTWARE END-USER LICENSE AGREEMENT)[9]

9.2.2 Free Software Licensing: Some Rights Reserved

Free software licensing turns this system on its head: instead of restricting users' rights to a limited set of "mere use" rights set out in the license, a free or open source software or "FOSS" license grants wide rights to exploit the work in question without requiring further authorization from the rights holder. Particularly, a FOSS license grants the rights of reproduction, transformation, distribution and public communication, often only subject to minimum conditions of attribution and liability disclaimer.

---

[7] Article I, Section 8, Clause 8 of the United States Constitution, known as the Copyright Clause, gives a rationale for this: "*To promote the Progress of Science and useful Arts, by securing for limited Times to Authors and Inventors the exclusive Right to their respective Writings and Discoveries*". For a review of an interesting old case in this respect, see Mitchell, 2009.

[8] *Central Processing Unit*, the portion of a computer system that carries out the instructions of a computer program and a means for measuring how much use is made of software.

[9] Available at http://www.adobe.com/products/eula/tools/ (last accessed 15 February 2011).

Permission is hereby granted, free of charge, to any person obtaining a copy of this software and associated documentation files (the "Software"), to deal in the Software without restriction, including without limitation the rights to use, copy, modify, merge, publish, distribute, sublicense, and/or sell copies of the Software, and to permit persons to whom the Software is furnished to do so, subject to the following conditions: [attribution] [disclaimer]....

("MIT" license[10]).

Thus the free software license, a "patch" on the legal framework, removes the basic limitations of copyright on third party users (and accessorily, though increasingly now expressly, patent rights) and permits rather than restricts. In particular, it permits the software to be used, studied, copied, modified and redistributed (in modified or unmodified form), without restriction or with minimal restrictions.

In an oft quoted essay, Richard Stallman considered the founder of the free software movement, explained the basic tenets of this movement and established the definition of *Free Software*[11]:

Free software is a matter of the users' freedom to run, copy, distribute, study, change and improve the software. More precisely, it means that the program's users have the four essential freedoms:

* The freedom to run the program, for any purpose (freedom 0).

* The freedom to study how the program works, and change it to make it do what you wish (freedom 1). Access to the source code is a precondition for this.

* The freedom to redistribute copies so you can help your neighbor (freedom 2).

* The freedom to distribute copies of your modified versions to others (freedom 3). By doing this you can give the whole community a chance to benefit from your changes. Access to the source code is a precondition for this.

The objectives of free software licensing match those of the legal copyright and patent regime: to promote the creation and distribution of works (not just software, as free licenses can and do also apply to other works such as texts, photographs, video or music). Thus while sharing the same objective, the *"promotion of the progress of science and useful arts"*, advocates of free software take the opposite view from the drafters of laws and believe that freedom rather than monopoly promotes creativity. As the Free Software Foundation states: *Free software is a matter of freedom: people should be free to use software in all the ways that are socially useful.*[12]

This is not to say that free software is "against" or contrary to the established legal regime: on the contrary, free software licenses are based in copyright and grant users wide rights to use the work on the basis of the current copyright regime (that initially gives the rights holders the exclusive right to grant such

---

[10] Available at http://www.opensource.org/licenses/mit-license.php (last accessed 15 February 2011).

[11] Stallman 1996a.

[12] Free Software Foundation 1996.

permissions). Violating the terms of a free software license entails a breach of copyright.[13]

"Open Source" software is software distributed under a license that complies with the Open Source Initiative's "Open Source Definition",[14] adapted from the Debian Free Software Guidelines. These criteria, including free distribution, access to source code, rights to make derivative works, nondiscrimination as to use and users, etc., establish the same basic principles (from a purely legal perspective) as those underpinning free software stated above. The definition states:

OSS licenses must meet 10 criteria so as to be considered open source:

1. **Free Redistribution**: The license shall not restrict any party from selling or giving away the software as a component of an aggregate software distribution containing programs from several different sources. The license shall not require a royalty or other fee for such sale.

2. **Source Code**: The program must include source code, and must allow distribution in source code as well as compiled form. Where some form of a product is not distributed with source code, there must be a well-publicized means of obtaining the source code for no more than a reasonable reproduction cost preferably, downloading via the Internet without charge. The source code must be the preferred form in which a programmer would modify the program. Deliberately obfuscated source code is not allowed. Intermediate forms such as the output of a preprocessor or translator are not allowed.

3. **Derived Works**: The license must allow modifications and derived works, and must allow them to be distributed under the same terms as the license of the original software.

4. **Integrity of the Author's Source Code**: The license may restrict source-code from being distributed in modified form only if the license allows the distribution of "patch files" with the source code for the purpose of modifying the program at build time. The license must explicitly permit distribution of software built from modified source code. The license may require derived works to carry a different name or version number from the original software.

5. **No Discrimination against Persons or Groups**: The license must not discriminate against any person or group of persons.

6. **No Discrimination against Fields of Endeavor**: The license must not restrict anyone from making use of the program in a specific field of endeavor. For example, it may not restrict the program from being used in a business, or from being used for genetic research.

7. **Distribution of License**: The rights attached to the program must apply to all to whom the program is redistributed without the need for execution of an additional license by those parties.

8. **License Must Not Be Specific to a Product**: The rights attached to the program must not depend on the program's being part of a particular software distribution. If the program is extracted from that distribution and used or distributed within the terms of the program's license, all parties to whom the program is redistributed should have the

---

[13] "*Jacobsen v. Katzer*", 535 F.3d 1373 (Fed. Cir. 2008), District Court of Munich, 19 May 2004, Case No. 21 O 6123/04 ("*Welte v. Sitecom Deutschland GmbH*"), District Court of Frankfurt, Docket Number 2-6 0 224/06. See Jaeger 2010; Jaeger and Gebert 2009 and Rosen 2009.

[14] Available at http://www.opensource.org/osd.html (last accessed 15 February 2011).

same rights as those that are granted in conjunction with the original software distribution.

9. **License Must Not Restrict Other Software**: The license must not place restrictions on other software that is distributed along with the licensed software. For example, the license must not insist that all other programs distributed on the same medium must be open-source software.

10. **License Must Be Technology-Neutral**: No provision of the license may be predicated on any individual technology or style of interface

So while the concept of *Open Source* software may differ from *Free Software* in political, ethical or organizational terms,[15] their basic legal premises—the granting of wide non-discriminatory rights to exploit software under minimal conditions—are the same, and in this chapter we will refer to both as *Free and Open Source Software*, or "FOSS".

Well-known examples of free software include the GNU/Linux operating system (in a variety of versions or "distributions", such as Red Hat, Fedora, Ubuntu, Knoppix, Gentoo), Mozilla Foundation's Firefox browser and Thunderbird email client, the Apache web server, OpenOffice.org and LibreOffice office tool suites, Google's Chromium and Android and a very long list of "etc." The principal online site hosting free software applications, Sourceforge.net, now lists more than 260,000 projects,[16] and this is only one repository of many, including Freshmeat, Github, and Google's own "code.google.com" project hosting site.[17]

What does this have to do with Google? Google uses a lot of FOSS, which has given it a high level of autonomy over its technology platform, something essential for hugely scaled systems such as Google's search platform.[18]

What are the most important open-source projects you ingest?
    The kernel, compilers–GCC, the Python interpreter. Python is very important to us. Google App Engine–it's a Python hosting system, basically. Java is very important to us, and that's become open-source now. We have some very good Java people working for us—Josh Block, Neil Gafter—they've got a great handle on that technology.
    Once you get past those three projects–the compilers, the languages, the kernel–then you go to the libraries. For us that's OpenSSL, zlib, PCRE. MySQL is hugely important to us. Past that, it starts tapering off pretty quick.[19]

Google also distributes under FOSS licenses a lot of the software it has created or contributed to, including Android, Chrome/Chromium, WebM and a series of other projects.[20]

---

[15] For the FSF's view, see Stallman 2007.

[16] Available at http://sourceforge.net/about (last accessed 15 February 2011).

[17] Code.google.com allegedly hosts more than 250,000 FOSS projects.

[18] Information technology autonomy is often argued for by Prof. Eben Moglen, Director of the Software Freedom Law Center.

[19] Chris DiBona, Google Open Source Program Manager in "*Q&A: Google's open-source balancing act*", CNET, 28 May, 2008. Shankland 2008b.

[20] A search for Google-led projects on the code.google repository http://code.google.com/hosting/search?q=label:Google provides 1063 answers (last accessed 15 February 2011). See also comment at Asay 2009b.

Android is a prime example of FOSS in which Google is involved. Android is a mobile operating system (or even a mobile Linux desktop) initially developed by Android Inc. (bought by Google in 2005) and now developed by Google and other members of the Open Handset Alliance (OHA), one of whose goals is to develop open standards for mobile devices.[21] Android is based upon a modified version of the Linux kernel, and includes the Dalvik virtual machine that is subject of the Oracle America claim. Version 1 of Android was first launched in September 2008, with further development leading up to the latest release, version 2.3 or "Gingerbread", in December 2010, and its success is such that it is said to have overtaken Blackberry in overall mobile operating system market share, and also Nokia's Symbian.[22] A key factor of this success, apart from support by the members of the OHA who include major players in the mobile market, is the open source nature of the program—which the OHA argues enables faster and greater innovation across the industry, and the ability to create many types of applications (delivered via Android online markets).

Chromium is another Google open source project, with its sister project Chrome. Chromium is an open source web browser project launched in 2008 and acquiring together with Chromium, by end of 2010, around 10% of browser usage.[23] Chromium is licensed under the BSD license,[24] a permissive FOSS license. Google Chrome includes this code and adds certain closed-source packages, such as Adobe Flash player, an auto-updater and other code, including for example support for "proprietary" media codecs such H.264 and AAC.[25]

The impact of FOSS licenses at a legal and practical level (regarding the use, development and integration of FOSS) is important. The direct consequence of using FOSS, and exercising the rights granted under the license, includes the ability to download and copy the program freely (usually from the Internet, for free); install, test and evaluate the software; modify it to suit different needs (or hire a developer/consultant to do so); implement the software in business (in as many machines or devices as necessary) and update it as new versions are released; and redistribute it (online or on a CD/DVD, etc.) so that others can also benefit from it and from any change or improvement which has been made.

---

[21] OHA press release: *Industry Leaders Announce Open Platform for Mobile Devices*, 5th November 2007, available at http://www.openhandsetalliance.com/press_110507.html (last accessed 15 February 2011).

[22] For statistics, see http://www.netmarketshare.com/operating-system-market-share.aspx?qprid=9&qpcustom=iOS,Android&sample=45; Reuters: *Google topples Nokia from smartphones top spot*, available at http://uk.reuters.com/article/2011/01/31/oukin-uk-google-nokia-idUKTRE70U1YT20110131 (last accessed 15 February 2011).

[23] See http://en.wikipedia.org/wiki/Usage_share_of_web_browsers (last accessed 15 February 2011).

[24] See http://code.google.com/chromium/terms.html (last accessed 15 February 2011).

[25] It also adds the Google bar, which collects keystroke data and provides significant behavioral data to Google, useful for behavioral targeting, an arrow in Google's quiver of advertising offerings (and which raises certain privacy concerns).

And here's the great thing about not running on Windows. If you want to change your operating system and you're using Linux, well, you can just do it. But imagine if we had to tell people with whom we're competing and who don't like us very much how many machines we were using, and how much we were using them, well... the thing is with open source and with Linux, we can control our own destiny. It's a very powerful position to be in.

We've never said how many machines we have, there are estimates out there but I'm not going to say if they're right or not, but you know, think of a big number, a big number, and then multiply that by $1,000 (£526) each for a copy of Windows Server. It's safe to say it would be hundreds of millions of dollars at least.[26]

For developers, this freedom has led to a new model or paradigm for distributed, Internet-enabled collaboration to develop software, creating what Yochai Benkler has called a *"quintessential instance of commons-based peer production"*[27] This has inspired other sectors of creativity, notably in the literature, music and audiovisual works, distributing these under "free content licenses", in particular the Creative Commons set of (free and non-free) licenses, which allow authors to select the degree of licensing freedom and type of sharing of their works.[28]

These rights, as you can imagine, have a significant impact in the uptake or "adoption" of FOSS, both by organizations and private users. Firefox 3, for example, had more than 8 million unique downloads the day it was released.[29] Google Chrome and Chromium have around 10% of browser usage after just 2 years of publication (in a market with a dominant software program such as Internet Explorer, Firefox, Safari and Opera as significant alternatives),[30] and the Apache web server held in December 2010 just under 60% percent of the web server market share.[31]

The impact of FOSS is significantly different from proprietary software, and not just on pricing. A comparison between the licensing and use of Microsoft Office suite and OpenOffice.org or LibreOffice is an easy example. While take-up or

---

[26] Chris DiBona, Google Open Source Program Manager, *Giving Google a licence to code*, The Guardian, November 2nd, 2006; Arthur 2006.

[27] Benkler 2006, p 63. Collaborative development models are also described in various articles in DiBona et al. 1999 and DiBona et al. 2006. For example Chris DiBona's *Open Source and Proprietary Software Development*. See also Feller and Fitzgerald 2002.

[28] *See* Creative Commons, http://creativecommons.org/ (last accessed 15 February 2011). Wikipedia is probably the most successful use of a free content license, the Creative Commons Attribution-ShareAlike 3.0 license (originally under GNU Free Document License).

[29] Mary Colvig in Mozilla Blog, *Over 8 million—way to go!* available at http://blog.mozilla.com/blog/2008/06/18/over-8-million-way-to-go/. Also commented at Ryan Pau: *Firefox 3 launch a success: 8 million downloads in 24 h*, on http://arstechnica.com/old/content/2008/06/firefox-3-launch-a-success-8-million-downloads-in-24-hours.ars (last accessed on 15 February 2011).

[30] Numbers from http://en.wikipedia.org/wiki/Usage_share_of_web_browsers (last accessed on 15 February 2011).

[31] Netcraft, *December 2010 Web Server Survey* at http://news.netcraft.com/archives/2010/12/01/december-2010-web-server-survey.html (last accessed on 15 February 2011).

migration to OpenOffice.org has not been significant with end-users in comparison to MSOffice usage,[32] the open source license of the office suite has enabled it to be used or bundled into other programs such as Alfresco or KnowledgeTree document managers or Ubuntu or openSUSE GNU/Linux operating systems and desktops, or adapted for markets such as China (RedOffice) or companies such as Oracle or OxygenOffice...[33]

Some of the main indirect consequences of the legal aspects of FOSS include:

- Reuse: The right to run, modify and redistribute FOSS gives rise to much higher level of reuse, both as regards components and complete applications for the end-user, leading to greater efficiency.
- Independence: Open access to source code, along with the right to run and modify it, gives the user a high level of independence from the provider, something that can be harnessed to demand higher quality of service.
- Collaboration: The same rights of access, implementation and modification foster collaborative creation of software (among developers who may never know each other) and error correction by users.[34]
- Business Models: being unable to "sell licenses", FOSS consulting and development firms tend to base their business on the sale of services (selection, integration and implementation, support and maintenance, training, guarantees, etc.).[35]
- Communities: Rights granted by licenses allow the intensive and massive dissemination of FOSS through Internet networks (especially from repositories like Sourceforge or Google Code) and encourage community building projects around FOSS.

These are impacts that are extremely attractive to Google: as a significant software developer that does not license software for fees (i.e. generally speaking it currently has no direct revenue stream from software distribution), creating and distributing applications that on the one hand are easily and freely distributable and on the other incentivise users to access Google's online platform (its revenue generator), is a key part of what could be called its overall "marketing" strategy: getting people into the "cloud" and simplifying access to online services. Open source code is thus not an end in itself.[36] Hence Google has contributed its open source browser (Chromium), the Google mobile OS/desktop with integrated browser (Android), and the Google operating system designed to work with web applications (ChromeOS or ChromiumOS). Google has also published a video

---

[32] OpenOffice.org announced 300 million downloads in February 2010, http://www.prweb.com/releases/2010/02/prweb3584404.htm, while the site's statistics page indicates nearly 90 million downloads of OpenOffice.org 3.2, the latest stable version. http://marketing.openoffice.org/marketing_bouncer.html (last accessed 15 February 2011).

[33] http://wiki.services.openoffice.org/wiki/OpenOffice.org_Solutions (last accessed on 15 February 2011).

[34] This has been described in the seminal publication, *The Cathedral and the Bazaar*, by Eric Raymond (Raymond 1999).

[35] Feller et al. 2005; DiBona et al., 1999 (in particular, Behlendorf 1999), and 2006.

[36] Keir 2009.

format (for publishing and accessing online video, such as YouTube). For Google, an important effect of FOSS seems to be, therefore, faster and better access to Google's online offerings, including email, document editing and sharing, video sharing, and other applications and its revenue-generating activities.

In addition, by opening up these programs, Google attracts third parties to develop and extend them and create businesses and communities around them, interoperating with and extending Google's business services, while granting independence in licensing terms.

The Android "mobile operating system" is distributed under the Apache Software License, one of the more commonly used FOSS licenses.[37] Under this permissive license, handset manufacturers and mobile operators not only have a free (gratis) software platform, but also can modify and adapt it to their hardware and to their target users' needs (larger or smaller footprint, included or excluded functionalities and applications, etc.) independently of Google, the principal copyright owner, i.e. without needing specific licensing terms or permission. In addition, the Android Open Source Project has created its own community of developers,[38] as well as there being independent developer communities,[39] and there is a market for Android applications created by independent parties.[40] This is similar, for example, to the Mozilla Foundation's Firefox and Thunderbird community and platform,[41] but it has to be said that this is not specific to open source, of course, for example as Apple has created similar communities and facilities.[42]

Google's Android project has not been without criticism, as for example the "app" to access Google's market is closed-source, and only devices that comply with Google's compatibility requirements are allowed to install the Android Market app and access the Market.[43] There are, however, other online markets for Android applications, something that the openness of the license has enabled.[44] Fragmentation is another problem: the ability to modify this software enables handset manufacturers and operators to create differentiated platforms—which, for third party developers creating mobile applications, may become a nightmare in

---

[37] Available at http://www.apache.org/licenses/LICENSE-2.0 (last accessed 15 February 2011).

[38] Available at http://source.android.com/, http://code.google.com/android/ and http://developer.android.com/index.html (last accessed 15 February 2011).

[39] Available at http://www.anddev.org/ (last accessed 15 February 2011).

[40] Available at http://market.android.com/ (last accessed 15 February 2011).

[41] Available at https://developer.mozilla.org/en-US/ (last accessed 15 February 2011).

[42] Available at http://developer.apple.com/devcenter/ios/index.action and http://www.apple.com/iphone/features/app-store.html (last accessed 15 February 2011).

[43] Available at http://source.android.com/compatibility/index.html; Commented by Dan Morrill, Google, on Android Developers Blog, "*A note for Google Apps for Android*", 25 September 2009, Available at http://android-developers.blogspot.com/2009/09/note-on-google-apps-for-android.html (last accessed 15 February 2011).

[44] *Priya Ganapati: Independent App Stores Take On Google's Android Market*, Wired Gadget Lab, 11 June 2010, available at http://www.wired.com/gadgetlab/2010/06/independent-app-stores-take-on-googles-android-market/ (last accessed 15 February 2011).

compatibility and version management.[45] In addition, while the code may be open source, there are also issues of interoperability and conforming to standards. Google's new java-like virtual machine, Dalvik, is not compliant with the (up to now) Java standard, as it does not use Sun's previously published Java SE or ME standards.[46] This prevents compatibility between Java applications written for those platforms and those for the Android platform. Finally, criticism has been levelled at Google for not really adopting an open source governance model, opening development and decision-making (regarding the code) to the "community",[47] criticisms that Google has attempted to answer by opening up the Android SDK and publishing "developer" and "canary" versions of its project code. However these criticisms have received further support from Google's announcement, in March 2011, not to "open up" the latest release of Android v3.0 named "Honeycomb", at least in the near future or at the same time as it provides the code to larger market players. I.e., the level playing field that FOSS licenses promote is not so level for Android.[48]

9.2.3 *Copyleft:* Share and Share Alike

Distributing software under a license such as the MIT license we have quoted above enables any third party to use and redistribute the software without restriction, having only to comply with fairly straightforward conditions. This means that a third party could take the code, improve it, incorporate it within another program and "close" the code by distributing it in binary form under a restrictive software license. This is perfectly legitimate and for example, Apple includes several programs licensed under such "permissive" licenses in its Mac OS X operating system.[49]

Using such permissive licenses is a specific organizational and/or strategic choice, one that Chris diBona, Open Source Programme Manager at Google has often stated.[50] A "permissive" software license is easy to manage, as it does not

---

[45] Cade Metz: Google: Android fragmentation not 'bad thing, The Register, 5th November 2009, February 2011).

[46] See below on the "*Oracle America Inc. v. Google Inc*" complaint.

[47] Cade Metz: *Google plays Hide and Seek with Android SDK*, The Register, 14th July 2008, available at http://www.theregister.co.uk/2008/07/14/android_developer_unrest/ (last accessed 15 February 2011).

[48] Commented on Bloomberg Businessweek, "*Google Holds Honeycomb Tight*", online at http://www.businessweek.com/technology/content/mar2011/tc20110324_269784.htm (last accessed 15 April 2011).

[49] Available at http://developer.apple.com/opensource/index.html.

[50] See, e.g. Chris DiBona video interview, in *Geek Time with Chris DiBona*, published in Google Open Source Blog, 28 December 2010, available at http://google-opensource.blogspot.com/2010/12/geek-time-with-chris-dibona.html (last accessed 15 February 2011).

really require "policing", or monitoring the market or sector for compliance (as it is very difficult to actually violate the license, and any technical violation will be simple to remedy). Permissive licenses are aligned with the policies and mission of many non-profit or academic institutions, such as the Apache Foundation or many universities, including e.g. the University of California, Berkeley, who drafted the original "BSD" (Berkeley Software Distribution) license.[51] If there is no commercial interest applying a restrictive license to the software—either because, as we have commented above, the software is not the main source of revenue, or because the licensor is a government or academic institution, there is little economic incentive to spend resources on monitoring for compliance (something which the GPL and other *copyleft* licenses commented below often require), and there is more incentive to promote user adoption and take-up through providing a "no strings attached" licensing regime.

> We prefer now to use the Apache licence; the BSD licence is pretty good, too. They are readily comprehensible. With open source you can use other licences; we have released code under the GPL, but we're not religious about using it.
>
> For example, we released a library to interact with Google Talk under the LGPL and BSD licences. The thing about the Apache licence, though, is that it's really easy to use. The GPL says that if you use it and link something to it, then you have to make that [thing you linked to] available as well.
>
> The Apache licence says here's some code, do whatever you want with it, but just preserve the notice in the program saying that you are using code from Apache. That's easy to comply with.[52]

Strategically, the permissiveness also enables third parties (specifically developers and integrators, ISVs and OEMs), to use the code without "substantive" conditions,[53] adapt the software to create innovative or customized versions or larger more sophisticated applications, or create added value extensions or versions that can be, if desired, distributed under a closed-source or proprietary license for a fee—something commercial software and hardware vendors (open source based or not) may be interested in.

Google Chromium is licensed under the BSD license, enabling it to be incorporated into a variety of platforms with near-total freedom for third party integrators, making Chromium versions available as part of Linux distributions or for use by Mac OS-X and Windows users.[54] Android is under the Apache Software License, a permissive license that means that in using Android, mobile phone

---

[51] Sakai project is an example of University sponsored project under a permissive license. The names of the two most emblematic permissive licenses "BSD" and MIT licenses, refer to academic institutions.

[52] Chris DiBona, *Giving Google a licence to code*, The Guardian, November 2nd, 2006.

[53] We say without "substantive" conditions, as most licenses, including permissive, at least require some form of attribution and inclusion of the liability disclaimer, while the copyright regime itself does not allow third parties to pass themselves off as authors/creators.

[54] See http://en.wikipedia.org/wiki/Chromium_%28web_browser%29 (last accessed 15 February 2011).

makers and operators do not need to worry about having to release the source code of their software (adapting and extending Android) to the public. Gears—a browser extension (BSD license), V8—a javascript engine (BSD) and GWT—Google Web Toolkit (Apache license) are other web-oriented projects of Google under permissive licenses.

The availability of the Android SDK[55] under this license has led to the creation of independent developer communities such as Anddev.org, and third party online App markets for Android users, with reports of over 200,000 applications available on the "official" Android Market in December 2010.[56]

That is to say, as software becomes a commodity, and indeed software goes online as a service, there is a greater incentive for companies like Google to provide the end-user "platform", whether mobile or fixed, in as free and unrestricted a manner as possible.[57] Both Google and third party intermediaries leveraging Google services can build on this to provide "for a fee" services (or software). This is also something that Sun did, on freeing the Java technology development kit, by adding a so-called "Classpath" exception to the GPL that permits developers to link to the GPL'd Java code without worrying whether that might require them to release it under the GPL (something we will come back to when commenting the current Oracle America Inc. v. Google Inc. case).

However, any "closing" of Free Software is contrary to the main principles of the Free Software movement, which is to foster its growth and availability. To prevent this, the mechanism of *copyleft*[58] was created, embodied in the GNU General Public License (GPL[59]) and certain other FOSS licenses. *Copyleft* licenses go beyond securing the four basic software freedoms set out above. With the aim of ensuring that any user of the software can enjoy these freedoms at all times, and not just the first licensee in the chain, *copyleft* licenses require that when unmodified or modified versions of the software are redistributed, they must be so under the same terms as the original software. In addition, the (re)distributor must ensure that all direct licensees have access to the source code of the program, so as to be able to exercise his or her rights. This dual condition, based on *"quid pro quo"* (reciprocity or share and share alike), is known as *copyleft* and removes the possibility of legally redistributing the software under a closed or proprietary license.

> Copyleft is a general method for making a program free software and requiring all modified and extended versions of the program to be free software as well....

---

[55] Under the Android SDK license at http://developer.android.com/sdk/terms.html (last accessed 15 February 2011).

[56] Available at http://www.androlib.com/appstats.aspx. (last accessed 15 February 2011).

[57] Commented at Asay 2009a.

[58] See GNU Foundation: *What is copyleft?* available at http://www.gnu.org/copyleft/ (last accessed 15 February 2011) and Stallman 1998.

[59] See http://www.gnu.org/licenses/gpl.html (last accessed 15 February 2011).

... In the GNU project, our aim is to give all users the freedom to redistribute and change GNU software. If middlemen could strip off the freedom, we might have many users, but those users would not have freedom. So instead of putting GNU software in the public domain, we "copyleft" it. Copyleft says that anyone who redistributes the software, with or without changes, must pass along the freedom to further copy and change it. Copyleft guarantees that every user has freedom.[60].

Copyleft is a licensing regime that is often confused with free software, but as we can see, is in fact a subset of the more general concept. On top of its original objective of keeping the original software and distributed modified versions "free", it is argued to promote collaborative development by pushing modifications and improvements out to the community.[61]

Significant free software projects distribute their software under *copyleft* licenses (mainly the GPL, in its versions 2 or 3). Examples include the GNU/Linux operating system, MySQL database, Java platform and libraries, the GIMP image processor, the Drupal content manager, Asterisk VoIP server or MediaWiki collaborative editing software. Other projects, under a weaker form of *copyleft* (LGPL or MPL licenses[62]), include Mozilla Firefox and Thunderbird, OpenOffice.org, JBoss and many more.

This reciprocal feature has not prevented important businesses to be built around *copyleft* software (Red Hat, Canonical, MySQL, Digium, JasperSoft, SugarCRM, to name just a few). These enterprises base their revenue on a variety of business models related to the software itself, principally the provision of services (support, updating, etc.) or the licensing for a fee of the same software under a license without *copyleft* obligations,[63] thus enabling intermediaries to keep private any of their software that interacts with the *copyleft* code or extends/modifies it.[64]

It is to be noted that the reciprocal obligations of the GPL only apply to the core code and its derivative works[65]: where the code is a "platform" (i.e. an operating system or application runtime engine), then the *copyleft* obligations would not extend to all the applications that run on the system. Therefore, many applications under a variety of licenses (including proprietary) run on GNU/Linux operating system or in the Java environment. Thus it is not necessarily the permissiveness of the licenses for Android or Chromium (Apache and BSD respectively) that promotes third party developers creating applications for these platforms. This is true of all FOSS licenses (and other platforms who publish a public API to access system functionalities, such as the Windows API). However, modifications to the core GPL'ed code, creating differentiated versions, would fall under *copyleft*, and require relicensing under the same license, with access to source code, on distribution.

---

[60] Stallman 1996b.

[61] Heffan 1997; Ravicher 2000; Stallman 1998.

[62] LGPL: Lesser GPL; MPL: Mozilla Public License, a license stewarded by the Mozilla Foundation and currently under review.

[63] What is known as "dual" or "multiple licensing". espoused by MySQL, Sleepycat, Trolltech. For a discussion of dual licensing, see Välimäki 2003.

[64] Daffara 2009.

[65] With a significant debate about derivative works in *copyleft* context, see Bain 2010.

> The thing that worries me about GPL is this: suppose Samsung wants to build a phone
> that's different in features and functionality than (one from) LG. If everything on the
> phone was GPL, any applications or user interface enhancements that Samsung did, they
> would have to contribute back.[66]

Google itself uses *copyleft* software, including the GNU/Linux-based servers which run its search engine services, the webservice platform and other Google applications, or the MySQL database engine software.[67] Google also creates a lot of software, which may often be a derivative work of these programs. But, as can be noted, this is not software that is actually distributed by Google. Thus a criticism often levelled at Google is that it does not play by the rules, because it does not share the software that it has improved and extended for its service platform, taking unfair advantage of publicly available software and community efforts.[68] This is because it does not have to and, as opposed to the other projects mentioned above, nor does it necessarily want to. *Copyleft* obligations arise on redistribution of the software code, and Google does not actually distribute the software that underlies its service platform: it only makes the user or technical interface and services available via the web. This has been called the "*Application Service Provider (ASP) loophole*" of the GPL.

The phenomenon of web services and remote network provision of software functionalities led, at the time of drafting the updated version of the GPL between 2006 and 2007, to calls for adding a provision for "*copyleft in the cloud*" to the GPL, i.e. including in the GPL additional *copyleft* obligations that arise not only on distribution but also on remotely making the software services available via networks. In the end, after consulting the software development and user community (including Google), the Free Software Foundation, steward of the GPL, decided not to add this clause to the GPLv3, but to publish an alternative *copyleft* license, called the Affero GPL or "AGPL", [69] that does so.

> ...if you modify the Program, your modified version must prominently offer all users
> interacting with it remotely through a computer network... an opportunity to receive the
> Corresponding Source of your version... at no charge, through some standard or customary means of facilitating copying of software. [70]

This license has been favorably received by the FOSS community and taken up by a number of projects, mainly those offering web-based or web-service-based software, such as EyeOS, a web operating system, or Funambol, a web-based synchronization platform.

---

[66] Andy Rubin, Android engineering director, Google. Shankland 2008a, http://news.cnet.com/8301-13580_3-9949793-39.html (last accessed 15 February 2011).

[67] Interview of Chris DiBona, Google Open Source Blog.

[68] This issue is commented in Vetter 2009 at 2119–2120.

[69] Named after the original FOSS project that had such a provision in its license, the Affero GPLv1. AGPLv3 was published in November 2007 and is Available at http://www.gnu.org/licenses/agpl.html (last accessed 15 February 2011). The additional obligation is at clause 13.

[70] AGPL cl13.

iText, a PDF creation library for Java (i.e. a software function for creating PDFs for different forms of content) that is often used in free software programs, has chosen as its license the AGPL.[71] This obliges users of the library to publish the source code of their application when the library functions are made available over the network.[72] The commercial company behind the project, iText Software Corp. offers a non-*copyleft* license alternative for those who do not want to have to do so. Thus its dual-license business model relies on third parties with web-based applications not wanting to be bound by these obligations and being ready to pay a license fee for more "traditional" licensing arrangements, e.g. per server or user-based.[73]

This type of license, if applicable to programs integrated by Google in its web platform, would probably force it to publish all or part of this platform, something that it is keen not to do. Indeed, Google bans using AGPL'ed code internally, and AGPL projects were initially not allowed on Google Code hosting (a policy change in 2010 now allows any OSI approved license).[74]

9.3   FOSS and Patents

As we have mentioned above, patents are a form of restriction of use, and patents over software processes are anathema to Free Software, which requires freedom to use software for any purposes without restrictions.[75] While within the European legal framework, patents over software are supposedly not available,[76] in the USA, however, they are a significant element of the software development and publishing landscape.[77] Patent law is becoming both a more important protection mechanism as well as a greater threat to freedom to operate for developers and users[78].

---

[71]   The project web page is at http://itextpdf.com/ (last accessed 15 February 2011).

[72]   Arguably, as there is a school of thought that dynamically linking libraries does not create a derivative work of the library subject to the *copyleft* terms of the license. See generally, Bain 2010.

[73]   Licensing terms at http://itextpdf.com/terms-of-use/index.php (last accessed 15 February 2011).

[74]   See recent comment in The Register: Google open source guru: 'Why we ban the AGPL', online at http://www.theregister.co.uk/2011/03/31/google_on_open_source_licenses/ (visited 15 April 2011).

[75]   See Stallman 2004a (Fighting software patents). Illustrated, for example, by the End Software Patents campaign of the FSF, Available at http://endsoftpatents.org/ (last accessed 15 February 2011).

[76]   Article 52 European Patent Convention, Shemtov 2010.

[77]   Recently slightly changed in the USA by the U.S. Supreme Court decision in Re. Bilski, 545 F.3d 943, 88 U.S.P.Q.2d 1385 (Fed. Cir. 2008).

[78]   Vetter 2009 at 2093. There are few FOSS projects that are likely to acquire patents for defensive purposes, although the Open Innovation Network (at http://www.open inventionnetwork.com/, last accessed 15 February 2011) was set up for this. Source code availability of FOSS allows a potential plaintiff to evaluate infringement easily (while a reverse evaluation would be more difficult).

Modern FOSS licenses, at least since the MPL was first published in 1998, include a patent grant over patent rights that a contributor to the software may have in his/her contribution, and complement this with one form or another of "patent peace" or "patent termination" clause,[79] terminating the license if litigation is filed alleging patent infringement with respect to the code. The objective here is to create an environment for developing software that is free of patent risks and restrictions.[80]

While this is not the place to comment on the whole debate of software patentability nor even free software and patents,[81] it is interesting to note that Google here seems to be aligned with most of the FOSS community with this issue.[82] As a user of free software, Google is interested in ensuring protection against patent claims in respect of the technologies it uses, and clearing the patent thicket in relation to technologies that it may sponsor, e.g. through Google Summer of Code or other Google FOSS projects, some of which are mentioned here. We note that Google tends to use the Apache Software License 2 for most of its code, which includes defensive patent provisions,[83] and recently its distribution of WebM, a video codec, under the BSD free software license, includes an explicit patent grant and termination clause.

WebM[84] is of interesting study. In August 2009, Google announced its acquisition of On2 Technologies, a company that had been developing an audio-visual codec for the last few years. A codec is a piece of software or device required to reproduce audiovisual content (through compression or encoding and decoding, hence its name), and codecs are used for editing, presenting and viewing video content (online or offline), including videostreaming and conferencing. There have been several standards or formats for audiovisual compression such as MPEG-1 and 2, MPEG-4 or H.264, improving over time the quality of compression and how much or little information is lost in the process. One of the issues surrounding codecs from a legal perspective is that they are encumbered by patents (over the data compression algorithms), requiring licensing in many countries which recognize such patents. Licensing is done through patent pools such as

---

[79] Apache Software License 2, MPL1.1, GPLv3, OSL 3.0, AFL 3.0, CDDL, CPL/EPL... All licenses are available at http://opensource.org/licenses/alphabetical (last accessed 15 February 2011).

[80] Other initiatives include the Open Innovation Network (www.openinventionnetwork.com), a form of patent pool for free software in relation to processes implemented in the GNU/Linux operating system, in parallel with projects such as "Linux Defenders" which aim to collect prior art against determined software patents (e.g. through defensive prior publication), or Peer to Patent (http://www.peertopatent.org/), a project to assist the USPTO find the information relevant to assessing the claims of pending patent applications.

[81] For this, for example, see Vetter 2009.

[82] E.g. Google is a licensee of OIN (http://www.openinventionnetwork.com/press_release 08_06_07.php, last accessed 15 February 2011).

[83] Arthur 2006 (*Interview with Chris DiBona*).

[84] The project is available at http://www.webmproject.org/ (last accessed 15 February 2011).

MPEG-LA[85] and VIA[86] and the cost and restrictions placed on licensing, it has been claimed, has stifled innovation[87] and, among other things, the development of video codecs—notably in the free software area.[88]

YouTube, one of Google "properties" since 2006, provides content in several video formats, including mainly the H.264 format since 2008. YouTube requires the Adobe Flash player for reproducing video, as does Vimeo and other online video sites, although since January 2010 YouTube also implements HTML5 format multimedia capabilities (that HTML5-compliant browsers can reproduce, without the need for the Adobe plug-in). While Adobe Flash Player can be used "for free", it is not free software and cannot be distributed directly as part of a truly free and open source platform.[89]

This brings us back to WebM, because this project offers a high quality audiovisual codec, VP8, under a FOSS license, the BSD, and thus allegedly outside the MPEG-LA licensing regime[90] and capable of being embedded in FOSS packages such as a Linux distribution or a browser. The use of the BSD license is in line with Google's strategy mentioned above, of opening up under permissive FOSS licenses certain "platform" technologies, in order to facilitate use and access to its services (in this case in particular, the YouTube video sharing site).

In addition, however, with WebM Google offers a patent grant in respect of its implementation of the video format.[91] This patent grant is in respect of Google's implementation of WebM, on the basis that Google may hold certain patents over the technologies, and provides any licensee with patent rights to use them. At the same time it includes a patent termination clause, similar to those used in more modern FOSS licenses (the Apache Software License in particular), which prevents licensees (users of the implementation) from bringing an infringement suit against this WebM technology based on patent rights.

"This implementation" means the copyrightable works distributed by Google as part of the WebM Project.

---

[85] See http://www.mpegla.com/ (last accessed 15 February 2011).

[86] See http://www.vialicensing.com/index.aspx (last accessed 15 February 2011).

[87] See for example, Red Hat's amicus curiae brief in the "*In re Bilski*" case, available at http://www.redhat.com/f/pdf/rh-supreme-court-brief.pdf (last accessed 15 February 2011). See also Torrance 2009.

[88] There are free software codec formats, such as Theora (video) and Vorbis (for audio), Pfeiffer 2010.

[89] Like the Adobe Reader, the Flash Player can either be subsequently downloaded by the end-user, or GNU/Linux distributers can enter into an agreement with Adobe for including the closed-source package with the Linux distribution (or in a "non-free" repository, as openSuse does).

[90] WebM includes audio streams compressed with the Vorbis audio codec.

[91] Originally, the patent grant was part of the WebM license, however this was split out after several complaints that the license was (a) not truly open source/free due to the limited patent grant, and (b) increases fragmentation of the community. Since June 2010, WebM software is licensed under the BSD license, and Google provides a separate patent grant for its implementation.

> Google hereby grants to you a perpetual, worldwide, non-exclusive, no-charge, royalty-free, irrevocable (except as stated in this section) patent license to make, have made, use, offer to sell, sell, import, transfer, and otherwise run, modify and propagate the contents of this implementation of VP8, where such license applies only to those patent claims, both currently owned by Google and acquired in the future, licensable by Google that are necessarily infringed by this implementation of VP8. This grant does not include claims that would be infringed only as a consequence of further modification of this implementation. If you or your agent or exclusive licensee institute or order or agree to the institution of patent litigation against any entity (including a cross-claim or counterclaim in a lawsuit) alleging that this implementation of VP8 or any code incorporated within this implementation of VP8 constitutes direct or contributory patent infringement, or inducement of patent infringement, then any patent rights granted to you under this License for this implementation of VP8 shall terminate as of the date such litigation is filed.[92]

The patent peace clause is not a perfect solution, as there is no guarantee that no other third party holds patents over technologies implemented in WebM.[93] Other criticisms of Google's publishing of WebM is the fact that an implementation under an open source license does not make the technology an open standard, something that has been called for in the interest of creating a truly open technology.[94] Google has submitted the specification of VP8 video codec to IETF as an Internet Draft,[95] however this is not part of a formal standardization process.

The interesting thing, however, is that Google has stated that as of beginning of 2011, Google's own browser Chrome (and thus also Chromium) no longer supports H.264 format for video, limiting itself to WebM (VP8) and Theora video codecs for HTML5.[96] This hints at a move on YouTube to do the same, i.e. remove videos encoded with the H.264 format. Until now, Google continued to use Flash on YouTube because Ogg cannot match the performance of H.264.[97]

---

[92] Additional IP Rights Grant (Patents). Patent grant Available at http://www.webmproject.org/license/additional/ (last accessed 15 February 2011).

[93] It is reported that the head of MPEG-LA is looking into creating a "a patent pool license for VP8 (http://digitaldaily.allthingsd.com/20100520/googles-royalty-free-webm-video-may-not-be-royalty-free-for-long/, last accessed 15 February 2011), and Steve Jobs allegedly has stated that Ogg/Theora might be encumbered by patents too (http://www.theregister.co.uk/2010/04/30/steve_jobs_claims_ogg_theora_attack/, last accessed 15 February 2011). Claims have also been made that VP8 is too similar to the H.264 for comfort (Garrett-Glaser 2010), claims that have been criticised if not fully rejected (Daffara 2010).

[94] Glidden 2010; Phipps 2010.

[95] VP8 Data Format and Decoding Guide, available at http://tools.ietf.org/html/draft-bankoski-vp8-bitstream-00 (last accessed 15 February 2011).

[96] Jazayeri 2010, available at http://blog.chromium.org/2011/01/html-video-codec-support-in-chrome.html and commented by Jon Brodkin in After dropping H.264, Google admits it's more popular than WebM, at http://www.networkworld.com/news/2011/011911-google-webm.html (last accessed 15 February 2011).

[97] According to Chris DiBona, reported by Cade Metz in The Register, 13 April 2010, available at http://www.theregister.co.uk/2010/04/13/reports_says_google_will_open_source_on2_codec_in_may/ (last accessed 15 February 2011).

9.4 "Oracle America Inc. v. Google Inc."

Before concluding on Google's involvement in FOSS, it is interesting to look at a few details of the *"Oracle America Inc. v. Google Inc."* case,[98] which is still very much undecided (so the comments here are tentative), but leads to some interesting comments regarding competitive and anticompetitive use of law and free software licensing in the information society.

Oracle has made eight claims, seven on patents and one for copyright infringement.[99]

Let us look at the copyright claim first, which includes direct infringement and inducement to infringe. The claim states that

> Without consent, authorization, approval, or license, Google knowingly, willingly, and unlawfully copied, prepared, published, and distributed Oracle America's copyrighted work, portions thereof, or derivative works and continues to do so. Google's Android infringes Oracle America's copyrights in Java and Google is not licensed to do so.
>
> Thus... users of Android, including device manufacturers, must obtain and use copyrightable portions of the Java platform or works derived therefrom to manufacture and use functioning Android devices. Such use is not licensed. Google has thus induced, caused, and materially contributed to the infringing acts of others by encouraging, inducing, allowing and assisting others to use, copy, and distribute Oracle America's copyrightable works, and works derived therefrom.

Initially, the infringed code was not specified, however Oracle later corrected this in its amended claim, filed in October 2010, claiming that Android's class libraries and documentation infringe on its copyrights, and that approximately one-third of Android's API packages are "derivative" of Oracle's copyrighted Java API packages, including examples of code that aim to prove its point.

A brief look at Android and its development helps understand the claims. Google developed most of the Android system, and it included a Java compatible technology called "Dalvik", a virtual machine optimized for mobile platforms. Java-based programs do not execute directly on the operating system, but use a "runtime engine" or "virtual machine", that provides the technical environment in which the Java-based program may run, including many support functions or class libraries. Sun Microsystems Inc. originally distributed the Java Runtime Engine

---

[98] *Complaint (with jury demand) for Patent and Copyright Infringement against Google Inc.* (Filing fee $350, receipt number 54611007901), filed by Oracle America, Inc. (Attachments: # (1) Civil Cover Sheet)(vlk, COURT STAFF) (Filed on 12-Aug-2010) Modified on 18-Aug-2010 (cjl, COURT STAFF). (Entered: 17-Aug-2010). Available at http://groklaw.net/pdf2/OrvGoogComplaint.pdf (last accessed 15 February 2011).

[99] James Gosling, the creator of Java, told Reuters in an interview that Oracle's lawsuit was filed only after the failure of protracted technology licensing negotiations with Google that began long before Sun sold itself to Oracle for $5.6 billion in January. Available at http://economictimes.indiatimes.com/infotech/internet/Lawsuit-may-signal-era-of-Oracle-Google-tensions/articleshow/6315161.cms (last accessed 15 February 2011).

(JRE) for free to all users,[100] and a Java Development Kit (JDK) for developers, so they could develop and distribute Java-based applications. Sun also released the specifications for Sun's Java platform, including Sun's Java virtual machine, under a free-of-charge license which allows developers to create "clean room" implementations[101] of Sun's Java specifications. If, however, you wanted to certify compliance, you needed to demonstrate compatibility with Sun's *Technology Compatibility Kit* ("TCK"), which while liberal in licensing terms, included field of use restrictions, notably for mobile platforms.[102]

Sun released most of the JDK under an open source license in May 2007, using the GPLv2 with certain exceptions, i.e. a *copyleft* license that does not affect applications that "use" the libraries.[103] There is now an independent project called OpenJDK,[104] but the TCKs are still under restrictive licensing terms. Note that "Java ME" (mobile or micro edition) is under the pure GPLv2, arguably because Sun envisaged a revenue stream from dual licensing Java ME, providing commercial mobile (i.e. non-desktop/server) licenses to those not wishing to be bound by the GPL.

Google's response to Oracle America alleges that Dalvik was developed as a clean room version of Java, without using any technology or intellectual property from Sun Microsystems. That is, Google has used the specification and syntax of Java, but not the Sun libraries that originally were included in the JDK or freed into the OpenJDK. Without entering into the detail of the implementation, which the court and experts may have to do to elucidate this case, the consequence of this is that device manufacturers do not need to include a copy of the Sun Java virtual machine on the Android devices: Android applications run in their own process with their own Dalvik instance.

Dalvik does, however, use some libraries originally included in a FOSS project called "Harmony" hosted by the Apache Software Foundation ("ASF"), for which the ASF requested Sun an unrestricted TCK license to verify its compatibility (license which was denied). It is these libraries that have come under scrutiny by Oracle and are the basis of part of its copyright infringement claim.

Looking at this situation in licensing terms, there seem to be at least three potential scenarios.

First, Dalvik is indeed a clean room implementation, as Google claims, or only uses non-copyrightable parts of Java or code expressions that, while being in Sun's Java code, result necessarily from the specification. If this were the case, Sun's

---

[100] This is included, for example, in the OpenOffice.org suite.

[101] A "clean room" implementation means developing a new alternative program from zero, without having access to the original program and thus be potentially liable for copyright infringement. Developing to an open specification is a form of clean room development.

[102] A short version of the history and background to Java is included in Google's response to Oracle America's claim (Factual Background, Section A), available at http://groklaw.net/pdf2/OraGoogle-51.pdf (last accessed 15 February 2011).

[103] Available at http://openjdk.java.net/legal/gplv2+ce.html (last accessed 15 February 2011).

[104] Available at http://openjdk.java.net/ (last accessed 15 February 2011).

copyright case would probably fail. The question of use of API information, "class names, definitions, organization, and parameters" as per Oracle America's amended complaint, is an interesting and ever more important one in copyright law and interoperable software. Copyright does not protect non-creative elements of a program (including, in the US legal framework, *"procedures, processes, systems, and methods of operation"* [105]), nor does it protect interoperability information or *"ideas and principles which underlie any element of a program, including those which underlie its interfaces"*, as per the European legal framework. [106] This is to ensure that copyright does not over extend itself to cover "ideas" (something more in the realm of patents) rather than a unique and original expression of those ideas, and to ensure that it does not encumber or restrict the interconnection and interaction between two independent programs. [107]

Second, Google has indeed incorporated copyright protected Java code from Sun in Dalvik. In this case, given the GPLv2 *copyleft* license on that code, Dalvik itself should be released under the same *copyleft* license. This is contrary to the permissive license strategy of Google we have already commented above, and releasing Dalvik under the Apache Software License is a breach of the GPL and Oracle America's copyright.

Third, there is Sun Java code in Dalvik, but this comes from third party contributions or components, such as the Apache Harmony libraries. If Apache Harmony had the right to incorporate the Java code, and the licensing is correct, then so does Google (this is the reusable nature and purpose of free software). If Harmony did not, then this scenario may also involve breach of Oracle America's rights. Whether Google has done this "knowingly" or not is at debate, as a third party could have incorporated original Java code from Sun in the Harmony libraries without others knowing (though Apache Software Foundation is usually rigorous in its IP management). However, on the basis of the more detailed claims filed subsequently by Oracle America, the Apache Software Foundation denies that the claimed infringing code comes from the Harmony project (even though it may have the Apache Software License). [108]

The patent claims against Google may be more complicated to determine and given the available information, our comments more summary. First, Oracle will have to get over the hurdle of Google's challenge to the validity of the patents that Google has allegedly infringed—validity that is under greater scrutiny and uncertainty since the US Supreme Court decision on *"re Bilski"* in 2010. [109] If these patents are found to be both enforceable and relevant to the Android code, there will also be the question of whether or not Sun/Oracle has granted a patent

---

[105] For more on this, see Omar et al. 2010; Samuelson 2007.

[106] Article 1.2 Directive 2001/29 on copyright in the information society.

[107] See Andrew Katz in this same volume, Chap. 10.

[108] ASF Blog, *Read beyond the headers*, https://blogs.apache.org/foundation/entry/read_beyond_the_headers (last accessed 15 February 2011).

[109] *"In re Bilski"*, 545 F.3d 943, 88 U.S.P.Q.2d 1385 (Fed. Cir. 2008).

license in respect of them. However here, Google may be in a "*Catch 22*" situation: it may be able to argue that it was granted a patent license under the Java GPLv2 license (an implicit grant, the GPLv3 has an explicit grant), however it could then fall foul of the copyright claim for breach of the GPL license (by releasing Dalvik and Android SDK under the Apache license), as we have commented above.

The lessons to be learned from this, over and above the need for clear code and license management in open source projects, relate to the strategic use of free and non-free copyright licensing in the Information Society. From both Google and Sun's (initial) point-of-view, there is a purpose to releasing their platform or infrastructure software under a FOSS license, so as to encourage take-up and the development of a community of developers and application providers around the platform. On the one hand it seems Google has no interest in licensing any part of its platform for a fee (as its revenue streams are in advertising, mainly), so it provides the Android code under a permissive license. Sun, on the other hand, may have perceived potential revenue streams from licensing its Java platform for mobile devices, so chose "to GPL" the Java platform and offer a dual licensing regime for those wishing to avoid *copyleft* obligations. This is reinforced by the terms of the Java TCK, which also would enable Sun to obtain revenue from compatibility testing and field of use restrictions.

Thus while Oracle, Sun's new owner, seems to be wanting to use its copyright and patent rights to obtain revenue from software innovations around its platform, Google is using them to rather promote use of its revenue-generating online service platform. The "freeing" of the Sun JDK could also seem to be misleading, as anyone who may want to create a Java alternative (one of the precepts of free software) could fall foul of Oracle's patents and licensing of the non-free parts, including its TCK.

9.5 Conclusions

Google is an example of how companies can use Free and Open Source Software in business as intended: to implement, improve and innovate extensively the software for furthering their own purposes, while also giving back to the community from which it takes the code.

One of the most interesting things about Google and FOSS is the way that the company leverages FOSS to drive and promote its revenue-generating businesses. On the one hand, FOSS is in the infrastructure of the core Google service, online searching, with its version of the GNU/Linux operating system running the servers where Google indexes and searches the web. On the other, the main free software projects promoted by Google, a browser (Chrome/Chromium), an operating system whose main, if not only, application is a browser (Chrome OS), and a mobile operating system platform (Android), all provide software whose main objective seems to be to get users on the web where Google's service offerings are centered.

Another project, WebM is a high quality video format that may eventually be the major if not only format supported by YouTube, and thus should drive the creation of FOSS video editing and publishing applications for users to create and post videos to YouTube, among other places.

This is not to say that all Google projects are self serving and it does not also make significant contributions to the FOSS community. Indeed, its Google Code platform is a great place to setup and run FOSS projects. The Google Summer of Code project generates interesting free and open source software (... while enabling Google to spot talent!). And Google also sponsors and contributes to important FOSS projects such as Python, Apache, Linux Kernel, GCC, etc., as commented above.

Yet Google has also been criticized that its balance on taking from and contributing to the FOSS community is tipped toward itself, as it uses more FOSS than it gives back to the general public, and that by offering "software as a service", it avoids the reciprocity obligations of *copyleft* software it extensively uses to provide such services. In addition, there have been claims that the development process for its main FOSS projects—Android, Chromium—is not really based on an open and transparent community development model but rather on something similar to a closed development model, opening up and releasing major version changes once every 6 months or so, before shutting its doors again.

However, the question of whether Google takes more than it gives back is a political and ethical one and not a legal one, which focuses on how Google complies with the applicable licenses and respects third party copyright and patent rights. From a more legal perspective, it seems that Google has espoused Free Software in a transparent and compliant manner. Licenses on Google Code are limited to recognized Open Source licenses, thus reducing license proliferation. Google's own code, when published, also uses these licenses, in particular the Apache Software License. Google even changed the original WebM license, a modified version of the "new BSD" license, so as to make it the standard version of this license, moving the specific patent right grant in relation to its own implementation of the format to a separate document.

The "*Oracle America Inc. v. Google Inc.*" case we have briefly commented here has shown that by actually distributing software (rather than offering software services and functionalities via the web), Google has opened itself up to another area of legal risk, that of infringing Intellectual Property Rights (copyright and patent rights) through the creation and distribution of software that is open to scrutiny to all. However, it remains to be seen if this case has a substantive legal basis or is essentially a legal move by Oracle Inc. to forestall competition in one of its revenue-generating business areas, the Java platform for mobile devices J2ME or Java ME (whereas other Java technologies, JRE, JDK and OpenJDK, can otherwise basically be used for free).

Taken out of context, the law suit could be said to be symptomatic of the risks of using and distributing Free and Open Source Software: the risk of incorporating software code that is or has been illegally copied, or using it in a manner that does not comply with the applicable license, thus infringing the rights of the owner of the code—or using code that implements methods or processes over which a third party has a patent monopoly, thus infringing the rights of the patent holder. The open nature of FOSS makes this easier to do, and easier to be spotted. However, within the context of FOSS as a whole, this type of case is exceptional: given the last 30 years' or more existence of FOSS and the widespread use of FOSS at personal, corporate, government and every other level one can think of,[110] the actual amount of litigation over free software is *de minimis*, if not totally absent in statistically relevant terms. The only other large case (in publicity terms) has been the "*SCO v. IBM*" suit, which has basically petered out.[111]

Free Software is a driving force of the Information Society, not only in the technological architecture of the web and increasingly inside organizations, with software such as GNU/Linux operating system or the Apache Web Server, but also crucially through its tenets of collaborative development and sharing of results— something anathema to the behemoths of the proprietary software world and also the media and content industry. This collaboration and sharing is underpinned by a legal trick, the Free Software license, which is a manner of privately (and increasingly publically) redressing the imbalance of modern copyright law which, according to many,[112] is more favorable to protecting the private interests of copyright holders to the detriment of the public interest. Public interest which copyright was initially supposed to defend.[113]

The success of these tenets has spread from software to other areas of licensing works protected by copyright, including in particular "content" licensing, promoted or supported by standardized free content licenses such as the Creative Commons suite of licenses, or the GNU Free Document License. Wikipedia is just one example of a successful project using these licenses, contributing to bring "peer reviewed" (and free) information to all. Flickr and Jamendo, respectively in the photographic and music sectors, are also examples of projects that make significant use of these licenses, enabling creators to provide their works to the public under terms that allow copying and redistribution and also—depending on the license—modifying or adapting them to the users' needs.[114]

However, open source licensing is just one ingredient of successfully advancing the information society: using open standards is now argued strongly to be another,

---

[110] See for example the numbers quoted by Wheeler, D, at http://www.dwheeler.com/oss_fs_why.html (last accessed 15 February 2011); "*FOSS market share*", at http://joomla.linux.lu/index.php?option=com_content&view=article&id=83&Itemid=85; Netcraft's June 2010 Web Server Survey, at http://news.netcraft.com/archives/2010/06/16/june-2010-web-server-survey.html; NetMarketshare's statistics at http://marketshare.hitslink.com/report.aspx?qprid=0; or Wikipedia: http://en.wikipedia.org/wiki/Usage_share_of_web_browsers (last accessed 15 February 2011).

[111] See http://en.wikipedia.org/wiki/SCO_v._IBM (last accessed 15 February 2011).

[112] Among others, Samuelson 2010.

[113] Mitchell 2009.

[114] Available at http://www.flickr.com/ and http://www.jamendo.com (last accessed 15 February 2011).

if not more important, factor, and more so when one's data and applications are "in the cloud". With source code transparency, FOSS has advantages for interoperability. Greater interoperability among information technology components typically enhances the value of any particular component. However, with cloud applications, such as Google's service offerings, interoperability requires open standards for data access, formats and transfers. This may be the main area of legal debate in the years to come.

References

Arthur C (2006) Interview: chris DiBona: giving Google a licence to code, the Guardian, Thursday 2 Nov 2006.   http://www.guardian.co.uk/technology/2006/nov/02/insideit.guardianweekly technologysection

Asay M (2009a) Google keeps tripping over Microsoft's grave, CNET news. http://news. cnet.com/8301-13505_3-10268180-16.html

Asay M (2009b) World's biggest open-source company? Google, CNET news. http:// news.cnet.com/8301-13505_3-10354530-16.html

Bain M (2010) Software interaction and the GNU general public license. IFOSS L Rev 2(2):165–180. doi:10.5033/ifosslr.v2i2.44

Behlendorf B (1999) Open source as a business strategy. In: DiBona C et al. Open sources: voices from the open source revolution. O'Reilly and Associates, California

Benkler Y (2006) The wealth of networks. Yale University Press, Yale

Daffara C (2009) Economic free software perspectives. open source business resource, Aug 2009: Tech entrepreneurship. http://www.osbr.ca/ojs/index.php/osbr/article/view/937/903

Daffara C (2010) An analysis of WebM and its patent risk—updated. http:// carlodaffara.conecta.it/an-analysis-of-webm-and-its-patent-risk/

DiBona C, Cooper D, Stone M (eds) (2006) Open sources 2.0: the continuing evolution, O'Reilly and Associates. http://commons.oreilly.com/wiki/index.php/Open_Sources_2

DiBona C, Ockman S, Stone M (eds) (1999) Open sources: voices from the open source revolution, O'Reilly and Associates. http://oreilly.com/catalog/opensources/book/toc.html

Feller J, Fitzgerald B, Hissam S, Lakhani K (eds) (2005) Perspectives on free and open source software. The MIT Press, Massachusetts, Cambridge

Feller J, Fitzgerald B (2002) Understanding open source software, development. Addison-Wesley, Reading

Free Software Foundation (1996) Philosophy of the GNU project. www.gun.org/philosophy

Garrett-Glaser J (2010) The first in-depth technical analysis of VP8. http://x264dev.multimedia. cx/archives/377

Glidden R (2010) How Google's open sourcing of VP8 harms the open web, 21 May 2010. http:// www.robglidden.com/2010/05/how-googles-open-sourcing-of-vp8-harms-the-open-web/

Heffan I (1997) Copyleft: Licensing collaborative works in the digital age, 49 stan. L Rev 1487:1508

Jaeger T (2010) Enforcement of the GNU GPL in Germany and Europe, 1 JIPITEC 34. http:// www.jipitec.eu/issues/jipitec-1-1-2010/2419/dippadm1268746871.43.pdf

Jaeger T, Gebert J (2009) Open source licensing—comment on "Jacobsen v. Katzer", IIC, pp 345 ff

Jazayeri M (2010) HTML Video codec support in chrome. http://blog.chromium.org/2011/01/ html-video-codec-support-in-chrome.html

Keir T (2009) How open source can beat the status quo, PCWorld. http://www.pcworld.com/ businesscenter/article/166551/how_open_source_can_beat_the_status_quo.html

Mitchell QC, Iain G (2009) Back to the future: Hinton v Donaldson, wood and Meurose (Court of Session, Scotland, 28th July 1773). IFOSS L Rev 1(2):111–122. doi:10.5033/ifosslr.v1i2.23

Omar J, Miller M, Webbink M (2010) Copyright in open source software—understanding the boundaries. IFOSS L Rev 2(1):13–38. doi:10.5033/ifosslr.v2i1.30

Pfeiffer S (2010) Patents and their effect on standards: Open video codecs for HTML5, IFOSSLR vol. 1, no 2 (2009). doi: 10.5033/ifosslr.v1i2.21

Phipps S (2010) WebM: missing the assurances open source needs? http://blogs.computerworlduk.com/simon-says/2010/05/webm-missing-the-assurances-open-source-needs/index.htm

Ravicher DB (2000) Facilitating collaborative software development: the enforceability of mass-market public software licenses. Virginia J L Tech 11(5). http://www.vjolt.net/vol5/issue3/v5i3a11-Ravicher.html

Raymond ES (1999) The cathedral the bazaar, O'Reilly and Associates. http://www.catb.org/~esr/writings/cathedral-bazaar/cathedral-bazaar/

Rosen L (2009) Bad facts make good law: The jacobsen case and open source. IFOSS L Rev et seq 1:27 (2009). http://www

Samuelson P (2007) Why copyright excludes systems and processes from the scope of its protection. Tex Law Rev 85:1921

Samuelson P (2010) The google book settlement as copyright reform, wisconsin law review, Forthcoming. http://papers.ssrn.com/sol3/papers.cfm?abstract_id=1683589

Shankland S (2008a) Google carves an android path through open-source world, CNET, 22 May 2008. http://news.cnet.com/8301-13580_3-9949793-39.html. Accessed 15 February 2011

Shankland S (2008b) Q&A: Google's open-source balancing act, CNET, 28 May 2008. http://news.cnet.com/8301-13580_3-9952719-39.html

Shemtov N (2010) Software patents and open source models in Europe: does the foss community need to worry about current attitudes at the EPO? IFOSS L Rev 2(2):151–164. doi:10.5033/ifosslr.v2i2.43

Stallman RM (1996a) The free software definition. In: Stallman RM, Lessig L (eds) (2002) Free software free society: selected essays of Richard M. Stallman. Free Software Free Society, Padova

Stallman RM (1996b) What is copyleft. In: Stallman RM, Lessig L (eds) (2002) Free software free society: selected essays of Richard M. Stallman. GNU Press, Boston

Stallman RM (1998) Copyleft: pragmatic idealism. In: free software, free society, selected essays of Richard M. Stallman, GNU Press. http://www.gnu.org/philosophy/pragmatic.html

Stallman RM (2004a) Fighting software patents—singly and together. http://www.gnu.org/philosophy/fighting-software-patents.html

Stallman RM (2007) Why open source misses the point of free software. In: Stallman RM, Lessig L (2002) Free Software Free Society. GNU Press, Boston

Stallman RM (2004b) Did you say "Intellectual property"? It's a seductive mirage. http://www.gnu.org/philosophy/not-ipr.xhtml

Torrance AW, Tomlinson W (2009) Patents and the regress of useful arts, Colum Sci Tech L Rev 10:130

Välimäki M (2003) Dual licensing in open source software industry. Systemes d'Information et Management 8(1):63–75

Vetter G (2009) Commercial free and open source software: knowledge production, hybrid appropriability, and patents. Fordham L Rev 77:2087

Chapter 10
Google, APIs and the Law. Use, Reuse and Lock-In

Andrew Katz

Contents

10.1 What is an API?

An API (or *application programming interface*) is the programmatic means by which a computer-based service (whether based on the cloud or elsewhere) can interact with other software and computer-based services.[1] In a sense, it is a user interface for machines to access machines. Open Office Writer has a user interface which consists of a white page, to mimic paper, icons representing the *save* and *print* functions and so-on, and a sequence of menus. This interface is designed to

---

The author would like to acknowledge the assistance of Rashi Nagpal (research) and Kate Bray (editorial support).

---

[1] Both "code", in Lawrence Lessig's terminology, see Lessig 2006.

A. Katz (✉)
Moorcrofts LLP, Marlow, UK
e-mail: andrew.katz@moorcrofts.com

A. Lopez-Tarruella (ed.), *Google and the Law*,
Information Technology and Law Series 22, DOI: 10.1007/978-90-6704-846-0_10,
© T.M.C. Asser press, The Hague, The Netherlands, and the author(s) 2012

balance power and ease of use for the human user.[2] An API performs a similar function for software to software communication.[3]

Examples are:

- the interfaces between an operating system and the programs that run on it (to allow the programs access to the computer's screen, keyboard and file system, for example);
- the interface allowing a program to accept plug-ins providing additional functionality, such a Photoshop or Mozilla Firefox;
- the interface allowing software programs to interact with Google Maps, Gmail, Facebook and Twitter

APIs may be unpublished, they may be published to enable third party access, or they may have published portions, but undocumented extensions.

By publishing an API, a provider is not only inviting developers to interact with their software programmatically, but they are also implying that the API will function to the published spec. What is not so clear is whether this implication extends to a promise that it will continue to function to that specification for a period of time. Developers have more commonly been concerned about initial functionality. However, as the quantity of data and applications in the cloud increases, they are increasingly concerned about that functionality remaining consistent over time.

A wise developer would require an API to be

- predictable (perform according to specification)
- stable (remain available over time)
- provide appropriate functionality (including the ability to migrate)

If an API is open (see below for one definition of this in the context of the European Interoperability Framework), then it is more likely to fulfill these criteria.

10.2 APIs and the Cloud

Without physical access to the computers and storage running the cloud services, the only access to data in the cloud—potentially your data—is through some form of API. This is true to a certain extent in respect of data on your own physical

---

[2] If an official API does not exist, programmers will occasionally resort to programmatically emulating a user in order to use the user interface as an API. Spammers frequently use this technique to post on bulletin boards, hence the increasing use of CAPTCHAs in an attempt to foil them.

[3] Sometimes, an interface straddles the two definitions. For example, the Simple Mail Transport Protocol does involve a "conversation" between the sender and recipient of email using English words like "send". The recipient is always a program. The sender is almost always a program as well, but may occasionally be a die-hard human hacker. Similarly, SQL queries are constructed in an English-based language, but are frequently generated programmatically behind the scenes.

server, but in practice, if you have physical possession of the disks on which the data is stored, it is much more difficult for a third party to render those data inaccessible even if they have tried to do so by obfuscation or even encrypting the file structure: you can take as many backup copies as you like, and analyse the file structure and content at your leisure. When your data is in the cloud, retrieving it is subject to the constraints of bandwidth between you and the cloud provider; constraints on the functionality of the API itself (for example, it may not allow bulk retrieval of records); constraints on the data that are capable of retrieval (it may be possible to retrieve the records themselves, but not useful metadata or index files); constraints imposed by the cloud provider in the name of protection (a barrage of single-record retrieval request in a short period of time may trigger some form of anti-distributed-denial-of-service protection), and so on. Finally, the cloud provider may intervene to make some functions unavailable.

Practical control over the API gives a cloud service provider immense power to constrain their users' activities, and in particular, to restrict, practically, movement to another provider.

Cloud service providers frequently also attempt to impose legal constraints. For example, the use of Google's APIs are subject to licences. In the case of Google maps, the user is granted the right to access the service, but also certain rights in relation to the use of the content generated by and contained within the service.[4] (We discuss the distinction between a service licence and a copyright licence below). There is also a limited trademark licence which restricts the way in which the user can use the various Google brands in relation to the service. One interesting characteristic of this licence is that the implementation of the service using Google Maps must be available free of charge to the public in general.[5]

10.3 Legal Constraints and APIs

"Licences" in a software context have historically tended to mean copyright licences. Accordingly, as the cloud has developed, licences to access online services and APIs have tended to look very similar to software licences, frequently inappropriately:

> The BBC grants to You a non-commercial, world-wide, payment-free, non-exclusive, non-sublicensable right to copy, reproduce, download and/or publish the API's and alter, adapt, edit, incorporate, modify, translate and create your own product or services based on the API's (a 'Work') provided that [...].[6]

---

[4] http://code.google.com/apis/maps/terms.html (last accessed 24 August 2011).

[5] Clause 9.1 of the terms.

[6] Taken from the BBC API licence, available at http://backstage.bbc.co.uk/archives/2005/05/api_licence.html (last accessed 1 September 2011).

In this case, although the API is not itself defined in the Agreement, there are links on the site which refer to them. Use of the APIs does not in any meaningful sense involve copying, reproducing for downloading them, but, rather requires the ability to *access* them, one right which is not, in fact, granted by the licence. We discuss this distinction later.

A refresher: a licence is defined as a permission to do something which would otherwise be unlawful. Therefore, there needs to be a potentially illegal act for the licence to impinge. In software, the act in question will generally be breach of copyright. Copying and running the software without the permission of the owner will be a breach of copyright. In this sense, the licence can *only* grant permissions (although the permissions may be highly conditional), and any restrictions which are imposed are additional obligations imposed by contract.[7] The licence from the owner provides the permission which prevents running and copying the software from being a breach of copyright. Lawyers have tried to create, for example, linking licences, which purport to restrict the extent and purposes for which people can link to their client's website. In doing so, they have assumed that linking to the web site is in itself an unlawful act, and that, therefore, their client is in a position to grant that right. It is by no means clear that this is the case. For example, the Practical Law Company provides resources for lawyers. The drafting notes accompanying its template website linking licence state that "permission to link to a website may not be legally required, *unless* the website terms expressly prohibit linking"[8] without making it clear on how it is possible (in the absence of a contractual obligation) for those terms to create an obligation out of nowhere.[9] Similarly, for an API licence to be effective, at law, it must permit the user to do something that would otherwise be unlawful.

Does access to an API violate copyright *per se*, such that the API owner is able to restrict access, and offer *copyright* licences to permit access?

The answer to this question is by no means straightforward, but in many cases is likely to be "no". APIs can be invoked in a broad number of programmatic means, but they tend to involve one program using a communication channel to request functions, and enable data to be passed back and forth. In order for this to amount to a breach of copyright, some act prohibited by copyright would need to happen, and that act would have to be undertaken by a party other than the copyright owner.

---

[7] A bare licence, therefore, cannot impose any restrictions on the user.

[8] See http://crossborder.practicallaw.com/2-200-2685?source=relatedcontent#sect1pos1res1 (paywall) (last accessed 1 September 2011).

[9] It is disturbing that lawyers are effectively capable of creating law where there was previously none, by allowing these behavioural norms to develop. This appears to be more prevalent in the sphere of intellectual property than anywhere else, and Cory Doctorow has written eloquently on his concern at being asked permission by people who want to make use of his works within the permissions clearly granted by a Creative Commons Licence, even if they are just doing it to "be polite". Available at http://craphound.com/?p=3063 (last accessed 1 September 2011) (although there's no harm in saying "I made use of your work—thanks for making it available").

The main acts restricted by copyright we are concerned with here are copying[10] and distribution. The mere invocation of an API does not generally (subject to some exceptions discussed below) involve the copying of any data of the provider presenting the API. It may involve the passing of a numerical value (which corresponds to a particular function requested) from one computer (the guest) to another (the host), together with some associated data. The host may respond by producing some data which are produced by it applying the requested function to the data supplied by the guest, or triggering the release of some data which it generates itself. The data returned may be copyright material, but that material is copied and distributed by the host computer.

Effective access to an API is greatly facilitated by access to the underlying documentation of that API as provided by the host, and functions and variable names may be labelled by the host API provider to facilitate programming. It may be argued that these function and variable names may themselves attract copyright. However, without examining the relevant law too closely, the following arguments militate against that:

1. The names themselves are too short to be regarded as literary works in their own right[11];
2. The publication of the variable names provides an implied licence to use them;
3. The use of the names is a necessary part of interoperability of one piece of software with another, a right which is protected under the European Computer Programs Directive,[12] US case law expressly excludes functional features from copyright protection.[13]

Having said that, it is worth examining the "modchip" cases brought by various games console manufacturers such as Nintendo,[14] which frequently also involve

---

[10] Transformation (or adaptation) is another primary right granted to copyright holders, but is not relevant to this discussion.

[11] It would be possible to design an API which only functions when a token is passed. The token itself may be a literary work which is designed to attract copyright protection.

[12] Directive 2009/24/EC on the legal protection of computer programs (OJ L 111, 5 May 2009). See, also, recital 11 which excludes protection of interfaces from this directive (although not necessarily from copyright generally): "For the avoidance of doubt, it has to be made clear that only the expression of a computer program is protected and that ideas and principles which underlie any element of a program, including those which underlie its interfaces, are not protected by copyright under this Directive";.

[13] "The exclusion of functional features from copyright protection grows out of the tension between copyright and patent laws. Functional features are generally within the domain of the patent laws.... [A]n item may be entirely original, but if the novel elements are functional, the item cannot be copyrighted: although it might be eligible for patent protection....". "*Incredible Technologies, Inc. v. Virtual Technologies, Inc*," 400 F.3d 1007, 1012 (7th Cir. 2005) (citing "*Pivot Point Intl., Inc. v. Charlene Prods., Inc.*", 372F.3d 913, 980 (7th Cir. 2004)) (emphasis omitted).

[14] "*Nintendo Company Ltd & Anor v Playables Ltd & Anor*" [2010] EWHC 1932 (Ch) (28 July 2010), available at http://www.bailii.org/ew/cases/EWHC/Ch/2010/1932.html (last accessed 24 August 2011).

criminal claims.[15] In one sense, modchips can be said to expose an API which the manufacturer wishes to remain concealed, and provisions of the Copyright, Designs and Patents Act 1988 as amended in the UK can be invoked when the exposure of those APIs facilitates copyright infringement.

A much more natural fit in terms of the legal wrong[16] that is committed by making unwarranted access to a cloud provider's API is provided by legislation prohibiting unauthorised access to computer systems.[17] For example, the Computer Misuse Act 1990[18] provides, in section 1(1), that:

> (1) A person is guilty of an offence if—
>   (a) he causes a computer to perform any function with intent to secure access to any program or data held in any computer, or to enable any such access to be secured
>   Thus it makes more sense from a jurisprudential perspective that the licence grants authorization to access the host's computer system under the Computer Misuse Act (or its equivalent in other jurisdictions) rather than to raise some sort of complex copyright-based argument as to access.

Google, for example, in its Google Maps licence[19] separates the two issues of use and content by having two separate licence clauses at 7.2—the *Service License* (for use authorization) and 7.3—the *Content License* (covering access to the geographical data returned by the service).

> 7.2 Service License. Subject to these Terms (including but not limited to Section 9 (License Requirements)), Google gives you a personal, worldwide, royalty-free, non-assignable and non-exclusive license to use the Service as provided by Google, in the manner permitted by the Terms.
> 7.3 Content License. Subject to these Terms (including but not limited to Section 9 (License Requirements)), Google gives you a personal, worldwide, royalty-free, non-assignable and non-exclusive license to access, use, publicly perform and publicly display the Content in your Maps API Implementation, as the Content is provided in the Service, and in the manner permitted by the Terms. Specifically, you understand the following:
>
> (a) Content (including but not limited to map data, traffic, and directions) is provided for planning purposes only. You may find that weather conditions, construction projects, closures, or other events may cause road conditions or directions to differ from the results depicted in the Content. You should exercise judgment in your use of the Content.
> (b) Certain Content is provided under license from third parties...

---

[15] "*Gilham v R*", [2009] EWCA Crim 2293 (09 November 2009) http://www.bailii.org/ew/cases/EWCA/Crim/2009/2293.html (last accessed 24 August 2011).

[16] Under UK Law, the Computer Misuse Act 1990 creates only criminal offences. Therefore, it is not clear that someone would immediately have a civil claim for unlawful access to their computer system in the UK. However, it may be possible to construct an argument in trespass to goods, by analogy with the similar US tort of trespass to chattels, referred to in Register.com v. Verio, Inc (see below).

[17] A difficulty in raising a claim of unauthorised access in modchip cases is that the console is likely to be owned by the person seeking access, meaning that the access would not be unauthorised.

[18] In the United Kingdom. Other jurisdictions have similar legislation.

[19] See http://code.google.com/apis/maps/terms.html, retrieved 24 August 2011.

A third possibility is the legal wrong committed by the user of the API is unlawful trespass to chattels, a tort. This issue was considered in *"Register.com, Inc. v. Verio, Inc."*,[20] a decision of the US Court of Appeals for the Second Circuit. Verio had been accessing Register's servers using an automated system which queried the domain name records held on Register's servers. Verio then used the information retrieved for marketing. Register commenced proceedings against Verio. Of interest in relation to this chapter is that one of Register's arguments[21] was that Verio was committing trespass to chattels by accessing Register's systems "in a manner likely to harm [them] by the use of Verio's automated robot software programs".

"A trespass to a chattel may be committed by intentionally... using or intermeddling with a chattel in the possession of another,"[22] where "the chattel is impaired as to its condition, quality, or value."[23]

The district court found that repeated access to Register's systems was of a different character to a single access. Repeated access would consume a significant proportion of the resources of Register's servers. Further, it would also encourage others to use similar programs to query Register's servers, and that even if Register's systems were able to cope with Verio's querying activities alone, they would not be able to cope with the parallel activities of a number of similar organisations. The Court of Appeals regarded that analysis by the district court as "not unreasonable".[24]

It is clear that access which was initially lawful may subsequently become unlawful, either because terms of access have subsequently come to the notice of the tortfeasor, or because the nature of the access (for example its volume and frequency), has brought it within the scope of activities which can cause harm to the chattel in question.

Thus, unlawful API access can be regarded as an actionable tort in the United States.[25] It is not clear whether such an analysis would be equally attractive to the courts of the United Kingdom.

It also seems logical to assume that for access to amount to unlawful trespass to chattels, those chattels have to belong to someone other than the person undertaking the access. This therefore suggests that where an entity is claiming unauthorised use of an API on the alleged tortfeasor's own equipment that trespass to chattels is not an appropriate legal theory upon which to proceed. This may arise,

[20] 356 F.3d 393 (2d Cir. 2004).

[21] Presented, incidentally, by William Patry, now counsel at Google.

[22] Restatement (Second) of Torts § 217(b) (1965), cited in the judgment with approval.

[23] ibid § 218(b).

[24] Judge Parker drafted the initial opinion of the court, but died before his opinion could be presented. The remainder of the panel disagreed with certain aspects of the opinion, but recognised its value nonetheless, and it is (unusually) appended to the judgment for reference.

[25] Footnote 54 to Judge Parker's opinion gives a useful summary of other cases on the point of extension of trespass to chattels to cover access to computer systems.

for example, where an entity has adopted an API developed by a third party and duplicated it in its own systems.[26]

10.4 Whose API Is It?

In the Google Maps example, it is clear that Google is operating the background software and presenting the API to the guest. With other cloud services, this may not be so clear. For example, if a user asks for a third party to provide a hosted web server on a standard, specified LAMP[27] stack, the user will be seeking to upload its content, for example, through an interface exposed by part of the stack like FTP.[28]

It may be helpful to imagine a computing service to be like an onion, with each layer representing a different service. The layers/services communicate with the layers/services immediately to either side of them through APIs. The outermost skin of the onion represents the user interface. In our example, the layers are from outside in, perl/php, MySQL, Apache and Linux. Deeper still are likely to be components of the virtualization infrastructure, for example Amazon's EC2 service.

This raises an important question. If someone accesses this LAMP stack, do they require the authorization of the host or the guest[29]? In other words, is the Host providing a hosting environment, probably an empty virtual machine, on which the LAMP stack is supplied as a convenience to the Guest, or is the Host providing the whole of the LAMP stack, inside its virtual machine, as a package? If the former, access to the LAMP stack would be granted by the Guest, in the latter, by the Host.

This has a number of practical consequences, not least in terms of software licensing and API licences. In this example, where the complete stack comprises free and open source software, it makes little practical difference whether the Host or the Guest is regarded as running the stack.[30] However, when components of the

---

[26] At the time of writing, Oracle has initiated a claim against Google against Google's alleged mis-appropriation of certain Java code, in particular its APIs. Unfortunately, the case has not yet produced any relevant case law, However, arguments of the parties are of interest, and Oracle, in particular, seems to be asserting that Google's own assertion of rights in relation to its own APIs is hypocritical. It is worth noting that Google's terms of use typically restrict the use of its own systems, and that therefore the trespass to chattels argument is relevant; Java, and any (allegedly) related APIs generated by Google (e.g. Dalvik), will in the overwhelming majority of cases be running on equipment not in the ownership of Oracle (for example, mobile consumer devices), and the trespass to chattels argument is therefore not relevant.

[27] Linux, Apache, MySQL, PHP/Perl. See http://en.wikipedia.org/wiki/LAMP_%28software_bundle%29 (last accessed 2 September 2011).

[28] File Transfer Protocol, see http://en.wikipedia.org/wiki/File_Transfer_Protocol (last accessed 2 September 2011).

[29] A reminder: we earlier in the chapter identified the host as the system providing the service which is made accessible by the API, and the guest as the system making use of that service.

[30] Assuming that the stack is a distribution of standard components. If, however, the stack contains elements released under a copyleft licence like GPL2, and those elements are modified, or, arguably, linked to other components of which the source code is not readily available, then this could, potentially, cause significant GPL violation issues. See Chap. 9.

stack are proprietary: for example, where the service is a hosted instance of Microsoft IIS where the barrier between host and guest lies is of significant importance in terms of licence compliance, and who is responsible for payment of licence fees.

It may also be relevant to data protection legislation, in terms of determining who is processing the data.

Frequently, this question of authorisation can be determined by asking "who has control over the API?" Thus, the Google Maps API is clearly controlled by Google, and therefore the boundary between Host code and Guest code lies at the API. In an example where the cloud provider is offering a LAMP stack, if the guest has access to the underlying operating system (Linux, in this example), and can, (at least in theory) change the API presenting, for example, the FTP service,[31] then the boundary between Host code and Guest code must lie elsewhere, more deeply into the system, possibly at the boundary between the operating system and the virtualisation infrastructure.[32] It is entirely possible (and not unusual) for different layers to be operated by different cloud providers: for example, the user may access a sales management system purchased from one provider, which itself hosts its system on virtualized infrastructure operated by another provider.[33]

Where the API boundary lies also impinges on the question of the ability of the provider to lock the user into its infrastructure.

10.5 APIs and Lock-In

Rufus Pollock shrewdly observed that the application of the law in the real world differs significantly from the application in the online world.[34] If you do not like the world provided by the makers of World of Warcraft, you can switch your allegiance to Linden Labs' Second Life. And if you cannot find an existing online world that's good for you, there is nothing stopping you from making one.

The real world, he argues, is much more constrained. Even assuming that you live in a regime that allows you to emigrate, there are obstacles to emigration:

---

[31] This example is not fanciful: the port used by the FTP service is frequently changed from the default as a form of security by obscurity.

[32] If the cloud provider is offering IIS hosting, then the user will clearly be unable to tinker with Microsoft's APIs. However, if the user is able to remove the whole of the IIS infrastructure, and replace it with, for example, a LAMP stack, then the boundary lies more deeply within the service. If the user is unable to do that, then the boundary must lie on the outside of IIS.

[33] The Data Protection Act 1998, in UK law, does not adequately address whether the operator of a cloud service in the deeper levels of a multi-level relationship would be regarded as a Data Processor.

[34] Talk at Law 2.0: Openness, Web 2.0 and the Ethic of Sharing, available at http://blog.okfn.org/2007/09/18/talk-at-law-20-openness-web-20-and-the-ethic-of-sharing/ (last accessed 2 September 2011).

severing ties with family and friends, disrupting children's education, a possible
language barrier, the cost of physically moving your possessions, finding suitable
employment and accommodation and meeting your chosen destination country's
immigration requirements and so on, present a major practical problem[35]:

That is, should the sovereign act in a way you do not like it is perfectly possible
for you at zero (or very low cost) to up sticks and head over the nearest border and
set up your own state. Consider then, the behaviour of a sovereign in this 'state of
anarchy'. While within his or her borders he or she may be a dictator, the fact that
any 'subject' who becomes unhappy can easily and simply leave greatly limits
their ability to abuse such power—though importantly it does not limit their ability
to do good, for in that case the "subjects" will be happy to stay. In this case, we
need to have little to fear from dictatorship, and by combining it with 'anarchy' we
obtain the best of both worlds.

Pollock's insight is that not only does a resident have the option to leave to a
more amenable environment, but that the threat of leaving has a normative effect
on the behavior of the "sovereign", making the domain more amenable to all
"subjects".[36]

Pollock discussed this in the context of online worlds like World of Warcraft
and Second Life, but the insight is as applicable to the providers of services in the
Cloud as it is to virtual worlds. A cloud provider which is aware that it is relatively
simple for a disgruntled user to transfer to another provider will be in the position
of Pollock's chastened sovereign: governed not only by the fear that a customer
may leave, but that competing cloud providers are actively seeking to provide
domains which will compel customer to switch. Pollock is an economist: his
prescription is vital to allow a market economy to develop in cloud service
provision.

Some service providers recognize that making a commitment to protect their
customers from lock-in is beneficial to their business. For example, Rackspace,
Canonical and others have established an organization called OpenStack[37] which
is intended to define an open standard for cloud services (and provide appropriate
open source code to implement it). Migration from one OpenStack compliant
vendor to another is intended to be straightforward. VMWare, likewise, has

---

[35] And, in contrast to the seventeenth and eighteenth centuries, it is no longer for an option to sail
west, hoping to find an uninhabited island on which one can establish a new independent
community. Current technology means that there are no habitable planets within reach of Earth at
all, let alone to intrepid bands of private adventurers.

[36] This effect does apply to a certain extent in the real world: large corporations, which are in a
sense virtual creatures of law and regulation anyway, can relatively easy to move to more fiscally
amenable jurisdictions. So can wealthy people. The poor are more tightly locked into their home
jurisdiction, which may be a factor behind the otherwise apparently bizarre decisions of some
governments who espouse progressive taxation one the one hand, and then make it easier for
corporations and the super-rich to avoid tax on the other.

[37] See http://openstack.org/ (last accessed 2 September 2011).

announced OpenPaaS,[38] intended to permit migration between OpenPaaS compliant platforms.

However, once a technology ecosystem has developed around an API, the controller of the API—often the cloud infrastructure or service provider—potentially has a great deal of market power to lock-in users in the following ways:

1. technically, by making it difficult for a user to extract data in bulk from the service provision or transfer it to another provider;
2. technically, by restricting access to metadata which have been established within the service;
3. legally, through terms of service restricting bulk downloads;
4. legally, through preventing third parties from implementing the same API.

Vint Cerf, in his role as Google's Chief Internet Evangelist, addresses the first two points by saying[39] that there should be a standard to allow data being migrated dynamically between cloud providers.[40]

We have discussed point 3 (terms of service). The last category deserves more analysis.

10.5.1 Copying APIs

If the API itself (essentially a specification) does not attract copyright protection, does its re-implementation in another context breach the copyright of the original provider? In Europe, the Computer Programs Directive[41] expressly provides a mechanism to permit software to be reverse-engineered for interoperability purposes. A similar principle subsists in the United States.[42]

---

[38] See http://blogs.vmware.com/console/2010/04/vmforce-and-vmwares-open-paas-strategy.html (last accessed 2 September 2011).

[39] See http://www.readwriteweb.com/enterprise/2010/01/vint-cerf-its-like-1973-for-mo.php (last accessed 2 September 2011).

[40] Which provides even more competitive pressure on providers, as it does not necessarily require a wholesale switch.

[41] Article 6 Directive 2009/24. This right may not be excluded by contract (it is not clear whether it can be restricted by a condition in a non-contractual copyright licence: something which is not, in general, known to the majority civil-law jurisdictions in the European Economic Area). It is also worth noting that there is a restriction on using interoperability information to create a competing product. However, this restriction is easily sidestepped in practice, for example by reverse engineering the lock to make the key, and then having a third part re-reverse engineer the key to make a compatible lock.

[42] See "Sega v. Accolade", US Court of Appeals, Ninth Circuit, October 20, 1992, 977 F.2d 1510, 24 USPQ2d 1561, available at http://digital-law-online.info/cases/24PQ2D1561.htm (last accessed 2 September 2011), and the related news item at http://www.eetimes.com/electronics-news/4073992/Ruling-for-Green-Hills-clears-way-for-copying-of-APIs. (last accessed 2 September 2011).

If a private API is reverse-engineered, and re-implemented in another product, the implementer of the original API may attempt to restrain the use of the re-implemented API. We have considered the effect of copyright on APIs. However, re-implementation of an API may also potentially violate patents.

SAMBA[43] is a project initiated by Andrew Tridgell in 1992. It was initially developed to enable non-Windows computers to share files and printers with Windows computers using the Microsoft SMB protocol (now called CIFS). Facilitating file and print sharing is intimately connected with security and permissions, and over time the project of necessity expanded to include Microsoft Active Directory compatibility. This enabled SAMBA-equipped servers (running, Linux, for example) to fulfill one of the essential roles of a Microsoft file server, acting as an Active Directory domain controller.

None of the SAMBA project team had access to any of Microsoft's underlying source code, and the implementation of the protocols was based on some remarkable reverse engineering (although, early in the project, Microsoft did co-operate with SAMBA in providing some protocol information).[44]

The existence of SAMBA posed a direct threat to Microsoft's server market, and despite the fact, the SAMBA code contained no Microsoft copyright code, Microsoft's threats of IPR infringement, and unwillingness to provide interoperability information, led to a case in the European Court of First Instance, in which Microsoft was found to be abusing its dominant position in the marketplace, and required to release interoperability information. It was also required to make certain promises in relation to its patents.[45]

While the outcome of the Microsoft case was hailed by the proponents of openness, it is worth bearing in mind that closure of an API and its protection by intellectual property claims may only be unlawful where that amounts to an abuse of a dominant position. Commercial pressure may, however, be placed on the providers of software which relies on closed standards (including APIs) by procurement rules which prevent public bodies from purchasing software or services which are reliant on closed standards.

10.5.2 Competition and Procurement Rules

Lock-in has been recognized as distorting the market process, creating unfair monopolies for the participants. Neelie Kroes, as EU Commission Vice President and Commissioner for the Digital Agenda, has recognised this, and has sought to

---

[43] See http://www.samba.org/ (last accessed 2 September 2011).

[44] See related news item at http://www.zdnet.com/blog/microsoft/microsoft-and-samba-finally-come-to-terms-over-windows-protocols/1064 (last accessed 2 September 2011).

[45] CFI Judgement of 17 September 2007, T-201/04, *"Microsoft Corp. v. Commission of the European Communities"*.

promote openness as a solution: "choosing open standards is a very smart business decision".[46] Lock-in can be created by closed file formats, data interchange specifications and even human elements like user interface familiarity. Closed APIs clearly provide one more opportunity for lock in. The law can try to promote openness by invoking specific procurement rules, as well as applying more general competition law principles.

In Europe, procurement rules perversely, permit requests for tenders which specify specific software (e.g. Microsoft Windows), but outlaw tenders requesting software from a specific manufacturer (e.g. software from Microsoft).[47] Organisations such as Open Forum Europe are lobbying for procurement rules to be amended such that no specific manufacturers or their products can be mentioned, and that tenders must be requested on the basis of specification only. The concern then shifts to whether a specification, because of lock-in, can effectively only be met by a single manufacturer.

In the US, Google has prevailed[48] over Microsoft by suing the US Government in a procurement action. The US Department of the Interior had issued a Request for Quotation requiring tenders to incorporate Microsoft's Business Productivity Online suite. A judge found that specifying a specific vendor's product contravened the US Competition in Contracting Act 1984.

The EU has promoted an Interoperability Framework, first issued in 2004.[49] It has no binding force, but recognizes the importance of interoperability of computer programs. In particular, it made the following statement about open standards:

> To attain interoperability in the context of pan-European eGovernment services, guidance needs to focus on open standards. The following are the minimal characteristics that a specification and its attendant documents must have in order to be considered an open standard:
>
> - The standard is adopted and will be maintained by a not-for-profit organisation, and its ongoing development occurs on the basis of an open decision-making procedure available to all interested parties (consensus or majority decision etc.).
> - The standard has been published and the standard specification document is available either freely or at a nominal charge. It must be permissible to all to copy, distribute and use it for no fee or at a nominal fee.
> - The intellectual property—i.e. patents possibly present—of (parts of) the standard is made irrevocably available on a royalty- free basis.
> - There are no constraints on the re-use of the standard.

---

[46] See her speech "Being open about standards" available at http://europa.eu/rapid/pressReleases Action.do?reference=SPEECH/08/317 (last accessed 2 September 2011).

[47] See related news item at http://www.computerweekly.com/blogs/public-sector/2010/11/procurement-perversities-stifl.html (last accessed 2 September 2011).

[48] See related news item at http://www.zdnet.com/blog/btl/googles-legal-victory-judge-stops-federal-agency-from-jumping-on-microsofts-cloud/43233 (last accessed 2 September 2011).

[49] European Interoperability Framework for pan-European eGovernment services, available at http://ec.europa.eu/idabc/en/document/2319/5938.html (last accessed 2 September 2011).

Interoperability proponents welcomed this formulation, and noted that although it acknowledged that the implementation of standards could require a patent licence, that the standard could only be described as "open" if a licence was made available on a royalty-free basis. There was, admittedly, concern that the existence of any patent protection in standards, even, where a licence to the patent for standards implementation was available on a royalty free basis, may make the implementation of standards-compliant software impossible if it contained components licensed under the GNU GPL. However, it was clear that the European Commission understood that lock-in was potentially dangerous and anti-competitive, and it was hoped that an update of the European Interoperability Framework published in 2010 would both pave the way for the framework being binding in certain circumstances, and also strengthen the definition of open standards.

The revised EIF[50] is, however, significantly vaguer. It establishes an openness principle:

If the openness principle is applied in full:

- All stakeholders have the same possibility of contributing to the development of the specification and public review is part of the decision-making process;
- The specification is available for everybody to study;
- Intellectual property rights related to the specification are licensed on FRAND terms or on a royalty-free basis in a way that allows implementation in both proprietary and open source software.[51]

The opening sentence of this extract suggests that the openness principle is not absolute, and indeed, several paragraphs down in that section, we find:

However, public administrations may decide to use less open specifications, if open specifications do not exist or do not meet functional interoperability needs.

It is not difficult, therefore, for any public administration to decide that a specific implementation does not meet its functional interoperability standard, and that therefore it is acceptable (under EIF2) to ignore the openness principle. Not surprisingly, commentators[52] have suggested that EIF2 is effectively toothless as a prescriptive document.

Despite EIF2, it may prove possible to raise an argument that by requiring providers to comply with closed standards, certain suppliers, particularly those using GPL code, are discriminated against. This is largely because, where use of a standard necessarily involves the implementation of a patented invention, the licence under which the use of the patent is permitted must be compatible with the

---

[50] Information available at http://ec.europa.eu/isa/strategy/index_en.htm (last accessed 24 August 2011).

[51] http://ec.europa.eu/isa/strategy/doc/annex_ii_eif_en.pdf section 5.2.1 Retrieved 24th August 2011 (last accessed 2 September 2011).

[52] G. Moody, European Interoperability Framework v2—The Great Defeat, available at http://blogs.computerworlduk.com/open-enterprise/2010/12/european-interoperability-framework-v2—the-great-defeat/ (last accessed 24 August 2011)-.

GPL's patent clause (clause 7, in GPL version 2, clause 11, GPL version 3). Because patent licences, even ones licensed on RAND or FRAND terms, are likely to extend solely to that implementer (in other words, do not permit sub-licensing), and are also likely to be limited in scope to implementations of that standard alone (and not to other uses), the GPL's patent clauses will not be satisfied.[53]

No cases, however, have been brought on this basis to date.[54] It will be interesting to see whether purchasing patterns change in the coming years.

10.6 Conclusion

Providers of cloud services such as Google wield an increasing amount of power, and there are a number of ways they can exercise that power, by employing both technological and legal means. The dangers of lock-in were previously underestimated, but awareness is increasing significantly, with providers increasingly using open standards as a key marketing message, to differentiate themselves from proprietary providers. Competition and procurement law provide some pressure to drive openness, but ultimately, it may be increased consumer awareness of the issues which drives the adoption of open APIs and standards.

Reference

Lessig L (2006) Code v2. Basic books, Cambridge

---

[53] See an article by Iain Mitchell Q.C. in the International Free and Open Source Law Review (http://www.ifosslr.org) 5th edition (September 2011) not yet published at the time of writing.

[54] In the US, a complaint was made the Federal Trade Commission in relation to Google's cloud services. However, this was not competition law related, and raised questions about whether Google's trade practices were deceptive, where they allegedly promised that their service was more secure than it was in practice. The complaint is available at http://epic.org/privacy/cloudcomputing/google/ftc031709.pdf (last accessed 24 August 2011).

Chapter 11
Paradoxes, Google and China: How Censorship can Harm and Intellectual Property can Harness Innovation

Danny Friedmann

Contents

11.1 Introduction

One could argue that Adam and Eve were exposed to censorship. The highest authority Himself deemed the first man and woman not ready to eat from the Tree of Good and Evil. Many governments, including the Chinese government, also do not want their citizens to decide for themselves and therefore filter their Internet

D. Friedmann (✉)
Chinese University of Hong Kong, Hong Kong, China
e-mail: dannyfriedmann@gmail.com

A. Lopez-Tarruella (ed.), *Google and the Law,*
Information Technology and Law Series 22, DOI: 10.1007/978-90-6704-846-0_11,
© T.M.C. Asser press, The Hague, The Netherlands, and the author(s) 2012

access. China has already the most Internet users in the world[1] while their Internet market remains far from saturated. This makes China the 'promised land' for online service providers. Google is such a provider and wants to be perceived as the freedom of choice champion. With its mission of "organizing all information and making it universally accessible and useful"[2] Google is similar to the snake. "Pssst Eve! Pssst Eve, eat the apple!"[3] While this is the path chosen by Google, the Chinese government asserts its sovereign rights and filters the Internet in the most extensive and sophisticated ways possible. From a utilitarian point of view the Chinese government believes this is the way to lead their citizens to prosperity. Due to their fundamental conceptual differences the collision course of these giants could be expected.

Mid December 2009, there were alleged cyber attacks on Google's corporate infrastructure that originated from China. The attacks on Google were not isolated cases. Other foreign companies in China were also attacked. Google believed the attacks were focused on getting access to Gmail accounts of human rights advocates. In combination with China's measures to limit free speech, this action made the US company threaten to leave China. However, Google came to the conclusion that China would not try to stop them, because, in any case, most Chinese use Baidu as their search engine. Google decided that they had more to gain by staying and redirecting the users of Google.cn to the Hong Kong site. This way Google cleansed its corporate conscience to some degree and some Chinese citizens, though not all the time, could see some uncensored search results. Did Google overplay its hand? Some considered that the Chinese government would expel Google from paradise. But in July 2010, China renewed Google's Internet Content Provider license.[4] So Google's adventure in China continues. This article deals with the snake and those trying to stop it from speaking up. It will also discuss intellectual property rights, a subject already topical since man was created in the image of the Creator himself. This article will look at these two important legal challenges presented by the Internet through the lens of innovation.

---

[1] China announced Thursday, December 31, 2010, that it has 450 million users, which is the most in the world. Wang G, 450 million Chinese use Internet, China Daily, December 31, 2010, via English Xinhua, available at http://news.xinhuanet.com/english2010/china/2010-12/31/c_13671684.htm. (last accessed 11 August 2011).

[2] Google's mission is stated on Google's corporate website. Google Corporate, available at http://www.google.com/corporate/. (last accessed 11 August 2011).

[3] Genesis 3:2-3:5: "The woman said to the snake: From the fruit of the (other) trees in the garden we may eat, but from the fruit of the tree that is in the midst of the garden, God has said: You are not to eat from it and you are not to touch it, lest you die. The snake said to the woman: Die, you will not die! Rather, God knows that on the day that you eat from it, your eyes will be opened and you will become like gods, knowing good and evil." Old Jewish English Bible 1917.

[4] China renewed Google's Internet Content Provider (ICP) on July 9, 2010. See Drummond D, An update on China, The Official Google Blog, July 9, 2010, available at http://googleblog.blogspot.com/2010/06/update-on-china.html. (last accessed 11 August 2011).

Officially China wants to lead its citizens to a socialist society and Google wants to make all information available to everyone, while not doing evil. These two ideals have respectively functioned for both China and Google as a magnet: both have become popular and powerful. However, China and Google are finding out that it is impossible to continue political and economic success without leaving the straight and narrow. They demonstrate their megalomania by thinking that if they digress a bit from their lofty goals to continue their power or expand their market position, they can make up for it by doing good in the longer run and remain faithful to their ideals at the same time.

In Sect. 11.2., it becomes clear that Google is involved in a growing number of litigation cases in which it is accused of infringing intellectual property rights. It is argued that online service providers are in the best position to enforce intellectual property rights and therefore they can provide solutions for the problems which they create (Google Paradox). The chapter discusses Google's adventure to give access to information to the people of China. It also illuminates the second Google paradox: Google wants to be perceived as the champion of freedom of information, while it practices censorship in most countries. Google has even filed a patent application for a methodology to censor depending on user location.

Section 11.3 takes a look at two World Trade Organization cases the U.S. has brought against China, in which the issues of censorship meet intellectual property rights. Then the legitimacy of censorship is assessed in light of China's international treaty obligations and its national law. The question arises whether foreign countries can do something to prevent their native industries becoming complicit in censorship by providing filtering products and services. In other words, the question will be asked as to whether domestic law can be exported to domestic companies that are operating abroad.

Section 11.4 is about transparency on censorship. The Chinese government has three narratives on the Internet. These narratives show the triple moral bookkeeping of China's policy. One of the narratives is directed abroad, one to its citizens and one to party officials. Because the Chinese government is censoring information about censorship, one needs to research the available research on censorship. This section will make use of the results of the OpenNet Initiative to paint a picture of the methodology of censorship in China and to identify which content is filtered. This section closes with an assessment of the effectiveness of censorship.

Section 11.5 will explore the relation between intellectual property and innovation, censorship and innovation and the crucial role innovation plays for the Chinese government.

11.2 Google Paradox: Freedom of Information Champion Executes Censorship

11.2.1 Censoring in the Name of Intellectual Property

What most of Google's innovative services have in common is that they are based on selling advertisements. Despite its corporate mantra, "Don't be evil",[5] Google has been frequently accused of intellectual property rights infringements by linking keywords of trademarked brands in advertisements to sites providing counterfeit goods and downloading pirated products, or of neglecting intellectual property rights in other ways.[6] Intellectual property infringements often concern copycats that free ride on the reputation and goodwill of a trademark or the creativity of an author. Besides these commercial damages, counterfeit goods can seriously harm the health or even be fatal to online purchasers. Google was invited for the February 2011 Senate Judiciary Committee hearing on "targeting websites dedicated to stealing American intellectual property" but refused to testify. In its absence, the company was labeled as a profiteer because of the nature of its relationship with sites that offer counterfeit goods and pirated products: Google gets paid each time links are clicked.[7] If the U.S. law proposal, "Combating Online Infringement Counterfeit Act (CO-ICA)",[8] will be adopted, Google will have to stop providing advertisement services and start filtering domestic and overseas domain names that are suspected of distributing counterfeit and pirated materials. Rights holders are constantly trying to make online service providers such as Google liable[9] for contributory copyright and trademark infringements. It makes sense, since they are in the best position to

---

[5] Code of conduct, Google investor relations, available at http://investor.google.com/corporate/code-of-conduct.html. (last accessed 11 August 2011).

[6] For example Google's Book/Library Project, a project whereby books are scanned and online indexed and searchable, whereby the copyright holders could opt-out (since August 2005) before a deadline, so that the work will be removed from the project. To apply here this kind of implied license theory is controversial. Google assumes that all copyright holders will join the project and if they do not want to, they have to opt-out, laying the burden to the right holders. Google Book Settlement, available at http://www.googlebooksettlement.com/r/enter_opt_out. (last accessed 11 August 2011).

[7] Tony Adams, CEO of Rosetta Stone: "Profit relationship between right now between illicit websites and Google. Because they pay them for every click." Senate Judiciary Committee (2011) 226 SD hearing on Targeting Websites Dedicated To Stealing American Intellectual Property, February 16, 2011, available at http://judiciary.senate.gov/hearings/hearing.cfm?id=4982 (last accessed 11 August 2011).

[8] U.S., Section 3804 (2010), Combating Online Infringement Counterfeit Act, introduced September 20, 2010 by Senator Patrick Leahy, available at http://www.govtrack.us/congress/bill.xpd?bill=s111-3804. (last accessed 11 August 2011).

[9] Contributory liability has a knowledge requirement and material contribution requirement. Ludwig 2006, p 478. There are "two prongs to contributory liability: (1) the defendant's knowledge of the infringing activity, and (2) the defendant's contribution to, or participation in, the infringing activity (Karnow 1999).

enforce. It could be difficult to locate the end users who might not even have the financial means to compensate for the damages. In Sect. 11.4.2 one can see a parallel development with China holding online service providers to have some contributory liability for filtering certain information. According to the Electronic Frontier Foundation, the COICA bill would *de facto* force search engines such as Google to censor some domain names. The targeting of domain names "that are dedicated to infringing activities", without judicial review, is considered a serious restriction to the freedom of speech.[10]

11.2.2 *"Freedom of Information Champion"*

Google cultivates an image of being a champion of the freedom of information. The freedom of expression is not absolute in any country. As a result Google filters in nearly all countries related to intellectual property infringements. in the U.S. it filtered information critical to Scientology in 2002[11] to comply with the Digital Millennium Copyright Act.[12] In France and Germany it is filtering search results relating to Nazi memorabilia, Holocaust deniers, white supremacists and sites that make propaganda against the democratic constitutional order.[13] In Thailand Google filters sites that allegedly insult its king.[14] In some countries adult pornography is blocked, and in almost all countries, child pornography[15] is blocked.

Google started its adventure in China in 2005.[16] Google learned a lesson from the controversy around Yahoo's conduct. Yahoo turned over information concerning subscribers, who were later imprisoned. The lesson was not to provide blogging and email services. In 2006 Google's senior policy council McLaughlin thought that Google.cn was the answer for the inaccessibility of Chinese citizens to

---

[10] Esguarra R, Censorship of the Internet Takes Center Stage in "Online Infringement" Bill, EFF, September 21, 2010, available at http://www.eff.org/deeplinks/2010/09/censorship-internet-takes-center-stage-online. (last accessed 11 August 2011).

[11] F.A.C.T. Net, Google, Censorship and Scientology, March 21, 2002., available at http://www.factnet.org/Scientology/Google_Scientology.html. Accessed 11 August 2011.

[12] Digital Millennium Copyright Act 1998.

[13] 113 white supremacist, antisemitic, Holocaust denial and Nazi memorabilia sites were excluded from the search results of Google.fr and Google.de. Zittrain J, Edelman B, Localized Google search result exclusions, Statement of issues and call for data, Harvard, October 26, 2002. http://cyber.law.harvard.edu/filtering/google/. (last accessed 11 August 2011).

[14] Greenberg A, Where Google Still Censors, Forbes, January 21, 2010., available at http://www.forbes.com/forbes/2010/0208/outfront-technology-china-where-google-still-censors.html. (last accessed 11 August 2011).

[15] "Most societies share the view that imagery of children under a certain age in a sexually compromising position is unlawful to produce, possess, or distribute." Zittrain and Palfrey 2008a, b, p 44.

[16] In 2005 Google opened its headquarters in Beijing and in 2007 opened an Research & Development office in Shanghai.

Google.com, Google News and Google Images. According to McLaughlin,
"Filtering our search results clearly compromises our mission. Failing to offer
Google search at all to a fifth of the world's population, however, does so far more
severely."[17] The next month Elliot Schrage, vice president, global communications and public affairs of Google, repeated this message during a testimony before
the subcommittee 'Asia and the Pacific, global human rights and international
operations'.[18] Schrage said Google's "(..) decision was based on a judgment that
Google.cn will make a meaningful—though imperfect—contribution to the overall
expansion of access to information in China."

However, after some cyber attacks that were allegedly aimed at Gmail accounts
of human rights advocates and originated from China, Google announced in
January 2010 that it would no longer censor its search results.[19] Further, Google
announced that if China would not agree it would leave the country. At the same
time Google called on the U.S. and other western governments to challenge
Internet censorship as a restraint on global trade. Bob Boorstin, Google's director
of Public Affairs said: "Governments that block the free flow of information not
only are breaking trade agreements in certain ways, but they're hurting their own
economies as well."[20] Did Google lose its patience? Eric Schmidt, CEO of Google
said: "We will take a long-term view to win in China. The Chinese have
5,000 years of history. Google has 5,000 years of patience in China."[21] Instead of
leaving China, Google relocated its Google Search, Google News and Google
Images from Google.cn to Google.com.hk.[22] However, since the relocation to
Google.com.hk,[23] results are not always and not everywhere available in China. So
Google.cn was not the answer for the inaccessibility of Google.com and the

---

[17] McLaughlin A, Google in China, the Official Google Blog, January 27, 2006., available at
http://googleblog.blogspot.com/2006/01/google-in-china.html. (last accessed 11 August 2011).

[18] Schrage E, Internet in China, testimony to the Subcommittee on Asia and the Pacific, and the
Subcommittee on Africa, Global Human Rights, and International Operations, Committee on
International Relations, United States House of Representatives, February 15, 2006, available at http://
googleblog.blogspot.com/2006/02/testimony-internet-in-china.html. (last accessed 11 August 2011).

[19] Johnson B, Google stops censoring Chinese search engine: How it happened, The Guardian,
March 22, 2010, available at http://www.guardian.co.uk/technology/blog/2010/mar/22/google-
china-live. (last accessed 11 August 2011).

[20] Waters R, Google opens new front in censorship battle, Financial Times, November 16, 2010,
available at http://www.ftchinese.com/story/001035559/en. (last accessed 11 August 2011).

[21] Lee K, Lecture: Google in China, Carnegie Mellon University, YouTube, February 27, 2008.,
available at http://www.youtube.com/watch?v=sgDGNPnb124&feature=player_embedded. (last
accessed 11 August 2011).

[22] "Users visiting Google.cn are being redirected to Google.com.hk, where we are offering
uncensored search in simplified Chinese, specifically designed for users in mainland China and
delivered via our servers in Hong Kong. On Google.cn users can use services such as music and
text translate, which are provided without filtering." See Drummond D, An update on China, The
Official Google Blog, July 9, 2010.

[23] Since no servers in China are used to generate search results it does not fall within the
jurisdiction of China.

relocation of Google.com.hk leads to the same accessibility challenges as to Google.com. Google is back where it started.

It is hard to believe that after five years in China Google suddenly realized that the extensive level of censorship it was forced to apply was incompatible with its mission statement. It is more likely that Google realized that its market share in China was dwarfed by the Chinese search engine Baidu, which is favored by the Chinese government. It is not unlikely to assume that a strong market position of Baidu in combination with the data integrity which Google could no longer guarantee pushed Google to a decision. This decision was whether Google would risk losing its license but gain the goodwill of the public.

After playing so explicitly the role of freedom of speech champion, it is ironic to find out that Google filed an application in the U.S. to patent censoring methodology that censors depending on the location of the user.[24] Actually the censoring methodology devised by Google goes beyond what countries ask of online service providers, namely to be more restrictive or less restrictive depending on the country of origin of the user. It almost seems that Google developed a product which they believed fulfills a gap in some host countries' needs.

11.3 Where Intellectual Property and Censorship Meet

11.3.1 Case Studies

The U.S. filed a case against China at the WTO for measures that allegedly affect the protection and enforcement of intellectual property rights negatively.[25] One of the complaints of the U.S. was that article 4 of China's Copyright Law[26] did not offer copyright protection to works of which publication or distribution are prohibited or under assessment by a censor. China's argument was that a censored work did have copyright, but that China did not have to protect it, based on article

---

[24] 'Variable user interface based on document access privileges', U.S. Patent application number: 10/953,496, filed: September 30, 2004, assignee: Google Inc. (Mountain View, CA), available at http://patft.uspto.gov/netacgi/nph-Parser?Sect1=PTO1&Sect2=HITOFF&d=PALL&p=1&u=/netahtml/PTO/srchnum.htm&r=1&f=G&l=50&s1=7,664,751.PN.&OS=PN/7,664,751&RS=PN/7,664,751. (last accessed 11 August 2011).

[25] *China—Measures Affecting the Protection and Enforcement of Intellectual Property Rights*, WT/DS362, WTO Panel Report, January 26, 2009. http://www.wto.org/english/tratop_e/dispu_e/cases_e/ds362_e.htm. (last accessed 11 August 2011).

[26] Article 4 Copyright Law 2001: "Works the publication or distribution of which is prohibited by law shall not be protected by this Law. Copyright owners, in exercising their copyright, shall not violate the Constitution or laws or prejudice the public interests." Amended Copyright Law 2001.

17 Berne Convention.[27] However, this provision states the opposite, namely that the protection of copyright cannot affect the possibility to control the circulation, presentation and exhibition of works. Therefore China's argument did not convince the panel. In the panel report it was determined that a denial of copyright protection based on article 4 Copyright Law was not compatible with China's obligations under the Agreement on Trade-related Aspects of Intellectual Property Rights (TRIPs)[28] and the Berne Convention. China amended its copyright law, which now includes a revised article 4 Copyright Law, which became effective on April 1, 2010.[29]

The U.S. brought another case against China at the WTO regarding market access.[30] The issue of market access brings censorship and intellectual property rights together. Censorship is not only a barrier to market access, but it is also a boon for pirated versions of movies or books.[31] So far only twenty foreign movies were allowed into the Chinese market,[32] each year handled by an importer with a distribution monopoly.[33] The reason given for this restrictive policy has been to protect the fledgling Chinese movie industry, or to protect the security of the state. Some are banned directly and the arrival of other films is delayed by lengthy

---

[27] Article 17 Berne Convention: 'The provisions of this Convention cannot in any way affect the right of the Government of each country of the Union to permit, to control, or to prohibit, by legislation or regulation, the circulation, presentation, or exhibition of any work or production in regard to which the competent authority may find it necessary to exercise that right'. The Berne Convention for the Protection of Literary and Artistic Works was established in 1886. China became a contracting party in October 15, 1992.

[28] China became a member of the World Trade Organization on December 12, 2001, and the Agreement on Trade-related Aspects of Intellectual Property Rights of 1994 is an integral part of this agreement.

[29] Article 4 Copyright Law: Copyright holders, when exercising their copyright, may not violate the Constitution and laws, and may not damage the public interest. The State implements supervision and management over publishing and dissemination according to the law. Article 4 Copyright Law amendment 2010.

[30] *China—Measures Affecting Trading Rights and Distribution Services for Certain Publication and Audiovisual Entertainment Products*, WT/DS363, WTO Panel Report, August 12, 2009. http://www.wto.org/english/news_e/news09_e/363r_e.htm. (last accessed 11 August 2011).

[31] "We cannot divorce the concept of market access from the question of piracy. In no case is that more apparent... [than] China", Bloomberg news agency quoted Pat Schroeder, president of the Association of American Publishers, as saying, InTheNews.co.uk, Chinese copyright piracy faces US threat, February 16, 2007, available at http://www.inthenews.co.uk/money/news/finance/chinese-copyright-piracy-faces-us-threat-$1053067.htm. (last accessed 11 August 2011).

[32] The number of foreign movies that can be shown in Chinese cinemas is limited to 20 movies per year. One can argue that this stimulated pirated DVDs to the point that only 7 per cent of the DVD's on the market are legitimate. Reuters, Market access key to piracy fight, via The Age, December 8, 2006, available at http://www.theage.com.au/news/World/Market-access-key-to-piracyfight/2006/12/08/1165081128349.html#. (last accessed 11 August 2011).

[33] *Film Distribution Company and Huaxia*, USTR (2005), Trade summary., available at http://www.ustr.gov/assets/Document_Library/Reports_Publications/2005/2005_NTE_Report/asset_upload_file469_7460.pdf, p 113. (last accessed 11 August 2011).

censorship reviews of Chinese authorities.[34] Because of this, censored Hollywood films are broadly pirated in China.[35] However, under the WTO ruling foreign producers will be able to contract private film companies as of March, 2011 to distribute their films in China. According to the state newspaper China Daily, it is expected that the number of foreign films allowed in Chinese cinemas will be increased.[36] Not only cannot legitimate foreign movies compete against pirated movies that pay no taxes and bear marginal production costs, but domestic movies also have the same problem.[37] This makes the argument that restricting foreign movies is in the interest of China's fledgling domestic film industry, less convincing.

11.3.2 Legitimacy of Censorship

11.3.2.1 International Law

Since the Peace of Westphalia[38] the following key principles are recognized as the foundations of international law: the principle of sovereignty,[39] the fundamental right of political self determination, the principle of legal equality between states

---

[34] The criteria for censorship are: the state advocates to create excellent films that have both ideological content and artistic quality". They should "get close to reality, life and the masses"; be of "benefit to the minors' healthy growth"; and "try to transform backward culture and combat firmly the decadent culture". And maybe most important no politics can be involved in entertainment, Toy M, Piracy still pays despite party line on what's fit for Chinese eyes, Sidney Morning Herald, February 10, 2007. http://www.smh.com.au/news/world/piracy-still-pays-despite-party-line-on-whats-fit-for-chineseeyes/2007/02/09/1170524304056.html. (last accessed 11 August 2011).

[35] "China's censorship process means that legitimate titles are a subset of all titles produced, i.e. producing pirated titles allows distributors to offer customers much wider choice; with no royalties and taxes to pay, and no quality control requirements to meet, pirated movies provide distributors with significantly higher profits, because sellers of pirated movies are generally unlicensed, the distribution network for pirated movies is far more developed than that for legally licensed movies", *Chinese Academy of Social Sciences report, Study of the Impact of Movie Piracy on China's Economy*, June 2006, available at http://www.uschina.org/public/documents/2006/07/cass_piracyimpact_e.pdf. (last accessed 11 August 2011).

[36] Zhao Y, Dawson KC, Opening-up of movie industry urged, China Daily, February 10, 2011, available at http://www.chinadaily.com.cn/china/2011-02/10/content_11977999.htm. (last accessed 11 August 2011).

[37] Legitimate foreign and domestic movies cannot compete with pirated movies "who endure no censorship, pay no taxes, and bear minimal production costs", Ranjard P, Misonne B, Study 12: Exploring China's IP Environment, Study on the Future Opportunities and Challenges of EU-China Investment Relations, February 15, 2007, available at http://trade.ec.europa.eu/doclib/docs/2007/february/tradoc_133314.pdf, p 13. (last accessed 11 August 2011).

[38] Peace of Westphalia in 1648, Wikipedia, available at http://en.wikipedia.org/wiki/Peace_of_Westphalia. (last accessed 11 August 2011).

[39] Westphalian sovereignty, Wikipedia, available at http://en.wikipedia.org/wiki/Westphalian_sovereignty. (last accessed 11 August 2011).

and the principle of non intervention of one state in the internal affairs of another state. Therefore, based on sovereignty a state can control its domestic matters, including those in cyberspace. Based on the principle of non intervention, other states cannot do much about it to stop it. Of course states can voluntarily bind themselves via treaties to standards of conduct. The Universal Declaration of Human Rights[40] was proclaimed in 1948 by 48 states, including the Republic of China. The word "universal" refers to the aspiration of the declaration to make it applicable to all people no matter in which country. But the declaration has no signatories and is not legally binding in any country. Even if it were binding, it was adopted by the Republic of China a year before the founding of the People's Republic. As a successor state, it is up to the People's Republic of China's discretion whether it will abide by the declaration.

China did sign the International Covenant on Civil and Political Rights (ICCPR)[41] on October 5, 1998.[42] Article 19.1 ICCPR states that everybody has the right to hold opinions without interference. And article 19.2 ICCPR articulates that everybody shall have the right to freedom of expression, which includes the freedom to seek, receive and impart information and ideas.[43] However, article 19.3 ICCPR states that the exercise of the rights carries special duties and responsibilities: "It may therefore be subject to certain restrictions, but these shall only be such as are provided by law and are necessary. (a) For respect of the rights or reputations of others; (b) For the protection of national security or of public order (ordre public), or of public health or morals." There is no controversy about respecting the rights or reputations of others, which includes intellectual property rights. But when exactly are certain restrictions necessary? And when does information or an idea fall under national security,[44] public order or morals? These undefined terms leave space for authoritarian regimes to justify any kind of censorship. China can use any kind of censorship, as long as it frames the justification

---

[40] Article 19: "Everyone has the right to freedom of opinion and expression; this right includes freedom to hold opinions without interference and to seek, receive and impart information and ideas through any media and regardless of frontiers." Universal Declaration of Human Rights, December 10, 1948, available at http://www.un.org/en/documents/udhr/index.shtml. (last accessed 11 August 2011).

[41] International Covenant on Civil and Political Rights, opened for signature, ratification and accession December 16, 1966, entered into force on March 23, 1976, available at http://www2.ohchr.org/english/law/ccpr.htm. (last accessed 11 August 2011).

[42] International Covenant on Civil and Political Rights, China's signature October 27, 1997 and ratification March 27, 2001. China's reservations about Macao, Hong Kong and Taiwan, available at http//treaties.un.org/Pages/ViewDetails.aspx?src=TREATY&mtdsg_no=IV-4&chapter=4&lang=en. (last accessed 11 August 2011).

[43] John Stuart Mill argued that freedom of speech should be understood as a multifaceted right. These include the right to seek, receive and impart information and ideas. Puddephatt 2005, p 128.

[44] "Put more simply, Internet filtering and surveillance, in an environment where the Internet is considered a form of territory alongside land or sea or air, are an expression of the unalterable right of a state to ensure its national security" Zittrain and Palfrey 2008a, b, p 45.

in the wording of article 19.3 ICCPR. Then again, even if China deviates from the ICCPR, it has not much to fear.

The Human Rights Committee, the treaty's enforcement mechanism, is *de facto* toothless. "Necessary" is a highly subjective term and is hard to examine, but one can peruse whether China provides law for restrictions, such as censoring the Internet.

11.3.2.2 National Law

China has a comprehensive system of online media control in place, which is built on principles already developed in controlling other forms of news and entertainment media.[45] Institutionally, it is implemented through party orders.[46] According to Chinese copyright/media scholar, Creemers, the Central Propaganda Department is at the central level the most important organ. It forms the Chinese Communist Party's trinity of power, together with the Organization Department and the Army. This organ controls all State media entities, such as the General Administration of Press and Publications, the State Administration of Radio, Film and Television (SARFT), the Ministry of Information Industry, and the Ministry of Culture. These in turn regulate the media, including online media.

Creemers explains that these media are mostly controlled through administrative regulations. In addition, some more egregious violations against social order are also included in the Criminal Law, for example, the provisions on subversion—Article 105—was one of the grounds on which Liu Xiaobo was convicted.[47] The administrative regulations provide the basic operating framework for works, but they also contain "safeguard provisions", which provide a legal basis for discretionary intervention that can be construed quite broadly. For example: in special circumstances, SARFT can order the withdrawal of an approved media product from the works. SARFT has the discretionary power to interpret.[48]

All regulations contain provisions on what cannot be published online, which internal safeguard mechanisms websites must have to avoid content problems, and penalization provisions.[49] The government keeps most control by giving licenses to products (films, television programmes, games, etc.), and companies. The State has a monopoly over market access. Creemers write that "[t]hose who are not doing what the Party-State requires of them, will lose their legal status and their possibility to earn a living".[50]

---

[45] Creemers 2011.

[46] Idem.

[47] Idem.

[48] Idem.

[49] An example is the Internet Audiovisual Programme Service Management Regulations, Creemers R, Internet Audiovisual Programme Service Management Regulations, China Copyright and Media, December 20, 2007, available at http://chinacopyrightandmedia.wordpress.com/2007/12/20/internet-audiovisual-programme-service-management-regulations/. (last accessed 11 August 2011).

[50] Creemers 2011.

11.3.3 How to Stop Domestic Companies Facilitating Censorship Abroad?

Can the U.S. companies such as Yahoo and Google do whatever they want when they operate abroad? Is there a way to hold them accountable for their conduct? Yahoo's behavior was described by the chairman of the House Foreign Affairs Committee at the 'Internet in China: A Tool for Freedom or Supression' hearing in 2006 as "at best inexcusably negligent".[51] But besides some scathing remarks and some public indignation, the company was not penalized. To avoid similar scenarios in the future some want to make it a crime for the U.S. companies to share personal user information with Internet restricting countries. the U.S. representative Christopher Smith proposed the Global Online Freedom Act (GOFA) in 2007 to no avail, and again in 2009.[52] But thus far the bill has not become law. Google proposed voluntary industry action in 2006[53] and endorsed the GOFA in 2008.[54] However, there already is a working example of a U.S. law that restricts domestic companies doing business abroad: the Foreign Corrupt Practices Act.[55] It prohibits corporations chartered in the U.S. to bribe foreign officials.[56] Also within the European Union there are now calls for export licenses to prevent European companies that facilitate Internet censorship.[57]

---

[51] "Let me be clear - this was no misunderstanding. This was inexcusably negligent behaviour at best, and deliberately deceptive behaviour at worst." Lantos T (2007), Yahoo! Inc.'s Provision of False Information to Congress, Hearing House Committee on Foreign Affairs, November 6, 2007, available at http://foreignaffairs.house.gov/110/lantos110607.htm. (last accessed 11 August 2011).

[52] Global Online Freedom Act, H.R. 2271, sponsored by Representative Christopher Smith in May 6, 2009, available at http://www.govtrack.us/congress/bill.xpd?bill=h111-2271. (last accessed 11 August 2011).

[53] Schrage E, Internet in China, testimony to the Subcommittee on Asia and the Pacific, and the Subcommittee on Africa, Global Human Rights, and International Operations, Committee on International Relations, United States House of Representatives, February 15, 2006.

[54] Smith C, Introducing the Global Internet Freedom Caucus, excerpts from his statement to the House of Representatives, March 9, 2010, available at http://chrissmith.house.gov/UploadedFiles/2010-03-09_Statement_on_Global_Internet_Freedom_Caucus.pdf. (last accessed 11 August 2011).

[55] Foreign Corrupt Practices Act, 15 U.S.C. §§ 78dd-1 and ff, 1977.

[56] "The analogy in the United States context runs to the Foreign Corrupt Practices Act, which disallows corporations chartered in the United States from bribing foreign officials and other business dealings that would violate U.S. law if carried out in the home market." Zittrain and Palfrey 2008a, b, p 117.

[57] Atzo Nicolaï and Han ten Broeke, two members of the Dutch House of Representatives, are advocating to implement European Union export licenses to prevent European companies to facilitate Internet censorship. Jong, S de, VVD: geen Internet filters meer naar dictaturen. NRC Handelsblad, February 21, 2011, available at http://www.nrc.nl/nieuws/2011/02/21/vvd-geen-internetfilters-meer-naar-dictaturen/(Dutch). (last accessed 11 August 2011).

11.4 Information About Censorship Censored

11.4.1 Transparency of Censorship

As can be read above, the International Covenant on Civil and Political Rights has two main prerequisites in order to tolerate censorship: it should be necessary and legitimized by positive law. A discussion about what is necessary is difficult if the participants of the discussion do not share one set of universal values. One could argue that in the West censorship is deemed necessary if it prevents the case where the individual freedom of one person harms the individual freedom of another. In China, where a stable society is deemed crucial for its continued economic growth, the same could be argued: if individual freedom is abused so that the harmonious society falls apart, conflicts will make economic growth impossible, which will make it impossible for individuals to enjoy their individual freedoms.

When Google agreed to censor so that at least they could give higher quality access to Chinese Internet users, it decided to provide a clear notice to the users indicating when one or more links had been removed from their search results. "The disclosure allows users to hold their legal systems accountable."[58] But holding legal systems of authoritarian regimes accountable is not without risks. One cannot accuse Google's public affairs vice president Schrage of not having chutzpah when he boasted that "Google's experience dealing with content restrictions in other countries provided some crucial insight as to how we might operate Google.cn in a way that would give modest but unprecedented disclosure to Chinese Internet users." In other words: "We have done so much censoring, now we know how to do it in the best way."

The second prerequisite for censorship is that this right should be written in laws. But these laws and regulations are a complex patchwork, and many have not been disclosed. In its Google Transparency Report, Google states, "Chinese officials consider censorship demands as state secrets, so we cannot disclose that information at this time."[59] The wording is interesting, since it does not mention Chinese law and it leaves room that it will disclose the information at a later moment in time. Thus, neither China nor Google make transparent what methodologies are used for censoring and what content is filtered. Fortunately, the scholars of the OpenNet Initiative have been measuring scope and depth of China's Internet filtering system, "the Great Firewall of China" in 2006–2007, and again in 2008–2010.[60] Their results shed light on the kind of filtering methods applied in China and who are involved in these activities.

---

[58] Schrage E, Internet in China, testimony to the Subcommittee on Asia and the Pacific, and the Subcommittee on Africa, Global Human Rights, and International Operations, Committee on International Relations, United States House of Representatives, February 15, 2006.

[59] Google Transparency Report 2011, available at http://www.google.com/transparencyreport/faq/#governmentrequestsfaq. (last accessed 11 August 2011).

[60] OpenNet Initiative, China Profile June 15, 2009. http://opennet.net/research/profiles/china. (last accessed 11 August 2011).

11.4.2 Methodologies to Filter

11.4.2.1 Filtering

The OpenNet Initiative report of 2009 describes the Great Firewall of China as the most sophisticated and extensive in the world. China has the most consistent record of responding to the shifting content of the Web.[61] China uses all kinds of filtering methods: from blocking whole general domain names, such as YouTube,[62] Blogger or Facebook,[63] to more keyword-based URL filtering to more precise filtering systems of content on a webpage.[64] The filtering can be done by the main Internet Service Providers. China Telecom provides Internet services to over 55 million people in the south of China and China Unicom to over 40 million people in the north of China.[65] If the filtering can be done locally, China chooses to do so from a corporate, university or school network or a local blog provider.[66] Or the filtering can be on local computers, as in the case of Green Dam Youth Escort. Filtering can be temporary[67] or permanent. The trend in censorship is just like intellectual property enforcement toward decentralization: holding local networks to have contributory liability[68] for noncompliance to the legal instruction to filter the Internet.

In 2009 the Ministry of Industry and Information Technology (MIIT) mandated that by July 1st of that year all computers sold in China must be preinstalled with a

---

[61] Zittrain and Palfrey suggest that this likely reflects a devotion of the most resources "to the filtering enterprise", Zittrain and Palfrey 2008a, b, p 35.

[62] Another reason to block a site as YouTube could be that is gives China's YouTube clone, Youku the opportunity to develop and become market leader in China.

[63] Mark Zuckerberg toured China. The amount of Chinese with Facebook went up from 300,000 to 700,000. "Facebook China" censor and who not? How would Facebook wall off the accounts of young Chinese who study overseas, set up accounts, and return to China? Would Facebook stop current news, like Nobel winner Liu Xiaobo, from spreading and trending? Would it turn over the personal details tied to accounts? Lukoff K, Why Mark Zuckerman Came to China and Why Facebook Will Not, December 27, 2010, available at http://techrice.com/2010/12/27/why-mark-zuckerberg-came-to-china-and-why-facebook-will-not/. (last accessed 11 August 2011).

[64] OpenNet Initiative researcher Steven Murdoch along with his colleagues Richard Clayton and Robert N. M. Watson have published a paper that describes in detail the workings of the "Great Firewall of China," including this dynamic filtering based on Web page content. As Clayton, Murdoch, and Watson note, "We have demonstrated that the 'Great Firewall of China' relies on inspecting packets for specific content." Zittrain and Palfrey 2008a, b, p 37.

[65] Anderson N, Just two Chinese ISPs serve 20% of world broadband users, Ars Technica, July 2010, available at http://arstechnica.com/tech-policy/news/2010/07/just-two-chinese-isps-serve-20-of-world-broadband-users.ars. (last accessed 11 August 2011).

[66] OpenNet Initiative (2005), Filtering by Domestic Blog Providers in China, January 20, 2005., available at http://www.opennetinitiative.net/bulletins/008/. (last accessed 11 August 2011).

[67] China allows CNN to be broadcast within the country with a form of time delay so the feed can be temporarily turned off when, in one case, stories about the death of political reformer Zhao Ziyang were broadcast. Zittrain and Palfrey 2008a, b, p 48.

[68] See Sect. 11.2.1 for contributory liability in the enforcement of intellectual property rights.

specific filter software: "Green Dam Youth Escort." Officially the purpose of "Green Dam" was to protect children. But researchers found out that it censored political and religious content as well. Moreover, it logged user activity and sent this information to the server of the software developer. It also made the user vulnerable to cyber attacks and it allegedly infringed the copyright of a U.S. company that develops filtering software. After a massive outcry by Chinese users and foreign computer manufacturers, MIIT withdrew its plan and made the pre installation of Green Dam voluntary.

By blocking[69] and then unblocking[70] some sites, such as Wikipedia, Zittrain and Palfrey suggest China is giving a signal, "that the state is watching in order to prompt self-censorship online."[71] The concept of Wikipedia, an online encyclopedia where users can add and edit content, might be threatening for a government whose legitimacy is dependent on official stories.[72] Not only because such a site offers alternative versions of the truth, but also because these are held by many users to be authoritative.

11.4.2.2 Removal of Content, Temporary Stop and Restrictions

Beside filtering, Chinese authorities can order online service providers, whether they are Internet service providers or blog platforms, to take down content or shut down a website, if the server is in China.[73] The spread of information during ethnic conflicts can exacerbate problems. To contain the conflict and stabilize the situation, China is willing and able "to pull the plug".[74] After ethnic riots in Xinjiang Uyghur Autonomous Region, in July 2009, China cut off the Internet, text messaging and international phone service for half a year. After that the Internet and phone service was restored, but with severe limitations: people have a limited

---

[69] Blocking of Wikipedia in mainland China, Wikipedia.

[70] "Wikipedia has grown so influential, in fact, that it has attracted the attention of China's censors at least three times between 2004 and 2006. The blocking and unblocking of Wikipedia in China—as with all other filtering in China, without announcement or acknowledgment—might also be grounded in a fear of the communal, critical process that Wikipedia represents." Zittrain and Palfrey 2008a, b, p 29.

[71] Zittrain and Palfrey 2008a, b, p 35.

[72] "While its decentralization creates well-known stability as a network, this decentralization reflected at the ''content layer'' for the purpose of ascertaining truth might give rise to radical instability at the social level in societies that depend on singular, official stories for their legitimacy." Zittrain and Palfrey 2008a, b, p 29.

[73] "In Anglo-European legal parlance, the legal mechanism used to implement such a system is called "intermediary liability." The Chinese government calls it "self-discipline," but it amounts to the same thing, and it is precisely the legal mechanism through which Google's Chinese search engine, Google.cn, was required to censor its search results." MacKinnon 2010.

[74] The possibility to shut down the Internet is sometimes referred to as the kill switch. Kill switch, Wikipedia,available at http://en.wikipedia.org/wiki/Kill_switch. (last accessed 11 August 2011).

number of text messages they can send, no access to non-Chinese websites and even limited access to Chinese websites.[75]

11.4.2.3 Cyber Attacks

The "highly sophisticated" cyber attacks targeted at Gmail accounts of human rights activists originated allegedly from China. But a causal link to the Chinese authorities could not be construed. One cannot categorize this as a form of censorship by the government, if the origin could not be established. The perpetrators could also be sympathizers with the government. MacKinnon observes that this example "serves as an important reminder that governments and corporations are not the only victims of cyber-warfare and cyber-espionage."[76]

11.4.2.4 Domain Name Controls

To control the Internet one can try to filter or delete content. Another method is to control the registration of domain names. In December 2009, the government-affiliated China Internet Network Information Center (CNNIC) announced that only companies and organizations could register websites with the country code toplevel domain name.cn. This to prevent registrations using a false name. The measure was sometimes explained as a way to clean up pornography, fraud and spam. An underlying reason could be that businesses, which can only operate with a license, can get a.cn domain name. This *de facto* resulted in two layers to control who could own a.cn domain name. After some protests, and probably some registrants choosing another toplevel domain name, CNNIC announced in February that individuals will again be allowed to register.cn domains. However, this time applicants have to appear in person to confirm their registration, show a government ID and submit a photo of themselves with their application. It is clear to applicants that they could easily be tracked and held responsible when compromising information is uploaded to a website connected to their domain name.

---

[75] "Xinjiang-based Internet users can only access specially watered-down versions of official Chinese news and information sites, with many of the functions such as blogging or comments disabled." MacKinnon 2010.

[76] MacKinnon points out that websites run by Chinese exiles, dissidents, and human rights defenders, journalists and academics have seen increasingly aggressive attacks over the past few years. "In other cases the effect is to compromise activists' internal computer networks and e-mail accounts to the point that it becomes too risky to use the Internet at all for certain kinds of organizing and communications because the dissidents don't feel confident that any of their digital communications are secure." MacKinnon 2010.

11.4.2.5 Surveillance

There is a difference between withholding information to users and giving information about the users to the authorities, the latter being far less passive. The technology used for filtering can be used to detect who wanted to see which content. Search engines are especially suited for this purpose. Internet users that have a sense of anxiety that their conduct online is under surveillance, real or imagined, are more likely to self-censor themselves. Cybercafes can be used as surveillance tools.[77] Cybercafes are required to monitor the visitors via, for example ID registration, login, surveillance cameras and monitoring software on the computers.

11.4.2.6 Fifty Cent Party Commentators

Chinese authorities realize that social media are not only risky, but also provide opportunities to make their side of the story heard and promote values endorsed by the Chinese Communist Party. According to an official white paper issued in September, the Internet is an important channel "for the Chinese government to get to know the public opinion and amass the people's wisdom.[78]" China's cultural ministries are training freelancers to channel the public opinion. Bandurski estimated in 2008 that in the whole of China there were at least 280,000 of these freelancers active.[79] These freelancers are derisively called Fifty Cent Party commentators, because they receive 50 cents (half a Renminbi) for each comment they make. Next to softening some online positions, and stressing propaganda points, they function also as the eyes and ears of the party.[80]

11.4.3 What Content is Filtered?

Google is prohibited to disclose what kind of content it is ordered to filter by the Chinese government. The OpenNet Initiative has done empirical testing of Internet blocking in 40 countries, including China, which started in 2006. It found evidence of technical filtering in 26 countries, including China.[81] The OpenNet Initiative's

---

[77] "One might also consider the cybercafe-based controls in China, say, as compared to the approach of setting up the "Great Firewall" at the state's geopolitical boundaries." Zittrain and Palfrey 2008a, b, p 43.

[78] Hewitt D, The March of the Netizens, BBC News, November 2, 2010. http://www.bbc.co.uk/news/world-asia-pacific-11576592. (last accessed 11 August 2011).

[79] Goldkorn J, More on the 50 cent army, Danwei, July 14, 2008., available at http://www.danwei.org/propaganda/more_on_the_50_cent_army.php. (last accessed 11 August 2011).

[80] China Media Project of the University of Hong Kong. See the interview to David Bandurski by Restall H, FEER, China's Guerilla War for the Web, YouTube video, July 31, 2008, available at http://www.youtube.com/watch?v=Zpomfqb3QVY. (last accessed 11 August 2011).

[81] Faris and Villeneuve 2008, p 5.

methodology was to compile lists of sites that cover a wide range of topics targeted
by Internet filtering, ranging from gambling, pornography, and crude humor to
political satire and sites that document human rights abuses and corruption. Subsequently, researchers test these lists to see which sites are available from different
locations within each country.[82] The results were illustrated in a figure, whereby
each country was positioned along a horizontal axis representing the scope of the
filtering (the ambition of the censoring country), and the vertical axis that depicted
the depth of the filtering (the success of the censorship in that country). Regarding
the breadth of filtering, only the Arab Emirates and Saudi Arabia scored higher than
China. In respect of depth of filtering only Iran scored higher than China.[83]

The keywords filtered in China can be categorized into 5 groups: (1) national
minorities' independence movements[84]; (2) all references to the Tiananmen
Square incident on June 4, 1989, including "6-4"; (3) Chinese communist leaders;
(4) the religious organization Falun Gong; and (5) keywords related to uprisings or
suppression.[85]

Compared to most authoritarian regimes, China is more engaged in filtering
political than social material. Like Vietnam and some countries in the Middle East
and North Africa, China is blocking sites related to religion and minority groups.
In China, sites that represent the Falun Gong and the Tibetan exile groups are
widely blocked. Just like Iran and Yemen, China blocks by keyword in the domain
or URL path. China filters by keywords that appear in the host header (domain
name) or URL path.[86]

China sometimes denies that it is even filtering. This was demonstrated by Chinese the official, Yang Xiaokun, who stated at the 2006 Internet Governance Forum:
"In China, we donot have software blocking Internet sites. Sometimes we have
trouble accessing them. But that's a different problem... We do not have restrictions
at all."[87] Or China justifies its filtering to help enforce intellectual property rights.[88]
Illustrative for China's perception of censorship are the statements of Wang Chen.
This deputy head of the Communist party's propaganda department and head of the
State Council Information Office said that by November 2010 about 350 million

---

[82] Idem, p 5.

[83] Idem, Fig. 1.1, p 8.

[84] National minorities' independence movements, in Tibet, Xinjiang and Inner Mongolia and
contacts with Taiwanese politicians known for their pro-independence standpoint.

[85] Deibert and Rohozinsky 2008, p 141.

[86] An example: the site http://archives.cnn.com/ is accessible, the URL http://archives.cnn.com/
2001/ASIANOW/east/01/11/falun.gong.factbox/ is not. When this URL is requested reset packets
are sent that disrupt the connection, because of the keyword falun.gong.

[87] Internet Governance Forum (2006), "Openness", transcription session, October 31, 2006,
available at http://www.intgovforum.org/IGF-Panel2-311006am.txt. (last accessed 11 August
2011).

[88] Rundle and Birdling 2008, p 83.

pieces of harmful information, including text, pictures and videos, had been deleted: "There was a notable improvement in the online cultural environment".[89]

The editors of the China Rights Forum present three narratives on how the Chinese government sees the Internet.[90] The history of the narratives is also illustrative that the topic of Internet censorship itself is not free of being censored.[91] The internal narrative shows that the government is very apprehensive about the open character of the Internet,[92] the distinction between the Chinese Internet and global Internet is also significant. The focus is on the flies that come in if you open the window for fresh air, to use the words of Deng Xiaoping.[93]

In the made-for-export narrative, China states that it is maintaining tight control over the Internet, because it is an important national infrastructure and it is just asserting its sovereignty. China wants to be perceived by the international community as a loyal and responsible member that behaves according to international law. Therefore it articulates that China guarantees its citizens' freedom of speech on the Internet as well as the public's right to know, to participate, to be heard and to oversee in accordance with the law. In other words it wants to show the world that in China there is freedom of expression, only limited by China's law. This narrative also states that China provides a safe environment in which businesses can operate. Hereby inviting foreign companies to do business in China and welcoming foreign direct investments.

---

[89] It is interesting that Wang cites the growing number of press releases as evidence of the government's and the party's increasing transparency. Hill K, Chinese Internet censors boast of good year, December 30, 2010, Financial Times, available at http://www.ft.com/cms/s/0/69baa762-1431-11e0-a21b-00144feabdc0.html#axzz1AzVjekLO. (last accessed 11 August 2011).

[90] The editors of the China Rights Forum make a distinction between three narratives on the Internet in China: (1) the internal narrative of the government; (2) the-made-for-export narrative; and (3) the official narrative. See China Rights Forum 2010.

[91] The internal narrative was the report by Wang Chen, Concerning the Development and Management of Our Country's Internet, April 29, 2010, and was posted on the website of the National People's Congress and was removed from the site shortly after. China Rights Forum 2010.

[92] "As long as our country's Internet is linked to the global Internet, there will be channels and means for all sorts of harmful foreign information to appear on our domestic Internet. As long as our Internet is open to the public, there will be channels and means for netizens to express all sorts of speech on the Internet." China Rights Forum 2010.

[93] Deng Xiaoping alluded with his winged words: "Open the windows, breath the fresh air and at the same time fight the flies and insects," to China's reform policy of 1979 of opening up to the world and taking some negative side effects for granted. Hays J (2008), China under Deng Xiaoping, Facts and Details, available at http://factsanddetails.com/china.php?itemid=80&catid=2&subcatid=7. (last accessed 11 August 2011).

The official narrative for the Chinese people is the internal narrative purified of any words about censorship.[94] The editors suggest that the Chinese authorities could be anxious about "the consequences of informed public debates or push back by netizens over such issues as implementation of real-name identification for forum moderators and an identity authentication system for bulletin boards." The editors might be right, as evidenced by the massive public outcry against Green Dam.[95]

11.4.4 Effectiveness of Censorship

Bob Marley sang: "You can fool people sometimes, but you cannot fool all the people all the time."[96] And this is also true for Chinese citizens, who are getting more Internet savvy and cynical toward government propaganda. Many have already manifested their online power, by participating in the "human flesh search engine"[97] phenomenon. The most effective filtering model is, according to Zittrain and Palfey, to require blog service publishers to block keywords in blog posts. However, "even this approach can be only a partial means of blocking subversive content over time. Chinese bloggers routinely turn to broadly understood code words to evade the censorship built into the tools".[98] A famous example is

---

[94] The deletions include everything related to censorship: "description of domestic propaganda and ideological work to guide public opinion online and unify public thinking and expansion of China's cultural soft power abroad via news and commercial channels and websites in foreign languages; description of the preliminary Internet information security protection system and the policy of "active defense and comprehensive prevention"; description of the need to construct a legal system for the Internet; and description of the overall allocation of responsibility and management structure that integrates regulation, supervision, industry self-regulation, and technological safeguards, and calls for a cross-department mechanism for preventing infiltration and handling harmful information from overseas." See China Rights Forum 2010.

[95] In the spring of 2009 the Ministry of Industry and Information Technology (MIIT) mandated that by July 1, 2009 all computers sold in China would be pre-installed with Green Dam Youth Escort. This software would filter pornography, but it censored additional political and religious content, it also logged user activity and sent this information to a central computer of the software's developer's company. In addition it was vulnerable to cyber-attacks. After a public outcry and protests of the U.S. computer industry and government, MITT withdraw its mandate and made the use voluntary. Green Dam Youth Escort, Wikipedia, available at http://en.wikipedia.org/wiki/Green_Dam_Youth_Escort. (last accessed 11 August 2011).

[96] Bob Marley and The Wailers, lyrics of the song Get up, stand up, 1973. Before Marley, Abraham Lincoln said: "You can fool some of the people all of the time, and all of the people some of the time, but you can not fool all the people all of the time."

[97] A crowd-sourced technique that Chinese netizens use to dig up personal information to locate someone, exposing government corruption or hit and run drivers. Human flesh search engine, Wikipedia, available at http://en.wikipedia.org/wiki/Human_flesh_search_engine. (last accessed 11 August 2011). (last accessed 11 August 2011).

[98] Zittrain and Palfrey 2008a, b, p 52.

the word "grass mud horse": it is a code word and metaphor for the power struggle over Internet expression. China Digital Times started in 2009 a comprehensive online glossary of translations of coded terms created by Chinese netizens and frequently encountered in online political discussions, called the Grass-Mud Horse Lexicon.[99] Another problem for the authorities is to find balance in filtering. If the authorities filter too much (overbreadth) they will include innocuous content. And if they filter too little (underbreadth) they do not achieve the government's goals. Then there are many ways to evade the Internet filter, for example with a virtual private network.[100] It will probably continue to be a cat and mouse game between censor and user. But there are many, many more mice and they are resourceful.[101]

11.5 Innovation Crucial for Chinese Government

11.5.1 Innovation and Intellectual Property

After the Olympic Games the level of China's resolve to enforce intellectual property rights appeared to have faded somewhat. In reality, this is not the case: the Chinese government realises how crucial intellectual property rights are for the survival of the Chinese Communist Party's hegemony. The only legitimacy the party has is continuing China's economic growth and lifting millions of people out of poverty. Since the labor costs are rising and the currency is appreciating, China's strategy to be the low cost producer of the world is not sustainable. Therefore Chinese companies need to climb the value ladder and add more value to their products and services. In other words innovation is the only way for the Chinese government to sustain economic growth. Intellectual property rights can harness innovation (patents), creativity (copyrights) and commerce (trademarks). Therefore, one can argue a crucial connection between the ability of China's industries to innovate and the survival of the one-party model in China.

---

[99] Qiang, CDT Launches the Grass-Mud Horse Lexicon, China Digital Times, December 7, 2010., available at http://chinadigitaltimes.net/2010/12/introducing-the-grass-mud-horse-lexicon/. (last accessed 11 August 2011).

[100] Dingledine R, Ten Things To Look For In Tools That Circumvent The Internet Censorship, In: "China's Internet": Staking Digital Ground, Human Rights in China, number 2, 2010, available at http://www.hrichina.org/public/contents/article?revision%5fid=175279&item%5fid=175276. (last accessed 11 August 2011).

[101] "The Chinese are very resourceful in this. A site about popular movie stars may become a vehicle for discussing delicate political issues. Among Chinese 'nerds' hacking systems are circulating that completely bypass censorship, but you must be knowledgeable enough to download these from non-blocked sites. And then there are weblogs that appear to discuss dogs but are in fact describing the political situation in China." Great Chinese Fire Wall of China (non-profit group of creatives). Great Chinese Fire Wall of China (undated). http://www.greatfirewallofchina.org/faq/14/How_do_the_people_of_China_counter_this? (last accessed 11 August 2011).

11.5.2 Innovation and Censorship

As explained in 11.5.1 the fate of the Chinese Communist Party are inextricably linked to its ability to bring economic prosperity to China. It believes that censorship is indispensable to keep social stability, so that the economy can grow in a harmonious way. However, censorship is not compatible with net neutrality, a word coined by Tim Wu.[102] Net neutrality is seen by many as the necessary architecture to make the Internet into such a varied, innovative ecosystem. It uses the end-to-end principle of network design, whereby the intelligence in the network should not be placed in the middle of the network, but at the fringes. By imposing control in the middle of the network, for example, via the Great Firewall of China, the censors are obstructing the growth of the network. Also censorship and surveillance of user-generated content could have serious chilling effects[103] on creativity and innovation.[104]

In this time and age the free flow of information via the Internet and innovation are intimately connected. It could be argued that the one cannot progress without the other. The assumption is often made that the creativity that is needed for innovation can only thrive in an environment with freedom of expression and the possibility to experiment. If this is true, the inverse might also be true. A country that is obstructing the free flow of information and where there is only marginal room for experimenting, might harm its ability to innovate and therefore its economic progress. Hillary Rodham Clinton put it this way: "When countries curtail Internet freedom, they place limits on their economic future".[105] Then there are intrinsic values attributed to the Internet: it could lead to a more open information environment, where there is greater access to information, more transparency, better governance and faster economic growth.[106] "All censorships exist to prevent any one from challenging current conceptions and existing institutions.

---

[102] Wu 2003.

[103] The term "chilling effect" was used by Paul Freund. Freund 1951. See also the site Chilling Effects Clearinghouse, available at http://www.chillingeffects.org/ ((last accessed 11 August 2011)0), a joint project of the Electronic Frontier Foundation, Harvard, Stanford, Berkely, University of San Francisco, University of Main, George Washington School of Law, Santa Clara University School of Law.

[104] Zittrain and Palfrey 2008a, b, p 51.

[105] "When countries curtail Internet freedom, they place limits on their economic future. Their young people don't have full access to the conversations and debates happening in the world or exposure to the kind of free inquiry that spurs people to question old ways of doing and invent new ones. And barring criticism of officials makes governments more susceptible to corruption, which create economic distortions with long-term effects. Freedom of thought and the level playing field made possible by the rule of law are part of what fuels innovation economies." Clinton HR, Internet Rights and Wrongs: Choices & Challenges in a Networked World, February 15, 2011, available at http://www.state.gov/secretary/rm/2011/02/156619.htm. (last accessed 11 August 2011).

[106] Zittrain and Palfrey suggest that this likely reflects a devotion of the most resources "to the filtering enterprise", Zittrain and Palfrey 2008a, b, p 51.

All progress is initiated by challenging current conceptions, and executed by supplanting existing institutions. Consequently the first condition of progress is the removal of censorships".[107] Although George Bernard Shaw wrote these words in 1905 they still sound plausible. Joseph Schumpeter stated that innovation "must be seen in its role in the perennial gale of creative destruction (..)."[108] The Internet has been a catalyst of innovation, and has disrupted many business models, such as the record, movie and publishing industries. And it is safe to say that the Internet will disrupt other industries[109] as well. Moreover, it is likely that completely new industries will emerge. If a country such as China wants to be competitive one can argue that it needs to make room for experiments. Then again, one could say that China already uses the Special Administrative Regions of Hong Kong and Macau and arguably Taiwan as test grounds where these greater freedoms are allowed. Within China, the Chinese government could experiment with greater freedom in Special Economic Zones, such as Shenzhen, and see whether greater freedom actually leads to more innovation.

Competition forces companies to come up with better products and services: in other words innovation. If China keeps shielding some companies from international competition by raising market barriers via censorship, it is not doing a service to these companies nor to its citizens. The companies stay less innovative, while counterfeit and pirated products will thrive.

11.6 Conclusions

The Chinese government started with the plan to create a more just and social society where the citizens share their resources. Now that the economic growth of China has continued for over thirty years, a big income gap between poor and rich and huge environmental problems have arisen. There is a lot of room for improvements of the individual online freedom of China's citizens.

Google started with the plan to give access to as many people as possible under the mantra of not doing evil. When it wanted to provide China's people with high quality access to its search results, it did not listen to its own mantra and condoned to become a tool of censorship in the hands of the Chinese government.

Trademark and copyright holders are trying to hold Google liable for contributory intellectual property rights infringements. One of the paradoxes is that if Google would empower others to apply its technology to enforce trademark and copyright infringements, it could solve more intellectual property-related problems

---

[107] Shaw 1905, p 41.

[108] Schumpeter 1942.

[109] This author foresees that 3D printers in combination with the Internet will have an unprecedented influence on intellectual property rights. See also Print me a Stradivarius, How a new manufacturing technology will change the world, The Economist, February 10, 2011, available at http://www.economist.com/node/18114327. (last accessed 11 August 2011).

than it causes by ignoring intellectual property rights in many of its initiatives. Google decided to provide users in China with a censored search engine Google.cn, so that it could guarantee the quality of its accessibility to the site. Only after Google experienced problems guaranteeing data-integrity and disappointing market expansion, did the company decide to provide uncensored search results. Because otherwise the Chinese government would not have continued their license, they decided to relocate the search results to the Hong Kong version: Google.com.hk. Google's stance against censorship and its mantra of not doing evil sounds laudable but is paradoxical. Google exaggerates when it is playing the role of freedom of information champion, because Google censors its search results in many countries. Google even filed an application to patent a methodology to censor, making the company actively involved in censorship.

While there are a lot of clear-cut international obligations for a country as China in the field of intellectual property rights, there are almost none in the field of censorship. One obligation based on the International Covenant on Civil and Political Rights prescribes that censoring measures should be necessary and codified by law. These terms are vague and hard to assess, since China makes these laws secret. Total lack of transparency gives a lot of uncertainty for Chinese Internet users about what is not allowed. This could have chilling effects on creativity. Furthermore it stimulates self-censorship, which might be the most effective form of censorship. So far, there are no laws, national or international, to prevent a U.S. company such as Google, to be involved in censorship in China.

Although the level of enforcement of intellectual property is insufficient, the Chinese government realizes how important intellectual property rights are, since they can harness innovation. And innovation is the way to continue China's economic growth spurt. China is censuring the Internet in the most sophisticated way of all countries, because it believes it is the only way to guarantee social stability needed for continued economic growth. The economic growth will lift millions of Chinese out of poverty and will consolidate the supreme position of the Chinese Communist Party.

Both China and Google have overshot their marks. Google will probably reach the borders of its arrogance soon, and will have to start respecting intellectual property rights more. Further, one should not have any illusions about the Google's moral leadership. It is more likely that the Internet behemoth will develop into a typical multinational that is mostly concerned in satisfying its shareholders' financial motifs. Like all countries and businesses, Beijing and Mountain View[110] are only listening to arguments that can help achieve their own goals. China's economic growth strategy to be the low cost producer and exporter to the world is not sustainable. Therefore innovation is crucial for China. It can be argued that balanced intellectual property rights and minimal censorship are best for innovation. And this might be the only argument China is willing to listen to.

---

[110] Google Inc., is headquartered in Mountain View, California, U.S.

References

Creemers R (2011) Unraveling China's Media Knot: Piracy, Copyright, Censorship and the WTO, forthcoming PH.D. Dissertation, Maastricht University

China Rights Forum (2010) How the Chinese authorities view the internet: three narratives. In: "China's Internet": Staking digital ground, human rights in China, number 2, 2010. http://www.hrichina.org/public/contents/article?revision_id=175069&item_id=175068. Accessed 11 Aug 2011

Deibert R, Rohozinsky R (2008) Chapter 6: good for liberty, bad for security? global civil society and the securitization of the internet. In: Deibert R et al (eds) Access denied: the practice and policy of global internet filtering. MIT Press, Cambridge, pp 123–150

Faris R, Villeneuve N (2008) Chapter 1: the scope and depth of internet filtering, In: Deibert R et al (eds.) Access denied: the practice and policy of global internet filtering, MIT Press, Cambridge, pp 5–28

Freund PA (1951) Supreme court and civil liberties, 4 vanderbilt law review 533 (1950–1951), at 539

Karnow C (1999) Indirect Liability on the Internet and the Loss of Control, INET'99, Internet Society, June 8, 1999. Available at http://www.isoc.org/inet99/proceedings/3e/3e_2.htm. Last accessed 11 August 2011

Ludwig D (2006) Shooting the messenger: ISP liability for contributory copyright liability, Boston College Intellectual Property & Technology Forum

MacKinnon R (2010) China's internet censorship and controls: the context of google's approach in China. In: "China's Internet": staking digital ground, china rights forum, human rights in China, number 2, 2010. http://www.hrichina.org/public/contents/article?revision_id=175187&item_id=175185. Accessed 11 Aug 2011

Puddephatt A (2005) Freedom of expression. The essentials of human rights. Hodder Arnold, London

Rundle M, Birdling M (2008) Chapter 4: filtering and the international system: a question of commitment. In: Deibert R. and al. (eds.), Access denied: the practice and policy of global internet filtering, MIT Press, Cambridge, pp 73–102

Schumpeter J (1942) The process of creative destruction. In: Capitalism, socialism, and democracy. Harper Torchbooks, New York

Shaw GB (1905) The author's apology from Mrs. Warren's profession, Brentano's, New York

Wu T (2003), Network neutrality, broadband discrimination. J Telecommun High Technol Law, vol. 2, p 141, http://ssrn.com/abstract=388863. Accessed 11 August 2011

Zittrain J, Palfrey J (2008a) Chapter 2: internet filtering: the politics and mechanisms of control. In: Deibert R et al (eds) Access denied: the practice and policy of global internet filtering. MIT Press, Cambridge, pp 29–56

Zittrain J, Palfrey J (2008b) Chapter 5: reluctant gatekeepers: corporate ethics on a filtered internet. In: Deibert R et al (eds) Access denied: the practice and policy of global internet filtering. MIT Press, Cambridge, pp 103–122

Chapter 12
The International Dimension of Google Activities: Private International Law and the Need of Legal Certainty

Aurelio Lopez-Tarruella

Contents

Senior Lecturer Privat International Law, Lecturer and Coordinator of the IT Module of the Magister Lvcentinvs on Intellectual Property.

A. Lopez-Tarruella (✉)
University of Alicante, 03690, Alicante, Spain
e-mail: Aurelio.lopez@ua.es

A. Lopez-Tarruella (ed.), *Google and the Law*,
Information Technology and Law Series 22, DOI: 10.1007/978-90-6704-846-0_12,
© T.M.C. ASSER PRESS, The Hague, The Netherlands, and the author(s) 2012

12.1 Introduction

As with many other Internet service providers (which we will refer to as ISPs), one of the characteristics of Google's activities is their international dimension. While the offer of some of its services might be restricted to certain countries—that is the case of Google eBook Store, only available in the US—or might be prohibited in certain States—that is the case of China—generally speaking, Google's services are available to Internet users located anywhere in the world.

From a business perspective, the international dimension of Google's activities is a blessing. It allows the company to maximize its revenues—as mentioned in Chap. 1, 52% of Google's incomes come from outside the US. However, from a legal perspective, this can be a nightmare. While Google's services are provided in a global market, there is no global Internet law or "cybercourt" with universal jurisdiction. The global market where Google provides its services is segmented into states with different jurisdictional systems and laws. As a consequence of this, Google's activities are subject to a great degree of legal uncertainty: while its activities might be considered legal in one country, they might be considered otherwise in other states. Furthermore, at first sight, Google should be ready to litigate before the courts of any state where there are users of its services.

The best mechanism to provide legal certainty for international commerce is the adoption of conventions of Private International Law (referred to as PIL). These are instruments providing a uniform set of rules according to which the courts of the contracting states can declare jurisdiction; or where a substantive regulation of the dispute is determined; or where a uniform body of conflict of law rules is provided so as to determine the law applicable to the dispute. Thanks to these conventions, companies doing businesses in the contracting states enjoy a higher level of legal certainty: they can easily know where they may be sued and what the law applicable to the dispute would be.

Unfortunately, international conventions governing activities such as those provided by Google and other ISPs are limited.[1] In today's world, each state determines the jurisdiction of its courts and the law applicable to the dispute in accordance with its domestic rules of private international law. This means that Google must consult the rules of each particular state to know when they can be sued there and what law would apply to determine whether their activities are legal. As can be imagined, in practice, this is almost impossible, which is why the level of the legal uncertainty of Google's activities is high. While this does not prevent the IT giant to provide services worldwide, the legal risks they incur are therefore high. This might be seen as one of the reasons why Google is involved in so much litigation around the globe.

---

[1] In other branches of commerce such as the international sales of goods, international conventions—e. g. the Vienna Convention on the international sales of goods of 1980—play a much more important role.

As an exception to the situation in the rest of the world, the Member States of the European Union share a common set of rules on jurisdiction and on applicable law. Of particular relevance to services provided by Google or any other ISP are the Brussels I Regulation[2]—in the field of jurisdiction—and the Rome I[3] and Rome II[4] Regulations—in the field of applicable law. The existence of these instruments should mean that Google has a higher level of legal certainty when providing services in the European Union. However, there are two reasons why this is not so.

First, the rules on jurisdiction under the Brussels I Regulation are not applicable in every case. In particular, they are not applicable in situations where the defendant is not domiciled in a Member State. In those cases, non-EU domiciled defendants doing business in Europe must consult the domestic rules of jurisdiction of each Member State to know in which cases they can be sued before their courts. That is the situation of Google and other US-based ISPs.[5]

Second, rules on jurisdiction and conflict of laws rules in the Regulations are not uniformly applied in the Member States. Even more: these rules are not even uniformly applied by the courts of a single Member State. This problem is shown in the French judgements that will be analysed in this chapter: judgements of the *Cour de Cassation* of 13 July 2010, *"Google v. Louis Vuitton"*,[6] and 23 November 2010, *"Axa c. Google"*[7]; judgements of the *Tribunal de Grande Instance* of Paris of 20 May 2008, *"SAIF v. Google"*,[8] 9 October 2009, *"H & K, André R. v. Google"*[9] and 18 December 2009, *"Editions du Seuil et autres v. Google Inc et France*

---

[2] Regulation 44/2001 on jurisdiction, recognition and enforcement of judgments in civil and commercial matters (OJ L 12, 16 January 2001). Denmark is not a Member State for the purpose of this Regulation. However, the Regulation applies in the Nordic country pursuant to an International Agreement signed between the European Union and Denmark (OJ L 299, 16 Nov 2005). In addition, in the relations between the European Union, Norway, Switzerland and Iceland, a similar regulation established in the Lugano Convention (OJ L 339, 21 Dec 2007) applies.

[3] Regulation 593/2008 on the law applicable to contractual obligations (Rome I) (OJ L 177, 4 Jul 2008).

[4] Regulation 864/2007 on the law applicable to non-contractual obligations (Rome II) (OJ L 199, 31 Jul 2007).

[5] This situation may change in the near future if the Commission Proposal to amend the Brussels I Regulation is adopted. The rules on jurisdiction in the Proposal cover not only disputes where the defendant is domiciled in a Member State but also those where the defendant is domiciled in a third State. Being so, legal certainty for non-EU domiciled companies will increase: they will only have to consult one body of rules to know in which case they can be sued in the European Union and before what courts. See *Proposal for a Regulation on jurisdiction and the recognition and enforcement of judgments in civil and commercial matters*, Doc COM (2010) 748 final.

[6] Available at http://legalis.net/spip.php?page=breves-article&id_article=3040 (last Accessed 22 Aug 2011).

[7] Available at http://www.legalis.net/spip.php?page=breves-article&id_article=3039 (last Accessed 22 Aug 2011).

[8] Available at http://www.legalis.net/spip.php?page=breves-article&id_article=2342 (last Accessed 22 Aug 2011).

[9] Available at http://www.legalis.net/spip.php?page=breves-article&id_article=2776 (last Accessed 22 Aug 2011).

(La Martiniere)"[10]; and Judgement of the *Cour d'Appel* of Paris of 26 January 2011, "*SAIF v. Google*".[11]

They all concern actions against Google for intellectual property (IP) infringement and they lead to different results despite the fact that they have all been adopted by courts in France and are related to very similar facts. The first two judgements are related to questions of jurisdiction and will be analysed in Sect. 8.2. The following three decisions concern conflict of law questions and will be dealt in Sect. 8.3.

The reason that I have chosen judgements adopted in France is not that French courts are particularly bad in applying PIL rules, but because litigation in France against Google is higher than in other countries, and new cases are constantly and accurately reported in blogs and websites. Actually, as with patent litigation in the Netherlands at the beginning of the century,[12] it looks like France is becoming the preferred *forum* to initiate actions for IP infringement on the Internet due to the willingness of French courts to take jurisdiction on the basis of *forum delicti commissi* (see below).

The problems that French courts face in applying PIL rules in these Google cases are shared by courts in other Member States. These problems exist due to the difficulty of adapting the application of PIL rules to the particularities of Internet relationships. The European Court of Justice (ECJ) has just started to receive preliminary questions concerning these matters. Its decisions will surely help national courts to apply the rules correctly and will ensure their uniform application. This is particularly important to increase the legal certainty for ISPs doing business in Europe.

12.2 Application of *Forum Delicti Commissi* in Disputes Related to Intellectual Property Infringements Committed on the Internet: The Consolidation of the "Directing Activities" Doctrine

As mentioned in the introduction, judgements of the French *Cour de Cassation* of 23 November 2010, "*Axa c. Google*" and 13th July 2010, "*Google v. Louis Vuitton*", concern questions of jurisdiction in infringements of intellectual property rights committed on the Internet.

---

[10] http://www.legalis.net/spip.php?page=jurisprudence-decision&id_article=2812 (last Accessed 22 Aug 2011).

[11] http://www.juriscom.net/documents/caparis20110126.pdf (last Accessed 22 Aug 2011).

[12] During that time, Dutch courts were open to adopting pan-European injunctions in cases of infringements of a European patent committed in multiple states by multiple companies belonging to the same group. Plaintiffs chose the Netherlands to benefit from the *Kort Geding*, a very fast summary procedure. The possibility to apply for those injunctions was restricted by the introduction of the "spider on the web" doctrine: in order to declare jurisdiction in those cases, the company of the group taking the decisions must be located in the Netherlands. Finally, the ECJ declared this doctrine incompatible with Article 6 (1) Brussels Convention in the Judgement of 13 Jul 2006, C-539/03, "*Roche Nederlanden c. Primus*".

For this category of actions,[13] when the defendant is domiciled in a Member State, the Brussels I Regulation states that the plaintiff may file the complaint before the courts of: (a) that Member State—Article 2; (b) the place where the harmful event occurred or may occur—*forum delicti commissi*; (c) in cases of multiple defendants, in the Member State where any of them is domiciled as far as certain conditions are met—Article 6 (1)[14]; (d) in cases where the infringement has been committed by an establishment of the defendant located in a different Member State, in that Member State—Article 5 (5).[15]

If the defendant is domiciled in a third country, Article 4 of the Regulation states that the courts of the Member State where the complaint is filed shall determine their jurisdiction in accordance to their domestic rules of PIL. In tort actions, it is generally established in national PIL systems that the courts of a state can declare jurisdiction when the harmful event occurred in the territory of that state. In this sense, Article 46 of the French New Code of Civil Procedure establishes the jurisdiction of the courts of the place of commission of the tortuous act or that where the damage occurs. PIL scholars understand that the interpretation of this provision should be guided by the ECJ case law on Article 5 (3) Brussels I Regulation.[16] However, nothing prevents national courts from adopting a different interpretation and, in practice, that is sometimes the case.

The main point of controversy in the judgements of the *Cour de Cassation* is the interpretation of *forum delicti commissi*. As Google Inc. is domiciled in the US, French courts could only declare jurisdiction on the basis of this ground for jurisdiction. The problem is that in both cases—and in many other Internet-based disputes—the harmful activity takes place in one State while the damages of that activity occur in another State: the administration of Google website takes place in the United States but the alleged infringement of intellectual property rights occurs in France. These situations raise three questions concerning *forum delicti commissi*:

(a) Which courts can declare jurisdiction: those of the place where the infringing activities took place, those of the place where the damage occurred, or both?
(b) Is it enough to consider that the damage occurred in a Member State is the fact that the website is accessible from that Member State? Or is it necessary to show that the website is directed towards that Member State?

---

[13] In cases where the action concerns the validity of an industrial property right, Article 22 (4) provides for the exclusive jurisdiction of the courts of the Member State where the right is registered.

[14] Two conditions must be met: (a) every defendant is domiciled in the Member States; (b) "the claims are so closely connected that it is expedient to hear and determine them together to avoid the risk of irreconcilable judgments resulting from separate proceedings".

[15] This is only applicable when the parent company is domiciled in a Member State. Furthermore, for the courts to declare jurisdiction the action shall be related to the business carried out by the establishment of that company.

[16] Ancel 2001, p 3.

(c) If the second option in (b) is answered in the affirmative, what evidence is
    needed to show that a website is directed towards a Member State?

The judgements of the *Cour de Cassation* are mainly concerned with the second
question: they show an evolution from the "simple accessibility" doctrine to the
"directing activities" doctrine. Furthermore, they partially answer the third
question. However, this latter answer is to be complemented by the recent and
future case law of the ECJ. Finally, the first question is settled case law, but a brief
explanation is needed to understand the evolution on the interpretation of *forum
delicti commissi*.

12.2.1 *"Fiona Shevill" and the Balancing of Interests in International Disputes Related to Infringement of Intellectual Property Rights*

The problem deriving from the different location of the place where the
infringing activity takes place and the place where the damage occurs is not
exclusive to the Internet. Actually, one of the first judgements of the ECJ on the
interpretation of the Brussels Convention, *"Bier c. Mines de Potasse d'Alsace"*,[17] relates to this problem. In this case, the company Mines de Potasse
d'Alsace had polluted the waters of the Rhine by the discharge of saline waste.
The damages of that pollution were suffered by companies engaged in horti-
culture in the Rhine basin located in the Netherlands. Could the action be filed
before the Dutch courts? According to the ECJ, the expression "place where the
harmful event occurred" in Article 5 (3) Brussels Convention, must be understood as being intended to cover both the place where the damage occurred and
the place of the event giving rise to it. Therefore the plaintiff could choose to file
the complaint in France or in the Netherlands.

Almost 20 years later, the ECJ further clarified the interpretation of *forum
delicti commissi* in *"Shevill c. Presse Alliance"*.[18] The case concerned an action
by a UK resident against a magazine, asking for damages for the publication of a
defamatory article. The magazine was edited in France by a French publisher
and distributed in several Member States including the United Kingdom. The
plaintiff sued in this latter Member State, but the UK court was not sure whether
to declare jurisdiction because only a very limited number of copies of the
magazine had been distributed there. The ECJ understood that, in such a case,
Article 5 (3) attributes jurisdiction to: (a) the courts of the Member State of the
place where the publisher of the defamatory publication is established, which
have jurisdiction to award damages for *all the harm caused by the defamation*;

---

[17] ECJ Judgment 30 Nov 1976, C-21/76, *"Bier c. Mines de Potasse d'Alsace"*.

[18] ECJ Judgment 7 Mar 1995, C-68/93, *"Shevill c. Presse Alliance"*.

(b) before the courts of each Member State in which the publication was distributed and where the victim claims to have suffered injury to his reputation, which have jurisdiction to rule solely in respect of *the harm caused in the territory of that Member State*.

Therefore, while the jurisdiction of the courts of any of the places where damages occur is kept, there is a limitation on the extent of their jurisdiction: they can only consider damages occurring in their territory.

At first sight, it is easy to apply this case law to actions for infringement of intellectual property rights committed on the Internet: (a) the plaintiff can file a complaint before the courts of the Member State where the defendant is domiciled—Article 2—or where the publisher of the infringing content is established—Article 5 (3)[19] for the damages deriving from the infringement regardless of the State where those damages occurred; (b) alternatively, the plaintiff can file a complaint before the courts of any of the Member States where the website was accessible and damages occurred—Article 5 (3), but only for the damages arising in the territory of that Member State.

In my opinion this interpretation ensures a balance between two conflicting interests: the obligation of the Member States to ensure an effective protection of intellectual property rights[20] and the need to guarantee for defendants their rights to a due process.[21] On the one hand, the decision makes it easier for right holders to start proceedings in defence of their rights: (a) they can choose between two *fora*—the courts of the defendant's domicile or the courts of the *forum delicti commissi*; and (b) if they want to sue for all the damages they can do so before the courts of the State where the defendant is domiciled. On the other hand, the defendant's right to a due process is also guaranteed: (a) they can only be sued for all the damages before the courts of their Member State of domicile; or (b) they can be sued in a Member State where the website was accessible and damages occurred, but only for the damages which occurred in the territory of that Member State. Thanks to the limitation of the competence of the courts of the *forum delicti commissi*[22] the danger of *forum shopping* is severely reduced. Furthermore, it

---

[19] This first ground of jurisdiction opened by the interpretation of Article 5 (3) in "*Fiona Shevill*" is seldom applied in practice. First, the place where the publisher is established usually coincides with the domicile of the defendant and, in those cases, Article 2—and not Article 5 (3)—applies. Second, if the publisher publishes the information through an establishment located in a Member State different to that of its domicile, the courts of the first Member State can declare jurisdiction to hear about all the harm caused by the infringement on the basis of Article 5 (5)— recourse to Article 5 (3) is not necessary either.

[20] Needless to say, this is one of the purposes of all legislative instruments adopted by the EU in this field and by international convention ratified by the EU and the Member States.

[21] See for example EJC Judgments of 10 February 2009, C-185/07, "*West Tankers*", of 13 Jul 2006, C-539/03, "*Roche Nederlanden c. Primus*" and of 13 Jul 2006, C-4/03, "*GAT c. LuK*".

[22] In this sense, it shall be recalled that both the Community Trade Mark Regulation and the Community Design Regulation establish the same limitation to the *forum delicti commissi* in Articles 98 (2) and 83 (2).

ensures that the defendant can only be sued before courts that are predictable and that show a close connection between the facts of the case and the court.

What the ECJ has not addressed yet is whether the simple accessibility of a website from a Member State is enough for their courts to declare jurisdiction on the basis of *forum delicti commissi*. Is the accessibility of a website from a Member State enough to understand that the harmful event occurred in that Member State in the sense of Article 5 (3) Brussels I Regulation?

12.2.2 The *Cour de Cassation Case Law on Forum Delicti Commissi: From the "Mere Accessibility" to the "Directing Activities" Doctrine*

In "*Axa v. Google*" and "*Google v. Louis Vuitton*", the French *Cour de Cassation* had to decide on a number of issues that were left open by the ECJ case law. The first is the question of whether the mere accessibility of a website from a Member State is enough to understand that damage has occurred in that Member State (in the meaning of Article 5 (3) Brussels I Regulation) or is it necessary to show that the website is targeted towards that Member State.

These are not the first decisions where the *Cour de Cassation* has been asked to answer this question. Actually, they show an evolution of the existing case law in "*Cristal*"[23] and "*HSM*".[24]

In "*Cristal*", the French company Louis Roederer filed an action for trade mark infringement against the Spanish company Castellblanch. The reason was that the latter was promoting sparkling wine in a ".es" website under the name "Cristal", a trade mark registered by L. Roederer in France. Castellblanch claimed before the *Cour de Cassation* that the first instance court should not have declared jurisdiction on the basis of Article 5 (3) Brussels I Regulation. According to Castellblanch, this provision requires for the court seized to declare jurisdiction that damages have effectively, not just theoretically, occurred. The court did not agree with the appellant. It considered that the *Cour d'Appel* had adequately justified its jurisdiction to consider damages committed in France by the use of a website in Spain. Despite the fact that it was a passive website—it provided information and no interaction with Internet users was possible—it was accessible from France. Therefore, the court stated that the alleged infringement existed. It was neither virtual nor eventual.

This interpretation was confirmed in "*HSM*". A French company sued HSM (Germany) for selling a counterfeited copy of one of its shoes on its website. HSM

---

[23] Judgement of 9 December 2003, "*Société Castellblanch c. Société Champagne Louis Roederer*", Rev. cr. dr. int. pr., vol 93, 2004, pp 632 ff, comments by O. Chacard.
[24] Judgement of 20 March 2007, "*Soc. HSM Schuhmarketing c. Soc. Gep Industries*", Rev. cr. dr. int. pr., vol 97, 2008, pp 323 ff, comments by E. Treppoz.

argued before the *Cour de Cassation* against the jurisdiction of French courts. According to HSM, the website was in German, it was targeted towards the German market and it was impossible for French residents to order shoes from it. The court did not agree with HSM. The display of the counterfeited shoes in the website was an act of unfair competition. Furthermore, the commercialization of those products in French territory could cause damages in France. Therefore the *Cour d'Appel* had adequately justified the jurisdiction of French courts.

Both judgements are the basis of the "mere accessibility" doctrine: the fact that a website is accessible from France is enough for French courts to declare jurisdiction on the basis of *forum delicti commissi*. A generalised adoption of this interpretation would mean that owners of websites that are accessible anywhere must be ready to face litigation before the courts of any country in the world. It can be argued that that is the price to pay for running a worldwide business. However, that argument is not valid: many ISPs want to do business in just some countries even though their websites are accessible anywhere. Even more, websites accessible anywhere may be administered by companies or physical persons that do not want to do business at all. For all these legal and physical persons, the "mere accessibility" doctrine increases legal uncertainty for Internet activities: a danger would exist of being sued in any country that follows the "mere accessibility" doctrine. Furthermore, the doctrine is exorbitant in the sense that it enables French courts to declare jurisdiction in cases where a connection with France is very weak, and this can harm a defendant's right of due process.[25]

Fortunately, the decisions in *"Google v. Louis Vuitton"* and especially *"Axa v. Google"* suggest an evolution in this case law.[26]

In the first case, Google was sued for trade mark infringement and passing off for offering advertisers in AdWords the possibility of selecting keywords which correspond to Vuitton's trade marks and those keywords in combination with expressions indicating imitation, such as "imitation" and "copy".[27] It should be recalled that this case was referred to the ECJ for a preliminary ruling that was the basis for the *"Google France"* Judgement, which is explained in another chapter of this book. What is important for the purpose of this chapter is that Google asked the *Cour de Cassation* to overturn the decisions of the *Tribunal de Grande Instance* (TGI) and the *Cour d'Appel* where French courts' jurisdiction to hear the

---

[25] One may say that because of this latter argument, the decision will never be recognised in the State where the defendant is domiciled. That is not the case: in the European Union courts of other Member States will not find in the Brussels I Regulation a ground to deny the recognition of these judgements. Furthermore, the plaintiff might not need to recognize the judgement in another country if his only purpose is to block the commercialisation of a product in the country where that website is accessible.

[26] Actually, there are several examples of lower level courts that did not follow this case law at all. See, for instance, Judgement of the *Cour d'Appel d'Orléans* of 6 May 2003, *"Les Folies Céramiques c. Mridul Enterprises et Trademark Tiles"*, Rev. cr. dr. int. pr., 2004, p 139 ff, comments Gaudemet Tallon.

[27] Further explanations on the substantive aspects of this case are provided in Chap. 3.

dispute was affirmed. It should be mentioned that in this case, the dispute did not concern Article 5 (3) Brussels I Regulation but Article 46 New French Code of Civil Procedure.

The courts in the first and second instances had followed the same reasoning as that of the *Cour de Cassation* in *"Cristal"* and *"HSM"*. Due to the way the Internet works, every website is accessible from French territory, thus the alleged acts of infringements could cause damages in France. The advertisements that constituted the alleged infringement could be viewed from France. As a consequence, French courts could declare jurisdiction. The fact that the products were offered in websites in a foreign language was considered irrelevant in so far as Internet users could use translation tools.

Surprisingly, the *Cour de Cassation* revoked the judgement. The reason was that the *Cour d'Appel* had declared jurisdiction without determining whether the infringing advertisements were targeted towards the public in France. The judgement is certainly a turning point in the *Cour de Cassation*'s case law: mere accessibility is not enough, French courts must determine whether the website is directed towards the public in France to declare jurisdiction. However, the judgement does not mention when a website can be said to be targeted towards the public in France.

Some light on this question is provided by *"Axa vs. Google"*. The facts of the case are very similar to those of *"Google vs. Louis Vuitton"*. Axa accused Google of trade mark infringement and unfair competition because AdWords provide users the possibility of selecting keywords which correspond to Axa's trade marks, so that sponsored links are displayed when a user introduces those keywords in the search engine. The *Cour d'Appel* had dismissed the claim because French courts were found not to have jurisdiction. Axa appealed. In its opinion, French courts did have jurisdiction. Following the *"Cristal/HSM"* case law, they argued that the jurisdiction of the court should be sustained on the fact that the website was accessible from France. The fact that the website was of a passive nature and was in a foreign language was irrelevant. The accessibility of the website from France caused damages which were neither virtual nor eventual. In their opinion the court was wrong in deciding that, despite the fact that "google.de", "google.co.uk" and "google.ca" were targeted towards the public in Germany, UK and Canada. The fact that they were accessible from France was sufficient to justify the jurisdiction of French courts and it could be implied that the websites had an economic impact on the French market.

The *Cour de Cassation* upheld part of the judgement of the *Cour d'Appel*. The latter had heard sufficient proof that the sponsored links were not targeted to the public in France. They were only displayed in Google websites that were targeted to the public in Germany ("google.de"), the UK ("google.co.uk") and Canada ("google.ca") and that were written in German and English. However, the *Cour de Cassation* overturned the part of the judgement concerning "google.fr": in this case, French courts could declare jurisdiction because that website was targeted to the French public. In any case, this was useless for the plaintiffs since the infringing sponsored links were not displayed in this website.

In "*Google v. Louis Vuitton*" and "*Axa v. Google*", the *Cour de Cassation* seems to have abandoned the "mere accessibility" doctrine in favour of the "directing activities" doctrine—that is, French courts can only declare jurisdiction if it is demonstrated that the website is targeted towards the public in France.[28] This is to be welcomed since it increases legal certainty for ISPs doing business worldwide. They can be sure they will not be sued in France unless their websites are directed towards the public in France. This is fair: if you do business in France, be ready to litigate in France. Furthermore, the defendant's due process right is safeguarded: the "directing activities" doctrine ensures that French courts can only declare jurisdiction in disputes closely connected with France, something that can be foreseen by defendants.

It should be noted that a short while after the adoption of these judgements, the ECJ endorsed the "directing activities" doctrine in the field of consumer contracts. In "*Pammer*",[29] the Court had to interpret Article 15 (1) (c) Brussels I Regulation. According to this provision, the special rules on jurisdiction on consumer contracts apply when the contract was concluded with a person who, by any means, directs commercial or professional activities in the Member State of the consumer's domicile or to several States including that Member State. In the decision, the Court clearly states that the mere fact that a website is accessible from the Member State where the consumer resides is not sufficient to consider that the owner of the website directs his activities to that Member State. The courts must also determine whether there is evidence demonstrating that the professional envisaged doing business with consumers domiciled in that Member State.[30]

Having adopted the "directing activities" doctrine in the field of consumer contracts, there is a question left open: will the ECJ adopt the doctrine for the interpretation of Article 5 (3) as well?

The ECJ will have the chance to answer this question in two forthcoming cases: C-523/10, "*Wintersteiger*" and joint cases C-509/09, "*eDate Advertising*" and C-161/10, "*Martinez*". In all of them, the ECJ is asked whether the phrase "the place where the harmful event may occur" in Article 5 (3) is to be interpreted as meaning that an action can be brought in the courts of any Member State in which the website may be accessed.

It is certainly true that the interests at stake in consumer contracts are not the same as in tort actions—on the one hand, the need to protect the consumer as the weaker party to the contract favours an interpretation that gives jurisdiction to the courts of the Member State where he is domiciled; on the other hand, for tort

---

[28] This new trend is confirmed in Judgement of *Cour de Cassation* of 29 Mar 2011, "*eBay Europe v. Maceo*", available at http://legalis.net/spip.php?page=jurisprudence-decision&id_article=3142 (last accessed 22 Aug 2011).

[29] ECJ Judgement of 7 Dec 2010, Joined cases C-585/08, "*Pammer*" and C-144/09, "*Hotel Alpenhof*".

[30] Paras 74–76. The ECJ makes reference to the joint declaration of the Council and the Commission on Articles 15 (1) (c) Brussels I Regulation, reproduced in Recital 24 of R. Rome II, where the same conclusion is reached.

actions it is settled case law that Article 5 (3) is neutral, in the sense that its aim is not to protect the victim. Nonetheless, it is my opinion that the ECJ should answer this question in the negative and endorse the "directing activities" doctrine for this latter category of actions as well.

This has been the case in the Opinion of the Advocate General (AG) in "*eDate Advertising*" and "*Martinez*".[31] While the disputes relate to infringements of personal rights (image, reputation), some conclusions might be applicable in the field of IP. First, in paras 51 and 56, the AG argues against giving value to the "mere accessibility" doctrine since it will automatically grant jurisdiction to the courts of all the Member States, potentially exposing publishers of content on the Internet to litigation in any state. The AG understands that this would open the door for plaintiffs to practice *forum shopping*, in a manner unsustainable for media providers, and it will imply a complete lack of predictability. Second, in para 55 and following, the AG justifies the adoption of a new criterion on the interpretation of Article 5 (3)—an evolution of the "*Fiona Shevill*" case law—for cases of infringement of personal rights: the criterion of the "centre of gravity of the conflict". According to this, Article 5 (3) should grant jurisdiction to the courts of the State where the centre of gravity of the conflict of the interests at stake in the dispute is located. In infringements of personal rights the centre of gravity is located in the place where the individual whose right has been infringed projects his life and the allegedly defamatory information is objectively and specifically relevant. In order to determine this second element, the court should look whether the media provider can reasonably foresee that the content of the information is interesting in that particular place, i.e. whether Internet users there will be attracted to access it.[32] In other words, it has to be proved that the website is directed towards that place.

This is precisely what the "directing activities" doctrine says. The AG even refers to "*Pammer*" when endorsing the doctrine, but two important clarifications are made. First, while in consumer contracts, it is the intention of the professional to direct his activities to the consumer's Member State of residence that counts, whereas when applying Article 5 (3), the application of the doctrine must be objective.[33] This should also be the case when applying the doctrine in IP infringements.

Second, the AG states that the courts of the place where the centre of gravity of the conflict is located shall have jurisdiction to know about all the damages deriving from the infringement.[34] While in disputes concerning the infringement of personal rights this interpretation might be justified on the fact that the most

---

[31] Opinion of the Advocate General of 29 Mar 2011. At the time of writing this article, the Opinion was not available in English.

[32] Para 63.

[33] "Information is not objectively relevant by the fact that the publisher is voluntarily directing it towards a particular Member State". Para 62.

[34] Para 57.

substantial harm is usually caused in the place where the victim lives, its application to IP infringements might be problematic[35]: the victim will usually enjoy his IP rights in several Member States, so it may be difficult to decide in which one the most substantial harm is caused. Furthermore, the limitation of the competence of the court of the *forum delicti commissi* to the acts committed or threatened within the territory of that Member State in the Community Trade Mark Regulation and the Community Design Regulation[36] points toward a similar limitation in cases of infringements of national IP rights.

To sum up, it can be affirmed that there are strong arguments for the ECJ to endorse the "directing activities" doctrine. A judgement in this sense will bind national courts of all Member States. As a consequence, legal certainty for ISPs doing business in Europe will increase. However, the application of this doctrine to consumer contracts, to infringements of personal rights and to infringements of IP rights may or will vary. Therefore, subsequent judgements might be needed to clarify the application of the doctrine to this latter category.

12.2.3 When Can It Be Considered that the Activities of a Website are Directed Towards the Member State of the Court Seized?

With the "directing activities" doctrine expected to be upheld by the ECJ soon, there is a final question to be answered: what evidence must be shown to demonstrate that a website is directing its activities towards the Member State of the court that has been seized?

"*Axa v. Google*" provides two criteria: (a) the use of the country code top-level domain name of the State of the court seized; (b) the information in the website is in the language of that State.

These two criteria are also mentioned by the ECJ in "*Pammer*". In relation to the first, the Court adds that the use of generic top-level domain names such as ".com" or ".eu" mean that the trader aims to target its activities internationally, including the State of the court seized. In relation to the second, the Court states that the language used might be relevant only when the website permits consumers to use one different to that of the Member State from which the trader pursues its activities, or the website is in a foreign language.

---

[35] Actually, this can also be problematic in infringements of personal rights. In certain cases the reputation of a person can be harm not in a place different from that where he lives. For instance, Cesc Fabregas plays football for Arsenal and lives in London. Any injurious information about him in a Spanish magazine will harm his reputation in Spain, not in the place where he lives. Or maybe the information harms his reputation both in Spain and the UK. Where would the "centre of gravity of the conflict" be located in these cases? Legal certainty is not really ensured with the new criterion on the interpretation of *forum delicti commissi*.

[36] See Articles 98 (2) and 83 (2).

In *"eDate Advertising"* and *"Martinez"*, the AG refers to these evidences as well. On the one hand, the Opinion states that the use of a domain name different from that where the publisher is domiciled shows that the information might be objectively relevant in other Member States. On the other hand, the language used in the website helps to delimit the geographic area where the information might be relevant.[37]

In *"Wintersteiger"*, a case that involves Google and the AdWords system, the Court will have to decide on the relevance of these two criteria as well. The question in this case is whether Austrian courts should have jurisdiction in a case where a non-Austrian advertiser uses an Austrian trade mark as keyword to trigger sponsored links in "google.de". While the top-level domain name is not that of the Member State of the court seized, the language (German) is. Should that be enough for Austrian courts to declare jurisdiction? According to *"Pammer"*, the answer should be negative since German is the language of the Member State from which the defendant pursues its activities. In my opinion, this should not be decisive: the Court should look whether other evidence points towards Austria. To start with, German is also spoken by Austrian consumers.

Other forms of evidence have been identified by the ECJ in *"Pammer"* which might also be useful for the application to the doctrine when applying Article 5(3). The first is the interactive character of the website. The Court is not very clear on this point. It seems to suggest that the possibility of residents of the Member State of the court seized to contact the trader or even to conclude a contract in the website is evidence to conclude that it is targeted towards that Member State. However, passive websites—those that only provide information and do not allow interaction with users—might also be considered as targeted towards the Member State of the court seized in so far as the trader provides its postal address or other data that allow consumers to contact him by non-electronic means.[38] The ECJ also mentions other evidence concerning the content of the website: the use of statements that express the intention to attract consumers from the Member State of the court seized[39]; the use of telephone numbers with an international code also states the intention of the trader to direct its activities to other Member States, including that of the court seized; the mention of an international clientele composed of customers domiciled in various Member States, including that of the court seized.[40] The currency used in the website is not decisive, unless prices are provided in a different currency to that of the Member State from which the trader pursues its activities[41]—e. g. if prices are expressed in euro and sterling pounds, this can be used as evidence that the website is directed towards the UK.

---

[37] Para 65.
[38] Para 79.
[39] Para 80.
[40] Para 83.
[41] Para 84.

Finally, despite the fact that the evidence identified in *"eDate Advertising"* and *"Martinez"* are related to the infringement of personal rights, they might be useful for IP infringement cases as well. As in *"Pammer"*, the Court makes reference to the content of the website: it has to be determined whether this has some relevance in the Member State of the court seized or the infringing information is published under a "heading" referring to that State. The metatags provided to search engines to identify the website are also evidence that show whether it is directed to the Member State of the court seized or not. Finally, the Court limits the value of the number of times the website has been accessed from that State.[42] Other criteria mentioned by the referring court in the preliminary question do not even deserve a word from the AG: the nationality of the person who complains of the infringement of his personal right or the place where the images published online were taken.

As mentioned before, these judgements should provide a uniform criteria to determine when a website is targeted towards the Member State of the court seized. Only in those cases should the court declare jurisdiction on the basis of Article 5 (3) Brussels I Regulation. A uniform interpretation of this provision will increase the legal certainty of the commercial activities of ISPs such as Google.

12.3 Applicable Law to Intellectual Property Infringements Committed on the Internet

In international disputes, once a court has declared its jurisdiction, it has to determine the law applicable to the dispute. Such law might be established by an international convention that provides for a uniform regulation. However, in most cases the applicable law is determined by the conflict-of-law rules established in an international convention, an instrument of EU Law or the PIL system of each State.

At present, the conflict-of-law rule that determines the law applicable to IP infringements is the so-called *lex loci protectionis*—i.e. the law of the country for which protection is sought. For the European Union's Member States, this rule is stated in Article 8 (1) Rome II Regulation. However, it is also established in Article 5 (2) Berne Convention, an international treaty that has been ratified by all the Member States. As explained in Sect. 8.3.2, it is not clear which provision Member States' courts should apply. As it will be seen in the judgements analysed in this section, sometimes French courts apply Article 5 (2) Berne Convention and at other times they apply the law of the place where the harmful event took place— *lex loci delicti commissi*. No reference to Article 8 (1) Rome II Regulation is made although it had already entered into force at the time most of those judgements were adopted.

---

[42] All these evidences are identified at para 65.

Conflict-of-law rules—*lex loci protectionis* among them—may determine the application of the law of the court with jurisdiction (*lex fori*) or a foreign law. This will depend on the situation and on the principles applicable to the subject matter that the conflict-of-law rule governs. However, national courts are usually tempted to directly apply their own law or to interpret conflict-of-law rules in such a way that the law applicable to the dispute ends up being the *lex fori*. While a *lex fori*-oriented interpretation makes national courts' work easier—they can solve the dispute according to a law they know and they do not have to wait until the proof of the foreign law is provided; this may lead to unfair results—the law applicable to the dispute ends up being one that does not provide the fairest solution—and to legal uncertainty, as the application of *lex fori* might not be the closest one to the dispute and thus its application cannot be predictable for the parties.

In the copyright infringement actions brought against Google in France, we observe an evolution of the interpretation of *lex loci protectionis*. While in the first case (Judgement of *TGI* Paris 20 May 2008, *"SAIF v. Google"*) the interpretation leads to the application of a foreign law—e. g. US law, in the latter cases (Judgements *TGI* Paris 9 October 2009, *"H & K, André R. v. Google"* and 18 December 2009, *"Editions du Seuil et autres v. Google"*, and Judgement of the *Cour d'Appel* of Paris of 26 January 2011, *"SAIF v. Google"*) the interpretation leads to the application of French law.

As analysed in Sect. 8.3.1, the determination of the law of the country where protection of the IP right is sought is extremely difficult in cases where the infringement took place on the Internet. Therefore, it is difficult to assess whether French courts have changed their interpretation of the rule in order to favour the application of French law or because it leads to the fairest solution of the cases in hand.

12.3.1 The Interpretation of Lex Loci Protectionis in Infringements of Intellectual Property Rights Committed on the Internet

The judgement of *TGI* Paris 20 May 2008, *"SAIF v. Google"*, is an example I use with my students to make them understand how important it is to have a good knowledge of conflict of laws. In this case, the TGI Paris heard of an action for infringement by the *Société des Auteurs des Arts Visuels et de l'Image Fixe* (*SAIF*) against Google. SAIF complained that the use of pictures authored by its members as thumbnails in Google Image constituted a copyright infringement in accordance with Articles. L 122-4 and L 335-2 French Intellectual Property Code.

Google answered that the claims should be dismissed because, according to Article 5 (2) Berne Convention, the law applicable to the dispute was US Law and the use of pictures as thumbnails was considered a fair use in the sense of the Section 107 Copyright Act.

The court upheld the arguments of Google and dismissed the claim. Article 5 (2) Berne Convention states that "the extent of protection, as well as the means of redress afforded to the author to protect his rights, shall be governed exclusively by the laws of the country where protection is claimed". It is generally accepted that this rule does not refer to the law of the country where the copyright infringement action is filed but to the law of the country where the copyright is allegedly infringed. That is why it is better to identify the *lex loci protection* as the law of the country where protection is sought. However, which is that law in the case of ubiquitous infringements? That is, when the infringing activity takes place in one state and the damages of that activity occur in other state(s), due to the ubiquitous character of the Internet. This is what happened in "*SAIF v. Google*". Google uploaded the pictures on their servers located in the United States, but they were accessible from France. Since both countries are parties to the Berne Convention, the pictures were protected by copyright in both countries. However, while the use of those pictures as thumbnails without permission from the right holders was considered legal in the US, it was not clear whether that conclusion might be reached in accordance with French law.[43] So an interpretation of Article 5 (2) in favour of the law where the infringing activities took place (*lex originis*) or the law of the country where the damages of the activity occur (*lex locus damni*) was decisive.

The court's decision to apply *lex originis* was based on the judgement of the *Cour de Cassation* 20 January 2007, "*Lamore*".[44] In that case it was argued that the movie "Waterworld" plagiarised the book "Tideworks". The court understood that, in such a case, Article 5 (2) Berne Convention led to the application of US Law, because the infringing activities took place there: the movie was conceived, filmed and released in that country and the book was published there. The court added that the damage caused to the author of the book in France was but a consequence of those activities.

Taking this judgement into consideration, in "*SAIF v. Google*" the court used the following reasoning. The infringing activities consisted of collecting images, indexing them and making them available on the "google.fr" server. These activities took place in Google's headquarters in the US. Furthermore, the decisions concerning the services of the ISP were taken there. Therefore, the law applicable to the dispute was that of the US.

The interpretation provided by the *TGI* benefits the interests of ISPs: determination of whether they incur in an infringement of intellectual property is to be decided by a unique law, that of the state from where they carry out their business.

---

[43] As we explain below, the *Cour d'Appel* understood that Google's use of images as thumbnails is legal in accordance with French Law as well, since the Safer Harbor principles of Directive 2000/31 on e-commerce apply.

[44] Available at http://legifrance.gouv.fr/telecharger_rtf.do?idTexte=JURITEXT000017627214& origine=juriJudi (last Accessed 22 Aug 2011).

This solution is highly beneficial for legal certainty for ISPs' international activities.

However, there are strong arguments against this interpretation that, although argued by SAIF, were not taken into consideration by the court. The main argument is that a generalisation of *lex originis* would allow IP infringers to easily "legalize" their activities by locating their servers in countries where the level of protection is very low. This is certainly a problem that the court in "*SAIF v. Google*" underestimated. Fortunately, as we explain next, the judgement was reversed by the *Cour d'Appel* in January 2011.

Application of *lex originis* is established in Directive 93/83 for satellite broadcasting and cable retransmissions.[45] Several proposals to expand the application of this solution to other activities—in particular to acts involving copyright on the Internet—have been discussed.[46] However all of them have failed, even in the restricted framework of the European Union where a high level of harmonisation exists among the legislation of the Member States.[47] The reason why states cannot accept such a solution seems to be that intellectual property regulations reflect each state's policy for the promotion of general objectives such as innovation, and the access to culture and creativity. Therefore they cannot admit that the exploitation of intellectual creations in their territories is governed by a foreign law.[48]

Just 16 months later, the members of the TGI had the chance to redeem themselves of the unfortunate interpretation of *lex loci protectionis* in "*H & K, André R. v. Google*". As in "*SAIF v. Google*", the US corporation was sued for the unauthorised use of a picture as a thumbnail in the Google Image service. Google argued that, according to Article 5 (2) Berne Convention and Artcle 8 Rome II, the law applicable to the dispute was US law and the use of images as thumbnails was covered by the "fair use" doctrine.

Surprisingly, although the facts of the dispute seem to be the same in both cases—the only difference being that in this case, the alleged infringed work is a picture and in the previous one there were several pictures—the interpretation of the law made by the court is completely different. In "*H & K, André R. v. Google*" the court understood that the infringing activity consisted of displaying the picture on the "google.fr" website and that such activity took place in France. Without mentioning any conflict-of-laws rule, the court concludes that Google's claim to apply US Law could not be upheld. French law was applicable.

Strictly speaking, it can be argued that this decision follows the same reasoning as "*SAIF v. Google*": The *lex loci protectionis* rule for infringements committed

---

[45] Directive 93/83/EEC of 27 Sept 1993 on the coordination of certain rules concerning copyright and rights related to copyright applicable to satellite broadcasting and cable retransmission (OJ L 248, 6.10.1993, pp 15–21). Article 1 (2).

[46] Ginburg 1998, p 325; Berge 2000, pp 384–388.

[47] European Commission, *Follow-up to the Green Paper on copyright and related rights in the information society*, Doc COM(96) 568 final.

[48] About these arguments, see Desurmont 2001, pp 17–27.

on the Internet leads to the application of the law of the country where the infringing activities take place. What changes is the interpretation of "infringing activities" and where they are committed. The legal consequences of the divergent interpretation of similar facts are enormous: in "*SAIF v. Google*", the complaint was dismissed, in "*H & K, André R. v. Google*", the US company was condemned for copyright infringement.

Having two divergent judgements adopted by the same court, one could imagine that a third decision would restore legal certainty. Such a decision would help ISPs to know which of the two interpretations should prevail. However, in "*La Martiniere*", the TGI Paris adopted an interpretation that had nothing to do with the previous ones. In this case, two publishers, the publishers' association and an association of authors of literary works sued Google for digitalising and making available in Google Books several works without authorisation from the authors and/or copyrights holders.

As in the previous cases, Google claimed that the application of Article 5 (2) Berne Convention leads to the law of the country where the infringing activities took place. That law was US law because the infringing activities—the digitisation of the works and the display of short extracts of them in Google Books—were carried out in the United States. Furthermore, Google argued that those acts were covered by the "fair use" doctrine in Section 107 Copyright Act.

The court did not uphold these arguments of Google. But its reasoning was completely different from that in "*H & K, André R. v. Google*". First, the court stated that the law applicable to non-contractual liability arising out of ubiquitous torts is that of the place where the harmful event occurred and that such place is located where the infringing activities took place (*lex originis*) and where the damage occured (*lex locus damni*). Then, the court decided that French law was applicable. But not because it was the *lex locus damni* but because it was the most *closely connected* to the dispute. It was the close connection to the facts of the case that justified the application of French law. In particular, the court identified the following links with France: the extracts from works of French authors in Google Books could be accessed by French Internet users located in French territory; the court where the complaint has been filed was French; the plaintiffs were French; the seat of Google France was located in France; the domain name "www.books.google.fr" included the country code ".fr"; the information in the website was in French.

As it can be observed, the case law of the TGI Paris shows an evolution from *lex originis* towards *lex locus damni*. This is confirmed in the Judgement of the *Cour d'Appel* of Paris, 26 January 2011. In this decision the Court reversed the judgement of the TGI in "*SAIF v. Google*". According to the *Cour d'Appel*, Article 5 (2) Berne Convention may be interpreted as the law of the place where the damage occurred or the law of the place where the infringing activities were carried out. In those cases where the facts of the dispute show a manifestly closer connection to the latter, such law should be applied. In the present dispute French law was applicable because it was the law of the place where users connect to a website and receive the information. Furthermore, such information was in French and was provided by a website with an ".fr" URL.

Is the case law of the TGI and the *Cour d'Appel* of Paris inconsistent with the *Cour de cassation* case law in "*Lamore*"? Not necessarily. In my opinion, the interpretation of *lex loci protectionis* seems to be well established: in Internet disputes, the rule leads to the application of *lex originis* or *lex locus damni* depending on which of those laws shows the closest connection to the dispute.[49] In "*Lamore*", the closest links were with the US—both parties were domiciled there and the works had been published there, and that is why the *Cour de Cassation* upheld the application of *lex originis*. But the situation in "*SAIF v. Google*" was not the same, since Google Images is a service provided in French to users in France (and thus the *lex locus damni* had the closer connection). The *Cour d'Appel* was right in reversing the decision of the TGI.

The same assessment can be made of the other decisions: the facts of the disputes show a closer connection to the law of the place where the damage occurs, so French law was applicable. Therefore, it can be affirmed that the interpretation of *lex loci protectionis* by French courts does not seem to be influenced by any "anxiety" for applying *lex fori* but for the need of adopting the fairest solution on the determination of the law applicable to disputes concerning copyright infringements on the Internet.

In addition to this, it should be mentioned that, apart from the Judgement of the TGI of Paris in "*SAIF v. Google*", there seems to be a uniform interpretation of *lex loci protectionis* in France. This ensures the legal certainty of ISP providing their IP-related services in France. However, does legal certainty also exist in Europe? I am afraid not. To start with, it is not clear whether Article 5 (2) Berne Convention is a conflict-of-laws rule or not. Furthermore, the application of *lex loci protectionis* to ubiquitous copyright infringements is certainly difficult and may lead to different interpretations. The possibility for the ECJ to adopt binding decisions on these questions would increase legal certainty for ISPs doing business in Europe. But is that possible?

12.3.2 What Provision Is Applicable to International Copyright Infringements: Article 5 (2) Berne Convention or Article 8 (1) Rome II Regulation?

The question raised in the last paragraph of the previous section is directly linked to the question of which provision is applicable to determine the law applicable to

---

[49] This is also sustained in previous judgements of the *Cour de cassation* such as Judgement of 5th Mar 2002, "*SISRO c. Ampersand Software BV*", Rev. cr. dr. int. pr., vol 92, 2003, pp 440–446, comments by Bischoff, J-M.

international copyright infringements: Article 5 (2) Berne Convention or Article 8 (1) Rome II Regulation.

In "*Lamore*", the French *Cour de Cassation* understood that Article 5 (2) Berne Convention was applicable. This interpretation is also sustained in "*SAIF v. Google*" by the TGI Paris and the *Cour d'Appel*. However, in "*H & K, André R. v. Google*" and "*La Martiniere*" this provision is not mentioned. The courts refer to the law of the place where the harmful event occurred (*lex loci delicti commissi*), and not to the place where protection is sought. Are these judgements compatible? What is the law applicable to copyright infringement: *lex loci protectionis* or *lex loci delicti commissi*? Does this question have any consequences in practice? The answers to these questions depend on the interpretation of Article 5 (2) Berne Convention. There are three possible alternatives.

For a first group of authors, this provision contains a conflict-of-laws rule that applies to determine the law applicable to the exploitation, protection and the non-contractual obligations deriving from the infringement of copyright.[50] It follows from this that Article 5 (2) Berne Convention prevails over Article 8 (1) Rome II Regulation in cases of copyright infringement. The reason is that Article 28 states that "the Regulation shall not prejudice the application of international conventions to which one or more Member States are parties at the time when this Regulation is adopted and which lay down conflict of laws rules relating to non-contractual obligations."

An argument against this interpretation is the fact that in a recent publication in the Official Journal of the notifications by the Member States of the international conventions referred to in Article 28 (1) Rome II Regulation,[51] none of them has notified the Berne Convention. While it might not have legal consequences, this omission can be interpreted in the sense that the Member States' governments do not consider that the Convention contains conflict-of-law rules related to non-contractual obligations.

This is precisely the position of a second group of authors. In their opinion, at the time of drafting the Berne Convention, the use of conflict-of-law rules in this field was not common. The drafters were inspired by existing bilateral treaties and none of them include this category of rules. The opinion of this group of authors is that the aim of Article 5 (2) Berne Convention is not to establish a conflict-of-laws rule but to reinforce the application of the national treatment principle. While the last part of the provision might be confused with a conflict-of-law rule, it is just a simple reference to the procedural rules of the place where the claim is filed.[52]

---

[50] Carrascosa 2004; Fernandez 1996; Esteve 2006.

[51] OJ 343, 17 December 2010.

[52] See Van Eechoud 2003, 125 and references in De Miguel 2007, p 380. A similar interpretation is established in the *WIPO Guide to the Berne Convention*, Geneva, 1978. If the complaint for copyright infringement is filed before the court where the damage occurred, the law of the court seized would be applied. If the complaint is filed before the court of a different country, such court should apply its conflict-of-law rules to determine the applicable law. (p 36).

In favour of this interpretation is the ECJ Judgement *"Tod's"*[53] where the Court *obiter dicta* states: "As is apparent from Article 5(1) of the Berne Convention, the purpose of that convention is not to determine the applicable law on the protection of literary and artistic works, but to establish, as a general rule, a system of national treatment of the rights appertaining to such works".

The consequence of the interpretation of this second group of authors is that the law applicable to the non-contractual obligations deriving from the infringement of copyright is to be determined always in accordance with Article 8 (1) Rome II Regulation. The law applicable to questions related to the authorship, ownership or protection of the copyright are to be determined by the conflict-of-law rules of each national PIL system.

Finally, a third group of authors understands that Artcle 5 (2) is a conflict-of-law rule, but its aim is exclusively to identify the law that must be applied to determine the extent and format of protection of the copyright. Other questions related to the copyright are not governed by Article 5 (2).[54] Among the aspects excluded are the non-contractual obligations arising out of copyright infringement.[55] At present, the law applicable to these aspects is determined in accordance with Article 8 (1) Rome II Regulation.[56]

It seems that French courts have followed this latter interpretation in the Google cases.[57] On the one hand, in *"SAIF v. Google"*—and in *"Lamore"* as well—the court applies *lex loci protectionis*, to determine whether the use of the work is protected by the law of the place where protection is sought. The question of determining the non-contractual obligation deriving from the infringement never appears because the court understands that there is no infringement. The only complaint about this judgement is that it contravenes the ECJ Judgement *"Tod's"* because Article 5 (2) is applied as a conflict-of-law rule. In any case, this does not have any consequence in practice.

On the other hand, in *"H & K, André R. v. Google"* and *"La Martiniere"* the court declares the existence of the infringement, thus *lex loci delicti commissi* is applied to determine the non-contractual obligation deriving from it. There are however, two elements to reproach the courts in these two cases: (a) they should

---

[53] EJC Judgement 30 june 2005, C-28/04, *"Tod's"*.

[54] According to Torremans and Fawcett 1998, p 467, "What is being determined in Article 5 is the substantive level of protection for those works that have previously qualified for protection under the Convention. The substantive right and the conditions under which the work can be used have to be determined first".

[55] In this sense Moura 2008, p 273: *"Il revient à la lex loci protectionis de régir la création, le contenu et l'extinction du droit d'auteur, sa cession et sa soumission à des charges, aussi bien que les sanctions de sa violation. La titularité du droit d'auteur, les droit contractuels d'utilisation de l'ouvre, la responsabilité civiles et les autres obligations extracontractuelles nées de l'utilisation illicite des biens en cause et les moyens juridictionnels de protection du droit violé sont cependant, au moins en partie, soumis à d'autres lois ».*

[56] Moura 2008, p 346.

[57] Actually, this is the established case law since Judgement of *Cour de cassation* of 22 Dec 1959, *"Le chant du monde"*, Rev. cr. dr. int. pr. 1960, p 361 ss.

have mentioned that French law was applicable in accordance with Article 5 (2) Berne Convention to determine whether a copyright infringement exists; (b) they should have applied French law as the law applicable to determine the non-contractual obligation deriving from that infringement pursuant to Artcle 8 (1) Rome II Regulation, because this instrument was already in force at the time the judgements were adopted.

While the first element does not have consequences in practice, the second does. As previously explained, Article 8 (1) Rome II leads to the application of the *lex loci protectionis*, and not to the *lex loci delicti commissi*. This second conflict-of-law rule is included in the Regulation in Article 4. Its application may lead to an outcome very different from that in Article 8 (1). According to Article 4 (2), when the residence of the parties is located in the same country, the law of that country will apply regardless of the place where the harmful event occurred. Furthermore, in cases where the tort is manifestly more closely connected with a country other than that of the place where the harmful event occurred, the law of that other country shall apply—Article 4 (3). One last aspect to bear in mind is the fact that Article 4 would not apply if the parties chose the law applicable to the dispute under the conditions of Article 14.

These exceptions to the application of *lex loci delicti commissi* do not exist in Article 8 (1) in relation to *lex loci protectionis*. This latter conflict-of-law rule cannot be derogated by choice of the parties—Article 8 (3), and no exception to its application exist. I am afraid, if French courts would have applied this provision—as they will have to do in the future—they would have had much less flexibility to determine French law as the law applicable to the disputes.

This is certainly a problem. It is to be seen how the ECJ will interpret this provision in situations of ubiquitous IP infringements. The lack of flexibility in the application of *lex loci protectionis* will probably lead to the application of the law of each of the countries where the infringement occurred. This solution is not efficient: it increases the costs for the parties—as far as they are obliged to prove the content of foreign law(s) in most Member States—and makes the resolution of the dispute more complex, since the judge would have to apply several laws.

Several authors have argued that *lex loci protectionis* should apply to determine whether an infringement exists, and *lex loci delicti commissi* should govern the consequences of that infringement. While the first question is informed by the territoriality principle and the public policy interests behind IP systems, its application is mandatory; the second question only concerns the parties so the application of the general conflict-of-law rule in the Rome II Regulation—including party autonomy—should apply. This would allow the court to apply exclusively one law: (a) the one chosen by the parties; (b) that of the State where the parties both reside; or (c) that which is, among the several potentially applicable laws, the one most closely connected to the dispute.

In any case, the solution is complicated: it implies the application of two conflict-of-law rules that may lead to the application of two different laws to the same facts. It would be better to have a single conflict-of-law rule that determines the law applicable to both aspects. That should be the *lex loci protectionis*.

But, which *lex loci protectionis*, that of Article 5 (2) Berne Convention or Article 8 (1) Rome II Regulation? Despite the fact that both provisions lead to the same outcome, the interpretation that the first is not a conflict-of-law rule and thus the second must apply, is highly beneficial for legal certainty: the second being a provision of EU Law, the ECJ will be able to interpret it. Thanks to this the Court in Luxembourg will have the chance to hear preliminary questions on the interpretation of Article 8 (1) and to facilitate its uniform application by the courts in the Member States.[58] Furthermore, besides the benefits that this has for legal certainty, the ECJ might also introduce some flexibility on the application of Article 8 (1) to make the conflict-of-law rule more efficient.

12.4 Conclusions

It is certainly the case that Google's success will not be compromised by the fact that Private International Law does not provide legal certainty to ISPs providing their activities internationally. However, this can be a problem for newcomers that try to find their niche in the Knowledge Economy.

As the Google cases analysed in this chapter show, the main reason for the existing legal uncertainty is the fact that traditional PIL rules are difficult to apply to Internet disputes. Preliminary questions have just started to arrive to the ECJ on these matters. Future decisions in these cases will help to overcome this problem. In this sense the following recommendation can be made.

For jurisdiction, the ECJ should endorse the "directing activities" doctrine on the interpretation of Article 5 (3) Brussels I Regulation in disputes related to IP infringements. According to this, the courts of a Member State can only declare jurisdiction on the basis of *forum delicti commissi* if it is shown that the website where the allegedly infringing information is contained is objectively directed towards Internet users in that Member State. The jurisdiction of those courts is limited to the damage caused within the territory of that Member State.

For applicable law, the ECJ should make it clear that Article 5 (2) Berne Convention is not a conflict-of-law rule and that Article 8 (1) Rome II Regulation is applicable to determine whether a copyright infringement exists and the non-contractual obligation deriving from that infringement. In cases of ubiquitous IP infringements, once the existence of the infringement has been determined in accordance with the laws of all the states where protection is sought, national courts should be allowed to select the most closely connected law to determine the consequences of such infringement between the parties.

---

[58] The ECJ also has competence to interpret the Berne Convention. However, this competence exclusively refers to the relationship between EU Law and the Convention, and not to the interpretation on how to apply its provisions.

References

Ancel M-E (2001) Contrefaçon de marque sur un site web: quelle competence intracommun-autaire pour les tribunaux français? In: Droit et Technique. Etudes a la mémoire du Xavier Linant de Bellefond, Paris, Licet, 2001, pp 1 and ff

Bergé J-S (2000) Droit d'auteur, conflits de lois et réseaux numériques: rétrospective et prospective. Rev. Crit. Droit Int. Privé, num 89, pp 357 and ff

Carrascosa Gonzalez J (2004) Conflicts of Laws in a Centenary Convention: Berne Convention 9th September 1886 for the Protection of Literary and Artistic Works. In: Feitschrift für Erik Jayme, Munich, Sellier pp 105 and ff

De Miguel Asensio P (2007) La *lex loci protectionis* tras el Reglamento Roma II. Anuario español Derecho internacional privado vol. 7, pp 376 and ff

Desurmont T (2001) La Communauté Européenne, les droits des auteurs et la Societé de l'information. RIDA vol 190, pp 3 and ff

Esteve González L (2006) Aspectos internacionales de las infracciones de derechos de autor en Internet. Granada, Comares

Fernandez Masiá F (1996) Protección internacional de los programas de ordenador. Granada, Comares

Ginsburg J C (1998) The Private International Law of Copyright in an Era of Technological Change. Recueil des cours de l'Academie de Droit international de La Haye vol 273, pp 243 and ff

Moura Vicente D (2008) La propriété intellectuelle en Droit international privé. Recueil des cours de l'Academie de Droit international de La Haye vol 335

Van Eechoud M (2003) Choice of Law in Copyright and Related Rights: Alternatives to the Lex Protectionis. Kluwer, The Hague

Chapter 13
In Search of Alterity: On Google, Neutrality and Otherness

Marcelo Thompson

Timeo hominem unius libri
—Aquinas.

Contents

M. Thompson (✉)
Faculty of Law, The University of Hong Kong, Hong Kong, People's Republic of China
e-mail: marcelo.thompson@hku.hk

M. Thompson
Oxford Internet Institute, University of Oxford, Oxford, UK

A. Lopez-Tarruella (ed.), *Google and the Law*,
Information Technology and Law Series 22, DOI: 10.1007/978-90-6704-846-0_13,
© T.M.C. Asser press, The Hague, The Netherlands, and the author(s) 2012

13.1 Search and Responsibility

'The King can do no wrong'—goes the proverbial saying whose contemporary equivalent can be found in the idea that 'Google does no evil'.[1] Both expressions convey, in their different ways and with regard to their different times, a description of a state of affairs and a normative directive ensuing from such a state. Descriptively, they reflect historical or contemporary beliefs in the righteousness of a sovereign. Normatively, they entail that the acts of such a sovereign ought to be judged by standards different from those under which the acts of ordinary people ought to be. If there is one forced element in such an analogy, that may be only that the first, ancient expression, even in legal systems where crown privileges have held strong throughout the centuries, has been widely attenuated by the historical developments of public law.[2] The authority of the second, contemporary motto, however, has been asserting itself ever more strongly.

When we speak of Google's position of sovereignty one can read such a claim as framed in figurative, metaphorical terms. Other works have advanced similar claims with more market-oriented tints. In his book *The Googlization of Everything*, Siva Vaidhyanathan notes, with fitting irony, that "we are not Google's customers: we are its product"[3]—our time, our attention, our preferences, our personal attributes, thus, these are the offerings on which Google builds its revenue. In this sense, we are not the persons who buy, we are the things that are sold. Vaidhyanathan's position cannot indeed be understood but in a metaphorical context. Lessened though our dignity may be through these commodifying bonds that link us to Google, our status as persons (and thus not products) still obtains.

And yet, we do contract out portions of our liberty; we transfer these to an overarching organization that purposes (or purports) to reflect the wider public interest—the "database of intentions",[4] in John Battelle's words—and to do so in a benevolent or at least non-malicious way. We become increasingly dependent on such an organization, at a very fundamental level, to navigate what Charles Taylor

---

[1] "Don't Be Evil" was a motto officially adopted by Google during an internal corporate meeting in 2001. According to accounts by Google's own personnel, it was chosen, together with other general principles, to reflect "what Google was all about"; it was adopted within an efficiency-oriented ethos, by engineers resistant to the excessive specificity of rules. *See* Battelle 2006, p. 138.

[2] Think of the United Kingdom. From the Magna Carta, in 1215, to date, in cases like *M* v *Home Office* [1994] 1 AC 377, the history of British constitutional law, though having mishaps and setbacks, has been one of control and subjection of the Crown. *See, e.g.*, Holt 1992, p. 29, *quoted in* Tomkins 2003, p. 40 (arguing that the Magna Carta was itself "based on a political theory of 'monarchical responsibility...'"). This, of course, is far from claiming that there is anything resembling a regime of perfect tripartite separation of powers in Britain, with the Crown entirely at check by the judicial power. *See, e.g.*, Adam Tomkins, *id.*, at 54–60.

[3] Vaidhyanathan 2011, p 3.

[4] Battelle 2006, p 1.

has suitably called the "space of questions"[5]—the ontologically basic framework-definition within which we find our ways and moral bearings in the world. The illusion that just to wish such a framework away and switch to a different provider is costless will be further addressed below—though it is, as I say, an illusion. Google *is* the sovereign, not only in metaphorical but in very real and unprecedentedly fundamental terms. It gives, it takes away the *reasons* whose number, variety, and relevance are increasingly determinant of the ways we author our lives—of our personal autonomy, hence. This will be ever more so in a society whose normative orientations come to be increasingly and explicitly articulated in the institutional orders of the information environment. Our liberty thus hinges upon the configurations of that framework and of an information environment which is remarkably influenced by it.[6] We are not Google's product: we are its subjects.

Now, whether or not one accepts as a fact this bold attribution of sovereignty to an Internet company, one may still accept the more modest remainder of the propositions introduced at the outset, that Google's motto reflects: (i) a belief in its (moral or cognitive) evaluative superiority—which gains strength when one notices that Google's self-assigned mission is that of "organizing all the world's information" and that this entails some degree of self-confidence in so doing; and (ii) an expectation that, due to its claimed superiority, the company should be judged by standards different from those by which ordinary people—or companies—should be.

Both these self-aggrandizing ascriptions come together in the main argument put forward in this article. In the pages that follow I will demonstrate, in the light of a concrete example, that Google seeks to establish an evaluative culture in which its possibilities of reasoning and acting upon its reasons assume a degree of priority with regard to those of other agents in the information environment. The pursuit of such a priority by Google, I will argue, presents itself as a call for the nullification, neutralization of equal possibilities of reasoning and action by other agents.[7] Having examined this argument and understood the problems it poses, we then discuss which, amongst different conceptions of the political system, is the

---

[5] Taylor 1991, p 29 ("[T]o speak of orientation is to presuppose a space-analogue within which one finds one's way. To understand our predicament in terms of finding or losing orientation in moral space is to take the space which our frameworks seek to define as ontologically basic. The issue is, through what framework-definition can I find my bearings in it? In other words, we take as basic that the human agent exists in a space of questions. And these are the questions to which our framework-definitions are answers, providing the horizon within which we know where we stand, and what meanings things have for us").

[6] Recent studies show that 6% of all global Internet traffic comes from Google (a number that may, depending on the variables, go up to 12%). See Labovitz 2010. This makes Google the largest source of traffic on the Internet. And yet, it is a measurement of traffic itself—not of Google's influence. Compared to Skype's, for instance, much of Google's type of traffic may be relatively light. Six percent, thus, is a very impressive number. But the real, unanswered question, is how much of the remaining traffic, though not carried by Google, arises directly or indirectly from information obtained through it.

[7] It is in this technical sense, which will get clear more ahead, that the word *neutralization* will be used in this article.

most suitable for dealing with such problems. Inquiring into all this, I believe, has immense relevance in a moment in which competition authorities, in Europe[8] and in the US alike,[9] seek to evaluate the regulatory implications of Google's practices in the realm of search. The conclusions reached in this article, however, also point to the limitations of a competition-based approach that focuses on search engines as particular ontological entities[10] and on search as a relevant market.

The article runs like this: The following section will focus on a very prominent instance in which the pursuit of neutralization of otherness, of alterity by Google presented itself to the fullest—the case of a call for the neutrality of Internet service providers (ISPs), also known as 'network neutrality' or, in other words, the idea that ISPs must not discriminate packets of data on the Internet based on their source, content or destination.[11]

Until it "changed" its position in August 2010,[12] Google had been one of the most vocal proponents of network neutrality. Its shift had less to do with normative repentance than with a pragmatic recognition of the regulatory difficulties in the implementation of its propositions—coupled, of course, with some degree of self-interestedness in the pursuit of alternative paths. In essence, however, Google continued to push a similar agenda of restraint for ISPs under a different terminology. We will discuss the almost incredible, indeed absolute form of restraint

---

[8] European Commission 2010.

[9] Editorial, N.Y. Times, 2011.

[10] A number of earlier works seem to adopt this ontological approach with regard to search. *See*, *e.g.*, Nissenbaum and Introna 2000, p. 169 (for a pioneer, normative account discussing how the ways search engines function are "at odds with the ... ideology of the Internet as a public good" (*id.* at 178)). *See also* Bracha and Pasquale 2008 and Grimmelmann 2007. Pasquale has recently expanded this perspective in a cogent piece. See Pasquale 2010.1, p.402, inviting "scholars and activists to move beyond the crabbed vocabulary of competition law to develop a richer normative critique of search engine dominance".

[11] I will not pursue here any comprehensive account of what network neutrality means in all its different flavours—if only because these so are varied and manifold that they make of network neutrality, to use Christopher Yoo's words, "a naked normative commitment". Yoo 2005, p. 26. I will, however, describe and evaluate that which I trust to be the archetypal stance on network neutrality; the stance most faithful to net neutrality's teleological foundations: Google's. Network neutrality here is mostly interesting for the world view it at the same times draws on and brings about.

[12] Google is widely believed to have shifted its stance on network neutrality in a joint proposal with *Verizon Communications Inc.*, sent to the US Federal Communications Commission in August 2010. See Davidson and Tauke 2010 [hereinafter *Joint Proposal*]. The proposal, in a nutshell, suggests a differentiated approach for providers of wireless and wireline Internet access—with a significant set of constraints applying to the latter but not to the former. The idea seems to be this: on the one hand, traditional broadband ISPs will be subject to neutralizing constraints that enable Google to ride freely upon them. On the other hand, the approach to wireless communications will be one that enables Google to be a first mover and, in partnership with Verizon, build upon its established dominance in the information environment. Doing so, Google can, in practice, neutralize other ISPs in ways it knows it would not be able to do through policy intervention by the FCC. Network neutrality, however, was overall abandoned by Google *as a term of art*. Below we understand why.

reflected in Google's formal calls for network neutrality and compare it with the position finally adopted by the Federal Communications Commission on the matter. I will highlight the incoherences of both these approaches—Google's more so than FCC's—and of the conceptions of law and action that they espouse.

Both FCC's and Google's approaches rely in part on the idea that search engines in particular and application and service providers in general should be judged by standards different from those applicable to ISPs. Part III addresses this misconception explaining how it amounts to an exclusion of ISPs from the normative whole that we call "the Internet" and relies on the false assumption that application and service providers cannot control the infrastructure of the information environment as ISPs are claimed to do. The article focuses, in particular, on the case of search and on the argument that customers are always free to switch away from Google's services.

Part IV revisits the overall claims of the article under the lights of contemporary liberal theory. It submits that, rather than providing support for the neutralization of any actor in the information environment, or overall requiring that stakeholders—ISPs, states, inter alia—keep away from people's evaluative pursuits on the Internet, liberalism actually requires that a range of substantive choices are made by stakeholders precisely to enable people to live autonomous lives. Here, the article engages with the most ambitious attempt so far to devise a political theory for the information environment, Yochai Benkler's. Benkler's thoughts lend remarkable—if contestable—authority to Google's world views and aspirations. But they also silently (and unfortunately) depart from the sounder political theory of Joseph Raz, which Benkler claims to embrace while only selectively doing so. The article draws on Raz's liberal perfectionist framework to propose a model for state action that moves us beyond neutrality and beyond overly optimistic accounts of self-regulatory possibilities of the information environment, in any of its layers. Part V concludes.

13.2   Neutralizing Alterity

There have been many instances—and one may argue this has happened systematically—in which Google sought to establish a framework of absolute social priority for its own reasons. At times this happened in defiance, in attempted exclusion of the dominant, exclusionary reasons of the law. That was the case, for example, when Google undertook to digitize all books in existence on earth (were these in the public domain or not) without seeking permission from their respective rights' holders.[13] Or when Google decided to challenge a legal regime with which it had been until then cooperating: that of China—in a process that continues to unfold. Indeed, having moved its search engine away from the Mainland,[14] Google now champions the use

---

[13] Having been challenged through a Class Action, Google pursued a settlement that, for the time being, has been struck by the Judge hearing the case. See, inter alia, Samuelson and Nimmer, 2011.

[14] Drummond 2010.

of the international trade system to nullify China's possibilities of choosing reasons which it trusts to be of worthy pursuit in the information environment.[15]

If effective, all those processes of prioritization of Google's own reasons—for reasons which I will elaborate on below—would threaten the prospects of contemporary liberalism. In short, those processes would impair the possibility that other actors but Google act upon reasons chosen by them. The liberal logic would be thus inverted, but to a company that expects to be judged as doing no evil and, paradoxically, as being a champion of values of liberal nature.

Nowhere does this problem appear more clearly and explicitly articulated than in the debates concerning the idea of network neutrality. The attempts to neutralize China's possibilities of regulating 'the Internet' and to establish exceptions for copyright in the Google Books case also challenge liberalism.[16] But they do so mainly by challenging the authority of the state and the law—and thus the possibility that these intervene to preserve, in the information environment, certain values that contemporary liberalism came to understand as worthy of protection. The challenge to individuals and the collective does not happen directly, by stripping these of possibilities for authoring their lives, pursuing goals they believe valuable.

Of course, in the Google Books case, though the biggest challenge had been to the institutions of copyright law, authors and publishers had their rights, to some extent, usurped by Google.[17] A normative inversion was attempted which would presume the righteousness of Google's behavior, resulting, to some extent, in the subjection of rights' holders to Google's will. And yet, serious though it is to have parts of one's books searchable against their will, rights' holders were not shackled, divested of their central reasons and pursuits.[18] But this is precisely what network neutrality does to ISPs.

---

[15] One of the main arguments used in recent World Trade Organization proceedings against China is precisely the idea of 'technological neutrality', which enjoins political authorities not to reflect specific choices in society's technological infrastructure. I have dealt with the merits of China's choices in this context in an earlier work. *See* Thompson 2011. For Google's approach, see Boorstin 2010.

[16] One may rush to claim that challenging China's policies with regard to the information environment is to do liberalism a favour. One should also note, however, that to nullify China's possibilities of making *any* choices on conceptions of the good in this regard—which is entailed in neutrality claims—is a self-defeating way of promoting liberalism. I enlarge on this point in Sect. 13.4.

[17] And this in spite of Google's expedient observations, somewhere else, that Copyright law in the US, including the DMCA, reflects "a delicate balance, carefully crafted by Congress and adjudicated through the courts". See Reply Comments of Google Inc., In re Preserving the Open Internet Broadband Indus. Practices, GN Docket No. 09-191, WC Docket No. 07-52 (Apr. 26, 2010). [See note 28].

[18] Were this to happen, it would be the product of a building up of different challenges to the law—and not as an absolutist, all-encompassing challenge to any individual actor in the information environment.

The idea of network neutrality hurts liberalism at its very core by establishing, for ISPs, a form of restraint that paradigmatically inverts the logic of the liberal principle. It does not merely impinge upon, it disfigures the idea of liberty by preventing important social agents from choosing their reasons for action—in this case, their criteria for managing their networks. And as the calls for neutrality extend, beyond ISPs, to other actors in the information environment, this othering of liberty threatens to become the normative touchstone of a remarkably individualistic age.

In effect, everywhere we see the Internet mob calling for the neutralization of states and economic actors. The underlying principle seems to be that no authority but that of the individual self should be recognized. As in a late reverberation of outworn liberal theory of the past centuries—which is embraced and bolstered by the scholarship and practical contrivances[19] developed by colleagues at the Berkman Center—the call of the time is for having "individuals as the bearers of the claims of political morality".[20] All this is all the most visible in the network neutrality movement.

Despite the ardency with which clamours for network neutrality have been echoed by the multitude, the principle is yet to see actual implementation. It is important however that we enlarge on its proposed contours so that we can understand the normative implications that would have accrued from the principle had it been implemented—and may still do if it ever is. Understanding these implications, as we will see further on, is of central importance when we seek to define the political destiny of our information environment.

13.2.1 Google's Manifesto

Google's original network neutrality defence can only be found today in the historical archives of the Internet.[21] Network neutrality is defined there through its effects as, "the principle that users should be in control of what content they view and what applications they use on the Internet". Interestingly though, the seeming kind-heartedness towards users, the only mentioned means to achieve the said effects, is reflected in the following precept: "broadband carriers should not be permitted to use their market power to discriminate against competing applications

---

[19] *See, e.g.*, StopBadware.org, Herdict.org and ChillingEffects.org—at least two of which count on Google as their foremost collaborator.

[20] Benkler 2006, p 281.

[21] Google's original evangelization page—"A Guide to Net Neutrality for Google Users"—can only, indeed, be found in the Internet Archive, its latest version being of Sept. 25, 2009. *See* Google 2009 [hereinafter *Guide*]. The paradox that Google would seek to remove information from public access is notable. When one queries the old URL one is simply redirected to Google's justifications for its changed position. For the old address, *see* http://goo.gl/PWLrY (Accessed 6 July 2011). For the new address, just look for the old at http://www.google.com/help/netneutrality.html (Accessed 6 July 2011).

or content". This shifts the focus, from protecting users, towards restraining ISPs. And, inspite of the chosen wording, it seems to aim at restraining ISPs even beyond competition aspects.

It is indeed difficult to disentangle the expression "use of market power" in the context above from the sheer performance of ISPs' core activities. ISPs hold the power of routing information through the Internet, which entails, by corollary, the power of not doing so. The making of decisions on if and how to route information seems thus to be enough to characterize the exercise of power in a market context. Similarly, "competing content" seems able to accommodate any content discriminated by an ISP—that is, any content which competes with content that has not been discriminated. Of course, the latter expression assumes more strength if the discriminated content is one which competes with that of the ISP itself or companies vertically integrated with the ISP's activities. In all the range of its meaning, however, Google's proposition seems to indicate, broadly and simply, that ISPs should not be permitted to discriminate applications or content on the Internet; that control of the flow of information on the Internet should not be entrusted to ISPs. As Google puts somewhere else in the now extinct document "broadband carriers should not be allowed to use their market power *to control activity online*".[22]

Two questions follow from this. First, if the objective is truly that of putting users in control, why should only ISPs be obliged by a rule that neutralizes their possibility of acting upon reasons chosen by them? Why are not application and service providers, in particular Google, equally constrained by a principle of neutrality? Second, is the idea of neutralizing any actor in the information environment compatible with the orientations of contemporary liberal politics? I will offer some tentative replies to these questions in Parts III and IV, respectively.

I will introduce, however, the first question in more detail in the lines below, as we seek to ascertain the normative boundaries of Google's more formal position on the regulation of ISPs. This position expands and precise Google's original orientations in its Guide to Net Neutrality under a new terminological orientation. In it, Google lays out its calls for ISPs' restraint in an awkward—and extremely telling—systematic perspective. Let us understand how.

13.2.2 The "Murkiness" of Justice

It is at the core of Google's activities—as it is of ISPs'—to make judgments about attributes of data it deals with. Should a principle of restraint neutralize Google's possibilities of doing so? The answer to such a question must go beyond Google itself and also include other application and service providers. After all, all of these are part of an Internet whose layers are in continuous interaction and whose actors

---

[22] Id.

have reciprocal impacts on the services of each other. However, given Google's prominent political role and its leadership in the network neutrality movement it seems but natural that scrutiny would at some point turn against Google itself—not only to test whether Google walks its own talk but also, and perhaps mainly, as a consequence of Google's immense possibilities of interfering with the individualistic desires of the Internet crowd. And indeed, by the time Google surprisingly "modified" its stance on the topic, in August 2010,[23] public calls for neutrality had more assertively started to include Google's activities as well.

On July 2010 the New York Times ran an editorial called "The Google Algorithm",[24] in which it noted the need to adopt regulation to ensure that Google's tweaks in its algorithms do not prevent Google from leading us where we want to go. While the Editorial did not explicitly contain a call for Google's neutrality it was widely read as containing such. As in acknowledgement of such a reading, a response to the Editorial was promptly published in the Financial Times by Marissa Mayer, Google's Vice-President of Search and Product Experience, in which she attempted to explain why regulators should not step in to enforce 'search neutrality'. In the piece, titled "Do not neutrali[z]e the web's endless Search",[25] Mayer claimed that neutrality rules "remove[…] the potential for innovation and turn[…] search into a commodity".[26]

Mayer's choice of words was not coincidental. Rather, the title and content of her short piece were pondered and reflective of an ongoing movement that started to become more material when Google first joined efforts with Verizon in October 2009. In a statement of common grounds issued at the time by both companies,[27] neither committed to neutrality, but rather to promoting an Open Internet. Shortly after, in January 2010, Google released its most official and important comments so far on the matter (Comments),[28] in the context of a Notice of Proposed Rulemaking (NPRM) issued by the Federal Communications Commission (FCC) in October 2009.[29] There, again, Google's notes on network neutrality were merely

---

[23] *Joint Proposal, supra* note 12.

[24] Editorial, N.Y. Times 2010.

[25] Mayer 2010.

[26] It is ironic, and we will come back to this point, that Google sees its own services as *innovating* while others'—those that should be neutralized—are seen as mere commodity.

[27] Schmidt and McAdam 2009

[28] Reply Comments of Google Inc., In re Preserving the Open Internet Broadband Indus. Practices, 6N Docket No. 09-191, WC Docket No. 07-52 (Jan. 14, 2010) [hereinafter Comments]. FCC's authority in this context was later challenged and found against in *Comcast Corp.* v. *FCC* 2010 [hereinafter *Comcast*], a case concerning the interruption of BitTorrent traffic by Comcast, whose behaviour was reprimanded in a 2008 Order issued by the FCC. *See* Federal Commmunications Commission 2008 [hereinafter Comcast Order]. For an analysis of the D.C. Circuit's decision finding against the FCC, see Thompson, 2010. See Google 2010, p. 72

[29] Federal Communications Commission 2009 [hereinafter NPRM].

tangential as the Comments moved from a neutrality-based approach towards a formal call for *awesomeness*.[30]

It might be tempting to think that the terminological shift represented a paradigmatic normative conversion—from a doctrine of neutral concern to a virtues-based approach; from the *neutral* towards the good, or the *awesome*. But the episode rather reveals the always all too close proximity between doctrines of neutrality and substantive world views about what the good, in political terms, is. Google's commitments have always been, in effect, to particular reasons, to conceptions of the good reflected in a political framework that enables it to avail its users with (only apparently) boundless informational choices. It is based on these views that Google seeks to neutralize alternative procedural and substantive possibilities for the information environment. But Google can still implement its world view while abandoning a terminology—that of neutrality—which was threatening to engulf its own services.

It was thus perhaps to close the terminological Pandora's box it had opened, perhaps to prepare the grounds for the broader partnership with Verizon it would soon announce, that Google decided to abandon neutrality as a term of art, conveying its policy propositions in different wordings. The spirit, however, was still the same. As put in its Comments:

> [Google's] interest in this proceeding is straightforward: to **keep the Internet awesome** for everybody.
>
>   The Internet was designed to empower users. They are in control of the applications and services they use and create. And they—**not network providers or anyone else—decide** what ultimately succeeds in the online market.[31]

Note that, on the one hand, Google reserves for itself the role of preserving awesomeness—which necessarily encompasses deciding upon whatever awesomeness is. On the other hand, Google sees the original design of the Internet as one for which no one but users—and, if the first sentence obtains, Google—makes choices of ultimate value. Such is the awesome model which Google believes should be preserved.

Now, it may seem that when the Comments mentioned that network providers—ISPs—should not be entitled to make decisions, this was meant as an exaggeration, something to be taken with a pinch of salt. That, however, does not happen to have been the case, for the Comments proposed what was called a "simple nondiscrimination" rule,[32] similar to the propositions of Google's earlier, more informal Guide. According to the "simple nondiscrimination rule" ISPs should be prevented from using their control over the network to favor or disadvantage particular sources of content or applications—in other words, ISPs should be prevented from using their position in the network to manage the network. As

---

[30] *See infra* note 31 and accompanying text.

[31] Comments, *supra* note 28, p i.

[32] Id. p ii, 3 and pp 60–63.

explained in the Comments, the "'simple nondiscrimination' rule prevents broadband providers from blocking, degrading, or prioritizing Internet traffic".[33]

Justifications given for such a rule were the critical nature of broadband access as a basic component of communications infrastructure, the scarce nature of broadband resources due to demand of enormous up-front investments, and the power held by ISPs to control the upper layers of the Internet[34]—where, to use FCC's terminology, Edge Providers[35] lie. Let us leave alone for now that all these same reasons could be applied, conversely, to Google itself. Let us also forget for a bit that, when highlighting the recent *bad* behavior by ISPs, Google gave as an example of its good behavior its commitment to openness through its investment in the Android operating system—which, ironically, Google has recently decided to close.[36]

What is important to be grasped at this point is the absolute nature of the restraints sought to be imposed to ISPs. This can be seen very eloquently in the Comments' endorsement of a statement in the NPRM which expresses, as a principle of "User Control of Content", that users should be *unconstrained* by broadband Internet access providers in their ability to participate in the marketplace of ideas".[37] It is important to note that the idea of unconstrained users implies completely constrained ISPs. The principle, thus, is that ISPs cannot choose reasons of their own in deciding upon how to manage their networks. The reasons available to ISPs would be fully heteronomous reasons, ex-ante defined by the FCC as valid and picked from a very narrow spectrum outlined in the Comments. It is in this sense that the Comments speak of "delineated permissible network management practices",[38] preferring the simplicity of absolute impossibility to the "murkiness" of justice as a standard. As it puts,

> Adopting an '**unjust** and unreasonable discrimination' standard and reasonable network management exception would establish a more **murky** [sic], complex, and likely ineffectual legal standard.[39]

To put it differently, it is not that ISPs should be allowed to operate within certain principles of justice and expected to make choices which are practically reasonable.[40] It is, rather, that such principles and choices are not available to ISPs

---

[33] Id. p 3.

[34] Id. pp 13–26.

[35] In its recently issued Open Internet Rules the FCC uses the expression 'edge providers' "to refer to content, application, service, and device providers, because they generally operate at the edge rather than the core of the network". See *infra* note 60, para. 3 n.2.

[36] *See* Paul 2011.

[37] Comments, *supra* note 28, at 56; NPRM, *supra* note 29, para 95.

[38] Comments, *id.* p 60.

[39] Id. p 62.

[40] Practical reason is here referred to in a technical sense, as "the general human capacity for resolving, through reflection, the question of what one is to do". Wallace 2003, and as involving all the normative elements, the comprehensive world-views that we discuss in the upcoming sections. For an insightful account on the requirements of practical reason, see Finnis 1980, 2005.

at all, except as narrowly dictated by the FCC. Autonomy is thus fully replaced by heteronomy.

The most patently absurd reason given in the Comments for such an absolute form of restraint is that a 'simple nondiscrimination' rule as the one proposed is "easier to understand and requires less enforcement expense and resources".[41] A reasoning in all similar to this would be one that is as unsubtle as Google's proposition: since bondage eliminates the normative uncertainty that could arise from entrusting bondsmen with the possibility of choosing their reasons for action, one can say that wider social benefits accrue from bondage than from liberty. We see well at which cost such sort of certainty would come.

Though the Comments do contemplate, as said, the possibility of the FCC defining a number of reasons according to which ISPs can manage their networks, these are restricted to a "narrow set of reasonable network management practices, limited solely to engineering practices legitimately related to network conges-tion".[42] But even here ISPs' possibilities are minimized as: (i) the "optimal solution" suggested by the Comments are, rather than reasoning, the sheer "addition of capacity on the network level"[43]; and, most importantly, (ii) ISPs are not even entitled to interpret the law, since compliance of content with the law is understood not to be an issue "related to network management at all".[44]

The latter restriction being true, one wonders what to make of the few possi-bilities in which the Comments do provide for the adoption of network manage-ment practices, such as to prevent "malware", block "spam" and "protect children from offensive materials (e.g., pornography)".[45] It is curious indeed that ISPs are in this sense allowed to address the intersection between the technological (engineering practices) and the ethical (the mal-, in malware), but need to interpret the ethical completely bereft of legal reasons. In other words, Google's strange liberalism leads it to agree with several (albeit narrow and predetermined) modalities of decision by ISPs on conceptions of the good for instance, deter-mining which software, in being harmful, is bad)[46] while denying to ISPs any possibility of decision on conceptions of the *right* (for instance, determining which software is illegal).

Not only is this a very unique kind of liberal philosophy, it is one that does not make sense at all, for to exclude any interpretation of lawfulness from the realm of

---

[41] Comments, *supra* note 28, p 63.

[42] Id. p 68.

[43] Id. p 69.

[44] "A separate network management exception for 'unlawful content' and the 'unlawful transfer of content' is unnecessary. (...) [T]hese issues are not related to network management at all, but rather are properly matters of law enforcement and compliance with the law". Comments, p. 72.

[45] Id.

[46] As the following lines will show, however differently one may understand the harm principle in other realms of practical reason, determining what is harmful *in relation to informational goods* inevitably engages our conceptions of the good in moral, political and otherwise cultural ways.

the ethical is to exclude from this same realm any possibility of reasoning upon those most severe forms of ethically deviant behavior that the law is concerned with. That is, while ISPs can manage their networks to prevent the trite, they may not do so spontaneously to avoid the atrocious when this is settled by the law.

It is here very important to notice that decisions on what constitutes "malware", for instance, are not merely engineering decisions. Google itself collaborates with a Harvard University-originated project called *Stop Badware*, a clearing house for stopping the spread of malware on the Internet.[47] One does not need to go very far to understand how normative the definition of badware is. According to Stop Badware, "[b]adware is software that fundamentally disregards a user's choice about how his or her computer or network connection will be used".[48] In other words, badware is software that imposes to users that same ideal that Google seeks to impose to ISPs and the world—heteronomy.

It is further evidence of badware's, beyond technological, normative nature that Stop Badware alludes to it as "a threat to the open Internet, one of our greatest political, economic, and cultural shared resources".[49] Hence, it is not surprising that Stop Badware would classify the Green Dam filtering software, whose installation in every PC in China was mandated by the government, as badware. The reason given for such a classification was that the software would "filter political speech without notice".[50] A fair question to ask in this regard would be: in light of the extensive regulatory framework of the Internet in China, can one really say that enough notice was not given that filtering would occur? More directly related to our inquiry, however, is to note that the classification of the Green Dam software as badware because of its filtering of political speech is tantamount to classifying the whole techno-regulatory framework of the Internet in China as badware. Given the extent to which such a framework is intertwined with China's political system and nation-building project[51] one can see how deeply political the definition of badware is.

It is thus a mistake to pretend that decisions on engineering of the Internet take place in separation from normative criteria—i.e. that ISPs may tackle network management as simply a matter of engineering. Elsewhere I have explained how the explicit articulation of normative expectations through technological artifacts renders it impossible for nation-states to ignore the processes by which these artifacts come into being—and thus the norms that they reflect and that are often

---

[47] *See supra* note 19.

[48] StopBadware 2011a.

[49] StopBadware 2011b.

[50] StopBadware 2009.

[51] *See, e.g.*, Zheng 2008, p. 17, arguing, on the one hand, that "the development of science and technology has long been embedded in the mind-set of the Chinese elite regarding nation-state building" and, on the other hand, that the policies and practices of nation-state building in China at the same time "provide opportunities for the rise of social movements". Both perspectives, for Zheng, interact in the constitution of what the political in contemporary China *is*, all this being "especially true in the case of … the Internet" (*id.*).

determined by large-scale, state-like enterprises.[52] States, hence, cannot commit to neutrality without risking the demise of their already fading authority and the nullification of conceptions of the good whose pursuit is worthy of protection. And as much as states need to interpret such normative realities in the most different realms of societal happening—against the odds of much of earlier centuries' liberal theories that would advocate for state neutrality—so need corporations, whose weaving of the technological infrastructure is constitutive of those realities.

It is tempting to move here towards more in-depth discussions on Science and Technology Studies to explain the relations between the technological and the social. We need not do so, however. We can settle the matter that the engineering of the Internet has politics—and is otherwise normative—just by looking at the standards that preside over the Internet's development. The Internet Engineering Task Force, for instance, adopts clearly politico-normative orientations in defining not only the process by which Internet standards are approved but also the value that these must embrace. It is in this sense that its RFC 2026—the meta-standard that sets the procedure for the making of standards—defines *fairness* as one of the goals of the Internet Standards Process.[53] Similarly, the Internet Society—IETF's organizational home—speaks of an "overarching principle of *openness*" and of *choice, access* and *transparency* as "underlying policy principles" for the Internet. At the same time, it criticizes the idea of network neutrality as a "broad and ill-defined term".[54]

The first organization in charge of Internet governance to formally adopt network neutrality as a principle was the Brazilian Internet Steering Committee (CGI.Br), in a Resolution of 2009[55]—albeit CGI.br's lack of any legally backed enforcement attributions.[56] Very interestingly, the way the principle was adopted in Brazil adds concrete weight to our discussions in this section. In its Resolution, CGI.br defined the principle as meaning that "Filtering or traffic privileges must meet *ethical and technical criteria only*, excluding any political, commercial, religious and cultural factors or any other form of discrimination or preferential treatment".[57] As Google's peculiar philosophy, CGI.br's implies a separation between two different normative realms—here, the ethical and the political, admitting of filtering to attend to the former while ruling it out entirely for the latter. Thus, while filtering for invasive ethical criteria would be allowed by the CGI.br Resolution—e.g. the filtering of homosexual content the assignment of privileges to content related to the political constitution of a society would be completely ruled out—e.g. quality of service assurances for traffic-intensive political material in times of presidential campaigning.

---

[52] *See supra* note 15.

[53] IETF, RFC 2026, Bradner 1996, para 1.2. The reference is not merely to fairness as a procedural criteria for approving standards—which appears in another part of the RFC—but, substantively, to fairness as a goal of the standards process. With a similar reading, see Kathy Bowrey, Law and Internet Cultures 1 (2007).

[54] Internet Society 2010.

[55] Brazilian Internet Steering Committee (CGI.br), 2009 [hereinafter CGI.br Resolution].

[56] *See* Falcão 2003, p 15.

[57] CGI.br Resolution, *supra* note 55, para 6.

An interesting answer to the ethical challenge posed above to the CGI.br Resolution could be that the filtering of homosexual content is not ethical, but rather anti-ethical and that ISPs cannot thus adopt homosexuality as a criterion for filtering content. But this then leaves with ISPs the power of deciding on the *validity* of ethical criteria adopted by them in the routing of Internet content. Granting ISPs the power of deciding so seems to be entirely at odds with the propositions of network neutrality advocates—and Google's proposition for an awesome Internet. And yet, it seems but natural that ISPs will examine the validity, the truth of the reasons they adopt. In effect, ISPs should be expected to do so, not only on ethical, but also on political, legal and any other normative grounds.

This is not to attribute to ISPs the role of gatekeepers of public morality. Especially, this is not to avail ISPs with the power of effacing the boundaries between the public and the private in the information environment. Privacy standards, for instance, will be amongst the reasons that should inform action by ISPs. Prohibitions against specific discriminatory practices, if enacted, will be valid reasons as well. If ISPs overstep, checks and balances should be in place to address their excesses. This is one thing. To exclude any specific normative realm—or normative realms altogether—from the scope of the valid reasons that an ISP can adopt is a completely different thing.

In sum, what should be taken from the lines above is, on the one hand, that the pretence that one can consider engineering criteria in isolation from other, normative criteria does not obtain. Network engineering, even in its own, typical standards, is informed by notions such as harm, fairness and openness, which render it much more subjective than one may think in the first place. On the other hand, the same thoughts can be applied to the pretence that network management can be limited to only one or more normative—e.g. ethical—criteria. Neither can the political be ruled out, as proposed by CGI.br, nor can the legal, inter alia,[58] be, as proposed by Google. Rather, reasoning in practical terms implies pursuing the truth amongst values that arise in the most diversified areas of societal happening. That some heteronomous criteria can be applied—for instance by the FCC—to ISPs does not mean that in any area ISPs should be precluded from reasoning or have their reasons presumed against.

At the core of such reasoning lies the idea of *justice*, weaving an orderly fabric with the different reasons that ISPs—as other actors of the information environment—may validly pursue. Google sought to exclude justice due to its arguable murky nature. And yet one cannot interpret ideas of *reasonable* network management without resorting to principles of justice. There are two points we should understand in this regard. One point is more practical; the other, more philosophical.

The practical point is that, from an FCC's earlier Internet Policy Statement of September 2005[59] to date, for instance in FCC's Open Internet Rules of December

---

[58] One note is due here. Amongst other murky criteria that go beyond engineering—e.g. fairness and lawfulness—Google seeks to rule out the political. In practice, however, the political is only ruled out at Google's own convenience, for it continues to play a strong role through Google's own affiliated projects, such as StopBadware.

[59] Federal Communications Commission, 2005 [hereinafter Policy Statement].

2010,[60] justice and reasonableness have neither been excluded nor treated by the FCC as exceptional elements in ISPs' reasoning. However differently Google may have wished in its Comments,[61] the requirement of reasonable network management was rightly placed by the FCC at the very core of every action to be lawfully undertaken by ISPs. In other words, reason was demanded—and thus *entrusted to*—rather than seized from ISPs.

It was in this sense that the Policy Statement mentioned that "[t]he principles [the FCC] adopt[s] are subject to reasonable network management".[62] FCC's Rules, similarly, coupled a prohibition of blocking *lawful* content[63] or *nonharmful* devices with a general requirement that every discriminating act be reasonable. There was, of course, no prohibition to interpret what the unlawful or the harmful are, for how could there be reasonableness without reason?[64] Use-agnosticism— the non-discrimination between specific uses of the network—was defined as an indication of reasonableness but by no means a requirement of it. In other words, ISPs can still (sometimes they must)[65] discriminate between different uses, as long as they do so reasonably. Reasonableness was understood broadly, encompassing the prevention of harm, enablement of parental control and guarantee of network integrity—whatever that turns out to be.[66]

And yet, somewhat disappointingly, albeit only topically, the FCC disentangled *reasonableness* from *lawfulness* in its definition of reasonable network management, noting: "[w]e conclude that the definition of reasonable network management omit elements that do not relate directly to network management functions and are therefore better handled elsewhere in the rules—for example, measures to

---

[60] Federal Communications Commission, 2010 [hereinafter Open Internet Rules or, simply, Rules].

[61] For Google, instead of a reasonable network management requirement at the core of every principle, there should be a general prohibition against network management practices not explicitly delineated. Such a prohibition would then be coupled with *a defence* for those cases where it can be established that a network management practice *is* reasonable. In its Rules, however, the FCC understood that "principles guiding case-by-case evaluations of network management practices are much the same as those that guide assessments of 'no unreasonable discrimination'". Rules, *supra* note 60, para. 87. In other words, these principles do not work merely as a *defence* of reasonable network management for presumably unjustified network management practices. They work as a general *rule* of "no unreasonable discrimination" for network management practices that are generally taken as reasonable, until otherwise established.

[62] Policy Statement, *supra* note 59, p 3 n.15.

[63] "The rule protects only transmissions of lawful content, and does not prevent or restrict a broadband provider from refusing to transmit unlawful material such as child pornography". Rules, *supra* note 60, para 64.

[64] The FCC noted its "disagree[ment] with commenters who argue that a standard based on "reasonableness" or "unreasonableness" is too vague to give broadband providers fair notice of what is expected of them". In its words, "[t]his is not so. Reasonableness" is a well-established standard for regulate conduct". Rules, id., para 77.

[65] Albeit the Rules (*id.*) establish no independent requirement that they do so.

[66] Does the *integrity* of networks encompass, for instance, IETF RFC 2026's goal of a *fair* Internet? *See supra* note 53.

prevent the transfer of unlawful content".[67] This does not mean, thus, that ISPs are prevented from evaluating the lawfulness or unlawfulness of content. It only means that this evaluation by ISPs will not be taken by the FCC as a criterion for deciding whether a network management practice is reasonable or not—which is a strange and indeed disappointing outcome, for, even if the factual effects of this policy will be limited, the normative significance of saying that understanding reasonableness prescinds from understanding lawfulness is worthy of notice.

This brings us to the second, more philosophical point that needs to be made about network management. This point speaks more widely to the nihilistic, arguably pragmatic posture of network neutralists in general—and may prompt them to question their anti-normative instance.

The idea is as follows: in much of contemporary legal theory, the understanding of law as *command* (the so-called command theory of law) has been replaced by another understanding according to which *law* provides people with *reasons* for action. Law, in this sense, mediates amongst different reasons we hold[68] in the process of thinking about what to choose and do—i.e. in the process of *practical reason*.[69] In mediating, law modifies the scope of other considerations,[70] impinging upon the reasons that people would otherwise hold. Legal reasoning cannot thus be dissociated from the overall process of practical reason. It modifies the normative order; as it is reflected in the common institutions of everyday life, law presents itself to us not merely episodically but every time we reason in practical terms. Thus how can *lawfulness* be thought of as something to be disentangled from *reasonableness*—by ISPs or by any other agent?

There are, of course, diverging views on the relations between legal reasons and other reasons upon which law impinges. Some see—rather than a process of exclusion—a process of confluence, of identity between the reasons of law and other reasons of practical nature. Under this view, the reasons provided by law are inherently connected with the reasons of morality, justice, politics—in effect, these are one and the same reasons in the central case of what we must understand by law. It is based on such 'central case viewpoint' that John Finnis presents his idealized, but nonetheless very persuasive thoughts:

> [T]he central case viewpoint itself is the viewpoint of those who not only appeal to practical reasonableness, but also *are* practically reasonable, that is to say: consistent; attentive to all aspects of human opportunity and flourishing, and aware of their limited commensurability; concerned to remedy deficiencies and breakdowns, and aware of their roots in the various aspects of human personality and in the economic and other material conditions of social interaction. What reason could the descriptive theorist have for

---

[67] Rules, *supra* note 60, para 82.

[68] In Joseph Raz's "service conception of authority", the authority of law stems from the service it provides in "*mediating* between people and the right reasons which apply to them". Raz 1994, p 214.

[69] *See supra* note 40.

[70] See Raz 2004, p 9 ("What happens ... is that law modifies the way morality applies to people. ... [L]aw modifies ... the way moral considerations apply").

rejecting the conceptual choices and discriminations of these persons, when he is selecting the concepts with which he will construct his description of [law's] central case and then of all the other instances of law as a specific social institution?.[71]

In sum, in *being* practically reasonable—in managing their networks reasonably, how can ISPs ignore all these aspects entailed by practical reason and, in its central case, by law?

One may frown, however, on ISPs adopting this more comprehensive view of the relations between law and other normative realms—in particular the relations between law and morality. And yet, this does not do away with the fact that ISPs will still need to identify what the law is when choosing their reasons for action. Whether there is an identity between the legal and the moral realms or not, law does translate the moral with its own, legal lenses—as it does with the political, the economic, and all other social systems which it, at the same time, functionally differentiates itself from and holds a functional relationship with—which Niklas Luhmann terms "structural coupling".[72] For Luhmann, the specific function performed by law is the stabilization of normative expectations,[73] which law translates from other social systems and reflects in a coding of its own.

It may be that Finnis or Luhmann, different as these authors' views may be, do not meet the pragmatic intents of those who want to advocate either the FCC's form of normative restraint—to say reasonableness does not encompass lawfulness—or Google's more wild version of it—to say that ISPs, besides not engaging with the law, must not adopt any murky, non-strictly engineering criteria either, such as those of justice, politics, amongst others.

It may be that network neutrality pragmatists still do not agree that it is not possible to exclude legal criteria from practical reason in general, and vice versa. They may not agree: (i) that ISPs can only exclude law from reasonableness if they ignore social institutions altogether—for legal reasons are always embedded in these; that, whereas Google is concerned with complexity, it may be more paralysing for ISPs to try to disentangle legal reasons from, inter alia, those based on harm than just to look for what is reasonable in these realms altogether; and (ii) that, if only legal criteria were admitted, ISPs still would have difficulties in excluding political or moral criteria from legal ones; that this would also be paralysing. We may close this section with a note in this regard.

Perhaps pragmatists of the sort above may be in pursuit of a more objective theory of law; one that rejects *incorporation* of other normative criteria—for instance, of moral criteria—by law. In other words, even if Google admit of the adoption of legal criteria by ISPs—which it currently does not—that should be as far as ISPs should be able to go. The most likely theoretical model for pragmatists

---

[71] Finnis 1980, p 15.

[72] See Luhmann 2004, p. 140 ("This does not mean, as one might suspect at first glance, that the legal system and the political system form one system together. But they do resort to special forms of structural coupling and are linked to each other through that coupling").

[73] Id., at 142–172.

of this sort to pursue is a form of legal positivism—exclusive legal positivism of a Razian kind, which both rejects the thesis of the incorporation of morality by law and, as a corollary, defends that the identification of law does not depend on the evaluation of its moral merits.[74]

But even here Google would still face two important challenges. The first is that not even exclusive legal positivists would deny that law reflects political criteria. As Joseph Raz notes, "legal positivists endorse the model of rules because of a political theory about the functions of law".[75] In effect, law's claims of authority to mediate amongst different reasons for action cannot but be political through and through. If ISPs are entitled to apply legal criteria as a matter of reasonableness it is unavoidable that political criteria will be applied as well.

A concrete example may help us to see this. Think of the GreenDam software, mentioned above. The classification of the GreenDam as badware necessarily relies on a disregard for the legitimacy of the regulations of the Chinese Communist Party; on a refutation of their validity as law. And challenging the validity of the laws of China is obviously a challenge of political nature. Even if one is unwilling to generally see the political in law, one cannot deny that if ISPs are allowed to filter the distribution of the GreenDam as badware—or, say, to facilitate the traffic of data in circumvention to the wider system of techno-political filtering in place in China—the challenge to the authority of the laws of China will not be but a political challenge as well.

The second, none the less important challenge here is that, whatever critiques one may level against legal positivism's separation between law and morality, it is wrong to assume that legal positivism invites any actor in society, from dutiful officials to anarchical programmers, to abandon the pursuits of moral criteria altogether in doing law or living life. Neither does legal positivism deny the incorporation of political criteria by law, nor does it invite us to, in living a successful life by the law, abandon the pursuit of moral values at all. These are rare theoretical privileges that only Google can claim for its own theory of law and action—or, rather, for its lack thereof.

---

[74] According to this view, as much as one can identify a service in the church, even being an agnostic, just by looking at its *important* features, so can the morally impious still understand what the law is just by looking at its sources, without sharing moral convictions of any sort (The example is given by Dickson 2001, pp. 68–69). Moral criteria, for Raz, concern law's legitimacy, the *acceptance* of its *legal* propositions, but are foreign to and modified by the legal propositions one accepts. In sum, law, in being accepted as law, impinges upon morality, but does not incorporate morality and can thus be identified without resort to it. *See* Joseph Raz, *supra* notes 68, 70.

[75] Raz 1994, p. 235. In this excerpt, as not very often happens, Raz is citing Ronald Dworkin approvingly, which shows just how much of a platitude the point is.

13.3 Subjugating Layers

In the lines above we have examined the internal incoherence of attempts to neutralize a category of actors of the Information environment—ISPs. We have demonstrated how these attempts are carried out and, hopefully, how nonsensical the undertaking, altogether, is. We can now advance towards our last claims in this article. These are, on the one hand, that there is no justification for treating ISPs differently from actors in other layers of the Information environment and, on the other hand, that the attempt to neutralize any actor of the information environment is incompatible with the orientations of contemporary liberal politics. We engage with the latter claim in Sect. 13.4. In the lines below we focus on the problem of differentiation.

13.3.1 Separate but Equal

In its Open Internet Rules, the Federal Communications Commission noted that "[t]here is one Internet, which should remain open for consumers and innovators alike".[76] The precise achievement of the neutralization of ISPs, however, would be a split of the Internet, as we know it, into two unknown ones. At the top, where edge providers, like Google, are, a layer of unconstrained possibilities; at the bottom, where ISPs labour, a sheet of serfdom. As a whole, an inversion of Newton's "standing in the shoulders of giants" allegory, for here ISPs have giants standing on theirs.

The division of the Internet in layers is but a thought exercise of engineers and policymakers.[77] The layers do not exist if not as a logical artefact for aiding our intuitions about the Internet and helping us set the standards for its development. The Internet is *a normative whole*. The loose and symbiotic *association* of different actors in a large-scale, world-encompassing informational grid gives the Internet a normative unity that enables us to recognize it as *the* Internet.[78] And such is a normative unity that at the same time allows us to navigate and reflects the structure of our relations in contemporary society—with all the same treats of fragmentation that are everywhere inherent to these relations.

---

[76] Rules, *supra* note 60, para 93.

[77] *See* Lessig 2001, p 23 (noting how the idea of layers helps us to organize our thoughts).

[78] As Searls and Weinberger argue, "[t]he Internet isn't a thing. It's an agreement". Searls and Weinberger 2003. Of course, we need to understand this as an exaggeration, for the Internet is enacted in different dimensions, including, beyond that of conventions, also the tangible dimension that John Law calls the Euclidean topology. It *is*, thus, a thing, an object in all these dimensions. *See* Law 2002. The unity of what we call the Internet, however, is indeed conventional. It is given by the syntactical network through which we *normatively* enact the Internet, as an agreement, a meeting of minds—and thus of reasons.

Now, if law intervenes to nullify the reasons of any of the agents in the eco-system it will be in effect ruling such an agent out of the central normative representation of our society and of ourselves that the Internet is. Of course, law does need to intervene to remedy normative perturbations that threaten to fragment the wider project of social cohesion. Law will need to regulate the activities of ISPs as it also needs to regulate the activities of every other actor of the information environment. This is one thing. But to nullify the prospects that ISPs will act with autonomy in choosing the reasons with which to contribute to this wider project of normative unity is another thing altogether.

The neutralization of ISPs thus excludes their membership to the information environment. It dissociates them from what we call the Internet—or at least it renders the division of the Internet in layers, more than a thought exercise, a tangible reality of domination. In other words, if ISPs are neutralized, either we term the space occupied by them as something that is "not the Internet"[79] or we indeed understand that there are two completely different layers in the Internet—one of dark, restricted boundaries within which ISPs wander, and other of luminous, endless possibilities that ISPs shoulder.

And such would be a heavy burden indeed. It is thus surprising to find in the scholarly literature the information that only the lower layers of the Internet are capable of constraining the upper layers, not the other way round.[80] Why would the need of managing networks even arise for ISPs if the upper layers had no effects upon their own?

An example may help us to make the point. One of the requirements recently imposed by FCC's Rules to ISPs was that of transparency.[81] In the realm of search, however, such is a requirement to which Google much objects with regard to its own engine. Google does so due to the possibility that linking farms, Google bombs and, in general, black hat "Search Engine Optimizers" will use such wealth

---

[79] Very symptomatically, in a submission to the FCC last year during a consultation following the Comcast decision, a group of influential academics and supporters of network neutrality invited the Commission to acknowledge that the transmission component of ISPs' services is not part of the Internet, opening way for the Commission to regulate these services. In the authors' words, "carriers' assertions that the Commission would be regulating 'the Internet' [by regulating the transmission component of their services] are deliberately misleading". Ammori, Crawford and Wu, 2010, p. 7–8. The FCC had considered this idea (abandoning it later) in the consultation, noting that, in regulating ISPs' transmissions, it would not be regulating the Internet: "[G]eneral agreement has developed about the agency's light-touch role with respect to broadband communications…. *The Commission does not regulate the Internet*". Schlick 2010, 2919. For a critique, see Thompson 2010.

[80] *See, e.g.*, Murray 2007, p 45 (noting, based on Benkler, that "vertical regulation is only effective from the bottom-up, that is regulation in a supporting layer is effective in the layers above, but does not affect the layers below").

[81] *See supra* note 60, paras 53 ff.

of information to game Google's algorithms and appear high in Google's Page Rank.[82] But can't the same be said of ISPs' networks?

Imagine if, besides a requirement of transparency, a full-blooded non-discrimination requirement had been established by the FCC, with no exceptions, for ISPs. Obviously, absent any constraints, application providers would be able to use the wealth of information available about ISPs' networks to game and exploit these to the fullest. One can think of Skype, Spotify, World of Warcraft and other bandwidth-harvesting applications deploying powerful algorithms to make complete use of available bandwidth. That would leave no choice to ISPs other than monitoring new entrants in the applications market and constantly increasing the capacity of their networks to meet the interests of these. That, as seen above, had in fact been precisely—if incredibly—Google's proposal for the regulation of ISPs, by electing "addition of capacity on the network level" as the "optimal solution" for solving network congestion.

The FCC hinted at this point in its 2008 Order to Comcast and yet has never addressed the contradiction ever since. In the Order, the FCC noted that Comcast could "work with the application vendors themselves" and quoted comments stating that "[i]f Comcast made 'available information on what it considers the peak periods of network traffic ... it would not be difficult for the authors of BitTorrent [– the application which was being blocked by Comcast –] to modify their programs to query a Comcast server to determine what is the best time to upload/download data"'.[83] It did not consider, however, perhaps due to its foreseeable lack of authority, the alternative of also regulating edge providers.

Republican Commissioner McDowell's Statement on the occasion, however—and for more democrat that that the ideals that run through this article may be—were much more in line with our notes above. He observed, on the one hand, that "applications providers could do a better job of designing software that works more efficiently on networks that were designed and built sometimes decades ago".[84] On the other hand, McDowell remarked that "we are witnessing a deepening division between some in the application industry and some network operators".[85]

---

[82] On Google's Transparency Report website, data related to transparency actually refers not to Google itself but to Governments who may create hurdles to the provision of Google's services—by means of user information requests, information filtering or infrastructure outage. *See* Google, 2011. *See also, e.g.*, Zittrain 2008, p. 220 ("Search engines are notoriously resistant to discussing how their rankings work, in part to avoid gaming—a form of security through obscurity. ... The most popular engines reserve the right to intervene in their automatic rankings processes—to administer the Google death penalty, for example—but otherwise suggest that they do not centrally adjust results").

[83] Comcast Order, *supra* note 28 para 49 and fn229.

[84] Order, *supra* note 28, p. 61 (Statement of Comm'r Robert M. McDowell). His example of P2P applications is particularly relevant: "The providers of certain peer-to-peer (P2P) applications, for example, could do a better job of making consumers aware that their applications require consumers' computers to work 24 by 7 in ways that can tie up their computing power and reduce broadband speeds for themselves and their neighbours" (*id.*).

[85] Id.

This was also possibly the view of the United States Court of Appeals for the District of Columbia Circuit in the decision that quashed FCC's Order in Comcast. In that case, the Court understood that, if the Commission were to regulate ISPs, it could not do so with regard to cable Internet services *per se*.[86] One of the avenues not ruled out by the D.C. Circuit, however, is the regulation of cable Internet services *for the impact these have on regulated, common carrier and broadcasting services.*[87] Currently, only dial-up access providers—i.e. providers of lower bandwidth Internet access through telephone lines—are regulated as common carriers. These are fading activities of no greater interest to our analysis. It is with regard to broadcasting services that the D.C. Circuit decision matters to our argument. The Commission's understanding on this issue had been that, since the provision of online video service providers (e.g. by Hulu) "has the potential to affect the broadcasting industry",[88] the ways ISPs such as Comcast manage their networks with regard to these services have direct regulatory implications. Such an argument, though brought before the Court, had not been invoked originally in the Commission's Order against Comcast and so the D.C. Circuit declined to consider it in the Comcast case. The appreciation of the matter, however, is left open for a future opportunity and it is thus telling that one of the only possible grounds still available for the Commission to invoke its authority upon ISPs involves the power of edge providers themselves (e.g. Hulu) to disturb regulated activities at a lower layer.

It is thus not surprising that the reciprocal influences between, on the one hand, the network layer, and, on the other hand, the applications and content layers were one of the foundations on which the Commission based its authority upon ISPs in its just recently issued rules.[89] And yet, the Commission decided to regulate the contours of network management by addressing only one level of the equation— that of ISPs—and disregarding the other level—that of edge providers—tout court. In the Commission's words, the Rules "apply only to the provision of broadband Internet access service and not to edge provider activities, such as the provision of content or applications over the Internet".[90] Perhaps the most stringent reason for the Commission to decide this way was that, in its view, ISPs are "distinguishable

---

[86] Those services had been earlier classified by the FCC itself as information services, due to the fact that their *"telecommunications* 'component' ... is 'functionally integrated' [with their *'computing* functionality'] into a single 'offering'". Comcast, *supra* note 28, p. 13 [applying *National Cable & Telecommunications Ass'n* v. *Brand X Internet Services*, 545 U.S. 967 (2005)]. In other words, those services were held to be not two different parts but a whole and thus not to be regulable as if telecommunication services, simply, they were. For instance, the Commission would not be able to impose a common carrier obligation to providers of information services— as such an obligation can only be imposed to services which the Commission has direct authority upon, which is not the case of information services.

[87] *See* Comcast, *supra* note 28, pp 33–34.

[88] Id., p 34.

[89] See Rules, *supra* note 60, paras 124 ff.

[90] Id., para 50.

from other participants in the Internet market-place"[91] in that they "control access to the Internet for their subscribers and for anyone wishing to reach those subscribers" and thus are "capable of blocking, degrading, or favoring any Internet traffic that flows to or from a particular subscriber".[92] But is that something that can only be said of ISPs? Can't we say the same of Google?

13.3.2 The Click-Away Delusion

The problems described above concern the digital arm wrestling between ISPs and edge providers. Edge providers, however, command the flow of communications on the Internet much beyond their influence over ISPs. It is important to understand how these actors gatekeep the information environment in ways that disprove the common assumption that at the content and application layers competition is just one click away. That being so, these actors consisting in such an essential part of the Internet infrastructure, there would be no reason to defend that ISPs are "distinguishable from other participants in the Internet market-place".[93] Given the scope of this article, we focus our argument on Google, drawing on research that demonstrates that network externalities surrounding Google's search platform restrict users' switching possibilities much beyond what is frequently assumed.

In his book *Information Rules*, Hal R. Varian, now Google's Chief Economist proposed: "we'll show you how to use lock-into your advantage, or at least to neutralize others who try to use it against you".[94] Nothing more natural, hence, than his own company becoming a master of such strategies. And even if lock-in has not been used by Google as a deliberate strategy, it is clear that a situation of lock-in has arisen in relation to Google's dominant position in the information environment.

It may be difficult to define precisely what Google's relevant market is—that is, in which respect Google is a dominant actor. Search is as ubiquitous a need in the information environment as it is in life in general. The search for valuable options is intrinsically connected with personal autonomy, for only those options which are somehow found enable one to author one's life. Google's dominance happens with regard to reasons, informational options of so many different sorts that it transcends any single economic realm. One may argue that what characterizes Google's dominant position is the tendency towards a monopoly of meaning in the information age—a semiotic monopoly. Of course, Google does not in fact monopolize all sources of meaning of our time. But it may be the agent that comes closest of doing so.

---

[91] Id., p 31 n.160.

[92] Id., para 50.

[93] *See supra* note 91 and accompanying text.

[94] Varian and Shapiro 1999, p 104.

As Google dominance unfolds even further, there will be the need for regulators to intervene. Competition law, however, would face difficulties in finding the right reason for so. The strongest difficulty, perhaps, would be to ascertain the defining characteristics of informational goods and services. In a society in which the basic economic good—information—has blurred the boundaries between all realms of life, competition law struggles to disentangle markets and, most importantly, to do so amidst the different degrees of depth of informational processes. It is important to understand this question of depth for it is at the root of the regulatory problem we are trying to solve. Let us here think of information in terms of a *deep structure* and of a *surface structure*.[95]

Deeper in the structure of information we find meaning. By ourselves or through our technological extensions we interpret information in ways that convey meaning. Some of these meanings will relate to the functions that information itself performs. It is here that information is an adventure game, that it is Windows or Linux, a novel or a viral Youtube video. We may look at information and find reflected in it some goods that competition law has traditionally dealt with. Information in this sense can be labeled, divided into categories, some of which will matter for competition law. But on the face of it, on its epithelial surface, information is just information—and yet an economic good in itself. It circulates economically. We trade it. We access it. But as we interpret it, as we decode it we travel towards deeper realms in which information conveys ever broader forms of meaning. Information is thus always in both these dimensions; it is both shallow and deep and the challenge of competition law is to ascertain at what level, at which of those dimensions to pursue the traditional categories of economic markets—or, perhaps, to recognize that the regulatory enterprise actually moves us towards broader problems that transcend those traditional categories altogether.

The perhaps hopeless struggle to find the boundaries between, on the one hand, information on its face and, on the other hand, the deeper meanings information conveys can be imperfectly summarized in McLuhan's famous expression that the medium is the message. Imperfectly because information itself is now medium and message. Gatekeepers no longer control merely something we can identify as Television or the Cinema. They control informational "equivalents" of these. They control access to information on its face and to the inner dimensions of information by controlling *processes which are themselves informational.*

And, very significantly, as these actors hold and impart information they add new information—in surface and meaning—to existing information. Even ISPs do so, for more that Google would wish them to inhabit only the surface structure of informational processes, dealing with meaning to no extent.

One may thus say that no single agent in the information environment would meet Jean-Baptiste Say's classical definition of the merchant as one who "giv[es] value to things to which [he] actually *communicate[s] no new quality, but that of*

---

[95] I use the expressions differently from Chomsky 1965, pp 64 ff.

approximation to the consumer"[96]—if any economic agent ever has met such a definition. Agents in the information environment do communicate new qualities to informational goods, even if for enabling the process of approximation Say refers to. ISPs, for instance, will verify if packets of data meet some core standards of network security. And, want it or not, as noted above, ISPs *will also* make some judgments of politics and morality that are inherent not only to such security checks (e.g. in the case of badware) but also to decisions on the legality of actions ISPs undertake in routing content through the net. "What are the boundaries of an injunction?" "Which authorities can prevent me from routing content?" "Is this information related to paedophilia?" "To terrorism?" "Is it fair to slow down pornographic material during peak hours?" "Would I need to have included a clause in this regard in my Terms of Service?"—these are all legitimate questions that may present themselves to an ISP. Hard cases, zones of penumbra inevitably call for interpretation and in doing so, in clearing packets before routing them, ISPs signal that these packets meet the criteria for being routed. Further value, further meaning is thus given to these packets.

The information environment, in effect, has no single agent working only at the surface structure of informational processes—not even ISPs. Actors situated at one informational level are situated at other levels as well.

As much as the deep structure of information will relate to ISPs activities so will the surface structure be very important for the regulation of search. So important that it should actually be the *starting point of regulatory activities*. This may seem counterfactual. Search seems to be virtually all about meaning. Page Ranks rely on outstandingly complex processes to classify and define the priority of information. Google's products only exist in what they mean to us. Looked at their very surface, Google Maps, Google Books are nothing but packets of data somewhere in the cloud. It is only because, through our computers and by ourselves, we interpret what information *means* that we can think of them in terms we are familiar with—as Maps, as Books. The natural, it seems, would be for competition law to regulate Google's activities by looking only into the deep structure where these processes *are*.

But when one looks at these processes in separation, through their different meanings, there seems to be no need to regulate Google's activities. Google Maps, Google Books are just isolated drops in the virtual seas of the information environment. They may seem to correspond, and in a way they do, to entirely different economic realms that regulators cannot systematically connect. Problems of horizontal concentration, in this sense, would be out of question given the apparent

---

[96] Say 1885, Book I, Chapter II, para 19.

distance between markets in which Google's products are situated.[97] And yet, the growing extent of Google's dominance in the information environment signals that there is something above and beyond such products whose economic contours we cannot systematically define.

One way of responding to that is by noting that Google's products seem to combine into something fundamentally different that we call "Search". But what is search if not something that has been offered by everyone, from the Church to libraries, throughout the centuries—the brokering of access to relevant information? Do not all Internet gatekeepers act as search engines—even when they also offer something else? While some provide purely logical forms of search (e.g. Wikipedia, Google Video, Hulu, Spotify), others connect information with the physical avenues where information materializes (which is what ISPs do).[98] All of these—ISPs, search engines "sensu stricto", application providers, "content" providers—offer us gateways to information that exists both in its surface and at the depths of its meanings. All of them make judgements of relevance and otherwise, in Say's words, "communicate new qualities"[99] to the information-things they approximate consumers to.

---

[97] As the U.S. Department of Justice and the Federal Trade Commission note in their Horizontal Merger Guidelines, even if competition agencies' analyses need not start with the definition of markets, "evaluation of competitive alternatives available to customers [– that is, of markets –] is always necessary at some point in the analysis". U.S. Dep't of Justice & Fed. Trade Comm'n 2010, p. 7 [hereinafter Guidelines]. The scholarly literature has also noted the insufficiency of market definition exercises with regard to informational goods. Gilbert and Rubinfeld, for instance, argue that technologies are often complementary to each other and thus that it is inadequate to define technology markets as those involving "technologies or goods that are close enough substitutes to constrain the exercise of market power with respect to the intellectual property that is licensed". Such definition can be found in U.S. Dep't of Justice and Fed. Trade Comm'n 1995, para. 3.2.2. *See* Gilbert and Rubinfeld, 2011, pp. 262, 269. The problem here would be to assume that there is even some degree of complementarity between Google's different services. That would lead to an overly elastic definition of markets that could very well encompass the whole web. On the other hand, adopting other starting points but the definition of markets may not be of much help to competition authorities either. Here, rather than looking into pricing dynamics within a defined market, what agencies will pursue are evidences of detrimental *competitive effects* of a merger (Guidelines, *id.*). These effects typically arise wherever reduced product quality, reduced product variety, reduced service, or diminished innovation (*id.* p. 1) are not followed by significant pressures of demand substitutability. None of these effects take place in Google's increasing dominance scenario—rather the opposite. Google passes all these tests with flying colours. The problems it prompts are of a completely different nature. They are externalities to the Pareto efficiencies and Nash equilibriums of economic analysis.

[98] One can find another example of this logical-cum-geographical type of services in the Domain Names System of the Internet, which maps mnemonically accessible names to logical locations associated to physically situated resources. IETF's RFC 1034 speaks of a *name space* in a logical sense but, ultimately, these logical entities that we call names identify resources. Thus, "[t]he primary goal [of the Domain Name System] is a consistent name space which will be used for referring to resources". Mockapetris, IETF, RFC 1034, 1997, para 2.2.

[99] *See supra* note 96 and accompanying text.

It is not search, as a particular service, that characterizes the form of dominance that Google, through its different activities, exerts in the information age. Difficult though it may be to define that dominance, however, one cannot deny the extent of Google's power over the flow of information in the information environment. It is perhaps to the quantitative extent of Google's dominance at the surface structure that we should look in the first place as an indication of the power of its qualitative decisions to influence the construction of meaning in our societies.

The clear tendency of such a process of dominance to continue to unfold invites the placement of checks and balances by regulatory authorities. Of course, these checks and balances must come at the level of meaning. They must address the lock-in effects that make switching from Google services so costly to consumers, and this is not something merely related to the topology of information flows.

Interestingly, from a regulatory standpoint, there may be no typical anticompetitive practice that Google is engaging in. And yet, the continuous densification of the surface structure of informational processes around Google's nodes on the Internet tells us that Google became a not always bright sun around which everything, irresistibly, swirls.

Some of Google's products grant it, visibly, powers very similar to those held by ISPs. They create a general purpose infrastructure to which applications connect—or from which applications can be banned. This challenges FCC's understanding, seen above, that what distinguishes ISPs from other economic agents on the Internet is that these "control access to the Internet for their subscribers and for anyone wishing to reach those subscribers" and thus are "capable of blocking, degrading, or favoring any Internet traffic that flows to or from a particular subscriber".[100] Android, Google's operating system for mobile devices, is one such example of a product that holds such a power, in a market that does not count on wide competition and in which competitors, like Apple iPad's iOS, do not have a very impressive track record of openness. Not only can Android block certain applications if so it wishes, it can have Google favour it through its other product offerings, furthering the ongoing process of lock-in. Microsoft has argued just so in a complaint recently filed before the European Commission in which it submits, inter alia, that Android, which is the dominant OS for mobiles, is being favoured by Youtube, a Google-owned company.[101]

Less visible, but way more significant, is the process of lock-in that Google has been able to carry forward with its search engine. Against the common assumption that users can easily shift to competitors such as Bing or Yahoo should Google abuse its dominant position, research has shown that Google's market displays low contestability.[102] In Argenton's and Prüfer's words, "the production of search

---

[100] See *supra* note 92 and accompanying text.

[101] Smith 2011 ("Unfortunately, Google has refused to allow Microsoft's new Windows Phones to access this YouTube metadata in the same way that Android phones and iPhones do").

[102] See Pollock 2010, p. 18, noting that a "strong contestability result... is unlikely to be robust [in the search market]". See Argenton and Prüfer 2011, pp. 1–2, arguing that "the search engine market displays a strong structural tendency towards monopolization".

quality is characterized by a peculiar (intertemporal) kind of indirect network externalities".[103] The quality of search is said to be a network externality because it results from the use of search engines by a network of consumers—the larger the network, the greater the quality and thus the value that the search engine, as a product, will acquire. As no search engine has accumulated the wealth of knowledge that Google has about users' clicking behaviour, no other search engine can offer the same experience in terms of accuracy that Google can.

Argenton and Prüfer also believe the market of search has reached a tipping point, promising to become ever more concentrated, monopolistic indeed, unless regulators intervene.[104] Such an increasing concentration, they demonstrate, has been taking place since 2003, evidencing that the market's tipping point had already been reached by then and pointing to a strong tendency towards monopolization. The solution, in the authors' view, would be an obligation for Google to share with its competitors the data related to users' clicking behaviour. In their words, "intense competition between search engines based alone on the merits of the search algorithm provides better incentives to the firms to produce high quality products than the rent enjoyed by a dominant firm that exploits a competitive advantage created by network externalities".[105]

Rufus Pollock also reaches the conclusion that, in theory, in a fixed zero-price scenario customers "will only use the search engine(s) with the maximum quality"[106]—a scenario of winner-takes-all competition. In practice, with regard to search, Pollock believes that it is likely that there will be some heterogeneity in the perception of quality—e.g. through brand preference, or specialization in a certain type of content (e.g. Baidu for MP3-related search). The situation is thus unlikely to be so stark as to lead to a monopoly, but still tends to lead to a firm being highly dominant in the search market. Heterogeneity in brand perception will also explain why certain search engines have a higher market share in certain markets than in others despite differences in quality—e.g. Yahoo's substantially low market share in the UK and Google's vis-à-vis Baidu's in China.[107]

On the other hand, however, and more importantly, brand perception also contributes to reinforce the adoption of the dominant search engine in the market and reduces the contestability of its market-share—in what it is joined by the adoption of search engine specific query strategies by users, personalization of search results[108] and, I would add, users' familiarity with a given search engine interface.[109] These are all factors that contribute to the non-negligible lock-in of users in

---

[103] Argenton and Prüfer, id. p 2.

[104] Id. p 9.

[105] Id. p 15.

[106] Pollock 2010, p 12.

[107] Id. pp 16–18.

[108] Id.

[109] See Argenton & Prüfer 2011, p. 7 (citing a survey showing that interface design plays a role in product differentiation of search engines).

the search market. Together with the very high up-front, fixed costs for challengers to invest in R&D and infrastructure[110]—costs which can always be topped up by Google—those factors lead to the continuous strengthening of Google's dominance in the search market. For reasons that Pollock explains well, the establishment of a monopoly tends towards—even purposefully—reduction of quality.[111]

The modality of regulatory intervention suggested by Pollock would be the decoupling of "software" (e.g. the ranking algorithms) and "service" (the facilities such as data-centres, support systems etc., which run the "software"). For him, decoupling the two would allow for greater competition, inclusively by fostering greater transparency on the software side. Regulation would happen over the service side, which would be provided through governmental intervention, in a monopoly or near-monopoly scheme, allowing companies to concentrate their investments on the software side.[112]

While Pollock's suggestion is interesting, it does not directly answer Argenton and Prüfer's concern with regard to monopoly on the information resulting from users' clicking behaviour. From a competition standpoint, lack of transparency seems to be much more a concern in that regard than with regard to ranking algorithms themselves. The transparency of ranking algorithms should be fostered not because of competition reasons—actually there is nothing harmful in secrecy in this regard.

Rather, criteria embedded in algorithms should be made available, at least to regulatory authorities, for more general public accountability reasons. After all, in determining which reasons to make available for their users, search engines will inevitably be guided by evaluative considerations of moral and political nature whose impact can be as far reaching in the public sphere as moral and political choices made by ISPs can be. If transparency is demanded from ISPs, there is no reason why the same standards should not be extended to search engines.

This demand for transparency does not seem to sit comfortably in Pollock's model. His proposals of regulatory intervention mostly concern the "service" component of search.[113] It seems that, in Pollock's view, transparency of the algorithms would arise as a natural outcome of regulatory decoupling rather than by regulatory fiat. At some point in his text, though, he does incidentally remark that regulators could handle distortions by requesting confidential access to the algorithms and functioning as a review panel for ranking 'appeals'.[114] Pollock does not, however, advance a proposal similar to that by Argenton and Prüfer, which seems a much more likely candidate to address his *competition concerns*. Ironically, though, Pollock's incidental suggestions with regard to search

---

[110] Pollock 2010, p 11.

[111] Id. pp 21–23.

[112] Id. pp 26–27.

[113] Id. p 26 ("[R]egulatory attention could be focused on the 'service' side which in many ways is simpler").

[114] Id. p 27.

algorithms seem to transcend pure competition matters and provide us with a viable solution to the problem of public accountability of dominant search engines.

But are these proposals enough to regulate Google's increasing dominance in the information environment? They concern only the problem of search engines "sensu stricto"—not Google's wider influence over the flow of information in what above we have called the surface structure of the information environment. In its recent complaint before the European Commission, Microsoft noted that Google's dominance in the search market is strengthened by Google's having exclusive deals with most website owners to display its search box with exclusivity for search by the users of these websites. It is true that Google's widespread search boxes further the process of lock-in.[115] They are, however, only a limited, visible part of a much larger problem. The problem of Google's dominance extends far beyond what we understand by its "search engine". Through the provision of services in the most diversified, even disconnected areas—ranging from Maps to Books, from News to Translation, from Videos to Shopping Tools, Blogs and Operating Systems, Google is increasingly everywhere information is.

One can see in Google's strategies plenty of the insights Hal Varian outlines in his work with regard to the recognition of lock-in effects. We know that, with regard to mass-market products, especially those characterized by zero-price models, "small consumer switching costs can constitute large barriers to entry".[116] We know that "[c]ustomer perceptions are paramount" and then that "a brand premium based on superior reputation or advertising is just as valuable as an equal premium based on truly superior quality".[117] We also know that "one of the distinctive features of information-based lock-in is that it tends to be so durable: equipment wears out, reducing switching costs, but specialized databases live on and grow, enhancing lock-in over time".[118] Or that "with brand-specific training, switching costs tend to *rise* with time, as personnel become more and more familiar with the existing system"[119]; that "[s]earch costs borne by consumers when switching brands include the psychological costs of changing ingrained habits".[120] Or, finally, that "[t]he easiest place to hop onto the lock-in cycle is at the *brand selection point*—that is, when the customer chooses a new brand"[121]—a brand with which she will be locked-in after an *entrenchment* phase, "when consumer really gets used to the new brand [and] develops a preference for that brand over others".[122] Paradoxical as it may seem, in zero-price markets all these effects are maximized.

---

[115] *See* Smith 2011.

[116] Varian & Shapiro 1999, p 109.

[117] Id. pp 113–114.

[118] Id. p 115.

[119] Id. p 121.

[120] Id. p 126.

[121] Id. p 131.

[122] Id. p 132.

It may, however, be unfair to characterize Google's profiting from these postulates as purely a deliberate plan to dominate the information environment. Of course, Google's practices come in a context. Altogether, they must be seen as intrinsic components of Google's overall political agenda. But, taken for their own, individualized properties, those strategies aren't simply ill intentioned attempts of domination. They are also characteristic traits of informational markets. That Google masters their knowledge so well is not just the result of some degree of malignity but also a demonstration of competence in understanding the social dynamics of our time. Hence, it would be odd to claim that simply because Google engages in those practices it is resorting to specific forms of anti-competitive behaviour.

This is not to say those practices should not be regulated. All that is meant here is that the justifications for regulatory intervention should move beyond the culpability of Google's individualized modes of conduct from a competition standpoint. Regulators must understand that Google's gigantic and ever-increasing influence over the surface structure of the information environment in effect sublimes the traditional categories of competition law and provides a distinctive justification for state action. It is thus fundamental to objectively measure the reach of this influence. Webometrics-like tools may be an important regulatory aid here.[123] They may help us to visualize the extent to which Google enframes the information environment and, by doing so, controls the construction of meaning in the most different realms of life in society.

And yet, because we are dealing with informational goods, our task as regulators cannot be purely objective. While the starting point of measuring the dynamics of information flows needs indeed to rely on objective parameters, the inherent subjectivity—the deep structure—of informational goods cannot be overlooked. It is actually this subjectivity that, by dissolving the boundaries between Google's activities, makes the reach of these so problematic.

The proposals by Argenton and Prüfer and by Pollock walk some way towards an objective direction. They take lock-in as a fact of life, rather than as a form of anti-competitive behaviour *tout court*, and they consider which policies can mitigate lock-in effects. But those authors seem still to rely on the idea of search as a relevant market and on the need to address lock-in effects related to search engines as a product. The objectivity of their proposals is thus limited by the ignored subjectivity of the object they focus on.

To think of search merely as *a* product to be regulated by disentangling *its* different components is a partial, still competition-based effort that does not factor in the polysemic nature of information—the capacity of information to convey the different meanings which and through which we are always searching for, be it by 'googling', clicking, dialling, twitting, opening, tapping, flipping and overall seeking to *access*. To search for information can thus mean as many things as the information we seek to access, the means we use for so and the ways we interpret such information ourselves or through our technological extensions.

---

[123] *See*, e.g., Thelwall 2009.

What we now call search is but a topical, contingent form of *procuring access*.

Of course, regulators must also be attentive to the different, contextual meanings of search; to the different forms through which search is carried out. Regulating these may mean to enact more granular, technology-specific rules—rules attentive to particular dimensions of social conventions surrounding technological artefacts. Above and beyond these fragmented dimensions, however, we must understand search as a foundational component of agency in the information environment—this space–time continuum that, today and for the foreseeable future, curves around Google's gravity.

We as regulators must understand that the dangerous monopoly that Google's activities *tend* towards is the monopoly of meaning itself—even if such is a tendency that will never be fully realized. In the end, there is no simple problem of competition here but a race to control the flow of information in a plethora of different possibilities. That is why we find Google interested in "competing" with ISPs, Cable TVs, Operating System developers, Encyclopaedias, Bookstores amongst many others. And that is why we find Google attempting to neutralize actors that in any way can threaten its overarching project of "organizing all the world's information". Such is indeed a project that, by its very nature, admits of no alterity.

13.4 Neutrality, Autonomy, and the Information Environment

In March 2010, when Google decided to pull its search engine away from Mainland China, the New York Times ran an article noting Google's state-like foreign policy attitude. The article quoted the following statement by New York University Professor Clay Shirky: "[w]hat forces Google to have a foreign policy is that what they're exporting isn't a product or a service, it's a freedom".[124] Shirky's statement in a way concurs with what has been said in our preceding section. As we have seen, the justifications for intervening on Google's activities are not purely economic. Regulation should ensue not merely because of competition aspects related to a product or a service. Rather, the problem is cognitive and evaluative in a broader sense. Regulation should ensue because of the tendency that Google, by controlling the structure of the information environment, will also control the construction of meaning and value in contemporary societies. Our concurrence with Shirky can thus only be partial. For it is not freedom what is exported by Google, but rather the lack thereof—a diminishing of our possibilities of living autonomous lives. And, as Yochai Benkler explains in his chef-d'oeuvre, *The Wealth of Networks*, "a concern with autonomy provides a distinct justification for the policy concern with media concentration" that move us beyond considering the limits of competitive markets.[125]

---

[124] Landler 2010.

[125] Benkler 2006, p 157.

From all we have seen in the lines above it should be clear that this article's concern with autonomy develops in two fronts. On the one hand, it relates to Google's attempt of, by influencing the development of law and policy, neutralizing other agents who threaten its overall project of "organizing" the information environment. This was our focus in Sect. 13.2, in which we looked in particular into the case of Internet Service Providers. On the other hand, our concern relates to Google's possibilities of increasingly controlling the global flow of information through the lock-in effects of its own services. This was our focus in Sect. 13.3. From the perspective of the economic agents that Google seeks to neutralize, it is beyond doubt that to have one's possibilities of choosing amongst available options neutralized—which the idea of network neutrality, in any of its flavours, imposes to ISPs—goes against freedom of enterprise and the foundations of any liberal model one can conceive of. With regard to the relationships between users and Google, however, the question is more nuanced.

Here one could argue that, by providing services that further number and diversity of options available to us, Google actually enhances our autonomy. This is the view held by Yochai Benkler, which merits our careful examination as we close our venture in this paper.

Benkler's body of work is undoubtedly the most sophisticated and profound thought-exercise on the political theory of the information environment. There is much we can learn from it but I will focus our discussions in this section on a single, overarching point, which is Benkler's understanding of what an ideal conception of the political system would look like if we are to further personal autonomy in the information environment. Understanding how the idea of neutrality can fit into such a conception—or why it cannot—is fundamental if we are to situate Google's prescriptions against the backdrop of a more refined account of the relations between state and society in the information age. Benkler's ideas shed important lights here. Though there is much to compliment Benkler for on his understanding of personal autonomy, I trust that, more broadly, there are also some acute shortcomings in his views of what a political system consists in, as well as some important lessons to be learned from these. Let us pursue the point further.

We should start by noting the prominence that filtering mechanisms rightly assume in Benkler's framework. According to Benkler, the decentralization and socialization[126] of earlier creative industries has caused an overload of information that threatens our prospects of self-authorship in the information environment.[127] Lost amidst so much, we need Google and (if there were) its like to redeem us from a life of ignorance in plenitude. The so-called Babel objection to the idea that social production furthers autonomy poses, in effect, that the cacophony of new

---

[126] In *The Wealth of Networks* and in earlier works, Benkler speaks of a new model of commons-based peer production or, more broadly, of social production, as a social-economic phenomenon that provides a third-way alternative to the traditional models of markets and firms—an alternative of systematic advantages for dealing with information and culture as objects of production. *See*, in particular, Benkler 2002.

[127] Benkler 2006, pp. 169 ff.

forms of production undermines our capacity of identifying those options that are available to us. Benkler's response is, in part, that filtering mechanisms like Google rescue us from our wandering around through the busy avenues of the information environment.[128]

The problem here, however, is the illusion that entrusting to a company the design of our possibilities of action in the information environment *furthers* our personal autonomy. In reality, the choices made by Google are *constitutive* of our personal autonomy—they are to a large extent what our autonomy amounts to or, precisely because of this, what our autonomy does not amount to at all. In other words, our normative sources here do not come from within, but rather from outside of us. The process is not one of autonomy, but of heteronomy[129] and, to the extent that a dominant entity seeks to "organize" all sources of normativity in the information environment, it is also a process of neutralization of other sources of normativity—of neutralization of alterity—in this same environment.

To be fair, there is a sense in which Benkler sees a role for the state in laying down the *structural* foundations that will enable personal autonomy to flourish in the information environment. But Benkler is also largely optimistic about the possibilities that these foundations will arise organically, from within the information environment itself. The role that he sees for the state is thus, correspondingly, a reduced role. It is with regard to this somewhat reductionist perspective, which I will note as a shortcoming of his theory, that Benkler's work invites our attention.

Benkler indeed seems to assume that a liberal model for our age demands a dissociation between the state and the substance of life plans chosen by individuals in the information environment. In assuming so, as I will discuss below, Benkler departs from the particular liberal model that, in his book and elsewhere, he claims to embrace—the model put forward by Joseph Raz, inter alia in his *The Morality of Freedom*.[130] It is unclear why Benkler departs from Raz so silently. Perhaps, though this is unlikely, he does so unconsciously. Perhaps he does so to render his theory more palatable to an audience traditionally resistant to the idea that the state may nose into the information environment beyond just supporting its development.[131] Whatever the reason, however, Benkler's departure from Raz is difficult

---

[128] Id.

[129] *See supra* p 9.

[130] Raz 1986. In one of his earlier articles, whose ideas are echoed in his book, Benkler draws more heavily and explicitly on Raz's work. *See* Benkler 2001

[131] That being so, Langdon Winner's words could not happen to be more opportune. Speaking of those who seek to advocate a broader normative agenda in a world dominated by anti-normative, efficiency-oriented stances, Winner notes: "Because the idea of efficiency attracts a wide consensus, it is sometimes used as a conceptual Trojan horse by those who have more challenging political agendas they hope to smuggle in. But victories won in this way are in other respects great losses. For they affirm in our words and in our methodologies that there are certain human ends that no longer dare to be spoken in public. Lingering in that stuffy Trojan horse too long, even soldiers of virtue eventually suffocate". Winner 1986, p 54.

to defend. Understanding how such a departure unfolds will allow us to reach important conclusions about the regulation of the information environment and of search as a foundational component of it.

On the one hand, and as we have just noted, Benkler does believe that state intervention is necessary to ensure the *structural* possibilities that enable personal autonomy to be furthered in the information environment. For him, we need to care for the effects that "law can have through the way it structures the relationships among people with regard to the information environment they occupy".[132] This is so as the structure of the information environment will itself enable or disable different configurations in social relationships. How more or less autonomous one will be within these relationships is tantamount to how the structure of the information environment is designed. In Benkler's words, "[t]he structure of our information environment is *constitutive* of our autonomy, not only functionally significant to it".[133] The state thus has a role in ensuring these structural foundations of personal autonomy.

On the other hand, precisely because in the information environment determining structure goes beyond form and transmutes into substance,[134] there is a delicate balance to be struck here. Benkler trusts that the empowerment of individuals—rather than the political system—to jointly and directly devise the structural contours of their environment is to be welcomed as the default option.

"[F]iltration and accreditation" tools are an important example, as a fundamental part of that structure. Due to their being "themselves information goods",[135] and thus as much substance as they are form, such tools can be devised through the same peer-production, social processes that Benkler sees as characterizing the production of knowledge in contemporary societies. Of course, to some extent the design of such tools will be reflective of boundaries outlined by the state. For Benkler, the setting of structural boundaries is necessary not as part of any program of positive liberty but as a condition of self-authorship in itself.[136] To a larger extent, however, the development of filtering and accreditation tools will mostly unfold as both an enabler and a produce of people's autonomous pursuit of their own walks of life. In fact, Benkler trusts this is the way things are happening right now. In his words,

> "From the discussions of Wikipedia to the moderation and metamoderation scheme of Slashdot, and from the sixty thousand volunteers that make up the Open Directory Project to the PageRank system used by Google, *the means of filtering data are being produced within the networked information economy using peer production* and the coordinate patterns of nonproprietary production more generally".[137]

---

[132] Benkler 2006, p 151.

[133] *Id.* p 146.

[134] We have discussed this point in section 13.3.

[135] Benkler 2006, p 169.

[136] Id. p 141.

[137] Id. pp 171–172.

It seems far-fetched, however—and it was so already in 2005, when his book was written—to include Google and the Wikipedia in the same group of socially produced filtering tools. Benkler seems to be widely carried by Google's rhetoric about the democratic properties of its search engine. This affinity with Google also appears very clearly in the antipathy reserved by the author towards the ways in which, according to him, the adoption of "policy routers" by Internet Service Providers[138] threatens to reduce individual autonomy. Why doesn't Benkler direct equivalent suspicions to that which is by far the hegemonic power in the information environment—Google? Most interestingly, while for the generality of gatekeepers the accumulation of power seems to be a concern in itself,[139] with regard to search engines, for Benkler, only monopoly and the masking of paid rankings seem to be so.[140]

As noted above, Benkler's liberal theory for the information environment draws widely on Joseph Raz's work. But it is from Benkler's peculiar departure from Raz that we can extract the most interesting lessons for our debates in this article. These lessons concern the interplay between the ideas of autonomy and neutrality.

It appears that, by criticizing ISPs' policy-based routing of data, Benkler is defending theories of network neutrality. Neutrality, however, is not something we can reconcile with liberal theory of a Razian orientation—if yet we can reconcile it with with contemporary liberalism at all. Raz is a *liberal perfectionist*. To a great extent, his work in political theory has focused on debunking earlier theories of political neutrality, such as John Rawls's and Robert Nozick's, under the premise that a truly liberal model founded on autonomy and value pluralism actually needs the political institutions of society to engage with conceptions of the good life. Without political engagement of this kind the state cannot ensure that people will have available to them the means necessary for authoring valuable lives. As Raz puts it,

> Political action should be concerned with providing individuals with the means by which they can develop, which enable them to choose and attempt to realize their own

---

[138] "It is fairly clear that the new router increases the capacity of cable operators to treat their subscribers as objects, and to manipulate their actions in order to make them act as the provider wills, rather than as they would have had they had perfect information" (id. p 148). This is not completely surprising, though, since much of Benkler's earlier scholarship had been directed to advocating commons-based forms of administration of communications resources. *See, e.g.,* Benkler 1998, with a view he continues to sustain in the book. See Benkler 2006, p. 161 ("The autonomy deficit of private communications and information systems is a result of the formal structure of property as an institutional device and the role of communications and information systems as basic requirements in the ability of individuals to formulate purposes and plan actions to fit their lives").

[139] "The extent to which information overload inhibits autonomy relative to the autonomy of an individual exposed to a well-edited information flow depends on how much the editor who whittles down the information flow thereby gains power over the life of the user of the editorial function, and how he or she uses that power" (id. p 169).

[140] "The problem would be with search engines that mix the two strategies and hide the mix, or with a monopolistic search engine" (id. p 157).

conception of the good. But there is nothing here which speaks for neutrality. For it is the goal of all political action to enable individuals to pursue valid conceptions of the good and *to discourage evil or empty ones.*[141]

Benkler, on the other hand, though welcoming a limited *structural* role for the state, notes that the structuring of social relationships "calls for no therapeutic agenda to educate adults in a wide range of options. It calls for no one to sit in front of educational programs".[142] Benkler seems to be reminding us that, precisely because the information environment conflates form and substance, the state should be mindful of its power of interfering in the content of people's conceptions of the good; that the state should embrace a posture of restraint with regard to these—a doctrine of *political neutrality*—deferring *substantive* choices to the new collaborative forces that characterize the information environment.

In his view, attempts to intervene on cultural discourse seem to be neither justifiable nor feasible. While Benkler does criticize the black-box approach of certain liberal theories—such as Rawls's—that ignore culture as a legitimate concern for the political constitution of a society,[143] he also cautions about the futility of attempting to regulate culture itself, beyond laying out the structural foundations upon which the cultural modes of the information age can thrive. We must take up a "systematic commitment to avoid direct intervention on cultural exchange".[144] In his words,

> "Understanding that culture is a matter of political concern even within a liberal framework does not... translate into an agenda of intervention in the culture sphere as an extension of legitimate decision making. Cultural discourse is systematically not amenable to formal regulation, management, or direction from the political system".[145]

The theory here is that the transparency and participatory possibilities of twenty first century liberal societies will increase reflexivity in cultural processes and enable people to make better and more autonomous decisions on how to author their life stories against an ever more refined cultural background. Fair enough and there surely are reasons to believe that *to a great extent* that will be so. But to move from here to the conclusion that people will wind up at such a liberating intellectual oasis even if left to their own devices by a state that has a merely structural role seems to be an unwarranted jump. Several challenges can be raised to this conclusion.

---

[141] Raz, *supra* note 130, p 133.

[142] Benkler, *supra* note 20, p 151.

[143] Id. pp. 279–280.

[144] Id. p. 298.

[145] Id.

First, research shows that cultural discourse tends towards polarization, where groups of individuals tend to get ever more extreme in their world views.[146] Will a framework to sort out disagreement between groups emerge even if no choices are made by the political system on aspects of such a framework that are themselves cultural and substantive?

Second, and related to this, are there frameworks that can evade cultural choices at all? The choice for a liberal framework for cultural decision making of the sort that Benkler envisions is already, in itself, a cultural choice of the kind he sets out to avoid. Different cultural traditions exist where possibilities of cultural dissent in the information environment are more tightly and substantively regulated—think of China. Conceptions of the state present themselves differently in these traditions and are reflected in different forms in the substance of their cultural discourses. The only way to live up to Benkler's aspirations is thus to eliminate any more ambitious image of the political system from the substance of cultural discourses in the information environment. But this, in itself, would amount to the elimination of dissenting voices, of alternative cultural conceptions within which a political system is formed. Culture pervades everything which is done in a society. To refrain from making substantive choices with regard to culture is to refrain from making substantive choices altogether. How can that be possible?

Third, Benkler's recipe says much about the framework that will enable us to jointly model the outer boundaries of a cultural clay man, but it says nothing about what to do, politically, when the clay man happen to embody a wicked soul. There is an underlying assumption in Benkler's work—in which he is certainly not alone—that the generative possibilities of the information environment, the forms of participation and collaboration that characterize it, must be cherished as intrinsically good.[147] This reflects an all too common creed in the auspicious properties of technological development—always to be preferred to the intractable substantive problems of normativity. But what to do when the mores and sentiments of a time happen to be different from what reason would advise?

---

[146] *See, e.g.*, Sunstein 2007. Benkler rejects Sunstein's theory but does not go to great lengths to disprove it. *See* Benkler, *supra* note 20, pp 238–239. The irony here is that the very visible polarization around net neutrality debates, and the twitter brouhahas that seem to feed these, lend remarkable persuasiveness to Sunstein's arguments. Further research on political polarization on Twitter notes that, while people do use that platform to engage with alternative world views, they find themselves unable to do so in a meaningful way—and, of course, tend to interact more with like-minded users. Boyd and Yardi seem to blame it on the constraints of the platform. That may be so. But then it is worth noticing that the major constraint presented by Twitter is not its brevity. More space will not *per se* add to consent. The major constraint is another which, especially after their recent victories in the spring revolutions, actors in the West may not be willing to sacrifice: *immediacy*. *See* Boyd and Yardi 2010. Noting, besides polarization, the frequently uncivil tone of the debates, *see* Conover et al., 2011.

[147] Generativity is, indeed, the happiness of contemporary utilitarianism—or at least its idiosyncrasy. *See* Zittrain 2008, p 90.

It is known that crowds can behave badly and the Internet gives us uncountable examples of that. Internet vigilantism is one such.[148] Aided by technological tools, crowds come together to hold individuals accountable beyond any proportionality or due process guarantees, if not to bully completely innocent people for the sheer fun of it. The Internet promises to forever 'remember' wrongdoers for their misdeeds and mocked individuals for their magnified traits.[149] The outputs of collaborative efforts are themselves inherently wrong in these cases. And one cannot endow ordeals with virtue just by correcting their procedural improprieties. The political system needs to address the substantive cultural assumptions upon which such processes hinge.

Fourth, and linked to the third, there is the challenge of adjudication. Who is going to settle disputes arising out of substantive cultural matters of the information environment? Benkler's only possible solution to this challenge is to say: information environment's very 'inhabitants'. He cannot say so, however, without resorting to the same Rawlsian rights-based discourse that he himself vilifies. That is, the only way Benkler can hold to this claim is to concede that adjudication by the state should be limited to legally-recognized rights *that are themselves of a different nature from that of substantive cultural affairs*, whose disputes should be settled by society. One could respond to this by saying that state adjudication, while not concerning cultural affairs, can *nonetheless* concern the *structure* that brings cultural affairs about. But this does not solve the problem. One still needs to clarify the nature of structural concerns themselves—the only possibility being to assign these the status of *rights*, in distinction from cultural *goods*.

However, if disputes concerning cultural goods are to be settled by society itself, who is going to mobilize the coercive apparatus? If these disputes—all that take place within the information environment—cannot mobilize the coercive apparatus, are we to restrict the use of coercion to the increasingly less frequent disputes that do not concern cultural matters? Furthermore, if society itself ends up devising alternative forms of coercion more compatible with cultural goods, can we still sustain the distinction between society and the state or, rather, Benkler's theory ends up engulfing itself?

The only way to answer these questions satisfactorily, it seems, is to admit that there isn't, after all, any difference of nature between *rights* and other cultural *conceptions of the good*. Rights-based disputes, in effect, arise in profoundly cultural settings. The difference that exists is one of degree. Rights are forms of good whose violation the law recognizes as having particular significance, assigning them, as a result, the power to invoke the coercive apparatus of the state—or at least to claim from the state different modalities of promotion and incentive that are inherent to their recognition and fulfilment. Normative, cultural as they are, rights exist within a wider practical universe. Together with other conceptions of the good, they form a system on whose contours our possibilities of

---

[148] *See* Cheung 2009.

[149] *See* Mayer-Schönberger 2009.

living an autonomous life will hinge. Nothing more natural, thus, than that the state engages with the system as a whole.

The idea of merely structural interventions by the state to further personal autonomy, though claiming to see what Rawls prevents us from seeing, namely culture, in effect resembles Robert Nozick's libertarian framework where the state provides people with nothing but a filter—a framework for reaching agreements that, politically, are conducive to no other political arrangement but that of a minimal state. Indeed, if the role of the state is to provide society with a framework for their own, autonomous cultural agreements in a world where culture is everything—staying away otherwise but to enforce the operation of the framework—the proposal is virtually identical (but in its claimed bounteousness) to that of Robert Nozick's framework for 'utopia'.[150]

Everything could not be more incompatible with Joseph Raz's liberal perfectionist model, which Benkler claims to embrace in his work—but which in reality he does not. Most importantly, if Raz is correct, Benkler's ruling out of more "positive" modalities of political action seems actually to be incompatible with Benkler's own agenda of furthering personal autonomy. For Raz, in effect, the substantive elimination of bad, autonomy-demeaning options is not incompatible with liberal pursuits—rather liberalism requires this.[151] While coercion should be reserved only for the morally repugnant options,[152] regulatory modalities that, for instance, subsidize the performance of valuable activities or discourage the pursuit of evil ones are nonetheless to be welcomed.[153] Education seems to be just a perfect example of these less direct forms of regulatory intervention.

The goal of liberalism, in sum, is to ensure the availability of valuable options for individuals and groups to author their lives. Modalities of state intervention that, by making substantive choices for the information environment, enhance the overall prospects that a wide range of options will be available for people to author their lives are to be preferred to the minimal and anti-idealistic conceptions of a state that practices a form of informational, cultural negligence under the flag of neutrality.

---

[150] *See* Nozick 1974, pp 297–333.

[151] It requires so even at the price of coercion to prevent the pursuit of morally repugnant options. For Raz, "[the] pursuit of the morally repugnant cannot be defended from coercive interference on the ground that being an autonomous choice endows it with any value". Raz 1986, p 418.

[152] "Perfectionist goals need not be pursued by the use of coercion. A government which subsidizes certain activities, rewards their pursuit, and advertises their availability encourages those activities without using coercion.... The government has an obligation to create an environment providing individuals with an adequate range of options and the opportunities to choose them.... Autonomy-based duties... require the use of public power to promote the conditions of autonomy, to secure an adequate range of options for their population" (*id.* pp 417–418).

[153] "[T]the autonomy principle is a perfectionist principle. Autonomous life is valuable only if it is spent in the pursuit of acceptable and valuable projects and relationships. The autonomy principle permits and even requires governments to create morally valuable opportunities, and to eliminate repugnant ones" (*id.* p 417).

Doctrines of neutrality rely on a fictitious and arbitrary distinction between goals that can be pursued by the state and those that cannot. They were characteristic of liberal theories of the industrial age—such as Rawls's, with which Benkler, in the end, has a somewhat uneasy relationship.[154] Such theories sustained the vision that the state must assign a lexical priority to individualistic forms of good (which they would call rights) while blinding itself as much as possible to more collective-oriented ones. To a large extent, doctrines of political neutrality have been put to rest by the communitarian critique and even by liberals' such as William Galston,[155] Thomas Hurka[156] and, above all, Joseph Raz. One of the most stringent reasons for so was precisely that evaluative arbitrariness about which John Finnis's words could not, once again, be more opportune:

> For the sake of a 'democratic' impartiality between differing conceptions of human good, Rawls insists that, in selecting principles of justice, one must treat as primary goods only liberty, opportunity, wealth, and self-respect, and that one must not attribute intrinsic value to such basic forms of good as truth, or play, or art, or friendship. Rawls gives no satisfactory reason for this radical emaciation of human good, and no satisfactory reason is available: [his] 'thin theory' is arbitrary.[157]

13.5 Conclusion

The main problem we have been exposed to throughout this article is none other than that which Finnis rightly attributes to Rawls—the arbitrary exclusion of important classes of reasons from the scope of political deliberation.

---

[154] Benkler does seem to have an uneasy relationship with Rawls. On the one hand, he criticizes Rawls's black-box approach with regard to culture. On the other hand, he does not seem to fully reject the political neutrality fundamentals upon which such an approach relies. But, beyond that, Benkler also trusts that his views of the networked information environment are compatible with the "difference principle" of Rawls's theory of justice—that is, with Rawls's views on distribution. Actually, Benkler trusts that his own views on the networked environment are compatible with *any* of the theories of justice he lists in his book—Rawls's, Dworkin's, Akerman's and Nozick's (Benkler, *id.* pp. 303–308). Is it a mere coincidence that all these authors have also espoused theories of liberal *neutrality*? (though the late Dworkin seems to have abandoned these, Benkler's reference seems to be still to the 1981 Dworkin). Or does Benkler's reliance upon neutralists actually tell us that it is not possible to disentangle those author's political views on autonomy and neutrality from their take on distribution—and that that is why perhaps Benkler is ready to refer to the latter? This being so, however, it would be important to point to a difficulty in Benkler's line of reasoning. Though Benkler seems ready to assume that Rawls's difference principle encompasses cultural goods, he can only do so by stretching Rawls's rather individualistic understanding of what primary goods amount to and the consequent (if arguable) neutrality of Rawls's political system towards culture. Other authors have explicitly tried this approach, but have also ignored the neutrality component of Rawls's theory, which renders the enterprise, in my view, equally problematic. *See* Van den Hoven and Rooksby 2008.

[155] *See, e.g.,* GALSTON 1991

[156] *See, e.g.,* Hurka 1996, 2003.

[157] Finnis 1980, p 106.

Network neutrality does so by enjoining the state to make sure that no questions involving such reasons arise at the network layer of the Internet. But neutrality here moves, thus, beyond the state, beyond the typical boundaries of the political constitution. It precludes, for certain actors, those political, normative contributions of their everyday life. Beyond—indeed, against—what liberals of Rawlsian orientation would admit, network neutrality annihilates the autonomy of actors whose core activities lie at the network layer—ISPs. In Google's advocacy, only those options which are merely related to engineering decisions should be left available to ISPs, which otherwise cannot act at all. No significant reasons exist for so. Nor could they. Here the arbitrariness that Finnis speaks about is radical and the violation of liberal principles, conspicuous.

Less ostensibly, the lenience with the extension of Google's dominance in the information environment is also founded upon an arbitrary decision of this sort. It reflects the understanding that only competition reasons—and not, for instance, moral reasons—would justify state action against "search engines". But traditional competition reasons, we have seen, are clearly not engaged by the new kind of monopolistic tendency displayed by the overall combination of Google's activities. Together, these activities tend to engender a regime of absolute organization that transcends the habitual considerations of market-based rationale. The call not to regulate Google's activities is thus a call to exclude other concerns—i.e. concerns with how truth is presented to people, with how knowledge is imparted and overall with the deeper, substantive aspects of the information environment. We have just seen Benkler's cautionary notes on going beyond the structure. But is it true that liberalism requires us to keep away from *substantive* forms of informational violence that may happen deep within the information environment?

Of course, structure matters. I was ready to note, in Sect. 13.3, how important it is to measure the extent of Google's dominance in the information environment and that this requires a careful examination of the very structure of information flows. Elsewhere I have noted that the regulation of social networking sites must not (and does not) ignore the ways in which the structure of these sites constrain how our relations of friendship are carried out.[158] But both in Google's case and in the case of, for instance, Facebook, we cannot blind ourselves to the fact that regulating structure matters precisely because of the *values* that the structure constrains. There is no reason to assume that states and the law should not directly engage and uphold such values in enabling us to follow more auspicious—and, indeed, autonomous—avenues in the information environment.

Equally importantly, there are no grounds to submit that law should forbid any agent in the information environment from engaging in evaluative pursuits either. Nor *can* law do so. Rather, within and in interaction with its boundaries, agents—ISPs inclusively—create the values that render law and life overall meaningful. Doing law is not an exclusive privilege of governments and legislators, but rather an essential part of the ways of all who reason in practical terms. And doing law

---

[158] *See* Thompson 2011.

entails the adoption of certain criteria of validation that "presuppose positions about what would be good for [a given community]"[159]; of certain general principles that articulate "what seem to one, *in one's legal thinking*—as they have seemed to many others—to be requirements of civilized, decent, humanly appropriate behaviour".[160] All of us engage with these principles and criteria as we live by the law in our everyday life. How can one not do so?

Truth, friendship, culture, for instance, are important evaluative criteria that are engaged when one thinks of *freedom, justice* and the *rule of law*.[161] These are not two completely different cognitive realms, one acceptable (the latter) and the other (the former) to be avoided at all costs by certain agents of the information environment. Rather, both realms compose a seamless web outside of which living a lawful life—or any life at all—is plainly impossible. While, of course, to outline the limits of our possible engagements with these criteria is an important function performed by law, the idea that one must be enjoined to act in partial or total disengagement from some or any of those criteria makes as much sense as the pretence that one can be forced to act in separation from law itself.

In his book *"Rights, Regulation and the Technological Revolution"*, Roger Brownsword speaks of a *community of rights* as the vantage point of a society which accepts that the "development and application of modern technologies should be compatible with respect for *individual rights*".[162] Amongst more specific characteristics of such a community would be its embeddedness of a formal moral standpoint and its reflective and interpretive nature—that is, its being a community that "constantly keeps under review the question of whether the current interpretation of its commitments is the best interpretation".[163] In a way, Brownsword's individual rights-based community is as restrictive as those of other, Rawlsian-style forms of liberalism we discussed above. It is a *community*, thus, just in a limited sense, for its reflective and interpretive commitments do not seem to encompass collective-oriented conceptions of the good that take us beyond the language of individual rights. It does not provide an explicit justification for concern by the political system with substantive cultural matters afflicting life in the information environment. It *is* a community, nonetheless, for it recognizes our possibilities of jointly devising the normative commitments (at least rights-based ones) under which to live by in our technological society.

We do well in expanding Brownsword's views. We must see to it that our substantive requirements for self-authorship in the information environment be furthered by the political system with regard to options that matter precisely

---

[159] Finnis 2005, p 110.

[160] Id.

[161] Some may disagree and defend that the identification of legal considerations can happen independently of moral criteria. Not even these, however, as noted above, would submit that successfully living a lawful life can happen in separation from a theory of morality that renders our legal pursuits meaningful and worth living by.

[162] Brownsword 2008, p. 24.

[163] *Id.* p 25.

because of their common nature—for instance, our possibilities of forming and revising our constitutive attachments, our relations of friendship, through social networking sites; or the priorities and degrees of relevance that we jointly attribute to different sources of knowledge and culture in the information environment. These, amongst others, are not projects that concern individuals as the exclusive bearer of claims of political morality. Rather they transcend individualisms and more authentically relate to our lives as members of a community.

But, most importantly, as Brownsword aptly recognizes, we must treat all these as options that we make and revise as *members* of a community. We must appreciate our common membership to the overall process by which our individual and collective life stories unfold. There is nothing that speaks for neutrality or for absolute forms of organization here. Rather, our membership to the wider community of the information environment demands that different voices—from individuals, for sure, but also from groups and organizations, inclusively of economic nature—be equally heard. It demands that all of us are able to daily re-enact the substantive normative commitments by which we live.

"I fear the man of a single book", Thomas Aquinas is said to have noted, in a possible reference to the dangers of fundamentalism. The normative evolution of the information environment demands indeed the teachings of many books. It objects to the overarching uniformity of standards predefined by any single company—as much as it objects to the exclusion of normative contributions by any other. Google's increasing and unified influence over the construction of meaning in the information environment, its belief in its own evaluative superiority, its mission of organizing all the world's information and its corresponding intent of neutralizing alternative sources of normative contribution speak to the heart of Aquinas's concerns. The boundaries between Google's different services tend to increasingly blur against the backdrop of its overall project. That Google's latest product is a social network called Google *Plus* is far from a coincidence. Rather, it denotes how a complete redefinition of Google's core services towards a social networking platform can in the end be seen as no more than an incremental addition, an upgrade, a *plus* in its overall plan. And as the pages of Google's single book unfold, more may very well amount to less.

Acknowledgments I am happy to acknowledge the generous support of the Alcatel-Lucent Foundation for my position as a Visiting Fellow at the Hans Bredow Institute for Media Research, University of Hamburg, where the first thoughts that led to this paper were conceived. The ideas expressed in the lines below, however, have to no extent been influenced by my institutional affiliation at that time beyond the boundaries of open (and discerning) academic exchange. I thank Wolfgang Schulz and Victoria Nash for thoughtful comments on earlier notes.

References

Ammori M, Crawford S, Wu T (2010) Submission to the Federal Communications Commission at 7-8. In re Preserving the Open Internet, GN Docket No. 09-191; Broadband Industry Practices, WC Docket No. 07-52; A National Broadband Plan for Our Future, GN Docket No. 09-51

Argenton C, Prüfer J (2011) Search engine competition with network externalities, TILEC Discussion Paper, DP 2011-024. http://extranet.isnie.org/uploads/isnie2011/argenton_prufer-.pdf. Accessed 1 Sept 2011

Battelle J (2006) The search: how Google and its rivals rewrote the rules of business and transformed our culture. Portfolio, New York

Benkler Y (1998) Overcoming agoraphobia: building the commons of the digitally networked environment. Harvard J Law & Technol 11:287–400

Benkler Y (2001) Siren songs and Amish children: autonomy, information, and law. N Y U L Rev 76:23

Benkler Y (2002) Coase's penguin, or, Linux and the nature of the firm. Yale L J 112:369

Benkler Y (2006) The wealth of networks: how social production transforms markets and freedom. Yale University Press, New Haven

Boorstin B (2010) Promoting free trade for the internet economy. http://google publicpolicy.blogspot.com/2010/11/promoting-free-trade-for-internet.html. Accessed 1 Sept 2011

Boyd D, Yardi S (2010) Dynamic debates: an analysis of group polarization over time on Twitter. Bull Sci Technol Soc 30(5):316–32

Bracha O, Pasquale F (2008) Accountability in the law of search. Cornell L Rev 93:1149–1210

Bradner S (1996) The internet standards practice—revision 3, IETF, RFC 2026, http://www.ietf.org/rfc/rfc2026.txt. Accessed 1 Sept 2011

Brazilian Internet Steering Committee (CGI.br) (2009) Principles for the Governance and use of the internet, Resolution CGI.br/RES/2009/003/P. http://cgi.br/regulamentacao/pdf/resolucao-2009-003-pt-en-es.pdf. Accessed 1 Sept 2011

Brownsword R (2008) Rights, regulation and the technological revolution. Oxford University Press, Oxford

Cheung A (2009) Rethinking public privacy in the internet era: a study of virtual persecution by the Internet crowd. The J Media Law 1(2):191–217

Chomsky N (1965) Aspects of the theory of Syntax. MIT Press, Cambridge

Comcast Corp. v. FCC, 600 F.3d 642 (D.C. Cir. 2010)

Conover M et al. (2011) Political polarization on Twitter, paper presented at the fifth international AAAI conference on weblogs and social media (Jul. 17–21), http://truthy.indiana.edu/site_media/pdfs/conover_icwsm2011_polarization.pdf

Davidson A and Tauke T (2010) A joint policy proposal for an open internet. http://googlepublicpolicy.blogspot.com/2010/08/joint-policy-proposal-for-open-internet.html. Accessed 1 Sept 2011

Dep't of Justice & Fed. Trade Comm'n (2010) Horizontal Merger. http://www.justice.gov/atr/public/guidelines/hmg-2010.pdf. Accessed 1 Sept 2011

Dep't of Justice and Fed. Trade Comm'n (1995) Antitrust Guidelines for the Licensing of Intellectual Property. http://www.justice.gov/atr/public/guidelines/0558.pdf. Accessed 1 Sept 2011

Dickson J (2001) Evaluation and legal theory. Hart Publishing, Oxford

Drummond D (2010) A new approach to China. http://googleblog.blogspot.com/2010/01/new-approach-to-china.html Accessed 1 Sept 2011

European Commission (2010) Press release, antitrust: commission probes allegations of antitrust violations by Google. http://europa.eu/rapid/pressReleasesAction.do?reference=IP/10/1624&format=HTML. Accessed 1 Sept 2011

Falcão J (2003) Globalização e judiciário: a internalização das normas de nomes de nomínio. In: Lemos R, Waisberg I (eds) Conflitos Sobre Nomes de Domínio: e Outras Questões Jurídicas da Internet. Revista dos Tribunais, São Paulo, p 15

Federal Communications Commission (2005) In re Appropriate framework for broadband access to the internet over wireline facilities; (…) appropriate regulatory treatment for broadband access to the internet over cable facilities, policy statement, 20 FCC Rcd at 14986

Federal Communications Commission (2008) Formal complaint of free press and public knowledge against Comcast Corporation for secretly degrading peer-to-peer applications, memorandum opinion and order, 23 F.C.C.R. 13028

Federal Communications Commission (2009) In re Preserving the open internet: broadband industry practices, notice of proposed rulemaking, 24 FCC Rcd. 13064

Federal Communications Commission (2010) In re Preserving the open internet: broadband industry practices, report and order, 25 FCC Rcd 17905

Finnis J (1980) Natural law and natural rights. Clarendon Press, Oxford

Finnis J (2005) The foundations of practical reason revisited. Am J Juris 50:109

Galston WA (1991) Liberal purposes: goods, virtues, and diversity in the liberal state. Cambridge University Press, Cambridge

Gilbert R, Rubinfeld D (2011) Revising the horizontal merger guidelines: lessons from the US and the EU. In: Faure M, Zhang X (eds) Competition policy and regulation: recent developments in China, Europe and the US. Edward Elgar, Cheltenham, p 262

Google Inc. (2009) A guide to net neutrality for Google users. http://web.archive.org/web/20090925074634/http://www.google.com/help/netneutrality.html. Accessed 1 Sept 2011

Google Inc. (2010) Comments of Google Inc., In re Preserving the open internet Broadband industry practices, GN Docket No. 09-191, WC Docket No. 07-52. http://www.openinternetcoalition.com/files/Google_Comments.pdf Accessed 1 Sept 2011

Google Inc. (2011) Transparency report. http://www.google.com/transparencyreport. Accessed 1 Sept 2011

Grimmelmann J (2007) The structure of search engine law. Iowa Law Rev 93:1–63

Holt J (1992) Magna Carta. Cambridge University Press, Cambridge

Hurka T (1996) Perfectionism. Oxford University Press, Oxford

Hurka T (2003) Vice, virtue, and value. Oxford University Press, Oxford

Internet Society (2010) Open inter-networking. http://www.isoc.org/pubpolpillar/usercentricity/20100222-Inter-Networking.pdf. Accessed 1 Sept 2011

Labovitz C (2010) Google sets new Internet traffic record. http://asert.arbornetworks.com/2010/10/google-breaks-traffic-record. Accessed 1 Sept 2011

Landler M (2010) Google searches for a foreign policy. http://www.nytimes.com/2010/03/28/weekinreview/28landler.html. Accessed 1 Sept 2011

Law J (2002) Objects and spaces. Theory, Cult & Soc 19(5–6):9

Lessig L (2001) The future of ideas: the fate of the commons in a connected world. Vintage Books, New York

Luhmann N (2004) Law as a social system. Oxford University Press, Oxford (Klaus A. Ziegert transl.; Fatima Kastner, Richard Nobles, David Schiff & Rosamund Ziegert eds.)M v Home Office [1994] 1 AC 377

Marissa Mayer (2010) Do not neutralize the web's endless search. http://www.ft.com/cms/s/0458b1a4-8f78-11df-8df0-00144feab49a,Authorised=   false.html?_i_location=http%3A%2F%2   Fwww.ft.com%2Fcms%2Fs%2F0%2F0458b1a4-11df-8df0-00144feab49a.html. Accessed 1 Sept 2011

Mayer-Schönberger V (2009) Delete: the virtue of forgetting in the digital age. Princeton University Press, Princeton

Murray A (2007) The regulation of cyberspace: control in the online environment. Routledge, London

N.Y. Times (2010) Editorial, The Google algorithm. http://www.nytimes.com/2010/07/15/opinion/15thu3.html. Accessed 1 Sept 2011

N.Y. Times (2011) Editorial, Investigating Google. http://www.nytimes.com/2011/07/05/opinion/05tue3.html?_r=2. Accessed 01 Sept 2011

National Cable & Telecommunications Ass'n v. Brand X Internet Services, 545 U.S. 967 (2005)

Nissenbaum H, Introna L (2000) Shapping the web: why the politics of search engines matters. The Inf Soc 16(3):169

Nozick R (1974) Anarchy, state, and Utopia. Basic Books, New York

Pasquale F (2010) Dominant search engines: an essential cultural & political facility. In: Szoka B, Marcus A (eds) The next digital decade: essays on the future of the internet. TechFreedom, Washington, D.C., p 401

Paul Mockapetris, Domain Names—Concepts and Facilities, IETF, RFC 1034 (Nov., 1997), http://goo.gl/BFppN

Paul R (2011) Android openness withering as Google withholds Honeycomb. http://arstechnica.com/open-source/news/2011/03/android-openness-withering-as-google-withhold-honeycomb-code.ars. Accessed 1 Sept 2011

Pollock R (2010) Is Google the next Microsoft: competition, welfare and regulation in online search. Rev Netw Econ 9:4–29 Article 4

Raz J (1986) The morality of freedom. Clarendon Press, Oxford

Raz J (1994) Ethics and the public domain. Oxford University Press, Oxford

Raz J (2004) Incorporation by law. Leg Theory 10(1):9

Samuelson P, Nimmer D (2011) The amended google book settlement: Judge Chin's decision. http://www.wipo.int/wipo_magazine/en/2011/03/article_0003.html. Accessed 1 Sept 2011

Say JB (1855) A Treatise on Political Economy. Longman, Hurst, Rees, Orme, and Brown, London

Schlick A (2010) A third-way legal framework for addressing the Comcast dilemma. http://www.broadband.gov/third-way-legal-framework-for-addressing-the-comcast-dilemma.html. Accessed 1 Sept 2011

Schmidt E, McAdam L (2009) Finding common ground in an open Internet. http://google-publicpolicy.blogspot.com/2009/10/finding-common-ground-on-open-internet.html. Accessed 1 Sept 2011

Searls D, Weinberger D (2003) World of ends: what the Internet is and how to stop mistaking it for something else. http://www.worldofends.com. Accessed 1 Sept 2011

Smith B, Microsoft Corporation (2011) Adding our voice to concerns about search in Europe. http://blogs.technet.com/b/microsoft_on_the_issues/archive/2011/03/30/adding-our-voice-to-concerns-about-search-in-europe.aspx. Accessed 1 Sept 2011

StopBadWare (2009) China's Green Dam is BadWare and So Much More. http://blog.stopbadware.org/2009/06/13/chinas-green-dam-is-badware-and-so-much-more. Accessed 1 Sept 2011

StopBadWare (2011a) Frequently asked questions. http://www.stopbadware.org/home/faq#what_is_badware. Accessed 1 Sept 2011

StopBadWare (2011b) About StopBadware, StopBadware. http://www.stopbadware.org/home/about Accessed 1 Sept 2011

Sunstein C (2007) Republic.com 2.0. Princeton University Press, Princeton

Taylor C (1991) Sources of the Self: The Making of Modern Identity. Cambridge University Press, Cambridge

Thelwall M (2009) Introduction to webometrics: quantitative web research for the social sciences. Synth Lect Inf Concepts Retr Serv 1(1):1

Thompson M (2010) The sheriff of 'not-the-Internet': reflections on Comcast Corp. v FCC, Communications Law. Review 1(1):201

Thompson, M (2011) The neutralization of harmony: whither the good information environment? (forthcoming)

Tomkins A (2003) Public Law. Clarendon Press, Oxford

Vaidhyanathan S (2011) The Googlization of everything : (and why we should worry). University of California Press, Berkeley

van den Hoven J, Rooksby E (2008) Distributive justice and the value of information: a (broadly) Rawlsian approach. In: van den Hoven J., Weckert J. (eds.) Information Technology and Moral Philosophy, p 376

Varian H, Shapiro C (1999) Information rules: a strategic guide to the network economy. Harvard Business School Press, Cambridge

Wallace R (2003) Stanford encyclopedia of philosophy: practical reason. http://plato.stanford.edu/entries/practical-reason. Accessed 1 Sept 2011

Winner L (1986) The whale and the reactor: a search for limits in an age of high technology. Chicago University Press, Chicago

Yoo C (2005) Beyond network neutrality. Harvard J Law & Technol 19(1):26

Zheng Y (2008) Technological empowerment: the internet, state, and society in China. Stanford University Press, Stanford

Zittrain J (2008) The future of the internet : and how to stop it. Yale University Press, New Haven